THIRD EDITION

CLINICAL MENTAL HEALTH COUNSELING IN COMMUNITY AND AGENCY SETTINGS

Samuel T. Gladding

Wake Forest University

Debbie W. Newsome

Wake Forest University

Merrill

Boston   Columbus   Indianapolis   New York   San Francisco   Upper Saddle River
Amsterdam   Cape Town   Dubai   London   Madrid   Milan   Munich   Paris
Montreal   Toronto   Delhi   Mexico City   Sao Paulo   Sydney
Hong Kong   Seoul   Singapore   Taipei   Tokyo

Vice President and Executive Publisher: Jeffery W. Johnston
Publisher: Kevin M. Davis
Acquisitions Editor: Meredith D. Fossel
Editorial Assistant: Nancy Holstein
Cover Design: Bruce Kenselaar
Cover Image: © Digital Vision Ltd./SuperStock
Operations Specialist: Fran Russello
Marketing Manager: Amanda L. Stedke

This book was set in 10/12 Garamond by Aptara®, Inc. It was printed and bound by Courier Companies, Inc.

Photo Credits: Alex Robinson © Dorling Kindersley, p. 2; Photodisc/Getty Images, pp. 22, 45; Michal Heron/PH College, p. 68; Anthony Magnacca/Merrill, p. 101; Charles Gatewood/PH College, p. 132; PH College, p. 165; Don Klumpp/Getty Images Inc.—Image Bank, p. 189; Anne Vega/Merrill, p. 218; George Dodson/PH College, p. 239; Getty Images—Photodisc, p. 260; Frank Siteman, p. 283; Steve Gorton © Dorling Kindersley, p. 320; John Serafin/SBG, p. 346.

Library of Congress Cataloging-in-Publication Data
Gladding, Samuel T.
 Clinical mental health counseling in community and agency settings / Samuel T. Gladding, Debbie W. Newsome.—3rd ed.
  p. cm.
 Prev. ed. has title: Community and agency counseling.
 ISBN-13: 978-0-13-173587-3
 ISBN-10: 0-13-173587-X
 1. Counseling. 2. Counseling—History. I. Newsome, Deborah W.
II. Gladding, Samuel T. Community and agency counseling. III. Title.
 BF637.C6G528 2009
 361'.06—dc22

2009013718

10 9 8 7 6 5 4 3 2 1

Merrill
is an imprint of

www.pearsonhighered.com

ISBN-10:   0-13-173587-X
ISBN-13: 978-0-13-173587-3

PREFACE

Counseling in community and agency settings has experienced much transformation during the past two decades. One of the most significant changes that occurred since the production of the second edition of this text was the adoption of the 2009 Council for the Accreditation of Counseling and Related Educational Programs (CACREP) Standards. The new standards no longer recognize *Community Counseling* and *Mental Health Counseling* as separate specialization areas. Instead, a new specialization area is recognized: that of *Clinical Mental Health Counseling*. The reason for this change, as stated by Dr. Tom Davis, chairman of the Standards Revision Committee, is that the community counseling and mental health counseling programs were essentially producing graduates who practiced in similar settings and who performed similar functions. Although there will be a time of transition before counselor education programs are required to make the necessary changes to their courses of study, the new standards "offer a solid preparation for our graduates, which will allow them to meet the complex mental health service delivery needs in our society" (Davis, personal communication, September 8, 2008). Hence, we changed the title and a large amount of content in this edition to reflect the new specialization area, as reflected in the text's title: *Clinical Mental Health Counseling in Community and Agency Settings* (3rd ed.).

Although many of the important concepts that are a part of the community and mental health counseling field have remained the same, some things have changed since the publication of the second edition of this text, including the adoption of the 2005 ACA *Code of Ethics*, the proliferation of issues (both positive and negative) connected with Internet use, an emphasis on the bio-psycho-social model of counseling, global events, and mental health service delivery systems. We recognize that the clinical mental health counseling profession will continue to evolve and that it is possible that by the time you read this text, even more changes will have taken place. Nonetheless, community and agency counselors will continue to perform a broad range of therapeutic services among diverse client populations and in a variety of settings. They will use evidence-based approaches that promote prevention, early intervention, wellness, and advocacy, taking into account the client, the environment, and the interaction between the two. They will continue to develop skills in working with clients dealing with crisis and trauma. Furthermore, they will continue to work with teams of other mental health and medical professionals to provide the best possible care for their clients.

In the third edition of this text, these and other topics are addressed. We examine the history and professional foundations of counseling, counseling with diverse populations, current influences on the field, roles and functions of clinical mental health counselors, and settings in which clinical mental health counselors practice.

NEW TO THIS EDITION

The third edition features much new content, including

- An expanded description of the professional identity of clinical mental health counselors
- Updated information regarding ethical and legal issues, particularly as they pertain to the 2005 ACA *Code of Ethics*

- A focus on the bio-psycho-social model of counseling and on holistic approaches to counseling
- An expanded chapter on counseling diverse populations to help counselors develop skills in working with a wide range of clientele
- Updated chapters that examine the settings in which clinical mental health counselors practice and the services they provide
- Case studies throughout the text that encourage students to apply what they have learned

ORGANIZATION OF THE TEXT

The content is designed to address pertinent topics in clinical mental health counseling. Contents are organized under four headings:

- **Part I: History and Professional Foundations of Counseling.** The history and foundations of counseling are outlined, beginning with a recounting of the historical roots of the profession (Chapter 1). In Chapter 2, the concept of professional identity is explored, including the specialty area of clinical mental health counseling. Special attention is given to credentialing associated with the profession. In Chapter 3, ethical and legal issues, particularly those that pertain to clinical mental health counseling, are explored. In Chapter 4, we address counseling issues related to diversity. In our society, it is crucial for counselors to develop skills in working with people of different racial backgrounds, sexual orientations, and levels of ability. Chapter 5 focuses on current and emerging influences on the counseling field, including managed care, technology, and holistic approaches to counseling.
- **Part II: Roles and Functions of Clinical Mental Health Counselors.** Clinical mental health counselors are responsible for developing the knowledge and skills needed to conduct a broad array of counseling services. Part II opens with a general description of the counseling process and specific descriptions of activities that occur during the initial, working, and termination stages of counseling. In the next chapter, specific attention is given to two general functions that counselors need to conduct skillfully: assessment and diagnosis. In Chapter 8, other essential counseling services are described, including crisis intervention, prevention, advocacy, and program evaluation.
- **Part III: Working with Specific Populations.** Clinical mental health counselors work with groups, couples, families, and individuals of varying ages. In Chapter 9, we discuss ways to work with groups, and in Chapter 10, we provide an introduction to working with couples and families. In Chapter 11, we describe issues related to counseling adults at different developmental stages. Attention is given to the specific counseling needs of men and women. We focus on children and adolescents in Chapter 12, giving attention to developmental issues, counseling techniques, and specific counseling concerns that face this age group.
- **Part IV: Clinical Mental Health Counseling: Settings and Services.** Clinical mental health counselors are employed in many different profit and nonprofit settings that operate in both the public and private sector. In Chapter 13, several settings in which counselors might be employed are described, including community mental health centers (CMHCs), community agencies, health-care facilities, child and family agencies, and other areas of service. More counseling settings and services are described

in Chapter 14, including career counseling, employee assistance programs, and private practices. We conclude the text with an Epilogue that focuses on the prevention of counselor burnout.

The content of the third edition is based on current research and practices germane to clinical mental health counseling. Information presented in the chapters is supplemented with narratives supplied by mental health professionals employed across counseling setting, who share their views of the rewards and challenges associated with the services they provide. In addition, case studies in each chapter, many of which were written by graduate students practicing in the field, provide opportunities for counselors-in-training to grapple with challenging issues.

ACKNOWLEDGMENTS

It takes the efforts of a community to create and revise a textbook. We want to thank our professional colleagues in the various communities in which we have worked—Wake Forest University, Rockingham Community Mental Health Center (NC), the Trinity Center, Rockingham Community College (NC), Fairfield University (CT), the University of Alabama at Birmingham, and the University of North Carolina at Greensboro. We also want to acknowledge the dedicated mental health professionals who supplied narratives or personal interviews for the text, including John Anderson, Tom Buffkin, Tania Castillero Hoeller, Kelli Coker, Robin Daniel, Pat DeChatelet, Ann Dixon Coppage, Paige Greason, Jay Hale, Peggy Haymes, Susanna Lund, Nick Mazza, Peg McEwen, Ellen Nicola, Mary Claire O'Brien, Peg Olson, Elizabeth Vaughan, Laura Veach, and Dorothy Walker.

Several of our graduate students contributed case studies for various chapters, including Elisabeth Harper, Lolly Hemphill, Katie Lee Hutson, Karen Kegel, Shahnaz Khawaja, Amanda Rich, and Kevin Varner. Throughout the course of the text revision, Wake Forest graduate assistants provided invaluable services, including Cassie Evans, Nathaniel Ivers, Brian Shaw, and Melissa Williams Snapp. A special word of gratitude goes to Elisabeth Harper, who worked tirelessly, sharing her time and expertise to ensure that we would complete the project in a timely manner. We would like to thank the reviewers who provided invaluable comments and suggestions. They are Thomas DeStefano, Northern Arizona University; Margery Shupe, Xavier University; Stephen R. Wester, University of Wisconsin–Milwaukee; and Susan E. Wycoff, California State University, Sacramento. We also thank Steve McCloskey, JD, who provided legal expertise for Chapter 3.

We recognize and are grateful for the contributions of the staff at Merrill/Prentice-Hall: Kevin Davis, Meredith Fossel, Mary Irvin, and Nancy Holstein, whose patience and flexibility made the project manageable.

We are especially thankful for the contributions of our spouses (Claire Gladding and David Newsome) for their patience, encouragement, and suggestions during the textbook revision. We appreciate our children, our families, and our friends for the humor, love, support, and sensitivity they provide on an ongoing basis. Finally, we are fortunate to work with several very special colleagues who listen, challenge, and inspire: John Anderson, Becki Fulton, Paige Greason, Donna Henderson, Pamela Karr, and Laura Veach.

ABOUT THE AUTHORS

Samuel T. Gladding is chair of and a professor in the Department of Counseling at Wake Forest University in Winston-Salem, North Carolina. He is a fellow in the American Counseling Association and its former president (2004–2005). He has also served as president of the Association for Counselor Education and Supervision (ACES), the Association for Specialists in Group Work (ASGW), and Chi Sigma Iota. He is the former editor of the *Journal for Specialists in Group Work* and a current member of the American Counseling Association Foundation and the North Carolina Board of Licensed Professional Counselors.

Dr. Gladding has authored numerous professional publications, including 29 books. In 1999, he was cited as being in the top 1% of contributors to the *Journal of Counseling and Development.* A National Loose spacing Certified Counselor (NCC), a Certified Clinical Mental Health Counselor (CCMHC), and a Licensed Professional Counselor (North Carolina), Dr. Gladding's specialty in counseling is creativity. He is married to Claire Tillson Gladding and is the father of three children—Ben, Nate, and Tim. In his spare time, he enjoys swimming, writing poetry, listening to music, and reading humor.

Deborah W. Newsome is an associate professor in the Department of Counseling at Wake Forest University in Winston-Salem, North Carolina. She served on the Executive Board of the Association for Assessment in Counseling and Education (AACE) for 6 years and is a member of several divisions of the American Counseling Association (ACA). She is a National Certified Counselor (NCC), a Licensed Professional Counselor (LPC), and a Licensed North Carolina School Counselor. She teaches courses in clinical mental health counseling, statistics, assessment, and career counseling. She also supervises graduate students' clinical experiences and volunteers at a local nonprofit counseling center.

Dr. Newsome has coauthored two books and over 20 book chapters and journal articles. In 2005, she received Wake Forest University's Graduate Student Association Faculty Excellence Award. She and her husband, David Newsome, are the parents of two young adults—David, Jr., and Jennifer. She is an avid runner and swimmer and enjoys playing the flute for various community organizations.

BRIEF CONTENTS

CONTENTS

Appendices

PART **1**

Historical and Professional Foundations of Clinical Mental Health Counseling

CHAPTER 1

Historical Overview of the Counseling Profession

There is a quietness that comes
  in the awareness of presenting names
  and recalling places
    in the history of persons
      who come seeking help.
Confusion and direction are a part of the process
  where in trying to sort out tracks
  that parallel into life
    a person's past is traveled.
Counseling is a complex riddle
  where the mind's lines are joined
  with scrambling and precision
    to make sense out of nonsense,
  a tedious process
  like piecing fragments of puzzle together
  until a picture is formed.

Gladding, S. T. (1978). In the midst of the puzzles and counseling journey. *Personnel and Guidance Journal, 57,* 148. © ACA. Reprinted with permission. No further reproduction authorized without written permission of ACA.

The following story was popular when I (Gladding) first entered the counseling profession: A young man took a stroll by a river. As he was walking, he noticed an old woman flailing her arms in the midst of the river and yelling for assistance. Without hesitation, he jumped into the water, swam out, grabbed her, and pulled her to safety. Just as she was recovering, a boy floated past in dire straits. Again, the young man dove into the water and rescued the boy in the same brave way he had done with the older woman. To the young man's chagrin and to the amazement of a small crowd that was gathering on the banks of the stream, a third person, a middle-aged executive, came floating by yelling for help. The young man was a hero once more with his rescue of the businessman.

Exhausted, he then started walking upstream. As he did, a bystander asked him, "Aren't you going to stay to rescue others who may fall in the river and need you?"

The young man replied, "No. I'm going farther up the river to find out why these people are falling in."

The story illustrates a key component of counseling in general and of community and agency counseling in particular: Counseling focuses on prevention whenever possible and on altering people's environments to make them hospitable as opposed to hostile.

The term *community counseling* was initially coined by Amos and Williams (1972) and later by Lewis and Lewis (1977) to identify counseling activities that took place outside other established domains, such as educational settings. In 1984, the Association of Counselor Educators and Supervisors (ACES) Committee on Community Counseling described community counseling as a process and orientation that:

- Favors using a multifaceted approach that is developmental and educative
- Emphasizes prevention
- Takes into account the effects of the community on the client
- Seeks to empower clients through advocacy (Hayes, 1984)

These basic premises, which highlight development, prevention, client–environment interaction, and empowerment, continue to characterize community counseling today, as well as the profession of counseling in general.

Remley and Herlihy (2010) summarized key points that provide the foundation for the professional identity of counselors. These guiding principles are

1. The best perspective for helping people resolve their personal and emotional issues is the wellness model for mental health. From a wellness perspective, mental health is viewed as occurring on a continuum, and the goal of counseling is to help the person move toward a higher level of wellness, rather than to cure an illness.
2. Many of the personal and emotional issues people experience can best be understood from a developmental perspective. Understanding the dynamics of human growth and development and addressing clients' concerns accordingly are key components of successful counseling.
3. Prevention and early intervention are preferable to remediation, whenever possible. Prevention activities include psychoeducational groups, training seminars, career exploration groups, and a host of other activities. Early intervention, which occurs when a client is at risk of experiencing personal or emotional problems, can help keep problems from escalating.
4. The goal of counseling is to empower clients to solve problems independently. Counseling is viewed as a transitory process through which clients increase their self-understanding and problem-solving ability.

In 1975, there was a push for establishing a division for counselors who worked in community and agency settings, and in June 1978, the American Mental Health Counselors Association was accepted as a division of American Personnel and Guidance Association (APGA; Weikel, 1996). The new division had 12,000 members and published a journal, *The Journal of Mental Health Counseling*. Mental health and community counselors both worked in community and agency settings; however, there continued to be a distinction between the two. Most notably, community counseling was not recognized as a separate division in APGA. The first training standards for mental health counselors were prepared by

Seiler, Brooks, and Beck (1987), and the 1988 Council for Accreditation of Counseling and Related Educational Programs (CACREP) Standards recognized mental health counseling as a specialty area. By 1994, CACREP had accredited four mental health counseling programs, and an additional six programs were included under community counseling accredited programs (Sweeney, 1995). Through the 1990s, the number of mental health specialty programs grew, although the number of accredited programs never approached that of community counseling accredited programs. Indeed, there was much debate regarding the distinctions between the two specialty areas, and in 2008, CACREP voted to approve a combined specialty area, clinical mental health counseling, which is discussed in more detail in the next chapter.

Today, community and mental health counselors provide services to a wide spectrum of people in a variety of settings. In some settings, the typical concerns expressed by clients may require short-term intervention. However, counselors also are trained to work with clients dealing with more serious concerns, requiring interventions of longer duration and an ability to implement evidenced-based practices. Counseling's emphasis on development, prevention, and treatment makes it attractive to those seeking healthy life-stage transitions and productive lives free from disorders (Romano, 1992).

BOX 1–1

"Practicing counselors are concerned about pathology, but not from a myopic perspective. People develop difficulties (and in many cases pathology) at various times during their developmental life span. Effectively dealing with pathology does not preclude using a developmental framework. Furthermore, an understanding of the developmental course of numerous disorders is an important aspect of prevention, accurate diagnosis, and treatment."

(Hinkle, 1999, p. 469)

The broad profession of counseling and its specialty areas have evolved over the years. Many people, unaware of that evolution, forget that the counseling profession has always stressed growth and focused on people in many stages of life. Therefore, it is important to examine the history of counseling in the broadest context possible. In the next section, the historical events and circumstances that have shaped the counseling profession are highlighted. Understanding the past can lead to a better appreciation of the present and future trends of the profession.

A CHRONOLOGICAL OVERVIEW OF PROFESSIONAL COUNSELING

One way to chart the evolution of counseling is to trace important events and personal influences through the decades of the 20th century and into the 21st century. Keep in mind that the development of professional counseling, like the activity itself, was and is a process. Therefore, some names and events will not fit neatly into a rigid chronology. Furthermore, changes in the profession continue to occur, even as this text is being revised. For example, the title of the book includes the term, *clinical mental health counselor*. This change in terminology reflects the recent adoption of the 2009 CACREP Standards. The 2009 Standards no longer include the specialty areas of community counseling and mental health counseling. Instead, the two areas have been merged into one specialty area: clinical mental health counseling. We discuss the change in more depth in Chapter 2. Throughout the text, we use a variety of terms to represent counselors who work in community and agency settings, including *clinical mental health counselors, community and agency counselors,* and *mental health practitioners.*

Before 1900

Counseling is a relatively new profession (Aubrey, 1977, 1982). It developed in the late 1890s and early 1900s and was interdisciplinary from its inception. Some of the roles carried out by counselors were and are shared by other individuals in the helping professions (Herr & Fabian, 1993).

Before the 1900s, most counseling was informal, characterized by sharing advice or information. In the United States, counseling developed from a humanitarian concern to improve people's lives in communities adversely affected by the Industrial Revolution of the mid- to late 1800s (Aubrey, 1983). The social welfare reform movement (now known as social justice), the spread of public education, and various changes in population makeup of the time (e.g., the influx of a large number of immigrants) also influenced the growth of the new profession (Aubrey, 1977; Goodyear, 1984).

Most of the pioneers in counseling identified themselves as social reformers and educators. They focused on teaching children and young adults about themselves, others, and the world of work. Initially, these helpers were involved primarily in child/adult welfare, educational/vocational guidance, and legal reform. Their work was built on specific information and lessons, such as moral instruction on being good and doing right and developing interpersonal skills (Nugent & Jones, 2005). They saw needs in American society and took steps to fulfill them. Classroom teachers and agency administrators were the main practitioners. These individuals were not called counselors; in fact, "no mention of counseling was made in the professional literature until 1931" (Aubrey, 1983, p. 78).

1900–1909

Community counseling began as an infant profession in the early 1900s, when the helping process was largely dominated by Freud's psychoanalytic theory and behaviorism. During this decade, three persons emerged as leaders: Frank Parsons, Jesse B. Davis, and Clifford Beers.

Frank Parsons, a Boston educator, focused on growth and prevention. Parsons has been characterized as a broad scholar, a persuasive writer, a tireless activist, and a great intellect (Davis, 1988; Zytowski, 1985). Parsons was a true "Renaissance man" with a colorful life career in multiple disciplines, including that of lawyer, engineer, college professor, social, worker, and social activist (Hartung & Blustein, 2002; Pope & Sweinsdottir, 2005). Often called the Father of Guidance, he is best known for having founded Boston's Vocational Bureau in 1908, which represented a major step in the development of vocational guidance.

Parsons worked with young people who were in the process of making career decisions. He theorized that choosing a vocation was a matter of relating three factors: a knowledge of the world of work, a knowledge of self, and the use of *true reasoning* to match the two (Drummond & Ryan, 1995). To facilitate this process, Parsons devised a number of procedures to help his clients learn more about themselves and the world of work. His efforts provided the foundation on which modern career counseling is based (Kiselica & Robinson, 2001).

Parsons's book, *Choosing a Vocation* (1909), published a year after his death, was quite influential, especially in Boston. For example, having been influenced by Parsons,

Boston's school superintendent, Stratton Brooks, designated 117 elementary and secondary teachers as "vocational counselors" (Nugent & Jones, 2005). The "Boston example" soon spread to other major cities as others recognized the need for vocational planning. By 1910, 35 cities were attempting to emulate Boston (Lee, 1966). Parsons's contributions as a scholar and as an activist had a profound influence on the evolution of community and agency counseling.

Jesse B. Davis was the first person to set up a systematized guidance program in the public schools (Aubrey, 1977). As superintendent of the Grand Rapids, Michigan, school system, he suggested in 1907 that classroom teachers of English composition teach their students lessons in guidance once a week to help prevent problems and build character. Influenced by such progressive American educators as Horace Mann and John Dewey, Davis believed that proper guidance would help cure the ills of American society. What he and other progressive educators advocated was not counseling in the modern sense but a forerunner of counseling: *school guidance* (a preventive educational means of teaching students how to deal effectively with life events). Davis's focus on prevention continues to be a key component of community and agency counseling in the 21st century.

A third figure who significantly affected the emerging counseling profession was Clifford Beers. Beers, a former Yale student, was hospitalized for mental illness several times during his lifetime. He found conditions in mental institutions deplorable and exposed them in his book, *A Mind That Found Itself* (1908), which became a popular best-seller. Beers used his book to advocate for better mental health facilities and reform in the treatment of the mentally ill. His work had an especially powerful influence on the fields of psychiatry and clinical psychology, where many of the practitioners referred to their activities as *counseling* (Hansen, Rossberg, & Cramer, 1994). Beers's work was the impetus for the mental health movement in the United States and for advocacy groups that exist today, including the National Mental Health Association and the National Alliance for the Mentally Ill.

1910s

The contributions of Parsons, Beers, and Davis during the initial decade of the century led to the emergence of several "firsts" during the next decade. The first university-level course in vocational guidance was offered at Harvard University in 1911. The first citywide school guidance program was established in Grand Rapids, Michigan, in 1912; and in 1913, the National Vocational Guidance Association (NVGA), the first national professional organization in the counseling field, was founded (Hershenson, Power, & Waldo, 1996).

The NVGA began publishing a bulletin in 1915 (Goodyear, 1984). In 1921, the *National Vocational Guidance Bulletin* started regular publication. It evolved in later years to become the *National Vocational Guidance Magazine* (1924–1933), *Occupations: The Vocational Guidance Magazine* (1933–1944), *Occupations: The Vocational Guidance Journal* (1944–1952), *Personnel and Guidance Journal* (1952–1984), and finally, the *Journal of Counseling and Development* (1984). NVGA was important because it established an association offering guidance literature, and it provided an organization for people interested in vocational counseling.

An interest in testing, especially group testing, emerged during this decade as a result of World War I. To screen its personnel, the U.S. Army commissioned the development of numerous psychological instruments, among them the *Army Alpha* and *Army Beta* intelligence tests. Several of the Army's screening devices were used in civilian populations after the war, and *psychometrics* (psychological testing) became a popular movement and an early foundation on which counseling was based.

Aubrey (1977) observed that because the vocational guidance movement developed without an explicit philosophy, it quickly embraced psychometrics to gain a legitimate foothold in psychology. Reliance on psychometrics had both positive and negative effects. On the positive side, it gave vocational guidance specialists a stronger and more "scientific" identity. On the negative side, it distracted many specialists from developments in other behavioral sciences, such as sociology, biology, and anthropology.

1920s

The 1920s were relatively quiet for the developing community counseling profession. This was a period of consolidation. Education courses for counselors, which had begun at Harvard in 1911, almost exclusively emphasized vocational guidance during the 1920s. The dominant influences on the emerging profession were the progressive theories of education and the federal government's use of guidance services with war veterans.

A notable event was the certification of counselors in Boston and New York in the mid-1920s. Another turning point was the development of the first standards for the preparation and evaluation of occupational materials (Lee, 1966). Along with these standards came the publication of new psychological instruments, including Edward Strong's *Strong Vocational Interest Inventory (SVII)* in 1927. The publication of this instrument set the stage for future directions for assessment in counseling (Strong, 1943).

A final noteworthy event of the decade was Abraham and Hannah Stone's 1929 establishment of the first marriage and family counseling center in New York City. Other centers soon developed throughout the nation, marking the beginning of the specialty of marriage and family counseling.

1930s

The 1930s were not as quiet as the 1920s, in part because the Great Depression influenced researchers and practitioners, especially in university and vocational settings, to emphasize helping strategies and counseling methods that related to employment. A highlight of the decade was the development of the first theory of counseling, which was formulated by E. G. Williamson and his colleagues (including John Darley and Donald Paterson) at the University of Minnesota. Williamson modified Parsons's theory and used it to work with students and the unemployed. His emphasis on a directive, counselor-centered approach came to be known by several names, including the *Minnesota point of view* and *trait-factor counseling*. Williamson's (1939) pragmatic approach promoted the counselor's teaching, mentoring, and influencing skills.

One premise of Williamson's theory was that persons had traits (e.g., aptitudes, interests, personalities, achievements) that could be integrated in a variety of ways to form factors (constellations of individual characteristics). Counseling was based on a scientific, problem-solving, empirical method that was individually tailored to each client to help him or her stop nonproductive thinking and become an effective decision maker (Lynch & Maki, 1981). Williamson's influence dominated counseling for the next two decades, and he continued to write about the theory into the 1970s (Williamson & Biggs, 1979).

Another major occurrence was the broadening of counseling beyond occupational concerns. The seeds of this development were sown in the 1920s, when Edward Thorndike and other psychologists began to challenge the vocational orientation of the guidance movement (Lee, 1966). The work of John Brewer paralleled this change in emphasis. His 1932 book, *Education as Guidance,* proposed that every teacher be a counselor and that guidance be incorporated into the school curriculum. Brewer believed that all education should focus on preparing students to live outside the school environment. His emphasis helped counselors see vocational decisions as just one part of their responsibilities. Although Brewer's work initially had the most relevance for counselors who worked in schools, it later affected counselors working in community settings.

During the 1930s, the U.S. government became more involved in counseling. For example, in 1938 Congress passed the George-Dean Act that created the Vocational Education Division of the U.S. Office of Education and an Occupational Information and Guidance Service (Sweeney, 2001). Furthermore, the government established the U.S. Employment Service, which published the first edition of the *Dictionary of Occupational Titles* (*DOT*) in 1939. The *DOT,* which became a major source of career information for vocational counselors, described known occupations in the United States and coded them according to job titles.

1940s

Three major events in the 1940s radically shaped the practice of counseling: the theory of Carl Rogers, World War II, and the government's involvement in post–World War II counseling.

Carl Rogers rose to prominence in 1942 with the publication of *Counseling and Psychotherapy,* which challenged the counselor-centered approach of Williamson as well as major tenets of Freudian psychoanalysis. Rogers espoused a nondirective approach to counseling that focused on the client. His ideas were both widely accepted and harshly criticized. Rogers advocated giving clients the responsibility for their own growth. He thought that if clients had an opportunity to be accepted and heard, then they would begin to know themselves better and become more congruent (genuine). The counselor, acting in a nonjudgmental, accepting role, served as a mirror, reflecting the verbal and emotional manifestations of the client.

Aubrey (1977) noted that before Rogers, the literature in counseling was very practical, dealing with topics such as testing, cumulative records, orientation procedures, vocational issues, and the goals and purposes of guidance. With Rogers, there was a new emphasis on the importance of the counseling relationship, skills, and goals. Guidance, for all intents and purposes, suddenly disappeared as a major consideration in the bulk of the literature and was replaced by a decade or more of concentration on counseling. The Rogers revolution had a major impact on both counseling and psychology. In addition to Rogers's nondirective, person-centered theory, a considerable number of alternative systems of psychotherapy emerged during this decade (Corsini, 2008).

With the advent of World War II, the U.S. government needed counselors and psychologists to help select and train specialists for the military and for industry (Ohlsen, 1983). The war also brought about a new way of looking at vocations for men and women. During the war, many women worked outside the home. Women's contributions to work and to the well-being of the United States during the crisis of war made a lasting impact. Traditional occupational sex roles began to be questioned, and greater emphasis was placed on personal freedom.

Also during the war, mental health professionals worked successfully with a large number of military personnel who suffered emotional breakdowns. The National Institute of

Mental Health was established, and in 1946, the National Mental Health Act was passed, which authorized funds for research and training to prevent and treat mental health disorders (Hershenson et al., 1996).

After the war, the U.S. Veterans Administration (VA) funded the training of counselors and psychologists by granting stipends and paid internships to students engaged in graduate study. Monies made available through the VA and the GI Bill (benefits for veterans) influenced teaching professionals in graduate education to define their curriculum offerings more precisely. Counseling, as a profession, began to move further away from its historical alliance with vocational development.

1950s

"If one decade in history had to be singled out for the most profound impact on counselors, it would be the 1950s" (Aubrey, 1977, p. 292). Indeed, the 1950s produced at least four major events that dramatically affected the history of counseling:

- The establishment of the American Personnel and Guidance Association (APGA)
- The establishment of Division 17 (Counseling Psychology) within the American Psychological Association (APA)
- The passage of the National Defense Education Act (NDEA)
- The introduction of new guidance and counseling theories

AMERICAN PERSONNEL AND GUIDANCE ASSOCIATION. APGA grew out of the Council of Guidance and Personnel Association (CGPA), a loose confederation of organizations "concerned with educational and vocational guidance and other personnel activities" (Harold, 1985, p. 4). CGPA operated from 1935 to 1951, but its major drawback was its inability to commit its members to any course of action. APGA was formed in 1952 with the purpose of formally organizing groups interested in guidance, counseling, and personnel matters. Its original four divisions were the American College Personnel Association (Division 1), the National Association of Guidance Supervisors and Counselor Trainers (Division 2), the NVGA (Division 3), and the Student Personnel Association for Teacher Education (Division 4). During its early history, APGA was more of an interest group than a professional organization, because it did not originate or enforce standards for membership (Super, 1955).

DIVISION 17. In 1952, the Society of Counseling Psychology (Division 17) of APA was formally established. It was initially known as the Division of Counseling Psychology. Its formation required dropping the term *guidance* from what had formerly been the association's Counseling and Guidance Division. Part of the impetus for the division's creation came from the VA, but the main impetus came from APA members interested in working with a more "normal" population than the one seen by clinical psychologists (Whitely, 1984).

Once created, Division 17 became more fully defined. Super (1955), for instance, distinguished between counseling psychology and clinical psychology, holding that counseling psychology was more concerned with normal human growth and development and was influenced in its approach by both vocational counseling and humanistic psychotherapy. Despite Super's work, counseling psychology had a difficult time establishing a clear identity within the APA (Whitely, 1984). Yet the division's existence has had a major impact on the growth and development of counseling as a profession. In fact, luminaries in the counseling profession such as Gilbert Wrenn and Donald Super held offices in both Division 17 and in APGA divisions for years and published in the periodicals of both.

NATIONAL DEFENSE EDUCATION ACT.   A third major event was the passage in 1958 of the National Defense Education Act (NDEA), which was enacted following the Soviet Union's launching of their first space satellite, *Sputnik I.* The act's primary purpose was to identify scientifically and academically talented students and promote their development. Through Titles V-A and V-B, funds were provided for upgrading school counseling programs and for training school counselors. In 1964, NDEA was extended to include elementary school counseling. By 1965, the number of school counselors exceeded 30,000 (Armour, 1969). Because of NDEA, funding was provided for institutes designed to train school counselors. School counselors were plentiful, and it became possible for counselor educators to consider offering programs in community and agency settings.

NEW THEORIES.   Several new counseling theories emerged during the 1950s. Prior to that time, four main theories influenced the work of counselors: (a) psychoanalysis and insight theories (e.g., Sigmund Freud); (b) trait–factor or directive theories (e.g., E. G. Williamson); (c) humanistic and client-centered theories (e.g., Carl Rogers); and, to a lesser extent, (d) behavioral theories (e.g., B. F. Skinner). Debates among counselors usually centered on whether directive or nondirective counseling was more effective, and almost all counselors assumed that certain tenets of psychoanalysis (e.g., defense mechanisms) were true.

During the 1950s, debate gradually shifted away from this focus as new theories of helping began to emerge. Behavioral theories, such as Joseph Wolpe's systematic desensitization, began to gain influence. Cognitive theories made an appearance, as witnessed by the growth of Albert Ellis's rational-emotive therapy, Eric Berne's transactional analysis, and Aaron Beck's cognitive therapy. Learning theory, self-concept theory, and advances in developmental psychology made an impact as well (Aubrey, 1977). By the end of the decade, the number and complexity of theories associated with counseling had grown considerably and were applicable to settings outside the educational environment.

1960s

The initial focus of the 1960s was on counseling as a developmental profession. Gilbert Wrenn set the tone for the decade in his widely influential book, *The Counselor in a Changing World* (1962). His emphasis, reinforced by other prominent professionals such as Leona Tyler and Donald Blocher, was on working with others to resolve developmental needs. Wrenn's book was influential throughout the 1960s, and he, along with Tyler, became one of the strongest counseling advocates in the United States.

The impact of the developmental model in counseling lessened, however, as the decade continued, primarily because of three events: the Vietnam War, the civil rights movement, and the women's movement. Each event stirred up passions and pointed out particular needs within our society. Many counselors directed their attention to social issues related to these events.

Other powerful influences that emerged during the decade were the humanistic counseling theories of Dugald Arbuckle, Abraham Maslow, and Sidney Jourard. Also important was the phenomenal growth of the group movement (Gladding, 2008). The emphasis of counseling shifted from a one-on-one encounter to small-group interaction. Behavioral counseling grew in prominence with the appearance of John Krumboltz's *Revolution in Counseling* (1966), which promoted learning (beyond insight) as the root of change. Thus, the decade's initial focus on development shifted somewhat, although an awareness of the need for counseling throughout society had grown.

Professionalism within APGA increased during the 1960s. In 1961, APGA published a "sound code of ethics for counselors" (Nugent, 1981, p. 28). In 1969, Division 17 of APA, which had further clarified the definition of a counseling psychologist at the 1964 Greyston Conference, began publishing a professional journal, *The Counseling Psychologist,* with Gilbert Wrenn as its first editor. This journal, along with the *Personnel and Guidance Journal,* accepted articles representing a wide range of counseling interests.

Particularly important to the evolution of community and agency counseling was the passage of the 1963 Community Mental Health Centers Act. The goal of this landmark act was to establish a nationwide system of community mental health centers (CMHCs) that would serve the needs of America's newly deinstitutionalized mentally ill population by focusing on outpatient, community-based services (Winegar, 1993). These centers opened up new counseling employment opportunities outside educational settings. For instance, alcohol abuse counseling and addiction counseling (initially called drug abuse counseling) began in the 1960s and were offered in mental health centers. Marriage and family counseling became more prominent because of the increase in America's divorce rate (Hollis, 2000). Many counselor education programs changed their focus from preparing counselors for work in schools to preparing counselors for work in community agencies (Hershenson et al., 1996).

A final noteworthy milestone was the establishment of the ERIC Clearinghouse on Counseling and Personnel Services (ERIC/CAPS) at the University of Michigan. Founded in 1966 by Garry Walz and funded by the Office of Educational Research and Improvement at the U.S. Department of Education, ERIC/CAPS provided multiple sources of information about counseling activities and trends in the United States and throughout the world. It also sponsored conferences on leading topics in counseling that brought national leaders together.

1970s

The 1970s saw the emergence of several trends. Among the more important were the rapid growth of counseling outside educational settings, the formation of helping-skills programs, the beginning of licensure for counselors, and the further development of APGA as a professional organization for counselors.

DIVERSIFICATION IN COUNSELING SETTINGS.   The rapid growth of counseling outside educational institutions started in the 1970s, when mental health centers and community agencies began to employ significant numbers of counselors. Before this time, the majority of counselors had been employed in educational settings, usually public schools. But the demand for school counselors decreased as the economy underwent several recessions and the number of school-age children began to decline. In addition, the number of counselor education programs increased from 327 in 1964 to about 475 by 1980 (Hollis & Wantz, 1980). This dramatic rise in the number of counselor education programs meant that more counselors were competing for available jobs (Steinhauser, 1985).

The diversification of counseling resulted in specialized training in counselor education programs and in the development of new concepts of counseling. For example, Lewis and

Lewis (1977) used the term *community counselor* to describe a new type of counselor who could function in multidimensional roles regardless of employment setting. Many community counseling programs were established, and counselors became more common in such agencies as mental health clinics, hospices, employee assistance programs, psychiatric hospitals, and substance abuse centers. Equally as striking, and more dramatic in growth, was the formation of the American Mental Health Counselor Association (AMHCA) within APGA. Founded in 1976, AMHCA quickly became one of the largest divisions within APGA and united *mental health counselors* into a professional organization in which they defined their roles and goals.

HELPING-SKILLS PROGRAMS.   The 1970s saw the development of helping-skills programs that concentrated on relationship and communication skills. Initiated by Truax and Carkhuff (1967) and Ivey (1971), these programs taught basic counseling skills to professionals and nonprofessionals alike. The emphasis was humanistic and eclectic. It was assumed that certain fundamental skills should be mastered to establish satisfactory personal interaction. A bonus for counselors who received this type of training was that they could teach the skills to others rather easily. Thus, counselors could now consult by teaching some of their skills to their colleagues.

STATE LICENSURE.   By the mid-1970s, state boards of examiners for psychologists had become more restrictive. Some of their restrictions, such as barring graduates of counseling programs in education departments from taking the psychology licensure exam, caused considerable tension, not only between APA and APGA but also within the APA membership itself (Ohlsen, 1983). The result was APGA's move toward state and national licensure for counselors. In 1976, Virginia became the first state to adopt a counselor licensure law. It was followed quickly by Arkansas and Alabama before the decade ended.

A STRONG APGA.   During the 1970s, APGA emerged as an even stronger professional organization. Several changes altered its image and function, one of which was the building of its own headquarters in Alexandria, Virginia. APGA also began to question its professional identification because personnel and guidance seemed to be outmoded ways of defining the organization's emphases.

In 1973, the Association of Counselor Educators and Supervisors (ACES), a division of APGA, outlined the standards for a master's degree in counseling. In 1977, ACES approved guidelines for doctoral preparation in counseling (Stripling, 1978). During the decade, the membership of the organization increased to almost 40,000, and five new divisions (including AMHCA) were chartered.

1980s

The 1980s saw the continued growth of counseling as a profession, exemplified by proactive initiatives from counselors associated with APGA and Division 17. Among the most noteworthy events of the decade were those that standardized the training and certification of counselors, recognized counseling as a distinct profession, increased the diversification of counselor specialties, and emphasized human growth and development.

STANDARDIZATION OF TRAINING AND CERTIFICATION.   The move toward standardized training and certification of counselors began early in the decade and grew stronger yearly.

In 1981, the Council for Accreditation of Counseling and Related Educational Programs (CACREP) was formed as an affiliate organization of APGA. It refined the standards first proposed by ACES in the late 1970s and initially accredited four programs and grandparented programs already recognized as accredited by the California State Counselor Association and ACES (Steinhauser & Bradley, 1983). In 1987, CACREP achieved membership in the Council on Postsecondary Accreditation (COPA), thereby putting it on a par with such accreditation bodies as the APA (Herr, 1985). CACREP standardized counselor education programs for master's and doctoral programs in the areas of school, community/agency, mental health, marriage and family counseling/therapy, and personnel services for college students. The inclusion of community/agency counseling in CACREP accreditation further strengthened this specialty within the profession.

Complementing the work of CACREP, the National Board for Certified Counselors (NBCC), which was formed in 1982, began to certify counselors on a national level. The NBCC developed a standardized test and defined eight major subject areas in which counselors should be knowledgeable: (a) human growth and development, (b) social and cultural foundations, (c) helping relationships, (d) groups, (e) lifestyle and career development, (f) appraisal, (g) research and evaluation, and (h) professional orientation. To become a National Certified Counselor (NCC), examinees were required to pass a standardized test and meet experiential and character reference qualifications. In 1984, NBCC set up standards for certifying career counselors, and as a result, many individuals became National Certified Career Counselors (NCCC; Herr, 1985). By the end of the decade, there were approximately 17,000 NCC professionals.

Finally, in collaboration with CACREP, the National Academy of Certified Clinical Mental Health Counselors (NACCMHC), an affiliate of AMHCA, continued to define training standards and certify counselors in mental health counseling, a process it had begun in the late 1970s (Seiler et al., 1987; Wilmarth, 1985). It also began training supervisors of mental health counselors in 1988. Both programs attracted thousands of new professionals into counseling and upgraded the credentials of those already in the field.

COUNSELING AS A DISTINCT PROFESSION.   A profession is characterized by its "role statements, codes of ethics, accreditation guidelines, competency standards, licensure, certification and other standards of excellence" (VanZandt, 1990, p. 243). The evolution of counseling in the 1980s as a distinct mental health profession came as a result of events, issues, and forces, both inside and outside APGA (Heppner, 1990). Inside APGA, there was a growing awareness among its leaders that the words *personnel* and *guidance* no longer described the work of its members. In 1983, after considerable debate, APGA changed its name to the American Association for Counseling and Development (AACD) to "reflect the changing demographics of its membership and the settings in which they worked" (Herr, 1985, p. 395). The name change symbolized the rapid transformation in identity that APGA members had been experiencing through the implementation of policies regarding training, certification, and standards. External events that influenced APGA to change its name and ultimately its focus included legislation, especially on the federal level, that recognized mental health providers and actions by other mental health services associations.

Moreover, professional commitment among members of AACD increased. Chi Sigma Iota, an international academic and professional honor society, was formed in 1985 to promote excellence in the profession. By the end of the decade, it had grown to over 100 chapters and 5,000 members (Sweeney, 1989). Furthermore, liability insurance policies, new counseling specialty publications, legal defense funds, legislative initiatives, and a variety of other membership services were made available to AACD members (J. Myers, personal communication, 1990). By 1989, over 58,000 individuals had become members of AACD, an increase of over 18,000 members in 10 years.

DIVERSIFICATION OF COUNSELING.   During the 1980s, counselors became even more diversified. Large numbers of counselors continued to be employed in primary and secondary schools and in higher education in a variety of student personnel services. Mental health counselors and community/agency counselors were the two largest blocks of professionals outside formal educational environments. In addition, the number of counselors swelled in mental health settings for business employees, the aging, and married persons and families. Symbolic of that growth, the Association for Adult Development and Aging (AADA) and the International Association for Marriage and Family Counselors (IAMFC) were organized and chartered as divisions of the American Counseling Association (ACA) in 1987 and 1990, respectively.

Strong membership in AACD divisions dedicated to group work, counselor education, humanistic education, measurement and development, religious and value issues, employment and career development, rehabilitation, multicultural concerns, offender work, and military personnel further exemplified the diversity of counseling during the 1980s. Special issues of AACD journals focused on such topics as violence (*Journal of Counseling and Development,* March 1987), the gifted and talented (*Journal of Counseling and Development,* May 1986), the arts (*Journal of Mental Health Counseling,* January 1985), and prevention (*Elementary School Guidance and Counseling,* October 1989). These publications helped broaden the scope of counseling services and counselor awareness.

INCREASED EMPHASIS ON HUMAN GROWTH AND DEVELOPMENT.   Counseling's emphasis on human growth and development during the 1980s took several forms. For example, new emphasis was placed on developmental counseling across the life span (Gladstein & Apfel, 1987). New behavioral expressions associated with Erik Erikson's first five stages of life development were formulated (Hamachek, 1988). An increased emphasis on the development of adults and the elderly was most clearly represented by the formation of the Association for Adult Aging and Development (AAAD) and by the development of curriculum guides that infused gerontological counseling into counselor preparation programs.

A second way that human growth and development was stressed was through increased attention to gender issues and sexual orientation (see, for example, O'Neil & Carroll, 1988; Pearson, 1988; Weinrach, 1987). Carol Gilligan's (1982) landmark study on the development of moral values in females, which helped introduce feminist theory into the counseling arena, forced human growth specialists to examine the differences between genders more thoroughly. There was more of an emphasis on moral development as research in the area increased (Colangelo, 1985; Lapsley & Quintana, 1985).

Finally, the challenges of working with different ethnic and cultural groups were discussed intensely (Ponterotto & Casas, 1987). The Association for Multicultural Counseling and Development (AMCD) assumed a leadership role in these discussions, but multicultural themes, such as the importance of diversity, became a central issue among all groups, especially in light of the renewed racism that developed in the 1980s (Carter, 1990).

Overall, the increased emphasis on human growth and development highlighted the need for counseling in a variety of settings. The innovations of the 1980s enhanced the professional status of community counselors in a number of areas, and the actual number of community counselors graduating from counselor education programs began to exceed the number of school counselors for the first time in history.

1990s

Changes in the evolution of the counseling profession continued into the 1990s. One change that was significant was the 1992 decision by the American Association for Counseling and Development (AACD) to modify its name and become the American Counseling Association (ACA). The new name better reflected the membership and mission of the organization. Three new divisions within ACA were founded: the American College Counseling Association in 1991, the Association for Gay, Lesbian, and Bisexual Issues in Counseling in 1996, and Counselors for Social Justice in 1999. By the end of the decade, ACA was composed of 18 different divisions.

A second noteworthy event of the decade was the continued strong emphasis on counseling issues related to multiculturalism and diversity. In 1992, Sue, Arredondo, and McDavis published a set of multicultural competencies and standards to guide professionals who were working with people of different races. This important publication set the stage for a larger debate about the nature of multiculturalism. Some leaders in the field adopted a more inclusive definition of multicultural counseling, taking into account differences in language, socioeconomic status, gender, sexual orientation, physical abilities, race, culture, and ethnicity (Lee, 1997). Much discussion occurred, and continues to occur, about what diversity and counseling within a pluralistic society entail (Weinrach & Thomas, 1998).

A third noteworthy event that had particular significance for community and mental health counselors also occurred in 1992. For the first time, counseling was included as a primary mental health profession in the health care human resource statistics compiled by the Center for Mental Health Services and by the National Institute of Mental Health (Manderscheid & Sonnenschein, 1992). This recognition put counseling on a par with other mental health specialties such as psychology, social work, and psychiatry. By the beginning of the 21st century, there were approximately 100,000 certified or licensed counselors in the United States (Pope & Wedding, 2008).

The provision of health care in general, including mental health care, significantly affected the counseling profession during the 1990s. The explosive growth of managed care organizations during the decade has been described as a revolution in the private mental health care delivery system (Winegar, 1993). Conglomerates emerged, and many counselors became providers for health maintenance organizations (HMOs). Consequently, the number of independent counselors decreased, as did the number of sessions a counselor could offer under managed health care plans. A new emphasis on legislation connected with these organizations forced counselors to become increasingly informed and active as legislative proponents (Barstow, 1998).

In addition, there was a renewed focus within the decade on counseling issues related to the whole person. Counselors focused on a range of factors that affect mental health, including spirituality, prevention, wellness, social interaction, and socioeconomic status (Bemak, 1998).

Other developments within the decade included the following:

- The merger of NACCMHC with NBCC to credential counselors
- The growth of CACREP- and APA-accredited programs in counselor education and counseling psychology, both on the master's and doctoral levels

- An increase in the number of counseling-related publications by ACA, APA, commercial publishers, and the ERIC Clearinghouse on Counseling and Student Services (ERIC/CASS)
- The growth of Chi Sigma Iota to over 200 chapters and 20,000 members

CURRENT TRENDS IN THE NEW MILLENNIUM

In 2002, the counseling profession formally celebrated its 50th anniversary as a profession under the umbrella of the American Counseling Association. However, within the celebration was a realization that the profession is ever changing and that emphases during the 21st century would most likely change with the evolving needs of clients and society. A wide range of issues, including the changing roles of men and women, innovations in media and technology, trauma and crises, aging, poverty, and social justice, captured the profession's attention as the new century began and continues to be salient today (Lee & Walz, 1998; Webber, Bass, & Yep, 2005). For clinical mental health counselors, the manner in which mental health care is provided and funded, particularly as it relates to managed care organizations, continues to be a prominent area of concern.

Of particular importance to counselors in the 21st century is the need to select counseling interventions based on outcome research. Counselors need to select *evidence-based interventions* that answer Gordon Paul's well-known question: "What works best with this particular client, with this particular problem, with this particular counselor, in this particular setting?" Counselors are challenged to refine, implement, and evaluate interventions that are empirically based.

Counselors today are using a variety of therapies, some traditional, some alternative, and some that were developed earlier for use in other disciplines but have only recently become part of the counseling world. Examples of such therapies include Eye Movement Desensitization and Reprocessing (EMDR; especially useful for trauma victims and clients with posttraumatic stress disorder), hypnosis, neurofeedback (a form of brainwave feedback), and postmodern therapies, such as narrative approaches. As the worlds of science, psychology, and mental health and well-being continue to converge, we anticipate that counselors will receive training in psych-biological-social approaches that have demonstrated effectiveness.

Perhaps the most pressing concern of the 21st century is finding ways to deal with conflict, violence, and trauma. In the 1990s, heightened concern about conflict and safety emerged during a rash of school shootings and the Oklahoma City bombing, which resulted in the deaths of many innocent people (Daniels, 2002). A defining moment in conflict and violence occurred on September 11, 2001, when terrorists crashed commercial airliners into the World Trade Center towers in New York City and into the Pentagon in Washington, D.C. These acts signaled the beginning of an active, new emphasis in counseling on preparing and responding to trauma and tragedies such as those associated with Hurricane Katrina, the Iraq War, and the Virginia Tech shootings (Walz & Kirkman, 2002; Webber et al., 2005). Counselors have become increasingly aware of the need to develop crisis plans and strategies for working with different populations affected by violence and tragedy. As a response, ACA created a Crisis Response Planning Task Force to prepare counselors to implement disaster mental health services on a large scale (Kaplan, 2002). Many community and agency counselors have participated in disaster relief training coordinated by the American Red Cross, and others have made plans to do so. Perhaps now more than ever before, counselors recognize the need to develop skills in helping clients cope with violence, trauma, and tragedy.

The wars in Iraq and Afghanistan have created an increased need for counseling professionals to develop skills needed to work with military families and veterans. A military-funded study of the mental health of troops deployed in Iraq indicated that soldiers returning from deployment, particularly those who have been deployed more than once, often exhibit a range of mental health symptoms, ranging from anxiety and sleeplessness to severe depression and posttraumatic stress disorder (Shanker, 2008). Recent federal legislation has paved the way for more counselors to work with veterans, although their autonomy in working with the U.S. Department of Veteran Affairs and Department of Defense is tenuous. Thus, the importance of advocating for the counseling profession on the national level remains high.

Several other counseling-related issues have evolved during the first decade of the 21st century. Finding effective ways to work with elderly clients, people with addictions (including the Internet), refugees and immigrants, and the millennial generation represent just a few of the emerging issues that presently confront mental health professionals (Rollins, 2008). We discuss several of the current influences on the counseling profession in Chapter 5, including managed care challenges, influences of technology, and holistic approaches to counseling (e.g., the bio-psycho-social model, spirituality, wellness). Other topics, including crisis counseling, social justice, advocacy, and outcome-based research, are addressed in conjunction with relevant chapters elsewhere in the text.

Currently, the ACA has 19 specialty divisions, which provide clinical mental health counselors with opportunities to develop skills in specialty areas or in working with particular populations. The newest division of ACA, the Association for Creativity in Counseling, was founded in 2004. As the first decade of the 21st century draws to a close, the following divisions and affiliates now operate under ACA's structure:

1. *National Career Development Association (NCDA).* Founded in 1913; formerly the National Vocational Guidance Association.
2. *Counseling Association for Humanistic Education and Development (C-AHEAD).* Founded in 1931; formerly the Student Personnel Association for Teacher Education.
3. *Association for Counselor Education and Supervision (ACES).* Founded in 1938; formerly the National Association of Guidance Supervisors and Counselor Trainers.
4. *American School Counselor Association (ASCA).* Founded in 1953.
5. *American Rehabilitation Counseling Association (ARCA).* Founded in 1958; formerly the Division of Rehabilitation Counseling.
6. *Association for Assessment in Counseling and Education (AACE).* Founded in 1965; formerly the Association for Measurement and Evaluation in Guidance.
7. *National Employment Counseling Association (NECA).* Founded in 1966.
8. *Association for Multicultural Counseling and Development (AMCD).* Founded in 1972; formerly the Association for Non-White Concerns in Personnel and Guidance.
9. *International Association of Addictions and Offender Counselors (IAAOC).* Founded in 1972; formerly the Public Offender Counselor Association.
10. *Association for Specialists in Group Work (ASGW).* Founded in 1973.
11. *Association for Spiritual, Ethical, and Religious Values in Counseling (ASERVIC).* Founded in 1974; formerly the National Catholic Guidance Conference.
12. *American Mental Health Counselors Association (AMHCA).* Founded in 1976.

13. ***Association for Counselors and Educators in Government (ACEG).***   Founded in 1984; formerly the Military Educators and Counselors Association (MECA).
14. ***Association for Adult Development and Aging (AADA).***   Founded in 1986.
15. ***International Association of Marriage and Family Counselors (IAMFC).***   Founded in 1989.
16. ***American College Counseling Association (ACCA).***   Founded in 1991.
17. ***Association for Lesbian, Gay, Bisexual, and Transgender Issues in Counseling (ALGBTIC).***   Founded in 1996.
18. ***Counselors for Social Justice.***   Founded as an organizational affiliate in 1999. Gained divisional status in 2002.
19. ***Association for Creativity in Counseling.***   Founded in 2004.

Summary and Conclusion

This chapter began with the story of a hero who went from being a rescuer to becoming a deliverer of preventive services. The story illustrates the assumptions of those who work as community and agency counselors: that it is important to focus on people's environments as well as their symptoms, that a multifaceted approach to treatment is better than one that is based on a single-service plan, and that prevention is more efficient than remediation. The chapter then briefly reviewed other premises of the counseling profession and traced its evolution into the 21st century.

Clinical mental health counseling is concerned with wellness, development, and situational difficulties, as well as with helping people who have more serious mental health issues. The history of counseling shows that the profession has an interdisciplinary base. It began with the almost simultaneous actions of Frank Parsons, Jesse B. Davis, and Clifford Beers to provide, reform, and improve services in vocational guidance, mental health treatment, and character development of children. Counseling is interlinked with but distinct from psychometrics, psychology, and sociology. Noteworthy events in the history of counseling include the involvement of the government in counseling during and after World War I, the Great Depression, World War II, and the launching of Sputnik. Ideas from innovators such as John Brewer, E. G. Williamson, Carl Rogers, Gilbert Wrenn, Leona Tyler, Thomas Sweeney, and others have shaped the development of the profession and broadened its horizon. The emergence and growth of the American Counseling Association (rooted in the establishment of the National Vocational Guidance Association in 1913) has been a major factor in the growth of the profession, especially since the 1950s.

Community counseling programs emerged in universities in the 1970s. Community counseling was officially recognized as a specialty area in 1981, with the establishment of CACREP. Mental health counseling programs were recognized by CACREP in the early 1990s. With the adoption of the new CACREP standards (2009), the two specialty areas are now recognized as one: clinical mental health counseling. The number of counselors working in agency settings has dramatically increased since the beginning of the 1980s. In the first decade of the 21st century, clinical mental health counselors can be found working with many different populations in a wide range of settings, including community mental health centers, medical settings, correctional institutions, businesses, and private practice. In the next chapter, attention shifts from the history of the counseling profession to the importance of developing a professional identity as a clinical mental health counselor who practices in community and agency settings.

Summary Table

HIGHLIGHTS IN THE HISTORY OF PROFESSIONAL COUNSELING

1900s

Frank Parsons, the "Father of Guidance," establishes the Boston Vocational Bureau to help young people make career decisions; writes *Choosing a Vocation*.

Jesse B. Davis sets up first systematic guidance program in the public schools (Grand Rapids, Michigan).

Clifford Beers, a former mental patient, advocates for better treatment of the mentally ill; publishes influential book: *A Mind That Found Itself.*

Sigmund Freud's psychoanalytic theory becomes the basis for treating the mentally disturbed.

1910s

National Vocational Guidance Association (NVGA) is established; the forerunner of American Counseling Association (ACA).

The Smith-Hughes Act is passed, which provides funding for public schools to support vocational education.

Psychometrics is embraced by vocational guidance movement after World War I.

1920s

First certification of counselors is initiated in Boston and New York.

Publication of the *Strong Vocational Interest Inventory (SVII)* begins.

Abraham and Hannah Stone establish the first marriage and family counseling center in New York City.

Counselors begin broadening their focus beyond vocational interests.

1930s

E. G. Williamson and colleagues develop a counselor-centered trait-factor approach to work with the unemployed. This approach is the first theory of counseling, often called the Minnesota point of view.

John Brewer advocates education as guidance with vocational decision making as a part of the process.

The *Dictionary of Occupational Titles (DOT)* is published as the first government effort to systematically code job titles.

1940s

Carl Rogers develops the client-centered approach to counseling and publishes *Counseling and Psychotherapy*.

With the advent of World War II, traditional occupational roles are questioned publicly; personal freedom is emphasized over authority.

U.S. Veterans Administration (VA) funds the training of counselors and psychologists. It coins the term, *counseling psychologist,* which begins as a profession.

1950s

American Personnel and Guidance Association (APGA) is founded—the forerunner of the American Counseling Association.

Division 17 (Society of Counseling Psychology) of the American Psychological Association is created.

National Defense Education Act (NDEA) is enacted. Title V-B provides training for counselors.

New theories (such as transactional analysis and rational-emotive therapy) are formulated that challenge older theories (such as psychoanalysis, behaviorism, trait-factor, and client centered).

1960s

Emphasis in counseling on developmental issues is begun. Gilbert Wrenn publishes *The Counselor in a Changing World.*

Leona Tyler writes extensively about counseling.

Behavioral counseling, led by John Krumboltz's *Revolution in Counseling,* emerges as a strong counseling theory.

Upheaval is created by civil rights movements, feminism, and the Vietnam War. Counseling is sidetracked from a developmental emphasis; counselors are increasingly concerned with addressing social and crisis issues.

Community Mental Health Centers Act is passed, which establishes community mental health centers and future employment settings for community counselors.

Group counseling gains popularity as a way of resolving personal issues.

APGA publishes its first code of ethics.

ERIC/CAPS is founded and begins building a database of research in counseling.

The Greyston Conference helps define counseling psychology, and *The Counseling Psychologist* journal is published.

1970s

Greater diversification of counseling is developed outside educational settings. The term *community counseling* is coined.

American Mental Health Counseling Association (AMHCA) is formed.

Basic helping-skills programs are initiated by Robert Carkhuff, Allen Ivey, and colleagues.

State licensure of counselors begins; Virginia is first state to adopt a counselor licensure law.

APGA emerges as a strong professional association.

1980s

Council for Accreditation of Counseling and Related Educational Programs (CACREP) is formed to accredit counseling programs, including community counseling.

National Board of Certified Counselors (NBCC) is established.

Chi Sigma Iota (international academic and professional honor society) is begun.

Growing membership continues in counseling associations, and a new headquarters building for AACD is created.

Human growth and development is highlighted in counseling. *In a Different Voice* by Carol Gilligan focuses attention on the importance of studying women's issues in counseling.

1990s

AACD changes its name to the American Counseling Association (ACA) in 1992.

Diversity and multicultural issues in counseling are stressed.

Spiritual issues in counseling are addressed more openly.

Increased focus is placed on counselor regulations and accountability.

National Academy for Clinical Mental Health Counselors merges with NBCC.

Counselors seek to be recognized as core providers as national health care reform is discussed and enacted.

Community counseling is recognized more as a specialty within the counseling profession as agencies continue hiring a number of counselors.

2000 to Present

The counseling profession celebrates its 50th anniversary.
Primary areas of focus include:

- Diversity, advocacy, leadership, and social justice
- Health maintenance organizations, managed care, and counselors' roles as providers of mental health services
- Innovations in technology, especially the widespread use of the Internet
- An emphasis on holistic approaches, wellness, and spirituality
- The need for outcome-based research to determine "best practice" options
- Emergence of therapies such as EMDR, neurofeedback, hypnosis, and postmodern approaches to help clients with a range of issues, particularly those related to stress or to brain trauma.
- Crisis management: Finding ways to deal with conflict, violence, and trauma, both from a preventive and a treatment standpoint
- An increased need to meet the myriad needs of military families, accompanied by legislative activity to recognize counselors as service providers
- The adoption of new CACREP standards, which merge community counseling and mental health counseling specialty areas into one specialty area: clinical mental health counseling

CHAPTER 2

Professional Identity

In the midst of a day
that has brought only grey skies, hard rain,
and two cups of lukewarm coffee,
You come to me with Disney World wishes
Waiting for me to change into:
a Houdini figure with Daniel Boone's style
Prince Charming's grace and Abe Lincoln's wisdom
Who with magic words, a wand,
frontier spirit, and perhaps a smile
Can cure all troubles in a flash.
But reality sits in a green-cushioned chair—
lightning has struck a nearby tree,
Yesterday ended another month,
I'm uncomfortable sometimes in silence,
And unlike fantasy figures
I can't always be
what you see in your mind.

Gladding, S. T. (1973). Reality sits in a green-cushioned chair. *Personnel and Guidance Journal, 54,* 222. © ACA. Reprinted with permission. No further reproduction authorized without written permission of ACA.

In Chapter 1, a definition of counseling and a description of the historical foundations of the counseling profession were presented. In this chapter, we focus on the professional identity of community and mental health counselors, who we identify collectively as *clinical mental health counselors.* As noted in Chapter 1, at times we will use various terms, including *community and agency counselors, clinicians,* and *mental health practitioners,* to refer to this category of mental health professionals. *Professional identity* refers to the philosophy, training model, and scope of practice that characterize a particular profession (MacCluskie & Ingersoll, 2001). A critical task for all counselors, including clinical mental health counselors, is to assume a professional identity and be able to explain that identity to others (Remley & Herlihy, 2010).

At the beginning of this chapter, we present a general introduction to some of the therapeutic professionals with whom counselors work. Next, we examine more closely the specific professional identity of professional counselors, with a specific focus on community and mental health counselors. The chapter closes with a description of professional credentialing that further defines the roles and functions of professional counselors in general and community and mental health counselors in particular.

The Case of Latanya

Latanya recently graduated from a state university with an undergraduate degree in psychology. After working as a mental health technician in a local mental health agency for 2 years, Latanya has made the decision to apply to graduate school. She is unsure whether to apply to a program that prepares students to become clinical social workers, professional counselors, counseling psychologists, or marriage and family therapists. Latanya also has considered getting a degree in pastoral counseling. Although she has researched several programs online, she is uncertain of the advantages and disadvantages associated with each profession. She also is confused by what appears to be a strong overlap in the professions. How would you help her make an informed decision?

THERAPEUTIC PROFESSIONALS IN COMMUNITY AND AGENCY SETTINGS

Defining Therapeutic Professions

Counselors in mental health settings frequently work with several different therapeutic professionals. To facilitate collaboration among mental health practitioners, it is important to have an understanding of both one's own professional identity and the professional identity of colleagues whose credentials differ but who perform similar activities.

Therapeutic professionals can be defined as "mental health professionals trained to help people with problems that manifest behaviorally or psychologically and that may have roots in physical, psychological, or spiritual dimensions" (MacCluskie & Ingersoll, 2001, p. 3). The problems people experience may range from situational or developmental concerns to more severe psychological disorders. Traditionally, attempts have been made to define specific mental health professions based on the severity of client problems. However, professional definition based strictly on client diagnosis may be somewhat misleading. Although the counseling profession focuses on providing services that are developmental and preventive in nature, community and agency counselors also are trained to work with clients experiencing more serious concerns, including problems described in the *Diagnostic and Statistical Manual of Mental Disorders* (*DSM-IV-TR,* American Psychiatric Association [APA], 2000). Thus, it may be more helpful to categorize different therapeutic professions by their training emphases and requirements, recognizing that similarities as well as differences exist among the various professions. In this section, we provide a brief overview of the therapeutic professions of social work, psychiatry, psychology, and counseling.

SOCIAL WORK.   *Social workers* usually earn a master's of social work degree (MSW), although some universities award a bachelor's degree in social work. Some social workers elect to pursue additional training at the doctoral level. The National Association of Social Workers (NASW) offers credentials for members who demonstrate advanced clinical and educational competencies. The practice of clinical social work is regulated by licensure laws in all 50 states.

Regardless of their educational background, social workers on all levels have completed internships in social agency settings. Social workers participate in a variety of activities, including helping individuals, groups, and communities enhance social functioning. Important goals include negotiating social systems and advocating for change (MacCluskie & Ingersoll, 2001). Some social workers administer government programs for the underprivileged and disenfranchised. Others engage in individual, group, and family counseling, emphasizing a systems and contextual approach, rather than following a medical model. Social workers work in a variety of settings, including schools, medical and public health environments, and mental health and substance abuse settings.

PSYCHIATRY.   In contrast, psychiatry represents a specialty area within the school of medicine. Psychiatrists earn a medical degree (MD) and then complete a residency in psychiatry. To earn the license to practice, they must pass both a national and a state examination. Psychiatrists may specialize in areas such as child or geriatric psychiatry, psychopharmacology, or a particular mode of therapy (Gerig, 2007). Psychiatrists are represented by the American Psychiatric Association.

There is some dispute within the field of psychiatry related to preferred models of training. Some psychiatrists primarily follow a strict biomedical model and spend most of their time with clients prescribing medications and evaluating their effects (MacCluskie & Ingersoll, 2001). Other psychiatrists adhere to a biopsychosocial model, which acknowledges the interaction of behavioral, psychological, and social factors on development and mental health. In general, psychiatrists specialize in treating people who have major psychological disorders, and until recently, they were the only therapeutic professionals who had the authority to prescribe medication. In a few locations, some psychologists now have legal rights to prescribe psychopharmacological medications.

PSYCHOLOGY.   Psychology programs are accredited by the American Psychological Association (APA). Psychologists typically earn a PhD (doctor of philosophy), EdD (doctor of education), or PsyD (doctor of psychology), although some psychologists earn master's degrees but not doctorates. Areas of specialization within the field include clinical, social, cognitive, developmental, counseling, and school psychology. All states license psychologists, although requirements for licensure differ from state to state.

Since the 1940s, psychologists have been viewed as experts in psychological assessment (Exner, 1995)—a view that has led to disagreement among therapeutic professionals about who should have access to various assessment instruments. In February 1996, responding to attempts by state psychology licensure boards to restrict assessment practices of other trained professionals, the National Fair Access Coalition on Testing (FACT) was formed. FACT is a not-for-profit organization that advocates for equitable access to testing services for all appropriately trained professionals (National Fair Access Coalition on Testing, 2007). Most recently, in May 2007, FACT was instrumental in protecting the rights of counselors in supporting the rights of trained professionals other than psychologists to administer and interpret tests in Indiana.

Counseling psychology is a specialization area that is represented by Division 17 of the APA. Division 17 was founded in 1946 to facilitate personal, vocational, educational, and interpersonal adjustment (Society of Counseling Psychology, 2007). Counseling psychologists, like clinical psychologists, have doctoral degrees and are employed in universities as well as a range of human service settings. Counseling psychology shares common roots and emphases with the field of counselor education, which is described next.

COUNSELOR EDUCATION.   Professional counselors earn either a master's or a doctoral degree from a counselor education or closely related program. Programs are accredited by the Council for Accreditation of Counseling and Related Educational Programs (CACREP). CACREP-accredited master's programs range from a minimum of 48 to 60 semester hours, depending on the area of specialization. The doctoral program for counselor education and supervision requires at least 96 semester hours and prepares graduates to work as counselor educators, supervisors, researchers, and advanced practitioners in academic and clinical settings.

At the time this text was being prepared, the CACREP board voted to implement the draft of the 2009 CACREP Standards. The new standards have particular significance for community and mental health counselors. Until the new standards were passed, counselor education programs could prepare counselors for community counseling (a minimum of 48-hours) or mental health counseling (a minimum of 60 hours). As the mental health field has evolved, the distinctions between these two areas (community counseling and mental health counseling) have blurred. Consequently, the new standards combine the two programs into a new program: that of clinical mental health counseling. To help counselor education programs who accredit community and mental health counselors, a period of transition is built into the new standards and is described as follows:

> The hourly degree requirements for entry-level degree programs in Clinical Mental Health Counseling are in transition. Beginning July 1, 2009, all applicant programs must require a minimum of 54 semester credit hours or 81 quarter credit hours of all students. As of July 1, 2013, the applicants must require a minimum of 60 semester credit hours or 90 quarter credit hours required of all students.

> (Council for Accreditation of Counseling and Related Educational Programs [CACREP], 2009)

There are specific requirements for the accreditation of Clinical Mental Health Counseling programs. In Box 2–1, a rationale for the merging of the community and mental health specialty areas is provided by Dr. Tom Davis, a professor at Ohio University, who chaired the CACREP Standards Revision Committee.

BOX 2–1

The New Clinical Mental Health Counseling Specialty Area

A great deal of discussion surrounded the state of CACREP's Community Counseling and Mental Health Counseling Program areas. The Standards Revision Committee (SRC) members listened to feedback from around the country concerning the pros and cons of the existence of the two program areas. After significant reflection the SRC came to the conclusion that the two program areas were essentially producing graduates who were pursuing the same positions within the mental health field, and in fact were performing the same functions within the various forms of the mental health system. Great attention was given to fortifying gaps in clinical training that existed within both of the 2001 program areas. We are convinced that the 2009 Standards offer a solid preparation for our graduates, which will allow them to meet the complex clinical mental health service delivery needs that exist in our society.

Tom Davis, PhD, CACREP Standards Revision Chair (personal communication, September 8, 2008)

Changes have been made to other entry-level degree programs, as well, although many of the program tracks (e.g., school, career) have remained the same in name. In addition to clinical mental health counseling programs, CACREP provides accreditation options in career counseling, college counseling and student development, school counseling, addiction counseling, and marriage, couple, and family counseling. Addiction counseling is a new specialty accreditation area, and the college counseling and student development program combines programs in college counseling, student affairs, and student affairs practice (CACREP, 2009).

The number of accredited counselor preparation programs has increased steadily since 1981. As of February 2008, there were 530 accredited master's-level programs and 52 accredited doctoral programs. The majority of accredited master's-level programs were in school counseling (n = 189) and in community counseling (n = 149). An updated directory of accredited programs and of programs in the process of applying for initial accreditation or reaccreditation can be accessed through the CACREP Web site: www.CACREP.org.

As noted in Chapter 1, several features of counseling help distinguish it from other therapeutic professions. Although they may espouse different theoretical orientations, counselors from all specializations tend to work from a preventive, developmental, holistic framework, building on clients' strengths and assets. Counselors help clients with issues ranging from developmental concerns and problems in living to issues associated with pathology. Thus, although counselors are trained to work with clients from a developmental, wellness-oriented perspective, they often are involved in diagnosing and treating mental and emotional disorders, including addictions. They also use psychoeducational techniques designed to prevent such disorders (American Counseling Association [ACA], 2007).

BOX 2–2

I treat everyone developmentally, but I want to recognize pathology when it is in the room with me.

   Robin Daniel, PhD, LPC, Director of Counseling and Student Disability Services, Greensboro College

---

BOX 2–3

Who are Professional Counselors?

What makes professional counselors unique from their peers in other mental health disciplines is their "wellness" orientation. While trained to understand pathology and mental illness, professional counselors take a preventive approach to helping people and are trained to use counseling treatment interventions, which include principles of development, wellness, and pathology that reflect a pluralistic society.

American Counseling Association, 2003, www.counseling.org/resources/licensure.htm

---

Some of the specific topics clinical mental health counselors are trained to help with include career and lifestyle issues, marriage and family concerns, addictions, stress management, crisis issues, disaster relief, mental disorders, and grief and loss. They help people grow mentally, emotionally, socially, spiritually, and educationally. Counselors typically follow a nonmedical approach that emphasizes the importance of biological, social, emotional, and psychological interactions. Whereas other helping professions may include counseling as a service, the *primary* service counselors provide is counseling with individuals, groups, couples, and families (Remley & Herlihy, 2010). They also provide additional professional services, including assessment, teaching, diagnosing, referral, research, and case management.

Currently, 49 states and the District of Columbia legally regulate the counseling profession through licensure. Licensed, generalist practitioners are ethically bound to practice within their areas of competence and must participate in appropriate educational and supervision activities if they choose to add areas of specialization to their practice.

OTHER THERAPEUTIC PROFESSIONALS.   Clinical mental health counselors who work in hospital settings are likely to interact with psychiatric nurses, who have been trained in schools of nursing, are registered nurses (RNs), and typically hold a master's degree. Clinical mental health counselors also work with counselors in various specialization areas, such as rehabilitation counseling, career counseling, marriage and family therapy, or addictions counseling.

COLLABORATION AMONG PRACTITIONERS.   Although it is important to establish a specialized identity within the broad arena of therapeutic professions, it is equally important to recognize the ways in which professions interrelate. Ideally, understanding the differences and similarities among the various fields will enable professionals to collaborate and complement each other's work so that clients' needs are served effectively.

BOX 2–4

Working Collaboratively with Other Therapeutic Professionals

I am a counselor educator who volunteers several hours each week at a nonprofit counseling center, where I counsel with children and families. Several other therapeutic professionals also work at the center, including two clinical psychologists, a social worker, a substance abuse counselor, a grief counselor, and several community or mental health counselors. A psychiatrist acts as the center's medical director, and the agency director is a licensed professional counselor with a specialty in community counseling.

Each week, the clinicians participate in group supervision. During this time, we present case studies and receive feedback from others in the group. Our combined knowledge, experiences, and training backgrounds contribute to a rich time of interaction and present clinicians with new skills and perspectives. We also discuss recent intakes and make decisions about which therapeutic professional, based on area of specialization, is best suited to work with a particular client.

Debbie Newsome, PhD, LPC, NCC

COMMUNITY AND MENTAL HEALTH COUNSELING AS SPECIALTY AREAS

The second edition of this text focused on the specialty field of community counseling. However, to align with the new CACREP standards, we expand the focus to include community counseling and mental health counseling, which, as stated earlier, will be merged into one program of accreditation: Clinical Mental Health Counseling.

Evolution of Community Counseling

Prior to the 1960s, the settings most commonly associated with counseling were schools and universities. With President John F. Kennedy's endorsement of the Community Mental Health Centers Act in 1963, the demand for counselors in community settings increased. The new law provided funding for the delivery of preventive mental health interventions in communities as well as in schools (Scileppi, Teed, & Torres, 2000). Responding to this need, counselor education programs began preparing students to work in community settings, with most community counseling programs beginning after 1970 (Hershenson & Berger, 2001). With the establishment of CACREP in 1981, master's programs in community and other agency settings, as well as programs in school counseling and college student personnel, were eligible to apply for accreditation. As of February 2008, 149 community counseling programs and 53 mental health counseling programs were accredited by CACREP. In addition, many universities house community or mental health counseling programs that are not CACREP accredited.

Although no specialized division for community counseling was formed in what was then the American Association for Counseling and Development (AACD), a Committee on Community Counseling was developed in 1983 within the Association for Counselor Educators and Supervisors (ACES) (Hershenson & Berger, 2001). The committee proposed that community counseling be viewed as a *process* and an *orientation,* rather than as a specialized work setting (Hayes, 1984). It was suggested that community counselors take into account the effects of the community environment on individuals and seek to empower individuals by serving as advocates, thereby affecting the community as a whole. Training of community counselors emphasized the delivery of preventive and rehabilitative services to a diverse clientele, and graduates of community counseling programs were employed in various positions and in many different settings (Hershenson & Berger, 2001).

Throughout the 1980s, no definitive criterion for community counseling programs was provided in the CACREP standards; instead, it was left up to each counseling program to define its own area of specialization (Hershenson & Berger, 2001). Consequently, there was a great deal of variation in course titles and content. Specific requirements for community counseling programs were delineated in the 1994 CACREP standards and were refined in 2002. The 2009 CACREP standards represent a merging of the community counseling and mental health counseling specialties into the specialty of clinical mental health counseling. The new standards are listed in Figure 2–1.

Defining Community Counseling

During its evolution, community counseling has been defined in several different ways. Early in its formation, community counseling was viewed as counseling that took place in any setting other than schools or universities. Prior to the establishment of the 1994 CACREP standards, concern was expressed about the lack of a clear definition of community counseling and the lack of consistency across programs (Cowger, Hinkle, DeRidder, & Erk, 1991). Since that time, a clearer definition of community counseling has emerged. Two of the more widely accepted definitions of community counseling are presented next.

Hershenson, Power, and Waldo (1996) defined *community counseling* as "the application of counseling principles and practices in agency, organizational, or individual practice

CLINICAL MENTAL HEALTH COUNSELING

Students who are preparing to work as clinical mental health counselors will demonstrate the professional knowledge, skills, and practices necessary to address a wide variety of circumstances within the clinical mental health counseling context. In addition to the common core curricular experiences outlined in Section II.F, programs must provide evidence that student learning has occurred in the following domains:

FOUNDATIONS

A. Knowledge

1. Understands the history, philosophy, and trends in clinical mental health counseling.
2. Understands ethical and legal considerations specifically related to the practice of clinical mental health counseling.
3. Understands the roles and functions of clinical mental health counselors in various practice settings and the importance of relationships between counselors and other professionals, including interdisciplinary treatment teams.
4. Knows the professional organizations, preparation standards, and credentials relevant to the practice of clinical mental health counseling.
5. Understands a variety of models and theories related to clinical mental health counseling, including the methods, models, and principles of clinical supervision.
6. Recognizes the potential for substance use disorders to mimic and coexist with a variety of medical and psychological disorders.
7. Is aware of professional issues that affect clinical mental health counselors (e.g., core provider status, expert witness status, access to and practice privileges within managed care systems).
8. Understands the management of mental health services and programs, including areas such as administration, finance, and accountability.
9. Understands the impact of crises, disasters, and other trauma-causing events on people.
10. Understands the operation of an emergency management system within clinical mental health agencies and in the community.

B. Skills and Practices

1. Demonstrates the ability to apply and adhere to ethical and legal standards in clinical mental health counseling.
2. Applies knowledge of public mental health policy, financing, and regulatory processes to improve service delivery opportunities in clinical mental health counseling.

COUNSELING, PREVENTION, AND INTERVENTION

C. Knowledge

1. Describes the principles of mental health, including prevention, intervention, consultation, education, and advocacy, as well as the operation of programs and networks that promote mental health in a multicultural society.
2. Knows the etiology, the diagnostic process and nomenclature, treatment, referral, and prevention of mental and emotional disorders.
3. Knows the models, methods, and principles of program development and service delivery (e.g., support groups, peer facilitation training, parent education, self-help).
4. Knows the disease concept and etiology of addiction and co-occurring disorders.
5. Understands the range of mental health service delivery—such as inpatient, outpatient, partial treatment and aftercare—and the clinical mental health counseling services network.

FIGURE 2–1   Standards for clinical mental health counselors (*Continued*)

6. Understands the principles of crisis intervention for people during crises, disasters, and other trauma-causing events.
7. Knows the principles, models, and documentation formats of biopsychosocial case conceptualization and treatment planning.
8. Recognizes the importance of family, social networks, and community systems in the treatment of mental and emotional disorders.
9. Understands professional issues relevant to the practice of clinical mental health counseling.

D. Skills and Practices

1. Uses the principles and practices of diagnosis, treatment, referral, and prevention of mental and emotional disorders to initiate, maintain, and terminate counseling.
2. Applies multicultural competencies to clinical mental health counseling involving case conceptualization, diagnosis, treatment, referral, and prevention of mental and emotional disorders.
3. Promotes optimal human development, wellness, and mental health through prevention, education, and advocacy activities.
4. Applies effective strategies to promote client understanding of and access to a variety of community resources.
5. Demonstrates appropriate use of culturally responsive individual, couple, family, group, and systems modalities for initiating, maintaining, and terminating counseling.
6. Demonstrates the ability to use procedures for assessing and managing suicide risk.
7. Applies current record-keeping standards related to clinical mental health counseling.
8. Provides appropriate counseling strategies when working with clients with addiction and co-occurring disorders.
9. Demonstrates the ability to recognize his or her own limitations as a clinical mental health counselor and to seek supervision or refer clients when appropriate.

DIVERSITY AND ADVOCACY

E. Knowledge

1. Understands how living in a multicultural society affects clients who are seeking clinical mental health counseling services.
2. Understands the effects of racism, discrimination, sexism, power, privilege, and oppression on one's own life and career and those of the client.
3. Understands current literature that outlines theories, approaches, strategies, and techniques shown to be effective when working with specific populations of clients with mental and emotional disorders.
4. Understands effective strategies to support client advocacy and influence public policy and government relations on local, state, and national levels to enhance equity, increase funding, and promote programs that affect the practice of clinical mental health counseling.
5. Understands the implications of concepts such as internalized oppression and institutional racism, as well as the historical and current political climate regarding immigration, poverty, and welfare.
6. Knows public policies on the local, state, and national levels that affect the quality and accessibility of mental health services.

FIGURE 2–1   **Standards for clinical mental health counselors** *(Continued)*

F. Skills and Practices

1. Maintains information regarding community resources to make appropriate referrals.
2. Advocates for policies, programs, and services that are equitable and responsive to the unique needs of clients.
3. Demonstrates the ability to modify counseling systems, theories, techniques, and interventions to make them culturally appropriate for diverse populations.

ASSESSMENT

G. Knowledge

1. Knows the principles and models of assessment, case conceptualization, theories of human development, and concepts of normalcy and psychopathology leading to diagnoses and appropriate counseling treatment plans.
2. Understands various models and approaches to clinical evaluation and their appropriate uses, including diagnostic interviews, mental status examinations, symptom inventories, and psychoeducational and personality assessments.
3. Understands basic classifications, indications, and contraindications of commonly prescribed psychopharmacological medications so that appropriate referrals can be made for medication evaluations and so that the side effects of such medications can be identified.
4. Identifies standard screening and assessment instruments for substance use disorders and process addictions.

H. Skills and Practices

1. Selects appropriate comprehensive assessment interventions to assist in diagnosis and treatment planning, with an awareness of cultural bias in the implementation and interpretation of assessment protocols.
2. Demonstrates skill in conducting an intake interview, a mental status evaluation, a biopsychosocial history, a mental health history, and a psychological assessment for treatment planning and caseload management.
3. Screens for addiction, aggression, and danger to self and/or others, as well as co-occurring mental disorders.
4. Applies the assessment of a client's stage of dependence, change, or recovery to determine the appropriate treatment modality and placement criteria within the continuum of care.

RESEARCH AND EVALUATION

I. Knowledge

1. Understands how to critically evaluate research relevant to the practice of clinical mental health counseling.
2. Knows models of program evaluation for clinical mental health programs.
3. Knows evidence-based treatments and basic strategies for evaluating counseling outcomes in clinical mental health counseling.

J. Skills and Practices

1. Applies relevant research findings to inform the practice of clinical mental health counseling.
2. Develops measurable outcomes for clinical mental health counseling programs, interventions, and treatments.
3. Analyzes and uses data to increase the effectiveness of clinical mental health counseling interventions and programs.

FIGURE 2–1 **Standards for clinical mental health counselors** *(Continued)*

DIAGNOSIS

K. Knowledge

    1. Knows the principles of the diagnostic process, including differential diagnosis, and the use of current diagnostic tools, such as the current edition of the *Diagnostic and Statistical Manual of Mental Disorders* (DSM).

    2. Understands the established diagnostic criteria for mental and emotional disorders, and describes treatment modalities and placement criteria within the continuum of care.

    3. Knows the impact of co-occurring substance use disorders on medical and psychological disorders.

    4. Understands the relevance and potential biases of commonly used diagnostic tools with multicultural populations.

    5. Understands appropriate use of diagnosis during a crisis, disaster, or other trauma-causing event.

L. Skills and Practices

    1. Demonstrates appropriate use of diagnostic tools, including the current edition of the *DSM*, to describe the symptoms and clinical presentation of clients with mental and emotional impairments.

    2. Is able to conceptualize an accurate multi-axial diagnosis of disorders presented by a client and discuss the differential diagnosis with collaborating professionals.

    3. Differentiates between diagnosis and developmentally appropriate reactions during crises, disasters, and other trauma-causing events.

FIGURE 2–1   Standards for clinical mental health counselors *(Continued)*

Note. Reprinted with permission of the Council for Accreditation of Counseling and Related Educational Programs (www.cacrep.org/2009standards.html)

settings that are located in and interact with their surrounding community" (p. 26). They suggested that community counseling is based on the following suppositions:

- The focus of assessment and intervention needs to include the community as well as the client.
- Interventions should take a proactive, health-promoting approach that is educative and empowering.
- Interventions are based on the principle of building on strengths, which include client and community resources.
- Community counselors working with specific populations or with particular issues may have to use skills developed by other counseling specialties (e.g., career, gerontological, or mental health counseling).
- Central functions of community counselors include counseling, coordinating, consulting, educating, programming, and advocacy.

Lewis, Lewis, Daniels, and D'Andrea (2003) also emphasized a multifaceted approach to community counseling that recognizes the importance of client–environment interaction. They defined *community counseling* as "a comprehensive helping framework of intervention strategies and services that promotes the personal development and well-being of all

	Client Services	**Community Services**
Direct	• Individual counseling • Crisis intervention • Substance abuse counseling • Family counseling	• Parent education programs • Stress management workshops • Conflict mediation workshops • Lobbying for social change
Indirect	• Advocating for clients • Referring clients to appropriate human service agencies	• Influencing public policy • Influencing public policy • Influencing systems that affect clients

FIGURE 2–2 **Examples illustrating components of community counseling**

Note. From *Community Counseling: Empowerment Strategies for a Diverse Society* (3rd ed.), by J. A. Lewis, M. D. Lewis, J. A. Daniels, and M. J. D'Andrea, 2003, Pacific Grove, CA: Brooks/Cole. Adapted with permission of Wadsworth, a division of Thomson Learning: www.thomsonrights.com. Fax 800 730-2215.

individuals and communities" (p. 6). They presented a model of community counseling comprised of four service components: (a) direct client services, (b) indirect client services, (c) direct community services, and (d) indirect community services. Examples of each service component are illustrated in Figure 2–2.

According to Lewis et al. (2003), effective community counselors reflect an awareness of society's effects on its members. They strive to understand the unique needs and experiences of people from diverse backgrounds and seek to prevent debilitating problems that occur in the community. Clients are viewed holistically, possessing strengths, resources, and limitations.

When clients learn to help themselves, they and their communities are strengthened. A common set of assumptions guides the work of community counselors, including the following:

• People's environments either nurture or limit them.
• The goal of counseling is to facilitate individual and community empowerment.
• A multifaceted approach to counseling is more effective than a single-service approach.
• Attention to the multicultural nature of clients' development is essential to the planning and delivery of counseling services.
• Prevention is more efficient than remediation.
• The community counseling model can be used in a variety of human service, educational, and business settings (Lewis et al., 2003, p. 20).

The community counseling definitions provided by both Hershenson et al. (1996) and Lewis et al. (2003) address the fact that community counselors perform a broad range of therapeutic interventions among diverse client populations and in a variety of settings. Community counselors embrace multifaceted approaches that promote prevention, early intervention, and wellness, taking into account the client, the community, and the interactions between the two. *Community* can be conceptualized as the larger set of social systems in which the client lives and which directly affect functioning and development (Hershenson et al., 1996). A theoretical paradigm, or frame of reference, that is particularly suited to this

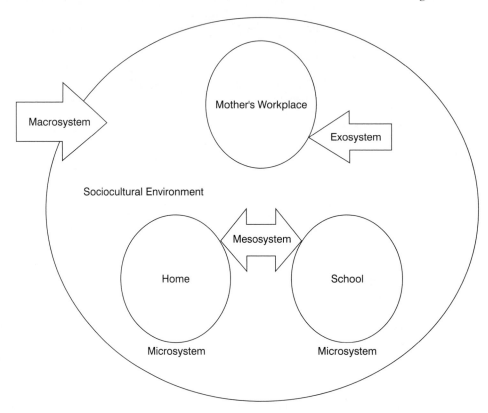

FIGURE 2–3   Multiple systems of interaction. Bronfenbrenner's Bioecological Model

conceptualization of community counseling is the bioecological model proposed by Uri Bronfenbrenner (1979, 1995). In the next section, a brief description of the environmental components of Bronfenbrenner's model is provided.

The Bioecological Model

The bioecological model of human development (Figure 2–3) focuses on the settings in which development occurs and on the interaction of individuals within and across those settings. According to the model, people grow and change through processes of progressively more complex reciprocal interactions between an active evolving individual and the persons, objects, and symbols in his or her immediate external environment (Bronfenbrenner, 1995). Specifically, the model integrates the various components that contribute to developmental outcomes, including the individual, the environment, and the processes of interaction that affect the individual in that environment.

People grow and develop within multiple environments that can be categorized into four nested systems: the microsystem, the mesosystem, the exosystem, and the macrosystem (Bronfenbrenner, 1979, 1995). The *microsystem* represents the most proximal environment within which an individual develops. Family, school, the peer group, and the workplace are all examples of specific microsystems. The next system, the *mesosystem,* is defined by interrelations among two or more microsystems at a particular point in an individual's development.

An example of the dynamic interactions of a mesosystem would be a situation in which a child's parents are going through a divorce. The child begins acting out at school, and the child's peers begin to reject him. In this case, the child's family, school, and peer group represent interacting microsystems, classified as a mesosystem.

A more distal system, the *exosystem,* refers to a context that exerts indirect influence on an individual. For example, a parent's workplace may affect the parent in ways that then indirectly affect the child. More specifically, a mother may be experiencing a high level of stress at work, which affects her interactions with her child at home. In this example, the mother's workplace represents an exosystem.

At the fourth level of Bronfenbrenner's taxonomy is the *macrosystem,* which refers to an overarching belief system or culture. This broad, inclusive system exerts its effects indirectly through cultural tools and institutions. The macrosystem affects the way society is structured and warrants special consideration when counseling with diverse populations.

Later in his life, Bronfenbrenner described a fifth system, the *chronosystem.* The chronosystem represents the evolution of the other four systems over time. An awareness of the chronosystem allows counselors to take into account ways the particular systems and their interactions develop and change throughout a client's life span. Of particular importance are life transitions, such as getting married, having children, and retiring from a career.

Community counselors recognize that a client's development is affected both by the immediate systems in which he or she participates and by the broader sociocultural forces that have a more global impact. Consequently, all systems and their interactions need to be considered when community counselors work with clients.

Defining Mental Health Counseling

According to the American Mental Health Counselor Association (AMHCA) (2009), mental health counseling is a distinct profession with national standards for education, training, and clinical practice. AMHCA's Web site (www.AMHCA.org) states the following about mental health counselors:

> Mental health counselors practice in a variety of settings, including independent practice, community agencies, managed behavioral health care organizations, integrated delivery systems, hospitals, employee assistance programs and substance abuse treatment centers. Mental health counselors are highly skilled professionals who provide a full range of services including:
>
> - Assessment and diagnosis
> - Psychotherapy
> - Treatment planning and utilization review
> - Brief and solution-focused therapy
> - Alcoholism and substance abuse treatment
> - Psychoeducational and prevention programs
> - Crisis management

In today's managed care environment, mental health counselors are uniquely qualified to meet the challenges of providing high-quality care in a cost-effective manner. Mental health counselors provide flexible, consumer-oriented therapy. They combine traditional psychotherapy with a practical problem-solving approach that creates a dynamic and efficient path for change and problem resolution.

Community and Mental Health Counseling Settings

A common denominator shared by community and mental health counselors is that they work outside educational settings, although there are some exceptions to this generalization. Community and mental health practice settings include mental health centers, work sites, hospital environments, substance abuse settings, employee assistance programs, and individual practices. Other settings that currently employ community counselors include geriatric centers, employee assistance programs, government programs, businesses and industries, religious institutions, health maintenance organizations, shelters for domestic violence victims, hospice programs, and programs for people living with HIV/AIDS. In Part IV of this text, we describe counseling practices in some of the more common settings in which community and mental health counselors are employed.

CHALLENGES TO THE SCOPE OF PRACTICE OF COMMUNITY AND MENTAL HEALTH COUNSELORS.   Professional counselors are qualified to perform a number of professional services for their clients, based on their training and expertise. Two areas in which counselors have been challenged by psychologists and other mental health professionals are *testing* and *diagnosis and treatment* of mental and emotional disorders. Some psychologists and social workers claim that they are prepared to deliver those services and that counselors are not. You will learn more about the services of assessment, diagnosis, and treatment in the remaining chapters of this text. In particular, assessment and diagnosis are described in depth in Chapter 7.

An economic component drives the professional turf disputes. Counselors who test and diagnose and treat mental and emotional disorders often compete in the marketplace with psychologists and social workers. Many health insurance companies and health management organizations require that mental health professionals be qualified to perform these two important tasks before they will reimburse for services. Therefore, there is an economic advantage for psychologists and social workers to claim that counselors are not qualified to perform these services.

Debates over who is qualified to perform and be reimbursed for services has taken place in state and national legislatures, particularly in regard to the way in which language is used in state statutes. In most states, counselors have been successful in inserting language into their licensing statutes that attests to their competence. However, in some states, those issues remain unresolved. Clinical mental health counselors need to keep up with legislation monitoring their scope of practice and be willing to serve as advocates for their professional rights.

PROFESSIONAL IDENTIFICATION THROUGH CREDENTIALING

Legal Recognition of Counseling

Professional credentialing is an essential part of professional recognition and identification. One of the first steps toward professional credentialing is legal recognition. As recently as 1960, counseling did not have a strong enough identity as a profession to be recognized legally. In that year, a judge ruled in the case of *Bogust v. Iverson* that a counselor with a doctoral degree could not be held liable for the suicide of one of his clients because counselors were "mere teachers" who received training in a department of education.

It was not until 1971, in an *Iowa Law Review Note,* that counselors were legally recognized as professionals who provided personal as well as vocational and educational counseling. The profession was even more clearly defined in 1974 in *Weldon v. Virginia State Board of Psychologists Examiners.* The judgment rendered stated that counseling was a profession distinct from psychology. The U.S. House of Representatives further refined the definition of counseling and recognized the profession in H. R. 3270 (94th Congress, 1976) by stating that *counseling* is "the process through which a trained counselor assists an individual or group to make satisfactory and responsible decisions concerning personal, educational and career development."

The initial state laws that regulated counseling, such as the one passed in Virginia in 1976, classified counseling as a generic profession with specialties, such as community or school counseling (Swanson, 1983b). Further impetus for defining counseling as a profession came in 1981 with the establishment of CACREP, which provided professional standards and review procedures for training programs (Hershenson et al., 1996).

Professional Credentialing

With the recognition of counseling as a separate professional entity, a need developed for regulation through credentialing procedures. The process of credentialing counselors has evolved over the years. Obtaining professional credentials, especially certification and licensure, has become increasingly important in the counseling profession (Glosoff, 1992). Some credentials are conferred by the counseling profession, and others are provided by states to regulate who can legally practice in that state. Both types of credentialing are designed to protect the public and the profession. To be credentialed, applicants must successfully complete appropriate academic programs in counseling (Gerig, 2007).

NATIONAL VOLUNTARY CERTIFICATION. The National Board for Certified Counselors (NBCC), the leading national organization that certifies counselors, was established by the counseling profession in 1982 to certify counselors who have met requirements in training, experience, and performance on the National Counselor Examination for Licensure and Certification (NCE; NBCC, 2007). By 2007, over 42,000 counselors were recognized as National Certified Counselors (NCCs). NCCs are certified for a period of 5 years, adhere to the NBCC *Code of Ethics,* and pay an annual maintenance fee. Specific requirements for initial certification are listed in Figure 2–4. At the end of each 5-year cycle, NCCs can apply for certification renewal by providing documentation of successful completion of a prescribed number of continuing education credits. For qualified counselors who hold the NCC credential, NBCC offers certification specialties in the following areas:

- Certified Clinical Mental Health Counselor (CCMHC) credential, which bases its standards on professional clinical mental health counselor competencies
- National Certified School Counselor (NCSC) credential, which identifies to the public those who have met national professional school counseling standards
- Master Addictions Counselor (MAC) credential, which identifies those counselors who have met national professional addictions counseling standards

Specific requirements for specialty credentials can be obtained by contacting NBCC at www.nbcc.org.

What is the National Board for Certified Counselors?

The National Board for Certified Counselors, Inc., and Affiliates (NBCC), an independent not-for-profit credentialing body for counselors, was incorporated in 1982 to establish and monitor a national certification system, to identify those counselors who have voluntarily sought and obtained certification, and to maintain a register of those counselors.

NBCC's certification program recognizes counselors who have met predetermined standards in their training, experience, and performance on the National Counselor Examination for Licensure and Certification (NCE), the most portable credentialing examination in counseling. NBCC has approximately 42,000 certified counselors. These counselors live and work in the US and over 50 countries. Our examinations are used by more than 48 states, the District of Columbia, and Guam to credential counselors on a state level.

 NBCC's flagship credential is the National Certified Counselor (NCC). NBCC also offers specialty certification in several areas:

- School counseling—The National Certified School Counselor (NCSC)
- Clinical mental health counseling—The Certified Clinical Mental Health Counselor (CCMHC)
- Addictions counseling—The Master Addictions Counselor (MAC)

The NCC is a prerequisite or co-requisite for the specialty credentials.

What are the requirements?

The three basic components of the requirements for the NCC credential are education, supervised experience, and examination.

- Candidates for the NCC credential must hold an advanced degree with a major study in counseling from a regionally accredited college or university. They also must meet specific semester or quarter hour requirements and content area requirements.
- Candidates for national certification must meet the supervised experience requirements specific to the option under which they qualify and apply.
- Candidates for national certification must achieve a national passing score on the National Counselor Examination for Licensure and Certification (NCE). You may be exempt from examination if you have already taken the NCE or NCMHCE or one of the state licensure examinations accepted by NBCC.

What the NCC Credential Does for You:

- Generates client referrals for you through CounselorFind, NBCC's referral service linking potential clients to nearby NCCs.
- Travels with you when you relocate in or outside the US.
- Keeps you in touch with current professional credentialing issues and events through The National Certified Counselor, NBCC's newsletter.
- Advances your professional accountability and visibility.
- Ensures a national standard developed by counselors, not legislators.
- Supports the rights of NCCs to use testing instruments in practice through NBCC's participation in the National Fair Access Coalition on Testing (FACT).
- Offers, through Lockton Affinity, liability insurance to NCCs at bargain rates.
- Allows online access to verification of national certification through the NBCC Registry.

FIGURE 2–4   The National Board for Certified Counselors
Note. Reprinted with permission of the National Board for Certified Counselors (NBCC, 2008).

The Center for Credentialing and Education (CCE) is an organization closely associated with NBCC that assists with credentialing, assessment, and credential management (Center for Credentialing and Education [CCE], 2008). CCE offers four certifications to professional counselors and other qualified professionals, including the Global Career Development Facilitator (GCDF), the Approved Clinical Supervisor (ACS), the Distance Crendentialed Counselor (DCC), and the Distance Credentialed Facilitator (DCF). Specific requirements for obtaining these credentials can be obtained by contacting CCE at www.ccc-global.org.

Professional certification is important because it ensures that counselors, rather than independent state legislators, set the national standards and minimum requirements for being a professional counselor. National certification also provides referral sources and networking across state lines. However, possessing the national counseling certification credential does not regulate professional practice; it is not a license to practice. Therefore, counselors need to be aware of state licensure statutes before they begin to practice professionally.

STATE REGULATIONS: LICENSURE, CERTIFICATION, AND REGISTRATION. Occupational licensure is one of the most important ways of defining an occupation as a profession (Hosie, 1991). Licensing defines scope of practice and determines who can and cannot offer certain services. Licensure is a governmentally sanctioned form of credentialing based on the concept of the regulatory power of the state (ACA, 2007). Currently, 49 states, including the District of Columbia, Guam, and Puerto Rico, legally regulate the practice of counseling. As of 2008, the only state that does not provide licensure for professional counselors is California, although California does offer licensure to qualified marriage and family therapists, and professional counselors continue to serve as advocates for counselor licensure in that state.

State laws that dictate requirements for licensure to practice counseling differ from state to state, especially with regard to training, experience, examinations, and even titles (Bradley, 1995). Once licensure requirements have been established, an individual cannot practice a profession legally without obtaining a license (Anderson & Swanson, 1994). There are some exceptions to this rule, depending on the setting in which one is practicing. For example, counselors who practice in educational institutions, nonprofit corporations, or in local, state, or federal agencies may be exempt from the licensure requirement (Remley & Herlihy, 2010). However, this exemption does not relate to reimbursement, and many third-party payors will not reimburse counselors who are not licensed.

States that have licensure statutes have established boards to oversee the issuing of credentials. Information about state credentials is presented in Table 2–1. Legal regulation can take the form of *licensure, certification,* or *registration*. The Council on Licensure, Enforcement and Regulation (1993) defines these three credentials in the following manner:

> *Licensure* is the most restrictive form of state regulation. Under licensure laws, it is illegal for a person to practice a profession without first meeting state-imposed standards. Under *certification,* the state grants title protection to persons meeting predetermined standards. Those without title may perform the services of the occupation, but may not use the title. *Registration* is the least restrictive form of regulation, usually taking the form of requiring individuals to file their names, addresses, and qualifications with a governmental agency before practicing the occupation. (p. 1)

TABLE 2–1   State licensure legislation

State	Year	Credentials	Exam
Alabama	1979	LPC, ALC	NCE
Alaska	1998	LPC	NCE
Arizona	1988	LPC, LAC	NCE, NCMHCE, or CRCE
Arkansas	1979	LPC, LAC	NCE and an oral exam
California	No licensure law at this time	In registry	NCE
Colorado	1988	LPC	NCE and CO Jurisprudence Exam
Connecticut	1997	LPC	NCE or NCMHCE
Delaware	1987	LPCMH	NCE or NCMHCE
District of Columbia	1992	LPC	NCE, NCMHCE, or CRCE
Florida	1981 (Revised 1987)	LMHC PMHC	NCMHCE
Georgia	1984	LPC, ALPC	NCE
Hawaii	2004	LMHC	NCE
Idaho	1982	LPC	NCE
		LCPC	NCMHCE
Illinois	1992	LPC	NCE or CRCE
		LCPC	NCE and NCMHCE or ECCP or CRCE
Indiana	1997	LMHC	NCMHCE
Iowa	1991	LMHC	NCE, NCMHCE, or CRCE
Kansas	1987	LPC	NCE
	(Legislature law passed 1996)	LCPC	NCMHCE
Kentucky	1996	LPCC	NCE
Louisiana	1987	LPC	NCE
Maine	1989	LPC	NCE
		LCPC (Also provides Conditional LPC and LCPC)	NCE and NCMHCE
Maryland	1985 and 1998	LCPC	NCE and Maryland Professional Counselors and Therapists Act Exam
Massachusetts	1987	LMHC	NCMHCE
Michigan	1988	LPC, LLPC	NCE or CRCE
Minnesota	2003	LPC	NCE
		LPCC	NCMHCI (ECCP accepted if NCE was already taken)
Mississippi	1985	LPC	NCE
Missouri	1985	LPC PLPC (provisional)	NCE
Montana	1985	LCPC	NCE or NCMHCE and Montana LCPC Jurisprudence exam

TABLE 2–1 State licensure legislation *(continued)*

State	Year	Credentials	Exam
Nebraska	1986	LMHP-CPC/LPC LMHP-CPC/LPC LMHP PLMHP (provisional)	NCE or NCMHCE NCE or NCMHCE
Nevada	2007	LCPC	NCE or NCMHCE (until 01/10/01, when only the NCMHCE will be accepted)
New Hampshire	1992	LCMHC	NCMHCE and essay exam provided by the board
New Jersey	1993	LPC, LAC	NCE
New Mexico	1993	LPCMH LMHC	NCE and NCMHCE NCE
New York	2002	LMHC Limited Permit also provided (2 years under supervision)	NCMHCE
North Carolina	Registry law 1983 (licensure law 1993)	LPC	NCE, NCMHCE, or CRCE
North Dakota	1989	LPC, LAPC LPCC	NCE NCMHCE and a videotaped clinical counseling session
Ohio	1984	LPC LPCC	NCE NCMHCE
Oklahoma	1985	LPC	NCE and Oklahoma Legal and Ethical Responsibilities Exam
Oregon	1989	LPC	NCE, NCMHCE, CRCE, or other approved exam and Oregon Law and Rules Exam
Pennsylvania	1998	LPC	NCE, EMAC, CRCE, ATCB, CBMT, PEPK, AAODA (Any one of the exams)
Rhode Island	1987	LCMHC	NCMHCE
South Carolina	1985	LPC LPC/I (intern)	NCE or NCMHCE
South Dakota	1990	LPC LPC-MH	NCE NCMHCE
Tennessee	1984	LPC	NCE and the TN Jurisprudence Exam

TABLE 2-1   State licensure legislation (continued)

State	Year	Credentials	Exam
		LPC/MHSP	NCE, NCMHCE, and the TN Jurisprudence Exam
Texas	1981	LPC LPC-I (Intern)	NCE and the Texas Jurisprudence Exam
Utah	1994	LPC Internship credential; check state law	NCE and NCMHCE Utah Professional Counselor Law, Rules and Ethics Exam
Vermont	1988	LCMHC	NCE and NCMHCE
Virginia	1976	LPC	NCMHCE
Washington	1987	LMHC	NCE or NCMHCE
West Virginia	1986	LPC	NCE or CRCE
Wisconsin	1992	LPC (LPC Trainee)	NCE, NCMHCE, CRCE, or equivalent exam and Wisconsin Jurisprudence Exam
Wyoming	1987	LPC	NCE

Note. Some states also require additional state specific exams.

Note. LPC = Licensed Professional Counselor; CPC = Certified Professional Counselor; LAC = Licensed Associate Counselor; LPCMH = Licensed Professional Counselor of Mental Health; LMHC = Licensed Mental Health Counselor; LCPC = Licensed Clinical Professional Counselor; LPCC = Licensed Professional Clinical Counselor; LAPC = Licensed Associate Professional Counselor; LCMHC = Licensed Clinical Mental Health Counselor; CMHC = Certified Mental Health Counselor; LPC/MHSP = Licensed Professional Counselor/Mental Health Service Provider; LMHP = Licensed Mental Health Practitioner; CCMH = Clinical Counselor in Mental Health; NCE = National Counselor Examination for Licensure and Certification; NCMHCE = National Clinical Mental Health Counseling Examination; EMAC = Examination for Master Addictions Counselor; CRCE = Certified Rehabilitation Counselor Examination; AAODA = Advanced Alcohol and Other Drug Abuse Counselor Exam; PEPK = Practice Examination of Psychological Knowledge.

Based on information in *Licensure Requirements for Professional Counselors: A state-by-state report* (2008 report). American Counseling Association.

Because legal regulation of the counseling profession currently is not uniform among the 50 states, counselors who want to practice in a particular state need to research that state's laws to understand which credential(s) the state recognizes and what the state authorizes the credentialed person to do (Remley & Herlihy, 2010). To coordinate efforts at uniformity in licensure policies among states, the American Association of State Counseling Boards (AASCB) was created in 1986. One of the missions of AASCB is to implement a *portability plan* so that states develop common standards and nationwide portability of licenses (American Association of State Counseling Boards, 2008).

Professional Affiliation

Another way community counselors establish and maintain a professional identity is through their affiliation with professional organizations. Being active in professional associations provides a number of benefits for community counselors. Through an association, members of a profession can address issues as a group rather than independently. Professional associations provide opportunities for continuing education, which is critical for maintaining credentials and updating skills. Professional associations also establish and enforce codes of ethics for their members, which provide consistent guidelines for conduct (Remley & Herlihy, 2010). The leading professional association for counseling is the American Counseling Association (ACA), which has over 40,500 members.

In addition to joining ACA, clinical mental health counselors may choose to join one or more of its 19 divisions, which are listed at the end of Chapter 1. Whereas community counseling is not represented by a specialized division in ACA, many counselors who practice in community and agency settings belong to the American Mental Health Counselor Association (AMHCA). AMHCA currently has approximately 6,000 members. It publishes the *Journal of Mental Health Counseling* quarterly, which focuses on theory, research, and practice in the field of mental health counseling. Other divisions that clinical mental health counselors might join include the Association for Assessment in Counseling and Education (AACE), the Association for Specialists in Group Work (ASGW), the International Association of Addictions and Offender Counselors (IAAOC), the International Association of Marriage and Family Counselors (IAMFC), or the National Career Development Association (NCDA). Also, clinical mental health counselors can join state branches of ACA, which hold annual conventions, represent counselors in legislative matters, publish newsletters, and often provide workshops and training for members.

Summary and Conclusion

In this chapter, we examined the professional identification of community and mental health counselors, both in relation to other therapeutic professionals and within the counseling profession itself. We discussed professional identification in relation to CACREP accreditation and the new area of program certification—clinical mental health counseling—that will replace the two tracks of community counseling and mental health counseling. We went on to describe some of the specific characteristics of community counseling, including the use of multifaceted approaches to promote prevention, early intervention, and wellness. Interactions between people and their environments are of particular interest to community counselors because of the way those interactions affect functioning and development. Consequently, counseling interventions include services to individuals, groups, families, and communities. We also described the speciality of mental health counseling. At the time this text was revised, the 2009 Standards had been adopted, but not enough time had elapsed to determine implications for its implementation. Perhaps by the time this text is revised again, counseling programs will have had opportunities to make the switch from community counseling or mental health counseling to the combined specialty of clinical mental health counseling.

An important component of professional identification is credentialing, which includes professional certification and licensure. Community counselors are encouraged to earn the credentials needed to represent themselves professionally to the public. The credential conferred by the counseling profession is that of National Certified Counselor (NCC). Licensure and other forms of legal regulation are conferred by the state to define the scope of practice and to determine who is allowed to offer certain services. Community and mental health counselors need to be familiar with the specific regulatory requirements dictated by the state in which they live and practice.

Another way to promote professional identification, interact with other counselors, and update knowledge and skills is through professional affiliation. Many community counselors choose to join the ACA. Depending on their interests and specializations, they also may choose to join one of ACA's 19 divisions. ACA and several of its divisions have established codes of ethics, which provide guidelines for conduct and are discussed in the next chapter.

CHAPTER **3**

Ethical and Legal Aspects of Counseling

In the cool grey dawn of early September,
I place the final suitcase into my Mustang
And silently say "good-bye"
   to the quiet beauty of North Carolina.
Hesitantly, I head for the blue ocean-lined coast
   of Connecticut.
Bound for a new position and the unknown.
Traveling with me are a sheltie named "Eli"
   and the still fresh memories of our last counseling session.
You, who wrestled so long with fears
   that I kiddingly started calling you "Jacob,"
   are as much a part of me as my luggage.
Moving in life is bittersweet—
like giving up friends and fears.
The taste is like smooth, orange, fall persimmons,
   deceptively delicious but tart.

Gladding, S. T. (1984). Bittersweet. *Counseling and Values, 28*, 146. © ACA. Reprinted with permission. No further reproduction authorized without written permission of ACA.

———————

Counseling is not a value-free or neutral activity (Cottone & Tarvydas, 2007; Welfel, 2006). Rather, it is an active profession based on values, which are "orienting beliefs about what is good . . . and how that good should be achieved" (Bergin, 1985, p. 99). Values are at the core of counseling relationships. All goals in counseling, whether for lifestyle modification or symptom relief, are undergirded by values systems (Bergin, 1992). On the basis of the values they hold, counselors and clients take directions in the counseling process and make decisions. Clinical mental health counselors need to be aware of their personal and professional values and beliefs if they are to act responsibly, ethically, and legally.

Counselors who are not clear about their personal values, ethics, and legal responsibilities, as well as about those of their clients, can cause harm despite their best intentions (Remley & Herlihy, 2010). Therefore, it is vital for counselors to be knowledgeable about their own values and beliefs as well as professional counseling guidelines before attempting to work with others. Ethical counselors demonstrate professional knowledge, concern, and good judgment in their work with clients. They are cautiously prudent in what they suggest and proactive in seeking consultation from other professionals when questionable circumstances arise. In this chapter, we explore ethical standards as well as legal constraints and mandates under which counselors operate.

DEFINITIONS: ETHICS, MORALITY, AND LAW

The terms *ethics* and *morality* are often used synonymously, and in some ways their meanings are similar. Both deal with "what is good and bad or the study of human conduct and values" (Van Hoose & Kottler, 1985, p. 2). However, each term has a distinct meaning.

Ethics can be defined as "a philosophical discipline that is concerned with human conduct and moral decision making" (Van Hoose & Kottler, 1985, p. 3). Ethics are normative in nature and focus on principles and standards that govern relationships between individuals, such as between counselors and clients. *Morality,* on the other hand, involves judgment or evaluation of action. It is associated with the use of such words as *good, bad, right, wrong, ought,* and *should* (Brandt, 1959; Grant, 1992). Even though some moral principles tend to be universally shared, moral conduct is defined within the context of a culture or society (Remley & Herlihy, 2010).

Kitchener (1984) described five moral principles that form the foundation for ethical guidelines and provide clarification for ethical decision making (Forester-Miller & Davis, 1998). These principles are as follows:

- *Autonomy,* which allows an individual the freedom of choice and action. Counselors are responsible for helping clients make their own decisions and act on their own values. Counselors also are responsible for helping clients consider the ramifications of their decisions and protect them from actions that may lead to harm of self or others.
- *Nonmaleficence,* which refers to not harming other people. Nonmaleficence, which is one of the oldest moral principles in the profession (Cottone & Tarvydas, 2007), is defined by the dictate followed by ancient Greek physicians to "above all, do no harm." Counselors are to refrain from actions that may intentionally or unintentionally harm others.
- *Beneficence,* which is a proactive concept implying doing things that contribute to the welfare of the client. When practicing beneficence, it is important for counselors to avoid taking a paternalistic approach toward clients that undermines their autonomy (Cottone & Tarvydas, 2007).
- *Justice,* which refers to treating all people fairly. The concept of justice implies that counselors should not discriminate on the basis of race, gender, sexual orientation, or any other factor. Counselors need to examine the degree to which justice is carried out

through the policies of agencies, institutions, and laws that affect mental health practices (Cottone & Tarvydas, 2007).

- *Fidelity,* which means that counselors are loyal to their clients, honor their commitments, and fulfill their obligations.

These five principles provide a fundamental framework for guiding community counselors in making judgments about what actions they should take to promote their clients' welfare (Granello & Witmer, 1998).

The concept of professional ethics can be further clarified by differentiating between *mandatory ethics* and *aspirational ethics* (Corey, Corey, & Callanan, 2007). *Mandatory ethics* refers to a level of ethical functioning characterized by required compliance with basic, minimal standards. *Aspirational ethics,* in contrast, describes the highest level of conduct toward which counselors may aspire. Community counselors are guided by aspirational ethics when they make choices in accordance with the higher principles behind the literal meaning of ethical codes.

Law, which differs from ethics and morality, is the precise codification of governing standards that are established to ensure legal and moral justice (Hummell, Talbutt, & Alexander, 1985). Law is created by legislation, court decision, and tradition, as in English common law. Laws codify the minimum standards of behavior that society will tolerate, whereas ethics represent ideal standards (Remley & Herlihy, 2010). The practice of community counselors is guided by ethical and legal standards, and it is important to be well informed about both.

The law does not dictate what is ethical in a given situation; rather, it dictates what is legal. Sometimes what is legal at a given time—for example, matters of race, age, or sex—is considered unethical or immoral by some significant segments of society. A classic example of such a controversy is found in the segregation patterns that people of color endured in the United States between the end of the Civil War and the 1950s. This practice was legal; however, it was without ethical or moral rationale.

Ethical codes are not intended to supersede the law; instead, they typically clarify existing law and policy (Cottone & Tarvydas, 2007). At times, however, conflicts between the legal and the ethical codes of conduct occur (see Figures 3–1). Although laws tend to be more objective and specific than ethical or moral codes, interpretations of laws change over time and are often situationally dependent (Vacc & Loesch, 2000).

Therefore, community counselors need to be aware of legal issues that are applicable to their counseling situations and work to reconcile differences in legislative and ethical standards. Furthermore, when community counselors act as consultants or advocates for clients, they need to be aware of the potential for legal change and have sound principles on which to advocate for modification of existing systems.

Remley and Herlihy (2010) provided a model for professional practice that integrates moral and ethical principles, ethical and legal codes, and outside sources of help. The model, depicted in Figures 3–2, illustrates the balance between the internal beliefs and values that drive the counselor and the external forces that guide and support counseling practice. Professional community counselors are committed to developing a deep awareness of personal values and professional moral and ethical principles, a thorough understanding of ethical and legal codes, and a willingness to participate in consultation, supervision, and professional development activities.

Interactions Between Ethics and the Law		
		Example
1. Ethical & Legal	Following a just law	Keeping a client's confidences that are also protected by law from disclosure
2. Ethical & Illegal	Disobeying an unjust law	Refusing to breach promised confidentiality even though ordered to do so by court
3. Ethical & Alegal	Doing good where no law applies	Offering free service to poor clients
4. Unethical & Legal	Following an unjust law	Following the Federal Trade Commission's edict that ethical codes cannot prohibit the use of testimonials in ads for counseling services
5. Unethical & Illegal	Breaking a just law	Disclosing confidential information protected by law from disclosure
6. Unethical & Alegal	Doing harm that no law prohibits	Promoting client dependency to enhance one's own feeling of power

FIGURE 3–1   Interactions between ethics and the law

Source: Adapted from *Ethical and Professional Issues in Counseling* (3rd ed.) (p. 50), by R. R. Cottone and V. M. Tarvydas, 2007, Upper Saddle River, NJ: Prentice Hall; and *Guide to Ethical Practice in Psychotherapy* by A. Thompson, 1990, New York: John Wiley & Sons. Copyright 1990 by John Wiley & Sons. This material is used by permission of John Wiley & Sons, Inc.

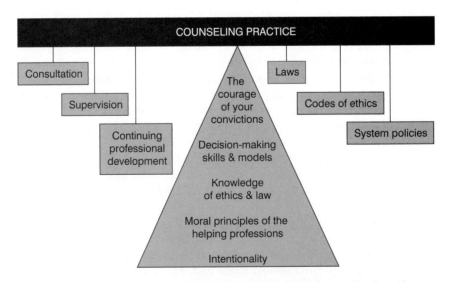

FIGURE 3–2   Professional practice—Built from within and balanced from outside the self

Source: From "Ethical, Legal, and Professional Issues in Counseling," by T. P. Remley, Jr., and B. Herlihy, © 2010. Reprinted by permission of Pearson Education, Inc., Upper Saddle River, NJ.

ETHICS AND COUNSELING

Purpose of Ethical Codes

Many mental health professions have established codes of ethics that provide guidelines for practitioners, including the American Counseling Association (ACA, 2005), the National Board of Certified Counselors (NBCC, 2005), the American Psychological Association (APA, 2003), and the National Association of Social Work (NASW, 1999). Typically, ethical codes consist of general statements that stipulate counseling duties to enhance client welfare (Granello & Witmer, 1998). Codes of ethics serve several purposes. They help promote ethical behavior by educating practitioners about sound ethical conduct, providing a mechanism for accountability, and serving as catalysts for improving practice (Herlihy & Corey, 2006). They help clarify professionals' responsibilities to clients and society and protect clients and members of the profession from unethical or incompetent practice. Also, the establishment of codes and standards helps protect a profession from outside regulation by providing a method for self-regulation.

The ACA (2005) *Code of Ethics* represents the sixth version of the counseling profession's ethical code. The original version was initiated by Donald Super and was adopted by the American Personnel and Guidance Association (APGA) in 1961. It has been revised periodically since then. In addition to the *Code of Ethics,* ACA produces *A Practitioner's Guide to Ethical Decision Making* (Forester-Miller & Davis, 1998) and an ACA *Ethical Standards Casebook* (Herlihy & Corey, 2006).

Within the ACA, several divisions have developed separate codes of ethics, a practice that potentially can create confusion among practitioners (Remley & Herlihy, 2010). Community counseling is not represented as a separate ACA division, and with the new Council for Accreditation of Counseling and Related Educational Programs (CACREP) standards, it is likely that CACREP-accredited community counseling programs will be moving toward meeting the requirements of clinical mental health counseling programs. Many clinical mental health counselors are members of the American Mental Health Counselors Association (AMHCA) or other ACA divisions that do have their own ethical codes, such as the American Association for Marriage and Family Therapy (AAMFT). Professional counselors who belong to multiple associations, hold national certifications, and are members of various divisions within the ACA are expected to comply with several different codes, which can be problematic and unwieldy. Remley and Herlihy (2010), as well as other counseling professionals, have recommended that a single, universally accepted code of ethics be established for the counseling profession. However, until this occurs, community and mental health counselors are responsible for understanding and adhering to the different ethical codes that govern the organizations to which they belong. In particular, counselors will want to be familiar with the ethical codes established by ACA (2005), AMHCA (2000), and NBCC (2005), as well as with any ethical standards created by the states in which they practice.

The ACA Code of Ethics

The ACA's latest *Code of Ethics* is a comprehensive document that indicates that counseling has developed into a major discipline. The *Code of Ethics* consists of eight sectional headings that address specific counseling issues.

• *Section A, The Counseling Relationship,* focuses on the nature of the relationship between counselors and clients. This section emphasizes client welfare as the counselor's primary responsibility. Twelve topics related to the counseling relationship are addressed, including the necessity to respect diversity, provide informed consent, and avoid dual relationships. The section also addresses the importance of recognizing the personal needs and values of the client and their effects on the counseling relationship. Sexual intimacies with clients are prohibited, and guidance is provided on issues such as fees, multiple clients, termination, and the use of computer technology. In this section, end-of-life care issues for terminally ill clients are addressed, which were not addressed specifically in earlier codes.

- *Section B, Confidentiality,* outlines the client's right to privacy in a counselor–client relationship. Limitations to confidentiality are addressed, as are considerations in working with groups, families, children, and incompetent clients. Requirements regarding client records are described, and guidelines are prescribed to protect client confidentiality when conducting research and training or consulting.

- *Section C, Professional Responsibility,* provides guidelines related to professional knowledge and competence, advertising and solicitation, presentation of credentials, public responsibility, and respect for others who work in the mental health field.

- *Section D, Relationships with Other Professionals,* elaborates further on the counselor's interactions with other mental health workers. The section focuses on relationships with colleagues, employers, and employees. It also describes ethical considerations related to consultation.

- *Section E, Evaluation, Assessment, and Interpretation,* presents guidelines on selecting, using, and interpreting assessment instruments. The section also addresses expectations related to informed consent, disclosure of test results, testing conditions and security, proper diagnosis of mental disorders, multicultural issues in assessment, forensic evaluation, and test scoring and interpretation.

- *Section F, Teaching, Training, and Supervision,* provides guidelines for counselor educators and trainers, counselor education programs, and students and supervisees. It addresses expectations and responsibilities of counselor educators, students, and counselor education programs.

- *Section G, Research and Publication,* describes the responsibilities of researchers. Included among those responsibilities are providing informed consent and protecting the rights of research participants. Section B also deals with the reporting of research results and guidelines for publication.

- *Section H, Resolving Ethical Issues,* addresses ways to resolve ethical issues, including how to handle conflicts between ethics and the law, suspected violations, and cooperation with ethics committees.

NBCC Code of Ethics

Many community counselors choose to become nationally certified. A prerequisite for becoming a Nationally Certified Counselor (NCC) is formally agreeing to abide by the NBCC *Code of Ethics.* The NBCC *Code of Ethics* was developed in 1982 and revised in 1987, 1989, 1997, and 2005. It can be accessed through the NBCC Web site (www.nbcc.org). The NBCC ethical code consists of seven sections, many of which parallel the sections of the ACA code. Unlike the ACA code, guidelines for consulting and private practice are each discussed in their own sections of the NBCC *Code of Ethics.* Counseling over the Internet is addressed, with further elaboration provided in NBCC's *Standards for the Ethical Practice of Internet*

Counseling (2007). We give more attention to the topic of ethics and Internet counseling in Chapter 5.

Limitations of Ethical Codes

Ethical codes are necessary but not sufficient for promoting ethical behavior (Pederson, 1997). Ethical standards are general and idealistic in nature, seldom answering specific questions (Remley & Herlihy, 2010). No ethical code can address every situation, and interpretation within the context of particular situations is crucial. Consequently, community and mental health counselors are responsible for exercising sound judgment and decision-making skills in their work with clients. They are guided by ethical guidelines but do not rely on them exclusively.

Several limitations exist in any ethical code. The following are among those most frequently listed (Corey et al., 2007; Mabe & Rollin, 1986):

- Some issues cannot be resolved by a code of ethics.
- Some codes are ambiguous, making them open to interpretation.
- Enforcing ethical codes is difficult.
- There may be conflicts within the ethics codes as well as among different organizations' codes.
- Some legal and ethical issues are not covered in codes.
- Sometimes conflicts arise between ethical and legal codes.
- Ethical codes need to be examined from a cultural perspective, recognizing that some may be adapted to specific cultures.
- Ethical codes do not address every possible situation, nor do they provide solutions for all situations.
- Ethical codes are historical documents. Thus, what may be acceptable practice at one time may be considered unethical later.
- There may be difficulty in bringing the interests of all parties involved in an ethical dispute together systematically.
- Knowledge of ethical codes does not necessarily equate with ethical practice.

Thus, ethical codes are useful in many ways, but they have their limitations. Counselors need to be aware that they will not always find all the guidance they want when consulting these documents. Nevertheless, anytime an ethical issue arises in counseling, the counselor should first consult ethical codes to see whether the situation is addressed.

OVERVIEW OF 2005 ACA *CODE OF ETHICS* CHANGES.   The ACA Ethics Committee took into account several emerging issues in the counseling profession when revising the 1995 *Code of Ethics.* Of particular importance was making the 2005 *Code* more applicable to the multicultural world in which counselors practice. According to Pedersen (1997), the 1995 ethical guidelines represented "a culturally biased perspective that minimalizes the importance of worldviews of ethnocultural minorities" (p. 27). Changes designed to protect the public and reflect emerging issues were also instituted. The following points represent an overview of the changes made to the ACA *Code of Ethics* during the 2005 revision, which supersedes the 1995 version (ACA, 2007; Briggs, 2008).

- There is an increased focus on cultural sensitivity throughout the 2005 *Code.*
- Counseling interventions grounded in theory and/or empirical foundations are mandated.

- The term *serious and foreseeable harm,* in regard to a counselor's duty to warn, replaces the term *clear and imminent danger.*
- Additional guidelines regarding the ethical use of technology are established.
- In some cases, dual relationships, when they are beneficial to the client, are allowed.
- Counselors are restricted from engaging in romantic or sexual relationships with clients for at least 5 years after the termination of the counseling relationship. (The 1995 *Code* specified 2 years.)
- Protection for the confidentiality of deceased clients is provided.
- Ethical guidelines related to end-of-life care for terminally ill clients are delineated.
- Counselors have permission to refrain from diagnosing clients, preferably in collaboration with the client, when such an action is in the client's best interest.
- Counselors need to have a transfer plan in place for assisting clients as they transition to a new counselor. They need to allow the new counselor to obtain their records if the counselor leaves the practice, becomes incapacitated, or dies.
- The 2005 *Code* does not include an additional *Standards of Practice,* which was part of the 1995 *Code.*

Ten interviews highlighting the major changes in the 2005 *Code,* which provide specific information about each change, can be accessed through ACA's Web site at www.counseling.org/ethics.

Making Ethical Decisions

It is not unusual for counselors to experience situations in which ethical guidelines are less than clear and an ethical decision must be made. In the absence of clear ethical guidelines, relying strictly on personal value judgments or doing what "seems right" is not adequate because not all value judgments are equally valid (Kitchener, 1984). Ethics is a critical component of counseling practice, and counselors need to be taught competent ways of making ethical decisions (Cottone & Claus, 2000). Numerous models have been developed to help counselors with the decision-making process (see Cottone & Claus for a review), although surprisingly little research has been conducted on the effectiveness of these models.

Kitchener's (1984) seminal work on ethical decision making in counseling and counseling psychology precipitated an increased interest in the topic among practitioners and educators. In her article, Kitchener emphasized the need for counseling professionals to develop a deeper understanding of the foundations of ethical decision making. Fundamental to the decision-making process are the five moral/ethical principles of **autonomy, beneficence, nonmaleficence, justice,** and **fidelity.** All these principles involve conscious decision making by counselors throughout the counseling process. Of these principles, some experts identify nonmaleficence as primary. Nonmaleficence involves removing present harm as well as preventing future harm (Thompson, 1990). It is the basis on which counselors respond to clients who may endanger themselves or others. It also underlies the mandate to respond to colleagues' unethical behavior (Daniluk & Haverkamp, 1993).

Among the many existing decision-making models, some are theoretically or philosophically based, others are practice based, and some draw from both theory and practice. Decision-making models bring order and clarity to the reasoning process, thereby helping counselors resolve ethical dilemmas more effectively. A model that is grounded in the five moral principles described earlier and that provides pragmatic, practice-oriented procedures was developed by Forester-Miller and Davis (1998) and is presented next. The seven-step decision-making model can be accessed through ACA's Web site at www.counseling.org.

ETHICAL DECISION-MAKING MODEL

1. *Identify the problem.* Gather information, being as specific and objective as possible, to help clarify the situation. Ask questions such as, "Is this an ethical, legal, professional or clinical problem, or some combination of each?" and "Is the issue related to my actions, the client's actions, or the agency and its policies?" Examine the problem from many different perspectives, and avoid searching for an easy solution. If legal questions exist, seek advice from legal experts.

2. *Apply the ACA Code of Ethics.* After the problem is identified, refer to the *Code of Ethics* (2005) to determine which ethical guidelines apply. If one or more guidelines apply and the course of action is clearly delineated, follow that course of action. If the problem is more complex, then there probably is a true ethical dilemma, and it will be necessary to take additional steps.

3. *Determine the nature and dimensions of the dilemma.* Several avenues should be followed to ensure that the problem has been fully examined, including these:

- Consider the principles of autonomy, beneficence, nonmaleficence, justice, and fidelity. Which principles apply to the situation? Which principle takes priority in this case if two or more principles are in conflict?
- Review the relevant professional literature.
- Consult with experienced colleagues or supervisors. They may be able to identify aspects of the dilemma that are not readily apparent.
- Consult with state or national professional associations.

4. *Generate potential courses of action.* If possible, work with at least one colleague to brainstorm as many options as possible.

5. *Consider the potential consequences of all options and determine a course of action.* Evaluate each option and its potential consequences. What are the implications for the client, yourself, and others? Eliminate options with problematic consequences and determine which option best addresses the situation and the priorities you have identified.

6. *Evaluate the selected course of action.* Evaluate the selected course of action to determine whether it presents any new ethical considerations. Stadler (1986) suggested applying three simple tests:

- Would you treat others in this situation the same way?
- Would you want your behavior reported by the media?
- Would you recommend the same course of action to another counselor in the same situation?

If the answer to any of these questions is negative, reevaluate the problem and the course of action selected. If the answers are affirmative, thus passing the tests of justice, publicity, and universality, move on to implementing a course of action.

7. *Implement the course of action.* Taking the final step involves courage and strength of conviction. Document the action and include a rationale for selecting the particular course of action (Watts, 1999). After implementing the plan, follow up on the situation to determine whether your actions resulted in the anticipated consequences.

It is important to remember that different professionals may arrive at different solutions to the same ethical dilemma, particularly if it is complex. Forester-Miller and Davis (1998) reminded us that following a systematic model to arrive at a decision provides a professional explanation for the course of action implemented. By evidencing good intentions, the knowledge and skill to make ethical decisions, and the moral courage to see those decisions through, community and mental health counselors are better able to engage consistently in ethical counseling behaviors.

OTHER GUIDELINES FOR ACTING ETHICALLY.   Swanson (1983a) listed four guidelines deemed important in assessing whether counselors act in ethically responsible ways. The first is that counselors *act with personal and professional honesty*. Counselors must operate openly with themselves and those with whom they work. Hidden agendas and unacknowledged feelings hinder relationships and place counselors on shaky ethical ground. One way to overcome personal or professional honesty problems that may get in the way of acting ethically is to receive supervision (Kitchener, 1994).

A second guideline is that counselors *act in the best interest of clients*. This ideal is easier to discuss than to achieve. At times, a counselor may impose personal values on clients and ignore what the client really wants. At other times, a counselor may fail to recognize an emergency and too readily accept the idea that the best interest of the client is served by doing nothing.

A third guideline is that counselors *act without malice or personal gain*. Some clients are difficult to like or deal with, and counselors must be especially careful with these individuals. However, counselors must also be careful to avoid relationships with likeable clients on either a personal or a professional basis. Errors in judgment are most likely to occur when the counselor's self-interest becomes a part of the relationship with a client (St. Germaine, 1993).

A final guideline is whether counselors can *justify an action* "as *the best judgment of what should be done based upon the current state of the profession*" (Swanson, 1983a, p. 59). To make such a decision, counselors must keep up with current trends by reading the professional literature, attending in-service workshops and conventions, and becoming actively involved in local, state, and national counseling activities.

The ACA *Ethical Standards Casebook* (Herlihy & Corey, 2006) can be especially helpful in many counseling situations. It presents case studies describing questionable ethical situations and provides guidelines and questions for reflection to assist counselors in making ethical responses. The text and case studies examine a wide range of ethical issues, including client rights and informed consent, multicultural counseling concerns, confidentiality, competence, working with multiple clients, counseling minor clients, working with clients who may harm themselves, counselor education and supervision, and the relationship between law and ethics.

As helpful as the casebook may be, in many counseling situations the proper course of action may not be obvious (Wilcoxon, Remley, Gladding, & Huber, 2007). For example, the question of confidentiality as it pertains to the individual rights of a person with AIDS and society's right to be protected from the spread of the disease is one with which some counselors struggle (Harding, Gray, & Neal, 1993). Likewise, there are multiple ethical dilemmas involved in counseling adult survivors of incest, including issues of confidentiality and the consequences of reporting abuse (Daniluk & Haverkamp, 1993). Therefore, when in doubt about what to do in a given situation, it is crucial for counselors to consult with colleagues and/or seek supervision, in addition to referring to principles, guidelines, casebooks, and professional codes of ethics. Also, ACA members can contact the ACA Ethics and Standards Department at 1-800-347-6647, ext. 314, or e-mail the director of the department, Larry Freeman, at lfreeman@counseling.org for a free professional consultation.

Unethical Behavior

Although most counselors strive to adhere to ethical standards, situations occasionally arise when such is not the case. In these circumstances, counselors must take some action. To do otherwise condones the unethical behavior and can be detrimental to both the clients and the profession. Whereas the primary purpose of the ACA *Code of Ethics* is to guide our own behavior, not to judge the behavior of others, as professionals we are mandated to address unethical behavior appropriately (Remley & Herlihy, 2010). The caution against judging too quickly must be balanced against the obligation to address practices of peers that are viewed as unethical.

The ACA *Code of Ethics* (2005) states, "When counselors possess knowledge that raises doubts as to whether another counselor is acting in an unethical manner, they take appropriate action" (Standard H.2.a.). The phrases "possesses knowledge" and "appropriate action" require careful attention. First, it is important to avoid making decisions based on secondhand information or rumors. Only direct knowledge of unethical behavior obligates a counselor to take action. Second, the procedures for determining what to do in situations when ethical conduct is in question vary according to the seriousness of the misconduct (Welfel, 2006). Minor breaches of conduct typically are more amenable to informal resolution than serious violations.

According to the ACA guidelines, a counselor should initially attempt to address issues of misconduct informally with the counselor whose behavior is in question. In many cases, especially if the privacy of an involved party is at risk, it is best to consult with a trusted professional before taking this step (Remley & Herlihy, 2010). Addressing the issue informally involves confrontation in a caring context, which ideally will lead to the counselor in question seeking help. If an informal approach is unsuccessful or unfeasible, it may be necessary to report the offense. According to the 2005 *Code*, *"If an apparent violation has substantially harmed, or is likely to harm a person or organization and is not appropriate for informal resolution or is not resolved properly, counselors take further action appropriate to the action"* (Standard H.2.c). Examples of appropriate action include reporting the perceived violation to state or national ethics committees, voluntary national certification bodies, state licensure boards, or the appropriate institutional authorities.

Prior to making a decision to report a suspected ethical violation, community and mental health counselors are advised to consult with other professionals. Remley and Herlihy (2010, p. 381) recommend that the following conditions have been met:

- The issue cannot be resolved directly with the counselor due to the circumstances or because attempts at resolution have been unsuccessful.
- You have direct knowledge that a serious violation has occurred that is causing substantial harm or has caused substantial harm.
- You have consulted with colleagues who agree that a report must be made.
- You are willing to participate in a hearing and testify, if a hearing is conducted.
- You are prepared to defend yourself if a counterclaim is filed against you.

The ACA Ethics Committee is responsible for managing formal reports of unethical practice on the part of ACA members. Responsibilities of the Ethics Committee include educating members about the ACA *Code of Ethics,* periodically reviewing and recommending revisions to the code, receiving and processing complaints of reported ethical violations of ACA members, providing interpretations of the ACA ethical guidelines, and recommending appropriate disciplinary actions in cases where ethical violations are substantiated (ACA Governing Council, 2005).

BOX 3–1

No one knows how often counselors actually engage in unprofessional, unethical, or illegal practice-related behaviors. However, the relative infrequency of censure by ethics committee, licensing board discipline, lawsuit, or criminal arrest when compared to the estimated 250,000-plus practicing counselors in America suggests that formal accusations of questionable behavior are rare. In our experience, even when there is an accusation against a mental health professional, things often turn out in favor of the practitioner.

(Wheeler & Bertram, 2008, p. 1)

Counselors are responsible not only for acting in ways that are personally and professionally ethical but also for engaging in behavior that is lawful. At times, ethical and legal standards are in conflict. In the next section, we explore legal issues that affect the mental health profession, followed by descriptions of some of the more common ethical and/or legal issues that community and mental health counselors encounter.

THE LAW AND COUNSELING

The profession of counseling is governed by legal standards as well as by ethical ones. *Legal* refers to "law or the state of being lawful," and *law* refers to "a body of rules recognized by a state or community as binding on its members" (Shertzer & Stone, 1980, p. 386). The law plays a pervasive role in the personal and professional lives of counselors and affects almost all areas of counselor practice. Wheeler and Bertram (2008) reminded us, "It is important that counselors understand the basic concepts of the legal system, the general body of law affecting professional practice, and the impact of professional conduct and ethical standards so they are prepared to address potential problems as they arise in practice" (p. 25).

The legal system of the United States is not static. Interpretations of law evolve over time and frequently are situationally contingent. Also, no general, comprehensive body of law regulates mental health professions (Van Hoose & Kottler, 1985). However, a number of court decisions and statutes influence legal opinions on counseling. Court decisions based on rulings that interpret a law according to a specific case establish what is known as *case law* (Cottone & Tarvydas, 2007). The 1993 Napa County, California, case involving Gary Ramona illustrates a legal decision of this nature. In a widely publicized trial, Ramona sued his daughter's therapists, "charging that by implanting false memories of sexual abuse in her mind they had destroyed his life" (Butler, 1994, p. 10). Ramona was awarded $475,000 after the jury "found the therapists had negligently reinforced false memories" (Butler, p. 11). The legal concept on which the case was decided was *duty to care*—a legal obligation of health providers to not act negligently.

Another important legal case in recent years was the 1996 U.S. Supreme Court decision in *Jaffee v. Redmond,* which maintained that communications between licensed psychotherapists and their patients are privileged and do not have to be disclosed in cases held in federal court (Remley, Herlihy, & Herlihy, 1997). The importance of the case for counseling is that a legal precedent was set regarding privileged communication between a master's-level clinician (in this case, a social worker) and her client. The court decision affirmed the importance of protecting confidential communications between "psychotherapists" (the term used in this particular ruling) and their clients, thereby establishing a precedent that makes it more likely for judges to extend privilege in cases involving licensed counselors and clients (Glosoff, Herlihy, & Spence, 2000).

Stude and McKelvey (1979) observed that the law is "generally supportive or neutral" (p. 454) toward professional codes of ethics and toward counseling in general. The law supports licensure or certification of counselors as a means of ensuring that those who enter the profession attain at least minimal standards. It also supports the general "confidentiality of statements and records provided by clients during therapy" (p. 454). In addition, the law is neutral "in that it allows the profession to police itself and govern counselors' relations with their clients and fellow counselors" (p. 454). The only time the law overrides a professional code of ethics is when it is necessary "to protect the public health, safety, and welfare" (p. 454). This necessity is most likely to occur in situations concerning confidentiality, when disclosure of information is necessary to prevent harm. In such cases, counselors have a *duty to warn* potential victims about the possibility of a client's violent behavior (Costa & Altekruse, 1994).

Legal Mechanisms That Affect Counselors

CREDENTIALING.   One way the mental health profession is affected by our legal system is through credentialing. As explained in Chapter 2, legal regulation can take the form of licensure, certification, or registration, with licensure being the most powerful form of credentialing (Remley & Herlihy, 2010). Currently, 49 states license counselors. Licensure statutes specify minimum standards for becoming licensed to practice in a particular state. They also provide legal definitions of counselors' roles and legal recourse for alleged violations (Hershenson, Power, & Waldo, 1996). Community and mental health counselors will want to be aware of credentialing requirements and legal ramifications associated with credentialing that may affect their practice.

CRIMINAL, CIVIL, AND ADMINISTRATIVE LAW.   Community and mental health counselors are affected by the legal system through criminal, civil, and administrative law, in addition to case law, which was discussed earlier. *Criminal law* applies to acts that are considered crimes against society and are prosecuted by the government, not by individuals (Wheeler & Bertram, 2008). Such acts are punishable by fines, imprisonment, or, in extreme cases, the death penalty. Fraud, civil disobedience, being an accessory to a crime, and contributing to the delinquency of a minor are examples of criminal offenses for which some mental health professionals have been found liable (Anderson, 1996; Vacc & Loesch, 2000).

Civil law applies to acts committed that affect the civil rights of individuals or other bodies (Anderson, 1996). Civil matters are settled in court when one individual brings suit against another, with sanctions applied to compensate the wronged individual. Civil liability is based on the concept of *tort*—a term that refers to a wrong that legal action is designed to set right (Wheeler & Bertram, 2008). Intentional torts include such things as battery, defamation of character, and invasion of privacy. Unintentional torts often involve *negligence,* which refers to situations in which the mental health professional does not carry out his or her responsibilities in accordance with the standards of care outlined by the profession. The most common cause of legal liability for mental health professionals is *malpractice,* a term that refers to negligence in carrying out professional responsibilities or duties (Cottone & Tarvydas, 2007).

Administrative law is created by government agencies that develop regulations to help define the laws, or statutes, that are passed by a legislative body (Wheeler & Bertram, 2008). A federal regulation that was instigated in 2003, which has many implications for mental health professionals, is the Health Insurance Portability and Accountability Act (HIPAA). HIPAA includes a variety of standards and rules that address client and patient privacy and security. The HIPAA Privacy Rule was instated on the federal level to address concerns related to the transmission of health care information, either electronically or on paper. The HIPAA Security Rule "dovetails with the HIPAA Privacy Rule and requires technical, administrative, and physical safeguards to protect the security of protected health information in electronic form" (Wheeler & Bertram, 2008, p. 69). To determine whether they are *covered entities* under HIPAA, community and mental health counselors can visit the Web site for the Centers for Medicare and Medicaid Services at ww.cms.hhs.gov/aps/hipaa2decisionssupport/default.asp.

MALPRACTICE.   Professional malpractice is regulated by state law and therefore usually applies only when a person is credentialed according to state statute. However, counselors can still be held legally negligible or guilty of intentional infliction of distress, even in cases when the term *malpractice* does not technically apply (Anderson, 1996). Community and mental health counselors are expected to exercise *due care* or face potential liability for failing to perform their professional duties (Wheeler & Bertram, 2008).

Areas of potential malpractice for counselors include, but are not limited to (Vacc & Loesch, 2000, pp. 249–250):

- Making a faulty diagnosis (e.g., attributing a physically based problem to a psychological condition)
- Failing to take action when someone other than the client is in danger
- Improperly certifying a client in a commitment hearing
- Engaging in behavior inappropriate to the accepted standards of the profession
- Failing to take adequate precautions for a suicidal client
- Providing services for which competence has not been established
- Breaching confidentiality
- Promising a "cure"
- Taking advantage of the counseling relationship for personal gain, monetary or otherwise
- Failing to use a technique that would have been more helpful
- Failing to provide informed consent
- Failing to explain the possible consequences of counseling interventions.

Until recently, there were relatively few counselor malpractice suits. However, with the increased number of licensed, certified, and practicing counselors, malpractice suits have become more common. Therefore, community counselors must make sure they protect themselves from such possibilities.

There are several proactive ways to avoid malpractice and protect oneself from liability. To avoid malpractice, community counselors will want to adhere to professional codes of ethics and provide counseling services viewed as acceptable by the profession (Anderson, 1996; Granello & Witmer, 1998). Regardless of how careful counselors are, however, malpractice lawsuits can still occur. Therefore, carrying professional liability insurance is essential. *Avoiding Counselor Malpractice* (Crawford, 1994) is an excellent book explaining the nature and scope of malpractice and ways to take reasonable precautions to avoid being implicated in lawsuits. *The Counselor and the Law: A Guide to Legal and Ethical Practice* (Wheeler & Bertram, 2008) is another text that provides vital information regarding legal issues affecting mental health professionals, including malpractice. Being cognizant of legal issues and obtaining legal advice when questions arise can help counselors protect themselves should their actions be challenged (Remley & Herlihy, 2010).

OTHER REASONS FOR COURT APPEARANCES.   A relatively small number of counselors have to appear in court to face liability charges. More frequently, counselors find themselves in court for other reasons. For example, a counselor may be asked to serve as an expert witness. An *expert witness* is "an objective and unbiased person with specialized knowledge, skills, or information, who can assist a judge or jury in reaching an appropriate legal decision" (Remley, 1992, p. 33). A counselor who serves as an expert witness is compensated for his or her time financially. Counselors who plan to serve as expert witnesses are advised to take courses, observe other experts in court, and read pertinent written materials to be prepared to serve in that capacity (Remley & Herlihy, 2010).

A counselor may also be summoned to appear in court through a *court order* (i.e., a subpoena to appear in court at a certain time in regard to a specific case). Such a summons is issued with the intent of having the counselor testify on behalf of or against a present or former client. Because the legal system is adversarial, counselors are wise to seek the advice of attorneys before responding to court orders (Remley, 1991). In so doing, counselors may come to understand the law, court proceedings, and options they have in response to legal requests. Role-playing possible scenarios before appearing in court may also help counselors function better in such situations.

To prepare for legal encounters, counselors should read some or all of the 12 volumes in the *American Counseling Association Legal Series*. These volumes, edited by Theodore P. Remley, Jr., are written by counseling experts who have either legal degrees or expert knowledge on important legal issues such as preparing for court appearances, documentation of counseling records, counseling minors, confidentiality and privileged communication, third-party payments, and managing a counseling agency.

The Case of Luke

Luke is a 6-year-old boy whose parents separated 11 months ago. He has been seeing you for counseling at a mental health agency for 6 months. Luke is living with his mother, who brought him to counseling after he began wetting the bed and withdrawing from friends and other activities. You have met with Luke for eight sessions, using nondirective play therapy as a primary intervention tool. During the course of therapy, Luke reveals that when his father was home, he was much happier. He draws a picture of his mother with an angry face and then he draws a large black X over her face. He says that he is angry with his mother and wants to live with his father.

You have kept careful records of each session, following HIPAA guidelines and the guidelines of your agency. Last week, you received a subpoena to appear in court next month, when the divorce will be finalized and custody decisions will be made. What concerns do you have? Will you reveal all of your written documents? What responsibilities do you have to Luke, his mother, his father, and the legal system?

COMMON ETHICAL AND LEGAL CONCERNS

Counselors in all settings deal with many issues that have ethical and legal ramifications. A number of authors (e.g., Corey et al., 2007; Cottone & Tarvydas, 2007; Remley & Herlihy, 2010; Welfel, 2006; Wheeler & Bertram, 2008) have written texts that describe ethical and legal concerns that affect mental health practitioners. Also, these topics are frequently addressed in professional development and continuing education activities. The purpose of this section is not to provide a comprehensive overview of all the ethical and legal issues community and mental health counselors may encounter; instead, it is to provide information about some of the more common concerns that affect the practice of community counseling: shared communication, informed consent, dual relationships, and professional competence. Other issues, including record keeping, mandated counseling, payment issues, professional responsibilities, counseling minors, and issues related to managed care and technology, are addressed in other chapters.

Privacy, Confidentiality, and Privileged Communication

The relationship between counselors and clients is based on trust. For communication to occur freely, clients must have both their privacy and the information shared in session protected. Ethical and legal issues related to communication and trust include privacy, confidentiality, and privileged communication.

DEFINITIONS. *Privacy* is the client's right to determine what information about themselves will be shared with others (Remley & Herlihy, 2010). It is a broad term that includes not only the confidences shared during counseling sessions but also the fact that the client is participating in counseling. Several factors can jeopardize a client's privacy right, including waiting in a general reception area, using credit cards for billing, disposing of records, taping sessions, and other documentary or business activities associated with the counseling setting (Cottone & Tarvydas, 2007). Professional mental health counselors must use foresight and take the necessary steps to respect and protect the dignity and privacy of their clients.

Confidentiality is a professional's promise not to disclose information revealed during the privacy of the counselor–client relationship, except under the conditions agreed on (Cottone & Tarvydas, 2007; Glosoff, 2001). The assurance of confidentiality is considered one of the most fundamental obligations of counselors. Counselors should discuss confidentiality and its limits with clients before counseling begins. Except in certain situations, which are described later, counselors may share confidential information only with the direct written consent of clients or their legal guardians (Cottone & Tarvydas, 2007). If confidence is broken, either intentionally or unintentionally, the concern becomes a potentially legal as well as an ethical issue for counselors.

Privileged communication, a narrower concept, regulates privacy protection and confidentiality by protecting clients from having their confidential communications disclosed without their permission. For privilege to be recognized, the communication "must have been made in confidence, with the indicated desire that it remain so" (Wheeler & Bertram, 2008, p. 66). Typically, state law governs whether privilege exists in a counselor–client relationship (Glosoff et al., 2000). On the federal level, the U.S. Supreme Court set a precedent for protecting confidential communications by ruling that the confidences shared between a social worker and her client were privileged and not subject to disclosure (*Jaffee v. Redmond*).

Although the concept of privilege appears to be relatively straightforward, in reality it is complex and somewhat confusing. One major reason for the confusion is that laws regulating privilege, particularly in regard to exemptions, vary from state to state. Furthermore, new laws are enacted and existing statutes are modified on a regular basis. Consequently, counselors must be familiar with statutes and case law and participate in continuing education offerings to stay abreast of new developments (Glosoff et al., 2000). Counselors also need to be aware of situations in which privilege is considered waived. Examples include when a client initiates a malpractice suit or licensure board procedure against a counselor or when a defendant claims insanity as a defense in a criminal case (Wheeler & Bertram, 2008).

Privacy, confidentiality, and privilege are among the most inquired about ethical and legal concerns received by the ACA Ethics Committee. Between October 2003 and October 2005, 24% of the total number of inquiries received by ACA's Risk Management Helpline related to these issues (Wheeler & Bertram, 2008). Specific areas of inquiry include subpoenas, counseling minors, substance abuse records, group and family counseling, counseling public offenders, confidentiality after a client's death, and issues related to technology (Wheeler & Bertram, 2008).

LIMITS OF CONFIDENTIALITY. Confidentiality is not absolute: There are times when obligations to other individuals and society override the ethical responsibility of confidentiality. It is the counselor's responsibility to clarify for clients the exceptional circumstances when breaching confidentiality is either permissible or required (Corey et al., 2007).

A landmark court case that reflects the importance of limiting confidentiality is *Tarasoff v. Board of Regents of the University of California* (1976). In this case, a student, Prosenjit Poddar, who was a voluntary outpatient at the student health services on the Berkeley campus of the University of California, informed the psychologist who was counseling him that he intended to kill his former girlfriend, Tatiana Tarasoff, when she arrived back on campus. The psychologist notified the campus police, who detained and questioned the student about his proposed activities. The student denied any intention of killing Tarasoff, acted rationally, and was released. Poddar refused further treatment by the psychologist, and no further steps were taken to deter him from his intended action. Two months later, he killed Tarasoff. Her parents sued the Board of Regents of the University of California for failing to notify the intended victim of a threat against her. The California Supreme Court ruled in their favor, indicating that a therapist has a duty to protect the public that overrides any obligation to maintain client confidentiality.

Thus, there is a limit to how much confidentiality a counselor can or should maintain. The ruling in the *Tarasoff* case, sometimes called *duty to warn,* implies that counselors need to take reasonable action to help protect potential victims from dangerous clients. Subsequent court decisions have expanded on the *Tarasoff* doctrine of *duty to warn,* by extending the *duty to warn* to persons, bystanders who might be injured by a negligent act, and individuals whose property has been threatened (Remley & Herlihy, 2010).

If a counselor determines that a client is dangerous (either to himself/herself or to others), choices of action range from relatively unintrusive (e.g., asking the client to sign a no-harm contract) to highly intrusive (e.g., having the client involuntarily committed to a psychiatric facility), with many other options existing between these two extremes. In situations where counselors are faced with the duty to warn, they should consult with colleagues and supervisors to determine the course of action that is ethically and legally sound.

A number of additional limitations to confidentiality and privileged communication have been cited in the literature. A summary of the more common exceptions is presented in Figures 3–3. Because of the differences in state statutes and individual circumstances, community counselors will want to verify the limitations that are applicable to their counseling practice. Also, if confidentiality must be broken, it is good practice to talk with the client about the need to share information and to invite the client to participate in the process when feasible (Remley & Herlihy, 2010).

Potential Exceptions to Confidentiality and Privileged Communication	
To protect others from harm	• When there is suspected abuse or neglect of a child, an elderly person, a resident of an institution, or another vulnerable individual • When the client poses a clear and imminent danger to self or others • When the client has a fatal, communicable disease and the client's behavior is putting others at risk of contracting the disease
To help improve client services	• When working under supervision (Let the client know you are being supervised.) • When consulting with colleagues or peers (e.g., treatment teams) • When clerical assistants handle confidential information (e.g., managed care) • When other mental health professionals request information and the client has provided written consent to share
Other possible exceptions	• When clients raise the issue of their mental health in legal proceedings • When counselors need to defend themselves against a complaint made to a licensure or certifying board or in a court of law • When the client is involved in civil commitment proceedings • When ordered by a court (The counselor should request privilege on behalf of the client, although the right to privilege may be legally overridden, depending on the circumstances.)

FIGURE 3–3   Potential exceptions to confidentiality and privileged communication
(*Sources:* Corey et al., 1998; Glosoff, 2001)

Informed Consent

Clients have a number of legal as well as ethical rights in counseling, but they frequently do not know about them. One of the counselor's first tasks is to learn what rights clients have and to inform the clients of those rights. The process of informed consent refers to clients' right to know what they are getting into when they engage in counseling. It allows them to make informed decisions about their treatment and the release of confidential information (Glosoff, 2001). Informed consent provides clients with information about how the counseling process works and makes them active partners in the counseling relationship (Remley & Herlihy, 2010).

In most cases, informed consent is both verbal and written. The ACA *Code of Ethics* specifies the nature of informed consent as follows:

> A.2.a. Informed Consent. Clients have the freedom to choose whether to enter into or remain in a counseling relationship and need adequate information about the counseling process and the counselor. Counselors have an obligation to review in writing and verbally with clients the rights and responsibilities of both the counselor and the client. Informed consent is an ongoing part of the counseling process, and counselors appropriately document discussions of informed consent throughout the counseling relationship. (ACA, 2005, p. 4)

Two criteria are central to the concept of informed consent: *disclosure* and *free consent* (Glosoff, 2001). *Disclosure* refers to providing clients with the information they need to make informed decisions about entering into counseling, remaining in counseling, and sharing personal information. *Free consent* means that clients choose to engage in an activity without undue pressure or coercion. For informed consent to be legally recognized, clients must demonstrate *capacity* (the ability to make rational decisions) and know that they are free to withdraw consent at any time, except in court-ordered situations. When working with minors and others unable to legally provide informed consent, special considerations, such as those discussed in Chapter 12, are necessary.

Professional disclosure statements prepared by counselors are contracts that formalize the informed consent process. Disclosure statements are described in more detail in Chapter 5. The ACA *Code of Ethics* (2005) specifies the elements that ethically are part of informed consent procedures and therefore need to be included in disclosure statements:

- The purposes, goals, techniques, procedures, limitations, potential risks, and benefits of the proposed services
- The counselor's qualifications, including relevant degrees held, licenses and certifications, areas of specialization, and experience
- Arrangements for continuation of services if the counselor dies or becomes incapacitated
- The implications of diagnosis and the intended use of tests and reports
- Information about fees and billing
- Confidentiality and its limitations
- Clients' rights to obtain information about their records and to participate in ongoing counseling plans
- Clients' rights to refuse any recommended services and be advised of the consequences of refusal

In addition to preparing a comprehensive, understandable professional disclosure statement for clients to sign, counselors need to talk with clients face-to-face to clarify any information that may be confusing. Also, ongoing discussion throughout the counseling process helps ensure that client and counselor are working together effectively. Informed consent begins when counseling is initiated, but the process should continue throughout the time the client is in counseling (Glosoff, 2001; Remley & Herlihy, 2010).

Because of the requirements of HIPAA, informed consent represents a legal as well as an ethical concern. Therefore, mental health professionals need to be familiar with HIPAA requirements for informed consent disclosure statements and ensure that their procedures are in compliance with the law (Remley & Herlihy, 2010).

Professional Boundaries and Multiple Relationships

A key aspect of acting ethically and legally as a counselor includes defining, maintaining, and respecting professional boundaries. As Wheeler and Bertram (2008) pointed out, counselors have a "unique responsibility, defined both ethically and legally, to manage the boundary between the role of professional counselor and client, including any other co-occurring roles that connect the counselor and the client" (p. 97). Whereas the most obvious boundary violation occurs when counselors engage in a sexual relationship with a client, a wide range of boundary issues exist (Gerig, 2007). Mental health professionals need to exercise caution to ensure that professional boundaries are maintained and not blurred. Boundaries help provide structure to the professional relationship and protect the welfare of clients, particularly in regard to vulnerability (Remley & Herlihy, 2010).

Often, boundary issues can be viewed in the context of dual or multiple relationships. The 2005 ACA *Code of Ethics* no longer uses the term *dual relationships;* instead, in Standard A.5.c., the *Code* focuses on *Nonprofessional Interactions or Relationships.* The standard indicates that nonprofessional relationships (e.g., friendships, romantic partners, family members) should be avoided, except when the interaction is **potentially beneficial to the client.** The reason is that "no matter how harmless such relationships may seem, a conflict of interest almost always exists, and any professional counselor's judgment is likely to be affected" (St. Germaine, 1993, p. 27). What follows is potentially harmful, because counselors lose their objectivity, and clients may be placed in situations in which they cannot be assertive and take care of themselves. For example, if a business transaction takes place between a counselor and a client at the same time that counseling is occurring, either party may be negatively affected if the product involved does not meet expectations. The resulting emotions will most likely affect the therapeutic relationship. This means refraining from entering into counseling relationships with friends, family members, students, fellow workers, and others with whom one has a preexisting relationship. To maintain healthy boundaries in existing counseling relationships, mental health professionals are advised to avoid socializing, exchanging gifts, or conducting business with clients.

Although the principles underlying the ethics of dual relationships seem clear, implementing them is sometimes difficult. Indeed, it may be impossible to avoid all forms of multiple relationships, particularly in small isolated communities (Glosoff, 2001). Remley and Herlihy (2010) noted that many "small worlds" exist, even in urban environments, and that people's political affiliation, ethnic identity, sexual orientation, and substance-dependence recovery status all can potentially lead to dual-relationship dilemmas. To avoid exploitation or other difficulties that may result from unavoidable multiple relationships, Glosoff (1997) suggested that counselors recognize the complexity of therapeutic relationships, exercise sound clinical judgment, attend to self-care, and engage in ongoing self-evaluation and peer consultation.

Professional Competence

Another area that has particular legal and ethical significance for community counselors is that of professional competence. Section C.2.a. of the ACA *Code of Ethics* (2005) addresses professional competence in this manner:

> Counselors practice only within the boundaries of their competence, based on their education, training, supervised experience, state and national professional credentials, and appropriate professional experience. Counselors gain knowledge, personal awareness, sensitivity, and skills pertinent to working with a diverse client population. (p. 9)

The concept of counselor competence is multidimensional. On one hand, it can be defined according to minimum requirements and minimum performance levels required by outside sources (e.g., licensure boards or counseling graduate programs). It also can be viewed as an ideal state of maximum knowledge and skills toward which counselors strive. Remley and Herlihy (2010) reminded us that competence is not an either/or concept; rather, it is multileveled and spans a continuum.

Counselors are required to practice within their boundaries of competence; however, those boundaries are not always easy to delineate. Boundaries of competence involve the levels of training, experience, and credentialing required to perform certain procedures or interventions (Cottone & Tarvydas, 2007). From a legal standpoint, competence refers to the capability of providing the accepted *standards of care* required for working in a particular situation. *Standards of care* can be defined as "the professional conduct as practiced by reasonable and prudent practitioners who have special knowledge and ability for the diagnosis and treatment of clinical conditions" (Granello & Witmer, 1998, pp. 371–372). For example, standards of care procedures are demonstrated when a mental health counselor with trained, supervised experience in cognitive–behavioral therapy and anxiety disorders selects a cognitive–behavioral intervention to use with a client dealing with panic disorder.

Professional competence can be developed and maintained through education, formal training, and supervised practice in particular areas. It is important to recognize the impossibility of universal competence: No single professional counselor will be competent in all areas (Welfel, 2006). When counselors attempt to expand their competencies, whether in a new practice area or with a new population of individuals, they need to evaluate the time, training, and supervision that will be required to develop the skills needed to work effectively with their clients.

Competent practice also involves an ability to work with a diverse population of clients. Both the ACA and the NBCC codes of ethics state that counselors have the responsibility to respect the diversity of their clients and act in ways that are nondiscriminatory. If a counselor does not have the training and supervised practice needed for working with culturally diverse clients, he or she may be practicing unethically by providing services to them (Remley & Herlihy, 2010). Community and mental health counselors have an ethical obligation to develop the knowledge and skills needed to work in a culturally diverse society. The *Multicultural Competencies and Standards* (Sue, Arredondo, & McDavis, 1992) provide guidelines for practicing culturally sensitive counseling with diverse populations. Mental health professionals need to be aware of their own cultural values and biases and also learn ways to work effectively with clients from different cultural backgrounds.

Often, counselors will find themselves in situations in which the needs of a particular client are greater than their professional competence. When this occurs, the best course of action is to refer that client to someone with the necessary training. At other times, counselors may need to refer clients on the basis of personal factors affecting competence, such as stress, illness, or some form of impairment (Remley & Herlihy, 2010). The key to practicing responsibly is being aware of one's capabilities and level of functioning and making sound judgments based on that awareness.

End-of-Life Decisions

Issues related to *end-of-life decisions,* particularly as they apply to physician-assisted suicide when individuals request a hastened death, raise both legal and ethical concerns. As stated earlier, even though the ACA *Code of Ethics* (2005) provides support for a client's right to choose options to end suffering caused by terminal illness, as well as support for counselor involvement in working with these clients, end-of-life issues present a plethora of moral, ethical, and legal questions (Wheeler & Bertram, 2008). As stated in the Purpose Statement in the 2005 ACA *Code of Ethics,* "Reasonable differences of opinion can and do exist among counselors with respect to the ways in which values, ethical principles, and ethical standards would be applied when they conflict." Even when a counselor is fully aware of his or her own stance on the issue, it is clouded by a number of factors, including (a) who the client is (the patient or the family members), (b) who has legal competence to determine what course of action is in the best interest of the family, (c) state laws, (d) the values of the client and other caretakers, and (e) the values of the counselor who is providing services (Wheeler & Bertram, 2008). Standard A.9.c states that counselors have the *option* of breaking or not breaking confidentiality. Before taking any course of action, community and mental health counselors who work with clients who are considering end-of-life options need to seek competent consultation throughout the decision-making process.

Concerns related to confidentiality, informed consent, dual relationships, professional competence, and end-of-life decisions are only a few of the many ethical and legal issues that community and mental health counselors are likely to encounter. To practice in ways that are ethically and legally sound, mental health professionals will want to participate actively in self-examination, consultation, supervision, and continuing education.

The Case of Daniel

Your client is an 18-year-old Japanese-American male named Daniel Hayashi who was referred to you by his high school counselor. Daniel has been diagnosed with an incurable cancer. Though his cancer can be treated with chemotherapy and radiation to extend his life for an indefinite amount of time, Daniel feels hopeless about his future. He has stopped doing schoolwork and looking forward to going to college. He told his school counselor of his plans to take his life, which in his culture is not forbidden and has historically been seen as an honorable decision, although he has not told his parents of his plan. Daniel's cultural background also leads him to be inexperienced with and skeptical of counseling. He is satisfied with his choice to take his life and is seeing you reluctantly.

Your own Judeo-Christian background leads you to view suicide as morally unacceptable. Your personal beliefs are that life should be protected at all costs. How can you honor Daniel's cultural beliefs while maintaining your own sense of morality? Where is the line between morals and ethics? Does this situation present an ethical dilemma? If so, what ethical principles are at odds? How does the ACA Code of Ethics address this situation? How would you proceed ethically?

Summary and Conclusion

The mental health profession is influenced by ethical and legal constructs that affect the counselor–client relationship and the practice of counseling. Counselors, like other mental health professionals, have established codes of ethics to guide them in the practice of helping others. The ACA *Code of Ethics* and the NBCC *Code of Ethics* are the main documents professional counselors should consult when they face ethical dilemmas, and clinical mental health counselors also need to consult the AMHCA *Code of Ethics*. Acting ethically is not always easy, comfortable, or clear, but it is a crucial part of maintaining professional integrity and of protecting the rights and welfare of clients.

In making ethical decisions, counselors rely on personal values as well as on ethical standards and legal precedents. Following a decision-making model and documenting reasons for selecting certain actions can promote ethical practice. To help with ethical dilemmas, community counselors can consult with professional colleagues and refer to casebooks and other professional literature. It is imperative that counselors become well informed in the area of ethics for the sake of their own well-being and for that of their clients.

In addition, it is crucial that counselors be informed about state and national legislation and legal decisions. These will affect the ways in which counselors work. Counselors are liable for civil and criminal malpractice suits if they violate client rights or societal rules. One way to protect themselves legally is for counselors to review and follow the ethical standards of the professional organizations with which they are affiliated and to operate according to recognized standard practices. Community and mental health counselors also need to have professional liability insurance in the event that their practices are questioned.

Ethical standards and legal codes reflect current conditions and are ever-evolving documents. They do not cover all situations, but they do offer help to counselors beyond that found in their own personal beliefs and values. Community and mental health counselors will want to be especially aware of ethical and legal obligations that relate to confidentiality, informed consent, professional boundaries and multiple relationships, professional competence, and end-of-life issues. They also will want to be knowledgeable about evolving ethical and legal standards that relate to managed care and the use of technology, topics that are addressed in the next chapter.

CHAPTER 4

Clinical Mental Health Counseling in a Diverse Society

I walk among groups of uniformed people
in a bustling, well-planned, unfamiliar land
   that looks in many ways like my own.
As I hear the sound of language
  alien to my ear
    I futilely search for meaningful words
     but end up with disappointments.
I am a foreigner
  different from the rest
   in looks, in style, and in expectations,
I stand out as a visitor in Osaka
  who still veers right instead of left
   to avoid the crowds in subways.
Amidst it all, I am filled with new awareness
  as I step from cultural shelters
   into a driving rain
    to become drenched in falling water
     and flooded with a rush of feelings.
The challenge of understanding
  both myself and others
   comes with each encounter.

From "Visitor in Osaka," by S. T. Gladding. Copyright 2002 by S. T. Gladding. Reprinted by permission.

———————————

The effectiveness of counseling depends on many factors, but among the most important is for the counselor and client to be able to understand and relate to each other. Effective clinical mental health counselors acknowledge differences among people and seek to improve their competence with diverse populations (Robinson-Wood, 2009).

Ethnicity, race, gender, religion, sexual orientation, age, a
represent some of the factors in which people differ. Understa
with differences is a matter of developing both self-awareness (fro
awareness of others (from the outside in; Okun, Fried, & Okun, 1999).

In this chapter, issues related to counseling distinct populations i
verse world are addressed. As Coleman (1998) pointed out, "Culturally neut
does not exist" (p. 153). As the U.S. population becomes increasingly more div
imperative for clinicians to develop the awareness, knowledge, and skills needed to
act successfully with people from different backgrounds. Methods that work well with o
client may be irrelevant or even inappropriate for other clients. Indeed, what may be valued and viewed as a strength in certain cultures may be devalued and viewed as a weak-
ness in others (Harris, Thoresen, & Lopez, 2007). Therefore, counselors must be lifelong
learners and implementers of new and effective methods of working with a wide range of
clients. Topics covered in this chapter include working with culturally and ethnically distinct clients, sexual minority clients, and clients with disabilities. We address the topics of
gender, age, socioeconomic, and other differences in Chapters 11 and 13, as well as in
other sections of this textbook.

COUNSELING ACROSS CULTURE AND ETHNICITY

Many distinct cultural and ethnic groups live in the United States. Currently, European Americans make up the largest group (approximately 70%), with four other distinct groups—
African Americans, Native Americans, Asian Americans, and Latino/(a)s—composing the
majority of the rest of the population (approximately 30%; U.S. Census Bureau, 2000). In addition to these groups, a small but significant number of Arab Americans and many people
who classify themselves as biracial or multiracial make up our population. Since the 2000
census, the number of Latinos surpassed that of African Americans, making this group the
largest ethnic minority group in the United States (U.S. Census Bureau, 2007).

Several factors influence the counseling of cultural and ethnic groups, such as understanding a client's identity, education, age, religion, socioeconomic status, and experiences with racism (Brinson, 1996). An understanding of these factors is especially
important when the counselor's and the client's cultural backgrounds differ. A guide that
can help counselors systematically consider various cultural influences is the ADRESSING
model (Hayes, 1996), shown in Figure 4–1. Letters of the model stand for "Age and generational influences, Disability, Religion, Ethnicity (which may include race), Social status,
Sexual orientation, Indigenous heritage, National origin, and Gender" (p. 332). This model
is transcultural specific, placing an emphasis both on culture-specific expertise and on a
wide range of cross-cultural issues.

About a quarter of those who initially use mental health facilities are from minority
cultural and ethnic groups (Cheung, 1991). Yet researchers have consistently found that
clients from minority groups who enter counseling tend to be less satisfied with the services they receive than are clients from majority groups. Some 50% of minority-culture
group members who begin counseling terminate after one session, as compared with
about 30% of majority-culture clients (Sue & Sue, 2003). Several hypotheses have been
proposed to explain why minority-culture clients underutilize counseling services. One
explanation is that minority clients do not find traditional settings or psychotherapy helpful. They may distrust the counseling process, considering it intrusive, dehumanizing, or

Minority Group	Biases with Power
...er adults	Ageism
...ple with disabilities	___ [a]
...ligious minorities	___ [b]
...hnic minorities	Racism
...eople of lower status	Classism
...Sexual minorities	Heterosexism
Native peoples	Racism
Refugees, immigrants, and international students	Racism and colonialism
Women	Sexism

[a] ...against people with disabilities.
[b] ...s anti-Semitism (i.e., against both Jewish and Muslim people) and ...minorities (e.g., Buddhists, Hindus, Mormons).

FIGURE 4–1 The ADRESSING model: Nine cultural factors, related minority groups, and forms of oppression

Source: From "Addressing the Complexities of Culture and Gender in Counseling," by P. A. Hayes, 1996, *Journal of Counseling and Development, 74,* p. 334. © ACA. Reprinted with permission. No further reproduction authorized without written permission of the American Counseling Association.

stigmatizing (West-Olatunji, 2001). To meet the needs of racial and ethnic minority populations more effectively, community counselors need to develop cultural competencies characterized by respect for and understanding of ethnic and racial groups, including their histories, traditions, beliefs, and value systems.

Defining Culture and Multicultural Counseling

Culture may be defined in several ways. The term can be conceptualized as a combination of "*ethnographic variables* such as ethnicity, nationality, religion, and language, as well as *demographic variables* of age, gender, place of residence, etc., *status variables* such as social, economic, and educational background and a wide range of formal or informal memberships and affiliations" (Pedersen, 1990, p. 550; emphasis added). Either consciously or unconsciously, our cultural backgrounds structure our behaviors, thoughts, perceptions, values, and goals (Cohen, 1998).

A broad, inclusive definition of *culture* is "any group of people who identify or associate with one another on the basis of some common purpose, need, or similarity of background" (Axelson, 1999, p. 2). Common cultural elements include heritage, experiences, beliefs, and values. These aspects of culture are "webs of significance" that give coherence and meaning to life (Geertz, 1973). They help create the lenses through which people view and experience the world.

An individual's cultural identity is often complex and not readily apparent. People's identities are embedded in multiple levels of experiences and contexts (Robinson-Wood, 2009; Sue, Ivey, & Pedersen, 1996). The salience of various cultural elements differs from person to person. For example, one person may base his or her cultural identity on shared physical characteristics, whereas another person may identify more with shared history and beliefs. Furthermore, many people have multiple group-referenced identities, such as being a physically challenged African-American female. To facilitate empathic understanding, clinical mental health counselors can intentionally help clients articulate their cultural identity and the associated values and beliefs they consider important.

Just as the word *culture* is multifaceted, the terms *multicultural* and *multicultural counseling* have been conceptualized in numerous ways. There is no universal definition of *multicultural,* although accrediting groups such as the Council for Accreditation of Counseling and Related Programs (CACREP) have chosen to define the term broadly. Defined broadly, *multiculturalism* takes into account differences in areas such as language, social class, race, ethnicity, gender, sexual orientation, and physical ability (C. Lee, 2006b). Multiculturalism takes into account the unique qualities of various groups as well individual differences within groups. West-Olatunji (2001) emphasized that multicultural counseling refers to "multiple perspectives or multiple cultural viewpoints within the counseling relationship in which none are dominant or considered more 'normal' than others" (p. 418).

Recognizing that all people are unique cultural beings and that no two people experience culture in exactly the same way, how, then, do counselors approach multicultural counseling? Historically, counselors have taken either an *etic* or an *emic* approach to the issue. The etic perspective emphasizes the universal qualities of counseling that are culturally generalizable. In contrast, the emic perspective focuses on the indigenous characteristics of each cultural group that influence the counseling process and consequently emphasizes counseling approaches that are culturally specific. Neither approach is singularly sufficient. The etic approach has been criticized for emphasizing universality to the extent of ignoring important cultural differences. The emic approach has been criticized for overemphasizing specific, culturally appropriate techniques to facilitate client change. Conceivably, the most constructive approach to multicultural counseling is one that merges etic and emic perspectives by focusing on both universal themes and specific cultural considerations.

As counseling professionals and researchers continue to build on the foundation of multicultural knowledge, one point remains clear: Clinical mental health counselors need to develop cultural sensitivity and competency to work effectively with clients who differ from them. Counselors who disregard cultural differences and operate under the assumption that all counseling theories and techniques are equally applicable to all clients are, according to Wrenn (1962b), *culturally encapsulated.* Insensitivity to the actual experiences of clients from different cultural backgrounds can lead to discrimination as well as to ethical misconduct.

Recently (summer 2008), *The Journal of Counseling and Development* published a special issue on the ongoing multicultural counseling movement. The guest editors, Michael D'Andrea and Elizabeth Foster Heckman, indicated that "the multicultural counseling movement has taken center stage in the counseling profession" (2008, p. 259). To that end, they identified five themes that have emerged from multicultural counseling publications during the past two decades:

1. Sensitivity to the significant ways that cultural factors affect human development,
2. Awareness of the competencies practitioners need to acquire to promote the healthy development of clients from diverse populations,
3. Giving consideration to the professional training strategies that help foster the development of cultural competence among professionals,
4. Having a broad knowledge of the research findings related to multicultural findings, and
5. Understanding present and future challenges that the counseling profession faces with a society that continues to be in a state of rapid flux in its racial/cultural demography. (p. 259)

Challenges and Issues in Multicultural Counseling

Becoming competent multicultural counselors can present both challenges and opportunities for practitioners. Skillful multicultural counseling involves being sensitive and flexible, tolerating ambiguity, and understanding and accepting different *worldviews* (Locke, 2001). *Worldview* refers to the way people perceive their relationship to the world, including nature, other people, objects, and religion (Sue, 1981). Worldviews, which are grounded in culture-based attitudes and experiences, influence people's thoughts, feelings, behaviors, and perceptions.

One challenge related to multicultural counseling is the ability to recognize difficulties that arise from living in poverty and discrimination. Such difficulties may be associated with, but do not define, an individual's cultural identity. A failure to distinguish between cultural identity and systemic oppression can lead to *overculturalizing*—that is, "mistaking people's reactions to poverty and discrimination for their cultural pattern" (Smith & Vasquez, 1985, p. 533). Historically, members of ethnic minority groups in the United States have an average income that is lower than the average income of majority group members. A disproportionate number of minority group families have limited financial resources (Surgeon General, 2002). When people live in an environment characterized by poverty and powerlessness, they may exhibit behaviors and attitudes that appear dysfunctional but are, in fact, healthy coping mechanisms for living in that environment (West-Olatunji, 2001). Clinical mental health counselors need to be aware of the multiple environmental and societal factors that affect their clients, some of which are culturally based and others that are not.

BOX 4–1

We cannot assume that racism will disappear just by our being good people, or by leaving people of color to deal with it. We cannot assume that sexism will disappear just by our being good people, or by leaving women to deal with it. We cannot assume that homophobia will disappear just by our being good people, or by leaving lesbians and gay men to deal with it. We cannot assume that discrimination against the "differently-abled" will disappear just by our being good people, or by leaving people who are differently-abled to deal with it. We can no longer tolerate the barriers that have kept us separate for so long. To take pleasure and strength in the particular heritage to which we were born is fine; to buttress our own identities by humiliating or demonizing or rendering invisible those of other heritages is a sure recipe for our own disaster. Alone, we will be mystified, silenced, invalidated; we will burn out in the struggle. But together, we can help each other pull down the walls that separate us and demolish the invisible barriers that keep us from the connection that is our human birthright.

(Locke, 2001, pp. 245–246)

A pressing issue that affects counseling in a diverse society is *racism.* Prejudice and racism are closely related, but have been defined differently. *Prejudice*, according to Allport's (1954) classic definition, is a negative bias toward a particular group of people. *Racism* is based on prejudicial beliefs, which maintain that racial groups other than one's own are inferior (Casas, 2005). Prejudice is mainly attitudinal in nature, whereas "racism extends the negative attitude into behavior that discriminates against a particular group" (Utsey, Ponterotto, & Porter, 2008, p. 339). Racism demeans all who participate in it and is a form of projection usually displayed out of fear or ignorance. *Cultural racism* occurs when one cultural group considers another group inferior, and the first group has the power to impose its standards on the other group. *Institutionalized racism* refers to the established use of policies, laws, customs, and norms to perpetuate discrimination and prejudice. It may be difficult for someone who is part of a majority group to recognize his or her own racism, although doing so is vital to the development of cultural self-awareness (W. Lee, 2007).

Another challenge in multicultural counseling is the dominance of theoretical approaches based on Euro-American philosophical assumptions and cultural values (Sue & Sue, 2003). Some of the predominant Euro-American assumptions and values include individualism, autonomy, an action-oriented approach to problem solving, the work ethic, the scientific method, and an emphasis on rigid time schedules (Axelson, 1999; Sue et al., 1996). A liability of these values in counseling is that theories built around them may not always be applicable to clients from other cultural traditions. Indeed, such culture-bound values may contradict the value systems of other cultural groups, and imposing them on racial/ethnic minorities may be detrimental. Clinical and mental health counselors are challenged to move beyond Eurocentric biases that characterize traditional counseling theories and develop new conceptual frameworks that provide a "more complete, accurate, and culturally respectful understanding of human development" (D'Andrea & Daniels, 2001, p. 537).

A fourth factor that affects multicultural counseling is the client's level of *acculturation,* which is a process of socialization in which members of one cultural group adopt the beliefs and behaviors of another group. Whereas we often refer to acculturation as a process through which a minority group adopts the beliefs and behaviors of the dominant group, the process may be reciprocal. During the acculturation process, individuals are simultaneously influenced by elements of more than one culture. Coping with the conflict created by this experience can be difficult. Research indicates that challenges in trying to balance contrasting values of two or more different cultures include "psychological stress, guilt, apathy, depression, delinquency, resentment, disorientation, and poor self-esteem" (Yeh & Hwang, 2000, p. 425). People navigate these stressors differently, particularly in the case of first-generation immigrants (Cuellar, 2000). Culturally sensitive counselors are aware of the different ways in which acculturation can influence client issues and the counseling process.

Socioeconomic status, racism, value differences, and acculturation all can potentially influence the client–counselor relationship and the effectiveness of counseling. We challenge you to remain abreast of the myriad issues related to multicultural counseling and to serve as advocates for social change, a topic that is addressed further in Chapter 8.

Developing Multicultural Counseling Competencies

In 1996, the Association for Multicultural Counseling and Development (AMCD) published a document, *Operationalization of the Multicultural Counseling Competencies* (Arredondo et al., 1996), designed to help counselors work effectively in an ethnically diverse society. These competencies were originally posited in an article by Sue, Arredondo, and McDavis in their well-known article, "Multicultural Counseling Competencies and Standards: A Call to the Profession" (1992). The multicultural counseling competencies (MCC) have been endorsed by many professional counseling associations and have contributed to changes in ACA's *Code of Ethics* (2005) and counseling accreditation standards (Council for Accreditation of Counseling and Related Educational Programs [CACREP], 2009). Clinical mental health counselors will want to be familiar with the multicultural competencies outlined in the publication and strive to implement them in their work with clients.

Specifically, the 31 competencies are organized into three categories: (a) *awareness* of one's own personal worldview and the effect of cultural conditioning on personal development, (b) *knowledge* of the worldviews of culturally different clients, and (c) *skills* needed to work with culturally different clients (Arredondo et al., 1996). Ethnically responsive counselors are professionals who have intentionally found ways to grow and develop in each of these three categories (C. Lee, 2006b).

SELF-AWARENESS.   For counselors to work successfully with clients from diverse backgrounds, counselors need to be aware of their own beliefs, attitudes, and feelings associated with cultural differences such as racism, sexism, heterosexism, and other areas of difference (Sue & Sue, 2003). They need to be aware of their own cultural values and biases before they can work effectively with people from different cultures. To develop self-awareness, counselors and counselors-in-training need to examine their own cultural heritage and personal ethnic identity development. This process is facilitated when counselors ask themselves questions such as, "How do I see myself as a member of my cultural group?" "How do I see other people in my cultural group?" and "How do I perceive people different from me in regard to race, ethnicity, sexuality, and other areas?" Self-exploration leads to self-awareness, which enables counselors to become cognizant of ways their worldviews and biases might influence the counseling process.

KNOWLEDGE.   In addition to developing self-awareness, counselors and counselors-in-training need to acquire a knowledge base that guides their work in a diverse society. To that end, C. Lee (2001) offered the following suggestions:

- Acquire an understanding of how economic, social, and political systems affect the psychosocial development of ethnic and other minority groups.
- Acquire general knowledge about the histories, experiences, customs, and values of people from diverse groups. Understand how these contexts influence personal and social development.
- Read the literature and use the media to learn about the lifestyles, customs, values, and traditions of different ethnic groups. For example, view diversity-focused films about specific cultures, such as the ones listed in Figure 4–2, to understand and experience these cultures vicariously. Also, literature can provide tremendous insight into a wide range of cultural experiences.
- Experience ethnic diversity firsthand by interacting with people in their cultural environments (e.g., attend festivals and ceremonies). In counselor-training programs, invite people from other cultures to speak, either individually or as part of a panel.

Although it is unrealistic to expect counselors to be knowledgeable about all cultures, they can intentionally learn about different ethnic groups, particularly those that they are most likely to encounter in counseling. By developing knowledge about different cultural groups, counselors are better prepared to work with clients in an ethnically responsive manner.

African American
Autobiography of Miss Jane Pittman
Boyz'n the Hood
The Color Purple
Colors
Do the Right Thing
Driving Miss Daisy
Eye on the Prize
Guess Who's Coming to Dinner
I Know Why the Caged Bird Sings
Jungle Fever
Long Walk Home
Malcolm X
Matewan
Mississippi Masala
Mo' Better Blues
Remember the Titans
Raisin in the Sun
Roots I & II
Sounder
To Kill a Mockingbird
Jungle Fever
White Man's Burden

Asian and Asian American
Come See the Paradise
Dim Sum
Double Happiness
Farewell to Manzanar
The Namesake (Bangladesh)
Joy Luck Club
The Kite Runner (Afghanistan)
The Wash
Wedding Banquet
Come See the Paradise
Crouching Tiger, Hidden Dragon

Latino/Latina
American Me
Ballad of Gregorio Cortez
Born in East L.A.
El Norte
Like Water for Chocolate
Mi Familia

Milagro Bean Field War
Romero
Stand and Deliver
American Me
Ballad of Gregorio Cortez
Spanglish

Multiethnic Films
Crash
Pleasantville
The Color of Fear

People with Disabilities
Born on the Fourth of July
Children of a Lesser God
Coming Home
Edward Scissorhands
Frankie Starlight
If You Can See What I Can Hear
Miracle Worker
My Left Foot
One Flew over the Cuckoo's Nest
The Other Side of the Mountain
Ray
A Patch of Blue
Waterdance
What's Eating Gilbert Grape

Gay, Lesbian, and Bisexual
And the Band Played On
Brokeback Mountain
For the Bible Tells Me So
Long Time Companion
Personal Best
Philadelphia
Priest
Strawberries and Chocolate
Torch Song Trilogy

Transgender
Boys Don't Cry
Beautiful Boxer
Normal
The Crying Game
Transamerica

FIGURE 4–2 Sample list of films focusing on diverse populations

Source: Adapted from *The Diversity Video Forum: An Adjunct to Diversity Sensitive Training in the Classroom,"* by E. J. Pinterits and D. R. Atkinson, 1998, *Counselor Education and Supervision, 37,* pp. 213–214. © 1998 by ACA. Reprinted with permission. No further reproduction authorized without written permission of the American Counseling Association.

Note: films that have been produced since 1998 have been added to the original list.

Native American	**Seniors**
Dances With Wolves	*Away from Her*
The Last of the Mohicans	*Cocoon*
The Mission	*Driving Miss Daisy*
Never Cry Wolf	*Foxfire*
Pow Wow Highway	*Fried Green Tomatoes*
Thunderheart	*Nobody's Fool*
Asian Indian	*On Golden Pond*
Mississippi Masala	*The Bucket List*
Slumdog Millionaire	

FIGURE 4–2   Sample list of films focusing on diverse populations (*Continued*)

SKILLS.   Ethnically responsive counselors are able to help people resolve problems or make decisions in ways that are consistent with the realities of their cultural experiences (C. Lee, 2001). Lee suggested that skills should be grounded in three premises:

1. Ethnic diversity is real and should not be ignored.
2. Ethnic differences are not deficiencies. Counselors need to meet clients where they are, recognizing differences and responding accordingly.
3. Counselors need to avoid stereotypes and consider the multiple contexts that affect client development.

With these premises in mind, Lee went on to describe five influences and attitudes that need to be taken into account when counseling people from diverse ethnic groups (pp. 586–587).

• **Kinship Influences.**   Kinship influences refer to the roles played by immediate and extended family, friends, and the community itself. Ethnically responsive counselors understand and appreciate those roles and, when appropriate, find ways to involve the kinship system in the counseling process. For example, in *network therapy* (Attneave, 1982), counseling takes place during a network meeting that includes the client, his or her immediate and extended family, and any significant people in the community who might be able to help with problem resolution.

• **Language Preference.**   Ethnically responsive counselors appreciate and are sensitive to a client's language preference. Differences in language can refer to dialect, style, fluency, and nonverbal communication. The language used in counseling may or may not be the language used in the client's home. When possible, counselors should communicate with clients in their preferred language. When this is not feasible, a referral to a bilingual counselor may be appropriate.

• **Gender-Role Socialization.**   Gender is a multifaceted construct that encompasses more than just biological sex. Gender roles are socially constructed and affect expectations, behaviors, and attitudes. An awareness of gender-role socialization can facilitate the counselor's ability to respond sensitively.

• **Religious/Spiritual Influences.**   As with kinship influences, the roles played by religion and spirituality differ both within and between ethnic groups. Counseling may be enhanced if the influences of these forces are recognized and, when appropriate, included as a dynamic in the counseling process.

• **Help-Seeking Attitudes and Behaviors.**   In some cultures, seeking outside help from a professional is neither understood nor valued. It may be necessary to offer services in nontraditional ways, perhaps outside the counseling setting.

BOX 4–2

As a new bilingual practitioner working with Latino/a clients and their families, I learned that I was expected not only to be a counselor but also to serve as advocate for clients who were not able at times to speak for themselves; that is, to speak English. I was faced with the dual challenges of es-tablishing myself as a beginning counselor and creating a safe environment for my clients. Being a bilingual counselor allows me the opportunity to use my language skills to counsel Spanish-speaking clients in a more direct and empathic way than would occur through using a translator. A blessing indeed, but it also has proved to be a bit of a struggle getting my peers to view me as a trained ther-apist. They initially viewed me as a *translator*, asking "What are they [the family members] saying?" rather than as a *counselor*, asking, "What do you think is going on with this family?"

As an advocate for my clients, I often must help them understand that my role is to help them with mental health issues, not to pass judgment regarding their immigration status in the United States. Through my continued work with Latino/a clients, I have experienced the joy of facilitating the removal of cultural and emotional *paredes* (walls) within individuals and families.

(Tania Castillero Hoeller, M.A. Ed., LPC, NCC, *Casa Guadalupe,* Catholic Social Services)

Becoming Ethnically Responsive Counselors: Integrating Awareness, Knowledge, and Skills

Developing multicultural counseling competencies is a complex process that integrates per-sonal growth with learning and skill development (W. Lee, 2007). One training technique that helps counselors improve their multicultural counseling skills while increasing sensitivity and understanding is Pedersen's (2002) triad role-play model. In the role-play, participants take the roles of counselor, client, and problem. They simulate a counseling session in which they strive to

- Articulate the problem from the client's cultural perspective
- Anticipate resistance from a culturally diverse client
- Diminish defensiveness by studying one's personal defensive responses
- Learn and practice recovery skills when culturally related problems occur

Pedersen (2002) recommended that counselors-in-training videotape their role-plays to facilitate greater learning. By discussing the videotaped role-plays, students can enhance their under-standing of how cultural differences can affect the counseling process.

USE OF THEORIES.   Another way counselors can develop skills in working with people from different cultures is by intentionally examining and implementing existing theories that have cross-cultural applications (e.g., Corsini & Wedding, 2008; Sue et al., 1996; Vontress, 1996). For example, existential counseling is a holistic approach that has appli-cations across cultures and socioeconomic groups (Epp, 1998). Existential theory deals with the meaning of life, freedom, human relationships, and the ultimate realities of life and death. These basic human conditions transcend culture and, for many clients, are primary counseling concerns.

An exciting development in multicultural counseling is the renewed emphasis on theories specifically designed for different cultures (C. Lee, 1997). For example, traditional Asian psychotherapies (e.g., yoga, meditation), which have existed for more than 3,000 years, have recently become more popular in the West (Walsh, 2000). Many of these Eastern traditions stress existential and transpersonal health and development, rather than pathology, using such techniques as meditation and yoga. They can have beneficial effects on wellness and psychological growth, whether used alone or in concert with other approaches.

CONVEYING CULTURAL EMPATHY.   An essential component of working effectively with culturally diverse clients is the counselor's ability to communicate cultural empathy (Chung & Bemak, 2002). For cultural empathy to be conveyed, Chung and Bemak (pp. 156–157) made the following recommendations:

- Demonstrate a genuine interest in learning more about the client's culture. Become knowledgeable about the historical and sociopolitical background of clients and demonstrate sensitivity about specific cultural issues.
- Convey genuine appreciation for cultural differences between the client and counselor.
- Incorporate culturally appropriate interventions and outcome expectations into the counseling process. Implement indigenous healing practices from the client's culture when possible.
- Understand and accept the context of family and community for clients of different backgrounds.
- Recognize the psychosocial adjustment that must be made by clients who have moved from one environment to another.
- Be sensitive to oppression, discrimination, and racism that are encountered by many people, often on a regular basis.
- Be prepared to advocate for and empower clients who feel underprivileged and devalued.

Counselors who are able to convey cultural empathy are more likely to develop therapeutic relationships with clients from different cultural backgrounds, thus increasing the likelihood of positive counseling outcomes.

The Case of Khadijah

Khadijah is a 30-year-old Muslim woman who is a recent refugee from Iraq. She lost her father and two brothers in the Iraq war. She has been in the United States for 2 months. Last week, she was harassed because of her head covering and long dress (traditional Muslim attire in Iraq). She was taunted for being a terrorist and was told that she should go back to her jihadist despotic relatives. All of this occurred in the presence of her 13-year-old daughter, who was dressed similarly. Since that incident, her daughter has refused to dress in an appropriate Islamic manner and has started challenging her parents when they insist that she do so. Khadijah has sought counseling to try to deal with the familial conflict, the anger she feels regarding the incident, the trauma of losing her father and brothers in the war, the culture shock of being in America, and general feelings of helplessness and depression.

What are your initial impressions about Khadijah? What aspects of her story have you come in contact with before? What, if anything, makes you feel uncomfortable or nervous? If you were Khadijah's counselor, what are some things you might do at the outset?

Summary

As community and mental health counselors develop ethnically responsive counseling skills, it is crucial to remember that *each individual, like each counseling session, is unique.* There are probably more within-group differences than between-group differences among different ethnic groups (Swartz-Kulstad & Martin, 1999). To counsel effectively, counselors must take steps to understand their clients and their specific concerns, taking into account their unique experiences as well as the broader contexts in which they live and interact.

As stated earlier, people frequently have multiple identities, some of which are more visible than others. In addition to focusing on ways to become an ethnically responsive counselor, it is also important to consider other issues related to counseling in a diverse society. In Chapter 11, counseling issues related to gender differences and working with older adults are addressed. In this next section, however, we turn our attention to counseling issues related to sexual orientation and gender identity.

SEXUAL ORIENTATION AND GENDER IDENTITY

Sexual orientation represents one of many dimensions that comprise an individual's identity. Unlike ethnicity, sexual orientation is, in many ways, an "invisible identity" (Bringaze & White, 2001). Consequently, counselors may not be aware of a client's sexual orientation unless the client chooses to reveal it. It is believed that approximately 15 million people in the United States are of sexual minority status (i.e., nonheterosexual; Survey Says, 2005). Percentages, which are difficult to determine precisely, range from 5 to 15% of the population (Miller & House, 2005; Moursund & Kenny, 2002). Because of the stigmatization that continues to be associated with sexual minority identity in our society, many lesbians, gays, and bisexuals experience discrimination and lack of acceptance. Whereas nonheterosexual individuals are more likely to seek counseling than their heterosexual counterparts, they report being less satisfied with their experiences in counseling and are more likely to terminate early (Miller & House, 2005).

Professional mental health organizations, including the American Counseling Association (ACA), the American Psychological Association (APA), and the National Association of Social Workers (NASW), forbid discrimination based on sexual orientation. For example, the ACA *Code of Ethics* (2005) mandates that professional counselors do not condone or engage in discrimination against clients based on their "age, culture, disability, ethnicity, race, religion/ spirituality, gender, gender identity, sexual orientation, marital status/partnership, language preference, socioeconomic status, or any basis proscribed by law" (Standard C.5.) To work effectively with lesbian, gay, or bisexual clients (hereafter referred to as *LGB*), practitioners need to develop a clear understanding of their own sexual identity, knowledge about issues related to LGB identity development and lifestyles, and skills for working competently with this population. In this section, information is presented about sexual orientation and sexual identity, special concerns related to working with LGB clients, and implications for counseling. Later in the section, we address counseling issues related to working with *transgender* individuals. Transgender individuals are persons whose gender identity differs from their biological identity. Although transgender persons may have experiences similar to LGB populations, they also have "social and psychological dimensions unique to their identity" (Palma & Stanley, 2002, p. 74).

Definitions and Terminology

Although research strongly indicates that sexual orientation is biological in origin, some people continue to refer to sexual orientation as *sexual preference,* a term that is vague and unhelpful (Chen-Hayes, 2000). The suggested terminology is *sexual orientation,* which refers to past, present, and ideal feelings about who is attractive and desirable in sexual and/or romantic ways (Chen-Hayes, 2000). Sexual orientation—which can be heterosexual, homosexual, bisexual, or questioning—is a multidimensional construct that many researchers believe exists on a continuum ranging from exclusively homosexual to exclusively heterosexual. The classic Kinsey studies (Kinsey, Pomeroy, & Martin, 1948) were among the first studies to purport that that people endorse sexual orientation along a continuum rather than "strictly in a bipolar fashion" (Savage, Harley, & Nowak, 2005). It is important to avoid making generalizations about sexual orientation because those generalities may not necessarily represent the experience of a specific client (W. Lee, 2007). For the sake of clarity, in this chapter the term *gay* refers to men who are sexually oriented to other men, *lesbian* refers to women who are sexually oriented to other women, and *bisexual* refers to individuals who are sexually oriented to both men and women. *Questioning,* which represents a more recent addition to sexuality terminology, refers to "individuals who are beginning to explore their sexual understanding" (Falkner & Starkey, 2009, p. 502).

Counselors will want to select terminology prudently in their work with all clients, regardless of their sexual orientation. In particular, referring to someone as *homosexual* is discouraged because of the psychopathological connotations ascribed to that term in early editions of the *Diagnostic and Statistical Manual of Mental Disorders* (American Psychiatric Association [APA], 1968), when homosexuality was classified as a mental illness. Because the use of language can affect self-esteem, stigmatize, and be offensive, it is important for counselors to be cognizant of their use of language and check with clients to determine their preferences in regard to terminology (Miller & House, 2005).

Researchers distinguish among the terms *sexual attraction, sexual behavior,* and *sexual identity.* A person may be erotically attracted to someone of the same sex but engage exclusively in heterosexual behavior. *Sexual identity,* on the other hand, includes both the affectional and sexual dimensions of self that are evidenced by thoughts, feelings, and behaviors (Palma & Stanley, 2002). It is based on attraction, interests, and self-identification and can be viewed across a life span of development rather than as a constant in a person's life (Falkner & Starkey, 2009). The development of sexual identity is a dynamic process that is influenced by personal and cultural experiences. Issues related to sexual identity development are often of particular concern to LGB clients, particularly when they have experienced prejudice, oppression, discrimination, and/or rejection.

Homophobia and Heterosexism

Prejudicial beliefs and attitudes, principally homophobia and heterosexism, have pervasive adverse effects on sexual minority clients, as well as on society as a whole. *Homophobia* refers to an antigay bias, or fear of individuals who are perceived as lesbian, gay, or bisexual. Homophobic attitudes are evidenced by stereotyping and denigrating LGB individuals. In extreme cases, these negative, derogatory responses become violent, resulting in harassment and hate crimes. As many as 92% of gay men and lesbian women have experienced antigay verbal abuse, and some 24% report being victims of physical violence (W. Lee, 2007). The fatal beating of Matthew Sheppard, a Wyoming college student, is a tragic but well-known example of a hate crime perpetrated against someone because he was gay. An important role of community and mental counselors is to combat homophobia when it is evidenced in any form.

Perhaps a more insidious form of discrimination and prejudice is *heterosexism,* which refers to the viewpoint that heterosexuality is the only acceptable sexual orientation (Miller & House, 2005). Heterosexism has been further defined as a pervasively oppressive institutional preference for heterosexuality (Ritter & Terndrup, 2002). The heterosexist stance continues to be the societal norm in the United States, as evidenced by prevailing attitudes that reinforce heterosexuality as the only acceptable life option. Heterosexism is evidenced when, for example, workplaces do not provide health care or bereavement benefits for same-sex partners or states fail to recognize same-sex life commitments as legal. Even more subtle forms of heterosexism may be evidenced in counseling agencies, when intake forms include blanks for *spouse,* or when counselors assume that their clients are heterosexual. Some researchers (e.g., Ross, 1990) use the term *homonegativity* to encompass the concepts of both *homophobia* and *heterosexism.* More succinctly, *homonegativity* can be defined as negative thoughts and feelings about sexual minorities (Worthington, Dillon, & Becker-Schutte, 2005).

Although general trends indicate that people are more accepting of minority sexual identities than they have been in past years, many LGB individuals continue to encounter homonegativity on a regular basis. Counselors need to be aware of their own beliefs and responses, avoid discrimination, and instead affirm clients and acquire the knowledge and skills for counseling effectively with LGB clients. Indeed, legal and ethical issues abound when a counselor refuses to counsel homosexual clients, which is considered a violation of the *standard of care* in the counseling community. For example, in *Bruff v. North Mississippi Health Services, Inc.* (2001), a federal appeals court upheld the job termination of a counselor who asked to be excused from counseling a lesbian client on relationship issues because the client's sexual orientation conflicted with the client's religious beliefs (Hermann & Herlihy, 2006).

BOX 4–3

When society categorizes an individual using only one dimension of humanness, a significant part of that person is omitted. This omission leads to stereotyping and labeling, which have a significant and detrimental impact on the individual. Examples of such stereotyping and labeling include, "He is a dumb jock; what is he doing with a philosophy major?" "She's a woman; she shouldn't do that kind of work." "He's gay; he should not be working with children." "She is married; she couldn't possibly be bisexual." All of these statements focus on only one aspect of the individual. By focusing on an isolated aspect, the person in each of these examples is minimized and reduced to that one aspect—an unfair and inaccurate characterization of the whole person. The more holistic approach to human behavior focuses on the integration of all aspects of the individual, including the emotional, social, intellectual, spiritual, and physical dimensions of each person.

(Miller & House, 2005, pp. 435–436)

Sexual Identity Development and Coming Out

MODELS OF IDENTITY DEVELOPMENT.   Several theoretical explanations of minority sexual identity development have been proposed, each with unique counseling implications. Identity models explain the cognitive, emotional, and behavioral changes that occur as an individual moves toward identifying him- or herself as gay, lesbian, or bisexual. One of the first models was published by Cass (1979, 1984), whose six-stage model provided a framework for understanding sexual minority identity development while also influencing mental health professionals to move away from a pathological view of homosexuality (Degges-White, Rice, & Myers, 2000). Cass's model includes six phases: Identity Confusion, Identity Comparison, Identity Tolerance, Identity Acceptance, Identity Pride, and Identity Synthesis.

Whereas Cass's model was based on a study of gay men, other models have been developed that point out different developmental paths experienced by women. In particular, lesbians often experience feelings of connectedness and attraction to women before associating those feelings with a specific sexual orientation (Bringaze & White, 2001). McCarn and Fassinger (1996) developed a model of lesbian identity development, which occurs over four phases: Awareness, Exploration, Deepening Commitment, and Internalization/Synthesis. Bisexual identity development, which has not been researched as extensively as gay or lesbian identity development, involves dimensions that are unique to the bisexual experience and need to be taken into consideration during counseling (Horowitz & Newcomb, 1999). Being sensitive to issues that affect sexual minority identity development, as well as to issues that affect overall identity development, is crucial to counseling effectively.

It is helpful to view sexual identity development as a process that is unique for each individual and is influenced by personal and cultural factors (Palma & Stanley, 2002). Movement from one stage of development to another may be fluid and nonlinear, with no one formula or path that is "best." Bringaze and White (2001) emphasized that the process of achieving a positive lesbian, gay, or bisexual identity can take many years, with some people getting stuck during the process and never developing a positive, integrated identity. Counselors will want to take into account each client's unique sociocultural background, experiences, and perspectives and meet that client where he or she is in regard to sexual identity formation.

SEXUAL AND ETHNIC MINORITY IDENTITY.   Lesbian, gay, and bisexual individuals from ethnic minority groups may face a unique set of issues that differ from those facing other LGB clients. In some ways, LGB people of color face particular struggles they attempt to function in several communities simultaneously (W. Lee, 2007). They may be more likely to face social discrimination on many levels, which can lead to psychological distress. For example, Latino communities largely reject sexual minority identities (Sager, 2001). In Latino communities, *familism,* or the primary importance of family, is often valued above individual needs. Coming out in a Latino family may accentuate feelings of guilt and alienate clients from their family, church, and community. Consequently, LGB Latino clients may "face the difficult choice of remaining closeted in the heterosexist Latin American community or dealing with racism in the LGB and European American communities" (Sager, p. 25). The fear of rejection, cultural disinheritance, and loss of ties to one's ethnic community can make it especially difficult for clients from Latino and other ethnic groups to develop healthy, integrated sexual identities.

COMING OUT.   A key component of minority sexual identity development is the *coming out process. Coming out,* or letting other people know that one is lesbian, gay, or bisexual, is not a one-time event, but instead is an ongoing process, affected largely by an individual's life circumstances. The process may begin at any age and can be especially difficult for adolescents, who may be more vulnerable and subject to ridicule. At any age, making the decision

1. What kind of reactions do you expect when you tell family members, friends, co-workers, etc.?
2. How can you determine what the reactions might be?
3. What would be the worst possible reaction?
4. What can you do to prepare yourself against that reaction?
5. What happens when or if you tell your parents?
6. Should you tell your parents together or individually?
7. Should you tell both of your parents?
8. What happens if you do not tell certain people?
9. Is it necessary to tell everyone?
10. What are the best ways to tell people?
11. Can you think of alternative ways to tell people?
12. Are you aware that responses may change over time?

FIGURE 4–3 The Consequences of Coming Out: Questions to Consider

Source: From *Introduction to the Counseling Profession* (4th ed., p. 445), by D. Capuzzi and D. R. Gross. Published by Allyn & Bacon, Boston, MA. Copyright © 2005 by Pearson Education. Reprinted by permission of the publisher.

to reveal one's sexual orientation to others can have serious consequences, both positive and negative (Winter, 2002). Community and mental health counselors can help clients sort through the various issues associated with that decision and examine the risks and benefits associated with coming out (Figure 4–3).

It is generally accepted that coming out is positively associated with mental health and relationship satisfaction (W. Lee, 2007). Coming out contributes to identity acceptance, integration, and authenticity. However, coming out also carries with it the risk of abandonment, ridicule, and disapproval. Practitioners have an obligation to assist clients to carefully assess potential risks as they consider the option of disclosure to others in their lives (Lemoire & Chen, 2005). The process may be psychologically painful, as the old sense of self is grieved before the new sense of self emerges. Practitioners can help clients cope with coming-out issues by providing emotional support, a safe space, and a nonjudgmental attitude, exhibiting a genuine "being with" the client, wherever he or she may happen to be (Harper & Varner, 2008). Counselors can take concrete steps to help clients with the coming-out process through the use of role-play, cognitive rehearsal, and bibliotherapy. Providing information about support groups, hotlines, churches that are "gay-affirming" (i.e., full acceptance), and other community resources can also benefit LBG clients struggling with coming-out issues.

Other Counseling Issues and Implications

Because of the pervasiveness of homonegativity in our society, LGB clients often enter counseling to help them come to terms with their orientation. However, the issues clients bring to counseling may or may not be related to sexual identity, and counselors need to avoid making premature assumptions about presenting concerns. With this caution in mind, some specific issues are unique to sexual minority clients. Often, LGB clients struggle to understand themselves and their relationships within a predominantly heterosexual society. Internalized homophobia and self-image, interpersonal relationships, career-related concerns, and conflicted religious values are just a few of the issues that LGB clients may choose to work on in counseling.

INTERNALIZED HOMOPHOBIA AND SELF-IMAGE.   Internalized homophobia occurs when a lesbian, gay, or bisexual individual internalizes negative societal attitudes about homosexuality (Miller & House, 2005; Sophie, 1987). Such internalization can result in cognitive dissonance, low self-esteem, depression, and other forms of psychological distress. Typically, a person's internalized messages are tied to childhood experiences, family roles, religious beliefs, and societal expectations. LGB individuals often receive negative messages from many sources, including friends, family members, church, school, and the media. Counselors can help clients explore and articulate the internalized messages they have received about being gay, lesbian, or bisexual. By encouraging the exploration of thoughts and feelings, counselors can then help clients challenge inaccuracies and reconstruct meanings about sexuality that are more positive and acceptable (Bringaze & White, 2001).

For clients to explore thoughts and feelings about their sexual orientation, they need to sense unconditional positive regard on the part of the counselor. They may test the counselor to determine his or her stance toward sexual minorities (Palma & Stanley, 2002). Clinical mental health counselors can be proactive in establishing an environment in which clients feel safe exploring issues related to sexual identity. Suggestions for counselors include the following (Black & Underwood, 1998; Miller & House, 2005; Palma & Stanley, 2002; Robinson-Wood, 2009; Winter, 2002):

- Demonstrate respect for the client's current experiences and presenting issues. These issues may or may not be related to sexual orientation.
- Be sincere, open, genuine, and ethical, respecting confidentiality and honoring differences.
- Explore personal issues related to sexuality and heterosexism. Covert, unexplored issues or attitudes are likely to affect the counseling experience negatively.
- Be aware of societal prejudices and oppression and advocate for an LGB-affirmative environment. Offices with books, brochures, and symbols that are relevant to LGB individuals suggest that the counselor is affirmative and nonjudgmental.
- Be sensitive to nonverbal or covert client messages that may signal permission for the counselor to address issues related to sexual identity.
- Be knowledgeable about sexual identity development issues. Provide support, normalize feelings, and anticipate confusion and ambiguity. Validate confusion.
- Help clients explore feelings. Many LGB clients, especially adolescents, feel isolated, guilty, afraid, ashamed, and angry. Listen empathically, providing them with a safe space in which feelings can be validated.
- Use role-play to help clients handle a variety of situations, including coming out to family members and friends, if clients choose to do so.
- Be aware of the potential for depression and self-esteem issues and address them accordingly.
- Provide accurate information about sexually transmitted diseases, including HIV and AIDS.
- Be informed about community resources and support groups and share that information with LGB clients.
- Attend seminars and workshops on counseling sexual minorities.

FAMILY RELATIONSHIPS.   Relationships with family members, particularly in regard to disclosure, can present unique sources of concern for LGB clients. When family members are supportive and accepting of sexual minority clients, relationships are enhanced, and clients report a higher degree of life satisfaction and adjustment (Bringaze & White, 2001). Unfortunately, however, many families do not support nonheterosexual orientations, and counselors need to help clients evaluate whether or not disclosure is advisable. Disadvantages associated with not coming out to family members include having to monitor and censor one's interactions and guilt associated with being unauthentic. On the other hand, when family values and cultural messages are such that an "out" sexual minority client will be alienated from his or her family, it may be in the client's best interest to avoid disclosure. Clinical mental health counselors can help clients explore the realistic consequences of coming out to family, and if the client decides to disclose, the counselor can facilitate the process through rehearsal, empty-chair activities, and/or letter writing (Bringaze & White, 2001). Counselors also may be in a position to help families work through questions and confusion that arise in relation to their family member's sexual orientation.

OTHER RELATIONSHIPS. Relationships with heterosexual friends and colleagues also may be sources of concern for LGB clients. Palma and Stanley (2002) pointed out that there often is a time lag between disclosure of one's sexual identity and the acceptance and/or affirmation that friends and colleagues are capable of providing. Counselors can help clients develop appropriate expectations of others by reminding them of the time it took for them to acknowledge their own sexual identity.

Associating with other people who are gay, lesbian, or bisexual can be especially helpful for LGB clients. Social and professional groups that provide support have been established in most urban areas and can serve as powerful resources for LGB clients. Groups exist that address multiple issues, including heterosexism, legal concerns, aging, health, and religion. Counselors in rural communities may have less local resources and therefore will want to be aware of resources available nationally, in nearby cities, and online.

LGB couples may seek counseling to work through relationship issues. Although some issues are common to same-sex and heterosexual couples (e.g., finances and communication problems) and are responsive to traditional therapeutic interventions, others are unique to gay and lesbian couples. For example, in many states, same-sex couples are denied most of the legal, religious, economic, and social benefits typically received by heterosexual couples. Likewise, same-sex couples do not have the social, legal, and moral sanctions that sustain heterosexual couples. Same-sex couples have fewer visible role models and may experience unique difficulties in regard to role definition. Gay men may have difficulty with competition and may be prone to seek isolation when problems arise. Lesbians may have difficulty with autonomy, differentiation, and maintaining a sense of self (W. Lee, 2007). Attempting to define roles in the same ways they are defined in heterosexual relationships can be counterproductive or detrimental. Practitioners who work with same-sex couples are advised to participate in education, training, and supervision to meet the needs of their clients.

RELIGIOUS CONCERNS. Often, LGB individuals struggle with conflicting values between their sexuality and their religious beliefs. Many religious communities, particularly conservative Christian denominations, Mormons, and Muslims, view homosexuality as sinful, and it may be difficult for LGB clients to find a place of worship where they are accepted. It may be especially difficult for LGB clients to reconcile their sexual orientation with the beliefs of their faith. As such, LGB clients may perceive it impossible to be a sexual minority and also religious, leading to an identity struggle referred to as *cognitive dissonance* (Mahaffy, 1996). When places of worship exhibit homonegativity, either actively or passively, LGB clients are likely to experience *religious rejection* (Harper, 2007), which may result in high levels of psychological distress (Berecz & Helm, 1998; Ritter & Terndrup, 2002). Feelings of shame, guilt, unworthiness, isolation, and loss, as well as feeling cut off from one's religious community, can be devastating and demoralizing.

There are several ways in which LGB individuals cope with religious rejection. They may choose to leave their church or other place of worship, deny or compartmentalize their sexual identity, change their sexual identity, or integrate their faith with their sexuality (Harper, 2007; Lease, Horne, & Noffsinger-Frazier, 2005; Mahaffy, 1996). Ideally, LGB persons are able to achieve identity integration so that they can embrace their sexual orientation in an affirming faith-based community. Counselors can help LGB clients discuss their religious beliefs and religious concerns. They also can share resources within the religious community that affirm sexual minorities.

BOX 4–4

Reparative or Conversion Therapy

Clients may ask for a specific treatment from counseling professionals because they have heard about it from either their religious community or from popular culture. A counselor, however, only provides treatment that is scientifically indicated to be effective or has a theoretical framework supported by the profession. Otherwise, counselors inform clients that the treatment is "unproven" or "developing" and provide an explanation of the "potential risks and ethical considerations of using such techniques/procedures and take steps to protect clients from possible harm" (ACA *Code of Ethics* [2005]. *Standard* C.6.e., "Scientific Bases for Treatment Modalities").

Considering all the above deliberation, the ACA Ethics Committee strongly suggests that ethical professional counselors do not refer clients to someone who engages in conversion therapy or, if they do so, to proceed cautiously only when they are certain that the referral counselor fully informs clients of the unproven nature of the treatment and the potential risks and takes steps to minimize harm to clients (also see Standard A.2.b., "Types of Information Needed"). This information also must be included in written informed consent material by those counselors who offer conversion therapy despite ACA's position and the Ethics Committee's statement in opposition to the treatment. To do otherwise violates the spirit and specifics of the ACA Code of Ethics.

From Ethical Issues Related to Conversion or Reparative Therapy (Whitman, Glosoff, Kocet, & Tarvydas, 2006). ACA In The News. (retrieved on July 24, 2008, from www.counseling.org/PressRoom/NewsReleases)

CAREER CONCERNS.   Career choice, workplace benefits and stresses, and career advancement may present unique challenges to LGB clients (W. Lee, 2007). Sexual minority clients may not be able to integrate their personal lives into the workplace as easily as their heterosexual counterparts. They also may be more likely to face work discrimination, which refers to unfair and negative treatment based on personal attributes that are unrelated to job performance (Chung & Bemak, 2002). Although many companies have adopted corporate nondiscrimination policies, discrimination in the workplace is still a reality faced by many sexual minority individuals. Counselors can help LGB clients examine their perceptions of discrimination and evaluate potential coping strategies, which may include open confrontation or changing jobs. In other situations, clients may decide not to come out in the workplace, in which case counselors can help the client cope with the additional stress that accompanies nondisclosure (W. Lee, 2007). Counselors are encouraged to engage in social advocacy for LGB clients, including lobbying for the inclusion of sexual orientation in companies' nondiscrimination policies (Pope et al., 2004).

OTHER ISSUES.   Just as heterosexual clients may enter counseling with one or more of many different issues, so may LGB clients. Some of the issues we have not yet discussed include parenting issues, domestic violence, substance abuse and addiction, sexual addiction and compulsive behavior, and HIV/AIDS. Counselors will want to engage in workshops and other training opportunities to be able to effectively work with LGB clients.

Myriad counseling-related issues are associated with HIV and AIDS. Although there have been tremendous advances in the medical treatment of persons with HIV/AIDS, numerous challenges continue to be associated with being diagnosed HIV-positive. Often, clients with HIV/AIDS "are dealing with frequent losses and unpredictability in career, partner relationships, their ability to parent minor children, and health status" (Falkner & Starkey, 2009, p. 520). Counselors can address issues related to HIV/AIDS by challenging uninformed opinions, providing psychoeducation for the larger community, and assisting with the multiple needs that afflict clients, friends, and family members living with HIV/AIDS. It also is important for counselors to be aware of the profound effect AIDS-related bereavement has had on gay men. Often, feelings associated with multiple losses, including denial, anger, depression, and guilt, need to be worked through in counseling sessions.

Working with Transgender Clients

The term *transgender,* sometimes called *transgendered,* was coined in the late 1980s by gay men as a way to describe their desire to live as women (Prosser, 1997). The definition of *transgender* is evolving, but in this section, we will refer to transgender individuals as those people who possess a gender identity that conflicts with his or her manifestation of sex. Male-to-female (MTF) transgender persons are born with male genitalia but experience their lives "gendered primarily as females" (Mostade, 2009, p. 308). For female-to-male (FTM) transgender individuals, the reverse is true. *Transsexual* individuals pursue hormonal treatment and/or sex reassignment surgery so that their externalized gender identification will match their internal gender identification.

Media attention has provided visibility for transgender persons. Movies such as *Midnight in the Garden of Good and Evil, Boys Don't Cry, Normal,* and *Transamerica* have "enabled activists to challenge public intolerance and grow in self-confidence and affirmation" (Carroll, Gilroy, & Ryan, 2002, p. 131). Watching movies like these can help build empathy for and understanding of the issues and prejudices faced by transgender individuals.

The *DSM-IV-TR* (2000) uses the term *Gender Identity Disorder* to describe a mental health condition in which a member of one sex wishes to be a member of another sex. However, as pointed out in Chapter 7, controversy surrounds its inclusion as a medical disorder. At the time this book was written, the *DSM-V* had not yet been published. Whether or not Gender Identity Disorder will be included in that manual has yet to be determined.

For counselors to work effectively with transgender clients, they need to build a knowledge base that will help them understand transgender issues. This base can be developed by reading academic materials devoted to the topic, attending workshops and training sessions, and seeking out resources that reach out to the transgender community. In addition, counselors need to examine their own values, beliefs, and biases. Working with transgender individuals where they are, recognizing that their main issue may not involve their gender identification, is crucial. When a client is considering hormonal and surgical intervention, trained mental health professionals can help the client explore options. Helping clients who are struggling with the decision about whether to pursue hormonal and/or surgical interventions can be an especially challenging issue (Mostade, 2009).

Clinical mental health counselors are in a position to serve as advocates for LGBT clients. Joining the Association of Lesbian, Gay, Bisexual, and Transgender Issues in Counseling (ALGBTIC), a division of ACA, is one way counselors can advocate for sexual minority clients. Counselors also can take proactive steps to counteract bias on all fronts, whether it exists in relation to a person's sexual orientation, gender, ethnicity, or any other characteristic subject to discrimination.

COUNSELING PEOPLE WITH DISABILITIES OVERVIEW

BOX 4–5

People with disabilities, like all people, want to participate fully in the society in which they live. The desire to achieve and to be successful is not diminished by a disability; indeed, the opportunity to work and contribute to the support of self and family is considered a basic right in a free, democratic society, and as American citizens, people with disabilities have a right to equality of opportunity of education, employment, transportation, housing, health care, and leisure. A person's disability should not interfere with full participation in any of these activities.

(Martin, 1999, p. 25)

People with disabilities constitute our nation's largest minority group (W. Lee, 2000). Approximately 54 million Americans (about one in five) report some level of disability, and 26 million Americans describe their disability as severe (Holmes, 1999; Livneh & Antonak, 2005). Disabilities are manifested in a variety of ways and may be physical, emotional, cognitive, and/or behavioral in nature. Examples of specific disabilities include orthopedic, visual, speech, and hearing impairments; cerebral palsy; chronic diseases; developmental disabilities; neurological disorders; psychiatric illness; and substance addiction. Because of the increasing number of people with disabilities, clinical mental health counselors are likely to provide services to clients with disabilities (Smart & Smart, 2006). In this section, we provide a general overview for counselors who work with people with disabilities.

In addition to variation in types of disabilities, there is much divergence in regard to age of onset, cause, severity, and manifestation of the disability. Consequently, the population of individuals with disabilities comprises one of the most diverse groups discussed thus far. Furthermore, people with disabilities represent the only minority group of which a person may unexpectedly become a member at any time (Foster, 1996).

Definitions and Terminology

The Americans with Disabilities Act of 1990 (ADA) defines *disability* as a physical or mental impairment that substantially limits a major life activity. Recently, the Supreme Court narrowed the ADA definition of disability by ruling that for a person to be considered substantially limited, the impairment must prevent or severely restrict the individual from doing activities that are of central importance to most people's daily lives, and that the impairment must be permanent or long term (Thomas, 2002). Disability status is dynamic, due to the transitory nature of health and to the connection between a person's level of functioning and the barriers in his or her environment (Fujiura, 2001). Furthermore, disability is a "common and natural fact of life" and should be considered within the context of the multiple identities and roles that constitute an individual's life span (Smart & Smart, 2006, p. 29).

When working with people who are disabled, counselors must put the client first, not the disability (Martin, 1999). One way to accomplish this is by avoiding labels and stereotyping. Related to this concept is the need to choose language respectfully, making sure that terms are not pejorative or dehumanizing. For example, it is better to refer to someone as a "person with a disability" rather than as a "disabled person" (Martin, 1999). Similarly, terms like "physically or mentally challenged" should be avoided. Because there are literally hundreds of physical and mental conditions that qualify as disabilities, no single source of information on terminology provides suggestions that are appropriate for all people. Therefore, as in other counseling situations, counselors will want to check with clients to determine their preferences regarding terminology and language use.

The degree to which a disability impedes an individual's functioning is situational. The presence of a disability and its subsequent effects vary, depending on the individual and the circumstances. For example, two people may have the same type of spinal cord injury but react and adapt to the injury differently. Or someone may have epilepsy that is well controlled by medication, so that the disease does not pose a major impediment to the activities of daily living. Counselors can determine the degree to which a disability poses a barrier by carefully assessing and evaluating the client and the environment(s) in which he or she lives and works. Through careful assessment, stereotyping and overgeneralization can be avoided. Indeed, many individuals view their disability as a valued part of their identity and would not choose to eliminate the disability if such an option were viable (Smart & Smart, 2006).

Factors Associated with Increased Rates of Disability

According to the U.S. Census Bureau's Survey of Income and Program Participation (SIPP), nearly 20% of Americans have specific functional losses or limitations classified as disabilities (cited in Fujiura, 2001). A number of demographic, socioeconomic, and medical trends have been linked with rising rates of disabilities. These factors, which include aging, poverty, medical advances, and emerging medical conditions, are summarized in Figure 4–4. To meet the minimum standards of practice, mental health practitioners in addition to rehabilitation counselors, will need to become proficient in working with clients with disabilities (Smart & Smart, 2006).

Attitudes and Myths about Disabilities

Misconceptions and biases toward individuals with disabilities often reflect lack of knowledge and negative stereotyping. Such societal attitudes are often subtle and may include reactions of disgust, pity, or discomfort expressed verbally or nonverbally. Some of the negative attitudes and myths that may be held by members of society who are not currently

- **Aging.** Approximately three out of every four Americans over the age of 80 has a disability of some type, and over half of this age group has a disability classified as "severe." With longevity continuing to increase, there also comes an increase in disabilities associated with the aging process.
- **Poverty.** Poverty has been linked to disability as both a consequence and a cause. According to 1997 SIPP data, nearly 28 percent of adults with a severe disability live in poverty, in contrast to 8 percent of the general population. Americans with disabilities are at a substantial disadvantage in regard to employment, access to private health insurance, and levels of educational achievement.
- **Medical Advances.** Due to medical advances, survival rates for spinal cord and severe brain injury, as well as other medical conditions, have improved dramatically. Also, survival rates for low-birth-rate infants have increased 70-fold during the past 25 years, affecting the prevalence of developmental disabilities.
- **Emerging conditions.** Over the past years, certain medical conditions have either emerged as new syndromes (e.g., chronic fatigue syndrome) or increased in incidence (e.g., asthma, autism, attention-deficit/hyperactivity disorder, bipolar disorder). It is unclear whether the higher numbers represent an increase in prevalence or an increase in the recognition and reporting of such conditions.

FIGURE 4–4   **Factors associated with increased disability**
From Fujiura, 2001.

disabled include the following (W. Lee, 2007; Martin, 1999; National Victim Assistance Academy [NVAA], 2002; Tyiska, 1998):

- **The Charity or Helplessness Myth.**   People with disabilities are suffering and should be extended charity instead of rights and responsibilities. Such an attitude also implies that people with disabilities are not capable of making decisions for themselves and need others to manage their lives.
- **The Spread Phenomenon Myth.**   If one disability is present, there must be other disabilities as well.
- **The Dehumanization or Damaged Merchandise Myth.**   A person with a disability is less than a full member of society or is inferior in some way.
- **The Feeling No Pain Myth.**   People with disabilities are immune from pain and suffering or have no feelings.
- **The Disabled Menace Myth.**   Because they are perceived as "different," people with disabilities are considered unpredictable and dangerous (e.g., people who fear having group homes for adults with mental retardation in their neighborhoods).

BOX 4–6

I want people to know that we are human. We live, we love, we hurt, we laugh, we cry . . . we just want to be seen and heard as human beings.

Shay (Study Participant) Moore, 2005, p. 343

Negative attitudes and perceptions tend to undermine self-advocacy efforts and increase the vulnerability of people with disabilities. To counteract this effect, counselors and

- Treat the person with dignity and respect.
- Ask the person how to communicate most effectively with him or her.
- Address and speak directly to the person, even if he or she is accompanied by a third party.
- When introduced to a person with a disability, you may shake hands. People with limited hand use or who wear an artificial limb can usually shake hands.
- If you offer assistance, wait until the offer is accepted, then listen to or ask for instructions.
- With regard to most accommodations, take your cue from the individual.
- Do not tell the person that you admire his or her courage or determination for living with the disability.
- When speaking to a person who uses a wheelchair or crutches, place yourself at eye level in front of the person to facilitate the conversation.
- When communicating with a person who is hard of hearing and who prefers to lip-read, face the person. Make sure you have the person's attention before you begin speaking. Speak slowly and distinctly, in a normal tone of voice without shouting.
- When using a sign language interpreter, have him or her sit next to you so that the hearing-impaired person can easily shift his or her gaze back and forth.
- When meeting with someone who is visually impaired, indicate your presence verbally, identify yourself by name, and speak in a normal tone of voice. If other people are present, ask them to identify themselves.
- If someone has a developmental disability, give that person time to respond. Talk slowly and calmly, using easy-to-understand language.
- Obtain expert consultation on how to communicate effectively with individual victims with developmental disabilities and people with serious mental illness.

FIGURE 4–5 **Suggestions for interacting with people who have disabilities**
From NVAA, 2002; and Tyiska, 1998.

others who work with people with disabilities need to take lead roles in helping change negative societal attitudes, beginning with an examination of any personal attitudes that might interfere with effective interactions and interventions (Figure 4–5).

Federal Regulation Related to Disability

Through the years, federal legislation has taken a key role in protecting the civil rights of people with disabilities. During the past two decades, several federal initiatives to provide education and related services to individuals with disabilities have been enacted as laws. The Americans with Disabilities Act of 1990 (ADA) provided a clear, comprehensive mandate for the elimination of discrimination against individuals with disabilities (Middleton, Rollins, & Harley, 1999). Specifically, the ADA was enacted to protect people with disabilities from discrimination in employment, public accommodations, transportation, and telecommunication. Other important legislative measures that have been implemented during the past two decades are outlined in Figure 4–6.

To provide effective preventive and remedial services, counselors must actively seek to understand the laws, regulations, and programs that affect people with disabilities. By being aware of the legislation and policy issues that shape the alternatives available to individuals with disabilities, counselors will be better prepared to meet the specific needs of the clients they serve.

- *Americans with Disabilities Act* (ADA, PL 101–336, 1990): A wide-ranging legislation in-tended to make American society more accessible to people with disabilities and to protect them from discrimination.
- *Individuals with Disabilities Education Act* (IDEA, PL 101–476, 1990) and the 1997 reautho-rization of IDEA (PL 105–17, 1997): A set of laws mandating that all individuals between the ages of 0 and 21 receive a free and appropriate public education with access to a wide range of services. IDEA helps ensure that the rights of children with disabilities and their parents or guardians are protected.
- *Workforce Investment Act* (WIA, PL 105–220, 1998): Legislation intended to guide the im-plementation of One-Stop Career Centers. One-Stop Career Centers provide a single loca-tion where an applicant can gain information needed to choose an occupation, find access to training, be placed in a job, and have access to all public services needed to continue in employment. Under the WIA, all services available through a One-Stop Career Center must be accessible to everyone who uses them.
- *Ticket to Work and Work Incentives Improvement Act* (WIAA, H.R. 1180, 1999): Legisla-tion designed to enhance the rights of consumers with disabilities to make a choice of service providers between private nonprofit, state rehabilitation agency, and private pro-prietary providers.

FIGURE 4–6   **Examples of legislation protecting the rights of individuals with disabilities**

Note: A helpful resource about legislation that affects people with disabilities, which is free to this popu-lation, is *Everything your need to know about Disability Acts & Laws*. Information about this resource can be accessed at www.disabilitybenefitsguide.com/DisabilityActs-Laws

COUNSELING CONSIDERATIONS

Overview of Goals and Interventions

The provision of counseling services to clients with disabilities can be categorized into three phases: *prevention* or *primary intervention, intervention,* and *postvention* or *rehabilitation* (Livneh & Wosley-George, 2001). In *prevention,* the emphasis is on preventing disease or disability before it occurs. Programmatic efforts are levied at increasing public awareness of specific activities or situations that are likely to lead to physical and/or emotional problems (e.g., stress, unhealthy behaviors, etc.). *Intervention* refers to direct, time-limited strategies that often are implemented with crisislike situations, such as spinal cord injury, myocardial infarction, or severe psychological distress. *Postvention,* also called *rehabilitation counsel-ing,* focuses on helping people with permanent or chronic physical, psychiatric, and mental disabilities cope successfully and adjust to life with that disability. Clinical mental health counselors may be involved in each of these three phases of service. In this section, primary attention is given to the rehabilitation phase of counseling.

The major goal of rehabilitation counseling is to help individuals with disabilities maxi-mize their potential in terms of acceptance, independence, productivity, and inclusion (Martin, 1999). Interventions can be targeted toward the individual client or toward the environment in which the client lives and works. Client-aimed interventions include personal adjustment counseling, vocational counseling, behavioral modification, and skill development in perform-ance of the *activities of daily living* (ADLs). In contrast, environment-aimed interventions are targeted toward barriers in the external environment that may need modification to meet the client's goals. Examples may include helping the client find ways to use assistive aids (e.g., hearing aids, prostheses, and wheelchairs), facilitating the removal of architectural barriers, and placing the client in a group home (Livneh & Wosley-George, 2001). Both types of intervention often are carried out by counselors involved in rehabilitation work.

BOX 4–7

One of the counseling students I (Newsome) supervised was working in a community agency with a client who was blind. The client was also an undocumented immigrant who had very few financial resources. The client wanted to contact resources in the community that would provide opportunities for work. Eager to help, the intern called *The Blind Factory* to inquire about working opportunities and other resources. Much to the intern's surprise, the place he called did not work with visually impaired individuals; instead, it was a business that specialized in making window coverings! Our best intentions can sometimes have unexpected outcomes.

Training, Roles, and Functions of Rehabilitation Counselors

Most counselors whose primary work is with clients with disabilities have participated in rehabilitation education counselor education (RCE) programs. The Council of Rehabilitation Education (CORE) accredits institutions that offer rehabilitation counseling. Rehabilitation counselors receive certification through the Commission on Rehabilitation Counselor Certification (CRCC; www.crccertification.com). The duration of the initial certificate is 5 years, after which the Certified Rehabilitation Counselor (CRC) is required to accumulate 100 continuing education contact hours to remain certified.

Many rehabilitation counselors belong to the American Rehabilitation Counseling Association (ARCA), a division of ACA, whose mission is to enhance the development of people with disabilities and promote excellence in the rehabilitation counseling profession (see Figure 4–7). Other professional organizations for counselors who specialize in working with clients with disabilities include the National Rehabilitation Counseling Association (NRCA) and the National Association of Rehabilitation Professionals in the Private Sector (NARPPS).

Rehabilitation counselors carry out several roles and functions in serving clients with disabilities. Initially, the role of the counselor is to assess the client's current level of functioning and the surrounding environmental influences that either hinder or assist functionality. Based on the results of that assessment, counselors help clients formulate goals. Depending on the nature of the goals, counselors may need to carry out several different roles. Versatility is important, as the counselor will not only provide services directly but also coordinate services with other professionals and monitor clients' progress in gaining independence and self-control.

Hershenson (1998) describes five different functions of rehabilitation counselors: counseling, consulting, coordinating services, case management, and critiquing effectiveness. In making decisions about what services to provide, Hershenson suggests that counselors take into account the client's personality (e.g., motivation, outlook on life, and reaction to the disability), interpersonal skills and socialized behavior, learning capacities, personal and work goals, and the extent of available supports and barriers. To achieve desired goals, the rehabilitation counselor may need to *counsel* with the client about specific coping issues, *consult* with the client's family and employer about expectations, *coordinate* a skills training program, engage in *case management* to monitor the delivery of services, and conduct an ongoing *critique* (*evaluation*) of the effectiveness of the interventions. Throughout the process, the counselor needs to be aware of the various systems and subsystems that influence the client's well-being. How do those systems and subsystems promote or impede

What is ARCA?

ARCA is an organization of rehabilitation counseling practitioners, educators, and students who are concerned with improving the lives of people with disabilities.

Its mission is to enhance the development of people with disabilities throughout their life span and to promote excellence in the rehabilitation counseling profession.

ARCA's goal is to provide the type of leadership that encourages excellence in the areas of rehabilitation counseling practice, research, consultation, and professional development. ARCA is equally interested in eliminating environmental and attitudinal barriers so that more opportunities are available with regard to education, employment, and community activities to people with disabilities. These goals are addressed by ARCA through public education and legislative activities.

One of ARCA's primary goals is to increase public awareness of rehabilitation counseling as a profession and to extend its influence by encouraging members to become involved in the association's outreach and educational efforts. Other goals are to help members develop their leadership skills through participation in ARCA's organizational activities and to work with state officials to develop appropriate licensure requirements.

DIVISION OF

AMERICAN COUNSELING ASSOCIATION

Scope of Practice for Rehabilitation Counseling

I. Assumptions

- The Scope of Practice Statement identifies knowledge and skills required for the provision of effective rehabilitation counseling services to persons with physical, mental, developmental, cognitive, and emotional disabilities as embodied in the standards of the profession's credentialing organizations.
- The several rehabilitation disciplines and related processes (e.g., vocational evaluation, job development and job placement, work adjustment, case management) are tied to the central field of rehabilitation profession with counseling as its core, and is differentiated from other related counseling fields.
- The professional scope of rehabilitation counseling practice is also differentiated from an individual scope of practice, which may overlap, but is more specializing than the professional scope. An individual scope of practice is based on one's own knowledge of the abilities and skills that have been gained through a program of education and professional experience. A person is ethically bound to limit his/her practice to that individual scope of practice.

II. Underlying Values

- Facilitation of independence, integration, and inclusion of people with disabilities in employment and the community.
- Belief in the dignity and worth of all people.
- Commitment to a sense of equal justice based on a model of accommodation to provide and equalize the opportunities to participate in all rights and privileges available to all

FIGURE 4–7

people; and a commitment to supporting persons with disabilities in advocacy activities to achieve this status and empower themselves.
- Emphasis on the holistic nature of human function which is procedurally facilitated by the utilization of such techniques as:
  1. interdisciplinary teamwork.
  2. counseling to assist in maintaining a holistic perspective.
  3. a commitment to considering individuals within the context of their family systems and communities.
  4. recognition of the importance of focusing on the assets of the person.
  5. commitment to models of service delivery that emphasize integrated, comprehensive services which are mutually planned by the consumer and the rehabilitation counselor.

III. Scope of Practice Statement

Rehabilitation counseling is a systematic process which assists persons with physical, mental, developmental, cognitive, and emotional disabilities to achieve their personal, career, and independent living goals in the most integrated settings possible through the application of the counseling process. The counseling process involves communication, goal setting, and beneficial growth or change through self-advocacy, psychological, vocational, social, and behavioral interventions. The specific techniques and modalities utilized within this rehabilitation counseling process may include, but are not limited to:

- assessment and appraisal;
- diagnosis and treatment planning;
- career (vocational) counseling;
- individual and group counseling treatment interventions focused on facilitating adjustments to the medical and psychosocial impact of disability;
- case management, referral, and service coordination;
- program evaluation and research;
- interventions to remove environmental, employment, and attitudinal barriers;
- consultation service among multiple parties and regulatory systems;
- job analysis, job development, and placement services, including assistance with employment and job accommodations; and
- the provision of consultation about access to rehabilitation technology.

FIGURE 4–7 *(Continued)*

Source: The American Rehabilitation Counseling Association (ARCA, 2005), Homepage: www.arcaweb.org/. Reprinted with permission.

rehabilitation? What physical and attitudinal resources or barriers do they present? It may be necessary to work with the client's friends, family, and employers to redesign the environment to maximize access and opportunities (Wright & Martin, 1999).

Counseling Issues and Implications

Whereas it would be inappropriate and inaccurate to make any all-encompassing statements regarding counseling people with disabilities, the nature of the issues presented may differ from those presented in other counseling situations. Livneh and Wosley-George (2001) noted the prevalence of specific themes that may emerge during the process, such as independence versus dependence, personal loss, coping with crises, and maintaining employment. Some of the common problems that arise in the personal and interpersonal domains are illustrated in Figure 4–8. Other counseling issues

Personal Domain	Interpersonal Domain
• Lack of motivation	• Increased dependence (financial, medical, psychosocial, other)
• Reluctance to participate in rehabilitation tasks	• Impaired social and/or vocational roles
• Increased depression and/or anxiety	• Changing family dynamics and relationships
• Damaged body image	• Disruption of social life
• Insult to self-concept	• Negative attitudes toward disability
• Loss of sense of control	• Societal rejection and/or social isolation
• Loss of reward and pleasure sources	• Disuse or lack of appropriate social skills
• Loss of physical and economic independence	• Decreased sexual activity
• Difficulty accepting and adjusting to the disability	
• Inability to access the environment	

FIGURE 4–8   **Common issues in the personal and interpersonal domains**
Based on information in Livneh and Wosley-George, 2001.

that may confront people with disabilities include coping and adjusting to an acquired disability, family concerns, career-related concerns, and abuse.

COPING WITH AN ACQUIRED DISABILITY.   When someone sustains an unexpected disability, whether through bodily injury or the onset of a disease, that individual is suddenly faced with an array of physical and emotional challenges. Individuals who become disabled may feel lost, terrified, and confused about what the future holds. In such cases, a primary counseling goal is to help the client make order out of chaos, recognizing that acceptance and adjustment take time. Frequently, the client is faced with grief and loss issues, much like those experienced after a death. Livneh and Evans (1984) outlined 12 phases of adjustment associated with an acquired disability: shock, anxiety, bargaining, denial, mourning, depression, withdrawal, internalized anger, externalized aggression, acknowledgment, acceptance, and adjustment/adaptation. Different interventions are appropriate for different phases. It is important for counselors to be aware of the adjustment process and work with it rather than against it. At times, client behaviors may seem bizarre or confusing, but that may be necessary for progress (Rothrock, 1999).

During the initial stages after a disability is sustained, crisis intervention and supportive counseling are often called for. Offering support and reassurance, listening and attending, and allowing the client to ventilate feelings can be especially helpful. Also, it is important to recognize that the client may be using defense mechanisms and that those mechanisms serve a purpose. Without them, "reality could overwhelm the individual, and the situation could be perceived as being impossible to address" (Rothrock, 1999, p. 210). In time, the client can deal more effectively with the reality of the disability.

As counseling continues, the counselor will want to help the client develop resources for accepting, coping, and adjusting to life with a disability. One way to encourage clients to draw from their own coping abilities is to find out what helped them cope with difficult events in the past. Modifications of previously successful coping behaviors can facilitate adjustment to the new lifestyle (Rothrock, 1999). For example, if a client has a supportive family, inviting the family to participate in counseling sessions could help with decision making and make life more manageable.

Cognitive therapy may help a client with a disability reinterpret life experiences in a manner that enhances resilience and a sense of coherence (Lustig, Rosenthal, Strauser, & Haynes, 2000). A strong sense of coherence increases the chances that a person will mobilize available resources and seek new resources when handling stressful situations. A client's sense of coherence is determined by his or her perceptions of (a) comprehensibility (the degree to which the world is perceived as predictable, ordered, and explicable); (b) manageability (the degree to which a person believes that he or she has the resources needed to handle a demand); and (c) meaningfulness (the belief that demands are worthy of investment and commitment). People with a strong sense of coherence are able to cope more effectively with stressors and thereby are more likely to adjust better to life with a disability (Lustig et al., 2000). Perceptions associated with a sense of coherence may be either adaptive or dysfunctional. The goal of cognitive therapy is to help clients modify assumptions and perceptions that are maladaptive so that adjustment and quality of life are enhanced.

Adjusting to an acquired disability takes time and perseverance. Counselors can facilitate the process by fostering independence rather than dependence, finding ways to turn failures into learning experiences, respecting their clients as fellow human beings, and helping them take ownership of their rehabilitation.

BOX 4–8

In the summer of 2004, my sister was diagnosed with primary progressive multiple sclerosis. The diagnosis affected my sister, my mother, and me in different ways. I was devastated, worried about my sister's future, and depressed. My sister, in contrast, took the diagnosis in stride. My mother's emotional reactions were somewhere between my sister's and mine. I made arrangements for my sister to pursue counseling, but her primary issue focused more on career issues than on the MS diagnosis itself. I also pursued counseling to deal with the anxiety and depression I felt about her diagnosis. My mother consulted with friends and read materials about MS so as to be more familiar with the disease and its prognosis. In other words, we each reacted to the diagnosis differently.

It has now been four years since my sister's diagnosis. She uses a cane for balance, becomes fatigued easily, and gets frustrated when the weather is either very warm or very cool. However, she has adopted an "it is what it is" attitude and has made various adjustments to accommodate the MS. She took a job as a salesperson that requires her to make numerous phone calls each day but does not require much walking. She moved into a one-story townhouse development, where she pays a fee for maintenance but no longer has to take care of a lawn. Most recently, she began doing her grocery shopping online so as to avoid the fatiguing process of walking down grocery store aisles and waiting in check-out lines.

Because I am the worrier in the family, meeting with a counselor served an invaluable purpose for me. My counselor's father, who was deceased, lived with MS for many years. *He did not let the disability define him.* Perhaps one of the most significant things my counselor told me was to allow my sister to determine what she could and could not do—to respect her independence, letting her know that I was there to help when she asked. My sister does not like to ask for help, so I cannot say that this has been an easy process. However, her sense of humor and ability to "play the cards she has been dealt" have helped tremendously as she and our extended family learn how to live with MS.

Debbie Newsome, Ph.D., LPC

FAMILY ISSUES.   Disabilities in family members can affect family functioning in numerous ways. Family responses to disability vary, depending in part on which phase of adaptation the family is in. Three common phases include the *crisis phase,* the *chronic phase,* and the *terminal phase* (W. Lee, 2007; Roland, 1994).

Families in the *crisis phase* are either waiting for a diagnosis or have just received information about a family member's disability. In this phase, family members often deal with feelings of shock, denial, anger, and depression. During this phase, counselors can provide the family with supportive counseling characterized by empathic listening and attending. A primary goal during the crisis phase is to help the family consider what will remain the same and what will need to change as a consequence of the disability and then determine how to manage that change as it occurs (Roland, 1994).

Families in the *chronic phase* are coping with the day-to-day issues related to the disability (Roland, 1994). The degree to which adjustment and coping are needed is affected by numerous factors, including the nature and severity of the disability and the temperament and stamina of family members. Useful counseling interventions during this phase include helping family members find ways to manage stress, building on strengths, developing realistic expectations, and anticipating problems before they arise so that they can be managed more effectively.

Certain disabilities, such as some types of cancer and amyotrophic lateral sclerosis (ALS), have a prognosis different from that of other disabilities, and in some cases, the condition is terminal. Family members typically need support as they deal with the many different emotions associated with anticipated loss. Counselors also can help families prepare for their loved one's death by making connections with hospice and other community resources. During the terminal phase, the primary caretakers frequently are under a tremendous amount of stress, and family interactions may be strained. Counselors can normalize the tension and encourage family members to find ways to take care of themselves as well as their loved one during this difficult time.

CAREER ISSUES.   Although two out of three people with disabilities want to work, only 50% of those individuals are employed (W. Lee, 2007). Indeed, individuals with disabilities are likely to have the highest rate of unemployment or underemployment in the United States (National Organization on Disability [NOD], 2004). Consider the following 2004 NOD/Harris Survey of Americans with Disabilities:

- **Only 35%** of people with disabilities report being **employed full- or part-time,** compared to 78% of those who do not have disabilities.
- **Three times as many live in poverty** with annual household incomes below $15,000 (26% versus 9%).
- People with disabilities remain **twice as likely to drop out of high school** (21% versus 10%).
- They are **twice as likely to have inadequate transportation** (31% versus 13%), and a much higher percentage **go without needed health care** (18% versus 7%).

The statistics represent more than numbers. Although many people with disabilities are unable to work for medical reasons, other individuals are able to pursue meaningful work if necessary accommodations are provided. Also, the construct of *work* needs to be examined closely by the counselor in conjunction with the client. Professional counselors who counsel clients with disabilities need to be skilled in career counseling, cognizant of the types of skills that can be acquired through rehabilitation training, and open to reconstructing traditional definitions of *work,* in relation to meaningfulness and purpose.

The specific nature of a client's disability affects the type of career counseling that needs to take place. For example, if a person has emotional or communicative disabilities, he or she may not interview well. In such cases, nontraditional job-seeking strategies, such as networking, may be helpful. Also, skills training that includes role-play and fantasy enactment may help the client become more adept at interpersonal interactions. In other situations, a client may have a disability that would not keep him or her from performing a particular job if adaptations are provided. Then the counselor's role may include increasing client awareness of vocational options, particularly as they relate to the Americans with Disabilities Act.

Rehabilitation counselors and clinical mental health counselors work with an increasing number of people with severe psychiatric disabilities. Severe psychiatric disabilities can result for people experiencing major psychoses, such as chronic schizophrenia, chronic recurrent affective disorders, and severe personality disorders. These individuals may experience deficits in social skills, personal management, symptom and medication management, cognition, and coping with stress. Many of them have not been successful in seeking employment; in fact, around 85% of working-age people with severe psychiatric disabilities are unemployed (McReynolds & Garske, 1999). The demands of working with this population are complex and can present a strong challenge to mental health workers. To help people with severe mental illness become and remain contributing members of society, rehabilitation, vocational training, and assistance in work settings are essential. Counselors who work in settings for psychiatric rehabilitation need additional training to meet the myriad needs of people with severe psychiatric disabilities.

ABUSE.   Unfortunately, individuals with disabilities are victimized at a higher rate than that of the general population. Women with disabilities, regardless of age, race, or class, are assaulted, raped, and abused at a rate two times greater than women without a disability, and the risk of being physically or sexually assaulted for adults with developmental disabilities is 4 to 10 times higher than it is for other adults (NVAA, 2002). Also, children with disabilities, regardless of the specific type, are approximately twice as likely to be physically or sexually abused as children without disabilities (National Clearinghouse on Child Abuse and Neglect Information, 2002). Counselors working with people with disabilities need to be alert to any signs indicating abuse and advocate for the rights of their clients.

OTHER ISSUES.   Cultural values and expectations influence beliefs about disabilities. In some cultures, mistaken beliefs about causal factors can lead to greater stigmatization of people with disabilities. For example, some Latino/a families have a fatalistic view about their lives, which may make rehabilitation more difficult. Also, some Asian cultures attribute disability to the behavior of one's ancestors, making the disability a source of shame. Within certain Native American tribes (e.g., the Dine'h), attributional beliefs may be attached to specific disabilities, such as the belief that seizures are caused by incest between siblings (W. Lee, 2007). Culturally based beliefs and attitudes like these can complicate the counseling process and need to be addressed sensitively.

Although people with disabilities share some common concerns, specific needs and counseling goals relate directly to the nature, duration, and severity of the disability. Although it is beyond the scope of this chapter to describe specific disabling conditions and recommended interventions, readers are encouraged to consult additional sources to gain more in-depth knowledge about counseling people with particular disabilities.

Summary and Conclusion

In this chapter, we have examined counseling issues related to three areas of diversity: culture and ethnicity, sexual orientation, and disability. A wealth of material in the professional literature portrays the general concerns of each group and describes the counseling theories and techniques most appropriate for cross-cultural counseling. Indeed, specialty courses and counseling concentrations that focus on one or more of these groups are offered in many graduate counselor education programs.

Although information about a particular population may appear unrelated to other populations, it is not. A common theme is that counselors who work with a variety of clients must be knowledgeable about them collectively and individually to deal effectively with their common and unique concerns. All too often, stereotypes and prescribed roles are assigned to members of distinct ethnic and racial groups, sexual minorities, and people with disabilities. To be a culturally responsive counselor, it is important to develop multicultural competencies in three primary areas: awareness, knowledge, and skills. Overcoming prejudices, fears, and anxieties and learning new skills based on accurate information and sensitivity are major challenges of counseling in a multicultural and pluralistic society.

When working with diverse populations, counselors need to be sensitive to the range of concerns that affect their clients. They must also realize the limitations and appropriateness of the counseling interventions they employ. Counselors must constantly ask themselves how each of their clients is similar to and different from others. Effective counselors concentrate on increasing their sensitivity to global issues as well as to individual concerns. By intentionally being culturally responsive, clinical mental health counselors have a unique opportunity to serve as advocates for their clients by denouncing all forms of stigmatization, marginalization, and oppression while finding ways to facilitate individual and collective empowerment.

CHAPTER 5

Current and Emerging Influences

I feel at times that I'm wasting my mind
as we wade through your thoughts and emotions.
With my skills I could be in a world-renowned clinic
with a plush, private office, soft padded chairs,
and a sharp secretary at my command.
Instead of here in a pink cinderblock room
where it leaks when it rains
and the noise seeps under the door like water.
But in leaving, you pause for a moment
as your voice spills out in a whisper:
"Thanks for being here when I hurt."
With those words my fantasies end, as reality,
like a wellspring begins filling me
with life-giving knowledge, as it cascades through my mind,
That in meeting you, when you're flooded with pain,
I discover myself.

Gladding, S. T. (1975). Here and now. *Personnel and Guidance Journal, 53,* 746. © ACA. Reprinted with permission. No further reproduction authorized without written permission of ACA.

I n the last section of Chapter 1, we described some of the current issues and trends that are influencing the counseling profession in general and the clinical mental health counseling profession in particular. Among those influences are multiculturalism and diversity, professional recognition, evidence-based treatment protocols, and advocacy and social justice issues. Although these topics are all significant, they are not addressed in Chapter 5 because attention is given to them in other sections of the book. In this chapter, we focus on topics that are not addressed in as much depth in other chapters but have had a widespread influence on our profession: managed care, technological innovations, and holistic approaches to mental health, including the bio-psycho-social model, spirituality, and wellness. Although these topics may seem unrelated, they are consistently listed as significant issues in the mental health profession (e. g., Patrick, 2007a; Rollins, 2008). Hence, addressing them in a chapter entitled "Current and Emerging Influences" is fitting.

Managed care has had a pervasive impact on the delivery of mental health services. It has profoundly affected the manner in which counseling is provided, with the majority of practitioners who work in managed care environments reporting an increased use of brief-term and solution-focused interventions (Mitchell, 1998). Working in managed care organizations has led to the rise of ethical concerns in regard to client care, confidentiality, competence, and integrity. In this chapter, we examine the development of managed care organizations, their influence on community counseling, ethical issues associated with managed care practices, and recommendations for counselors who work in managed care environments.

Innovations in technology also have created opportunities and challenges for community counselors. In particular, the widespread use of the Internet has led to new options for individual and group counseling, as well as to increased access to mental health resources for the general public. Advances in technology come with a cost, however, and with new technological advances also come ethical concerns about a host of issues, including confidentiality, accountability, and viability of online resources. Thus, a second topic explored in this chapter is that of computer applications in counseling.

Finally, during the past decade there has been a renewed interest in holistic approaches to counseling. Mental health professionals are encouraged to consider psychological, physical, social, emotional, spiritual, and environmental factors as they assess clients, develop treatment plans, and implement interventions. As we focus on holistic approaches, we describe the bio-psycho-social model, discuss issues related to spirituality and counseling, and address wellness models and interventions that continue to gain prominence in the counseling field.

Each of these topics—managed care, technological innovations, and holistic approaches to counseling—has had a distinct effect on the current practice of counseling in community and agency settings. It is likely that they will continue to affect counselors and the services they provide in the years that lie ahead. As counselors provide services in a dynamic, changing society, they will want to be aware of factors that influence clients and the counseling profession and make informed decisions about how to respond professionally to those influences.

MANAGED CARE

The explosive growth of managed health care organizations (MCOs), especially during the past two decades, has had a tremendous impact on the counseling profession. *Managed care* is a general term used to describe the systems of businesses and organizations that arrange for the financing and delivery of health services, including medical and mental health practices (Phelps, Eisman, & Kohout, 1998). *Managed behavioral health care,* which represents a growing segment of the managed care industry, specializes in mental health and substance abuse treatment.

The influx of managed care has caused significant changes in the manner in which mental health treatment is provided and financed. Indeed, according to some mental health professionals, managed care has emerged as the "single most important influence on the practice of counseling and psychotherapy" (Davis & Meier, 2001, p. vii). To function effectively as a professional counselor in contemporary society, an understanding of key concepts and implications associated with managed care is essential. In this section, we describe the development and key functions of managed care systems and discuss some of the implications for counselors, particularly in regard to ethical considerations.

The Development of Managed Care Systems

In many ways, health care today is equated with managed care. Prior to the 1980s, however, managed care organizations were uncommon. Mental health care was generally funded by major medical insurance, which utilized a fee-for-service system. Within such a system, insurance companies paid for services rendered by practitioners after consumers met specified deductible amounts. These third-party health care systems were founded on the premise that a large group of persons would pay a premium to offset the cost of care for those who were ill (Cooper & Gottlieb, 2000).

When third-party insurance systems such as Blue Cross were first established, mental health benefits were not included in their plans. Indeed, it was not until the 1950s that such insurance plans began to include mental health benefits, with services being provided more frequently on an outpatient, rather than on an inpatient, basis (Austad & Berman, 1991).

With more employers offering insurance coverage, and with the establishment of federally funded programs such as Medicare and Medicaid in 1965, the cost and the utilization of medical and mental health services increased dramatically. Escalating costs and growing demands for coverage and service led to increasingly greater portions of the federal budget and corporate profits being earmarked for health insurance costs (Mitchell, 1998).

In response to the rising cost of health coverage associated with existing plans, insurance companies, employers, and the federal government began to grapple with ways to curb expenses. Managed care provided an alternative to the traditional fee-for-service system. The Health Maintenance Organization Act of 1973 designated federal funding for the development of managed care programs and required employers to offer managed care options to employees (Cooper & Gottlieb, 2000). Health maintenance organizations (HMOs) are one of several forms of managed care systems designed to reduce total health care costs by shifting care to less-expensive forms of treatment (Luck, 1999; Madonna, 2000). By the late 1990s, 75% of Americans with health insurance were enrolled in some type of managed care plan (Kiesler, 2000). In the 21st century, managed health care has emerged as a major factor influencing health care in general and mental health services in particular (Cooper & Gottlieb, 2000).

What Is Managed Care?

Managed care can be described as "a way of providing care, a philosophy of care, a way to finance care, and a way to control costs" (Talbott, 2001, p. 279). It refers to the administration of health care services by a party other than the client or practitioner. Managed care systems assume the financial risks as well as oversee the services provided by practitioners to clients. Generally speaking, the two primary goals of managed care systems are to (a) contain costs and (b) ensure quality of care. Costs are controlled by limiting the amount and type of services, monitoring services, and changing the nature of services offered (Foos, Ottens, & Hill, 1991). Managed care systems typically use treatment guidelines, peer review, and financial incentives and penalties to influence providers, payors, and financial intermediaries to manage the cost, financing, utilization, and quality of health care services (Luck, 1999).

Most of today's mental health professionals have at least some degree of involvement with managed care systems (Glosoff, 1998). Consequently, counselors need to be familiar with terms and procedures associated with managed care environments. The three most common models of managed care are HMOs, preferred provider organizations (PPOs), and government-funded health programs (i.e., Medicaid, Medicare, and Civilian Health and Medical Programs of the Uniformed Services). Descriptions of various managed care systems and terms associated with those systems are presented in Figures 5–1 and 5–2.

Today, hundreds of managed care companies are operating in both the public and the private sectors. These companies contract with approved mental health providers and facilities to provide mental health services for consumers at reduced fees. Providers and facilities that contract with MCOs agree to comply with company procedures, including preadmission screening and utilization reviews. Some companies are more restrictive than others, so prospective providers are encouraged to explore the potential effects the policies may have on their work with clients (Glosoff, 1998).

Term	Definition
Managed Care Organization (MCO)	The oversight of health care delivery by a third party whose purpose is to limit costs and monitor and influence services. The term refers to any HMO or managed behavioral care entity.
Health Maintenance Organization (HMO)	An organization that provides comprehensive health care to its members in return for a fixed monthly membership fee. Health services are coordinated by a primary care physician, who serves as the gatekeeper and makes all decisions regarding referral for specialty examinations and services.
Individual or Independent Practice Association (IPA)	An organization that typically is created by physicians and marketed to employers. An IPA may contract services with several different HMOs. Practitioners in the IPA serve clients from the HMOs as well as their individual clients.
Preferred Provider Organization (PPO)	Groups of hospitals, physicians, or other practitioners who contract with employers, insurance companies, or third-party groups to provide comprehensive medical care for a fee that is typically discounted. This plan allows patients to visit specialists outside the plan's network, but at a higher cost.
Health Care Finance Agency (HCFA)	The federal agency that oversees health financing policies for Medicare and the Office of Prepaid Health Care
Joint Commission on Accreditation of Health care Organizations (JCAHO)	A nonprofit organization whose goal is to improve the quality of health care services.
National Committee for Quality Assurance (NCQA)	A private, nonprofit group composed primarily of representatives from managed care companies and employers whose purpose is to evaluate the quality of managed care plans and accredit MCOs based on standardized reviews.

FIGURE 5–1   Types of managed care organizations and managed care regulators

Note. Definitions compiled from various sources, including Davis; Meier, 2001; Lawless, Ginter, & Kelly, 1999; and Winegar & Hayter, 1998.

Term	Definition
Capitation	A form of payment in which the provider is paid on a per-member basis.
Carve-outs	The separation or carving out of specific types of health care from the overall benefit package. For example, the mental health and substance abuse portion of health care benefits may be "carved out" of the overall package, with separate contracts being made with managed behavioral care organizations.
Case/Care Management	A coordinated set of professional activities focused on treatment planning and assurance of treatment delivery that addresses the clients' needs while maintaining quality, cost-effective outcomes.
Case Rate	A preestablished fee paid for the entire course of treatment for one case.
Clinical Review Criteria	The written protocols or decision trees used by a utilization review organization to determine medical necessity and level of care decisions.
Closed Panel Health Plan	The managed care organization (MCO) requires participants to utilize practitioners, facilities, and pharmacies with which it has a contractual relationship.
Covered Services	Professional services of health care providers that have been authorized by the health care plan or HMO.
Gatekeeper	An individual (usually a clinician) who controls the access to health care services for members of a specific group. Often, the gatekeeper is the *primary care physician (PCP)*. In some health care delivery systems, the gatekeeper is a case manager.
Gag Clause	A stipulation made by an MCO that prevents counselors from discussing alternative treatments outside the boundaries of approved services (gag clauses are less common now than in the past after having been successfully challenged in court).
Intensive Outpatient Program (IOP)	In behavioral health care, IOP refers to an outpatient treatment program that provides 2 to 4 hours of care two or more times per week (both individual and group counseling).
Level of Care	Refers to treatment alternatives on a continuum of care (e.g., inpatient, partial hospitalization, outpatient, long-term residential treatment).
Medically Necessary	When a particular treatment or evaluation is required, appropriate, and in agreement with acceptable standards of medical practice and cannot be provided in a less intensive setting.
Network	Contracts made by an HMO with two or more independent group practices to provide services to HMO members.

FIGURE 5–2   Terms associated with managed care systems

Note. Definitions compiled from various sources, including Davis; Meier, 2001; Lawless, Ginter, & Kelly, 1999; and Winegar & Hayter, 1998.

Term	Definition
Open Panel (HMO)	The HMO allows members to receive services outside of the provider network without referral authorization. Members usually pay an additional deductible and/or co-pay for these services.
Primary Care Physician (PCP)	Physician who oversees the provision of health care for defined subsets of HMO members. Some managed care plans require PCP screening and referral for mental health or substance abuse treatment as well as for other types of health care.
Practice Guidelines	Recommended interventions and procedures for treatments of specific conditions so as to achieve optimum results as efficiently as possible.
Provider Contract	A written agreement between a licensed health care provider (e.g., physician, counselor, facility) and a health plan.
Utilization Review	Process by which the MCO reviews the diagnosis, treatment plan, and response to treatment before authorizing the use or extension of the client's benefit plan.

FIGURE 5–2 *(Continued)*

Implications for Counselors

How has managed care affected the work of professional counselors? According to Anderson (2000), working within managed care systems has changed the way mental health professionals perform clinical duties. Short-term, highly focused interventions that follow treatment guidelines and protocols are the norm. The emphasis is on demonstrating the efficacy of services while containing costs. Counselors working in managed care environments are expected to write specific treatment plans, participate in utilization reviews, and comply with the limits placed on the amount of therapy authorized by managed care organizations. Cooper and Gottlieb (2000), citing several sources, highlighted the defining characteristics of counseling and psychotherapy in a managed care system:

- Brief therapy is mandated and characterized by immediate assessment of the client's presenting problem, clearly delineated treatment goals, and an active counselor.
- The counselor forms a pragmatic therapeutic relationship with the client for the purpose of providing the most efficient and effective treatment.
- Required communication with the client's PCP is usually required, as well as increased interaction with other health care professionals.
- The counseling process is monitored by the MCO and typically includes documentation of treatment necessity and regular submission of treatment plans. The process of monitoring the therapeutic process is called *utilization review* (UR) and may occur before, during, and after treatment.

Advantages and Disadvantages of Managed Care

Proponents of managed care assert that managed care services contain costs while simultaneously maintaining quality service (Paulson, 1996; Winegar, 1993). Supporters claim that time-limited treatment is a research-supported practice that is as effective as traditional treatment for most clients (see Austad & Berman, 1991; Hoyt, 1995). Other potential advantages associated with managed care include greater access to mental health services, increased numbers of referrals for some practitioners, and the implementation of quality control and standards of practice (Lawless, Ginter, & Kelly, 1999). Accredited managed behavioral care organizations typically require providers to document the quality of their work in several areas, including client satisfaction, clinical outcomes, and adherence to best-practice guidelines, thus increasing practitioner accountability.

Even though working in managed care settings may benefit practitioners and clients in some ways, recent studies indicate that most mental health professionals believe that managed care has negatively affected their work with clients and presents significant ethical challenges (see Cohen, Marecek, & Gillham, 2006; Cooper & Gottlieb, 2000; Danzinger & Welfel, 2001; Phelps et al., 1998). Practitioners have expressed several concerns related to counseling in managed care environments. One concern is that standardized treatment guidelines fail to take into account the unique nature of clients' needs and compromise counselors' autonomy in determining specific interventions (Mitchell, 1998). The systems that set up treatment protocols usurp much of the clinical judgment and professionalism of the practitioner (Smith, 1999). Other concerns include arbitrary time limits, caps on the number of sessions approved, increased paperwork, difficulties in being placed on provider lists, and insufficient qualified personnel acting as gatekeepers (Glosoff, Garcia, Herlihy, & Remley, 1999). Managed mental health care systems are based on a medical model, which requires the labeling of pathology before services are authorized (Glosoff, 1998), rather than on a growth-based developmental model, which characterizes the counseling profession. Services that do not constitute a medical necessity will not be reimbursed, and many policies exclude coverage for certain types of counseling and mental health conditions, including marriage counseling, career counseling, educational services, experimental interventions, and personality disorders (Braun & Cox, 2005; Luck, 1999). Particularly distressing to many clinicians are the ethical dilemmas encountered when attempting to balance managed care dictums with professional codes of ethics. Indeed, Phelps et al. (1998) reported that negative appraisals of managed care organizations often stem from the difficult ethical issues with which practitioners are faced.

Ethical Considerations

A growing body of literature addresses ethical dilemmas that face community counselors working in managed care environments (e. g., Braun & Cox, 2005; Cooper & Gottlieb, 2000; Daniels, 2001; Danzinger & Welfel, 2001; Davis & Meier, 2001; Glosoff et al., 1999; Smith, 1999). Ethical concerns related to client welfare, confidentiality, informed consent, counselor competence, and integrity are among the issues frequently encountered in managed care environments, requiring counselors to engage in thoughtful decision-making practices.

CLIENT WELFARE. A professional counselor's first and foremost responsibility is to respect the dignity and promote the welfare of clients (American Counseling Association [ACA], 2005). At times, counselors working in managed care environments are faced with the difficulty of supporting the client's right to quality care as a priority over the counselor's relationship with the reimburser. According to the ACA (2005) *Code of Ethics,* treatment plans should be clinically viable, offer a reasonable likelihood of effectiveness, be consistent with the client's abilities and situations, and respect the client's freedom of

choice (Standard A.1.c.). However, because treatment plans must conform to MCO protocols and be approved by MCO representatives, counselors may not be free to plan and implement treatments independently. When professional judgments differ from MCO
mandates, practitioners must decide whether to implement the approved but less-suitable
treatment plans or risk denial of reimbursement (Danzinger & Welfel, 2001).

Time-limited treatment imposed by MCOs also can affect client welfare in that it may
compromise quality, providing the client with partial treatment, which may result in early
termination. Miller (1996) referred to this practice as *rationing* and cautioned that it is
imperative for counselors to inform clients in advance about the possibility of rationed
services. In some cases, clinicians may determine that clients will benefit from brief therapy.
Even so, the number of sessions recommended by the clinician for a satisfactory outcome
may be greater than the number allocated by the MCO (Davis & Meier, 2001). When this is
the case, counselors need to make appropriate arrangements for those who cannot be
served effectively following MCO guidelines. Such arrangements may include negotiating
longer treatment with MCOs, having clients pay out of pocket, referring clients to alternative
treatment sources, and working pro bono (Glosoff et al., 1999). Standard A.11.a. of the ACA
(2005) *Code of Ethics* addresses the issue of early termination by stating that counselors are
not to abandon their clients and are responsible for making arrangements for continuation
of care.

There are legal as well as ethical ramifications of time-limited treatment and early termination. In court cases dealing with the issue of responsible treatment of clients, most decisions have found the practitioners primarily responsible for their clients' care, regardless of
MCO guidelines (Glosoff et al., 1999). For example, in *Wickline v. State of California* (1987),
the service provider was held liable for the HMO's decision to limit hospitalization, even
though the provider had recommended additional treatment. In this case, which dealt with
the delivery of medical services rather than of needed mental health services, the court
maintained that the provider did not protest the HMO's denial of services aggressively
enough (Davis & Meier, 2001). In another case, *Muse v. Charter Hospital of Winston-Salem,
Inc.* (117 N.C. App. 468 [1995]), the court ruled that it was the duty of the mental health
facility to provide care to patients based on patients' medical conditions, not on the needs of
insurance companies.

BOX 5–1

Muse v. Charter Hospital of Winston-Salem, Inc.

In *Muse*, plaintiffs brought an action for the wrongful death of their son, Joe, who was an inpatient
in a psychiatric hospital for treatment of depression with suicidal thoughts. When Joe's insurance
was about to expire, the hospital sought a promissory note of payment from the parents. The parents agreed to pay for 2 extra days, after which Joe was released as an outpatient. Shortly thereafter,
Joe took an overdose of drugs and killed himself. In this case, the court held that the hospital "had
a duty not to institute a policy or practice which required that patients be discharged when their insurance expired and which interfered with the medical judgment of [the doctor]" (117 N. C. App.
468 [1995], LEXIS at *2).

(Madonna, 2000, p. 26)

CONFIDENTIALITY.   Assurance of confidentiality is at the heart of the counseling relationship. Without this assurance, many clients would not feel safe discussing private, intimate aspects of their lives (Remley & Herlihy, 2010). Section B of ACA's (2005) *Code of Ethics* extensively addresses the issue of confidentiality. Traditionally, counselors have been able to assure clients of confidentiality, with certain exceptions (i.e., threat of harm to self or others). With the advent of managed care, however, the issue of confidentiality has become much more complex (Barnett, 1998). Danzinger and Welfel (2001) reported that one of the most frequently listed ethical challenges associated with managed care was that of confidentiality. Eighty percent of the counselors and counselor educators surveyed in their study stated that interactions with MCOs either often or occasionally compromised client confidentiality.

MCOs often request extensive, personal information about clients and detailed reports of their treatment (Cooper & Gottlieb, 2000). Once information is shared with MCOs, counselors have little control over what happens to that information (Danzinger & Welfel, 2001). Cooper and Gottlieb offered several recommendations to practitioners to help them address ethically the issue of confidentiality:

- Provide a comprehensive informed consent form to help clients understand the ramifications of MCO reimbursement policies.
- Only release the minimal amount of information needed so that the client's privacy is protected.
- Make sure clients understand the nature of any release forms signed.
- Avoid sending case notes to MCOs; instead, send treatment summaries.
- Exercise caution when transmitting information via e-mail, fax machines, and cellular phones. Whenever possible, mail requested paperwork to the MCO.

INFORMED CONSENT.   Standard A.2.b. of the ACA (2005) *Code of Ethics* states that counselors are to inform clients of the purposes, goals, procedures, limitations, risks, and benefits of counseling, both at the onset of the counseling relationship and throughout the process as necessary. The *Code of Ethics* also states that counselors should take steps to make sure clients understand the implications of diagnosis; the use of tests, reports, fees, and billing arrangements; and the limits of confidentiality. Counselors working within a managed care context may need to expand their informed consent procedures to ensure that clients are aware of their benefit plans, MCO-related limits to confidentiality, and potential limits to treatment (Daniels, 2001). It is helpful for practitioners view informed consent as an *ongoing process* rather than as a single event (Cooper & Gottlieb, 2000). When clients begin counseling, they may not be fully able to understand what they are told, especially if they are experiencing stress, anxiety, or depression. Revisiting issues related to informed consent ensures that the client truly comprehends the information that was presented initially.

COMPETENCE.   Most MCOs endorse brief-therapy models of treatment. Although many counselor education programs now include brief-therapy models as part of their curricula, some counselors have not been adequately trained or prepared to practice brief therapy. Standard C.2.a. of the *Code of Ethics* states that counselors are to practice only within the boundaries of their competence, based on their training, experience, and credentialing. If counselors are not adequately trained to provide treatments authorized by an MCO, then they must either receive proper training or refrain from joining particular managed care panels (Cooper & Gottlieb, 2000; Daniels, 2001).

INTEGRITY.   *Integrity* refers to honesty and fairness and includes being accurate and unbiased when reporting to other parties, including to MCOs (Cooper & Gottlieb, 2000). Honesty in diagnosing and reporting is addressed in Standard E.5.a. and Standard C.5.c. of ACA's ethical code. However, when client diagnoses do not fall within reimbursement guidelines, counselors may be tempted to diagnose inappropriately to gain reimbursement (Danzinger & Welfel, 2001). For example, a practitioner might assign a more serious diagnosis than is warranted to obtain more authorized sessions, a process known as *upcoding* (Cooper & Gottlieb, 2000). In other situations, the counselor may be tempted to *downcode,* or apply a less-serious diagnosis, so that the client is able to receive treatment. For example, if a client presents with borderline personality disorder—an Axis II condition that typically is not reimbursable—a counselor who downcodes would record only an Axis I condition, such as depression (Cooper & Gottlieb, 2000). In a national survey of clinical counselors, over 70% of the respondents stated that they were aware of at least occasional occurrences of downcoding, and over 60% indicated awareness of upcoding (Mead, Hohenshil, & Singh, 1997). Both practices, sometimes called "diagnosing for dollars" (Wylie, 1995, p. 22), are unethical and constitute insurance fraud.

Recommendations for Counselors

Providing quality care without compromising ethical and legal concerns is a challenging but necessary goal for all counselors who work in managed care environments (Braun & Cox, 2005). If an ethical dilemma does arise, it is important to have a decision-making plan in place. One example of an ethical decision-making model was presented in Chapter 3. In solving ethical dilemmas related to managed care, Cooper and Gottlieb (2000) suggested using Haas and Malouf's model of ethical decision making, which includes the following steps:

1. Gather information about the problem.
2. Consult with colleagues and look at relevant literature to consider pertinent legal and ethical principles.
3. Create a list of appropriate responses.
4. Conduct a cost–benefit analysis of each potential response.
5. Choose the option that best resolves the dilemma.
6. Act on that option and evaluate its effectiveness.

In addition to knowing how to solve ethical dilemmas effectively, counselors can do several things to facilitate their work with clients affiliated with MCOs. Counselors are encouraged to gain a complete understanding of the terms and functions of MCOs, including preauthorization, cost containment, clinical criteria requirements, and use review procedures (Glosoff et al., 1999). Counselors also need to be aware of client benefits, referral procedures, criteria for medical necessity, procedures for completing claim forms, and emergency procedures (Anderson, 2000). Other ways to prepare for work in a managed care environment include developing knowledge and skills related to *DSM-IV* categories, treatment-plan writing (Figure 5–3), brief and solution-focused counseling, and procedures for getting on provider panels (Lawless et al., 1999). Combining clinical expertise with knowledge of MCO procedures and skill in working collaboratively with MCO personnel can help practitioners provide quality mental health services in the age of managed care.

- A clear statement of the client's problem
- A statement of goals with specific, measurable criteria to measure goal attainment
  - Goals can be listed as short term, intermediate, and long term, depending on the issues that are addressed.
- A clear statement of objectives or activities that will be implemented to help the client meet the established goals
  - Ask yourself, "How will I know if the client accomplished the objective?"
- A time frame within which goals and objectives will be accomplished

Example:

The client currently exhibits flat affect, depressed mood, and reports disturbed sleep (no more than 4 hours a night for the past month) and decreased appetite (has been eating one meal a day for the past 2 weeks). The goals are (1) to make a list of three pleasurable activities from which client will choose one and perform 3 days out of the week, (2) to eat two well-balanced meals a day for one week, and (3) to identify triggers to depression by writing in a journal three times a week. I plan to see the client in weekly individual sessions. I will be using cognitive behavioral techniques to help identify triggers to depression as well as client-centered therapy to enhance the therapeutic relationship. I am requesting 12 sessions. At the end of these sessions, the client's progress will be reevaluated.

(Anderson, 2000, p. 345)

FIGURE 5–3 **What to include in a treatment plan written for an MCO**
Reprinted with permission of AMHCA.

BOX 5–2

How are Mental Health Professionals Placed on Provider Panels?

- A given geographic region must have a need for additional providers. If a particular region already has enough providers, the MCO has no need to recruit new counselors. MCOs estimate that one provider of mental health services is needed for every 1000 people they insure (Polkinghorne, 2001).
- Counselors must show that they follow acceptable diagnosis and treatment procedures and be willing to accept reduced fees. They must be willing to abide by the protocols of the MCO and demonstrate achievement of desired treatment outcomes.
- Counselors must be able to use therapeutic approaches that are brief and goal oriented in order to provide efficient, time-limited services.

(Gerig, 2007, p. 209)

Just as managed care has precipitated changes in the delivery of mental health services, technological advances have brought about new options regarding counseling service delivery. In the next section, we direct our attention to computer applications in counseling, focusing in particular on counseling and the Internet.

INNOVATIONS IN TECHONOLOGY

Of the many developments that have profoundly influenced the mental health profession, those related to technology have been especially salient. The widespread availability of computer networking and the Internet in the 1990 s dramatically increased the use of computers in counseling (Oravec, 2000). Mental health professionals are challenged to make decisions about ways they will choose to use, or not use, computers in their work. As noted by Walz (2000), "All counselors must come to grips with this exponentially expanding medium and decide for themselves what to do and what not to do" (p. xii). It has been nearly a decade since Walz issued that statement, and issues related to technological applications in counseling continue to abound.

Throughout the past several decades, efforts to integrate technology into mental health care have increased significantly. The impact of technology in general and computers in particular on the counseling profession accelerated with the advent of the microcomputer in the 1970s. During the 1970s and 1980s, computer applications were developed for a variety of counseling-related activities, including assessment and test interpretation, career guidance, and client data management (Granello, 2000). By 1994, more than 70 computer-assisted guidance systems and software programs were in use. Currently, a wide range of technologies influence counseling, including software to aid in treatment planning and report writing, statistical packages for analyzing client date, online assessment, and software for marketing and client recruitment (Haley & Vazquez, 2009). Even more pervasive is the influence of the Internet, which provides options for online counseling, advertising, and mental health resources for clients, to name just a few. The accelerated use of technologies presents counselors with new opportunities as well as potential challenges. Consequently, "healthy management of technological tools may be one of the most critical competencies a counseling professional can model and teach" (Casey, 2000, p. 18).

The Internet and Clinical Mental Health Counseling

Whereas technological applications in the mental health field are widespread and numerous, the evolution of the Internet in the 1990s has had, perhaps, the greatest impact on the counseling profession. According to a May 2008 survey, 73% of American adults use the Internet (Pew Internet & American Life Project, 2008). It is likely that this percentage is even higher among adolescents and even children, who represent a generation that is growing up in a time of rapidly expanding technology (Maples & Han, 2008). For students of the millennial generation (born after 1982), using computers, cell phones, and other technological tools represent standard forms of communication. Whereas much debate and speculation has taken place regarding the effects this rapid worldwide communication system will have on the way people interact, it is clear that the Internet and other forms of technological communication will have ongoing global implications (Skinner & Zack, 2004).

BOX 5–3

The boom in Internet access and use, first in academic circles and then with the general public, has created an entire new chapter in the computer-counseling relationship.

(Granello, 2000, p. 11)

Although its origins date back to post–World War II days, the Internet became accessible to the general public in the 1990s. The development of the World Wide Web (WWW, or "the Web") transformed the Internet into an information highway (Sampson & Bloom, 2001), providing the general public with global interconnection and instantly accessible information. Counseling-related Internet applications include electronic mail (e-mail) counseling, list servers, computer conferencing, chat rooms, and bulletin board systems, and electronic coaching (E-coaching). Assessments, information, and instruction also are delivered in a wide array of formats on the Internet.

As individuals spend more time interacting with each other online, mental health services that make use of the Internet are becoming increasingly more widespread. In this section, attention will be given to two emerging forms of online mental health applications: *Internet (online) counseling services* and *computer-assisted counseling* (Haley & Vazquez, 2009). *Internet counseling services* refer to situations in which an online professional relationship has been established between a counselor and a client over time for the purpose of helping the client (Sampson & Bloom, 2001). *Computer-assisted counseling* includes Internet-based information resources, online assessment, online journals, software for managing client data, software for treatment planning, and other resources that can be accessed via the computer, either through the Internet or through software applications.

Online Counseling

Online counseling, Internet therapy, cybercounseling, and *technology-assisted distance counseling* are commonly used terms to describe the process of counseling with individuals, families, or groups over distance using the Internet (Haley & Vazquez, 2009; Oravec, 2000). Online counseling can occur through e-mail interaction, chat room counseling, and bulletin board counseling. Web-telephony counseling (real-time speaking over the Internet using a microphone) and videoconferencing (real-time counseling using audio and video technology that usually involves a camera, monitor, and computer processor) are other example of cybercounseling (Haley & Vasquez, 2009). These two methods, as well as chat room counseling, are examples of *synchronous counseling* (i.e., the interaction takes place during the moment of connection). However, these methods are not used as frequently at this point because many people do not have the necessary technological equipment. In contrast, the use of e-mail is quite common in the United States and other countries (Maples & Han, 2008) and thus is a more viable option for most clients and counselors. E-mail counseling and bulletin board counseling are examples of *asynchronous counseling* because there is a time lapse in communication between the counselor and the client.

ONLINE E-MAIL COUNSELING.   Many people are quite adept at using e-mail as a primary means of communication. For some, using e-mail for therapeutic purposes is a logical next step. In situations where face-to-face contact is geographically or physically not feasible, or when it creates excessive anxiety for the client, online counseling using e-mail may provide access to mental health services that otherwise would not be a possibility (Shaw & Shaw, 2006; Tait, 1999).

Online individual counseling can take several different forms. In some cases, a question-and-answer format is used: An individual states a problem, and the mental health professional responds within a fixed time period with information, recommendations, or a counseling referral (Sampson, Kolodinsky, & Greeno, 1997). In other situations, the online counseling acquires a more formal structure, in which client and counselor make arrangements to communicate therapeutically, using e-mail as the mode of communication for each session. *Therapy Online* is an example of an e-mail counseling and therapy practice initiated by Murphy and Mitchell (1998). Depending on the client's needs, counseling can range from a few brief exchanges to more long-term interactions. The client–counselor relationship is initiated when the client completes a worksheet available at the *Therapy Online* Web site (www.therapyonline.ca). If online counseling seems to be an appropriate option, the counselor(s) and client design a plan to structure future correspondence.

BOX 5–4

Therapy Online: About Us

Therapy Online began offering its services in 1995 on a modem-accessed local bulletin board service. Since the beginning, we have worked hard to be leaders in the field of online counselling by:

- carefully examining existing ethical codes for counselling
- applying those codes to our online counselling practice
- developing new ethics specifically for online counselling
- taking leadership in the field of counselling by developing effective online counselling skills
- publishing professional articles on online counselling skills and practical issues
- offering training to other counsellors at conferences and workshops

From D. Mitchell, 2007 (www.therapyonline.ca/aboutclt.htm)

In an online interview discussing their e-mail counseling practice (Collie, Mitchell, & Murphy, 2000), Mitchell and Murphy noted several benefits associated with electronic counseling, including "convenience, privacy, schedule flexibility, the possibility of communicating thoughts and feelings right away rather than waiting until the weekly appointment, and the potential for leveling the power imbalances" (p. 234). Murphy and Mitchell described the importance of developing specific online counseling skills to compensate for the lack of visual cues. These skills, which include the use of metaphorical language, the use of special fonts, and descriptive immediacy, enable the counselor to contextualize and enhance the meaning of the printed word, thus enabling the counselor to convey warmth and caring to the client. Murphy and Mitchell also emphasized the importance of informing clients at the outset of the possibility of technical glitches interfering with communication pathways. They suggested providing clients with a window of time in which they should expect a response, and if no response is forthcoming, to contact the counselor.

Online support groups and *online group counseling* represent other ways to offer computer-assisted mental health services (Oravec, 2000). Online support groups provide opportunities for global communication among individuals dealing with issues such as grief, depression, and chronic illness. Many participants perceive these computer-based support groups as helpful and validating, although research about their efficacy is limited (Gary & Remolino, 2000). Online group counseling also has received some support in the literature (Riemer-Reiss, 2000). With online group counseling, the counselor coordinates exchanges among members, sets ground rules, and takes steps to ensure that all participants have the opportunity to benefit from the proceedings. Until more research is conducted on these and other online services, counselors need to be alert to potential dangers and complications associated with their uses.

How prevalent is the practice of online counseling? Obtaining an accurate number of fee-based online mental health counseling sites is challenging because the number is constantly changing. Additionally, sites that may be accessible at one point in time may disappear from the Internet at a later date. Skinner and Zack (2004) noted that "the business of online counseling is relegated primarily to modest Web sites with limited staffs and low overhead," certain counselor networks, small group practices, and individual practitioners (p. 41). They emphasized the importance of increasing consumer and professional awareness of what online therapy is and what it is not.

The credentials of counselors offering online services vary greatly. Because the bond of trust between counselor and client is a central value in counseling ethics, it is imperative that online counselors are able to exemplify trustworthiness (Shaw & Shaw, 2006). Online counselors need to accurately identify themselves and their qualifications (Shaw & Shaw, 2006). This issue raises concerns in regard to unlicensed people promoting themselves as counselors (Hughes, 2000). Some Web sites include disclaimers stating all information provided is advice (or education), not "therapy"; however, even with the disclaimer, the implications are problematic. Prior to 2001, clients could check the credentials of online mental health service providers by accessing the *Credential Check* Web site. However, that site is no longer available, and finding ways to check the credibility of e-therapists raises a challenging ethical concern.

In response to some of the professional, ethical, and legal issues potentially associated with online counseling, the National Board of Certified Counselors (NBCC) organized a task force in 1995 to develop a set of technology-assisted counseling guidelines. These guidelines evolved into the *Standards for the Ethical Practice of WebCounseling,* which were adopted formally in 1997 and then updated in 2001 and 2007 (National Board for Certified Counselors [NBCC], 2007). Now called the *Standards for the Practice of Internet Counseling,* the guidelines address practices that are unique to Internet counseling and are based on the principles of ethical practice that embody the NBCC *Code of Ethics* (NBCC, 2007). Specific areas that are addressed include the counseling relationship, confidentiality, data security, licensure, and certification. The *Standards for the Ethical Practice of Internet Counseling* are listed in Figure 5–4 and also can be accessed through the NBCC Web site (www.nbcc.org/webethics2).

In October 1999, the ACA Governing Council approved a separate set of ethical guidelines for online counseling. These guidelines, *Ethical Standards for Internet Online Counseling,* address many of the same issues that the NBCC *Standards* address and can be accessed through ACA's homepage (www.counseling.org). A third set of guidelines was approved by the International Society for Mental Health Online (ISMHO) in 2000: *Suggested Principles for the Online Provision of Mental Health Services* (www.ismho.org). Even with the passage of ethical standards and principles by these organizations, major challenges exist regarding the use of online counseling services. Results of a recent study assessing the practices of 88 online counseling Web sites showed that fewer than half of online counselors were following accepted standards of practice on 8 of the 16 ethical items evaluated (Shaw & Shaw, 2006). Issues related to certification and licensure, safeguarding clients' rights (e. g., informed consent, counseling minors), dealing with emergency

Internet Counseling Relationship

1. In situations where it is difficult to verify the identity of the Internet client, steps are taken to address impostor concerns, such as by using code words or numbers.

2. Internet counselors determine if a client is a minor and therefore in need of parental/guardian consent. When parent/guardian consent is required to provide Internet counseling to minors, the identity of the consenting person is verified.

3. As part of the counseling orientation process, the Internet counselor explains to clients the procedures for contacting the Internet counselor when he or she is offline and, in the case of asynchronous counseling, how often e-mail messages will be checked by the Internet counselor.

4. As part of the counseling orientation process, the Internet counselor explains to clients the possibility of technology failure and discusses the alternative modes of communication, if that failure occurs.

5. As part of the counseling orientation process, the Internet counselor explains to clients how to cope with potential misunderstandings when visual cues do not exist.

6. As a part of the counseling orientation process, the Internet counselor collaborates with the Internet client to identify an appropriately trained professional who can provide local assistance, including crisis intervention, if needed. The Internet counselor and Internet client should also collaborate to determine the local crisis hotline telephone number and the local emergency telephone number.

7. The Internet counselor has an obligation, when appropriate, to make clients aware of free public access points to the Internet within the community for accessing Internet counseling or Web-based assessment, information, and instructional resources.

8. Within the limits of readily available technology, Internet counselors have an obligation to make their Web site a barrier-free environment to clients with disabilities.

9. Internet counselors are aware that some clients may communicate in different languages, live in different time zones, and have unique cultural perspectives. Internet counselors are also aware that local conditions and events may impact the client.

Confidentiality in Internet Counseling

10. The Internet counselor informs Internet clients of encryption methods being used to help ensure the security of client/counselor/supervisor communication. Encryption methods should be used whenever possible. If encryption is not made available to clients, clients must be informed of the potential hazards of unsecured communication on the Internet. Hazards may include unauthorized monitoring of transmissions and/or records of Internet counseling sessions.

11. The Internet counselor informs Internet clients if, how, and how long session data are being preserved. Session data may include Internet counselor/Internet client e-mail, test results, audio/video session recordings, session notes, and counselor/supervisor communications. The likelihood of electronic sessions being preserved is greater because of the ease and decreased costs involved in recording. Thus, its potential use in supervision, research, and legal proceedings increases.

FIGURE 5–4   Standards for the ethical practice of Internet counseling
© 2007 NBCC
Note. Reprinted with permission of the National Board for Certified Counselors (NBCC, 2007, www.nbcc.org/webethics2).

12. Internet counselors follow appropriate procedures regarding the release of information for sharing Internet client information with other electronic sources. Because of the relative ease with which e-mail messages can be forwarded to formal and casual referral sources, Internet counselors must work to ensure the confidentiality of the Internet counseling relationship.

13. Internet counselors review pertinent legal and ethical codes for guidance on the practice of Internet counseling and supervision. Local, state, and national statutes, as well as codes of professional membership organizations, professional certifying bodies, and state or provincial licensing boards need to be reviewed. Also, as varying state rules and opinions exist on questions pertaining to whether Internet counseling takes place in the Internet counselor's location or in the Internet client's location, it is important to review codes in the counselor's home jurisdiction as well as in that of the client. Internet counselors also consider carefully local customs regarding age of consent and child abuse reporting, and liability insurance policies need to be reviewed to determine if the practice of Internet counseling is a covered activity.

14. The Internet counselor's Web site provides links to Web sites of all appropriate certification bodies and licensure boards to facilitate consumer protection.

FIGURE 5–4 (*Continued*)

situations, third-party payments, and online security have yet to be resolved. One of our duties as counseling professionals is to take an active role in guiding the development and implementation of Internet-based service delivery, both now and in the future (Shaw & Shaw, 2006; Sussman, 1998).

Computer-Assisted Counseling

Computer-assisted counseling can include a number of applications that facilitate the work of counselors (Haley & Vazquez, 2009). For example, the Internet provides people with quick access to multimedia-based psychoeducational resources (Riemer-Reiss, 2000; Sampson & Bloom, 2001). These resources can be used without counselor assistance for self-help purposes, or they may be prescribed to supplement traditional counseling. Online psychoeducational resources address a wide range of topics, including mental illness, parenting, conflict resolution, stress management, child development, and career-related issues. Often, the Internet sites allow people to select media formats that best suit their individual learning styles (Sampson & Bloom, 2001). They typically include links to other Web sites, making it possible to access multiple sources of information very rapidly. A downside of the proliferation of information is that Internet-based "assessments, information, and instruction may be attractively presented but inherently invalid and potentially harmful" (Sampson & Bloom, 2001, pp. 623–624).

A specialty area that has many useful computer-based applications, both for personalized computer-based software and for online use, is that of career development. The first computer-based career planning systems were developed in the 1960s (Casey, 2001). Since that time, numerous comprehensive computer-assisted career guidance systems, such as the SIGI-PLUS and DISCOVER, have been created to help people learn about their career interests, skills, and values. More recently, a plethora of career-related materials has been made available online. Either on their own or with the help of a counselor, people can use the Internet to

- Get information about employment opportunities, job resources, and occupational outlooks.
- Get information about company profiles.
- Get information about graduate schools and financial aid.
- Create and submit electronic resumes.
- Complete assessments of interests, personality, skills, and values.
- Visit virtual career centers.

As with other psychoeducational material available online, some sources are more reputable than others. Potential problems associated with online career resources include varied qualities of services, the possibility of invalid or unreliable assessment tools, lack of follow-up and support, misinformation, and in some cases, compromised confidentiality.

The National Career Development Association (NCDA, 1997) developed the NCDA *Guidelines for the Use of the Internet for Provision of Career Information and Planning Services.* These guidelines, which can be accessed through the NCDA Web site (www.ncda .org), provide detailed information for counselors who use Internet-based career services in their practices. The NCDA Web site also provides an extensive list of Internet resources for career development and career planning.

Issues and Implications for Counselors

Technology in general and the Internet in particular have led to a broad spectrum of counseling-related computer applications (Casey, 2001). Computer applications, when used prudently, can enhance counseling services in multiple ways and lead to professional growth. However, there are also are costs associated with technology. Some of the major concerns that have accompanied increased Internet access include Internet addiction, cybersex addiction, Internet pornography, cyberbullying, and online predators. In a recent issue of *Counseling Today* (Rollins, 2008), leaders in the counseling profession were asked to describe their perspectives on major new or evolving issues that they expect counselors to confront in the years ahead. The emerging client issues mentioned most frequently were related to technology: Internet addiction, online pornography addictions, cyberbullying, cyber-affairs, and information overload. Thus, in addition to developing skills for using technology effectively in counseling, counselors need to be aware of the signs and symptoms associated with Internet-related disorders and develop the skills needed for intervention.

Another issue related to mental health services and technology is that of equality of access. Although the number of people with access to computers at home or at work has increased, there is still a *digital divide* (the gap between those people with effective access to information technology and those without access to the technology and/or those who do not have the skills needed to use the technology). One way efforts have been made to close the divide is by providing free access to computers in public libraries (Pew Internet & American Life Project, 2008). However, using a computer in a library compromises individual privacy and is less convenient than logging on to a computer in one's home. Counselors are encouraged to take necessary steps to ensure that computer-related counseling services are available to all clients, regardless of their socioeconomic, geographic, racial, or generational status.

To work effectively in our rapidly advancing technological society, counselors need to stay abreast of emerging developments. Engaging in research, participating in ongoing technological training, being familiar with the resources available online, and being involved in continued refinement of guidelines for Internet use in counseling are just a few of the ways counselors can responsibly manage the opportunities and challenges that accompany the inevitable expansion of computer use that will continue to influence the provision of mental health services.

THINK ABOUT IT

- What issues related to Internet counseling concern you most?
- Which would you prefer: online counseling or face-to-face counseling (as a counselor and/or as a client)?
- What safeguards can be put in place to ensure that people claiming to be professional counselors really are who they say they are?
- What are some ways to deal effectively with licensure and jurisdiction issues related to online counseling?
- As a counselor, how can you help clients evaluate online mental health resources for credibility?

As advancements are made in technology, accompanied by increased access to data and communication options, many Americans have found themselves on communication and accessibility overload. With progress comes a pushing of personal and professional limits, which can result in fatigue, frustration, and disorganization. Finding ways to balance progress with a respect for limits is essential to maintaining physical and psychological health. It is not surprising, then, that holistic approaches to counseling, which encourage optimizing wellness and all its dimensions, have emerged as strong influences on the counseling profession. It is to those influences that we direct our attention next.

HOLISTIC APPROACHES TO MENTAL HEALTH

Approaching mental health holistically (i.e., considering the whole person, including mental, physical, emotional, spiritual, and environmental factors) is not a new phenomenon. Clinical mental health counselors address these factors to enhance wellness, personal growth, and development. They also have skills in assessing multiple dimensions of client development and in developing treatment plans to address client needs and, in some cases, pathology. Providing services from a holistic approach complements the philosophical foundations of the counseling profession (Myers & Sweeney, 2008). In this section, we address several areas that apply to holistic approaches. We begin with an introduction to the bio-psycho-social model. We then address topics of spirituality, mindfulness, and wellness.

The Bio-Psycho-Social Model

The counseling profession finally has a model sophisticated enough to use across all specialties, modalities, and presenting problems.

(Kaplan & Coogan, 2005, p. 23).

The bio-psycho-social (BPS) model is an approach to medicine and mental health that recognizes the interrelated, integrated roles played by biology, psychology, and social/cultural factors in the maintenance of wellness and the understanding of illness. Although the concept does not appear novel, the BPS model has only recently begun to appear in counseling literature. The model was proposed in 1977 by George Engel, a cardiologist, who viewed the prevailing biomedical model as narrow, reductionist, and linear. He proposed the BPS model as a holistic alternative (Borrell-Carrió, Suchman, & Epstein, 2004). Engel believed that to adequately respond to people's distress and suffering and to help them feel understood, clinicians need to attend to the biological, psychological, and social dimensions that affect overall health (Borrell-Carrió et al., 2004). The model proposed by Engel represents a worldview that includes patients' and clients' subjective experiences as well as biomedical data.

So how does the work of a cardiologist that began over three decades ago affect the clinical work conducted by mental health practitioners in contemporary society? Kaplan and Coogan (2005) stated that counseling needs a comprehensive paradigm that allows assessment and intervention across a range of modalities and specialties. The BPS model represents such a paradigm. Certainly, recognizing the importance of holistic approaches to counseling practice is not a new phenomenon. However, the BPS model provides a framework for understanding three essential, interrelated, integrated components that affect overall health as well as mental health.

The recently approved Council for Accreditation of Counseling and Related Educational Programs (CACREP) standards (2009) highlight the importance of the BPS model to the work of clinical mental health counselors. In Section 2 of the Clinical Mental Health Counselor Standards—*Counseling, Prevention, and Intervention*—clinical mental health counselors are expected to know the principles, models, and documentation formats of biopsychosocial case conceptualization and treatment planning. To that end, we provide a brief overview of the three major components of the model, suggestions for assessment and treatment, and a case study that challenges the reader to utilize the BPS model in practice.

BIOLOGICAL COMPONENTS. Biological components of the BPS model include physical, biochemical, and genetic factors that influence mental health (Kaplan & Coogan, 2005). Thanks to scientific advances, we have a much better understanding of biogenetics, mind–body interconnections, neurochemicals, and neurodevelopment. Although counselors are not expected to be neuroscientists, we do need a fundamental knowledge of neurological and physiological factors that affect human behavior. In particular, an understanding of the functions of the brain, its development, the role of neurotransmitters, and the effects of psychotropic medications (medications that affect the mind, emotions, and/or behavior) is imperative. Counselors can gain knowledge in this field, which continues to develop at a rapid pace, through continuing education and training. Whereas it would beyond the scope of this chapter (or of our expertise) to describe these factors in depth, we will explain a few of the more pertinent biological factors that affect mental health: neurotransmitters, the limbic system, and biogenetics.

Neurotransmitters are the chemicals in the brain that account for the transmission of signals from one neuron to the next across synapses. They are produced by glands, such as the pituitary gland and the adrenal glands (Boeree, 2003). Neurotransmitters, which are chemicals, are released from one neuron to another. They either excite or inhibit the message being sent by the brain across the neurons.

Several neurotransmitters have been identified and are known to affect mental health, including regulation, inhibition, and stability. Examples include *acetylcholine, serotonin, dopamine, norepinephrine, epinephrine,* and *gamma-amino butyric acid* (cited in Oestmann, 2007). Though interactions among the billions of neurons that comprise the human brain make it difficult to determine exactly what affects what, we do know certain things about some neurotransmitters. For example, a decrease in dopamine is linked to an increase in hyperactivity and irritability (Matthews, 2001). Norepinephrine modulates other transmitters and shares some similarities with dopamine. Serotonin is an inhibitory neurotransmitter that is closely associated with emotion and mood. Too little serotonin can lead to depression, problems with anger control, obsessive-compulsive disorder, other emotional disorders, and suicide. Too little serotonin also leads to an increased appetite for carbohydrates and sleeping difficulties and has been associated with migraines, irritable bowel syndrome, and fibromyalgia (Boeree, 2003).

Counselors who have a basic understanding of brain chemistry are in a better position to understand how psychotropic medications work. They can then confer intelligently with psychiatrists and other physicians who work with their clients and who have prescription privileges. Therefore, it is important for counselors to be informed about a client's medication practices and be well versed in the roles played by pharmacology in relation to clients' well-being (Oestmann, 2007).

The *limbic system,* also located in the brain, plays a key role in the way clients feel and express emotions such as rage, fear, and aggression. The limbic system is also linked to sexuality (Matthews, 2001). It affects memory, the way a person responds to threats, emotional expression, physical health, and well-being. George Boeree (2002) described this "emotional nervous system" as follows:

> The limbic system is a complex set of structures that lies on both sides and underneath the thalamus, just under the cerebrum. It includes the hypothalamus, the hippocampus, the amygdala, and several other nearby areas. It appears to be primarily responsible for our emotional life, and has a lot to do with the formation of memories. In this drawing, you are looking at the brain cut in half, but with the brain stem intact. The part of the limbic system shown is that which is along the left side of the thalamus (hippocampus and amygdala) and just under the front of the thalamus (hypothalamus):

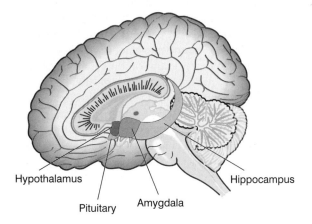

Hypothalamus   Hippocampus

Pituitary   Amygdala

Clients dealing with chronic pain, stress, or struggling with cognitive functioning may be especially affected by limbic system responses (Oestmann, 2007). Because clinicians are likely to work with clients experiencing these and other conditions, understanding the relationship between stress and the limbic system is especially pertinent.

Stress results in emotional reactions that may include intense anxiety, an inability to concentrate, irritability, and a range of physical symptoms. Responses to stressors can "jolt the body out of homeostasis" (Oestmann, 2007, p. 131). Two hormones secreted by the adrenal glands are epinephrine (adrenalin) and glucocorticoids (cortisol or hydrocortisone). A recent UCLA study indicates that the decline in an individual's immune system after facing chronic stress is due to the stress hormone cortisol (Nauert, 2008). Buffers such as outlets for frustration, a sense of control over events or sources of stress, social support, and a belief that things will improve can help clients cope with stress more effectively (Oestmann, 2007).

Genetics play another key role in the biological component of the BPS model. We realize that an in-depth or even cursory overview of genetics at this point would likely put the reader to sleep, but it is important for mental health professionals to recognize the roles genetics plays in mental health. Many psychiatric conditions have a genetic component that puts individuals at a higher risk for developing certain disorders (e.g., autism, Asperger's disorder, anxiety disorders, bipolar disorder, Parkinson's disease, schizophrenia, ADHD, Tourette's syndrome, and alcoholism, to name a few; Oestmann, 2007). In many cases the specific genes related to the disorders are not yet known, and environmental factors are believed to "activate" the genes in some conditions. Study of genetics and the human genome continues to be an important part of scientific research, and counselors will want to stay abreast of the newest developments in the field. Also, it is important to note that only a few of the biological factors that influence overall health have been discussed in this section. However, because this section is merely an overview of the biological components of the BPS model, we now turn our attention to the *psychological components* of the model.

PSYCHOLOGICAL COMPONENTS.   Psychological components of the BPS model include patterns of thinking, coping skills, judgment, perceptions, and emotional intelligence (the ability to perceive, understand, and express emotions). Additional psychological factors include general temperament and personality characteristics. Many of the factors included under the psychological umbrella represent areas that mental health professionals are well versed in. For example, several factors addressed during a Mental Status Exam, which is described in Chapter 7, are categorized as psychological components.

The BPS model proposes that psychological components can influence biological components and vice versa. For example, a client who is experiencing depression may demonstrate all-or-nothing thinking, concentration difficulties, and a sense of helplessness. Symptoms of the depression may be evidenced physiologically, including sleeplessness, appetite disturbance, and a decreased energy level. Both the psychological and physical manifestations of the depression may be connected to neurotransmitter imbalances, such as decreased levels of dopamine and serotonin. A thorough assessment of the client's circumstances may indicate that she and her husband had recently separated, her mother had died of cancer within the past year, and her job is about to be outsourced—social factors, which will be discussed next. The combination of biological, psychological, and social factors coalesced in a way that threatened the client's mental well-being.

SOCIAL COMPONENTS.   Social components, which also may be conceptualized as sociocultural components, include family relationships, support systems, work relationships, and the broader cultural environment as it intersects one's personal cultural identity. Oestmann (2007) also listed several other factors in the social component, including values and beliefs, environmental conditions, lifestyle factors, changes in mental health practices associated with managed care, and reproductive challenges. Whereas some mental health professionals might argue that some of these additional factors are not really "social factors" (e.g., reproductive challenges can also be classified as biological or physiological factors), it still is important to consider them when conducting a thorough BPS assessment.

ASSESSMENT AND TREATMENT PLANNING.   The purpose of the BPS model is to provide health professionals a way to assess elements of human behavior within a comprehensive whole (Kaplan & Coogan, 2005). As noted earlier, the components of the model, as well as factors within those components, interrelate and interact. Clinical mental health counselors can enhance their work with clients by taking each of the three primary components into account when conducting an assessment and designing a treatment plan. Although we provide more in-depth attention to assessment and treatment planning in other chapters, we want to make you aware of one example of an assessment method that enables the clinician to access the major domains of the BPS model: the BATHE technique (Lieberman & Stuart, 1999; McCulloch, Ramesar, & Peterson, 1998; Rodriguez, 2004).

The BATHE technique focuses on five specific areas that lay the groundwork for working collaboratively with a client and for beginning to examine the biological, psychological, and social systems that influence the client's well-being. We briefly describe each area and provide examples of questions that a clinician might ask during the assessment interview. The areas addressed in the interview do not need to be addressed linearly. (Note: We appreciate Chris Rodriguez's [2004] contributions to the sample questions.)

- **Background**—The counselor begins to build rapport and establish a collaborative relationship. The general questions suggested here can lead to further examination of biological, psychological, and social factors affecting the client's condition.
  - What are your current circumstances?
  - What do you believe is the reason for your visit today?
  - What do you feel comfortable sharing with me today?
  - What can you tell me that would help me understand your circumstances?
- **Affect**—The counselor attempts to understand the client's current emotional state.
  - How do you feel about what you have shared with me today?
  - What *effect* does (the presenting problem) have on you?
- **Trouble**—What is the client's presenting problem? What additional factors might underlie the problem?
  - What troubles you most today?
  - What disturbs you about your current circumstances?
  - What is unsettling you?
  - What physical symptoms are you having?
- **Handling**—The counselor assesses the client's coping style and support systems.
  - How are you handling this situation?
  - How are you coping with your circumstances?
  - Who do you turn to for support?
  - How do you find relief?
- **Empathy**—Empathy is conveyed by the counselor to the client in a manner that is perceived by the client. The counselor seeks to convey the message that under the circumstances, the client's response is understandable.
  - This [situation] must be quite difficult for you.
  - You are dealing with some really challenging circumstances.

Oestmann (2007) noted that counseling professionals work in collaboration with a health team, not solely with the client, and that efforts are made to coordinate care. Through this process, the counselor's perceptions and treatment are integrated into a holistic approach to care.

Treatment planning within the BPS framework varies according to the presenting concerns, taking into account mind, body, and social environments that affect the client. For example, consider the case of Khun Prasong.

The Case of Khun Prasong (Praz)

Khun Prasong is a 30-year-old second-generation Thai American. His parents immigrated to the United States 40 years ago. Khun Prasong goes by the name "Praz," although his parents still call him by his given name. Praz is a civil engineer who often feels anxious about his job performance and about social interactions. His English is excellent; however, he does not have many close friends. He has never married and does not belong to any recreational clubs. Nor has he had a physical checkup in the past 10 years.

Praz reports that he feels sad most of the time. During the past 3 months, he has lost his appetite, and the activities he used to enjoy are no longer pleasurable to him. He is getting about 4 hours of sleep a night and says that he feels chronically tired. Praz's parents and only sibling live in Texas, which is 600 miles away.

Using the BPS model as a framework, how would you conceptualize Praz's case? Which issues are most pressing? How would you consider addressing them? What other information would you like to have? What other health professionals would you collaborate with? How would you use the BATHE model to assess Praz?

Clinicians who are guided by a BPS framework recognize that mental health is a dynamic balance. It is not feasible to treat one component of the model without taking into account the other components. In the case of Khun Prasong, it will probably be important to encourage him to get a physical checkup to rule out specific physiological issues. It will also be important to find out more about his social support system and his relationship with his family. What is his connection with the Thai culture? Another important issue is his work: Does he find his job as a civil engineer rewarding? What led him to that field? Are there people in his company with whom he feels comfortable socializing? Certainly, it will be important to evaluate the level of his depression, including suicidal ideation. Due to the presenting symptoms associated with depression and anxiety, referring Praz to a reputable psychiatrist is advised. Throughout the process, you will want to continue to assess the biological, psychological, and social factors—positive and negative—that are affecting Khun Prasong's mental health. You will want to work collaboratively with him, determining which areas of concern to address first.

Spirituality

The bio-psycho-social model described in the previous section does not include a specifically spiritual component. However, for hundreds of years, theologians, philosophers, physicians, and, more recently, mental health professionals, have debated the relationship among the mind, body, and spirit (Meyers, 2007). It can be argued that a truly holistic approach to counseling follows a *bio-psycho-social-spiritual* model.

Research suggests that the majority of Americans value spirituality and religion (e.g., Cashwell & Young, 2005; Simpson, 2009). In recent years "a burgeoning literature has emerged concerning religion and psychotherapy" (Ottens & Klein, 2005, p. 32). Religious and/or spiritual connections can serve as sources of wisdom, community, strength, and health (Harris, Thoresen, & Lopez, 2007). Many mental health professionals recognize spirituality as a cultural and coping factor that has the potential to affect counseling relationships, processes, and outcomes. They also recognize the need for training to address religious and spiritual issues in counseling (Burke, Chauvin, & Miranti, 2005).

Within the counseling field, there is a long tradition of including spirituality as an important dimension of human life. For example, such luminaries as Victor Frankl, Abraham Maslow, and Rollo May emphasized the importance of spirituality in living. In addition, Adler believed that besides the three main tasks of life—society, work, and sexuality—there are two other challenges of life: spirituality and coping with self (Dreikurs & Mosak, 1966). Furthermore, Jung believed spirituality is a vital part of life, with those over the age of 40 uniquely qualified to explore its many dimensions. Lest that comment be misinterpreted, we do not espouse waiting until one is age 40 or older to explore spiritual issues; however, Jung recognized the developmental process of spiritual growth.

Though some theorists integrated spirituality and counseling, others argued to keep the topics separate. Historically, the topics of spirituality and religion were not embraced by the fields of counseling and psychology (Burke et al., 1999; Cadwallader, 1991; Myers & Williard, 2003). Several reasons help explain the separation between spirituality and counseling. For example, mental health professionals have been "taught to adopt a stance of neutrality and remain objective and unbiased" (Burke et al., 2005). Some professionals have expressed concern that counselors who incorporate spirituality into their clinical work may violate ethical guidelines by imposing their values on clients (Richards & Bergin, 1997). Furthermore, certain well-known theorists, including Sigmund Freud and Albert Ellis, equated religiosity with mental illness (Myers & Williard, 2003). Consequently, it has been difficult for some clients to bring their spiritual concerns to counseling and difficult for counselors to ask clients about their beliefs (Cadwallader, 1991). However, being open with clients about spirituality gives them the opportunity to bring spiritual issues into the therapeutic alliance if they choose to do so.

TERMINOLOGY.   What, exactly, is *spirituality*, and how is it similar to and different from *religion*? Defining the two terms is not an easy task. Although multiple definitions of spirituality and religion have been proposed, any definition must be accompanied by qualifications. The Association for Spiritual, Ethical, and Religious Values in Counseling (ASERVIC), which focuses of spiritual, ethical, and religious values, conducted a "Summit on Spirituality" in 1995. During the Summit, a description of spirituality was generated, and a list of competencies for integrating spirituality into counseling was devised (Young, Wiggins-Frame, & Cashwell, 2007). The description of spirituality that was constructed during the Summit follows.

> [Spirituality is a] capacity and tendency that is innate and unique to all persons. The spiritual tendency moves the individual toward knowledge, love, meaning, peace, hope, transcendence, connectedness, compassion, wellness, and wholeness. Spirituality includes one's capacity for creativity, growth, and the development of a value system.
>
> ("Summit Results," 1995, p. 30)

Religion has also been defined in multiple ways. It can be referred to as the social or organized means by which a person expresses spirituality (Burke et al., 2005; Young et al., 2007). The two terms are interrelated but are not identical. It is possible for someone to be spiritual without being religious. It also is possible to abide by religious traditions without being spiritual. In this section, we focus primarily on spirituality, recognizing that for many people, the two terms go hand in hand.

BENEFITS ASSOCIATED WITH SPIRITUALITY.   "A growing body of research has established a relationship between diverse spiritual principles and multiple aspects of health" (Simpson, 2009, p. 299). Studies have demonstrated links between spirituality and physical health, including coping with illness, facilitating recovery, and immune function (Matthews, McCullough et al., 1998; Meisenhelder & Chandler, 2002; Woods, Antoni, Ironson, & Kling, 1999). Research also supports links between spirituality and mental well-being. Examples include higher self-esteem, decreased alcohol use, and less depression (cited in Simpson, 2009). Certainly, the 12-step programs for addictions, which were initiated in 1935 through Alcoholic Anonymous, incorporate spirituality into the recovery process. Many wellness models include spiritual wellness as an important component, with some models conceptualizing spirituality as the core characteristic of a healthy person (Simpson, 2009).

Although positive links between spirituality and well-being have been documented, there also are concerns associated with certain religious beliefs. Cadwallader (1991) describes religion as existing on a continuum between life-affirming and life-constricting. In her view, religion can either benefit or damage mental health, depending on the way it functions in a person's life (cited in Harper, 2007). Healthy religion can lead to self-actualization and positive self-esteem, whereas unhealthy religion can lead to self-castigation and despair (Cadwallader, 1991). Because religion may have either positive or negative effects on mental health, depending on the context, it is the counselor's obligation to be willing to discuss the topic and provide support for the client whose religion has a negative impact on psychological well-being (Cadwallader, 1991; Yakushko, 2005).

SPIRITUALITY AND THE COUNSELING PROCESS.   During the 1995 Summit on Spirituality and throughout subsequent discussions with counselors, counselor educators, and supervisors, ASERVIC generated a list of nine competencies for integrating spirituality into counseling (Young et al., 2007). These competencies can be accessed through the ASERVIC Web site (www.aservic.org/Competencies.html) and read as follows:

1. The professional counselor can explain the difference between religion and spirituality, including similarities and differences.
2. The professional counselor can describe religious and spiritual beliefs and practices in a cultural context.
3. The professional counselor engages in self-exploration of religious and spiritual beliefs in order to increase sensitivity, understanding, and acceptance of diverse belief systems.
4. The professional counselor can describe her/his religious and/or spiritual belief system and explain various models of religious or spiritual development across the life span.
5. The professional counselor can demonstrate sensitivity and acceptance of a variety of religious and/or spiritual expressions in client communication.
6. The professional counselor can identify limits of her/his understanding of a client's religious or spiritual expression, and demonstrate appropriate referral skills and generate possible referral sources.

7. The professional counselor can assess the relevance of the religious and/or spiritual domains in the client's therapeutic issues.

8. The professional counselor is sensitive to and receptive to religious and/or spiritual themes in the counseling process as befits the expressed preference of each client.

9. The professional counselor uses a client's religious and/or spiritual beliefs in the pursuit of the client's therapeutic goals as befits the client's expressed preference.

To what degree do counselors endorse the competencies for integrating spirituality into counseling? During a recent survey, a random sample of 505 American Counseling Association members responded to a questionnaire that evaluated their ratings of the importance of the competencies. Results indicated that ACA members strongly support the importance of the competencies for effective counseling practice, with an overall mean rating of 4.2 on a 5-point Likert scale. Sixty-eight percent of the participants strongly agreed that formal training in the area of spirituality was important. On another note, however, 43.5% either strongly disagreed, disagreed, or were neutral in regard to their current ability to integrate those competencies into their practice (Young et. al, 2007). The researchers recommend extending counselor training competencies beyond self-awareness, providing counselors-in-training with more direction about how to address spiritual issues within the counseling relationship.

Generally speaking, it is best to encourage the client to take the lead in addressing spiritual issues. Some general assessment questions that can open the door to discussing spiritual issues, if the client chooses to go in that direction, include the following:

- Do you have any spiritual or religious beliefs? Help me understand them.
- How do these beliefs affect your relationships?
- Are there religious practices that you follow? What do you like about them, and how are they helpful?
- When you think about the presenting issues for counseling, what personal values or spiritual convictions seem to apply?
- Considering the issue you are facing, what do you imagine (Buddha, Jesus, Muhammad, Moses, Lao Tzu, etc.) might have said about it?
- Are you aware of any ways in which your beliefs may be contributing to the problem?

(Cashwell & Young, 2005; Nations, 2006)

Ingersoll (1994) stated that counselors interested in working effectively with clients committed to a particular spiritual view can best do so by affirming the importance of spirituality in the client's life, using language and imagery in problem solving and treatment that is congruent with the client's worldview, and consulting with other "healers," such as ministers and other spiritual leaders. This process calls for cultural sensitivity as well as for ethical practices of the highest standards. When spirituality is evidenced in the form of particular religious beliefs, such as Buddhism, Confucianism, or Christianity, counselors need to be respectful and work with clients to maximize the positive nature of their beliefs and values in connection with the difficulties they are experiencing.

For mental health professionals to work effectively with clients, they need to be aware of their own spiritual beliefs. In a nationally representative sample of ACA-affiliated counselors, the majority of respondents valued spirituality in their lives (Kelly, 1995). However, not all counselors consider spirituality a priority. Therefore, counselors should first assess their own spiritual beliefs before assessing the beliefs of their clients. Then their job is to assist clients in dealing with psychosocial tasks, such as maintaining a meaningful quality of life, coping with loss of function, and confronting existential or spiritual issues as they arise.

MINDFULNESS.   Mindfulness is a unique approach that has rapidly attracted attention among health care professionals (Rajeski, 2008). The practice of mindfulness to enhance well-being has been part of the Buddhist tradition for over 2500 years (Wallace & Shapiro, 2006) and can be considered within the context of spirituality. A simplified definition of mindfulness is paying attention to the here and now, in a purposeful, nonjudgmental manner (Kabat-Zinn, 1994). Mindfulness has been demonstrated to reduce stress, treat depression, control chronic pain, and treat substance abuse (Kabat-Zinn, 1990; Schure, Christopher, & Christopher, 2008). A person can practice mindfulness without using formal meditation, although many individuals find regular meditation practice helpful. Although it would be beyond the scope of this chapter to describe the practice of mindfulness in depth, interested readers are encouraged to read the many books and articles that focus on the practice of mindfulness as a way to promote mental balance, well-being, and inner peace.

BOX 5–5
The Power of Mindfulness

I first was exposed to the power of mindfulness in my own life. As a yoga practitioner and instructor, I saw how being present for the moment and allowing that moment to be exactly as it was could transform the most ugly, dark place into something that would fill me with wonderment and even awe. In graduate school, when stressed about a sticky conversation or fretting about the upcoming dissertation, I reminded myself to pay attention to the feeling of my feet on the ground, to walk with awareness, to be connected to the now. Slowly, the fears and worries would lose their power. They were still there—just with less of a grip on my mind.

As a counselor, I use mindfulness techniques with my clients both informally and formally through Dialectical Behavior Therapy and mindfulness-based stress reduction groups. Informally, I try to infuse my all sessions with mindful awareness. I am always surprised how much more intuitive and empathic I feel when I am intentionally present in a mindful way.

Formally, I have found that clients respond quite favorable to being taught mindfulness tools. One client experience always stands out for me—Sarah. When I first met Sarah, she was classically depressed. She hung her head, didn't make eye contact, and saw the world through very, very dark lenses. During an early session, we discussed the possibility of finding little moments to enjoy in her day. She didn't think it was possible, but was so desperate for relief that she was willing to try. I was incredibly surprised when she returned the next week to report that after a fight with her partner when she was feeling completely overwhelmed and afraid, she took the moment to practice mindfulness. She sat on the picnic table outside her kitchen and paid attention the feeling of the sun on her face. As she described the moment to me, she made eye contact and, for the first time in our relationship, smiled.

Paige B. Greason, Ph.D., LPC, Counselor and Counselor Educator

---

The increased attention given to spirituality in counseling complements the growing emphasis our profession is placing on enhancing individual wellness. We discuss specific models of wellness in Chapter 8. However, prior to that discussion, we want to direct your attention to some general concepts related to the wellness movement.

Wellness

The emphasis on promoting wellness within the mental health field has expanded during recent years. The American Counseling Association emphasized the promotion of wellness as "the foundation to the counseling profession" (Tanigoshi, Kontos, & Remley, 2008, p. 72). Wellness involves many aspects of life, including the physical, intellectual, social, psychological, emotional, spiritual, and environmental. Myers, Sweeney, and Witmer (2000) defined wellness as:

> a way of life oriented toward optimal health and well-being in which body, mind, and spirit are integrated by the individual to live life more fully within the human and natural community. Ideally, it is the optimum state of health and well-being that each individual is capable of achieving. (p. 252)

In an interview printed in *Counseling Today* (Rollins, 2008), Thomas Sweeney elaborated on the significance of a wellness approach to counseling. He stated, "We need to look at how to enrich instead of fixing that which is broken. Being healthy is to be normal, but being 'well' is to optimize that" (p. 33). In other words, the emphasis in counseling is not just on wellness but on *positive wellness*.

A holistic approach to counseling, which addresses the biological, psychological, social, and spiritual components described earlier, focuses on wellness. Wellness-based counseling has been described as *salutogenic* (i.e., health enhancing). A wellness perspective involves assessing all dimensions that affect health and well-being and recognizing the balance of those dimensions. Perhaps in response to the interest in wellness expressed by the general public, an increasing number of mental health practitioners and physicians are adopting holistic practices in their work with clients and patients (Savolaine & Granello, 2002).

Models of counseling-based wellness were introduced over 15 years ago and have evolved from theoretical models to empirically based models that provide an evidence base for practice (Myers & Sweeney, 2008). In Chapter 8, we discuss wellness in conjunction with prevention, which is an essential service of the counseling profession. In that chapter, we present the Indivisible Self Model (Myers & Sweeney, 2005) and explain its components. We also describe how the Indivisible Self Model developed from its predecessor, the Wheel of Wellness (Myers, Sweeney, & Witmer, 2000). Another well-known wellness model is Bill Hettler's (1984) six-dimensional hexagon, which includes spiritual, emotional/social, physical, occupation/leisure, environmental, and intellectual components. Hettler's model emphasizes the importance of striving for a high level of wellness among each of the six dimensions as well as balancing them effectively to optimize wellness (National Wellness Institute, n.d.).

A large body of research supports the importance of exercise to overall wellness (Okonski, 2003). Exercise has both physical and psychological benefits. In an extensive review of the literature on the effectiveness of physical fitness on measures of personality, Doan and Scherman (1987) found strong support for the relationship between regular exercise on both physical and psychological health. Chung and Baird's (1999) review of the literature found that exercise can positively affect mood state, anxiety level, and self-esteem. These reviews and others support counselors who prescribe exercise and other positive health habits as treatment interventions. Okonski (2003) suggested several ways counselors can implement exercise in mental health counseling, including helping clients set reasonable, attainable goals; helping clients find types of exercise that are enjoyable; encouraging clients from trying too much too soon; and educating clients on the physiological and psychological effects of exercise.

Overall, a cornerstone of the wellness approach is an emphasis on prevention and education in addition to treatment interventions. Wellness emphasizes the positive nature and health of human beings (Myers, 1992). Counselors help clients focus on strengths and assets and also find ways to help them make changes in dimensions of wellness that need strengthening. Ideally, mental health professionals who implement a holistic approach to practice use evidence-supported theory to achieve counseling goals (Harris et al., 2007).

Summary and Conclusion

As the field of counseling continues to evolve, it is essential to respond to the diverse and dynamic needs of clients, organizations, and society in general. In this chapter, we have examined three distinct forces that influence the counseling profession and the delivery of counseling services.

Managed care is a term used to describe the systems of organizations that arrange for the delivery of health services. The expansion of managed care has changed the way mental health care services are provided and financed. Practitioners who work in managed care environments are likely to employ brief, highly focused interventions that follow treatment guidelines. Both advantages and disadvantages are associated with the proliferation of managed care organizations. Among the advantages that have been cited are increased access to mental health services, higher rates of referrals, controlled costs, and the implementation of quality control and standards of practice. However, many mental health practitioners indicate that managed care has negatively affected their work with clients and created significant ethical challenges. Clinical mental health counselors who work in managed care environments need to be aware of potential ethical concerns and engage in thoughtful, informed decision-making practices as they confront those concerns.

Technological innovations have precipitated rapid changes in American society—changes that will continue to influence education and lifestyles in ways that cannot yet be envisioned. The increased availability and use of computers and the Internet have brought additional opportunities and challenges to the counseling profession. In particular, online computer applications, including counseling and guidance, have created new possibilities for mental health services. As with managed care, advances in technology have been accompanied by ethical challenges that warrant careful consideration. Clinical mental health counselors will want to stay informed about technological developments and make well-informed decisions about integrating technology into their counseling practices.

Holistic approaches, which focus on caring for the whole person in all dimensions, have taken on increased importance in counseling over the years. Clinical mental health counselors are expected to be skilled in biopsychosocial case conceptualization and treatment planning (CACREP, 2009). In addition, spirituality has gained more prominence in the counseling profession and can be incorporated into counseling practice. Although not all clients will want to explore spirituality or religion, many will want to include them in the counseling process. Finally, the wellness paradigm represents a state of positive well-being and continues to influence the practice of mental health professionals.

The counseling profession will continue to evolve and be challenged to adapt to societal and technological changes (Patrick, 2007a). Counseling professionals will face issues that, at this point, we cannot yet envision. Consequently, it is imperative that clinical mental health counselors, as well as other mental health professionals, engage in lifelong learning and training to address the challenges and opportunities that affect our professional practice.

PART **2**

Roles and Functions of Clinical Mental Health Counselors

CHAPTER **6**

The Counseling Process

Your words splash heavily upon my mind
  like early cold October rain
    falling on my roof at dusk.
The patterns change like an Autumn storm
  from violent, rumbling, crashing sounds
    to clear, steady streams of expression.
Through it all I look at you
  soaked in past fears and turmoil;
Then patiently I watch with you in the darkness
  for the breaking of black clouds
    that linger in your turbulent mind
And the dawning of your smile
  that comes in the light of new beginnings.

Gladding, S. T. (1975). Autumn storm. *Personnel and Guidance Journal, 54,* 149. © 1975 by ACA. Reprinted with permission. No further reproduction authorized without written permission of ACA.

———————————

Community and mental health counselors promote client well-being on multiple levels by providing prevention services and treatment for a wide range of clients in diverse settings. They are trained to assess and diagnose, provide crisis intervention, and work with individuals, groups, couples, and families. In this section, we provide an overview of the roles and functions of community and mental health counselors. Much of the information is general, and you will need to adapt it to meet the needs of clients in the particular environments in which you work. Also, we encourage you to read materials and attend workshops that focus on specific services provided by counselors, including those that are overviewed in this section of the text.

In Chapter 6, we focus on a general description of the counseling process. We begin with a brief description of physical factors that affect the counseling environment and thus the counseling process. Next, we turn our attention to the initial, working, and termination stages of counseling. We highlight counselor and client behaviors associated with each stage, including establishing rapport, developing treatment plans, and ending the counseling relationship.

A key component of working effectively with clients is maintaining careful records of counseling activities. Throughout the chapter, specific documentation procedures associated with the different stages of counseling are addressed, including professional disclosure statements, intake interviews, treatment plans, and case notes.

As you read this chapter, keep in mind that assessment and diagnosis, two primary skills used by community and mental health counselors, often begin at the onset of the counseling process. We address these two skills in depth in Chapter 7.

BOX 6–1

What Do You Think?

Some people are attuned to their physical surroundings and are affected by the environments in which they are living or working. Other people are relatively oblivious to physical surroundings. Whereas the degree of sensitivity people have toward their surroundings is neither a positive or negative trait—it is just a predisposition—it behooves counselors to be aware that some of their clients will be affected by the physical setting in which counseling occurs. Which type of person are you? Are you affected by the sights, smells, and sounds that surround you, or do you tend to be less aware of your immediate physical environment? As a clinical mental health counselor, what factors related to the physical setting in which you practice are within your control?

THE PHYSICAL SETTING OF COUNSELING

The physical settings in which community counselors work vary in size, comfort, and appearance. How much control counselors have over their working environments varies as well, depending on the agency or organization. Counseling can occur almost anywhere, but some physical settings help promote the process better than others. Environmental factors can influence individuals physically, psychologically, and emotionally. Thus, it is important to consider physical elements that enhance or detract from the counseling process.

Pressly and Heesacker (2001) reviewed counseling-relevant literature on various physical conditions that affect counseling, including accessories, color, room design, and other factors. Although there are no universal qualities that compose the "ideal" counseling setting, certain features appear to be more conducive to the counseling process than others. Therefore, it is helpful to be aware of different environmental elements that can affect the counseling process.

Aesthetic Qualities and Room Design

People are influenced by room appearance in different ways. Although a few people may be oblivious to their surroundings, it is likely that both counselors and clients will be affected by room décor at some level. Artwork, photographs, and objects that counselors consider meaningful or attractive can help make the counseling environment more appealing. In regard to wall hangings, research has shown that people prefer texturally complex images of natural settings to posters of people, urban life, or abstract works (Pressly & Heesacker, 2001). Plants, which represent growth, can enhance the office's appeal. Preference for office colors varies, depending on the age and sex of clients. Children and young adults tend to associate light colors with positive emotions and dark colors with negative emotions. Neutral colors may be soothing as well as practical and may be preferred when space is shared with other counselors.

Lighting research indicates that brightly lit rooms may enhance general conversation, whereas softer light is more conducive to intimate conversation. Lighting that highlights furniture, artwork, and plants can be especially effective. In addition to lighting, room temperature influences the mental concentration of counselors and clients. In places where community counselors can control the thermostat, keeping the temperature within a comfortable range, while being sensitive to client differences, is preferable (Pressly & Heesacker, 2001).

The room design itself also affects the counseling process. Whenever possible, the counseling room should be private and free from distracting sounds or smells. Research on furniture placement indicates that most clients prefer an intermediate distance between themselves and the counselor. What is considered optimal, however, is influenced by a number of factors, including cultural background, gender, and the nature of the relationship. Pressly and Heesacker (2001) cited studies that suggest clients may feel a greater degree of autonomy and comfort in offices where they have some control over the furniture arrangement. For example, couches and movable chairs allow clients to place themselves in positions that are comfortable. Also, it is important for counseling offices to be physically accessible to individuals with disabilities.

The arrangement of the furniture depends on what the counselor is trying to accomplish. Some counselors prefer to sit behind a desk during sessions, but most do not. A desk can be a physical and symbolic barrier to the development of a close relationship. Benjamin (1987) recommended that counselors include two chairs and a nearby table in the setting. The chairs should be set at a 90-degree angle from each other so that clients can look either at their counselors or straight ahead. The table can be used for many purposes, such as a place for a box of tissues. Benjamin's ideas are strictly his own; each counselor must find a physical arrangement that is comfortable for him or her.

Regardless of the arrangement within the room, counselors should not be interrupted during counseling sessions. Phone calls should be held, cell phones turned off, and in some cases, a Do Not Disturb sign should be hung on the door. Auditory and visual privacy are mandated by professional codes of ethics and facilitate maximum self-disclosure.

THE COUNSELING PROCESS

Initial Sessions: Building a Counseling Relationship

Counseling by its very nature is a process that occurs over time. Although counseling is not a linear process, it can be helpful conceptually to divide the process into three stages: initial, working, and termination. Various tasks and responsibilities are associated with each stage, including securing informed consent, conducting intake interviews, and record keeping. Also, different client factors, including motivation for change and responsiveness to treatment, need to be considered. Throughout the counseling process, practitioners continually work to establish and maintain a positive counseling alliance with their clients.

During the first few sessions of the counseling process, counselors focus on building a therapeutic relationship and helping clients explore issues that directly affect them. In initial sessions, counselors spend time assessing the seriousness of the concern presented, providing structure to the counseling process, and helping clients take initiative in the change process.

The Case of Anne

Anne, a 35-year-old accountant, has recently been feeling unfulfilled at work and in her marriage of 10 years. The activities she used to enjoy, such as listening to music and going on walks, are no longer appealing to her. She finds herself withdrawing from social interactions, experiencing sleeping difficulties, and feeling constantly agitated during the day. One of her friends has recommended that she seek counseling. Anne is skeptical but is willing to do what it takes to start feeling like herself again. She has never been to counseling before and is a little nervous about the first appointment. She does not know what to expect from the process and is concerned that the counselor will think she is unstable.

If you were Anne's counselor, what are some things you would take into consideration during the initial counseling sessions? What steps might you take to help alleviate her anxiety about the counseling process? What will you need to do in regard to issues of confidentiality?

Seriousness of the Presenting Problem

The counseling process and the direction it will take are influenced by the seriousness of the client's presenting problem. The seriousness of the presenting concern is assessed throughout the counseling process; however, often the degree to which a client is struggling can be determined during initial sessions. In particular, the *intake interview*, which is discussed in depth later in this chapter, can help counselors determine the nature, severity, and duration of the presenting issue.

Evidence indicates that there is a relationship between initial self-reported disturbance level and treatment course. "Clients who report higher initial levels of distress take more sessions to reach clinically significant improvement than clients reporting lower levels of distress" (Leibert, 2006, p. 109). In addition, research shows that the largest gains in improvement occur early in treatment. Clients dealing with more serious levels of disturbance benefit from longer term treatment. Furthermore, some conditions (e.g., schizophrenia, antisocial personality disorder, some other personality disorders) are more resistant to treatment and are unlikely to improve through traditional talk therapies (Leibert, 2006).

Structure

Clients and counselors sometimes have different perceptions about the purpose and nature of counseling. Clients often do not know what to expect from the process or what is expected of them. By providing structure to the process, counselors can help clarify expectations and prevent misunderstandings. Structure in counseling, which also is called *role induction,* refers to counselor–client understanding about the conditions, procedures, and nature of counseling. It helps protect rights, define roles, provide direction, and verify obligations of both parties.

Structure is provided throughout all the stages of counseling, but it is especially important at the beginning. Clients often seek counseling when they are in a state of crisis or flux, which can leave them feeling out of control. To help clients regain stability and find new directions in their lives, counselors provide constructive guidelines. Counselors' decisions about how to establish structure are based on their theoretical orientation to counseling, their areas of expertise, and the personalities of their clients. Finding a balance between too much and too little structure can be challenging. It helps for counselors to be flexible and to negotiate the nature of the structure with their clients on an ongoing basis.

Establishing practical guidelines is essential to the structure-building process. Guidelines include *time limits* (such as a 50-minute session), *action limits* (for the prevention of destructive behavior), *role limits* (what will be expected of each participant), and *procedural limits* (in which the client is given the responsibility to work on specific goals or needs; Brammer, 1993; Goodyear & Bradley, 1980; Kelly & Stone, 1982). Guidelines also provide information on fee schedules and other important concerns of clients. In general, structure promotes counseling development by providing a framework in which the process can take place.

At the outset, counselors will want to provide clients with an opportunity to give informed consent to participate in counseling. Informed consent has ethical and legal implications that are discussed in depth in Chapter 3. Glosoff (2001), citing several sources, suggested using an informed consent content checklist to guide the counseling process, which includes the following topics:

- **Counselor's Background and Professional Affiliations.** Include education, areas of specialization, licensure and certification, professional affiliations, and contact information for appropriate regulatory or certification boards and professional organizations.
- **Therapeutic Process Issues.** Describe the nature of the counseling process and counseling relationships, boundaries of the professional relationship, your theoretical orientation and how that affects the counseling process, and clients' rights to participate in ongoing counseling plans.
- **Risks, Benefits, and Alternatives.** Make sure clients understand that results cannot be guaranteed. Discuss the limitations, potential risks, and benefits of counseling. Explain the client's right to refuse recommended services and to be advised of potential consequences of that refusal.
- **Fees.** Describe fees associated with services, cancellation and "no-show" policies, arrangements with any managed care organizations, and issues related to insurance reimbursement.
- **Confidentiality and Privileged Communication.** Describe confidentiality and its limits, information that may need to be shared with insurance companies, plans for dealing with any exceptions to confidentiality that may arise, and clients' rights to obtain information about their records. Also include information about any supervisory or peer consultation arrangements.
- **Structure of the Counseling Relationship.** Describe the frequency and length of sessions, approximate duration of counseling, any known limitations to the length of treatment, and procedures for termination.
- **Diagnostic Labels.** How will diagnostic labels be used? How do insurance companies use diagnostic labels to determine reimbursement? What are the potential ramifications of diagnostic labels (e.g., preexisting conditions)? What are your limitations to control what insurance companies do with the information you provide them?
- **Emergency Situations and Interruptions in Counseling.** What are the normal hours of operation? What constitutes an "emergency," and what should clients do if you cannot be reached? Explain what happens when you are on vacation and the

possibility of unexpected interruptions in counseling services, as well as ways to handle those interruptions.

• **Involuntary Clients.**   What information will be shared, with whom, and for what purposes? How will participation in counseling affect legal issues (e.g., parole)? Involuntary clients have the right to refuse treatment but need to be informed of the legal consequences if that action is taken.

To help ensure the provision of informed consent, clinical mental health counselors will want to prepare a *professional disclosure statement,* which provides information to clients about the counselor and about the counseling process. Such statements, like the one in Figure 6–1, often define a counselor's qualifications and theoretical orientation as well as the purposes, expectations, responsibilities, methods, and ethics of counseling. Professional disclosure statements differ, depending on the counseling setting and the clientele (e.g., adult or child, agency or private practice, involuntary or voluntary clients). As counselors develop new competencies, they will want to modify their disclosure statements to reflect the new areas of expertise.

Initiative

Initiative can be thought of as the motivation to change. Most counselors and counseling theories assume that clients will be cooperative. Indeed, many clients come to counseling on a voluntary or self-referred basis. They experience tension and concern about themselves or others, but they are willing to work hard in counseling sessions. Other clients, however, are more reserved about participating in counseling. Vriend and Dyer (1973) estimated that the majority of clients who visit counselors are reluctant to some degree. When counselors meet clients who seem to lack initiative, they often do not know what to do with them, much less how to go about doing it. Therefore, some counselors are impatient, irritated, insensitive, and may ultimately give up on working with these clients. They may end up blaming themselves or their clients if counseling is not successful. Such recriminations need not occur if counselors understand the dynamics involved in working with reluctant or resistant clients. Part of this understanding involves assuming the role of an involuntary client and imagining how it would feel to come for counseling. A role-reversal exercise in which counselors act out this process can increase counselor empathy.

The Case of Luke

Luke, who is 57 years old, has been feeling irritable and tired for about 6 weeks. His wife, Carmen, suggested that he go see a counselor. Luke is skeptical about counseling and blames his irritability on his job. However, he is willing to go to counseling to appease Carmen, who continues to suggest that he get help.

During the first two counseling sessions, Luke spends most of the time talking about his dislike for his job. He also says that he is frustrated by his wife's insistence on pursuing counseling. He does not see any reason to try to examine his personal issues. He says that if he can just hold onto the job for a few more years, he will be able to retire and then everything will be "fine." He does not want to talk about his feelings or about options for change.

As Luke's counselor, what could you do to help with the counseling process? Read the next section about reluctant and resistant clients and see if you have any additional ideas about how to proceed.

A COUNSELOR–CLIENT CONTRACT

By Joseph Wittmer, Ph.D., NCC, and Theodore P. Remley, J.D., Ph.D., NCC

The following statement was written by Joe Wittmer, Ph.D., NCC, and Theodore P. Remley, J.D., Ph.D., NCC.

Our profession is becoming more attuned to client rights as well as to counselor accountability. The client–counselor contract given here addresses both of these important issues. Please feel free to change and use the contract as you deem appropriate. However, be aware of the laws in your state, the uniqueness of your own setting, and your own competencies in your use of the contract. NBCC considers this document particularly helpful to those formulating state-mandated disclosure statements used in most licensure states.

INFORMATION AND CONSENT

Qualification/Experience:

I am pleased you have selected me as your counselor. This document is designed to inform you about my background and to ensure that you understand our professional relationship.

I am licensed by (your state) as a Professional Counselor. In addition, I am certified by the National Board for Certified Counselors, a private national counselor certifying agency. My counseling practice is limited to (types of clients, i.e., adolescents, personal, career, marriage, etc.).

Nature of Counseling:

I hold a (your postgraduate degree or degrees relevant to counseling) from (name of institution[s]) and have been a professional counselor since (year of your master's degree in counseling or related field.)

I accept only clients who I believe have the capacity to resolve their own problems with my assistance. I believe that as people become more accepting of themselves, they are more capable of finding happiness and contentment in their lives. However, self-awareness and self-acceptance are goals that sometimes take a long time to achieve. Some clients need only a few counseling sessions to achieve these goals, while others may require months or even years of counseling. Should you decide to end our counseling relationship at any point, I will be supportive of that decision. If counseling is successful, you should feel that you are able to face life's challenges in the future without my support or intervention.

Although our sessions may be very intimate emotionally and psychologically, it is important for you to realize that we have a professional relationship rather than a personal one. Our contact will be limited to the paid sessions you have with me. Please do not invite me to social gatherings, offer gifts, or ask me to relate to you in any way other than in the professional context of our counseling sessions. You will be best served if our relationship remains strictly professional and if our sessions concentrate exclusively on your concerns. You will learn a great deal about me as we work together during your counseling experience. However, it is important for you to remember that you are experiencing me only in my professional role.

Referrals:

If at any time for any reason you are dissatisfied with my services, please let me know. If I am not able to resolve your concerns, you may report your complaints to the Board for

FIGURE 6–1   Professional disclosure statement

Note. From "A Counselor–Client Contract," by J. Wittmer and T. P. Remley, 1994 (Summer), NBCC *News Notes, 2*, 12–13. Reprinted with permission of NBCC.

Professional Counselors in (your state) at (phone number) or the National Board for Certified Counselors in Greensboro, NC, at 336-547-0607.

Fees, Cancellation and Insurance Reimbursement:

In return for a fee of $_____ per individual session, $_____ per couple/family session, and/or $_____ per group session, I agree to provide services for you. The fee for each session will be due and must be paid at the conclusion of each session. Cash or personal checks are acceptable for payment. In the event that you will not be able to keep an appointment, you must notify me 24 hours in advance. If I do not receive such advance notice, you will be responsible for paying for the session that you missed.

Some health insurance companies will reimburse clients for my counseling services and some will not. In addition, most will require that I diagnose your mental health condition and indicate that you have an "illness" before they will agree to reimburse you. Some conditions for which people seek counseling do not qualify for reimbursement. If a qualifying diagnosis is appropriate in your case, I will inform you of the diagnosis I plan to render before I submit it to the health insurance company. Any diagnosis made will become part of your permanent insurance records.

If you wish to seek reimbursement for my services from your health insurance company, I will be happy to complete any forms related to your reimbursement provided by you or the insurance company. Because you will be paying me each session for my services, any later reimbursement from the insurance company should be sent directly to you. Please do not assign any payments to me.

Those insurance companies that do reimburse for counselors usually require that a standard amount be paid (a "deductible") by you before reimbursement is allowed, and then usually only a percentage of my fee is reimbursable. You should contact a company representative to determine whether your insurance company will reimburse you and what schedule of reimbursement is used.

Records and Confidentiality:

All of our communication becomes part of the clinical record, which is accessible to you on request. I will keep confidential anything you say to me, with the following exceptions: a) you direct me to tell someone else, b) I determine that you are a danger to yourself or others, or c) I am ordered by a court to disclose information.

By your signature below (please sign both copies, keep one for your files and return the other copy to me), you are indicating that you have read and understood this statement, and/or that any questions you have had about this statement have been answered to your satisfaction.

(Counselor's Name and Signature)

Date:

(Client's Name and Signature)

Date:

FIGURE 6–1 (*Continued*)

RELUCTANT AND RESISTANT CLIENTS.   A *reluctant client* is one who has been referred by a third party and is frequently "unmotivated to seek help" (Ritchie, 1986, p. 516). Many children, adolescents, and court-referred clients are good examples. They do not wish to be in counseling, let alone talk about themselves. Many reluctant clients terminate counseling prematurely and report dissatisfaction with the process.

A *resistant client* is a person in counseling who is unwilling or opposed to change. Such an individual may actively seek counseling but does not wish to go through the emotional pain, change in perspective, or enhanced awareness that counseling demands (Cowan & Presbury, 2000). Instead, the client clings to the certainty of present behavior, even when those behaviors are dysfunctional or counterproductive. Some resistant clients refuse to make decisions, are superficial in dealing with problems, and may agree to try something different but not carry out the plan. According to Sack (1988), "the most common form of resistance is the simple statement 'I don't know'" (p. 180). Such a response makes the counselor's next move difficult and protects the client from having to take any action.

Resistance can take many forms and may be active or passive. Otani (1989, p. 459) proposed four broad categories of resistance: "(1) amount of verbalization; (2) content of message; (3) style of communication; and (4) attitude toward counselors and counseling sessions." The 22 forms of resistance included in these categories are represented in Figure 6–2.

Resistance can also be considered within the context of clients' motivation for change. The *transtheoretical model of change,* developed by Prochaska and associates (e.g., Prochaska & Norcross, 2003; Prochaska, DiClemente, & Norcross, 1992), provides a way to conceptualize different levels of readiness for change: *precontemplation, contemplation, preparation, action,* and *maintenance.* A description of each level is provided in Figure 6–3. Assessing a client's readiness for change according to these levels informs decisions regarding treatment and interventions. Although the model was originally designed for clients dealing with addictions, it has relevance for a wide range of clients because it helps the counselor assess the client's motivation to change.

Whereas some clients enter counseling already in the preparation stage, others may still be in the precontemplation or contemplation stage, where they are denying either the existence or the seriousness of a problem. Reluctant clients, including people who have been court-ordered to participate in counseling, typically are in one of these two stages of readiness. For such clients, processes that increase arousal and provide support are more likely to be effective than are approaches that focus on tasks or behavioral schedules (Petrocelli, 2002). To be effective, community counselors need to be aware of a client's level of readiness and motivation for change, as well as specific tasks and interventions that are most suitable for that level.

WINNING THE BATTLE FOR INITIATIVE.   There are several ways counselors can help clients win the battle for initiative and achieve success in counseling. One way is to anticipate the anger, frustration, defensiveness, or ambivalence that some clients display (Ritchie, 1986). Indeed, such responses are to be expected with involuntary clients, as well as other clients who are fearful of the helping process. Counselors who anticipate client resistance are better prepared to deal effectively with it when it is encountered (Young, 2009).

A second way to deal with a lack of initiative is to show acceptance, patience, understanding, and a general nonjudgmental stance. Demonstrating these supportive attitudes helps build and strengthen the therapeutic relationship, which is perhaps the most powerful predictor of successful client outcome (Seligman, 2006). An empathic, nonjudgmental approach helps promote trust and open communication. When open communication exists, clients are more likely to be honest with themselves and the counselor and better able to recognize and express reasons for resistance or noncompliance (Young, 2009).

Category A: Response quantity resistance

Definition: The client limits the amount of information to be communicated to the counselor.
Forms
Silence
Minimum talk
Verbosity

Category B: Response content resistance

Definition: The client restricts the type of information to be communicated to the counselor.
Forms
Intellectual talk
Symptom preoccupation
Small talk
Emotional display
Future/past preoccupation
Rhetorical question

Category C: Response style resistance

Definition: The client manipulates the manner of communicating information to the counselor.
Forms
Discounting
Thought censoring/editing
Second-guessing
Seductiveness
Last-minute disclosure
Limit setting
Externalization
Counselor focusing/stroking
Forgetting
False promising

Category D: Logistic management resistance

Definition: The client violates basic rules of counseling.
Forms
Poor appointment keeping
Payment delay/refusal
Personal favor-asking

FIGURE 6–2 Twenty-two forms of resistance

Source: From "Client Resistance in Counseling: Its Theoretical Rationale and Taxonomic Classification," by A. Otani, 1989, *Journal of Counseling and Development, 67,* 459. © 1989 by ACA. Reprinted with permission. No further reproduction authorized without written permission of the American Counseling Association.

A third way to win the battle for initiative is through the use of persuasion (Kerr, Claiborn, & Dixon, 1982). All counselors have some influence on clients and vice versa (Dorn, 1984; Strong, 1982). How a counselor responds to the client, directly or indirectly, can make a significant difference in whether the client takes the initiative in working to produce change. *Persuasiveness,* also referred to as *social influence,* is "the process of encouraging clients to take reasonable and growth-producing risks, to make thoughtful decisions and healthy choices, to disclose and process feelings and experiences, and to move forward toward their goals"

Stage of Change	Characteristics	Possible Interventions
Precontemplation	Client is unaware that a problem exists.	Awareness exercises Support Motivational interviewing Feedback Education
Contemplation	Client is aware that a problem exists but denies that the problem is serious or requires treatment.	Exploration of values, personal goals, and desired changes Motivational interviewing Exploration of strategies for making changes Promoting ownership and responsibility
Preparation	Client has taken small steps toward change, indicating potential commitment.	Explore reasons for and against changing Strengths and weaknesses inventory Gestalt techniques
Action	Client has demonstrated commitment to change through overt behaviors. Client has made positive changes in the desired area and is attempting to change his or her lifestyle to maintain the changes.	Behavioral strategies (e.g., rehearsal, reinforcement, tasks, ordeals, and homework) Continuing support Reinforcement management Follow-up contracts Support groups Relapse prevention
Maintenance		

FIGURE 6–3   The stages of change

Note. Based on Petrocelli, 2002; Prochaska, DiClemente, & Norcross, 1992; Young, 2009.

(Seligman, 2006, p. 23). When clients view the counselor as reliable, credible, and competent, they are more likely to respond positively to counselor persuasiveness.

A fourth way counselors can assist clients in gaining the initiative is through confrontation. *Confrontation* involves pointing out discrepancies in clients' beliefs, actions, words, or nonverbal behaviors (Young, 2009). Clients then take responsibility for responding to the confrontation. There are three primary ways of responding: denial, accepting some aspect of the confrontation as true, and fully accepting the confrontation and agreeing to try to resolve the inconsistency. Doing something differently or gaining a new perspective on a problem can be a beneficial result of confrontation, especially if what the client has tried in the past has not worked.

Counselors can also use language, especially metaphors, to break through resistance or reluctance. Metaphors can help reduce threat levels by providing images, by offering fresh insights, by challenging rigidity, and by overcoming tension (James & Hazler, 1998). For example, a counselor might say, "Carrying that heavy bag of guilt must really be taking its toll on you. I wonder what it would be like to put it down?"

Although helping clients take the initiative for their personal growth and change ideally occurs during initial sessions (or the initial session), client resistance can be evidenced at any point during the counseling process. Counselors can help clients move forward by recognizing resistance when it is evidenced and helping clients assume ownership for the change process.

Initial Counseling Interviews

The counseling process begins with the initial session, which serves as the foundation for subsequent interventions. Initial sessions set the tone for the counseling process and strongly influence the likelihood of future sessions.

In the first session, both counselors and clients work to determine whether it is reasonable to build and continue a counseling relationship. Counselors should quickly assess whether they are capable of working with the client's issues through being honest, open, and appropriately confrontational (Okun & Kantrowitz, 2008). Also, clients must ask themselves if they feel comfortable with and trust the counselor before they can enter into the relationship wholeheartedly. Although the client–counselor relationship evolves over time, clients are likely to form perceptions about the quality of the relationship early, and those perceptions tend to be stable (Seligman, 2006).

Frequently in clinical settings, the initial session is used primarily to gather information about the client for the purpose of *assessment* and *diagnosis,* topics that are discussed more extensively in Chapter 7. Counselors who are employed by medical, mental health, correctional, rehabilitation, and social agencies are likely to conduct formal intake interviews to gather information and form diagnostic impressions. Usually, these agencies have intake questionnaires designated for initial session use (see Figure 6–4). Examples of topics addressed during intake interviews include the following:

- **Identifying information about the client** (age, race, birth date, marital status, occupation, contact information)
- **The presenting concern(s) and level of client distress** (intensity or severity of concern)
- **History of the presenting concern** (onset of concern, duration and frequency, surrounding events)
- **Family background** (marital status, number of children, other relatives in the home, influences of family on presenting concern)
- **Personal history** (educational, medical, vocational, other)
- **Previous counseling experiences** (duration, outcome, what was helpful or not helpful)
- **Risk assessment** (suicidal or homicidal ideation)
- **Clinical impression and/or diagnosis** (case conceptualization, current level of functioning)
- **Client's goals for counseling** (What does the client want to happen in counseling? To what degree does he or she believe the problem is changeable?)

Although intake interviews tend to be structured and focused, counselors will want to be attentive to relationship-building skills throughout the session. In some settings, the intake forms are lengthy and may prohibit building rapport, unless the counselor takes definite steps to counteract that possibility. For example, the counselor may begin the interview by stating something like:

> During the first session, it is important for me to ask several questions to get a clearer picture of what brings you here and to be able to make decisions about what might be most helpful for you. So please bear with me through the process, even though it may seem rather formal and structured. At times, I will ask you to explain things in more detail. If there are questions you would rather not answer, please let me know and we'll move on to another question.

I. **Identifying data**

   A. Client's name, address, telephone number through which client can be reached. This information is important in the event the counselor needs to contact the client between sessions. The client's address also gives some hint about the conditions under which the client lives (e.g., large apartment complex, student dormitory, private home, etc.).

   B. Age, sex, marital status, occupation (or school class and year). Again, this is information that can be important. It lets you know when the client is still legally a minor and provides a basis for understanding information that will come out in later sessions.

II. **Presenting problems, both primary and secondary**

   It is best when these are presented in exactly the way the client reported them. If the problem has behavioral components, these should be recorded as well. Questions that help reveal this type of information include

   A. How much does the problem interfere with the client's everyday functioning?

   B. How does the problem manifest itself? What are the thoughts, feelings, etc., that are associated with it? What observable behavior is associated with it?

   C. How often does the problem arise? How long has the problem existed?

   D. Can the client identify a pattern of events that surround the problem? When does it occur? With whom? What happens before and after its occurrence?

   E. What caused the client to decide to enter counseling at this time?

III. **Client's current life setting**

   How does the client spend a typical day or week? What social and religious activities, recreational activities, etc., are present? What is the nature of the client's vocational and/or educational situation?

IV. **Family history**

   A. Father's and mother's ages, occupations, descriptions of their personalities, relationships of each to the other and each to the client and other siblings.

   B. Names, ages, and order of brothers and sisters; relationship between client and siblings.

   C. Is there any history of mental disturbance in the family?

   D. Descriptions of family stability, including number of jobs held, number of family moves, etc. (This information provides insights in later sessions when issues related to client stability and/or relationships emerge.)

V. **Personal history**

   A. Medical history: any unusual or relevant illness or injury from prenatal period to present.

   B. Educational history: academic progress through grade school, high school, and post–high school. This includes extracurricular interests and relationships with peers.

   C. Military service record.

   D. Vocational history: Where has the client worked, at what types of jobs, for what duration, and what were the relationships with fellow workers?

   E. Sexual and marital history: Where did the client receive sexual information? What was the client's dating history? Any engagements and/or marriages? Other serious

FIGURE 6–4 Sample intake interview

Source: From *Counseling Strategies and Interventions* (pp. 66–68), by H. Hackney and L. S. Cormier, 1999, Boston, MA: Allyn & Bacon. © 1999 by Pearson Education. Reprinted by permission of the publisher.

emotional involvements prior to the present? Reasons that previous relationships terminated? What was the courtship like with present spouse? What were the reasons (spouse's characteristics, personal thoughts) that led to marriage? What has been the relationship with spouse since marriage? Are there any children?

F. What experience has the client had with counseling, and what were the client's reactions?

G. What are the client's personal goals in life?

VI. Description of the client during the interview

Here you might want to indicate the client's physical appearance, including dress, posture, gestures, facial expressions, voice quality, tensions; how the client seemed to relate to you in the session; client's readiness of response, motivation, warmth, distance, passivity, etc. Did there appear to be any perceptual or sensory functions that intruded upon the interaction? (Document your observations.) What was the general level of information, vocabulary, judgment, abstraction abilities displayed by the client? What was the stream of thought, regularity, and rate of talking? Were the client's remarks logical? Connected to one another?

VII. Summary and recommendations

In this section you will want to acknowledge any connections that appear to exist between the client's statement of a problem and other information collected in this session. What type of counselor do you think would best fit this client? If you are to be this client's counselor, which of your characteristics might be particularly helpful? Which might be particularly unhelpful? How realistic are the client's goals for counseling? How long do you think counseling might continue?

FIGURE 6–4   (*Continued*)

Another way to deal with lengthy intake forms is to ask the client to complete the forms before coming to the first session. In such cases, the forms can be mailed directly to the client (with his or her permission) or the client can go to the community or agency site prior to the appointment date. If counselors ask clients to complete forms in advance, they will want to read those forms prior to meeting with the client and be sure to clarify the information the client has provided.

In other community and clinical settings, the intake interview is less structured. In an unstructured interview, the counselor has a general concept of topics to cover, but the questions are geared toward the individual needs of the client. With less-formal initial interviews, it often is not necessary to follow a particular sequence in gathering the needed information; instead, the counselor follows the client's lead. An advantage to a less-structured interview is that it can be intentionally adapted to meet the client's unique needs. However, unstructured interviews have more room for error and may result in spending too much time on relatively minor issues (Whiston, 2009). To help counteract this problem, it is helpful for the counselor to prepare an informal form with major headings, such identifying information, presenting concern, history of the concern, and other topics that are typically covered in an initial interview. Having something tangible to refer to helps ensure that no major topics are inadvertently omitted.

Regardless of the type of intake interview conducted, counselors will use a combination of closed and open questions to gather information about the client. *Closed questions* can be effective in eliciting a large amount of information in a short time, but they do not encourage elaboration, which might be needed. An example of a closed question is, "How long have you been separated from your husband?" In contrast to the closed question is the *open question,* which typically begins with words such as *what, how,* or *could* and allows the client more latitude to respond. "I wonder how you feel about that," "Help me understand what you mean," and "Could you tell me more?" are examples of open questions. Both types of questions can be used effectively by counselors during intake interviews to gain information and spur the client's thinking (Young, 2009).

Another form of communication used by counselors during initial sessions is a *request for clarification,* which helps the counselor make sure that he or she understands what the client is saying. These requests require the client to repeat or elaborate on material just covered. For example, a counselor might say, "Please help me understand this relationship" or "I don't see the connection here."

When counselors are working with clients who differ from them in regard to ethnicity, gender, sexual orientation, or other areas of diversity, it is especially important to ensure that the counselor understands what the client means. An example that highlights the importance of clarifying meaning occurred when I (Newsome) was preparing to visit the site of a counseling intern. Although I wasn't conducting an intake interview in this case, the illustration still is applicable. The intern, who was Japanese, told me that he would have his cell phone on and would meet me outside the front door of the site "for safety." I was a little taken aback because I had worked at this site several years ago and never had concerns about personal safety. Later I asked the intern to help me understand what he meant by "safety." He stated that he meant that he wanted to be available in case I got lost or didn't know where to park! There was no danger implied in his interpretation of the word.

Building a Relationship During Initial Sessions

During the initial interview, it is important to take the steps needed to make clients feel comfortable, respected, supported, and heard. For this to occur, counselors need to set aside their own agendas and focus exclusively on the client, including listening to the client's story and presenting issues (Myers, 2000). This type of behavior, in which the counselor shows genuine interest in and acceptance of the client, helps establish *rapport.*

The counselor can help build rapport by intentionally using specific helping skills, such as reflecting feelings, summarizing, clarifying, and encouraging. It is critical for counselors to develop a repertoire of helping skills and an ability to use them appropriately throughout the counseling process. Ivey and Ivey (2007) stated that the two most important skills for rapport building are basic attending behavior and client-observation skills. A counselor needs to focus on what the client is thinking and feeling and how the client is behaving. Establishing and maintaining rapport is vital for the disclosure of information, the initiation of change, and the ultimate success of counseling.

Inviting clients to talk about their reasons for seeking help is one way to initiate rapport. These noncoercive invitations to talk are called *door openers,* which contrast with judgmental or evaluative responses known as *door closers* (Bolton, 1979). Appropriate door openers include inquiries and observations such as "What brings you to see me?" "What would you like to talk about?" and "You look like you are in a lot of pain. Tell me about it." These unstructured, open-ended invitations allow clients to take the initiative in the session (Cormier & Hackney, 2008). In such situations, clients are more likely to talk about priority topics.

The amount of talking that clients engage in and the insight and benefits derived from the initial interview can be enhanced when the counselor appropriately conveys empathy, encouragement, support, caring, attentiveness, acceptance, and genuineness. Of all these qualities, *empathy* is the most important.

Empathy

Empathic counselors are able to share a client's experiences through deep and subjective understanding (Vacc & Loesch, 2000). Of particular importance is being able to perceive the cultural frame of reference from which the client operates. An effective counselor perceives the cultural frame of reference that guides the client's perceptions. When this type of empathy bridges the cultural gap between the counselor and the client, it is known as *culturally sensitive empathy* (Chung & Bemak, 2002).

Carl Rogers (1987) described two factors that make empathy possible: (a) realizing that "an infinite number of feelings" do not exist and (b) having a personal security where "you can let yourself go into the world of this other person and still know that you can return to your own world. Everything you are feeling is 'as if'" (pp. 45–46). Being able to empathize with clients at this level involves a combination of innate skill, intentionality, and learned skills.

Empathy is expressed through active listening, which is the intentional use of attending abilities that enable the counselor to respond to the client's verbal and nonverbal messages and emotional experiences (Vacc & Loesch, 2000). Counselors can make responses at several levels that reflect different degrees of empathy. A scale formulated by Carkhuff (1969), Empathic Understanding in Interpersonal Process, provides a classic measure of these levels. Each of the five levels either adds to or subtracts from the meaning and feeling tone of a client's statement:

1. The verbal and behavioral expressions of the counselor either do not attend to or detract significantly from the verbal and behavioral expressions of the client.
2. Although the counselor responds to the expressed feelings of the client, he or she does so in a way that subtracts noticeable affect from the communications of the client.
3. The expressions of the counselor in response to the expressions of the client are essentially interchangeable.
4. The responses of the counselor add noticeably to the expressions of the client in a way that expresses feelings a level deeper than the client was able to express.
5. The counselor's responses add significantly to the feeling and meaning of the expressions of the client in a way that accurately expresses feeling levels deeper than what the client is able to express.

Responses at the first two levels are not considered empathic; in fact, they inhibit the creation of an empathic environment. For example, if a client expresses distress over the loss of a job, a counselor operating on either of the first two levels might reply, "Well, you might be better off in a different line of work." Such a response misses the pain that the client is feeling.

At Level 3, a counselor's response is rated as "interchangeable" with that of a client. For example, the client might say, "It's been 5 years since Jim died, and I still find myself crying when I think about him," and the counselor responds, "You still get sad when you think about Jim."

At Levels 4 and 5, a counselor either "adds noticeably" or "adds significantly" to what a client says. It is this ability to *go beyond* what clients say that distinguishes counseling from conversation or other less-therapeutic forms of behavior (Carkhuff, 1972). For example, in response to the client who describes crying about Jim, a Level 4 response might be, "You cared deeply about Jim. It sounds as though you miss him a lot." Level 5 responses typically are made during long-term therapeutic relationships (Neukrug, 2007). They express to the client a deep understanding of the feelings—or the feelings behind the feelings—that are contributing to the client's current situation. The client's reaction determines whether or not a counselor's response accurately reflects the client's implicit message.

During the initial phase of counseling, counselors are involved in developing a therapeutic relationship and assessing the client's problems and possible causes of those problems. During the initial sessions, counselors work with clients to determine what will help them heal, change, and cope more effectively with life. The work carried out during the initial sessions leads to the collaborative establishment of therapeutic goals, which are recorded in the form of a treatment plan.

Throughout the counseling process, an important part of a clinical mental health counselor's work is documenting what goes on during intake interviews and subsequent sessions. Because careful, intentional record keeping is an essential skill, information about keeping client records is presented next.

Client Records

There are a number of helpful sources community and mental health counselors can refer to for assistance in record keeping and documentation. Also, most agencies have guidelines for maintaining client records, and counselors need to familiarize themselves with those guidelines. One book that is particularly pertinent to record keeping is *Documentation in Counseling Records* (3rd ed.; Mitchell, 2007). Much of the material that follows comes from that source.

WHAT ARE CLIENT RECORDS?   The term *client records* refers to all client information that is needed for effective service delivery (R. Mitchell, 2007). Although most client records are in printed or electronic form, client records also include any video- or audiotapes of client–counselor interactions. The number and types of forms vary depending on the needs of the client, agency, and practitioner. Piazza and Baruth (1990) noted that most client records fall within one of the following six categories: (a) identifying or intake information, (b) assessment and diagnostic information, (c) the treatment plan, (d) case notes (also called *staff notes*), (e) the termination summary, and (f) other data (e.g., signed consent for treatment, copies of correspondence, consent for release of information forms). Identifying information, assessment information, and treatment plans are usually documented during initial counseling sessions; case notes provide a written record of treatment and intervention; and termination documentation is compiled at the end of the counseling process. Client records provide documentation of what transpires between a counselor and a client. They protect the interests of both parties and promote continuity of care.

REASONS FOR CAREFUL RECORD KEEPING.   For many counselors, completing paperwork can be tedious and less fulfilling than actually working with clients. However, professional documentation is a key component of the counseling process. Well-organized, accurate records "are the most effective tool counselors have for establishing client treatment plans, ensuring continuity of care in the event of absence, and proving that quality care was provided" (Wheeler & Bertram, 2008, p. 115).

Whereas many years ago, it was not uncommon for mental health professionals to refrain from keeping client records, accurate and complete records are now considered the professional standard of care (Wheeler & Bertram, 2008). R. Mitchell (2007) pointed out several reasons careful record keeping is essential:

- The American Counseling Association (ACA) *Code of Ethics* (2005) requires counselors to "maintain records necessary for rendering professional services to their clients and as required by laws, regulations, or agency or institution procedures" (Section A.1.b.)
- Careful documentation helps protect counselors if malpractice allegations are made.
- Inadequate or incomplete documentation may be harmful to the client as well as to the counselor.
- In the event that the primary counselor is unable to provide services, client records can ensure appropriate continuity of care.
- Funding sources require documentation that verifies the need for services as well as the nature of the services rendered.
- Utilization review, peer review, and quality assurance review, which often are based on client records, are essential to the work that occurs in many clinical settings.

CONFIDENTIALITY AND ACCESS TO CLIENT RECORDS.   Counselors are responsible for ensuring the safety and confidentiality of any client records they create, maintain, or destroy. This means that counselors make sure client documents are secured in locked files or saved in protected computer programs. Efforts should be made to ensure that all client charts and other client information remain in the agency. Also, when client records are disposed of because they are outdated or invalid, they should be shredded before being thrown away or recycled (Welfel, 2006).

The 2005 *ACA Code* stipulated that "counselors take precautions to ensure the confidentiality of information transmitted through the use of computers, electronic mail, facsimile machines, telephones, voicemail, answering machines, and other electronic or computer technology (Standard B.3.e.). When case notes and other client records are created and/or stored on a computer, there needs to be a security component that ensures the protection of information (R. Mitchell, 2007). In addition to basic concerns related to electronic storage and transmittal of data, counselors need to be aware of regulations related to the Health Insurance Portability and Accountability Act (HIPAA). Since the passage of HIPAA in 1996, "there has been an ongoing controversy about the storage and transmission of electronic data as well as various interpretations of pertinent law" (R. Mitchell, 2007, p. 41). We encourage you to review the HIPAA document online to increase your awareness of issues related to the confidentiality of records and transmittal of data (HIPAA Web site: www.hipaa.org).

Although ownership of the content of client records technically belongs to the mental health professional, clients have the right to access copies of their records and control their dissemination (Welfel, 2006). Therefore, counselors have an ethical and a legal obligation to provide competent clients access to their records if requested, unless the content would be detrimental to client welfare. Also, clients have the right to demand that copies of clinical records be transferred to other professionals. It is important for clinicians to keep clients' access rights in mind as client records are created.

If counselors need to transfer or disclose client records to legitimate third parties, written consent should be obtained from the client. In such cases, it is preferable to mail documents rather than to fax them, unless the situation is critical (R. Mitchell, 2007). If records must be faxed, the cover letter needs to indicate that the information is confidential, intended for use only by the designated person, and that receipt must be acknowledged. The original cover letter and the subsequent acknowledgment of receipt should be filed in the client's record.

Client records can be subpoenaed in litigation situations, sometimes despite client objection and/or claims of privilege. Subpoenas are court orders that cannot be ignored. When subpoenas are issued, counselors should consult with a lawyer before turning over records or appearing in court (Remley & Herlihy, 2010). If records must be turned over, copies of the originals should be sent and should not include documentation from other professionals. In some cases, the attorney who issued the subpoena will allow counselors to write and submit treatment summaries rather than submit copies of the actual case notes themselves. Because it is possible that you will be subpoenaed at some point during your counseling career, it is important to keep up to date on state and federal regulations regarding subpoenas. Remley and Herlihy (2010, pp. 148–152) provided specific information about responding to subpoenas that can help you know how to act if your records are subpoenaed.

SUGGESTIONS FOR RECORD KEEPING.   R. Mitchell (2007) provided several recommendations for documenting intake sessions, treatment plans, and case notes. Among those suggestions are

- Make notes grammatically clear and correct.
- Use precise language, avoiding jargon, clichés, and qualifiers.
- Enter only the information that is pertinent to the client's situation. The record should be logical, beginning with assessment and moving to a plan, case notes, case reviews, and a termination.
- Write legibly and in an organized manner.
- Eliminate unfounded opinions or assumptions.
- Logically relate the recorded intervention to the treatment plan.
- Avoid including personal feelings in client records.
- Describe the client's behavior or quote what was said during the session.
- Do not use Wite-Out. If you need to alter a document, use a pen to draw a single line through the entry. Above the line, write *error* and *corrected entry,* then add the correct information.
- Write notes within 24 to 48 hours of the session.
- Document outcomes of sessions.
- Sign each record, including your full name and credentials. In some cases, it is necessary to obtain a cosignature (e.g., supervisor or medical director).

In addition to these suggestions, Remley and Herlihy (2010) suggested writing notes with the assumption that they will become public information at some later date. However, the counselor should not be so cautious that insufficient information is recorded.

Careful record-keeping procedures will serve counselors well in any of the clinical settings in which they work. Although the process is somewhat time consuming, it benefits the counselor and the client in many ways. In particular, keeping accurate professional records facilitates the provision of quality services to clients and provides self-protection for the counselor (Remley & Herlihy, 2010). Treatment plans and case notes, which represent the most common form of documentation kept by community and mental health counselors, are discussed in the next section, which focuses on the working phase of counseling.

THE WORKING PHASE OF COUNSELING

In the initial phase of counseling, counselors concentrate on gathering information and getting their clients involved in the helping process. The initial sessions of counseling conclude with a treatment plan that serves as the basis for the next phase of counseling—the action or working phase. During this phase, specific objectives are refined and interventions for achieving those objectives are implemented. It is important to remember that the division between the *initial phase* and the *working phase* is arbitrary. For example, assessment, although associated with the initial phase of counseling, continues through all phases of counseling. Treatment plans, which usually come at the conclusion of the initial phase of counseling, also signify the beginning of the working phase of counseling and are described next.

Treatment Plans

Treatment plans help set the course for further counseling interventions. They are required by managed care organizations and many insurance companies for service approval and reimbursement. A *treatment plan* explains why the client is receiving services and what is going to take place in counseling. It lists measurable and desired outcomes of treatment and is sometimes called a *plan of care, service plan, habitation plan, residential plan,* or *case management plan,* depending on the type of services provided and the agency providing those services (R. Mitchell, 2007).

R. Mitchell (2007, pp. 22–23) recommended including the following components in a treatment plan:

- **Problem statement.** The presenting problem or concern is clearly described. *Example: depression due to marital difficulties.*
- **Goal statement and expected date of achievement.** List specific, measurable goals that relate to the presenting problem(s). Include expected dates that goals will be accomplished. *Example: Keep a journal describing thoughts, feelings, and behaviors for the next 2 weeks. Address partner with "I messages" when disputes occur rather than walking out of the room.*
- **Treatment modality.** Describe the interventions that will be used to help meet the stated goals. To be a billable service, the intervention must be provided by a professional who is considered qualified by the funding source. *Example: Meet weekly with a group of women experiencing relationship-related depression.*
- **Clinical impression or diagnosis.** Clinical impressions need to accurately reflect the client's mental health as described in the assessment. Diagnostic terms, when used, should be listed according to *DSM* (*Diagnostic and Statistical Manual of Mental Disorders*) or *ICD* (*International Classification of Diseases*) codes. A client's condition must not be overstated or understated. *Example: 309.0 Adjustment Disorder with Depressed Mood.*
- **Names and credentials.** List the names and credentials of people who participated in the development of the treatment plan. Also list the name of the assigned clinician. The person who writes the plan needs to sign and date it.

Treatment plans should represent a collaborative, ongoing effort between client and counselor. The ACA *Code of Ethics* (2005) stipulates the following:

> Counselors and their clients work jointly in devising integrated counseling plans that offer reasonable promise of success and are consistent with abilities and circumstances of clients. Counselors and clients regularly review counseling plans to assess their continued viability and effectiveness, respecting the freedom of choice of clients. Standard A.1.c., *Counseling Plans*

Interventions, Skills, and Techniques

Counseling interventions are outlined in the treatment plan and are determined by several factors, including the nature of the presenting problem, client characteristics (e.g., cultural background, age, gender, personality); counselor characteristics, theoretical orientation, and training; and the organization in which the counselor works. For example, a counselor with a strong existential orientation is likely to interact and intervene differently with clients than a counselor with a cognitive–behavioral orientation (Granello & Witmer, 1998).

Within the mental health profession, there is a push to determine what interventions tend to yield the best outcomes for specific conditions. There is a demand from consumers and professionals to provide empirical evidence of the efficacy of counseling. Pressure from managed care companies also has prompted a focus on evaluating treatment outcomes (Hill & Beamish, 2007).

Outcome research indicates that, in general, counseling is effective across settings and theoretical orientations (see Sexton, Whiston, Bleuer, & Walz, 1997, for a review). What, then, leads to successful outcomes? A summary of counseling research reveals that client outcome is determined by client variables, a set of *common curative factors,* and specific interventions applied to particular problems (Granello & Witmer, 1998). It is important for counselors to provide the most effective treatments possible by selecting interventions and techniques that have been demonstrated as effective.

Following in the tradition of the medical profession, which adopts procedures or protocols based on research for treatment of specific problems, the American Psychiatric Association, American Psychological Association, psychiatric nursing profession, and American Counseling Association have independently made strong efforts to summarize outcome research to guide mental health practices. One responsibility of clinical mental health counselors is to find ways to integrate research and practice so that the interventions they select coincide with professional standards of care (Granello & Witmer, 1998). When interventions are informed by research, successful outcomes during the working phase of counseling are more likely. For example, Hill and Beamish (2007) summarized outcome research reviewing treatment outcomes for obsessive-compulsive disorder. Delineating standards of care, based on outcome research, enhances the professional credibility of clinical mental health counselors. At the same time, however, it is important to remember that not all clients experience the same problem in the same way, and focusing too much on immediate problem resolution rather than taking a more broad-based approach to healthy emotional functioning may be counterindicated (Vacc & Loesch, 2000).

Lambert and Bergin (1994) suggested that the common curative factors of effective counseling can be organized into three categories (Table 6–1): (a) *support factors* (e.g., the

TABLE 6–1 Common Factors across Therapies Associated with Positive Outcomes		
Support Factors	**Learning Factors**	**Action Factors**
Catharsis	Advice	Behavioral regulation
Identification with therapist	Affective experiencing	Cognitive mastery
Mitigation of isolation	Assimilation of problematic experiences	Encouragement of facing fears
Positive relationship	Changing expectations for personal	Taking risks
Reassurance	effectiveness	Mastery efforts:
Release of tension	Cognitive learning	• Modeling
Structure	Corrective emotional experience	• Practice
Therapeutic alliance	Exploration of internal frame of reference	• Reality testing
Therapist/client active	Feedback	Success experience
participation	Insight	Working through
Therapist expertness	Rationale	
Therapist warmth, respect,		
empathy, acceptance,		
genuineness		
Trust		

Note. From "The Effectiveness of Psychotherapy," by M. J. Lambert and A. E. Bergin, 1994, in A. E. Bergin and S. L. Garfield (Eds.), *Handbook of Psychotherapy and Behavior Change* (4th ed., pp. 143–189). New York: Wiley. Copyright © 1994 by John Wiley & Sons. Reprinted with permission. This material is used by permission of John Wiley & Sons, Inc.

therapeutic alliance, trust, empathy, catharsis), (b) *learning factors* (e.g., cognitive learning, affective experiencing, feedback), and (c) *action factors* (e.g., reality testing, rehearsal, mastery efforts). During the working phase, counselors may find it beneficial to use various combinations of these factors to help clients make positive changes. Earlier in the chapter, we examined support factors that facilitate the development of a therapeutic client–counselor relationship. In this section, particular attention will be given to three of the learning and action factors: cognitive learning (ways of thinking), affective experiencing (ways of feeling), and rehearsal (ways of behaving).

COGNITIVE LEARNING.   Often, clients come to counseling with distorted or dysfunctional cognitions, making them more susceptible to problems related to life events (Seligman, 2006). Cognitive distortions affect the way people think, feel, and act on multiple levels. Counselors can help clients change distorted or unrealistic cognitions by offering them the opportunity to explore thoughts and beliefs within a safe, accepting, and nonjudgmental environment.

Cognitive distortions are negative, inaccurate biases that can result in unhealthy misperceptions of events. For example, a worker may assume that his or her boss considers him or her less capable than others, when in reality, the boss is pleased with the worker's performance. Cognitive theorists have identified several types of distortions, including exaggerating the negative, minimizing the positive, overgeneralizing, catastrophizing, and personalizing. Cognitive distortions also are evidenced when people engage in all-or-nothing thinking or *selective abstraction* (taking a detail out of context and using it to negate an entire experience). Such perceptions can result in negative automatic thoughts, which then negatively affect emotions and mood states. Counselors can teach clients to evaluate and challenge the validity of their cognitions (Beamish, Granello, & Belcastro, 2002). Teaching clients ways to correct faulty information processing can help them view situations from a more realistic perspective and react accordingly.

The goal of cognitive learning and restructuring is to help clients formulate new cognitions that are more realistic and adaptive (Beck, 1995). One way counselors can help clients modify cognitions is through the process of *reframing*, which offers the client another probable and positive viewpoint of what a situation is or why an event might have happened. Such a changed point of view provides the client with an opportunity to respond differently to the situation. For example, if an adolescent client insists that his mother is always worrying and nagging him, the counselor might be able to help the client reframe the situation by suggesting that it sounds like his mother is concerned about his well-being and appears to care about him very much.

AFFECTIVE EXPERIENCING.   Just as it is important to help clients examine their cognitions, or to think about their thinking patterns, it also is important to help clients recognize and explore the emotions they experience. Although numerous emotions are common to the human experience, people experience emotions uniquely. Seligman (2006, pp. 157–159) describes eight dimensions that characterize emotions:

- **Emotional, physical, or a combination.** Emotions are physically embedded. For example, worry (an emotion) can lead to nausea and/or headaches (physical symptoms).
- **Overt, covert, or a combination of both.** Overt feelings are evident to other people, whereas covert feelings are kept inside and not revealed.
- **Positive, negative, or neutral.** Joy, happiness, and amusement are positive emotions. Shame, worry, and fear are negative emotions. Curiosity is an example of a neutral emotion. Emotions that typically fall into one category may be experienced differently by certain people. For instance, John's emotion of anger may result behaviorally in intimidation, which gives him a feeling of power and control. In contrast, Courtney may turn her anger inward, believing that outward expressions of anger will result in disapproval by others.
- **In or out of awareness.** Some people are more aware of their emotional states than are others. People who are unaware of their emotions often experience problems in relationships. Feelings that are considered "unacceptable" (e.g., envy, shame) may be particularly challenging in treatment.
- **Level of intensity.** The intensity with which emotions are felt varies, depending on the person and the circumstances. Intense expression of negative emotions can lead to misunderstandings and relationship difficulties.
- **Appropriateness for context and stimulus.** Emotional expression that may be appropriate in one context may not be appropriate in another context. For example, expressing anger when an infant is crying in a restaurant may be inappropriate, whereas expressing anger toward someone who has put you down may be both healthy and appropriate.
- **Congruence.** When emotions are expressed congruently, verbal and nonverbal behaviors match. People can unknowingly sabotage their communication efforts when emotions and behaviors are incongruent.
- **Helpful or harmful.** Depending on the way and the context in which they are expressed, emotions may enhance lives and relationships or contribute to struggles intrapersonally and interpersonally.

Counselors can use a number of skills and techniques to increase clients' emotional awareness. The skill of accurately reflecting feelings is used by many counselors to help clients focus on emotions they may be avoiding (Young, 2009). Helping clients identify the feeling associated with a particular incident, reflecting the feeling back to them, and then encouraging them to determine where in their body that feeling is experienced can help clients develop emotional awareness. By asking them to think of a time in their lives when they had the same bodily sensations and emotional feelings that were just experienced, counselors can assist clients in exploring patterns of emotional responses. Also, many Gestalt techniques, when used properly, provide powerful ways for clients to connect with their emotions. However, in some cases, interventions that focus on emotions are not recommended, particularly when clients are in high levels of pretreatment distress (Sexton et al., 1997).

Simply releasing emotions, also called *catharsis,* can have some value in counseling, but it should not be the final goal. When clients experience emotional release in counseling, counselors will want to work through underlying beliefs, thoughts, and patterns of behavior (Corey, 2009). The goal of increasing affective experiencing, then, is to help clients connect their emotions with cognitions and behaviors in a way that leads to new insights and changed behavior.

REHEARSAL.   Whereas cognitive learning focuses on thoughts and affective experiencing focuses on emotions, *rehearsal* focuses on client behavior. Counselors can help clients maximize the possibility of accomplishing their goals by giving them opportunities to rehearse or practice new behaviors. Just as practicing benefits athletes and performance artists, so can it benefit clients dealing with particular issues such as assertiveness and social skill deficits. Clients can rehearse in two ways: overtly and covertly (Cormier & Cormier, 1998). *Overt rehearsal* requires clients to verbalize or act out what they are going to do. For example, if an adult daughter is working on becoming more assertive with her overbearing parent, she can rehearse what she is going to say and how she is going to act before she actually encounters the parent. *Covert rehearsal* involves mentally preparing for a specific course of action through imagination and reflection. For example, individuals who have to give a speech can first imagine the conditions under which they will perform and then reflect on how to organize the subject matter for presentation. Imagining the situation beforehand can alleviate unnecessary anxiety and help improve performance.

Sometimes a client needs counselor coaching during the rehearsal period. Coaching may involve providing temporary written or visual aids to help clients remember what to do next in a given situation. At times, it may simply involve giving clients corrective feedback. Feedback provides clients with accurate information about the behavior they are practicing. For feedback to be received, it is helpful to talk about the feedback process ahead of time and share observations in a nonthreatening, objective manner. To maximize its effectiveness, feedback can be given both orally and in writing.

Another way to help clients practice and generalize the skills learned in counseling sessions is by assigning homework. Homework provides clients with opportunities to work on particular skills outside the counseling session. Homework has numerous advantages, including:

- Keeping clients focused on relevant behavior between sessions.
- Helping them see clearly what kind of progress they are making.
- Motivating clients to change behaviors.
- Helping them evaluate and modify their activities.

- Helping clients assume more responsibility for their own behaviors.
- Celebrating a breakthrough achieved in counseling (Hay & Kinnier, 1998; Hutchins & Vaught, 1997).

Many counselors use homework at some time to get clients to help themselves. For homework to be most effective, it needs to be relevant to the situation and specifically tied to some measurable behavior change (Okun & Kantrowitz, 2008; Young, 2009). Counselors will want to follow up with clients to ensure that homework assignments are completed, determine their level of effectiveness, and modify assignments as needed.

Cognitive learning, affective experiencing, and rehearsal are just a few of the many interventions counselors use during the working phase of counseling. Throughout the process, effective counselors will continue to employ basic helping skills (e.g., clarifying, summarizing, probing, immediacy, confrontation, reflecting content and feeling) and specific theory-grounded techniques (e.g., the empty-chair technique) to help clients make progress toward their goals. As counseling progresses, it is important to work with the client to reevaluate goals and progress, making changes when necessary.

An important task that accompanies all phases of counseling, including the working phase, is documenting counselor–client interactions. After each counseling session, counselors will need to write case notes to document what occurred. Information about writing case notes is presented next.

Case Notes

Each time a counselor meets with a client, he or she is responsible for documenting the activity. This documentation is sometimes referred to as a *case note, clinical entry, staff note, progress note, group note,* or *service log.* Prior to the advent of managed care services, the primary purpose of case notes was to enable counselors to record information about the content of the counseling session and to guide professional practice. This purpose still is paramount. However, 21st-century community counselors operating in managed care environments must write case notes with the understanding that the content may be used to determine reimbursement for services. Furthermore, as stated earlier in regard to record keeping, case notes are required by the *ACA Code of Ethics* (2005), protect counselors from litigation issues, and are in keeping with professional expectations. Some of the general information included in most case notes includes:

- **Confirmation of a Service.**   What did the counselor do during the session? What did the client do? Use verbs to describe the services rendered (e.g., *focused, identified, discussed, recommended*).
- **Verification of the Information Implied Within the Billing Code.**   The content of the case note should confirm the date of service, length of session, and type of service provided.
- **An Original, Legible Signature.**   Some notes need cosignatures. To determine whether a cosignature is necessary, counselors need to read and comply with the state licensure and funding source regulations.

Many acceptable formats can be followed when writing case notes. Examples of three useful formats are presented in Figure 6–5. In many instances, the agency for which a counselor works will have a predetermined outline that is to be followed when writing case notes, and it is incumbent on the counselor to adhere to that format. Remley and Herlihy (2010) remind us that the primary purposes of keeping case notes are to provide quality services to clients and to document decisions made and actions taken as a counselor.

STIPS Format (from Prieto & Scheel, 2002)	
Signs and symptoms	Record the client's current level of functioning and clinical signs and symptoms, especially as they relate to the presenting issues. Record any changes from previous level of functioning. Note observable client behaviors (e.g., appearance, affect, speech).
Topics of discussion	Describe the major issues discussed in the session. Include any developments that have occurred since the previous session.
Interventions	Record specific interventions used during the session. Interventions should relate to the identified problem and treatment goals. Track client's completion of "homework" assignments and record any new assignments. Summarize progress clients have made toward established goals.
Progress and plans	Record plans for the next session, including specific topics of discussion, planned interventions, and anticipated outcomes. Note any changes to the overall treatment plan.
Special issues	Record any newly developed or ongoing critical issues that need to be tracked (e.g., suicidal ideation, homicidal threats, concerns about referrals, suspected abuse). Document ways these issues are being handled (e.g., consultation, supervision, reporting to outside agencies).

Goals and Action Plan Format (from Piazza & Baruth, 1990)	
Goals for the session	State goals for the session that relate to the client's treatment plan and are connected to previous sessions. (Goals should be flexible to accommodate more pressing concerns when necessary.)
Goal attainment	Describe the techniques and interventions used in the session and evaluate their effectiveness. If the interventions were ineffective, what could have been done differently?
Clinical impressions	Record clinical impressions based on client behavior and statements. Avoid recording subjective impressions that are not supported by data.
Action plan	State plans for the next session. These plans will be used to provide the goal statement for that session.

SOAP Format (from Cameron & Turtle-song, 2002)	
Subjective	Record information about the problem from the client's perspective (and from that of significant others). Include the client's feelings, thoughts, and goals. Describe the intensity of the problem and its effect on relationships.
Objective	Record factual observations made by the counselor. Observations include any physical, interpersonal, or psychological findings noted by the counselor (e.g., appearance, affect, client strengths, mental status, responses to the counseling process).
Assessment	Summarize clinical thinking about the client's issues. This section synthesizes and analyzes data from the subjective and objective observations. When appropriate, include the DSM-IV-TR diagnosis. (Section may also include clinical impressions used to make a diagnosis.)
Plan	Record plans for future interventions and a prognosis. Include the date of the next session, proposed interventions, and anticipated gains from treatment.

FIGURE 6–5   Three sample formats for case notes

Documenting Work With High-Risk Clients

Special considerations need to be taken when counselors work with clients classified as *high risk*. Examples of high-risk cases include clients who are potentially violent, suicidal, homicidal, or engaged in criminal behavior. Clients who have experienced or committed abuse also are considered high risk. Some of the legal and ethical considerations counselors are faced with when working with such clients are explored in Chapter 3. Suicide assessment and crisis intervention are described in Chapters 7 and 8. In this section, the focus is on documentation issues that need to be taken into account for the counselor's self-protection.

If a counselor determines that a client is potentially dangerous, three things must be done: (a) explain how the conclusion was reached, (b) take action, and (c) document the action (R. Mitchell, 2007). There are a number of actions a counselor might take, depending on the situation. In some cases, it is necessary to notify the potential target and/or appropriate law enforcement agencies. Other action options include consulting with a psychiatrist and taking steps toward an involuntary hospitalization. Before taking action, it is advisable to consult with coworkers, a supervisor, and a lawyer and then document those consultations. Take any threat of suicide or homicide seriously and write down the client's exact words (as closely as possible) when documenting the threats. In some cases, suicidal and homicidal contracts can be clinically useful; however, in litigation, a contract does not always protect the clinician (R. Mitchell, 2007). If a client threatens to kill or harm someone, the counselor has a *duty to warn* (see Chapter 3). If confidentiality is broken for this reason, counselors need to document that decision and its justification. Practitioners should involve clients in the documentation process when feasible because it can "enhance the service relationship [and] promote empowerment" (R. Mitchell, 2007, p. 68).

If a counselor suspects abuse, neglect, or criminal behavior, it is advisable to discuss the case with a lawyer and contact the proper authority if a report is required (R. Mitchell, 2007). When documenting concerns about abuse, be sure to record the client's words and behaviors rather than express unsubstantiated opinions. By sticking to the facts and avoiding impressionistic or defamatory statements, objectivity is maintained and the counselor is in a better position to carry out the next step. A general rule of thumb is to be precise and specific in all documentation, especially in cases of high risk. When an abused child is in

---

BOX 6–2

Recommendations for Risk Management Documentation (Wheeler & Bertram, 2008)

Document what the client did or said that implied he or she was engaging in, or considering engaging in, high-risk behavior.

- Document the severity level of any threat of high-risk behavior, based on your clinical expertise.
- Record options you considered as responses, based on your assessment.
- Explain what options you ruled out and why, thereby explaining your clinical decision making.
- Consult with colleagues, supervisors, and/or attorneys whenever possible, and document that consultation.
- Document the option you chose, including specific actions you took to implement that option.
- Document what occurs after that action is taken.

therapy, R. Mitchell (2007) recommended that clinicians work with the child's attorney and make attempts to have records sealed or reviewed only by the judge involved in the case.

TERMINATION

Why Termination Is Important

Termination is the last phase of counseling and refers to the decision made by the client, counselor, or both parties to stop counseling. It is probably the least researched and most neglected phase of counseling. Many counselors assume that termination with a client will occur naturally, with satisfying outcomes for both parties. Goodyear (1981) stated that "it is almost as though we operate from a myth that termination is a process from which the counselor remains aloof and to which the client alone is responsive" (p. 347).

But the termination of a counseling relationship has an impact on all involved, and it is often complex and difficult. Termination may well produce mixed feelings on the part of both the counselor and the client (Kottler, Sexton, & Whiston, 1994). For example, a client may be both appreciative and regretful when the time comes to end a particular counseling relationship. Unless it is handled properly, termination has the power to harm as well as heal.

Historically, addressing the process of termination directly has been avoided for several reasons. Ward (1984) suggested two of the most prominent reasons. First, termination is associated with loss, which on the surface may seem contradictive to counseling's emphasis on growth and development. Second, termination is not directly related to the microskills that facilitate counseling relationships. Therefore, counselors may not be prepared to attend fully to the ending of a counseling relationship.

However, termination serves several important functions. First, termination signals that something has been completed. Throughout life, individuals enter into and leave a succession of experiences, including jobs, relationships, and life stages. Growth and adjustment depend on an ability to make the most of these experiences and learn from them. To begin something new, a former experience must be completed and resolved (Perls, 1969). Termination provides the opportunity to end a learning experience properly, whether on a personal or professional level (Hulse-Killacky, 1993). Counselors who manage the termination process appropriately can help clients learn healthy ways to end relationships for the purpose of moving on to the next stage of life.

Second, termination gives clients the opportunity to maintain changes already achieved and generalize problem-solving skills to new areas. Successful counseling results in significant changes in the ways clients think, feel, or act. These changes are rehearsed in counseling, but they must be practiced in the real world. Termination provides an opportunity for such practice. The client can always go back to the counselor for any needed follow-up, but termination is the natural point for the practice of independence to begin. It is a potentially empowering experience for the client that enables him or her to address the present in an entirely new or modified way. At termination, the opportunity to put "insights into actions" (Gladding, 1990, p. 130) is created. In other words, what seems like an exit becomes an entrance.

Finally, termination serves as a reminder that the client has matured (Vickio, 1990). Besides offering clients new skills or different ways of thinking about themselves, effective counseling termination marks a time in clients' lives when they are less absorbed by and preoccupied with personal problems and better able to deal with outside people and events. This ability to handle external situations may result in more interdependent relationships that are mutually supportive and that consequently lead to a life that is more balanced and satisfying. Having achieved a successful resolution to a problem, a client now has new insights and abilities that are stored in memory and may be recalled and used in the future.

Timing of Termination

When to terminate a relationship is a question that has no definite answer. If the relationship is ended too soon, clients may lose the ground they gained in counseling and regress to earlier behaviors. If termination is never addressed, clients can become dependent on the counselor and fail to resolve difficulties and grow as persons. There are, however, several pragmatic considerations related to the timing of termination (Cormier & Hackney, 2008; Young, 2009):

• *Have clients achieved behavioral, cognitive, or affective goals?* When both clients and counselors have a reason to believe that particular goals have been reached, the timing of termination is easier to determine. The key to this consideration is setting up a mutually agreed-upon contract before counseling begins.

• *Can clients concretely show where they have made progress in what they wanted to accomplish?* In this situation, specific progress may be the basis for making a decision about termination.

• *Is the counseling relationship helpful?* If either client or counselor senses that what is occurring in counseling sessions is not helpful, termination is appropriate.

• *Has the context of the initial counseling arrangement changed?* In cases where there is, for example, a move or a prolonged illness, termination (as well as a referral) should be considered.

Overall, there is no one right time to terminate a counseling relationship. The "when" of termination must be determined in accordance with the uniqueness of the situation and with overall ethical and professional guidelines.

EARLY TERMINATION. Issues related to termination for counselors working in managed care environments are explored in Chapter 5. In many cases, counselors may be expected to provide time-limited services to clients. In these situations, counselors need to explain the time limits at the outset of counseling. If the client reaches the end of an HMO-imposed time limit before he or she is ready to terminate, the counselor will want to negotiate for additional sessions with the service provider, refer the client to alternative sources for help, ask the client to pay out-of-pocket, or provide pro bono services (Glosoff, 1998). The ACA *Code of Ethics* (2005) makes it clear that counselors cannot abandon their clients (Section A.11.). However, the *Code of Ethics* also stipulates that it is permissible for counselors to discontinue services in the following circumstances:

• It is clear that the client is no longer benefiting from counseling.
• The client does not pay the designated fees.
• The counselor is in jeopardy of harm by the client or another person with whom the client has a relationship.
• Agency limits do not allow services to continue.
• An appropriate referral is made, but the client declines the referral.

Standard A.11.d. states, "When counselors transfer or refer clients to other practitioners, they ensure that appropriate clinical and administrative processes are completed and open communication is maintained with both clients and practitioners" (*ACA Code of Ethics*, 2005). Although counselors cannot insist that a client accept a transfer or referral for services, they can talk with the client about options, demonstrate respect for the client's opinions, and honor the client's decision in a professional manner.

Facilitating the Termination Process

Counseling relationships vary in length and purpose. It is vital to the health and well-being of everyone involved that the subject of termination be brought up early so that the time in counseling is used as effectively as possible. Individuals need time to prepare for the end of meaningful relationships. There may be some sadness even if the relationship ends in a positive way. Thus, termination should not necessarily be presented as the zenith of the counseling experience. It is better to play down the importance of termination rather than to play it up (Cormier & Hackney, 2008).

Ideally, counselor and client should agree on when it is time to end the counseling relationship (Young, 2009). Often, verbal messages may indicate a readiness to terminate. For example, a client may say, "I really think I've made a lot of progress over the past few months"; or a counselor may state, "You appear to be well on your way to no longer needing my services." Statements of this nature suggest client recognition of growth or resolution. At other times, client behaviors signal that it is time to end the counseling relationship. Examples include a decrease in the intensity of work; more humor; consistent reports of improved coping skills; verbal commitments to the future; and less denial, withdrawal, anger, mourning, or dependence (Shulman, 1999; Welfel & Patterson, 2005).

How much time should counselors and clients devote to the termination process? Cormier and Hackney (2008) believe that when a relationship has lasted more than 3 months, the final 3 to 4 weeks should be spent discussing the impact of termination. During this time, counselors can help clients review their accomplishments, giving them credit for the gains they have made (Seligman, 2009). Counselors may also ask clients for feedback about the counseling process, especially if the client has initiated the termination. Although the exact amount of time termination should take is a matter of judgment, there needs to be a time of preparation before ending a counseling relationship. Ideally, when the counseling relationship ends, clients will feel confident about living effectively without the support of the counseling relationship (Young, 2009).

To help with the termination process, counselors can use a procedure called *fading,* in which counseling appointments are spaced over increasing lengths of time. Counselors can also help with termination by encouraging clients to articulate ways they will utilize their newly developed coping skills in upcoming life experiences.

The Case of Heather

Heather, a 17-year-old adolescent, has been in counseling with you for 12 sessions. Her counseling goals included managing test-taking anxiety and overcoming her fear of public speaking. You and Heather have used several strategies to help her accomplish her goals, including deep breathing exercises, cognitive and behavioral rehearsal, and thought-stopping techniques. Heather has made a lot of progress during the 12 sessions, and your last two sessions have seemed to be more conversation-oriented than therapy-oriented. You believe that it is time to move toward termination. What issues will you want to consider? How will you approach these issues with Heather? Will the fact that Heather is a minor affect the way you enter into the termination process? How do you think Heather will react to ending the counseling relationship? In what ways might you follow up with her after the termination process is complete?

Termination Documentation

When the counseling process is over, a closing statement, or termination summary, needs to be written and added to the client's record. R. Mitchell (2007) listed two reasons for carefully documenting termination: (a) the client may return for additional services, and (b) a client or the legal representative may initiate a malpractice suit. Well-written termination summaries, particularly in cases of premature termination, can protect counselors against the accusation of abandonment.

Termination documentation provides a clinical summary of the course of treatment and its outcomes. Piazza and Baruth (1990) and R. Mitchell (2007) recommended including the following information in the termination summary:

- A synopsis of the initial assessment, treatment plan, interventions, and outcomes
- An evaluation of the client's current level of functioning
- Reasons for termination
- Summary of progress toward goals, including fff final diagnostic impressions
- Follow-up plan (When clients are moving from inpatient to outpatient care, an after-care plan is needed that states identifying information about the new counselor and a plan for services.)
- Other pertinent information (Whether or not additional information is documented is determined on a client-by-client basis.)

As with case notes, the format of the termination summary may be determined by the organization in which a counselor practices. Community counselors will want to be familiar with all record-keeping procedures associated with their work sites.

Follow-Up

Follow-up entails checking to see how the client is doing, with respect to the presenting issue, sometime after counseling has ended (Okun & Kantrowitz, 2008). In essence, it is a type of positive monitoring process that encourages client growth (Egan, 2007). Although some counselors neglect following up on clients, the process is important because it reinforces the gains clients have made in counseling and helps both the counselor and the client reevaluate the counseling experience. Follow-up also emphasizes the genuine care and concern counselors have for their clients. Short-term follow-up is usually conducted 3 to 6 months after a counseling relationship terminates. Long-term follow-up is conducted at least 6 months after termination.

Follow-up may take many forms, but there are four main ways in which it is usually conducted (Cormier & Cormier, 1998). The first is to invite the client in for a session to discuss any progress the client has continued to make in achieving desired goals. A second way is through a telephone call to the client. A call allows the client to report directly to the counselor, although only verbal interaction is possible. A third way is for the counselor to send the client a letter asking about the client's current status. A fourth and more impersonal way is for the counselor to mail the client a questionnaire dealing with current levels of functioning. Many public agencies use this type of follow-up as a way of demonstrating accountability. The latter two procedures do not preclude the use of more personal follow-up procedures by individual counselors. Although time consuming, a personal follow-up is probably the most effective way of evaluating past counseling experiences. It helps assure clients that they are cared about as individuals and are more than just statistics.

Referral and Recycling

Counselors are not able to help everyone who seeks assistance. When a counselor realizes that a situation is unproductive, it is important for him or her to either terminate the relationship or make a referral. A *referral* involves arranging other assistance for clients when the initial arrangements are not likely to be helpful (Okun & Kantrowitz, 2008). There are many reasons for referral, including the following (Goldstein, 1971):

- The client has a problem the counselor does not know how to handle.
- The counselor is inexperienced in a particular area (e.g., substance abuse) and does not have the necessary skills to help the client.
- The counselor knows of a nearby expert who would be more helpful.
- The counselor and client have incompatible personalities.
- The relationship between counselor and client is stuck in the initial phase of counseling.

Referrals involve a *how,* a *when,* and a *who.* The *how* involves knowing how to make a referral in a manner that maximizes the possibility that clients will follow through with the referral process. Clients may resist a referral if they feel rejected by the counselor. Welfel and Patterson (2005) suggested spending at least one session with clients in preparation for referrals. Some clients will need several sessions.

The *when* of making a referral involves timing. The longer clients work with a counselor, the more reluctant they may be to see someone else. Thus, timing is crucial. If a counselor reaches an impasse with a certain client, the counselor should refer that client as soon as possible. On the other hand, if the counselor has worked with a client for a while, the counselor should demonstrate sensitivity by giving the client enough time to get used to the idea of working with someone else.

The *who* of making a referral involves the person you are recommending to a client. The interpersonal ability of that professional may be as important initially as his or her skills if the referral is going to be successful. A helpful question to ask is whether the new counselor is someone you would feel comfortable sending a family member to see (MacCluskie & Ingersoll, 2001). Another consideration in regard to whom a client should be referred involves insurance panels. When appropriate, counselors can check to ensure that the new counselor will be covered under the client's insurance policy.

Recycling is an alternative when the counselor thinks the counseling process has not yet worked but can be made to do so. *Recycling* involves the reexamination of all phases of the therapeutic process (Baruth & Huber, 1985). Perhaps the goals were not properly defined or an inappropriate strategy was chosen. Whatever the case, by reexamining the counseling process, counselor and client can decide how or whether to revise and reinvest in the counseling process. Counseling, like other experiences, is not always successful on the first attempt. Recycling gives both counselor and client a second chance to achieve what each wants: positive change.

Summary and Conclusion

This chapter covered a wealth of material, ranging from the physical settings in which counselors work to specific activities that occur during the actual counseling process. Clinical mental health counselors know how to work with clients throughout the counseling process, including the initial phase, the working phase, and termination.

In the initial counseling sessions, counselors work to establish rapport and set up a structure for success. During this stage, issues related to informed consent are addressed, including the nature of counseling, the counselor's background, fees, and expectations. Counselors also make efforts to get clients to take the initiative in the change process. Clients enter counseling for different reasons, and many are reluctant or resistant. Counselors accept clients where they are, establish rapport, and provide motivation. During the initial sessions, counselors gather information about clients either formally (e.g., structured intake interviews) or less formally for the purpose of assessment. At the end of the initial phase, the counselor and client work collaboratively to set goals and design a treatment plan for change.

During the working phase of counseling, clients move toward achieving goals. The emphasis therefore shifts from understanding to activity. In selecting interventions, effective counselors integrate research with practice so that they can implement counseling procedures that are most likely to produce positive outcomes. Various common curative factors have been linked with effective counseling, including cognitive learning, affective experiencing, and rehearsal.

In the termination phase, counselors and clients gradually end their relationship, and clients leave counseling. An important part of termination is follow-up. In follow-up, client progress is monitored through phone calls, personal interviews, or the mail.

Throughout the counseling process, practitioners need to document their interactions with clients. In this chapter, several recommendations associated with careful record keeping were made, particularly as they apply to writing treatment plans, case notes, and termination summaries. As community counselors provide quality services to their clients, they simultaneously manage the necessary documentation with a high degree of professionalism.

CHAPTER 7

Client Assessment and Diagnosis

She works in a world I have never known
Full of rainbow pills and lilac candles
Woven together with simple time-stitches
A pattern of color in a gray fabric factory
Where she spends her days
spinning threads
that go to Chicago by night.
Once with a little girl smile and a giggle
She flew to Atlanta in her mind,
Opening the door to instant adventures
far from her present fatigue,
That was a journal we shared
arranging her thoughts in a patchwork pattern
until the designs and desires came together.

Gladding, S. T. (1974). Patchwork. *Personnel and Guidance Journal, 53,* 39. © ACA. Reprinted with permission. No further reproduction authorized without written permission of ACA.

———————————

Community and mental health counselors are responsible for carrying out many different functions, some of which may depend on the settings in which they work. Two general functions that clinical mental health counselors need to conduct skillfully are assessment and diagnosis. Assessment is an ongoing process in which counselors gather information about clients from several different sources and use that information to make decisions about treatment planning. Diagnosis is closely related to assessment, and although the topic continues to be somewhat controversial, diagnosis is used by counselors in many private and public settings to describe clients' conditions, guide treatment planning, and apply for third-party reimbursement. This chapter provides information about assessment and diagnosis and examines issues related to the two processes.

The Case of Michelle

Michelle is a 24-year-old medical student. Recently she was driving home from a spring break vacation with her two best friends when she fell asleep at the wheel. Unable to regain control of the car, she swerved into another lane, colliding head-on with an oncoming car and leaving her friends in serious condition. Michelle survived with minimal injuries but her two friends have been in the hospital for 4 weeks. Unable to overcome the guilt of her role in the accident, Michelle has withdrawn from her social network. She is having trouble sleeping at night and often experiences flashbacks during the day. She has lost much of her appetite and states that she does not remember anything from the accident. Her medical doctors believe she may have amnesia from the accident, but those close to her believe she is avoiding any discussion of the accident because of the guilt she feels. She refuses to visit her friends in the hospital because she believes she will be plagued by great anxiety and flashbacks. Since the accident, she has had a sudden and seemingly intractable change in personality, often wishing to spend time alone in her room. Her family worries she may be experiencing post-traumatic stress symptoms following the accident but are unable to get her to open up about her feelings.

If Michelle agreed to go to counseling, how would you begin to assess her situation? What hypotheses would you make about her behavior? What else might be going on? What diagnosis or diagnoses might apply? What would a multiaxial diagnosis look like if your agency required you to complete one? Think about these and other questions as you read this chapter on assessment and diagnosis.

ASSESSMENT IN COUNSELING

Assessment is a multifaceted activity that is integral to the counseling process. Although some people associate assessment with the early stages of counseling, it actually is an ongoing activity that takes place throughout the counseling process, from referral to follow-up (Hohenshil, 1996). Formal and informal methods of assessment help counselors gather information to determine the nature of clients' issues, the prevalence of their problems, their strengths and skills, and whether counseling is likely to be beneficial. Conducting systematic assessment helps counselors and clients develop a better understanding of the presenting problems and issues, select and implement effective interventions, and evaluate progress made in counseling (Whiston, 2009).

Assessment begins with the first counselor–client contact, as the counselor listens to the client's story and observes behaviors (Young, 2009). During this initial stage, important data about the client are collected, counselors begin to hypothesize about the nature of the client's concerns, and decisions are made about whether counseling will be beneficial. To gather information about clients, clinical mental health counselors typically conduct intake interviews, which were described in Chapter 6. In this section, additional information is provided about assessment in counseling, including methods and purposes of assessment, principles of sound assessment, and issues related to assessment and diagnosis.

Assessment Defined

The term *assessment* has been defined in numerous ways. The *Standards for Educational and Psychological Testing* (American Educational Research Association [AERA], American

Psychological Association [APA], & National Council on Measurement in Education [NCME], 1999, p. 172), a key authoritative source in the assessment field, defines *assessment* as "any systematic method of obtaining information from tests and other sources, used to draw inferences about characteristics of people, objects, or programs." Whiston (2009) uses the terms *appraisal* and *assessment* interchangeably because both processes utilize both formal and informal techniques, not just standardized tests. *Psychological testing,* a term often associated with assessment, is just one of several methods counselors use to collect client information. A psychological test is defined by Anatasi and Urbina (1997) as an objective, standardized measure of behavior. Other methods of assessment include interviews, checklists, rating scales, and qualitative or experiential approaches. Counselors integrate and interpret the results of these evaluation methods to increase their understanding of clients and their situations (Hood & Johnson, 2007).

As part of their training, community and mental health counselors take at least one course in appraisal procedures, in which they learn methods and principles of assessment. It would be beyond the scope and purpose of this chapter to describe those methods and principles in depth. However, a brief overview is presented here to highlight important factors related to assessment in counseling.

Methods of Assessment

Assessment procedures may be formal or informal, standardized or nonstandardized, and objective or subjective. They can be used to measure attributes and behaviors in many domains, including personality, cognition, affect, ability, interests, values, and relationships. Clinical mental health counselors can choose from a wide spectrum of methods for assessing clients, including the following:

• **Standardized Tests.**   Psychological tests that are standardized must meet certain requirements for test construction, administration, and interpretation. Such tests use representative norm groups for scoring and interpretation and typically have been evaluated for reliability and validity (Hood & Johnson, 2007). These tests also include uniform standards for administration. Examples of areas measured by standardized tests include aptitude, achievement, personality, interests, values, and skills.

• **Checklists and Rating Scales.**   Checklists and rating scales provide subjective estimates of behaviors or attitudes based on observations made by the client or other observers. With checklists, clients or observers simply mark words or phrases that apply to them or their situation. Such tools can provide valuable information to counselors in a relatively brief time. Some checklists are standardized, such as the Symptom Checklist-90–Revised (SCL-90–R; Derogatis, 1994) and the shorter version of the instrument, the Brief Symptom Inventory (BSI; Derogatis, 1993). These checklists, as well as less formal checklists, are often used during intake sessions in mental health settings (Whiston, 2009).

With rating scales, the rater indicates the degree or severity of the characteristic being measured (Whiston, 2009). For example, a client may be asked to rate his or her energy level on a graded scale, from lethargic (1) to energetic (5). Informal rating scales may be used to determine the client's perception of the intensity of the presenting problem. Standardized rating scales that are completed by the client and significant others can be especially helpful for measuring a wide spectrum of behaviors. For example, The Conners' Rating Scales–Revised (Conners, 1996) provide rating scales that are completed by parents and teachers (and by the adolescent, in the case of older children) and are used to help assess attention deficit/hyperactivity disorder (ADHD), as well as to assess other behavior problems, such as anxiety or oppositional behavior.

• **Other Inventories.**   Community and mental health counselors may use a number of other inventories besides rating scales and checklists to assess client concerns. For example, the Minnesota Multiphasic Personality Inventory–2 (MMPI–2; Butcher, Dahlstrom, Graham, Tellegen, & Kaemmer, 1989) is widely used by counselors in mental health settings (Bubenzer, Zimpfer, & Mahrle, 1990). The MMPI–2 consists of 567 affirmative statements that clients respond to in one of three ways: true, false, or cannot say. In addition to identifying individuals who may be experiencing psychiatric problems, the MMPI–2 is able to discern important characteristics such as anger, alienation, depression, and social insecurity. Counselors need extensive training and experience to use the instrument accurately and appropriately (Austin, 1994).

An instrument that community and mental health counselors frequently use with clients is the Myers-Briggs Type Indicator (MBTI; Myers, McCaulley, Quenk, & Hammer, 1998). The MBTI, which is based on the work of Carl Jung and Jungian theory, is the most widely used personality inventory for normal functioning (Quenk, 2000). The MBTI was initially developed by Katharine Briggs and her daughter, Isabel Briggs Myers. Currently, it is published by Consulting Psychologists Press (CPP) and frequently is taken on the computer, yielding a computer-generated report that is interpreted to clients by the counselor. This assessment instrument helps clients examine differences and similarities of personality types based on four dimensions, which are depicted in Figure 7–1.

• **Clinical Interviews.**   Interviews are commonly conducted by counselors to assess clients. Initial interviews, often called intake interviews, were discussed in Chapter 6. Interviews

EXTRAVERSION (E)	**INTROVERSION (I)**
• Draws energy from the outer world of people and things.	• Draws energy from the inner world of ideas and impressions.
SENSING (S)	**INTUITION (N)**
• Focuses on the present, on concrete information, and prefers to examine things using the 5 senses.	• Focuses on the future, with an emphasis on patterns and possibilities.
THINKING (T)	**FEELING (F)**
• Decisions are based primarily on logic and objective analysis.	• Decisions are based primarily on values and subjective evaluation of person-centered concerns.
JUDGING (J)	**PERCEIVING (P)**
• Prefers a planned, organized approach to life, where things are structured and settled.	• Prefers a flexible, spontaneous approach to life, where options are kept open.

FIGURE 7–1   The four Myers-Briggs Type Indicator dichotomies

can vary in format, ranging from relatively open and unstructured to highly structured. During the past several years, many structured clinical interviews have been published for research and practice purposes (see Vacc & Juhnke, 1997, for examples). Structured clinical interviews can be especially useful in the current era of managed care, which stresses precision, time-limited counseling, and demonstrated effectiveness.

A structured clinical interview consists of "a list of relevant behaviors, symptoms, and events to be addressed during an interview, guidelines for conducting the interview, and procedures for recording and analyzing the data" (Vacc & Juhnke, 1997, p. 471). The questions are usually asked in an ordered sequence and typically are either diagnostic (specifically related to the *Diagnostic and Statistical Manual*) or descriptive (providing data on emotional, behavioral, and social issues, but not for the purpose of diagnosis). Structured clinical interviews can be helpful in that they use preestablished questions to assess a wide range of behaviors in a consistent manner (Neukrug & Fawcett, 2006). However, the very structure of the interview may limit rapport building and may prevent the client from going into depth about important issues.

Whereas structured clinical interviews specify the order and wording of questions, semistructured interviews are less restrictive. Semistructured interviews address the same issues as structured interviews do, but they provide more flexibility in sequence, wording, and interpretation.

Unstructured interviews provide even more flexibility in those areas and can be very helpful in building rapport. However, they do not allow for the breadth of coverage provided by structured and semistructured interviews. Unstructured interviews also make it more likely that a clinician will spend excessive time focusing on certain items, thereby neglecting other items (Neukrug & Fawcett, 2006).

• **Mental Status Examination.** The mental status examination (MSE) has been used by psychiatrists, psychologists, and social workers for over 50 years (Hinkle, 1992). In recent years, the MSE has also been used by community and mental health counselors who work in settings in which mental disorders are diagnosed and treated (Polanski & Hinkle, 2000). A skillfully administered MSE provides information about a client's level of functioning and self-presentation. It may be conducted formally or informally during the initial interview and provides a format for organizing objective and subjective data gathered during the interview (Polanski & Hinkle, 2000). Data gathered during a Mental Status Exam is frequently used for initial diagnosis (Whiston, 2009).

The MSE assesses behaviors and attitudes that can be organized under the following six categories: (a) appearance, attitude, and activity; (b) mood and affect; (c) speech and language; (d) thought process, thought content, and perception; (e) cognition; and (f) insight and judgment (Trzepacz & Baker, 1993). A brief description of each category is presented in Figure 7–2. When conducted proficiently, the MSE provides biological, social, and psychological information about the client that facilitates diagnosis and treatment planning (Polanski & Hinkle, 2000).

• **Qualitative Methods.** Qualitative assessment procedures include card sorts, structured exercises, creative activities, genograms, timelines, and other open-ended approaches. These methods are usually less formal than quantitative techniques, allowing for greater counselor and client flexibility and adaptability, which may make them especially suitable for a diverse clientele (Goldman, 1990). Qualitative methods elicit active client participation and provide ways for the counselor to understand the client's current problems within the context of his or her unique developmental history.

What Is a Card Sort?

A card sort is a qualitative method of assessment, which also serves as an intervention. It is an activity in which the client sorts cards that contain words describing various possibilities (e.g., vocational options, college choices, other life choices). Clients are asked to separate the cards into categories, such as "yes," "no," or "maybe." In this way clients are able to organize their ideas and explain their decision-making processes. Through this process, the counselor can help the client explore thoughts and feelings about the topics written on the cards.

THE MENTAL STATUS EXAMINATION

- *Appearance: Appearance* refers to the client's physical presentation, dress, grooming, cleanliness, and presence or absence of any disabilities. It can also include body position, posture, and use of eye contact.
- *Attitude: Attitude* refers to the client's approach to the interview and interactions with the counselor. Observations about attitude include tone of voice, facial expressions, attentiveness, and degree of evasiveness in responses. Attitude may change during the course of the interview. Examples of terms used to describe attitude include *cooperative, uncooperative, suspicious, hostile,* and *open.*
- *Activity:* This category refers to the client's level and quality of motor activity. Any observation of tics, tremors, mannerisms, compulsions, and perseveration is documented. Physical manifestations of emotions (e.g., laughing, crying, fist clenching, and grunting) are documented, as well.
- *Mood and affect: Mood* refers to the client's predominant internal feeling state, as reported by the client. *Affect* refers to the client's outward expression of an emotional state, as observed by the counselor, and varies in range and intensity.
- *Speech and language: Language* refers to the client's ability to comprehend word meanings and express them through writing and speaking. Speech and language defects include *defects of association* (the way words are grouped to make phrases) and *defects of rate and rhythm of speech* (e.g., pressured or delayed speech patterns).
- *Thought process, thought content, and perception:* During the MSE, thought content and process are inferred from what the client says and what the counselor observes. Disturbances of thought process, content, and perception can include delusions and hallucinations. Appraising a client's thoughts of violence to self or others is a crucial part of thought content assessment.
- *Cognition: Cognition* refers to the client's ability to use logic, intellect, reasoning, memory, and other higher order cognitive functioning. During the MSE, cognition is assessed in a structured manner. Areas to be evaluated include attention, concentration, orientation, memory, and abstract thinking. Counselors can assess attention and concentration by asking the client to count backward by 7s or 3s from 100. Assessment of long- and short-term memory and orientation to person, place, time, and circumstance also help evaluate cognitive functioning.
- *Insight and judgment:* These are the most advanced areas of mental functioning. *Insight* refers to the degree to which a client is aware of how personal traits and behaviors contribute to his or her current situation. *Judgment* refers to the ability to make decisions about an appropriate course of action.

FIGURE 7–2 The mental status examination
(Information sources included Polanski & Hinkle, 2002, and Trzepacz & Baker, 1993)

The active nature of qualitative assessment promotes counselor–client interaction and client self-awareness while revealing information about that client that might otherwise remain unknown. Qualitative assessment activities can serve as interventions as well as tools for gathering data. Participation in such activities (e.g., creating and discussing a genogram) can help clients understand relationship patterns, reexamine premature decisions (e.g., card sorts for career guidance), and become more aware of personal challenges and strengths (e.g., timelines, ecomaps).

Purposes of Assessment

The primary goal of assessment is to collect data about clients' behaviors, characteristics, and contexts that will then facilitate clinical decision making and evaluation. With this general purpose in mind, it is helpful to look at some of the specific ways that assessment facilitates counseling throughout the different stages of the process: in early stages for treatment planning, during the treatment phase as an actual intervention, and throughout the process and after termination for evaluation (Whiston, 2009).

ASSESSMENT TO INFORM THE CLINICIAN AND GUIDE TREATMENT PLANNING.   At the outset of counseling, clients may talk about a wide spectrum of concerns. One of the goals of assessment during this early stage of counseling is to work with the client to clarify and prioritize the issues. A systematic assessment helps ensure that counselors are helping clients with the most important issues. In addition to helping clients prioritize their concerns, Young (2009) suggested eight other reasons counselors need to spend sufficient time assessing clients during initial sessions:

- Assessment provides crucial information that facilitates realistic goal planning. It informs treatment planning and often is used to provide a diagnosis.
- Assessment helps clients explore the problem and discover events that may be triggering it.
- Assessment helps counselors understand the impact of contextual factors, including family, culture, and socioeconomic status, on the client's mental health.
- Assessment helps counselors recognize the uniqueness of individuals. To this end, counselors need to recognize that we tend to view clients and their issues through our own cultural lenses and therefore need to take precautions to assess objectively, respecting differences in cultural backgrounds and values.
- Assessment uncovers the potential for self-harm or violence (i.e., suicidal or homicidal ideation. See Figure 7–3).
- Assessment reveals important historical data. For example, timelines can help counselors understand significant life events portrayed in sequential order.
- Assessment highlights strengths as well as concerns. Often, we think of assessment as a tool that helps mental health professionals diagnose pathology. However, assessing clients' strengths, resources, and abilities enables counselors to select interventions that capitalize on clients' skills and support systems.
- Assessment can help clients become more aware of the severity of a problem (e.g., substance abuse). Oftentimes, clients are either unaware or in denial about a particular issue. Assessment is one way to help clients break through denial and begin to recognize the severity of a problem.

In summary, a thorough assessment helps the counselor gain a more complete understanding of the client. Information provided through assessment helps the counselor make

---

A Suicide Risk Awareness Index

Check your knowledge by responding to the following true/false statements:

1. More women than men commit suicide.
2. In 2004, suicide was the 11th leading cause of death in the United States.
3. The group with the highest suicide rate is African American females over the age of 65.
4. Exposure to the suicidal behavior of others, including media figures, can increase the risk of suicide.
5. All depressed clients should be evaluated to determine suicidal ideation.
6. The state with the highest suicide rate is New Jersey.
7. One of the most important signs to look for in suicide assessment is a sense of hopelessness or helplessness.
8. The strongest risk factors for suicide in adults are depression, alcohol abuse, cocaine use, and separation or divorce.
9. Firearms are the most commonly used method of suicide, with men being more likely than women to use firearms.
10. Discussing suicide potential with a client increases the likelihood that it will be carried out.

Answers to Suicide Awareness Index:

1. False; Although women are more likely than men to attempt suicide, more men die by suicide at a ratio of 4:1.
2. True
3. False; The highest rate of suicide, when categorized by gender and race, is among white men over the age of 85.
4. True
5. True; It is important to evaluate all clients for suicidal ideation, and depression is a risk factor for suicide.
6. False; New Jersey has the lowest suicide rate. The state with the highest suicide rate is Nevada (Granello & Granello, 2007).
7. True; Most suicidal clients exhibit a degree of hopelessness and/or helplessness.
8. True
9. True; Firearms are used in more than half of all suicides. For men, 57% of suicides were by firearms.
10. False; All clients should be evaluated for suicidal ideation. (Statistics were obtained from the National Institute of Mental Health, 2008a.)

   Most counselors will, at some point, encounter the challenge of working with a suicidal client. One of the key areas counselors need to evaluate during the initial session, as well as at other points in the counseling process, is the risk of suicide. The risk of suicide can be assessed informally by asking the client about his or her thoughts. Hood and Johnson (2007, p. 181) suggest a series of graded questions, such as:

- How have you been feeling lately?
- How bad does it get?
- Has it ever been so bad that you wished you were dead?
- Have you ever had thoughts of suicide?

FIGURE 7–3 Suicide risk assessment and intervention

If the client indicates that he or she has thought about suicide, the counselor will want to conduct a more in-depth assessment, asking about the suicidal thoughts and following through with a suicide risk assessment. The suicide risk assessment becomes part of the treatment in that talking about suicidal thoughts validates the client's experiences and communicates hope that the problem can be addressed (Hood & Johnson, 2007).

There are several formal and informal ways to assess suicide risk. The strongest indicators of suicide risk are ideation, plan, intent, and means (Haley, 2004). Stelmachers' recommendation that clinicians focus on seven areas:

- *Verbal Communication.* What has the client verbalized or hinted at? It is important to listen closely; the client may couch the ideation as a joke. Themes of escape, reducing tension, or self-punishment can all be indications of suicidal ideation.
- *Plan.* If the client gives any indication of suicidal thoughts, the counselor should determine if there is an actual suicide plan by asking questions such as "Have you thought about how you might do it?" or "How would you do it?" Generally, more specific, thought-out plans indicate a greater risk of an attempt, although with impulsive clients, this may not be the case.
- *Method.* If the client has a plan, determine what has already been put in place to carry out the plan. What methods are being considered and how available are they? Is the plan feasible? Determine the exact location of any lethal means (e.g., firearms and drugs).
- *Preparation.* To what degree has the client already put plans in place? For example, has he or she written a note or secured the lethal means? Has a place been determined? Sometimes people who are considering suicide give away possessions or get financial matters in order. The amount of preparation usually relates directly to the level of client risk.
- *Stressors.* Assess past, present, and future stressors. Stressors associated with suicide include loss of a loved one, physical illness, and economic difficulties. Anniversaries or special dates related to the stressors may exacerbate the client's sense of loss or depression, increasing the risk of suicide. Also, multiple stressors can compound a client's sense of hopelessness.
- *Mental State.* Mental disorders such as depression, substance abuse, and schizophrenia heighten the risk of suicide. Evaluating the client's mental and emotional state is crucial. Does the client express despondence, helplessness, anger, guilt, or torment? If so, he or she will need to be monitored closely. On the other hand, a sudden improvement of mood can indicate that the client has decided to "end the pain," and may be a sign for further evaluation.
- *Hopelessness.* What are the client's thoughts about the future? A sense of hopelessness is strongly associated with attempted suicide (Stelmachers, 1995) and serves as a red flag for suicide risk.

In addition to the somewhat informal (but extremely useful) methods of suicide assessment listed above, several assessment instruments have been developed to assess suicide risk. Among those are (Granello & Granello):

- *Beck Scale for Suicidal Ideation,* available through the Psychological Corporation.
- *Inventory of Suicide Orientation,* available through National Computer Systems, Inc.
- *Suicide Probability Scale,* available through Western Psychological Services.
- *Suicidal Ideation Questionnaire* (adolescent and adult versions), available through Psychological Assessment Resources.

FIGURE 7–3 *(Continued)*

- *Firestone Assessment of Self-Destructive Thoughts* (Firestone & Firestone, 1998).
- *Lifetime Parasuicide Count* (Linehan & Comtois, 1997).
- *Positive and Negative Suicide Ideation Inventory* (Osman, Gutierrez, Kopper, Barrios, & Chiros, 1998).
- *Suicide Behaviors Questionnaire—Revised* (Linehan, 1996).
- *Suicide Ideation Scale* (Rudd, 1989).

These are just a few of the many instruments that are available to help clinicians who choose to use standardized instruments to evaluate suicide risk. However, it is important to remember that these instruments are only tools and do not take the place of interactive dialog.

Suicide Intervention: What To Do If a Client Appears Suicidal

In terms of immediate treatment, counselors need to do whatever is necessary to keep the client safe (MacCluskie & Ingersoll, 2001). Past history, current assessment of the client's condition, and prognosis will determine the type of intervention that needs to occur. MacCluskie and Ingersoll describe treatment options as either *inpatient treatment* or *outpatient treatment*.

Inpatient treatment. If it is determined that the client is of danger to self, the prospect of voluntary hospitalization should be discussed. Ideally, the client then is taken to the hospital, where he or she is signed in. In this case, the client should be accompanied by a family member, a trusted friend, or by the clinician to ensure safety. Under no circumstances should the suicidal client be left alone, even briefly.

In situations when the counselor has determined that the client is of immediate danger to self but the client will not agree to voluntary hospitalization, involuntary hospitalization may be necessary. Family members and friends can be helpful in this process, although at times it is necessary for the counselor to commit the client, even though taking such a step can be detrimental to the counseling relationship (MacCluskie & Ingersoll, 2001).

Outpatient treatment. When the danger to self is not immediately imminent, outpatient treatment may be the best option. In this situation, "the goal is to obtain follow-up counseling soon—preferably in the next 48 hours, to provide support and re-assess the client" (MacCluskie & Ingersoll, 2001, p. 174). If the counselor's agency cannot provide continued, ongoing services, the counselor is responsible for scheduling the client with another professional at another agency, and follow-up should occur within the next few days. The client needs to be given emergency contact information and asked to sign a no-harm contract. In many cases, family members need to be consulted, preferably with the client's permission. With both inpatient and outpatient treatment, the counselor should consult with other professionals and document activities and decisions.

When working with suicidal clients, counselors can engage in specific behaviors to help clients overcome suicidal ideation and behaviors. Helpful interventions include building a strong therapeutic relationship with the client, validating other relationships in the client's life, helping the client resolve intense emotions, confronting self-destructive behaviors, encouraging personal autonomy, and helping clients acknowledge and overcome feelings of helplessness and despair (Paulson & Worth, 2002). Collaborating with medical personnel to arrange for medical evaluation may also be indicated (Laux, 2002).

FIGURE 7–3 *(Continued)*

sound decisions about treatment goals and intervention strategies. In some settings, early assessment also is used to render a formal diagnosis.

ASSESSMENT AS AN INTERVENTION.   Beyond providing the counselor with information for diagnosis and treatment, assessment methods have the potential to serve directly as interventions. Formal and informal appraisal procedures can encourage client self-exploration and catalyze decision making. For example, discussing the results of a career interest inventory can help clients crystallize their understanding of personal interests, particularly as those interests relate to the world of work. Completing checklists of personal qualities can promote recognition and appreciation of strengths. Instruments like the *Five Factor Wellness Inventory* (*5F-WEL*; Myers & Sweeney, 2005b), which is designed to assist individuals in making healthier lifestyle choices based on a model for wellness, can help clients examine areas of their life that may be out of balance. Qualitative methods such as card sorts or timelines encourage clients to engage in self-reflection, which can then facilitate movement in new directions. It is the *interactive dialog between counselor and client,* either during an activity like a card sort or during the interpretation of the results of a psychological test, that transforms the assessment process from an information-gathering activity to a therapeutic intervention.

ASSESSMENT FOR EVALUATION AND ACCOUNTABILITY.   The need to evaluate the effectiveness of counseling has become increasingly more important as managed care organizations and other agencies demand accountability. For evaluation to occur, goals and objectives need to be specified clearly during the early stages of counseling. Follow-up assessment can take several forms, including goal attainment scaling, self-monitoring techniques, posttests, client satisfaction surveys, and outcome questionnaires (Hood & Johnson, 2007).

Using assessment for evaluation is not a straightforward activity. Counseling is a complex process, and its effectiveness depends on many variables. Also, demonstrating the effectiveness of counseling varies, depending on who completes the outcome measure (e.g., the client, the counselor, or an outside observer). For evaluation to be meaningful, counselors will want to consider measuring change from multiple perspectives, using several different methods.

In addition to outcome evaluation at the conclusion of counseling, assessment can be conducted at various points throughout the process to determine what has been helpful and what needs to be changed. By obtaining objective and subjective feedback from clients, counselors can modify interventions so that clients are more likely to meet their goals.

Principles of Sound Assessment

The process of psychological assessment is both a science and an art (Hood & Johnson, 2007). Counselors need to have comprehensive knowledge about psychological assessment instruments and their psychometric properties (e.g., reliability, validity, norming procedures). They also need to integrate that knowledge with strong communication and counseling skills as they select, administer, and interpret assessment instruments. To help counselors conduct assessment skillfully, Hood and Johnson (2007, pp. 6–7) have suggested several basic principles:

- Determine the purpose of assessment. Focusing on that purpose will help counselors identify which assessment procedures to conduct.
- Involve the client in selecting areas to be assessed and in the interpretation of assessment results.

- When using formal assessment instruments (e.g., standardized tests), make sure that the instruments demonstrate *test trustworthiness*, which includes validity, reliability, cross-cultural fairness, and practicality (Neukrug & Fawcett, 2006).
- Never rely on a single assessment tool; instead, use multiple methods of assessment. For example, a counselor may use information gained from an intake interview, the Beck Depression Inventory—II, an informal checklist, and outside observers to form an impression about whether a client is depressed.
- Consider the possibility of multiple issues, many of which may be interconnected (e.g., substance abuse, depression, and physical problems).
- Assess the client's environment. Problems occur in a social context and are rarely related to just one factor.
- Evaluate client strengths, as well as areas of concern. Identifying strengths and resources can help shift the focus from the problem to potential solutions (White, 2002).
- Consider alternative hypotheses, rather than simply looking for evidence to support a favorite hypothesis. What else might be going on with the client?
- Treat assessment results as tentative. As more information becomes available, initial assumptions may change.
- Be aware of the client's cultural and personal biases that may influence decisions. Incorporate cultural data, such as measures of acculturation levels, into the assessment process.
- Consider the influence of individual factors, including age, gender, and educational level, on assessment results. In some cases, (e.g., career interest inventories), gender-based norms should be used to interpret results.
- Consult with other professionals on a regular basis.
- Provide feedback about assessment results to clients. The feedback process can improve self-understanding and promote change.

Issues Related to Assessment

Counselors are responsible for conducting ethically sound assessment procedures. Several documents have been developed to help guide professionals who use assessment instruments with the public. The *Standards for Educational and Psychological Testing* (AERA, APA, NCME, 1999) was developed by experts in several fields, including research, measurement, psychology, and counseling. It addresses a wide range of issues related to assessment practices, including test–user competencies, assessing testing applications, and diversity considerations. A document prepared by the Association for Assessment in Counseling and Education, *Applying the Standards for Educational and Psychological Testing—What a Counselor Needs to Know* (2003), clarifies applications of the *Standards* (1999) for counselors. Both sources can help community and mental health counselors use assessment instruments responsibly and ethically.

COUNSELOR COMPETENCE.   Before using psychological assessment instruments, counselors need to consider their levels of training and experience. Competence to use assessment instruments accurately is stressed in professional codes of ethics and also has legal ramifications. Different instruments require different degrees of competence, and counselors need to be able to demonstrate skill in using a particular instrument before administering it. To monitor competence, many test publishers require professionals to provide a record of their educational background before allowing them to purchase assessment instruments. Although there some exceptions, tests traditionally are categorized by levels (i.e., Levels A, B, and C) and are sold only to those professionals who meet the requirements for a particular level (Hood & Johnson, 2007). Ultimately the responsibility to select and administer an assessment instrument correctly lies with the individual counselor (Whiston, 2009).

DIVERSITY CONSIDERATIONS.   A number of concerns have been raised about the misuse of assessment instruments with ethnic and racial minorities, people with disabilities, women, and other special populations. Indeed, one of the most controversial issues in assessment relates to whether appraisal instruments are fair to people from different racial or ethnic groups (Suzuki & Kugler, 2001). When selecting instruments, counselors need to consider the client's cultural background, gender, language, developmental level, and level of physical ability. Counselors can expect to work with diverse populations and need to be skilled in cross-cultural assessment (Whiston, 2009). Specific considerations related to assessing diverse clientele include the following:

- Select instruments that are appropriate for the population being tested by examining the purpose of the test, norming groups, and sensitivity of content. Be aware of cultural limitations of certain appraisal instruments.
- Determine the client's language proficiency, and when possible, use tests that are written in that language.
- When administering tests to individuals with disabilities, do everything possible to ensure that the instrument accurately measures the skills or aptitudes it is designed to measure, rather than any characteristics associated with the disability. Be aware of options available for clients with disabilities who require testing accommodations.
- Consider the potential effects of counselor–client cultural differences on the test-taking process and its results. Be culturally sensitive in establishing rapport, conducting the assessment, and interpreting the results.

Community and mental health counselors can refer to a number of resources to help them become more effective in cross-cultural assessment. One resource that is of particular importance to community and mental health counselors is the *Standards for Multicultural Assessment* (2nd ed.; Association for Assessment in Counseling, 2003). This document, which builds on an earlier version (Prediger, 1994), compiles standards associated with multicultural assessment from five other source documents. The compilation of standards are organized into four categories: Selection of Assessment Instruments: Content and Purpose; Selection of Instruments: Norming, Reliability, and Validity; Administration and Scoring of Assessment Instruments; and Interpretation and Application of Assessment Results. The source documents from which the standards were compiled include the following:

- *Code of Fair Testing Practices in Education* (2nd ed.; Joint Committee on Testing Practices [JCTP], 2002). Available for download at www.apa.org/science/jctpweb.html.
- *Responsibilities of Users of Standardized Tests* (3rd ed.; ACA & AAC, 2003). Available for download at www.apa.org/science/jctpweb.html.
- *Standards for Educational and Psychological Testing* (2nd ed.; American Educational Research Association, American Psychological Association, and National Counseling of Measurement in Education). Online information about ordering is available at www.apa.org/science/jctpweb.html.

- *Multicultural Counseling Competencies and Standards.* (Association for Multicultural Counseling and Development, 1992). These standards can be viewed in Arredondo et al.'s 1996 article.
- *Code of Ethics and Standards of Practice of the American Counseling Association.* (ACA, 1995). [*Note:* The 2005 *Code of Ethics* had not been implemented when the *Standards for Multicultural Assessment* were published. Counselors are advised to use the most current *Code of Ethics* when making decisions related to cross-cultural assessment].

Another helpful resource for developing competence in cross-cultural assessment is *The Handbook of Multicultural Assessment* (Suzuki, Ponterotto, & Meller, 2008). This handbook, which is in its third edition, provides information about general issues related to multicultural assessment as well as specific information related to ethical guidelines and clinical issues.

USE OF RESULTS. In all situations, client welfare is the counselor's primary consideration. In assessment, issues related to *privacy, confidentiality,* and *communication of results* are especially pertinent. Many of the documents listed in this chapter (e.g., the *ACA Code of Ethics* and the *Standards for Educational and Psychological Testing*) provide helpful guidelines for using assessment results. ACA's *Code of Ethics* (2005) addresses the use of assessment results in Section E: Evaluation, Assessment, and Interpretation. Section E provides standards in 13 areas of assessment:

- E.1. General (purpose of assessment, client welfare)
- E.2. Competence to Use and Interpret Assessment Instruments
- E.3. Informed Consent in Assessment
- E.4. Release of Data to Qualified Professionals
- E.5. Diagnosis of Mental Disorders
- E.6. Instrument Selection
- E.7. Conditions of Assessment Administration
- E.8. Multicultural Issues/Diversity in Assessment
- E.9. Scoring and Interpretation of Assessments
- E.10. Assessment Security
- E.11. Obsolete Assessments and Outdated Results
- E.12. Assessment Construction
- E.13. Forensic Evaluation: Evaluation for Legal Proceedings

An issue related to the use of assessment results that directly affects clinical mental health counselors on a regular basis is that of diagnosis. Clinical mental health counselors routinely diagnose and treat clients with problems ranging from developmental concerns to more serious mental health conditions (Hohenshil, 1996). Indeed, almost all settings in which community and mental health counselors work require a diagnosis for reimbursement of services (White, 2002). A *DSM-IV* multiaxial assessment and diagnosis provides essential information that helps counselors and clients with goal setting and treatment planning. However, diagnostic procedures have the potential for abuse, in that "an inappropriate label could follow a person throughout life, affecting family, social, educational, and occupational status" (Hohenshil, 1996, p. 65). Consequently, as we turn our attention to the diagnosis, it is important to remember that diagnosis is an ongoing process that is conducted not to label clients or for purposes of reimbursement but instead to aid in treatment planning and intervention.

DIAGNOSIS

Approximately 26.2% of Americans adults ages 18 and over suffer with mental health disorders in a given year (National Institute of Mental Health [NIMH], 2008b). That statistic translates into one out of four adults. When applied to U.S. Census information, the figure translates to 57.7 million adults (NIMH, 2008b).

To treat clients effectively, community and mental health counselors in the 21st century need to be skilled at assessing and diagnosing clients. Although some professionals believe that diagnosis contradicts a developmental approach to counseling (Ivey & Ivey, 1999), others maintain that "without an accurate diagnosis, counselors will probably have difficulty determining the proper treatment for a disorder and assessing whether a person is likely to benefit from counseling" (Seligman, 2009, p. 374). Hohenshil (1996) reminds us that many employers, licensing agencies, and insurance companies expect counselors to know how to formally diagnose mental disorders. He goes on to state that diagnosis, either formal or informal, has always been a part of counseling. For example, making a decision about whether a client's problem is a developmental issue or a form of pathology is, in fact, a form of diagnosis. In addition to making informal diagnoses, in recent years clinical mental health counselors have been expected to accrue skills in diagnosing using a formal diagnostic system, such as the *Diagnostic and Statistical Manual of Mental Disorders*, 4th edition, text revision (*DSM-IV-TR;* American Psychiatric Association, 2000).

Diagnosis is "the process of comparing the symptoms exhibited by the client with the diagnostic criteria of some type of classification system" (Hohenshil, 1996, p. 66). A diagnosis is a description of a person's condition and not a judgment of a person's worth (Rueth, Demmitt, & Burger, 1998). The purposes of diagnosis are to (a) define clinical entities so that clinicians have a common ground for understanding what a diagnostic category means and (b) help counselors determine appropriate treatment (Maxmen & Ward, 1995). Seligman (2009, pp. 374–375) outlined several reasons for becoming skilled in diagnosis:

- A diagnostic system provides a consistent framework and set of criteria for naming and describing mental disorders.
- Accurate diagnosis enables counselors to understand client symptoms and anticipate the typical course of a disorder.
- Diagnosis enables counselors to make use of the growing body of research on treatment effectiveness (e.g., what types of interventions are most likely to ameliorate a specific disorder) and develop a treatment plan that is likely to be effective.
- Diagnosis provides a common language for mental health professionals, which facilitates parity, credibility, communication, and collaboration.
  - Many diagnoses are linked to standardized assessment inventories, such as the MMPI-II and the Millon Clinical Multiaxial Inventory III, thus providing a direct link between assessment and diagnosis.
- When counselors make diagnoses and treatment plans according to an accepted system, they can more easily demonstrate accountability and are less vulnerable to malpractice suits.
  - Using a standardized, accepted system of diagnosis helps counselor obtain third-party reimbursement for services, thereby making counseling more affordable to those who might otherwise not be able to pay.

- Sharing diagnoses with clients, when appropriate, can help them understand their symptoms. Knowing that other people deal with the same symptoms and that information and treatment are available can be reassuring.
- Diagnosis can help counselors determine whether they have the skills and training needed to help a particular client or whether it would be better to refer that client to another mental health professional.

Although there certainly is justification for developing diagnostic skills, there also are risks and concerns associated with the diagnostic process. Some of those risks include (Ivey & Ivey, 1999; Seligman, 2009):

- Diagnostic labels can be stigmatizing if misused and may lead to misperceptions of that person if the diagnosis becomes known.
- Diagnosis is part of the medical illness–cure tradition and is not consistent with a holistic, developmental approach to counseling that emphasizes wellness, multicultural concerns, contextual influences, and strength-based approaches.
- Diagnosis is historically contingent and socially constructed, not absolute reality.
- Diagnosis can lead to pathologizing the client so that he or she is viewed "as" the disorder (e.g., schizophrenic, borderline), rather than as a person with particular concerns and symptoms.
- Diagnosis may have a negative impact on people's ability to obtain insurance and, in some situations, affect their employment opportunities.
- The most common diagnostic systems (i.e., the *DSM-IV-TR* and the *ICD-10* [*International Classification of Diseases*]) are steeped in the Western concept of mental illness and may not be relevant to people from other cultures.
- Attaching a diagnostic label to a client puts the focus of treatment on the individual rather than the family or the social system. In some cases, this can cause the family to pathologize the individual rather than work collectively on relationships and shared issues.

Although there are risks associated with the process of diagnosis, many of those risks can be avoided by conducting skillful and comprehensive assessments, presenting diagnostic information in such a way that it is understood by clients and families, and honoring client confidentiality (Seligman, 2009). To make proper diagnoses, counselors must receive extensive training and supervision. They should know diagnostic categories, particularly those described in the *DSM-IV-TR*. Therefore, it is to the *DSM-IV-TR* that we direct our attention next.

Using the *DSM-IV-TR* in Counseling

In the United States, the most widely used system for psychiatric diagnosis is the *Diagnostic and Statistical Manual of Mental Disorders* (*DSM*). Currently in its fourth edition, the *DSM-IV-TR* includes over 200 diagnoses, which are divided into 17 general categories and clearly defined by objective criteria (Maxmen & Ward, 1995). Whereas the *DSM-IV* was published in 1994, the text revision (*TR*) was published in 2000 to bridge the span between the *DSM-IV* and the *DSM-V,* which is scheduled for publication in the near future. The text revision includes some changes to text sections of the *DSM* (e.g., Associated Features and Disorders, Prevalence) but no substantive changes in criteria sets for mental disorders (APA, 2000).

WHAT IS A MENTAL DISORDER?   According to the *DSM-IV-TR* (2000), the term *mental disorder* can be defined as:

> a clinically significant behavior or psychological syndrome or pattern that occurs in an individual and that is associated with present distress (e.g., a painful symptom) or disability (i.e., impairment in one or more important areas of functioning) or with a significantly increased risk of suffering death, pain, disability, or an important loss of freedom. (p. xxxi)

It is important to note that behaviors that are culturally sanctioned are not considered mental disorders. Furthermore, for a condition to be classified as a disorder, according to the DSM, at least one of three feature—distress, impairment, and/or significant risk—must be evidenced (Seligman, 2009). As professionals in the counseling field know, many people who seek counseling do not have mental disorders. For example, if Heather is experiencing relationship problems with her partner of 5 years and is trying to make a decision about whether to stay in the relationship or leave, she does not have a mental disorder unless she exhibits distress, impairment, or significant risk to herself or others. In making a diagnosis, the counselor might state that Heather is experiencing a phase of life problem.

DSM diagnoses are made based on the clinician's evaluation of certain criteria. Counselors are not trained to work with all the disorders represented in the *DSM;* however, they are expected to be knowledgeable about the disorders and aware of their own areas of competence (Whiston, 2009). For instance, if a client presents with a cognitive disorder such as dementia, which is characterized by multiple cognitive impairments, the counselor may be part of a treatment team, but the primary treatment will usually come from a physician (Seligman, 2009).

MULTIAXIAL DIAGNOSIS.   The *DSM-IV-TR* uses a multiaxial diagnostic system that involves assessment on five different axes. The multiaxial system allows counselors to organize information based on clients' symptoms, their physical conditions, their levels of coping, and current stressors (Seligman, 2009). An overview of the five axes is presented in Table 7–1.

All clinical conditions or disorders are listed on Axis I or Axis II. Axis I disorders include all mental disorders and conditions except personality disorders, mental retardation, and borderline intellectual functioning, which are listed on Axis II. Clients may have one or more diagnoses listed on these two axes. The principal diagnosis is the first disorder listed on Axis I, unless otherwise specified. When a diagnosis is listed, clinicians include the name and code

TABLE 7–1   Multiaxial Assessment

Axis	What Is Rated	Example
Axis I	Clinical disorders, developmental disorders, and other conditions that may be a focus of clinical attention	305.00; Alcohol abuse; Moderate
Axis II	Personality disorders and mental retardation	317.00; Mild mental retardation
Axis III	General medical conditions	Chronic pain
Axis IV	Psychosocial and environmental problems	Divorced, unemployed, minimal social support
Axis V	Global assessment of functioning (GAF)	30 (present) 45 (highest level in past year)

number specified by the *DSM*. The severity of the disorder is specified as well, using the terms *Mild, Moderate, Severe, In Partial Remission,* or *In Full Remission* (Seligman, 2009).

Clinicians use Axis III to describe general medical conditions that may be related to the client's mental and emotional conditions. For example, recurring stomachaches or headaches might be related to an anxiety disorder. If the clinician does not have the client's medical records, he or she should specify that the medical conditions were self-reported.

On Axis IV, clinicians list psychosocial and environmental stressors that the client has experienced during the past year. Examples of stressors that may affect clients include family problems, finances, living situations, lack of social support, and negative life events (Maxmen & Ward, 1995).

Axis V is used to provide a global assessment of functioning (GAF) rating, which is based on a scale ranging from 1 to 100. Higher GAF ratings indicate higher levels of functioning. Scores below 50 usually indicate that the client is experiencing severe symptoms (Seligman, 2009). The rating typically depicts the client's current level of functioning, although sometimes clinicians also include the client's highest level of functioning within the past year. Although some research indicates that the GAF is an inadequate measure of adaptive functioning (Bacon, Collins, & Plake, 2002), in mental health settings the GAF is used more frequently than any other diagnostic tool to measure adaptive functioning and impairment.

Each of the five axes that comprise a DSM assessment and diagnosis contribute unique information about a client's overall situation. By examining all the information provided through multiaxial assessment, counselors can make decisions about diagnosis, treatment planning, and prognosis. When making a diagnosis, the counselor will want to begin with an initial broad observation and screening of the client. Next, he or she directs attention toward how the client's symptoms are evidenced. What type of symptom syndromes is the client experiencing (e.g., frequency, duration, and onset of symptoms)? The counselor then forms a tentative hypothesis about the type of disorder the client is experiencing, followed by a careful, diagnosis-specific inquiry to determine if the symptoms meet the specified criteria for a *DSM* diagnosis (Fong, 1995). A diagnosis should be given only if the specific criteria outlined in the *DSM* are met.

Overview of Mental Disorders and Conditions

It would be beyond the scope of this chapter to describe each of the 200-plus mental disorders and conditions contained in the *DSM-IV-TR*. Instead this section will review briefly each of the 17 sections used to categorize disorders and conditions within the *DSM*. People entering the field of clinical mental health counseling will want to master *DSM* terminology and differential diagnosis (i.e., distinguishing between disorders of similar character by comparing their signs and symptoms) by attending workshops and training courses and by consulting with experienced professionals.

• **Disorders Usually First Diagnosed in Infancy, Childhood, or Adolescence.** This large, comprehensive category includes disorders that usually originate early in life, with some disorders persisting into adulthood. Examples of early onset disorders include mental retardation (which is included in this section but listed as an Axis II disorder), learning disorders (e.g., dyslexia), communication disorders (difficulties in speech and language), and pervasive developmental disorders (e.g., autism, Asperger's disorder, and Rett's disorder). Also included in this category are attention-deficit and disruptive behavior disorders (e.g., oppositional-defiant disorder and conduct disorder), feeding and eating disorders of infancy or early childhood (e.g., pica), tic disorders (e.g., Tourettes syndrome), elimination disorders, and other disorders that are not included in the previous categories (e.g., separation anxiety). Clinical mental health counselors who work with children and adolescents can gain additional information on these disorders, including intervention suggestions, in books such as *Counseling Treatment for Children and Adolescents with DSM-IV-TR Disorders* (Erk, 2008).

- **Delirium, Dementia, and Amnestic and Other Cognitive Disorders.**   Each of these disorders is organic in nature and involves some form of impairment to the brain. The impairment may be temporary or permanent and is characterized by deficits in cognition or memory. Examples of cognitive disorders include delirium (characterized by a clouding of consciousness and reduced environmental awareness), dementia (characterized by a deterioration of intellectual functions), and amnestic disorders (characterized by memory impairment). As mentioned earlier, counselors do not diagnose or treat cognitive disorders, but they need to be familiar with the symptoms in order to refer clients who demonstrate such deficits (Seligman, 2009).

- **Mental Disorders Due to a General Medical Condition.**   At times, a medical condition that is described on Axis III manifests itself not only as a physical problem but also as a mental or emotional condition. For example, if catatonia results from encephalitis, the differential diagnosis would be Catatonic Disorder Due to a General Medical Condition. Technically, psychological problems that result from medical conditions are not considered *mental disorders,* but they are included for identification purposes.

- **Substance-Related Disorders.**   This category includes psychological and behavioral conditions related to substance use, including *substance dependence* and *substance abuse.* Substances associated with substance-related disorders are grouped into 11 classes, including alcohol, amphetamine, caffeine, cannabis, cocaine, and others. Prescribed and over-the-counter medications can cause substance-related disorders, as can certain toxins, such as heavy metals and pesticides.

In assessing for substance-related disorders, it is important to differentiate between *dependence* and *abuse.* Substance dependence involves regular use of the substance, resulting in impaired control over its use and continued use of the substance despite negative consequences. Substance abuse, in contrast, involves a pattern of substance use that leads to clinically significant impairment or distress. It may result in failure to fulfill major role obligations, legal problems, or being involved in physically hazardous situations (Whiston, 2009).

The *DSM-IV-TR* also includes substance-induced disorders in the general category of substance-related disorders. *Substance intoxication* and *substance withdrawal* are examples of substance-induced disorders.

Many community and mental health counselors specialize in working with clients with substance-related disorders. In keeping with the growing need for specialists in that area, the new CACREP Standards (2009) are now accrediting programs that train counselors to become addiction counselors.

- **Schizophrenia and Other Psychotic Disorders.**   The key feature of these disorders is a loss of contact with reality, including hallucinations and delusions (Seligman, 2009). Although community and mental health counselors typically are not specifically trained to work individually with clients who are psychotic, sometimes clinical mental health counselors are part of treatment teams that works with people dealing with various psychoses. According to Maxmen and Ward (1995), "Schizophrenia devastates as no other, for no other disorder causes as pervasive and profound an impact—socially, economically, and personally" (p. 173). Approximately 1% of adult Americans are affected by schizophrenia (National Institute of Mental Health [NIMH], 2008b). Some of the symptoms exhibited by people with psychotic disorders include hallucinations, delusions, disorganized speech, catatonia, grossly disorganized behavior, lack of insight, and flat affect.

Whereas earlier medications for schizophrenia and related psychotic disorders had many negative side effects, in recent years more effective medications and treatments have been developed. Consequently, many people diagnosed and treated are able to live rewarding and meaningful lives in their communities (NIMH, 2008b).

• **Mood Disorders.**   Mood disorders are characterized by manic or depressive episodes. Examples include major depressive disorder (severe depression lasting at least 2 weeks), dysthymic disorder (moderate but long-lasting depression), bipolar disorders (characterized by manic and depressive episodes), and seasonal affective disorder (characterized by depressive onset during winter months). In a given year, approximately 20.9 million American adults, or 9.5% of the population, have a depressive disorder, with women more likely to be diagnosed than men (NIMH, 2008b). The most commonly diagnosed mood disorder is major depressive disorder, which is the leading cause of disability for American adults between the ages of 15 and 44 (NIMH, 2008b). Cognitive–behavioral counseling, frequently in conjunction with medication, is often used to treat mood disorders.

• **Anxiety Disorders.**   Anxiety disorders are the second most commonly occurring category of mental disorders, following substance abuse (Fong & Silien, 1999). Each year, approximately 40 million American adults (18.1%) have an anxiety disorder (NIMH, 2008b). Anxiety is a multidimensional construct, characterized by feelings of apprehension, dysphoria (a general state of feeling unhappy or unwell), and/or symptoms of tension. Because anxiety is also a symptom of other mental disorders, counselors need to know how to diagnose anxiety disorders accurately. Examples of anxiety disorders include social phobia, agoraphobia, panic disorder, obsessive–compulsive disorder, generalized anxiety disorder, specific phobias (fear of a specific object or situation, such as spiders), posttraumatic stress disorder (PTSD), and acute stress disorder. Anxiety disorders often co-occur with other disorders, such as depression.

• **Somatoform Disorders.**   People with somatoform disorders present with physical symptoms that initially appear to be medical in nature but cannot fully be explained as medical conditions. The physical symptoms are not feigned in that physical symptoms of some sort do exist. Examples of somatoform disorders include somatization disorder, conversion disorder (e.g., blindness without a physical cause), hypochondriasis, and body dysmorphic disorder (characterized by an imagined or minimal flaw in one's appearance).

• **Factitious Disorders.**   Unlike clients with somatoform disorders, clients with factitious disorders feign illness or disability because they enjoy assuming the role of "patient." They may fabricate complaints or inflict injury on themselves. A particularly troublesome disorder in this category is Munchausen's syndrome by proxy, characterized by caregivers using a child to gain access to medical treatment, often by injuring or even killing the person in their care. People with factitious disorders usually are resistant to treatment and may leave counseling prematurely.

• **Dissociative Disorders.**   Dissociative disorders involve an alteration of consciousness that is neither organic nor psychotic. Dissociative identity disorder (DID) is the most familiar of these conditions. DID, previously called multiple personality disorder, was illustrated by the media through the cases of Eve and Sybil (Seligman, 2009). Other examples of dissociative disorders are dissociative fugue, dissociative amnesia, and depersonalization disorder.

• **Sexual and Gender Identity Disorders.** This category includes three subcategories: sexual dysfunction, paraphilias, and gender identity disorders. Sexual dysfunction refers to difficulties related to sexual desire, sexual arousal, orgasm, and sexual pain. Paraphilia refers to an abnormal or unnatural attraction, such as pedophilia (sexual activity with children). Gender identity disorder is characterized by intense discomfort with one's biological gender and is not to be confused with sexual orientation issues. Clients with gender identity disorder (GID) either view themselves as members of the opposite sex or they want to change physically to become members of the opposite sex (Whiston, 2009). In the 2006 movie, *Transamerica,* Felicity Huffman played the role of a man with gender identity disorder in the process of taking the final step to become a transgender woman. It is important to note that many people do not believe that GID should be classified as a mental health disorder and that it should be removed from the list of diagnoses in the *DSM-V,* when it is published. As stated by Dr. Madeline Wyndzen (2008), transgendered individuals and many clinicians "find the mental illness labels imposed on transgenderism just as disquieting as the label that used to be imposed on homosexuality" (www.genderpsychology.org/psychology/dsm_v_workgroup.html).

• **Eating Disorders.** This new section in the *DSM-IV-TR* is composed of two primary types of eating disorders: anorexia nervosa and bulimia nervosa. Subtypes within each of these main types include restricting, binge eating, and purging (anorexia nervosa) and purging and nonpurging types (bulimia nervosa). Females are much more likely to develop these disorders than are males. Clients with anorexia nervosa do not maintain a minimally normal body weight, although they tend to view themselves as "too fat." Clients with bulimia nervosa may not be underweight, but they engage in binge eating followed by purging (vomiting, using laxatives) or nonpurging activities (fasting or excessive exercise) to rid themselves of what they have eaten. "If left untreated, Eating Disorders can be physically harmful and even fatal" (Seligman, 2009, p. 387). Often, treatment of eating disorders occurs in group settings and involves treatment teams that include counselors, nutritionists, and other mental health or medical specialists.

• **Sleep Disorders.** This category is also new to the *DSM-IV-TR.* Sleep disorders are categorized as *Primary* (the cause is undetermined and unrelated to another condition), *Related to Another Mental Disorder, Due to a Medical Condition,* and *Substance Induced.* The inclusion of sleep disorders in the *DSM* reflects a growing awareness of the effects sleep deprivation can have on an individual's functioning (Seligman, 1999). Diagnosing sleep disorders is somewhat difficult and often takes place in sleep-disorder clinics.

• **Impulse–Control Disorders Not Elsewhere Classified.** The defining characteristic of impulse–control disorders is the client's difficulty in resisting impulses, drives, or temptations. For many of these disorders, the client feels a buildup of tension that is released when the act is committed but later may be followed by feelings of remorse or guilt. Examples include kleptomania (stealing objects that are not needed), pyromania (setting fires), pathological gambling, trichotillomania (recurrent pulling out of one's hair) and intermittent explosive disorder (characterized by engagement in aggressive or destructive behaviors). Although Internet addiction is not at this point classified as a mental disorder by the *DSM-IV-TR,* there has been much debate among professionals about the possibility that overuse of the Internet could be an impulse–control disorder. Stress management and behavioral approaches are often part of the treatment plan for impulse–control disorders (Seligman, 2009).

• **Adjustment Disorders.** Adjustment disorders are characterized by mild to moderate impairment associated with a stressor experienced within 3 months of the onset of symptoms. The disorder may develop as the result of a single stressor or multiple stressors (e.g., divorce, job loss, and moving). If the disorder lasts less than 6 months, it is described as acute. If it lasts longer, it is considered chronic. Adjustment disorders are among the mildest of the disorders listed in the *DSM* and generally are responsive to crisis intervention or solution-focused counseling (Seligman, 2009).

• **Personality Disorders.** Clients with personality disorders demonstrate enduring patterns of functioning that are maladaptive, are inflexible, and significantly impair social and occupational functioning or cause subjective distress (Maxmen & Ward, 1995). The maladaptive behavior is manifested in at least two of the following areas: cognition, interpersonal functioning, affectivity, or impulse control.

Personality disorders are coded on Axis II and can be difficult to diagnose and treat. Because clients' perceptions of their personality disorders typically are *egosyntonic* (the disorder is an integral part of the self), they may be less likely to believe that their problems are changeable (Whiston, 2009). Ten personality disorders are described in the *DSM-IV-TR* and are grouped into three clusters: Cluster A (paranoid, schizoid, and schizotypal personality disorders), Cluster B (antisocial, borderline, histrionic, and narcissistic personality disorders), and Cluster C (avoidant, dependent, and obsessive–compulsive personality disorders). People with Cluster A personality disorders often appear odd or eccentric. Clients with Cluster B disorders tend to appear dramatic, emotional, or erratic. In contrast, individuals diagnosed with Cluster C disorders appear anxious or fearful.

Diagnosis of a personality disorder involves evaluating the client's long-term patterns of functioning, with the particular characteristics of the disorder being evidenced by early adulthood (APA, 2000). It is important to take into account the client's ethnic, cultural, and social background to avoid misdiagnosis.

• **Other Conditions That May Be a Focus of Clinical Attention.** The conditions or problems coded in this category are not considered to be mental disorders, but they often are a focus in counseling. Some of the conditions are listed as V-Codes, and all are recorded on Axis I except for borderline intellectual functioning. Conditions listed in this category include relational problems (e.g., parent–child, sibling, or partner), problems related to abuse or neglect (physical and/or sexual abuse), and "additional conditions" such as bereavement, academic problems, or occupational problems. Often, people presenting with these conditions are emotionally healthy but are going through a difficult time, making counseling an especially suitable option.

Diagnosis and Treatment

Diagnosis is just one part of a comprehensive assessment that leads to treatment planning. It is a crucial part, however, in that it affects the delivery of counseling services, third-party reimbursement, and professional credibility.

Seligman (1996, 2009) has developed a model to help counselors integrate assessment, diagnosis, and treatment planning based on the *DSM-IV-TR* diagnostic system. The title of the model is a mnemonic device called DO A CLIENT MAP. Each letter of the mnemonic addresses one of the areas to be considered during diagnosis and treatment planning, thus providing a comprehensive organized guide for working with a client (Seligman, 2009, p. 309):

1. **D**iagnosis according to the *DSM-IV-TR* multiaxial system
2. **O**bjectives of treatment (written as treatment goals)
3. **A**ssessment procedures (formal and informal procedures)
4. **C**linician (considerations related to clinical background, gender, ethnicity, and other issues)
5. **L**ocation of treatment (inpatient or outpatient, site)
6. **I**nterventions (theoretical approach and specific interventions)
7. **E**mphasis of treatment (e.g., supportive, probing)
8. **N**umbers (individual, group, or family counseling)
9. **T**iming (duration and scheduling of sessions)
10. **M**edication (determine whether a referral for medication is needed)
11. **A**djunct services (additional activities to supplement the counseling process, such as tutoring)
12. **P**rognosis (based on the diagnosis, the GAF score, and levels of support)

Counselors will want to use the *DSM-IV-TR* responsibly, recognizing the importance of cultural influences and social context on client behaviors (Whiston, 2009). They will need to examine assessment information and diagnostic criteria critically, so that the diagnostic process is used for its intended purpose: to inform and guide treatment.

Using what you have learned in this chapter, hypothesize what might be going on with Rajesh. Follow Seligman's (2009) DO A CLIENT MAP model and determine how you would complete each of the 12 areas. What cultural issues need to be considered? What other issues need to be considered?

The Case of Rajesh

Rajesh is a 20-year-old, first-generation American of Pakistani parents. He is a sophomore at a large university. He is nearing the end of his sophomore year and has been a successful student until this past semester.

Rajesh's roommate, who is his older brother, Paresh, has noticed that he has been spending more and more time online—and his Internet use is beginning to affect his schoolwork and class attendance. He used to accompany his older brother home every weekend to visit their large extended family, but lately Rajesh has been making excuses to stay on campus and play the online game World of Warcraft, *often until the early hours of the morning. In general Rajesh seems irritable and depressed, spending more time alone and doing just enough to get by in his classes.*

Rajesh's mother is also concerned about his behavior. His conversations with her on the phone—formerly a weekly event—have become infrequent, and he seems preoccupied when he talks with her. His mother says she is disappointed and feels slighted. According to her, he avoids her questions about school and about his future plans. He has begun responding in English, refusing to speak in Urdu.

At the end of this semester, Rajesh will be expected to formally declare a major, and his parents are expecting him to pursue an undergraduate track that will lead him to medical school. Rajesh is a talented visual artist and spends time drawing elaborate pictures of characters and scenes from World of Warcraft. *His older brother has stated that his artwork is "fantastic and full of imagination," and that he talks about his online life and his love of comic book art more than he talks about his biology classes. Rajesh has expressed an interest in attending an art class, but has found that it conflicts with his hectic schedule as a biology major.*

Summary and Conclusions

In this chapter, assessment and diagnosis—two essential elements of counseling in most community and agency settings—were described. Assessment is a process that occurs throughout counseling and serves several purposes. It helps counselors and clients gain a better understanding of presenting problems, serves to guide treatment planning, acts as an intervention, and helps counselors evaluate progress and outcomes. Counselors can choose from a variety of assessment tools, including standardized tests, rating scales, interviews, the mental status examination, and qualitative approaches. There are a number of sound appraisal principles that counselors will want to follow, including the use of multiple methods to assess clients.

To help counselors conduct ethically sound assessments, several documents have been developed, including the *Standards for Educational and Psychological Testing* (AERA, APA, NCME, 1999). Some of the issues that affect the assessment process include counselor competence, assessing diverse populations, and use of assessment results.

Closely related to the process of assessment is diagnosis. Although the topic is somewhat controversial, diagnosis has become increasingly important for counselors over the course of the past few decades. Consequently, community and mental health counselors will want to be familiar with the most commonly used system of diagnosis of mental and emotional conditions: the *Diagnostic and Statistical Manual of Mental Disorders* (APA, 2000). The *DSM-IV-TR* provides a way for clinicians to assess clients on five broad dimensions, or axes. All mental disorders are recorded on Axis I or Axis II and are classified into 17 categories. Although professional mental health counselors do not treat all types of diagnoses, they will want to be familiar with signs and symptoms associated with each so that they can either plan appropriate interventions or make appropriate referrals.

Assessing and diagnosing are only two of several important functions carried out by clinical mental health counselors. In the next chapter, we consider other counseling roles, including crisis intervention, primary prevention, advocacy, and program evaluation.

CHAPTER **8**

Essential Counseling Services: Crisis Intervention, Prevention, Advocacy, and Evaluation

She stands
leaning on his outstretched arm
sobbing awkwardly
Almost suspended between
the air and his shoulder
like a leaf being blown
in the wind from a branch of a tree
at the end of summer.
He tries to give her comfort
offering soft words
and patting her head.
"It's okay," he whispers
realizing that as the words leave his mouth
he is lying
And that their life together has collapsed
like the South Tower of the World Trade Center
that killed their only son.

Sam Gladding, *September 27th*, 2002.

In Chapters 6 and 7, we focused primarily on individual counseling services: the counseling relationship, the counseling process, client assessment, and client diagnosis. Certainly, individual counseling is one of many important mental health services offered in community settings. Other essential services include crisis intervention, prevention programs, advocacy, and program evaluation. We begin this chapter by describing crisis intervention, which sometimes occurs with individual clients and other times is conducted with groups of people. We then focus on prevention, advocacy, and program evaluation—three key components of service delivery in community mental health organizations. Two other key services—group and family counseling—are discussed in the following two chapters.

Problems in living are an intrinsic part of life. Although the nature and intensity of problems faced by people vary, most individuals encounter crisis of some type during the course of their life journeys. Being able to work effectively with people facing crisis situations is a crucial counseling skill. Therefore, in the first part of the chapter, we focus on the important service of crisis intervention.

Whereas crises may be inevitable and community counselors need to know how to intervene appropriately, a proactive mental health service that can help people manage crises more effectively and perhaps avoid certain crises altogether is prevention. Indeed, one of the defining characteristics of the counseling profession is an emphasis on preventing mental health problems by building on strengths and developing resources. Primary prevention strategies provide the most efficient way to promote mental health among large numbers of people. Consequently, clinicians need to be skilled at designing and implementing prevention programs. In the second part of the chapter, we describe three prevention models and provide suggestions for implementing stress management programs.

Related to prevention is the service of advocacy, which steps outside the traditional role of counseling by focusing on injustices and environmental conditions that need to change for client welfare to be maximized (Kiselica & Robinson, 2001). The American Counseling Association (ACA) and other mental health organizations have made advocacy a priority in recent years. Advocates can engage in a spectrum of activities to address systemic needs, ranging from empowering clients to actively lobbying for social justice. Advocacy, both for clients and for the profession of counseling, has been described as a "professional imperative" (Myers, Sweeney, & White, 2002). Thus, in the third section of this chapter, we describe advocacy and outline skills and attributes needed to advocate successfully.

Although program evaluation is described at the end of the chapter, it does not occur only at the end of counseling service delivery. Instead, effective evaluation is an ongoing process that is integral to all aspects of community and agency counseling programs, from start to finish. Ongoing, systemic, well-planned evaluation is a vital component of effective mental health service delivery systems. Evaluation enables counselors to make decisions about which services are effective and which need to be changed. It provides ways to ensure that services are being implemented as planned and that specific goals and outcomes are being met. Evaluation provides a way for counselors and community agencies to be accountable to clients, other professionals, accrediting agencies, and the community at large. We close the chapter with an overview of program evaluation, focusing on process and outcome evaluation as they relate to clinical mental health counseling.

CRISIS INTERVENTION

During the past two decades, the need for crisis intervention services has increased significantly. One reason more services are needed is the recent upsurge of large-scale violent acts occurring in the United States, as evidenced by the terrorist attacks on New York City and Washington, DC, in 2001; the 2007 Virginia Tech massacre; the 1999 shootings at Columbine High School; and the 1995 bombing of the Federal Building in Oklahoma City, to name just a few of the more publicized catastrophic events. Violent acts occur "with such frequency and indiscriminateness that no one can consider him- or herself safe" (Myer, 2001, p. 3). Other disasters, including earthquakes, floods, fires, hurricanes, and tornadoes, result in tragic losses of lives and homes. For example, Hurricane Katrina struck the southern coast of the United States in August 2005, causing devastating, long-lasting effects. On an international level, tsunamis, earthquakes, and cyclones recently have had catastrophic effects on people in Southeast Asia, Pakistan, and China. Automobile and plane accidents, injury, illness, and disease are other examples of crisis situations that can have devastating effects on victims and their families.

Experiences of violence, disaster, and any form of trauma can leave people without the sufficient resources needed for coping. In such cases, crisis intervention services are needed. Crises may affect a large group of people, as with Hurricane Katrina, the 2008 cyclone in Myanmar (Burma), or the September 11 terrorist attacks, or they can be more individualized, as evidenced when people threaten or commit suicide. When people experience a crisis situation, either within their communities or intrapersonally, finding ways to resolve the crisis effectively is essential to mental health and well-being.

Definition of Crisis

BOX 8–1

When written in Chinese, the word *crisis* is composed of two characters. One represents danger, and the other represents opportunity.

crisis

Before discussing crisis intervention services, it is important to clarify what is meant by the term *crisis*. Many definitions have been proposed, including the following:

- Crisis is a perception or experiencing of an event or situation as an intolerable difficulty that exceeds the person's current resources and coping mechanisms. Unless the person obtains relief, the crisis has the potential to cause severe affective, behavioral, and cognitive malfunctioning. (James, 2008, p. 3)
- Crises are personal difficulties or situations that immobilize people and prevent them from consciously controlling their lives. (Belkin, 1984, p. 424)
- Crisis is a state of disorganization in which people face frustration of important life goals or profound disruption of their life cycles and methods of coping with stressors. The term *crisis* usually refers to a person's feelings of fear, shock, and distress *about* the disruption, not to the disruption itself. (Brammer, 1985, p. 94)
- A crisis is a critical phase in a person's life when his or her normal ways of dealing with the world are suddenly interrupted. (Lewis, Lewis, Daniels, & D'Andrea, 2003, p. 117)

The concept of crisis is not simple or straightforward. Although a single event may precipitate a crisis, a combination of personal traits, environmental factors, and interpersonal support systems affect the manner in which the event is perceived and managed. An event that is perceived as relatively minor by one individual, such as failing a final examination, may be perceived as a crisis by someone else. Also, the timing, intensity, and number of other stressors the person is experiencing can affect the complexity of the crisis situation.

James (2008, pp. 13–14) emphasized the importance of distinguishing between different types of crises. Building on the research of other crisis specialists, he described four crisis domains:

1. *Developmental Crises.* Developmental crises occur during the normal flow of human growth and maturation. As people move through different developmental stages in their lives, they may experience crisis during certain changes or shifts. For example, a developmental crisis may occur when the last child leaves home or when a person retires. When the event corresponds to culturally accepted patterns and timetables, it is less likely to be experienced as a crisis than when it does not (e.g., teenage pregnancy or forced early retirement; Myer, 2001). Developmental crises are considered normal; however, individuals perceive and respond to them in different ways and with varying degrees of success.

2. *Situational Crises.* A situational crisis occurs when an unexpected, extraordinary event occurs that the person had no way of anticipating or controlling. Examples include automobile accidents, rape, job loss, sudden illness, and death of a loved one. A situational crisis is "random, sudden, shocking, intense, and often catastrophic" (James, 2008, p. 13).

3. *Existential Crises.* An existential crisis is equated with intense, pervasive inner conflict and anxiety associated with the existential issues of purpose, meaning, responsibility, freedom, and commitment. At times, existential crises are precipitated by *nonevents,* such as realizing that one is never going to have children or make a significant difference in a particular field of work. Or it may occur when a spouse or partner of 25 years questions the value of the relationship and seriously considers moving in a different direction.

4. *Ecosystemic Crises.* Ecosytemic crises refer to natural or human-caused disasters that overtake a person or group of people who "find themselves, through no fault or action of their own, inundated in the aftermath of an event that may adversely affect virtually every member of the environment in which they live" (James, 2008, p. 14). In many ways, ecosystemic crises are situational crises that have widespread ramifications. The terrorist attacks of September 11, 2001, devastations of war, and suicide bombings exemplify human-caused ecosystemic crises with wide-reaching effects. Examples of ecosystemic crises caused by natural phenomena include hurricanes, tornadoes, tsunamis, wildfires, and earthquakes.

Although crises represent highly stressful and disruptive situations, they do not imply mental illness (Lewis et al., 2003). Many, but not all, crises are time limited, usually lasting somewhere between 6 and 8 weeks, after which the major symptoms of distress diminish. However, crises can have long-term physical and psychological outcomes, depending on how the crisis is resolved (James, 2008). In many instances, crisis intervention services are needed to help people resolve crises in ways that will prevent negative outcomes in the future. As our understanding of crisis theory and intervention has expanded, "it has become apparent that given the right combination of developmental, sociological, psychological, environmental, and situational determinants, anyone can fall victim to transient pathological symptoms (James, 2008).

Unresolved trauma can, in some instances, lead to the development of posttraumatic stress disorder (PTSD). With PTSD, the trauma lasts in an individual's mind long after the event itself has passed. People with PTSD may exhibit a number of symptoms, including reexperiencing the traumatic event through flashbacks, avoidance of trauma-related activities, emotional numbing, and a range of coexisting disorders (e.g., substance abuse, obsessive–compulsive disorder, and panic disorders; American Psychiatric Association [APA], 2000). Counselors who work with PTSD clients need specialized training in empirically validated treatments to help reduce the impact of the trauma and improve functioning. In particular, clinicians who work with veterans of foreign wars, such as military personnel who served in Vietnam, the Gulf War, Afghanistan, or Iraq, need to be familiar with the signs and symptoms of PTSD and be trained to work effectively with these individuals.

In contrast, when people experiencing crisis do manage to resolve their cognitive, affective, and behavioral reactions effectively, they can change and grow in a positive manner (James, 2008). As noted by Aguilera and Messick (1982):

> The Chinese characters that represent the word "crisis" mean both danger and opportunity. Crisis is a danger because it threatens to overwhelm the individual and may result in suicide or a psychotic break. It is also an opportunity because during times of crises, individuals are more receptive to therapeutic influence. Therefore, prompt and skillful intervention may not only prevent the development of a serious long-term disability but may allow new coping patterns to emerge that can help the individual function at a higher level of equilibrium than before the crisis. (p. 1)

Definition of Crisis Intervention

Crisis intervention differs from traditional counseling in that it is a "time-limited treatment directed at reactions to a specific event in order to help the client return to a precrisis level of functioning" (Myer, 2001, p. 5). It is an action-oriented approach used to help clients cope with a particular life situation that has thrown them off course. According to the National Organization for Victim Assistance (NOVA), goals of crisis response include helping the client defuse emotions, rearrange cognitive processes, organize and interpret what has happened, integrate the traumatic event into his or her life story, and interpret the traumatic event in a way that is meaningful (Bauer, 2001).

Crisis intervention, also called *crisis management,* typically does not last longer than 6 weeks and may be much briefer (Myer, 2001). It is not to be confused with more long-term postcrisis counseling, which can include the treatment of posttraumatic stress disorder (PTSD). *Postcrisis counseling,* which may be necessary, depending on the nature of the crisis and the client's psychological well-being, is another important mental health service, but it is not the focus of this section.

Because crisis intervention differs from traditional counseling, clinical mental health counselors need to be trained to intervene effectively in crisis situations. The overview of crisis intervention provided in this section is not designed to be exhaustive, nor will it sufficiently prepare counselors to become crisis workers. However, it is important to be knowledgeable about specific strategies and skills associated with crisis management. To that end, we review the six-step model of crisis intervention presented by James and Gilliland (2005). The model, which is depicted in Figure 8–1, has been used successfully by professionals and trained lay workers to help people cope with many different types of crises.

ASSESSING:

Overarching, continuous, and dynamically ongoing throughout the crisis; evaluating the client's present and past situational crises in terms of the client's ability to cope, personal threat, mobility or immobility, and making a judgment regarding type of action needed by the crisis worker. (See crisis worker's action continuum, below.)

Listening →

LISTENING: Attending, observing, understanding, and responding with empathy, genuineness, respect, acceptance, nonjudgment, and caring.

1. *Define the problem.* Explore and define the problem from the client's point of view. Use active listening, including open-ended questions. Attend to both verbal and nonverbal messages of the client.

2. *Ensure client safety.* Assess lethality, criticality, immobility, or seriousness of threat to the client's physical and psychological safety. Assess both the client's internal events and the situation surrounding the client, and, if necessary, ensure that the client is made aware of alternatives to impulsive, self-destructive actions.

3. *Provide support.* Communicate to the client that the crisis worker is a valid support person. Demonstrate (by words, voice, and body language) a caring, positive, nonpossessive, nonjudgmental, acceptant, personal involvement with the client.

Acting →

ACTING: Becoming involved in the intervention at a nondirective, collaborative, or directive level, according to the assessed needs of the client and the availability of environmental supports.

4. *Examine alternatives.* Assist client in exploring the choices he or she has available to him or her now. Facilitate a search for immediate situational supports, coping mechanisms, and positive thinking.

5. *Make plans.* Assist client in developing a realistic short-term plan that identifies additional resources and provides coping mechanisms —definite action steps that the client can own and comprehend.

6. *Obtain commitment.* Help client commit himself or herself to definite, positive action steps that the client can own and realistically accomplish or accept.

Crisis Worker's Action Continuum

| Crisis worker is nondirective | Crisis worker is collaborative | Crisis worker is directive |

(Threshold varies from client to client)   (Threshold varies from client to client)

Client is mobile   Client is partially mobile   Client is immobile

The crisis worker's level of action/involvement may be anywhere on the continuum according to a valid and realistic assessment of the client's level of mobility/immobility.

FIGURE 8–1 The Six-Step Model of Crisis Intervention

Source: From *Crisis Intervention Strategies* (5th ed.), by R. K. James and B. E. Gilliland, © 2005. Reprinted with permission of Wadsworth, a division of Thomson Learning: www.thomsonrights.com. Fax 800 730-2215.

As can be seen in Figure 8–1, three primary counselor functions are carried out at various stages of crisis intervention: (a) assessment, which occurs throughout crisis intervention; (b) listening, which is especially important during Steps 1, 2, and 3; and (c) acting, which varies in degrees of directiveness and occurs primarily during Steps 4, 5, and 6. Because assessment occurs throughout the intervention process and is the key to effective intervention, we address that topic first.

Crisis Assessment

The first step in crisis intervention is to assess the nature of the crisis. The purpose of crisis assessment is to provide information about (a) the severity of the crisis; (b) the client's current emotional, behavioral, and cognitive status; (c) the coping mechanisms, support systems, and additional resources available to the client; and (d) whether the client is of danger to self and others (James, 2008).

Crisis Intervention Terminology Associated with Assessment

Equilibrium: A state of emotion or mental stability and balance.

Disequilibrium: A lack of emotional stability or balance.

Mobility: A state of being able to autonomously change or cope in response to different moods, feelings, emotions, needs, and influences. Being flexible or adaptable to the surrounding environment.

Immobility: A state of being incapable of changing or coping in response to different moods, feelings, emotions, needs, and influences. Being unable to adapt to the immediate physical and social world.

James (2008), p. 41

One method of crisis assessment that provides an efficient model for obtaining information about the severity of the crisis and the client's range of responses is the Triage Assessment Model (Myer, Williams, Ottens, & Schmidt, 1992). The model provides a framework for assessing a client's reactions in three domains: affective, behavioral, and cognitive (ABC). Each domain is composed of three categories of reactions that represent the range of responses clients typically experience in crisis situations. To use the model effectively with diverse populations, counselors need to be sensitive to cultural differences, recognizing that reactions may have different meanings in certain cultures (Myer, 2001).

• Responses in the *affective domain* include anger/hostility, anxiety/fear, and sadness/melancholy. Clients are assessed to determine which of these emotions is being experienced by the client and which appears to be dominant. People in crisis may be experiencing intense emotions and may scream or sob uncontrollably (Myer, 2001). At the other extreme, clients may appear emotionally numb, withdrawn, or shut down. Impaired emotional expression is an indication of the *disequilibrium* that usually accompanies crisis experiences. Counselors can help reestablish *equilibrium* by demonstrating empathy and using reflective listening skills to validate feelings.

• Responses in the *cognitive domain* include client perceptions of transgression (i.e., violation), threat, and loss. According to Myer (2001), perception of transgression is focused on the present (what is happening now, during the crisis). Perception of threat is future oriented, and perceptions of loss are focused on the past (recognizing that something is irrevocably gone). Perceptions may occur in any of several life dimensions: (a) physical, (b) psychological, (c) social relationships, and (d) moral/spiritual.

• Reactions in the *behavioral domain* are approach, avoidance, and immobility. Clients usually adopt one of the three behaviors in reacting to the crisis. When clients try to implement strategies to address the crisis event, they are using *approach* behaviors. *Avoidance* behaviors are those by which the client tries to ignore, deny, or escape the crisis event. *Immobility* refers to a set of behaviors characterized by nonproductive, disorganized, or self-defeating attempts to cope with the crisis. Behavioral reactions may be constructive or maladaptive. To determine the helpfulness or harmfulness of the response, counselors can evaluate the potential outcome of the reaction by asking themselves, "Will the behavior aid or hinder the resolution of the crisis?" (Myer, 2001).

• During the assessment process, counselors need to be alert to any possibility of suicidal or homicidal ideation. Usually, the potential for violent reactions increases when the client's responses are intense or extreme. If a counselor has reason to believe that a client is a danger to self or others, he or she needs to assess the situation to determine *intent* (whether immediate or future), *availability of means, lethality of means,* and *whether there is a definite plan.* (See Chapter 7 for a more complete description of suicide assessment and intervention.)

When assessing each of the three domains, the counselor must determine not only the client's predominant response in each category but also the severity of the reactions on each scale. Myer (2001) suggested that crisis intervention should focus initially on the client's most severe reaction, realizing that the intensity of responses varies throughout the crisis experience, so continued assessment, flexibility, and adaptation are needed.

As stated earlier, assessment takes place throughout the crisis intervention process. Two other counselor functions that occur during crisis intervention are *listening* and *acting.* To explain how these functions are enacted, we next describe James and Gilliland's *Six-Step Model of Crisis Intervention* (cited in James, 2008).

Six-Step Model of Crisis Intervention

Step 1   Defining the Problem.   The first step in the model is to "define and understand the problem from the client's point of view" (James, 2008, p. 39). Core counseling skills, which include empathy, genuineness, and unconditional positive regard, are essential to this step of intervention. Giving clients a chance to tell their stories not only helps with assessment but also helps clients "turn down the volume" of powerful feelings and reengage cognitive processes (Bauer, 2001). An important purpose of crisis intervention is to help clients take steps toward stabilizing emotionally and reengaging cognitively.

BOX 8–2

Human beings are not wired to think after a crisis; we are wired to act and react. Unfortunately, many important decisions must be made and problems solved in post-crisis moments. Poor choices can complicate and increase the painful impact of surviving a tragedy. The sooner survivors have access to relatively clear thinking, the sooner they can begin making thoughtful decisions. Crisis responders facilitate this reconnection to thinking by helping survivors turn their experience from jumbled fragments into a coherent story.

(Bauer, 2001, p. 242)

Step 2 Ensuring Client Safety. Ensuring client safety means "minimizing the physical and psychological danger to self and others" (James, 2008, p. 39). Throughout crisis intervention, keeping clients safe must be of primary concern. Both the external environment and the client's internal processing of events need to be taken into account. Specific ways to assess the lethality of suicidal clients and provide for their safety are described in Chapter 7.

Step 3 Providing Support. Through words, actions, and body language, the counselor needs to convey to the client genuine caring and support. It is not sufficient for the counselor to simply think he or she is being supportive. Rather, a key goal is to find ways to ensure that *the client perceives the counselor* as supportive, nonjudgmental, and involved.

Step 4 Examining Alternatives. The next three steps of crisis intervention involve the use of strategies to help clients make appropriate choices and restore equilibrium. In Step 4 of the model, the counselor helps the client explore a range of options and alternatives. Part of the exploration includes encouraging the client to identify available support sources and coping mechanisms. Identifying resources and coping mechanisms and exercising constructive thinking patterns can help lessen clients' stress and anxiety.

Step 5 Making Plans. This step is the logical follow-up to Step 4. Clients are encouraged to select from the different alternatives that were explored and then make specific plans for implementing the selected option. In this step, it is important for the counselor to work collaboratively with clients, thereby supporting their independence, power, and self-respect. Clients need an opportunity to restore their personal sense of control, which often is severely shaken in crisis situations.

Step 6 Obtaining Commitment. In this step, the counselor encourages commitment to definite positive action steps that will help the client move toward precrisis equilibrium. It is important for action steps to be uncomplicated and clearly articulated, thereby increasing the probability of the steps being enacted. It also is essential to make plans for follow-up with the client. Depending on the situation, follow-up may include ongoing counseling or a referral to an appropriate source for continued assistance.

The six-step model of crisis intervention presents an organized framework to guide counselors as they work with clients who have experienced crisis or trauma. It provides a way to help clients manage the emerging feelings, concerns, and situations that they may experience.

Throughout the crisis intervention process, counselors assess the person and the situation to ensure that the client is safe, evaluate resources, and make decisions about how to intervene most effectively. Counselors use effective listening, communication, and problem-solving skills to help clients in crisis regain equilibrium, make sense of their situation, and resolve the crisis in a healthy manner.

Reflections on Counseling After Crisis

Crisis intervention is demanding, intensive work that requires specific skills, attributes, and attitudes on the part of the counselor. Prolonged exposure to clients who have experienced tragedy can lead to *compassion fatigue,* or *secondary traumatization* (James, 2008). Finding ways to prevent compassion fatigue or burnout are critical if counselors are going to provide crisis services effectively.

BOX 8–3

After the September 11 terrorist attacks, I (Gladding) was asked to go to New York to work as a "mental health technician" for the American Red Cross. For a week, I worked at the Family Assistance Center on Pier 94. There I saw survivors of the tragedy and worked with them to help process the wide range of feelings—from denial to grief—that they felt. My job was to assist individuals in making applications for death certificates of their loved ones. I was an escort who walked with families from the front of the building to the back and talked with them about what they were feeling, what they had felt, or what they were doing in regard to the emotions that would be coming. I also accompanied families to Ground Zero so they could see for themselves the horror and finality of the event. The view of the site helped many individuals begin the process of grieving in depth as they realized in a stark and striking way that those they had loved and cherished in so many ways were indeed dead and would not be coming back to be with them.

From these experiences and other related incidents, I learned a great deal more than I ever anticipated about the nature of counseling, clients, and even myself. The lessons I learned have some universal application for persons who enter almost any crisis situation. They are especially applicable to crises that may seem on the surface overwhelming. In the midst of working with people who are in a crisis, counselors need to make sure they:

- Are mentally healthy to begin with
- Interact in positive and professional ways with colleagues
- Stay flexible and prepare for the unexpected
- Find out about resources and support personnel in the community to whom they can make referrals
- Realize the power of small acts of kindness, such as a sympathetic word
- Be mindful of the influence of nonverbal actions that lend support to those in need, from giving them tissues to offering them symbols of comfort
- Take care of themselves through physical exercise, keeping a journal, taking in needed nourishment, and debriefing regularly

Counseling after a crisis is a time filled with heavy emotion. It is a time of opportunity as well as one of turmoil. It demands much of counselors. Knowing what to expect can make the experience both positive and productive. The lessons I took away from my experiences in New York can be applied to many types of crisis situations—both large-scale community trauma and individualized, personal crisis events.

Disaster Mental Health Training

Within recent years, increasing attention has been given to disaster mental health (DMH) and to DMH interventions. Although it would be beyond the scope of this text to describe the many components related to disaster mental health services, many clinical mental health counselors will choose to participate in DMH training. Morgan (1995) described DMH as the field application of crisis intervention. Workers in DMH are often called on to help with national and international disaster relief. The American Counseling Association, the American Red Cross, the International Critical Incident Stress Foundation (ICISF), the National Organization for Victim Assistance (NOVA), the Salvation Army, and other organizations assist in training thousands of people annually in crisis intervention services as they apply to large-scale disasters.

The types of training for emergency response vary from organization to organization. For example, *Crisis Incident Stress Debriefing*, also referred to as the *Mitchell Model* (Mitchell & Everly, 1996), is a seven-phase structured group approach that usually is provided 1 to 10 days after the crisis and is "designed to mitigate acute symptoms, assess the need for follow-up, and if possible provide a sense of post crisis psychological closure" (Everly & Mitchell, n.d., p. 1). The American Red Cross trains disaster mental health workers to respond across the continuum of disaster preparedness, response, and recovery. Clinicians interested in participating in this training should contact their local Red Cross division. The Salvation Army trains crisis responders to provide emotional and spiritual care to meet the needs of both disaster responders and disaster-affected families and individuals. Yet another form of disaster response, which is supported by mental health experts as the "acute intervention of choice," is Psychological First Aid (PFA; National Child Traumatic Stress Network and National Center for PTSD, 2006). A field operations guide describing PFA is available on www.nctsn.org and www.ncptsd.va.gov.

Whereas some crises are, to an extent, a part of life, the manner in which people cope with crises and other stressors depends largely on their ability to access resources and personal strengths. Certainly, many crises are unavoidable and have devastating effects on many individuals. For other crises, however, proactive, preventive actions can lead to the avoidance of a crisis event altogether and build resilience in people so that the unavoidable crises are managed more effectively. In the next section, we focus on the essential clinical mental health counseling service of prevention.

PREVENTION

Definition of Prevention

A primary philosophical emphasis throughout the history of the counseling profession has been on preventing psychological distress by building on strengths and facilitating healthy development. The term *prevention,* however, is somewhat ambiguous, and professionals in mental health fields have struggled with its definition (Romano & Hage, 2000). The literal definition of prevention is to stop something from happening (e.g., cancer, depression, or suicide). Gerald Caplan added to this definition as early as 1964 by differentiating among three types of prevention: *primary, secondary,* and *tertiary. Primary prevention* occurs "before the fact" and refers to prevention efforts that attempt to reduce the number of new occurrences of a disorder. The goal of primary prevention is to keep healthy people healthy by increasing environmental resources or bolstering personal competencies (Scileppi, Teed, & Torres, 2000).

Secondary prevention is targeted toward people at risk of developing a mental health problem or who are exhibiting early symptoms of a disorder. The goal is to work with these individuals to forestall or alleviate problems before they become more severe. *Tertiary prevention* refers to efforts aimed at reducing the debilitating effects of an existing disorder. Tertiary prevention can also be conceptualized as treatment, remediation, or reactive intervention.

BOX 8–4

Thus, a preventive perspective is not concerned with pathology but with health. It is not focused on reparation of existing problems but on helping people and human systems to avoid problems in living and more intractable dysfunctions. It is directed at larger numbers of people, not at individuals taken one at a time. And, it embraces an ecological, multicultural, systemic approach to help giving.

(Conyne, 2000, p. 840)

Although the lines differentiating among the three types of prevention are not always distinct, in this section we focus on primary prevention and its implementation. Primary prevention can include doing something in the present to prevent something undesirable from happening in the future, or doing something in the present that will permit or increase desirable outcomes in the future (Albee & Ryan-Finn, 1993). The following descriptions provide clarification about the nature of primary prevention (Conyne, 2000, p. 840):

- Primary prevention is intended to decrease the incidences of new cases of any designated disorder.
- Primary prevention occurs through intentionally and collaboratively planned programs that are comprehensive, multilevel, multimethod, and interdisciplinary.
- Primary prevention programs are designed and implemented from a contextual, ecological perspective, taking into account multicultural and societal variables.
- Primary prevention is conducted to reduce risk factors (e.g., stressors, exploitation) while building protective factors (e.g., self-esteem, career aspirations).
- Primary prevention results in an empowered concordance between people and systems. Efforts are made to help make the person–environmental fit more satisfying, effective, and productive.

Primary prevention promotes healthy lifestyles by introducing preventive maneuvers that reduce the chances that a health problem will occur (Kaplan, 2000). It involves reducing negative influences, such as toxic lifestyles and environments, and strengthening resistance to stress through the development of coping skills, interpersonal skills, intrapersonal strengths, and support systems. Prevention may involve direct services, aimed at helping people build competencies, and indirect services, targeted toward changing specific environmental factors (Lewis et al., 2003). Furthermore, prevention efforts can be population based, group based, or individually based (Capuzzi & Gross, 2004).

Rationale for Prevention

BOX 8–5

Comprehensive models of prevention must legitimize indirect services that enhance the lives of our client populations.

(Vera, 2000, p. 835)

Prevention provides the most efficient way of helping promote mental health among the largest number of people. Whereas unquestionably there will continue to be a need for reactive interventions—individuals will continue to experience emotional distress and direct counseling may be needed to help alleviate that distress—greater emphasis on proactive, primary prevention provides opportunities to reach more people before distress is experienced. Albee (2000) argued for increased attention to major preventive efforts for these reasons:

> The data are clear: At least a third of the population of the United States suffers debilitating emotional distress, yet the overwhelming majority of publications, public information, volunteer citizen's groups, news releases, presidential commissions, White House conferences, and so forth focus on individual treatment. To me, this whole situation is a flagrant example of denial. We have pitifully few resources with which to offer one-to-one treatment, yet we deny the importance of primary prevention. And too often when we discuss prevention, it is in terms of small-scale educational or inspirational programs, not major efforts. (p. 846)

Primary prevention is time efficient and cost efficient. It also is consistent with the bioecological approach to clinical mental health counseling outlined in Chapter 2. When primary prevention efforts are targeted toward the proximal and distal environments in which people live and work, the likelihood of promoting mental health among individuals, communities, and the society at large is enhanced.

Although the need for prevention is theoretically at the core of professional counseling, there has been a general resistance to implementing large-scale prevention efforts (Lewis et al., 2003). To illustrate, surveys of mental health journals (e.g., the *Journal of Mental Health Counseling*) reveal that considerably more attention is devoted to treatment of conditions than to preventive counseling (Kiselica & Look, 1993; Kleist, 1999). Several factors contribute to this resistance. First, only small portions of budgets for mental health services are allocated for prevention programs (Scileppi et al., 2000). Monetary resources are limited, and from a political perspective, it is difficult to divert scarce resources from people who are already suffering from mental disorders. Similarly, most third-party reimbursement is based on a medical diagnosis and typically does not cover preventive interventions. Also, it has been noted that many training programs for counselors and other mental health workers do not offer specific courses on preventive interventions (Kleist, 1999). Consequently, even though strong arguments have been made for primary prevention, agencies may lack the funds, and mental health workers may lack the knowledge and skills needed to implement comprehensive preventive programs (Romano & Hage, 2000).

Many scholars and practitioners have called for a renewed emphasis on prevention among counseling professionals (e.g., Albee, 2000; Conyne, 2000; Kleist, 1999; Romano & Hage, 2000). Prevention outcome research provides strong evidence that prevention is "a highly effective strategy for enhancing the quality of mental health in the community" (Scileppi et al., 2000, p. 80). Prevention efforts targeted toward wellness, health promotion, and resiliency can help people circumvent avoidable problems of living and navigate the unavoidable problems more effectively. For prevention programs to be successful, they need to be well designed, skillfully implemented, targeted toward a specific population and/or setting, and culturally sensitive. It also is important, after implementation, to evaluate their effectiveness (Conyne, 1991).

Prevention Models

Various models of effective primary prevention have been described in prevention literature. One such model is Bloom's (1996) *configural equation* of prevention, which focuses on three broad dimensions. Prevention efforts can be directed toward:

a. Increasing individual strengths and decreasing individual limitations (e.g., enhancing self-efficacy or teaching stress-reduction techniques)
b. Increasing social supports and decreasing social stresses (e.g., promoting self-help groups or drug information hotlines)
c. Enhancing environmental resources (e.g., community programs) and minimizing environmental pressures (e.g., targeting poverty, providing services following natural disasters)

Albee's *incidence formula* (Albee & Gullotta, 1997) provides another way to conceptualize the prevention of psychological difficulties. The incidence formula model emphasizes the need to bolster people's coping skills, self-esteem, and support systems. Prevention strategies also can be directed at reducing negative effects of certain biological conditions (e.g., predispositions to physical and mental conditions) and environmental stress. Lewis et al. (2003) adapted Albee's original formula, adding the variables of *personal power* and *powerlessness*. The adapted formula is depicted in Figure 8–2.

Preventive programs designed to increase personal attributes, skills, and support and decrease external and internal stressors may be directed toward individuals and/or the environments in which they live and work. Strategies to increase personal power and decrease powerlessness may involve systemic interventions directed at unjust social conditions, which we describe later in the section on advocacy.

THE WHEEL OF WELLNESS AND THE INDIVISIBLE SELF MODELS.   In Chapter 5 we described the renewed focus the counseling profession has placed on wellness, based on the assumption that optimal growth involves an active concentration on developing the body, mind, and spirit so that optimum health and well-being are achieved (Myers, Sweeney, & Witmer, 2000). Emphasizing wellness and helping people optimize personal wellness is one form of prevention. The *Wheel of Wellness* (Myers et al., 2000; Sweeney & Witmer, 1991; Witmer & Sweeney, 1992) is a holistic theoretical model of wellness that was designed to illustrate characteristics associated with healthy people.

As can be seen in Figure 8–3, the wheel consists of five major life tasks: *spirituality, self-direction, work and leisure, friendship,* and *love. Spirituality* is at the center of the wheel and is considered the most important component of well-being. Twelve subtasks associated with the five major tasks are listed in the spokes of the wheel: *sense of worth, sense of control, realistic beliefs, emotional awareness and coping, problem solving and creativity, sense of humor, nutrition, exercise, self-care, stress management, gender identity,* and *cultural identity.* Life tasks are influenced by life forces, including family, community, education, religion, and

$$\text{Psychological health} = \frac{\text{Coping Skills} + \text{Self-Esteem} + \text{Social Support} + \text{Personal Power}}{\text{Organic Factors} + \text{Stress} + \text{Powerlessness}}$$

FIGURE 8–2   An equation for psychological health

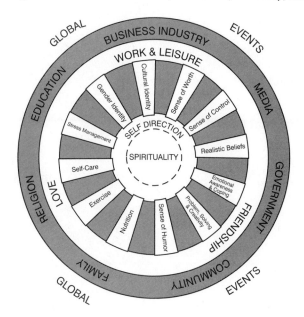

FIGURE 8–3   **The Wheel of Wellness**

Note. From *The Wheel of Wellness* (p. 10), by J. M. Witmer, T. J. Sweeney, and J. E. Myers, 1998, Greensboro, NC: Authors. Copyright 1998 by Witmer et al. Reprinted with permission.

government. Life forces and life tasks are influenced by external global factors, both natural (e.g., catastrophic events) and human (e.g., war; Myers et al., 2000).

Whereas the Wheel of Wellness model is theoretical in nature, statistical analyses did not support its structure. Consequently, Hattie, Myers, and Sweeney (2004) used findings from those analyses to devise an empirically supported model of wellness: *The Indivisible Self.* The model is grounded in Adlerian concepts, particularly the concept of holism (Myers & Sweeney, 2005). A model of *The Indivisible Self* (IS-Wel model) is presented in Figure 8–4. Counselors can use the model in counseling to help clients assess personal wellness and evaluate choices that they can make to enhance wellness. The five primary factors that comprise the IS-Wel are (a) the creative self, (b) the coping self, (c) the social self, (d) the essential self, and (e) the physical self. For definitions of all the components of the IS-Wel model, readers are referred to Myers and Sweeney's article, "Wellness Counseling: The Evidence Base for Practice" (2008).

Ways to Use the Indivisible Self Model in Counseling:

1. *Introduction of the Wellness Model.*   First the concept of wellness is defined, the model is introduced, and the connection between healthy living and overall well-being is described.

2. *Assessment of the Wellness Components.*   The Five Factor Wellness Inventory (5F-Wel; Myers & Sweeney, 2005) is used to provide information about levels of functioning in specific areas of wellness. Clients are encouraged to examine their scores, evaluate how those scores match their personal perceptions, and make decisions about what areas could be strengthened.

CONTEXTS:

Local (safety)
Family
Neighborhood
Community

Institutional (policies & laws)
Education
Religion
Government
Business/Industry

Global (world events)
Politics
Culture
Global Events
Environment
Media
Community

Chronometrical (lifespan)
Perpetual
Positive
Purposeful

FIGURE 8–4   **The Indivisible Self: An Evidenced-Based Model of Wellness**

3. *Development of a Personal Wellness Plan.* This step can be conducted individually when designing counseling interventions for a particular client. When designing prevention programs, counselors can use the information gained from the initial assessment to determine which areas of focus might benefit the most people and then design programs accordingly. In either case, the plan should include specific objectives for change, methods for accomplishing change, and resources available to facilitate the process (Myers & Sweeney, 2005).

4. *Evaluation and Follow-Up.* Plans for evaluation and follow-up need to accompany whatever prevention (or intervention) strategy is implemented. Counselors can help participants identify markers of change to indicate short- and long-term goal accomplishment and to evaluate the overall success of the program.

General prevention models, including those constructed by Bloom (1996), Albee and Gullotta (1997), and Myers and Sweeney (2005), serve as road maps for guiding the development of wellness and prevention programs. Although each model is distinct, the three share common characteristics, including a holistic emphasis that takes into account individual and environmental factors. Guided by these or other models, counselors will want to design prevention strategies based on the specific needs of the populations with which they are working.

Examples of exemplary prevention programs are numerous. Efficacious prevention programs have been implemented with preschoolers, children, adolescents, and adults. Many of the programs directed toward children and youth focus on life skills, such as interpersonal communication, problem solving and decision making, physical fitness and health maintenance, and identity development (e.g., Darden, Gazda, & Ginter, 1996; Ginter, 1999). Prevention programs for adults also address life skills, with some programs geared toward specific concerns, such as eating disorders, violence, parenting, and stress management. Because everyone suffers from physical and emotional stress of some nature, stress management is an especially important area to consider when designing prevention programs. Stress management programs can be adapted for all ages and provide a variety of physical and mental health benefits. For these reasons, a brief overview of stress, coping, and stress management is provided next.

Stress Management

The relationship among stress, coping, and well-being has received much attention during the past several decades (Romano, 2001). *Stress* is a construct that has been defined in multiple ways. It can be viewed as a relationship between the events that happen to us and our physical, cognitive, emotional (i.e., affective), and behavioral responses to them (McNamara, 2000). Stress can refer to an internal state, an external event, or the interaction between a person and the environment. A more formal definition, offered by Lazarus and Folkman (1984), describes stress as "a particular relationship between the person and the environment that is appraised by the person as taxing or exceeding his or her resources and endangering his or her well-being" (p. 19). Perceptions of what is stressful vary widely among individuals, with some people viewing certain events as quite stressful and others being nonplussed by them.

Anything perceived as a source of threat, harm, loss, or challenge has the potential to be stressful. Stressors may be chronic (e.g., living in poverty), acute (e.g., death of a spouse), or ongoing daily aggravations (e.g., arguing between siblings). Exposure to stress triggers several physical, emotional, and cognitive changes. Immediate, short-term reactions to stress can potentially motivate people toward action; however, long-term exposure can lead to physical and psychosocial difficulties (Sharrer & Ryan-Wenger, 2002). Coping with stress is the process by which a person handles stressful situations and the thoughts and emotions they generate.

Prevention programs to help people manage stress effectively typically focus on (a) identifying sources of stress, (b) recognizing the physical and emotional consequences of stress, and (c) learning and implementing adaptive coping responses. McNamara (2000) suggested that counselors include the following eight components in stress management programs:

1. ***Education about the causes and consequences of stress.*** Education includes helping people recognize sources of stress in their own lives and their cognitive, physical, and emotional responses to stress.
2. ***Training in methods to reduce psychological and physical arousal.*** Counselors can use deep breathing and relaxation exercises to help people reduce their reactions to stress.
3. ***General problem-solving and decision-making skills.*** Helping people construct a model for problem solving and decision making can help establish a healthy sense of control.

• Clarify your goals.	What is the most important and why?
• Avoid procrastination.	Establish a routine and reward yourself for completing tasks.
• Keep a calendar or day-timer.	Write down meetings, scheduled events, assignments, etc.
• Break down large tasks into manageable units.	Make plans for completing each unit.
• Keep a daily and weekly "to do" list.	Prioritize activities and tasks and check them off when they are completed.
• Recognize the need for balance and flexibility.	Include breaks and recreational times that coincide with your body clock.
• Keep things in perspective.	Worry saps time and energy and is nonproductive. If you find yourself getting anxious, take time to relax and practice deep breathing.

FIGURE 8–5   Time management tools

4. **General cognitive skills.**   Cognitive restructuring, including reducing negative or catastrophic thinking, can also provide a sense of control that helps reduce stress.

5. **Physical ways of coping with stress.**   Nutrition, physical activity, and sleep quality all affect people's psychological well-being. Developing and practicing good habits in each of these areas can help reduce stress.

6. **Time management.**   Time management tools are essential for handling stress effectively. Setting achievable goals, balancing work and leisure, and organizing tasks are examples of time management tools. Additional examples are listed in Figure 8–5.

7. **Skills for increasing self-control and self-esteem.**   Anger management skills can be taught to facilitate self-control. Counselors also can help people identify and develop personal strengths, thus building resilience.

8. **Social skills.**   Social skills training includes effective communication, conflict resolution, and assertiveness training.

Stress management programs are often implemented in schools, work settings, universities, and community agencies. It is important for clinical mental health counselors to be able to plan, implement, and evaluate stress management programs for the populations with which they work.

Many chronic stressors, including poverty, discrimination, and prejudice, are systemic in nature and need to be addressed accordingly. Albee (2000) stated, "The longer I work in the field of prevention, the more convinced I become that economic, social-class variables are most important in perpetuating stress, social injustice, and exploitation" (p. 850). Lewis et al. (2003) collectively referred to individuals who experience a similar kind of stress for an extended time as *vulnerable populations*. Examples of vulnerable populations include people who are poor, homeless, and unemployed; families undergoing divorce; pregnant teenagers; people with chronic diseases such as AIDS; and people victimized by discrimination. To address the needs of vulnerable populations, counselors are urged to engage in advocacy, outreach, and social action, which are described next.

ADVOCACY

The 1999 Presidential Theme for the American Counseling Association was *Advocacy: A Voice for Our Clients and Communities.* During recent years, much attention has been directed toward the advocacy role of counselors. Advocacy counseling expands the traditional role of individual counseling, which focuses on intrapersonal concerns, to a broader focus that addresses injustices and environmental conditions that need to improve for the benefit of an individual or group (Kiselica & Robinson, 2001). In this section, we define advocacy as it relates to community and agency counseling and discuss roles counselors can take to advocate for their clients.

What Is Advocacy?

Several definitions of advocacy have been proposed. For example, Toporek (2000) defined *advocacy* as actions taken by counseling professionals to help remove environmental barriers that hamper clients' well-being. Ezell (2001) described advocacy as "purposive efforts to change specific existing or proposed policies or practices on behalf of or with a specific client or group of clients" (p. 23). Lewis et al. (2003) noted that advocacy serves two purposes: (a) to increase clients' sense of personal power and (b) to foster environmental changes that reflect greater responsiveness to clients' personal needs. Lee (2006a) defined advocacy as "action a counselor takes to facilitate the removal of external and institutional barriers to clients' well-being" (p. 147).

Outreach, empowerment, social justice, and *social action* are all terms associated with advocacy. *Outreach* refers to initiating behaviors toward people in need for the purpose of making a helpful difference. It involves reaching out to vulnerable populations in their communities and helping them find new ways to cope with stressors (Lewis et al., 2003). *Empowerment* is a process through which clients gain the resources and skills needed to have more control over their environments and their lives (McWhirter, 1997). *Social justice* "involves promoting access and equity to ensure full participation of all people in the life of a society," particularly those members of society who have been marginalized (Lee, 2006a, p. xiv). *Social action* refers to behaviors designed to promote social justice. Social action can occur on behalf of a client or on the larger society in which we live. It is designed to eradicate social inequities, which may limit or obstruct vulnerable groups' access to basic societal rights. Whereas the terms *social justice* and *social action* are similar, *social justice* can be considered a belief system that values fair and equal treatment for all members of society. *Social action* derives from that belief system, resulting in actions taken to promote equal rights for all people. *Advocacy counseling* can include outreach, empowerment, and social action, which is rooted in the concept of social justice. Advocacy serves to enhance a client's sense of personal power and/or foster change in the broader sociopolitical environment.

As noted earlier, empowering individuals and diminishing societal forces that cause powerlessness among certain groups are ways to promote psychological health (refer back to Figure 8–2). Advocacy counseling can be conceptualized on a continuum, with empowerment of the individual client on one end of the continuum and social action to reduce oppression, discrimination, and other forms of injustice on the other end (Toporek, 2000). Consequently, the counselor's role as an advocate can range from designing interventions that empower individual clients to taking actions that influence public policy and institutional change.

EMPOWERMENT.   Facilitating empowerment in counseling is a way to focus on the individual client within the context of his or her sociopolitical environment. It may involve helping a woman who is being abused become aware of the inappropriate use of power and privilege that her partner is claiming. Or it may involve helping a client recognize an environmental barrier (e.g., discrimination in the workplace) and then make a plan to overcome it (Toporek, 2000). According to McWhirter (1994, 1997), empowerment is a lifelong process that involves critical self-reflection and action, an awareness of the power dynamics in the environment that affect diverse populations, and the development of skills to gain personal power and empower others.

To help counselors understand the concept of empowerment, McWhirter (1994, 1997) designed a "5 C's" model of empowerment for counseling, which includes the following components:

- *Collaboration,* which involves working collaboratively with clients to define the problem and plan for change. It also includes taking steps to decrease the inherent power differential between counselor and client.
- *Context,* which refers to acknowledging the role of factors such as poverty, racism, sexism, and other barriers in maintaining or exacerbating clients' problems.
- *Critical consciousness,* which is fostered by critical self-reflection and power analysis. The goal is to raise client awareness of the social, economic, and other power dynamics that affect their well-being.
- *Competence,* which focuses on clients' strengths, resources, and skills that can be used to help resolve the problem.
- *Community,* which may be defined broadly to include family, friends, ethnicity, faith, organizational affiliations, or other bonds. Connection with the community is essential to the empowerment process because it provides resources and support as well as opportunities for the client to "give back" by empowering others.

Key outcomes of empowerment are an enhanced sense of personal control and the ability to advocate for oneself. To facilitate self-advocacy in clients, counselors first need to be aware that counseling has the potential to encourage dependence in that it presupposes neediness (McWhirter, 1997). Rather than act as "rescuers," effective advocates help clients develop and utilize strengths and resources, both personally and in their communities.

BOX 8–7

My First Professional Role in a Community Counseling Setting: Counselor, Advocate, and Team Member

After graduating from Wake Forest University with a master's degree in counselor education with an emphasis on community counseling, I joined a county mental health agency as a mental health practitioner, serving clients who have severe and persistent mental illness (SPMI). I am part of a team modeled after PACT (Program for Assertive Community Treatment), a nationally known model developed by Deborah J. Allness, M.S.S.W.M.D. and William H. Knoedler, M.D. The program is designed specifically for mental health professionals serving the SPMI population within the communities in which they live. Our treatment team is multidisciplined, meeting each day to plan and coordinate care for clients, before going out into the community.

I realized early that I could apply the principles, theories, and counseling traditions learned during my educational training, practicum, and internship, as well as from my previous life experiences. My most challenging lesson to date is *patience*—not as much with clients, but rather with systems—the systems and agencies that must be choreographed and coerced in order to provide services. Building rapport and relationships among colleagues and others in the larger support system is especially important. It has taken little time to discover that I am not only a client's counselor, but also an advocate. Thus, I have also learned to advocate for myself as a professional counselor as well as ONE member of a dynamic mental health team.

Advocating for clients requires addressing stigmas every day, personal as well as those of the health, welfare, social services systems, and correctional facilities. In this environment, it is paramount to remember that ALL clients have rights, privileges, and expectations. Respecting differences and using power judiciously means sometimes adjusting MY counseling expectations to a new reality. In the classroom, diagnosis, treatment, and outcomes are stressed and garner importance. Working with the SPMI population teaches an additional lesson: Maintaining psychiatric stability is often an outcome to be celebrated.

Additional considerations that accompany the formidable tasks of effective assessment, diagnosing, and treatment planning are client issues of substance abuse, physical illness, intellectual functioning deficits, criminal history, and poor family support. A team approach incorporating biopsychosocial assessment that leads to the development of treatment plans that can be actualized is extremely important. The services we provide our clients are often their most consistent resources and activities available, thus demanding that each intervention encourage support and greater self-sufficiency rather than build dependence.

In summary, counseling in a community agency setting and working with SPMI clients has many unique and difficult challenges. In addition, the possibilities for personal and professional growth are tremendous. My decision to become a counselor is validated by the struggles and triumphs that I share each day with the clients, members of my team, and the larger pool of mental health professionals with whom I work.

Tom Buffkin, M.A. Ed., LPC, NCC

SOCIAL ACTION. Counselors committed to social action are involved in confronting barriers faced by clients or client groups in their sociopolitical context (Toporek, 2000). Social action may be directed toward agencies, communities, the legal system, and legislation (Ezell, 2001). Social action can address immediate environmental concerns (e.g., advocating for changes to make a specific facility more accessible to people with disabilities) or more global concerns (e.g., becoming actively involved in legislative or policy issues that adversely affect groups of people). Advocating for mental health parity to ensure that mental health-care benefits are covered in the same way as other health-care benefits is one form of social action. Other examples of social action include advocating for public policy changes on behalf of the homeless and making community presentations to advocate for fair and respectful treatment of lesbian, gay, and bisexual individuals.

Counselors for Social Justice, a division of the American Counseling Association, provides an organized forum through which counselors can advocate for oppressed populations. Counselors for Social Justice (CSJ) was established in 1999 as an organizational affiliate and officially became an ACA division in September 2002. The mission of CSJ is "to work to promote social justice in our society through confronting oppressive systems of power and privilege that affect professional counselors and our clients and to assist in the positive change in our society through the professional development of counselors." (CSJ, 2007). CSJ promotes individual and collective social responsibility, provides a support network for counselors engaged in social justice activities, and collaborates with other organizations in ACA and the larger community to implement social action strategies.

Advocacy Skills and Attributes

A number of skills and attributes are needed to engage in advocacy successfully. At the core of successful advocating is a compassionate spirit that is sensitive to human suffering and committed to helping alleviate that suffering (Kiselica & Robinson, 2001). Compassion and commitment provide the necessary motivation to take action related to an identified need (Myers et al., 2002). Once a need is identified, counselors need skills to identify specific areas to target, keeping the bigger picture in mind. Social change usually does not occur quickly, and when changes are made, it takes time to implement and evaluate those changes (Ezell, 2001). To this end, advocates demonstrate planfulness, persistence, and patience.

To advocate successfully, counselors use many of the same verbal and nonverbal communication skills that are essential to effective counseling. Advocates need to be able to listen and respond empathically to vulnerable clients so that they feel understood and heard. Beyond that, counselors need to develop strong skills in persuasion, conflict resolution, compromise, and negotiation (Ezell, 2001). Also, to advocate successfully, counselors need skills in communicating effectively with the power sources from which change will originate. For example, when communicating with legislators, it is important to be organized, concise, and concrete. The use of jargon, exaggeration, or rambling hurts a counselor's presentation.

Other skills associated with advocacy include integrity, flexibility, resourcefulness, and the ability to prioritize. In addition, advocates need skills in assessing situations accurately; knowledge of laws, policies, and legal processes; capabilities in using the media and technology; an understanding of community organization and development; and a commitment to ethical standards (Kurpius & Rozecki, 1992).

In summarizing skills and practices related to advocacy, Ezell (2001) stated that effective advocates do the following:

- Provide vigorous representation for their clients
- Use multiple methods to understand their clients' needs, issues, and problems
- Target specific policies or practices for change
- Map the decision systems responsible for targeted policies and practices
- Recast larger problems into solvable pieces
- Propose concrete solutions to problems

- Utilize several strategies and skills simultaneously and sequentially
- Actively counter negative stereotypes and misbeliefs
- Use the least conflictual tactics necessary to accomplish their objectives
- Exhibit cultural awareness and respect as they relate to colleagues, clients, and decision makers
- Place a high priority on influencing budgets
- Closely monitor the implementation of changed policies and practices (p. 193)

Challenges of Advocacy

Advocacy can be challenging work, particularly if efforts are not made to avoid certain pitfalls. Because of the personal investment involved, advocacy can be emotionally draining and lead to burnout if professionals do not set limits and boundaries (Ezell, 2001). Also, it is important for advocates to evaluate themselves and their motives, being careful to avoid overzealousness and blind idealism (Kiselica & Robinson, 2001). Out of the desire to help vulnerable populations, it is possible to move ahead too quickly, not respecting existing barriers and perhaps even creating additional ones. Similarly, in attempting to right a wrong, advocates may tend to exaggerate claims about specific problems, an action that is unethical.

In addition to moving too quickly, it also is possible to assume responsibility for too much. McWhirter (1997) noted that "the number of issues that lend themselves to social activism is virtually endless" (p. 10). Focusing on specific issues, such as violence against women, affordable housing, or community assistance for seniors, enables counselors to channel energies more effectively than attempting to address an assortment of societal ills. Albee (2000) reminded us that not everyone needs to become a revolutionary; there is room in the field for all levels of intervention.

Advocacy for the Profession

Although our primary purpose in this section is to describe advocacy for client well-being, a related form of advocacy is for the counseling profession itself, which, according to Myers et al. (2002), is a professional imperative. Professional advocacy includes contributing to the development of a strong professional identity, lobbying for professional recognition, and demonstrating professional pride and accountability. It may include working through the political process by influencing legislation that affects the profession of counseling, such as obtaining government-funded reimbursement for licensed professional counselors and lobbying for mental health parity. Engaging in professional advocacy benefits clients because it helps ensure that counselors are recognized as competent and credible mental health service providers.

To successfully advocate for the counseling profession, clinical mental health counselors need to stay abreast of public policy and take steps to influence the passage of laws when conditions adversely affect either their clients or the counseling profession. The ACA Office of Public Policy and Information is an excellent resource for federal legislative initiatives and can be accessed through the ACA Web site (www.counseling.org).

PROGRAM EVALUATION

Another key component of community counseling services is program evaluation. Evaluation enables counselors and administrators to know whether the planned services have taken place as expected and whether specific goals and outcomes were achieved (Lewis, Lewis,

Packard, & Soufleé, 2001). Evaluation results are used to make decisions about current and future services, including prevention programs; individual, group, and family counseling services; crisis programs; and outreach efforts. Systematic evaluation provides a way for counselors to reflect carefully on their counseling practices and make improvements as needed (Hadley & Mitchell, 1995; May, 1996).

Counselors who lack or fail to employ evaluation procedures place themselves and the counseling profession in jeopardy with the general public, third-party payers, and specific clients who rightfully demand accountability. A failure to evaluate counseling methods and related outcomes also puts counselors in danger of being unethical because they cannot prove that the counseling services implemented have a reasonable promise of success as the ethical codes of professional counseling associations require (Sexton & Whiston, 1996).

Purposes of Evaluation

Evaluation usually involves gathering meaningful information on various aspects of a counseling program and using those data to inform program planning and service delivery (Lewis et al., 2003; Loesch, 2001). Evaluation has a quality of immediate utility. In clinical settings, it gives counselors direct feedback on the services they provide and insight into what new services they need to offer. It also enables clients to have systematic, positive input into a counseling program. In describing counseling program evaluation (CPE), Loesch emphasized:

> The purpose of CPE is to maximize the efficiency and effectiveness of service delivery through careful and systematic examination of program components, methodologies, and outcomes. It is not the purpose of CPE simply to provide a rationale for what currently exists or is being done. Rather, CPE is used primarily to change counseling service delivery for the better. (2001, p. 513)

Lewis et al. (2001) suggested that program evaluation serves five specific purposes. First, it aids in administrative decision making. Information gathered about the outcomes of services helps administrators make informed decisions about which programs to continue and expand and which programs to eliminate or reduce. Second, evaluation can help service providers make improvements in current programs by comparing them with what was originally planned. Third, evaluation provides a way to demonstrate accountability to funding and accrediting agencies, clients, and other stakeholders. Demonstrated accountability through evaluation can help agencies gain increased support from the larger community, which is a fourth purpose of evaluation. Finally, outcome evaluation can add to the growing body of research relevant to *best practices,* also called empirically validated (or supported) treatments (Sexton, 2001). For these purposes to be accomplished, evaluation results need to be disseminated to policy makers, consumers, and service providers (Lewis et al., 2001).

Steps in Evaluation

For program evaluation to be effective, it needs to be comprehensive, systematic, and sequential. Plans for evaluation need to be made at the front end of program design, not afterward (Lewis et al., 2001). To plan and implement an effective evaluation program, it is helpful to follow a sequential process, such as the following five-step procedure outlined by Burck and Peterson (1975).

According to Burck and Peterson, the first step in formulating an evaluation program involves a needs assessment. If counselors are to be accountable, they must first identify problems or concerns within their programs. *Needs assessment* refers to a set of methods or approaches used to determine if there is a need for a certain program or intervention (Duffy & Wong, 2003). Assessments can be conducted through surveys, interviews, focus groups, and other observational or descriptive methods.

Information gathered through the needs assessment is used to identify program goals and performance objectives. Formulating goals and objectives represents the second step in program evaluation. Here, both *terminal program outcomes* (those that are most immediately recognizable) and *ultimate program outcomes* (those that are most enduring) are described in terms of measurable performance objectives. In formulating goals and objectives, it is important to identify current program strengths, limitations, and resources and prioritize within that framework.

The third step in evaluation is designing and implementing a program. Program activities are selected to address the specific goals and objectives that have been delineated. To be successful, a program needs "a well-developed plan that integrates content, methods, resources, services, marketing, and evaluation" (Lusky & Hayes, 2001, p. 32).

Program design and implementation leads to the fourth step, which is revising and improving the program. No matter how well a program is planned, responses and outcomes are not always predictable. Consequently, ongoing evaluation of the process is required, accompanied by program revisions when necessary.

The fifth and final step is assessing the program's effectiveness in relation to the stated goals and objectives. Burck and Peterson (1975) referred to this step as "noting and reporting program outcome" (p. 567). This task is performed primarily by disseminating the findings of the program evaluation to the general public. Such consumer information is vital for potential clients if they are to make informed decisions, and counselors within a clinical program need this kind of feedback to improve their skills and services. Specific ways to gather outcome information are described in a subsequent section.

Comprehensive evaluation involves many people, including service providers, administrators, clients, and often the larger community. Each of these stakeholders plays a part in determining how the evaluation is conducted. Their degree of involvement in the process varies, depending on their interests and needs, but "all help determine the nature of effective evaluation practices" (Loesch, 2001, p. 515).

Process and Outcome Evaluation

Several different models of evaluation have been described in counseling literature. Most comprehensive models provide ways to evaluate *processes* and *outcomes*. In process evaluation, the focus is on the manner in which services are being delivered. In outcome evaluation, the focus is on whether the programs produced the desired results. Both are essential components of comprehensive program evaluation.

Process evaluation, also called *formative evaluation,* provides information about how well a program is being implemented (Lewis et al., 2003). During process evaluation, evaluators determine whether the programs are operating in accordance with stated plans, objectives, and expectations. Process evaluation involves ongoing monitoring of what services are being provided, by whom, for whom, to how many, when, and at what cost (Lewis et al., 2001).

Results obtained through process evaluation inform service providers about potential changes that need to be made to enhance program delivery. For example, if a support group for battered women is not being well attended, perhaps the group is meeting at an inopportune time, or perhaps the content used during group meetings is not addressing the most pertinent needs of the participants. By conducting process evaluation, counselors can determine what is or is not working and adapt accordingly.

Outcome evaluation provides information about whether, and to what degree, the goals and objectives of the program have been achieved. Also called *summative evaluation,* outcome evaluation provides one way for counselors to demonstrate accountability for their services. *Outcomes* are the benefits that clients received as a result of participating in a particular program (Scileppi et al., 2000). Although both process and outcome evaluations rely on clearly specified objectives, process evaluation objectives usually relate to projected activities, whereas outcome evaluation objectives are stated in terms of expected results.

Outcomes can be measured in various ways, several of which are described in Figure 8–6. Some of the more common measures include goal attainment scaling, consumer satisfaction surveys, and standardized outcome assessment devices (Dougherty, 2008). Ideally, evaluators will use multiple methods of assessment that are selected to measure client changes in skills, knowledge, behaviors, or adjustment (Lewis et al., 2001). Formal, in-depth outcome evaluation that is part of a well-designed research plan can help counselors and program administrators distinguish between changes that are a result of treatment and those that are simply a result of chance occurrences. However, implementing a formal, research-oriented outcome evaluation can be very time consuming, and efforts often focus on only one program component at a time (Lewis et al., 2001). Less formal outcome evaluation methods can be implemented more efficiently but are less likely to yield definitive results about treatment effects.

In some agencies, data gathered through process and outcome evaluations are used to conduct an *efficiency evaluation*. An efficiency evaluation connects the costs of implementing a particular program with the benefits achieved by the participants. In analyzing costs, resources required for program implementation are assessed, including time, effort, and financial expenditures. A key goal of an efficiency evaluation is to determine whether the same results can be achieved by reducing time, effort, or financial cost (Lewis et al., 2001).

Quality Assurance

In many settings, *quality assurance* (QA) is an ongoing process by which the agency and outside groups monitor the quality of services offered (MacCluskie & Ingersoll, 2001). Because of the demands of accrediting organizations such as the Joint Committee of Accreditation of Healthcare Organizations (JCAHO) and the National Committee for Quality Assurance (NCQA), documented outcome evaluation that provides evidence of quality of care is crucial. Quality of care is a multidimensional construct that encompasses access and availability of care, client satisfaction with services, and adherence to recognized standards of care and service delivery (Steenbarger & Smith, 1996). It is in the best interest of community agencies to document evidence that quality services are being delivered and to seek external accreditation. External accreditation lets the public know that agencies have met certain minimum criteria for service delivery, thereby placing agencies in a better position to negotiate contracts with third-party providers (MacCluskie & Ingersoll, 2001).

Issues and Challenges of Evaluation

In principle, the concept of evaluation is relatively straightforward. In reality, however, evaluation is a complex process that can pose several challenges. One of the greatest challenges,

Measurement	Purpose	Examples
Client satisfaction surveys	To evaluate the degree to which clients feel they have received services that are useful	Client Satisfaction Questionnaire-8 (CSQ-8); (Attkisson & Greenfield, 1994)
		Service Satisfaction Scale-30 (SSS-30); (Attkisson & Greenfield, 1994)
Goal attainment scaling	To help determine the efficacy of services according to preestablished criteria	Clients evaluate their progress toward achieving specific goals using a 5-point Likert scale.
Assessments of client functioning	To measure functional status along general or specific dimensions	Global Assessment of Functioning (GAF); (*DSM-IV-TR;* APA, 2000)
		Life Functioning Scales (Howard, Orlinsky, & Bankoff, 1994)
Assessments of client symptomatology	To rate the frequency or intensity of presenting complaints	Brief Symptom Inventory (Derogatis & Lazarus, 1994)
		Brief Psychiatric Rating Scale (Faustman, 1994)
Alternative assessment approaches	To gather information about clients using methods other than traditional paper-and-pencil approaches	Performance assessment (evaluating how a person acts or behaves in given situations)

FIGURE 8–6   **Measuring outcomes: Examples of evaluation methods**

From Loesch, 2001; and Steenberger and Smith, 1996.

according to Steenbarger and Smith (1996), involves the logistics of data collection. Administration and scoring of paper-and-pencil measures can be tedious and time consuming, leading to delays in calculating and disseminating results. Another challenge relates to the gathering and interpretation of evaluation data. Finding valid and reliable methods of measuring program effectiveness is a difficult task, and method selection varies from setting to setting. Consequently, what one agency considers "effective service" may or may not be truly effective. In addition to methodological concerns, professionals may resist evaluation because of concerns about how the results are going to be used. People do not like to be judged, especially if the results of the evaluation may be used against them (Duffy & Wong, 2003). When evaluators take steps to use evaluations constructively rather than punitively and clarify the intended purposes of the evaluation from the outset, people are more likely to respond favorably.

Although the challenges described in the preceding paragraph can create barriers to program evaluation, they can be overcome if handled sensitively. When evaluation is viewed as an integral component of service delivery that benefits both staff and clients, resistance to the process is minimized and opportunities for growth and improvement are enhanced.

Summary and Conclusion

In this chapter, we have provided an overview of four essential counseling services: crisis intervention, prevention, advocacy, and evaluation. It is important for community counselors to develop skills in each of these areas. The demand for crisis intervention has risen during recent years. Many forms of trauma, including violence, natural disasters, and developmental crises, can leave people without sufficient resources to cope effectively. In such cases, counselors need to be prepared to offer services to help people navigate the uncertainty and confusion that ensue. The Six-Step Model of Crisis Intervention proposed by James and Gilliland (cited in James, 2008) provides a guide to help counselors work effectively in crisis situations.

Preventing psychological distress by helping people develop resources and strengths while reducing negative influences represents a fundamental value of the counseling profession. Primary prevention programs, which take into account individual and environmental influences, provide the most efficient way of promoting mental health among the largest number of people. The three prevention models described in the chapter emphasize the importance of enhancing individual strengths and environmental resources and decreasing individual limitations and social stresses. The Wheel of Wellness model (Myers et al., 2000) provides a theoretical guideline for optimizing health and well-being by enhancing specific life tasks, including spirituality, self-direction, work and leisure, friendship, and love. The Indivisible Self model (Myers & Sweeney, 2005a, 2008) is an evidence-based model that represents a reconfiguration of the original theoretical model.

A third service that is vital to community counseling is advocacy. Advocacy services go beyond the traditional role of individual counseling by focusing on ways to address social injustices and environmental conditions that impinge on the well-being of individuals or groups. There are many ways counselors can serve as advocates for their clients, ranging from facilitating personal empowerment to political involvement aimed at improving societal conditions. Advocating for the counseling profession also benefits clients by ensuring that the profession is recognized as a viable, credible provider of mental health services.

A fourth example of essential community counseling services is program evaluation. Evaluation provides information that is used to make decisions about current and future counseling services. Systematic evaluation, which occurs throughout the course of service delivery, provides a way to demonstrate accountability and maximize the quality of the services that are provided. Two common types of evaluation are process evaluation, which supplies information about how well a program is being implemented, and outcome evaluation, which indicates the degree to which service goals and objectives are being met.

Each of the services described in this chapter—crisis intervention, prevention, advocacy, and program evaluation—has been researched and written about extensively by professionals in the field. The information presented here provides only a brief overview of the four topics. As part of your professional preparation, we encourage you to examine some of the many excellent resources related to these service components to enhance your knowledge and skills.

Working with Specific Populations

CHAPTER 9

Working with Groups

Who am I in this pilgrim group
  whose members differ so in perception?
Am I timid like a Miles Standish,
  letting others speak for me
    because the experience of failure is softened
      if a risk is never personally taken?
Or am I more like a John Alden
  speaking boldly for others in the courting of beauty
    but not seeking such for myself?
Perhaps I am more than either man
  or maybe I'm both at different times!
In the silence and before others, I ponder the question anew.

Working in groups is a counseling specialty that is relatively new, but one that is often effective in helping individuals resolve personal and interpersonal concerns. Organized groups make use of people's natural tendency to gather and share thoughts and feelings as well as work and play cooperatively.

This chapter examines the following aspects of groups:

- Their place in counseling
- Types of groups most often used
- Realities and misperceptions about groups
- Uses of as well as advantages and limitations of groups
- The theoretical basis for conducting groups
- Stages and issues in groups
- Qualities of effective group leaders

Counselors, especially in community settings, who restrict their competencies to individual counseling and do not learn how to run groups limit their options for helping.

THE PLACE OF GROUPS IN COUNSELING

A *group* is generally considered to be "a collection of two or more individuals who meet in face-to-face interaction, interdependently, with the awareness that each belongs to the group and for the purpose of achieving individual and/or mutually agreed upon goals" (Gladding, 2006, p. 55). The exception to this definition is found in some groups who meet on the Internet, where there is no face-to-face interaction (Page et al., 2000).

Groups have a unique place in counseling. Everyone typically spends some time in group activities each day, for example, with colleagues, schoolmates, neighbors, or business associates. Gregariousness is a part of human nature, and many personal and professional skills are learned through group interactions. It is only natural, then, for counselors to make use of this primary way of human interaction. Groups are an economical and effective means of helping individuals who share similar problems and concerns.

Groups are not a new phenomenon in therapeutic work. They have a long and distinguished place in the service of counseling. Joseph Hersey Pratt is generally credited with starting the first psychologically oriented group. He did so in 1905 with tuberculosis outpatients at Massachusetts General in Boston. He found their regular group experience to be informative, supportive, and therapeutic. The following professionals were also pioneers in the group movement in the 20th century:

- Jacob L. Moreno, who introduced the term *group psychotherapy* into the counseling literature in the 1930s
- Kurt Lewin, whose field theory concepts in the 1930s and 1940s became the basis for the Tavistock small study groups in Britain and the T-group movement in the United States
- Fritz Perls, whose Gestalt approach to groups attracted new energy and interest in the field
- W. Edwards Deming, who conceptualized and implemented the idea of quality work groups to improve the processes and products people produced and to build morale among workers in businesses
- William Schutz and Jack Gibb, who emphasized a humanistic aspect to groups that focused on personal growth as a legitimate goal
- Carl Rogers, who devised the basic encounter group in the 1960s that became the model for growth-oriented group approaches

Thus, organized groups are over 100 years old. Those who have engineered and created ways of conducting them have established various types of groups as a main component within counseling.

TYPES OF GROUPS

Groups come in many forms: "There seems to be a group experience tailored to suit the interests and needs of virtually anyone who seeks psychotherapy, personal growth, or simply support and companionship from others" (Lynn & Frauman, 1985, p. 423). A number of group models are appropriate for a wide variety of situations. Although lively debate persists about how groups should be categorized, especially in regard to goals and process (Waldo &

FIGURE 9–1   The Group Work Rainbow

Note. From Robert K. Conyne, University of Cincinnati. Used with permission.

Bauman, 1998), the following types of groups have training standards developed by the Association for Specialists in Group Work (ASGW; 2000): psychoeducational, counseling, psychotherapy, and task/work (see Figure 9–1).

Psychoeducational Groups

Psychoeducational groups were originally developed for use in educational settings, specifically in schools. They are also known simply as "educational" or "guidance" groups. The primary function of these types of groups is the prevention of personal or societal disorders through the conveying of information and/or the examining of values. Psychoeducational groups stress growth through knowledge. Content includes, but is not limited to, personal, social, vocational, and educational information. For instance, group participants may be taught how to deal with a potential threat (e.g., AIDS), a developmental life event (e.g., growing older), or an immediate life crisis (e.g., the death of a loved one). Preventive and growth activities can take many forms but usually they are presented as nonthreatening exercises or group discussions (Carroll, Bates, & Johnson, 2004).

Psychoeducational group activities are offered throughout the life span in a variety of settings. Sometimes these groups take the form of life-skill development, especially for those who have a deficit of appropriate interpersonal behaviors (Gazda et al., 2005). This "how-to" approach may include the use of films, plays, demonstrations, role-plays, and guest speakers. The size of the group varies with the setting (e.g., a self-contained classroom), but the typical group size ranges from 10 to 40 individuals. The group leader has expertise in the topic being discussed and is in charge of group management and disseminating information. One of the most important parts of the process that goes on in such groups revolves around group discussions of how members will personalize the information presented in the group context. These groups are designed to meet the needs of generally well-functioning people.

Counseling Groups

Counseling groups focus on prevention, growth, and remediation. They seek to help group participants resolve the usual, yet often difficult, problems connected with interpersonal difficulties. An additional goal is to help participants develop their existing interpersonal problem-solving competencies so they may be better able to handle future problems. Nonsevere career, educational, personal, social, and developmental concerns are frequently addressed.

Because the focus of group counseling is on each person's behavior and growth or change within the group, the interaction among persons, especially in problem solving, is highlighted. Group dynamics and interpersonal relationships are emphasized. Whereas psychoeducational groups are recommended for everyone on a continuous basis, group counseling is more selective. It focuses on individuals experiencing "usual, but often difficult, problems of living" (ASGW, 1990, p. 14) that information alone will not solve.

The size of these groups varies with the ages of the individuals involved, ranging from 3 or 4 in a children's group to 8 to 12 in an adult group. The number of group meetings also fluctuates, but generally ranges from 6 to 16 sessions. The leader is in charge of facilitating the group interaction but becomes less directly involved as the group develops. Usually, the topics covered in group counseling are developmental or situational in nature, such as educational, social, career, and personal. Counseling groups tend not to be of long-standing duration. Compared with psychoeducational groups, this type of group offers a more direct approach to dealing with troublesome behaviors. The major advantages of group counseling are the interaction, feedback, and contribution of group members with each other over a period of time.

Psychotherapy Groups

Psychotherapy groups are set up to help individual group members resolve their in-depth psychological problems. They are described in the professional literature as remedial types of groups. "Because the depth and extent of the psychological disturbance is significant, the goal is to aid each individual to reconstruct major personality dimensions" (ASGW, 1992, p. 13).

At times, there is overlap in group counseling and group psychotherapy, but the emphasis on major reconstruction of personality dimensions usually distinguishes the two. The setting of group psychotherapy is often in inpatient facilities, such as hospitals or mental health facilities, because of greater control of the people involved. As an entity, psychotherapy groups may be either open ended (admitting new members at any time) or closed (not admitting new members after the first session). Certain types of individuals are poor candidates for outpatient, intensive group psychotherapy. Among these individuals are depressives, incessant talkers, paranoids, schizoid and sociopathic personalities, suicidal personalities, and extreme narcissists (Yalom & Leszcz, 2005). It may be easier to identify group psychotherapy candidates who should be excluded than to pick those who should be included. Regardless, group psychotherapy is an American form of treatment and has provided much of the rationale for group counseling.

One of the primary aims of the group psychotherapy process is to reconstruct, through in-depth analysis, the personalities of those involved (Gazda, Ginter, & Horne, 2001). The size of the group varies from two or three to a dozen. Members meet for a period of months, or even years. The group leader has expertise in one of the mental health disciplines (psychiatry, psychology, counseling, social work, or psychiatric nursing) as well as in training and expertise in dealing with people who have severe emotional problems. The responsibilities of the leader are to confront as well as to facilitate.

Task/Work Groups

Task/work groups assist their members in applying group dynamics principles and processes to improve work practices and to accomplishment identified work goals. "The task/work group specialist is able to assist groups such as task forces, committees, planning groups, community organizations, discussion groups, study circles, learning groups, and other similar groups to correct or develop their functions" (ASGW, 1992, p. 13). The prototype of a task/work group is a quality circle in which members of a work unit discuss the processes under which they operate and try to make continuous improvements.

There are as many types of task/work groups as there are kinds of tasks and work. Regardless of type or form, all such groups emphasize accomplishment and efficiency in completing identified work goals. They are united in their emphasis on achieving a successful performance or a finished product through collaborative efforts. Unlike other groups examined, there is no emphasis in task/work groups on changing individuals. Whether the group is successful or not depends on group dynamics, which are the interactions fostered through the relationships of members and leaders in connection with the complexity of the task involved. Because task/work groups run the gamut from informal subcommittee meetings to major film productions, the number of members within a task/work group may be large, but such a group usually works best when kept below 12. The length of a task/work group varies, but most are similar to other groups in that they have a beginning, a working period, and an ending. A difference in task/work groups compared with others is that often little attention is paid by members or leaders to the termination stage, and some of these groups end abruptly.

Mixed Groups

Most groups belong in one of the four categories of specialty groups just discussed. However, some do not fit well into any category. The most notable of these, so-called mixed groups, encompasses multiple ways of working with members and may change emphasis frequently. For example, some groups that are instructive are also simultaneously or consequentially therapeutic. The prototype for such a mixed type of group is a self-help group.

Self-help groups take two forms: those that are organized by an established professional-helping organization or individual (support groups) and those that originate spontaneously and stress their autonomy and internal group resources ("self-help" groups in the truest sense) (Riordan & Beggs, 1987). Although there are distinctions between support groups and self-help organizations, these groups share numerous common denominators, including the fact that they are composed of individuals who have a common focus and purpose. They are psychoeducational, therapeutic, and usually task driven as well. In addition, members of these groups frequently employ counseling techniques, such as reflection, active listening, and confrontation.

Many support and self-help groups seem to be successful in helping their members to take more control over their lives and to function well. Some that lack professional leadership make up for this deficiency in terms of experienced lay leaders. The narrow focus of these groups is both an asset in achieving a specific goal and a deficit in helping participants expand their horizons.

The Case of Cassie

Cassie has been a volunteer in a low-income neighborhood. She has mainly worked with children organizing them into teams that compete as well as cooperate with each other on various levels, from playing stickball to cleaning up trash on a street. The children seem to have thrived under Cassie's leadership, even though she is a young, white female, and they are predominantly people of color. Now Cassie's supervisor wants her to stretch herself and do more for the neighborhood. The supervisor specifically wants Cassie to lead a parent/child group and focus on family relationships. The kids she has worked with will be in the group.

Cassie is unsure she should switch roles. She is only 23 and is not a parent. Furthermore, her role as an educational leader will be quite different from her role now as a recreational leader. So the questions playing in Cassie's mind are: Can she switch roles and not alienate the children she has been working with? And does she know enough and have enough credibility as an outsider with no parental experience to help educate low-income parents on techniques that would be helpful in creating a healthy family environment? If you were Cassie, what would you do?

REALITIES AND MISPERCEPTIONS ABOUT GROUPS

Because group work is so important and prevalent in counseling and therapeutic circles, national organizations have been established for professionals engaged primarily in leading groups. Prominent group organizations include the American Group Psychotherapy Association (AGPA), the American Society of Group Psychotherapy and Psychodrama (ASGPP), and the Group Psychology and Group Psychotherapy division of the American Psychological Association (APA; Division 49). However, probably the most comprehensive of these organizations, and the one to which most professional counselors belong, is the Association for Specialists in Group Work (ASGW), a division of the American Counseling Association (ACA). This organization, which has a diverse membership, was chartered by the ACA in 1974 (Carroll & Levo, 1985). It has been a leader in the establishment of educational and best practices guidelines for group leaders (ASGW, 1998, 2000). It publishes a quarterly periodical, the *Journal for Specialists in Group Work.*

Despite these group organizations and the long history of different types of groups in society, certain misperceptions about groups are still prevalent in the general public (Gladding, 2008). Most misperceptions involve counseling and psychotherapy groups (as opposed to psychoeducational and task/work groups). The following are some prevalent myths about groups:

- They are artificial and unreal experiences.
- They are second-rate structures for dealing with problems.
- They force people to lose their identity by tearing down psychological defenses.
- They require that people become emotional and spill their guts.
- They are touchy-feely, confrontational, hostile, and brainwashing experiences (Childers & Couch, 1989).

The reality is that none of these myths are true, at least in well-run groups. Indeed, quite the contrary is actually the case. Therefore, it is important that individuals who are unsure about groups ask questions before they consider becoming members. In such a way, doubts and misperceptions can be addressed, anxiety may be lessened, and people may benefit significantly within a group environment.

USES, ADVANTAGES, AND LIMITATIONS OF GROUPS

Although there are specialty groups and best practices associated with such groups, whether a person is right for a group is always a question that should be asked. Furthermore, the advantages and limitations of groups should always be considered before establishing a group.

Uses of Groups

Most clinical counselors must make major decisions about when, where, and with whom to use groups. There are some situations in which groups are not appropriate. For instance, a counselor employed by a company would be unwise to use groups to counsel employees with personal problems who are unequal in rank and seniority in the corporate network. Likewise, a clinical mental health counselor would be foolish to use a group setting as a way of working with children who are all behaviorally disruptive. But a group may be ideal for helping people who are not too disruptive or unequal in status and who have common concerns. In such cases the procedure is for counselors to schedule a regular time in a quiet, uninterrupted setting for such people to meet and interact together.

Groups differ in purpose, composition, and length, but basically they all involve work. Gazda et al. (2001) described work as "the dynamic interaction between collections of individuals for prevention or remediation of difficulties or for the enhancement of personal growth/enrichment" (p. 297). Hence, the term *group work* is often used in connection with what goes on in groups. Group work is

> a broad professional practice involving the application of knowledge and skill in group facilitation to assist an interdependent collection of people to reach their mutual goals, which may be intrapersonal, interpersonal, or work related. The goals of the group may include the accomplishment of tasks related to work, education, personal development, personal and interpersonal problem solving, or remediation of mental and emotional disorders. (ASGW, 2000, p. 3)

Advantages of Groups

Groups have a number of general advantages. For example, group members can come to realize that they are not alone, unique, or abnormal in their problems and concerns. Through their interaction with one another, they learn more about themselves in social situations. In groups, clients can try out new behaviors and ways of interacting because the group atmosphere provides a safe environment to experiment with change and receive feedback. Members also observe how others attack and resolve problems, thereby picking up skills vicariously. Finally, the group may serve as a catalyst to help persons realize a want or a need for individual counseling or the accomplishment of a personal goal.

If set up properly, groups have specific advantages that can be beneficial in helping individuals with a variety of problems and concerns. For instance, research has shown that breast cancer patients live longer and have a better quality of life when they undergo group therapy as a part of their recovery (Sleek, 1995). Groups can also be powerful and effective experiences for clients dealing with social phobias, developmental disabilities, and insomnia. Literally hundreds of studies describe group approaches and statistically support the effectiveness of various forms of groups. Documentation of group experiences is occurring at such a fast rate that it is difficult to stay abreast of the latest developments.

Some researchers in the field regularly write comprehensive reviews on select group activities that help practitioners become better informed. The following are some relevant findings that are advantages of groups:

- Group counseling can be used to help improve the test scores and social skills of low-performing students. (Webb, Brigman, & Campbell, 2005)
- Groups can promote career development in general (Santos, 2004) and can be used effectively in vocational planning with some underserved populations, such as battered and abused women. (Peterson & Priour, 2000)
- Learning groups geared toward cooperative sharing can help participants achieve their goals more easily. (Avasthi, 1990)

- Support groups can be of benefit in helping older women cope with divorce and its aftermath. (Blatter & Jacobsen, 1993)
- Group intervention with female adolescent offenders can help them increase their self-confidence and self-esteem and achieve a sense of relationship with others. (Calhoun, Bartolomucci, & McLean, 2005)
- Group counseling and psychoeducational programs can help persons who have sustained a heart attack improve their quality of life. (Bagheri, Memarian, & Alhani, 2007)

Limitations of Groups

Yet despite their many uses and advantages, groups are not a panacea for all people and problems. They have definite limitations and disadvantages (Gladding, 2008). For example, many client concerns and personalities are not well suited for groups. The problems of individuals may not be dealt with in enough depth in groups. In addition, group pressure may force a client to take action, such as self-disclosure, before being ready. Groups may also lapse into a groupthink mentality, in which stereotypical, defensive, and stale thought processes become the norm while creativity and problem solving are squelched.

Another drawback to groups is that individuals may try to use them for escape or for selfish purposes and thereby disrupt the group process. Furthermore, it may be difficult for leaders to find a suitable time to conduct groups so that all who wish to can participate.

A sixth concern is whether groups will reflect the social milieu in which individual members normally operate. Otherwise, what is learned from the group experience may not be relevant. Finally, if groups do not work through their developmental stages successfully, they may become regressive and engage in nonproductive and even destructive behaviors such as scapegoating, group narcissism, and projection (McClure, 1994).

THEORETICAL APPROACHES IN CONDUCTING GROUPS

Theoretical approaches to counseling in groups vary as much as individual counseling approaches. In many cases, the theories are the same. For instance, within group work different approaches are based on psychoanalytic, Gestalt, person-centered, behavioral, rational-emotive behavior, transactional analysis, and cognitive theories. Yet, the implementation of any theoretical approach differs when employed with a group because of group dynamics (the interaction of members within the group).

In an evaluation of seven major theoretical approaches to groups, Ward (1982) analyzed the degree to which each approach pays attention to the (a) individual, (b) interpersonal, and (c) group levels of the process (Table 9–1). The psychoanalytic, Gestalt, and behavioral approaches to groups were strong in focusing on the individual but weak on the other two components of the group process. However, the Rogerian approach was strong on the individual level and medium on the interpersonal and group levels. Ward pointed out the limiting aspects of each approach and the importance of considering other factors, such as the group task and membership maturity, in conducting comprehensive group assignments.

In a similar way, Frey (1972) outlined how eight approaches to group work can be conceptualized on continuums from insight to action and from rational to affective (Figure 9–2), and Hansen, Warner, and Smith (1980) conceptualized group approaches on continuums from process to outcome and from leader centered to member centered

TABLE 9–1   Rating of theory strength at three group levels

| Theory | Levels | | | Limiting Factors |
	Individual	Interpersonal	Group	
Freud	Strong	Weak	Weak	Task, members, leader
Perls	Strong	Weak	Weak	Task, members, leader
Behavioral	Strong	Weak	Weak	Task, leader
Ellis	Strong	Medium	Weak	Task, leader
Berne	Strong	Strong	Weak	Task
Rogers	Strong	Medium	Medium	Style

Note. From "A Model for the More Effective Use of Theory in Group Work," by D. E. Ward, 1982, *Journal for Specialists in Group Work, 7*, 227. © 1982 by ACA. Reprinted with permission. No further reproduction authorized without written permission of the American Counseling Association.

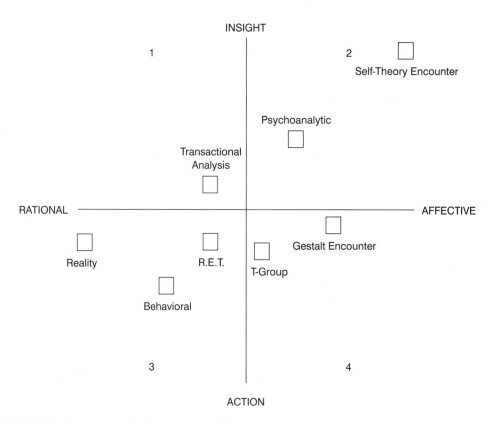

FIGURE 9–2   Group approaches conceptualized

Note. From "Conceptualizing Counseling Theories," by D. H. Frey, 1972, *Counselor Education and Supervision, 11*, 245. © 1972 by ACA. Reprinted with permission. No further reproduction authorized without written permission of the American Counseling Association.

FIGURE 9–3 **Group approaches conceptualized**

Note. From James C. Hansen, Richard W. Warner, and Elsie J. Smith, *Group Counseling: Theory and Process,* 2nd Ed., Copyright © 1980 by Houghton Mifflin Company. Reprinted with permission.

(Figure 9–3). Group leaders and potential group members must know how theories differ to make wise choices.

Overall, multiple theoretical models provide richness and diversity for conducting groups. Three additional factors are useful for group leaders to consider in arriving at a decision on what approach to take:

1. Does one need a theoretical base for conducting the group?
2. What uses will the theory best serve?
3. What criteria will be employed in the selection process?

A theory is a lot like a map. In a group, a theory provides direction and guidance in examining basic assumptions about human beings. Theory is also useful in determining goals for the group, in clarifying one's role and functions as a leader, and in explaining the group interactions. Finally, a theory can help in evaluating the outcomes of the group. Trying to lead a group without an explicit theoretical rationale is similar to attempting to fly an airplane without a map and knowledge of instruments. Either procedure is foolish, dangerous, and likely to lead to injury.

A good theory also serves practical functions (Gladding, 2008). For example, it gives meaning to and a framework for experiences and facts that occur within a setting. Good theory helps make logical sense out of what is happening and leads to productive research. With so

many theories from which to choose, the potential group leader is wise to be careful in selecting an approach.

Ford and Urban (1963) contended that four main factors should be considered when
selecting a theory: personal experience, consensus of experts, prestige, and a verified body
of knowledge. There are liabilities and advantages to all these criteria. Therefore, it is crucial
for counselors to listen to others and to read the professional literature critically to evaluate
the theories that are most verifiable and that fit in with their personality styles.

STAGES IN GROUPS

Groups, like other living systems, go through stages. If an individual or group leader is not
aware of these stages, the changes that occur within the group may appear confusing rather
than meaningful, and the benefits may be few. Leaders can maximize learning by setting up
conditions that facilitate the development of the group and "through using developmentally
based interventions, at both individual and group levels" (Saidla, 1990, p. 15). In either case,
the group, and those within it, benefit.

There is debate within the professional literature about what and when groups go through
stages. Developmental stages have been identified in various types of groups, such as learning
groups and training groups, yet much of the debate about stages focuses on group counseling.
The most agreed-on number of group counseling stages is four or five, but there are models for
as few as three and as many as six stages. Tuckman's stage model is considered mainstream.

Tuckman (1965) was one of the first theorists to design a stage process for group counseling. He believed there were four stages of group development: forming, storming, norming, and performing. This concept was later expanded to include a fifth stage of group
development: adjourning (Tuckman & Jensen, 1977), or mourning/morning (Waldo, 1985).
In each stage certain tasks are performed. For example, in the *forming stage,* the foundation
is usually laid for what is to come and who will be considered in or out of group delibera-
tions. In this stage (the group's infancy), members express anxiety and dependency. They
talk about nonproblematic issues. One way to ease the transition into the group at this stage
is to structure it so that members are relaxed and sure of what is expected of them. For example, prior to the first meeting, members may be told they will be expected to spend 3
minutes telling others who they are (McCoy, 1994).

In the *storming stage,* there is usually considerable turmoil, conflict, and unevenness
as in adolescence. Group members seek to establish themselves in the hierarchy of the
group and to deal successfully with issues concerning anxiety, power, and future expectations. Sometimes the group leader is attacked at this stage.

The *norming stage* is similar to young adulthood, where "having survived the storm the
group often generates enthusiasm and cohesion. Goals and ways of working together are decided on" (Saidla, 1990, p. 16). This stage is sometimes combined with the storming stage and
leads to the *performing stage,* which parallels adulthood in a developmental sense. At this stage,
the group members become involved with each other and with their individual and collective
goals. This is the time when the group, if it works well, is productive. Finally, in the *adjourning,*
or *mourning/morning stage,* the group comes to an end, and members say good-bye to one another and to the group experience. In this death stage, members feel either fulfilled or empty.
There is often a celebration experience at this point or at least a closure ceremony.

One of the easiest ways to conceptualize groups, regardless of the type being led, is
through the four-stage group model: forming, norming, working, and terminating. Table 9–2

TABLE 9–2   Four stages of groups

	FORMING	NORMING	WORKING	TERMINATING
Emphasis	Help members feel they are part of the group. Develop trust and inclusiveness.	Leader and members work through overt and covert tension, frustration, and conflict as they find their place in the group and develop a sense of cohesiveness (i.e., "we-ness").	Productivity, purposefulness, constructiveness, achievement, and action are highlighted.	Completeness, closure, and accomplishment of tasks/goals are highlighted along with celebration and ultimately the dismissal of the group.
Dynamics/ Characteristics	Members initiate conversations/ actions that are safe; interactions are superficial.	Energy, anxiety, and anticipation increase temporarily. Focus on functioning of group as an entity heightens. Cooperation and security increase toward end of this stage.	Members are more trusting of self and others. Increased risk taking, hopefulness, problem solving, and inclusiveness of others in achieving goals/objectives. Leader less involved in directing or structuring group. Members become increasingly responsible for running group.	About 15 percent of the group's time is spent concentrating and reflecting on events signifying the end of the group, such as completion of a task. Members deal with the issue of loss, as well as celebration, individually or collectively.
Role of Leader	Leader sets up a structured environment where members feel safe; clarifies purpose of group; establishes rules; makes introductions. Leader models appropriate behaviors; initiates ice-breaker activities; engages in limited self-disclosure; outlines vision of the group.	Leader manages conflict between members; emphasizes rules and regulations regularly; helps group become a more unified entity.	Leader concentrates on helping members and group as a whole achieve goals by encouraging interpersonal interactions. Prevention of problems through use of helping skills and renewed focus on reaching goal(s). Modeling of appropriate behavior(s) by leader.	The leader helps members assess what they have learned from the group and encourages them to be specific. Leader provides a structure for dealing with loss and celebration of group as well as its ending; arranges for follow-up and evaluation.

(continued)

TABLE 9–2   Four stages of groups *(Continued)*

	FORMING	**NORMING**	**WORKING**	**TERMINATING**
Role of Members	Members need to dedicate themselves to "owning" the group and becoming involved. They need to voice what they expect to get out of the group as well as what they plan to give to it.	Members seek and receive feedback from others, which changes from more negative to neutral/positive as group works through power issues and becomes more unified. "I statements" become more necessary and prevalent.	Members concentrate on individual and group accomplishments; give and receive input in the form of feedback about their ideas and behaviors.	Group members focus on the work they have accomplished and what they still need to achieve. Members celebrate their accomplishments, resolve unfinished business with others, and incorporate their group experiences in both unique and universal ways.
Problem Areas	Inactive, unfocused, or uninvolved group members will inhibit the group from progressing. Too much openness is also detrimental. Anxiety that is denied or unaddressed will surface again.	Group may deteriorate and become chaotic and conflictual with less involved members. Corrective feedback may be misunderstood and underused. A sense of cohesiveness may fail to develop, and group may regress and become more artificial.	Unresolved conflicts or issues may resurface. Inappropriate behaviors may be displayed and inhibit the growth of the group. Rules may be broken.	Members may deny the group is ending and be unprepared for its final session(s). Members may also be reluctant to end the group and may ask for an extension. Leaders may not prepare members for the ending and may in fact foster dependency.
Intervention Techniques	Set up the group room where it is conducive to interpersonal interaction, such as arranging chairs in a circle. Help group members feel relaxed, welcomed, and valued. Invest energy in giving group members a say or air time so they are energized and invested in the group.	Leader may introduce structured experiences, rely more on spontaneity, and use increased self-discloure. Leader may employ helping skills, such as active listening and linking, to build trust and sense of togetherness and purposefulness. Leader and members may take limited risks. Acknowledgment of differences as strengths.	More time may be allotted for discussion and interaction of goals and processes. Group may try acknowledgment of what is occurring and using the ideas of the group in reaching a resolution. A reminder to the group of agreed on goal(s) and the finiteness of the group's time may be helpful.	Both the group leader and members may actively remind each other of the conclusion of the process. Groups may be helped through good-bye events, such as celebrations, written or verbal feedback assignments on what they have learned from the group experience, and the joint planning of last sessions and the date of a follow-up.

TABLE 9–2   *(Continued)*

	FORMING	NORMING	WORKING	TERMINATING
Ideal Outcome	Leader and members are clear on purpose of group, dedicated to that purpose, and feel a sense of trust in the group and their ability to contribute to it. Anxiety within the group lessens as members get to know each other and the purposes of the group better. Enthusiasm and commitment are heightened.	Differences and similarities within group members are recognized and used. Group becomes cooperative and leader/members invest in it with shared goals/ objectives. Conflicts between members are resolved. Group becomes poised to begin the working stage.	Group stays focused and productive; works as a team. Risk taking, creativity, and pride in group and its accomplishments occur. Group makes a transition toward termination.	Group members will have pride in having accomplished planned projects/goals and be able to point to tangible results. Everyone in the group will have dealt successfully with the loss in ending the group. Everyone will leave the group stronger and better connected with other group participants. Everyone will make a successful transition back from the life of the group to everyday life.

gives a brief breakdown of the emphasis of each stage, its dynamics/characteristics, the role of the leader, the role of the members, possible problems, interventions, and ideal outcomes.

Overall, the developmental stages of a group are not readily or even clearly differentiated. "A group does not necessarily move step by step through life stages, but may move backward and forward as a part of its general development" (Hansen et al., 1980, p. 476). However, to be most effective it is necessary that a group have at least a beginning, a middle, and a closing (Jacobs, Masson, & Harvill, 2009). After that, the question of what stage a group is in and where it is heading is one that is primarily answerable through either retrospection or insightful perception.

ISSUES IN GROUPS

A number of issues are involved in conducting successful groups. Some deal with procedures for running groups; others deal with training and ethics.

Selection and Preparation of Group Members

Screening and preparation are essential procedures for conducting a successful group. Some individuals who wish to be members of groups are not appropriate for them. If such persons are allowed to join a group, they may end up being difficult group members (e.g., by monopolizing or manipulating) and cause the group leader considerable trouble (Kottler, 1994). They may also join with others, at an equally low level of functioning, and contribute to the regression of the group. When this happens, members become psychologically damaged, and the group is unable to accomplish its goals (McClure, 1990).

Screening and preparation are usually accomplished through pregroup interviews and training sessions that take place between the group leader and prospective members. During a pregroup interview, members should be selected whose needs and goals are compatible with the established goals of the group, whose functioning does not impede the group process, and whose well-being is not jeopardized by the group experience. Research indicates that pregroup training, where members learn more about a group and what is expected of them, provides important information for participants and gives them a chance to lower their anxiety (Sklare, Petrosko, & Howell, 1993).

In the process of setting up a group, certain individuals may need to be screened out or may elect to screen themselves out. Screening is a two-way process. Potential group members may not be appropriate for a certain group at a particular time with a designated leader. Prospective group members should be advised of their options if they are not selected for a group, such as joining another group or waiting for a group to form that is better able to address their needs or situation. In selecting group members, a group leader should select individuals in the group who can identify with other group members at least on some issues. In essence, the screening interview "lays the foundation upon which the group process will rest" (McCoy, 1994, p. 18).

Group members and leaders need to be informed as much as possible about group process before the group begins. Group process has to do with at least three basic questions: Who am I? Who am I with you? Who are we together? (Hulse-Killacky, Killacky, & Donigian, 2001). In other words, group process is the interaction of group members based on intrapersonal and interpersonal dynamics. Group process can be thought of as the chemistry between members; that is, how it attracts or repels. It is the process of the group, not the content, focus, or purpose, that will eventually determine whether a group succeeds. In other words, group process must be balanced with group content (Donigian, 1994). "When either the content or the process of . . . groups becomes disproportionate, the group may experience difficulty accomplishing work" (Nelligan, 1994, p. 8). Veterans of group experiences usually need minimal information about how a group will be conducted; novice participants may require extensive preparation. The point is that members who are informed about the procedures and focus of a group before they begin will do better in the group once it starts. This is true for any of the major types of groups, that is, psychoeducational, counseling, therapy, or task/work.

Before joining a group, potential members should check with the group organizer about what possibilities and outcomes are expected in a group experience. Corey (2008) listed a number of issues that potential participants have a right to expect clarification on before they enroll in a group. Among the most important of these, potential group members need the following information:

- A clear statement of the group's purpose
- A description of the group format, ground rules, and basic procedures
- A statement about the educational and training qualifications of the group leader(s)
- A pregroup interview to determine whether the potential group leader and members are suited for one's needs at the time

So, what's your problem tonight?

Sounds to me like you're angry!

Na! sounds jealous.

I think you are bottling up rage!

I appreciate your concern for me, but I'd really like to begin tonight's group with a round of how *you're* feeling.

K. L. K. © '95

The Group

FIGURE 9–4 The Group

Source: © 1995 by Kurt Kraus. Used with permission.

- A disclosure about the risks involved in being in a group and the rights and responsibilities of group members
- A discussion about the limitations of confidentiality and the roles group leaders and participants are expected to play within the group setting

Regardless of the perceived need for information, research supports the idea that "providing a set of expectations for participants prior to their initiation into a group improves the possibility of members having a successful group . . . experience" (Sklare, Keener, & Mas, 1990, p. 145). Specific ways group leaders can facilitate "here and now group counseling are by discouraging 'you' and 'we' language, questioning, speaking in the third person, seeking approval, rescuing, and analyzing." Group leaders must model the behaviors they wish others to emulate. They must be able to make the covert overt and do away with hidden agendas, as the cartoon by Kraus (1995) humorously shows in Figure 9–4.

Finally, group leaders must know how to handle resistance and challenges to their leadership. Sklare et al. (1990, pp. 146–147) give methods of productively dealing with these behaviors.

Group Size and Duration

The size of a group is determined by its purpose and preference. Large groups are less likely to spotlight the needs of individual members. Therefore, outside group guidance there is an optimal number of people that should be involved. A generally agreed-on number of group members is 6 to 8, though Gazda (1989) noted that if groups run as long as 6 months, up to 10 people may productively be included. Group size and duration affect each other. Corey (2008) stated that

> for ongoing groups with adults, about eight members with one leader seems to be a good size. Groups with children may be as small as three or four. In general, the group should have enough people to afford ample interaction so it doesn't drag and yet be small enough to give everyone a chance to participate frequently without . . . losing the sense of "group" (p. 72).

Open Versus Closed Groups

Open-ended groups admit new members after they have started; closed-ended groups do not. Open-ended groups are able to replace lost members rather quickly and maintain an optimal size. Many long-term outpatient groups are open-ended (Gladding, 2008). Closed-ended groups, though not as flexible in size, promote more cohesiveness among group members and may be very productive in helping members achieve stated goals.

Confidentiality

Groups function best when members feel a sense of confidentiality; that is, what has been said within the group setting will not be revealed outside. To promote this sense of confidentiality and build trust, a group leader must be active. The subject of confidentiality should be raised in the prescreening interview. The importance of confidentiality needs to be stressed during the first meeting of the group and on a regular basis thereafter (Corey, Corey, & Callanan, 2007). The ACA and a number of other professional groups have published guidelines on confidentiality that emphasize the role group leaders have in protecting their members by clearly defining what confidentiality is and the importance and difficulty of enforcing it. Whenever there is any question about the betrayal of confidentiality within a group, it should be dealt with immediately. Otherwise, the problem grows, and the cohesiveness of the group breaks down. Olsen (1971) pointed out that counselors must realize they can only guarantee their own adherence to the principles of confidentiality. Still, they must ensure the rights of all group members.

Physical Structure

Where a group is conducted is either an asset or a liability. Yalom and Leszcz (2005), among other prominent specialists in group work, emphasized the need for a physical structure (i.e., a room or setting) that ensures the safety and growth of group members. Groups within community agencies need to be conducted in places that promote the well-being of the group. Attractive furnishings and the way the group is assembled (preferably in a circle) can facilitate the functioning of the group.

Co-Leaders

It is not necessary for groups to have co-leaders (two leaders); however, such an arrangement can be beneficial to the group and to the leaders, especially if the group has over

10 members. With co-leaders, one leader can work with the group while the other monitors the group process. A co-leader arrangement may also be beneficial when an inexperienced leader and an experienced leader are working together. In such a setup, the inexperienced leader can learn from the experienced one. Many group specialists advocate that an inexperienced leader co-lead a group first before attempting the process alone (Ritter, 1982).

Dinkmeyer and Muro (1979) suggested that successful, experienced co-leaders (a) possess a similar philosophical and operational style, (b) have similar experience and competence, (c) establish a model relationship for effective human interaction, (d) be aware of splitting member loyalty ties to one leader or the other and help the group deal with this, and (e) agree on counseling goals and the processes to achieve them so that power struggles are avoided.

Pietrofesa, Hoffman, and Splete (1984) recommend that co-leaders sit opposite each other in a group so that leader responsibility and observation are maximized. They point out that it is not necessary for group co-leaders to be of the opposite sex; skills, not gender, matter most.

Case Study: Delilah's Dilemma

Delilah has been interested in self-growth all her life. She figured that with the wellness trend sweeping the nation that others would be too. She was right. Her friends therefore urged her to start a wellness group because they knew she was an expert in self-growth and wellness. Delilah gave in and succumbed to their wishes. She was sure there was much she could add to the lives of others.

Delilah thought it might be best if she ran her group according to a group counseling model instead of conducting it as a psychoeducational group. She also thought it best to keep the group open. To her surprise, Delilah found herself frustrated in her effort to steer the group in a positive way. New people kept asking old questions and members kept dropping in and out of the group as their schedules dictated.

What would you do in this situation now if you were Delilah? What do you think she should have done in the first place? Do you think this group is salvageable and if so, would it be worth the effort?

Self-Disclosure

Self-disclosure is defined as "here and now feelings, attitudes, and beliefs" (Shertzer & Stone, 1981, p. 206). The process of self-disclosure is dependent on the trust that group members have for one another (Bunch, Lund, & Wiggins, 1983). If there is high trust, there will be greater self-disclosure. An interesting aspect of this phenomenon is that self-disclosure builds on itself and also builds cohesion among group members (Forsyth, 2006). During the first stages of the group, self-disclosure may have to be encouraged. Morran (1982) suggested that in the beginning sessions of a group, leaders make self-disclosures often to serve as a model for others and to promote the process. As Stockton, Barr, and Klein (1981) documented, group members who make few verbal self-disclosures are more likely than others to drop out of a group or have a less positive experience in the group.

Feedback

Feedback is a multidimensional process that consists of group members' responding to the verbal messages and nonverbal behaviors of one another. It is one of the most important and abused parts of any group experience. When feedback is given honestly and with care, group members can gauge the impact of their actions on others and attempt new behaviors. Corey (2008) distinguished between group feedback given at the end of a session and that given at the termination of a group. During the latter process, Corey encourages group members to be clear, concise, and concrete with one another. Group members should give themselves feedback about how they have changed during the group experience. After processing feedback information, group members should record some of the things said during final feedback sessions so they will not forget and can make use of the experience in evaluating progress toward their goals.

To promote helpful feedback, the following criteria should be taken into consideration (Donigian & Hulse-Killacky, 1999; Gladding, 2008; Yalom & Leszcz, 2005):

- Feedback should be beneficial to the receiver and not serve the needs of the giver.
- Feedback is more effective when it is based on describable behavior.
- In the early stages of group development, positive feedback is more beneficial and more readily accepted than negative feedback.
- Feedback is most effective when it immediately follows a stimulus behavior and is validated by others.
- Feedback is of greater benefit when the receiver is open and trusts the giver.

Follow-Up

Follow-up is used to keep "in touch" with members after the group has terminated to determine how well individuals are progressing on personal or group goals. Often group leaders fail to conduct proper follow-up. This failure is especially prevalent in short-term counseling groups or in groups led by an outside leader (Gazda, 1989). Leaders should provide for follow-up of group members after termination of a group as needed or requested. Follow-up helps group members and leaders assess what they gained in the group experience and allows the group leader to make a referral of a group member for help, if appropriate. Follow-up sessions maximize the effects of a group experience and encourage members to keep pursuing original goals (Jacobs et al., 2009).

Corey (2008) suggested that a follow-up session for a short-term group be conducted about 3 months after termination of the group experience. He pointed out that the process of mutual feedback and support from other group members at this time can be very valuable. If group members are aware during the termination stage of their group that they will meet again for a follow-up, they are more likely than not to continue pursuing their goals. In addition to a whole group follow-up, individual follow-up between leaders and group members is important, even if these sessions are conducted by phone.

QUALITIES OF EFFECTIVE GROUP LEADERS

There are distinguishing qualities of effective and ineffective group leaders (Johnson & Johnson, 2009). For instance, group leaders who are authoritarian, aggressive, confrontational, or removed emotionally from the group are ineffective and produce group casualties (i.e., members who drop out or are worse after the group experience; Yalom & Lieberman, 1971). The following are four leadership qualities that have a positive effect on the outcome of groups, if not used excessively:

1. ***Caring:*** the more the better
2. ***Meaning attribution:*** includes clarifying, explaining, and providing a cognitive framework for change
3. ***Emotional stimulation:*** includes being active, challenging content, risk taking, and self-disclosure
4. ***Executive function:*** includes developing norms, structuring, and suggesting procedures (Yalom & Leszcz, 2005).

It is vital that group leaders find a position between the two extremes of emotional stimulation and executive function for the well-being of the group. Group leaders should not allow members to experience so much emotion that they are unable to process the material being discovered in the group; nor should they structure the situation so rigidly that no emotion is expressed.

Ohlsen (1977) stated that effective leaders are those who understand the forces operating within a group, recognize whether these forces are therapeutic, and if they are not, take steps to better manage the group with the assistance of its members. His assessment of leadership complements that of Yalom and Leszcz (2005), who believe that good group leaders behave with intentionality because they are able to anticipate where the group process is moving and recognize group needs. An example of this phenomenon is the ability of group leaders to treat the group homogeneously when there is a need to manage group tensions and protect group members and to treat them heterogeneously when the group has become too comfortable and is not working.

In addition, Corey (2008) maintains that effective group leaders are committed "to the never-ending struggle" to become more effective as human beings. He listed a number of personal qualities that are "vitally related to effective group leadership" (pp. 15–16). Among these qualities are presence, personal power, courage, willingness to confront oneself, sincerity, authenticity, enthusiasm, sense of identity, and inventiveness/creativity.

Gill and Barry (1982) agreed that group leadership skills are crucial to effectiveness. They traced the evolution of the emphasis on skills in groups through four classification systems (Dyer & Vriend, 1977; Ivey, 1973; Lieberman, Yalom, & Miles, 1973; Ohlsen, 1977). Gill and Barry's conceptualization of needed group skills is based on Egan's (2007) model of counseling, which involves three stages: group formation, group awareness, and group action.

A final quality of effective group leaders is that they are well educated in group theory and practice. In 1984, the Council for Accreditation of Counseling and Related Educational Programs (CACREP) adopted ASGW guidelines for the education of group leaders. These detailed guidelines, which were revised in both 1990 and 2000, are vital for potential group leaders to consult and follow.

Summary and Conclusion

Groups are an exciting, diversified, necessary, and effective way to help people and can take an educational, preventive, or remedial form. Standards have been formulated by the ASGW for psychoeducational groups, counseling groups, psychotherapy groups, and task/work groups. The theories used in groups are often the same as those used in working with individuals. There are differences in application, however, especially in regard to an emphasis on dynamics, process, and content.

Group leaders must be competent in dealing with individual as well as with group issues if they are to be maximally effective. Learning how to do this is a developmental process. Good group leaders know what types of groups they are leading and share this information with potential members. Group leaders follow ethical, legal, and procedural guidelines of professional organizations. They are concerned with the general well-being of their groups and the people in them. They anticipate problems before they occur and take proactive steps to correct them. They systematically follow up with group members after the group has terminated. They keep up with the professional literature about groups and are constantly striving to improve their personal and professional levels of functioning.

Overall, groups are a stage-based, effective, and expanding way of working with people to achieve individual and collective goals. Professional counselors, especially those in community settings, must acquire group skills if they are to be well rounded and versatile.

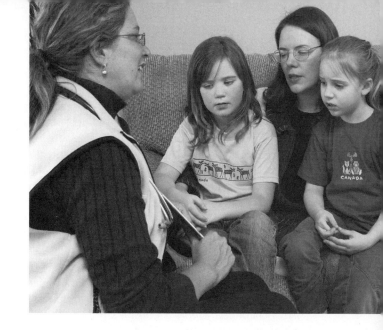

CHAPTER 10

Marriage, Family, and Couples Counseling

At thirty-five, with wife and child
   a Ph.D.
     and hopes as bright as a full moon
      on a warm August night,
He took a role as a healing man
   blending it with imagination,
     necessary change and common sense
To make more than an image on an eye lens
   of a small figure running quickly up steps;
Quietly he traveled
   like one who holds a candle to darkness
   and questions its power
So that with heavy years, long walks,
   shared love, and additional births
He became as a seasoned actor,
   who, forgetting his lines in the silence,
     stepped upstage and without prompting
      lived them.

Gladding, S. T. (1974). Without applause. *Personnel and Guidance Journal, 52,* 586. © 1974 by ACA. Reprinted with permission. No further reproduction authorized without written permission of ACA.

The profession of marriage and family counseling is relatively new. Its formal beginnings are traced to the 1940s and early 1950s, but its real growth occurred in the 1970s and 1980s (Nichols, 1993). It differs from individual counseling and group counseling in both its emphasis and its clientele (Gladding, 2008; Hines, 1988; Trotzer, 1988). For instance, marriage and family counseling usually concentrates on making changes in systems, whereas individual counseling and group counseling primarily focus on intrapersonal and interpersonal changes.

This chapter explores various aspects of marriage and family counseling as they relate to clinical community counselors. It begins with an examination of what a family is, the family life cycle, various family life forms, and the issues prevalent in each. It then looks at family stressors, outcome research, and the organizations and associations of those most involved in the profession. In addition, this chapter explains, briefly, some of the major theories used in both marriage counseling and family counseling, including those that are systemic as well as nonsystemic. The chapter then concludes with an overview of marriage and family enrichment.

Counselors who know how to work with couples and families are at a distinct advantage in offering services to a wide variety of clientele. It is essential for those who are employed in community settings to master the skills of helping those in various family life situations.

WHAT IS A FAMILY?

Families come in many forms (e.g., nuclear, single-parent, remarried, multigenerational, gay and lesbian) and may be defined in a number of ways (Goldenberg & Goldenberg, 2008). In this chapter, a *family* is considered to be those persons who are biologically and/or psychologically related through historical, emotional, or economic bonds and who perceive themselves to be a part of a household (Gladding, 2007). Such a definition allows for maximum flexibility in defining the boundaries of family life and fosters an understanding of the different forms of family life available without describing each in great detail. Furthermore, this definition engenders an appreciation of persons within family units and the roles they play.

Overall, families are characterized in multiple ways, and those that are healthy function efficiently according to form and need. Within most families there is a dual emphasis on fostering the development of individuals while simultaneously offering family members stability, protection, and preservation of the family unit structure (Strong, DeVault, & Sayad, 2008).

FAMILY LIFE AND THE FAMILY LIFE CYCLE

Family life and the optimal growth and development that take place within it are at the heart of marriage and family counseling. The *family life cycle* is the name given to the stages a family goes through as it evolves over the years (Walsh, 2003). These stages sometimes parallel and complement those in the individual life cycle (e.g., Erikson, 1959; Levinson, Darrow, Klein, Levinson, & McKee 1978), but often they are unique due to the number of people involved and to the diversity of tasks to be accomplished. In Table 10–1, a nine-stage family life cycle model, derived from several sources, is illustrated (see Becvar & Becvar, 2009). The cycle, which is primarily applicable to middle-class Americans, begins with the unattached adult and continues through the family into later life. In each stage of the family life cycle there are practical, emotional, and relational challenges as well as potential crises that need to be addressed in a timely and adequate way.

Some families and family members are more "on time" in achieving stage-critical tasks that go with the family cycle of life shown here. In such cases, a better sense of well-being is achieved (Carter & McGoldrick, 2005). Other families, such as those in poverty, the wealthy, or new immigrants, have different ways of navigating through the life cycle, and indeed their life cycle is usually quite different from that of the middle class. Regardless of timing, all families have to deal with family cohesion (i.e., emotional bonding) and family adaptability (i.e., ability to be flexible and change). Each of these two dimensions has four levels, as represented by Olson (1986; Olson & Gorall, 2003) in what is known as the Circumplex Model of

TABLE 10–1 Stages of the Family Life Cycle

Stage	Emotional Issues	Stage-Critical Tasks
1. Unattached adult	Accepting parent–offspring separation	a. Differentiation from family of origin b. Development of peer relations c. Initiation of career
2. Newly married adults	Commitment to the marriage	a. Formation of marital system b. Making room for spouse with family and friends c. Adjusting career demands
3. Childbearing adults	Accepting new members into the system	a. Adjusting marriage to make room for child b. Taking on parenting roles c. Making room for grandparents
4. Preschool-age child	Accepting the new personality	a. Adjusting family to the needs of specific child(ren) b. Coping with energy drain and lack of privacy c. Taking time out to be a couple
5. School-age child	Allowing child to establish relationships outside the family	a. Extending family/society interactions b. Encouraging the child's educational progress c. Dealing with increased activities and time demands
6. Teenage child	Increasing flexibility of family boundaries to allow independence	a. Shifting the balance in the parent–child relationship b. Refocusing on midlife career and marital issues c. Dealing with increasing concerns for older generation
7. Launching center	Accepting exits from and entries into the family	a. Releasing adult children into work, college, marriage b. Maintaining supportive home base c. Accepting occasional returns of adult children
8. Middle-aged adults	Letting go of children and facing each other again	a. Rebuilding the marriage b. Welcoming children's spouses, grandchildren into family c. Dealing with aging of one's own parents
9. Retired adults	Accepting retirement and old age	a. Maintaining individual and couple functioning b. Supporting middle generation c. Coping with death of parents, spouse d. Closing or adapting family home

Note. From *Family Therapy: A Systematic Integration* (7th ed.), by Dorothy Stroh Becvar and Raphael J. Becvar, 2009, Boston, MA: Allyn & Bacon. © 2009 by Allyn & Bacon. Reprinted with permission.

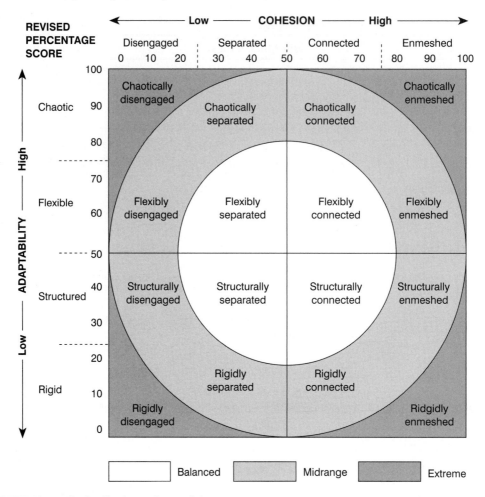

FIGURE 10–1   The family circumplex model

Note. From *Family Social Science,* by David H. Olson, Ph.D., Professor Emeritus, University of Minnesota, St. Paul, MN 55108. © 2006). Reprinted with permission.

Marital and Family Systems (see Figure 10–1). "The two dimensions are curvilinear in that families that apparently are very high or very low on both dimensions seem dysfunctional, whereas families that are balanced seem to function more adequately" (Maynard & Olson, 1987, p. 502).

Families that are most successful, functional, happy, and strong are not only balanced but are also highly social (Watts, Trusty, & Lim, 2000). According to researchers (Stinnett & DeFrain, 1985), healthy families (a) are committed to one another, (b) appreciate each other, (c) spend time together, (d) have good communication patterns, (e) have a high degree of religious or spiritual orientation, and (f) are able to deal with crisis in a positive manner.

Wilcoxon (1985) noted the importance of marriage and family counselors' being aware of the different stages within the family while being concurrently attuned to developmental tasks of its individual members. When counselors are sensitive to individual family members and to the family as a whole, they are able to realize that some individual manifestations, such as depression (Lopez, 1986; Weitzman, 2006), career indecisiveness (Kinnier, Brigman, & Noble, 1990), and/or substance abuse (Clark, 2003; Stanton, 1999), are related to family structure and functioning. Consequently, they are able to be more inclusive in their treatment plans.

When evaluating family patterns and the mental health of everyone involved, it is crucial that an assessment be based on the form and developmental stage of the family constellation. To facilitate this process, Carter and McGoldrick (2005) proposed sets of developmental tasks for traditional and nontraditional families. Bowen (1978, 1994) suggests terms, such as *enmeshment* and *triangulation,* to describe family dysfunctionality. (*Enmeshment* refers to family environments in which members are overly dependent on each other or are undifferentiated. *Triangulation* refers to family fusion situations in which one person is pulled in two different directions by the other members of the triangle.) Counselors who effectively work with couples and families have guidelines for determining how, where, when, or whether to intervene in the family process. They do not fail to act, such as neglecting to engage everyone in the therapeutic process, nor do they overreact, such as placing too much emphasis on verbal expression (Gladding, 2007).

DIFFERENT TYPES OF FAMILIES AND THEIR ISSUES

Prior to the 1980s, family therapy, with some notable exceptions, concentrated on working with traditional, middle-class nuclear families. Since that time, however, it has become evident that the future of the profession of family therapy is dependent on the ability and flexibility of professionals to work with a wide variety of families. Some of the most prevalent of these family forms are minority ethnic family groups, dual-career, single-parent, childless, remarried, gay/lesbian, aging, multigenerational, and military families.

Minority Ethnic Families

Past research has indicated that distinct and relatively small-sized ethnic family groups are often misunderstood by majority cultures. This misunderstanding is associated with cultural prejudices, flaws in collecting data about minorities, stereotyping, and unrecognized economic differences (Hampson, Beavers, & Hulgus, 1990; McGoldrick, Giordano, & Garcia-Preto, 2005; Thomas, 1990). Bias is unfortunate because it perpetuates myths that may cause harm. Ethnic families need to be seen in regard to their strengths and liabilities both collectively and individually.

One trend now is to study ethnic families from the perspective of their competencies, social class, and observed family styles (Hampson et al., 1990; McGoldrick et al., 2005). This type of approach makes it more likely that significant differences and similarities of families from various ethnic backgrounds will be reported accurately and fairly and that any treatment offered will be appropriate.

Dual-Career Families

Dual-career families are those in which both marital partners are engaged in work that is developmental in sequence and to which they have a high commitment (Hertz & Marshall, 2001). Over 50% of married couples in the United States are pursuing careers, and the likelihood is that their numbers will continue to increase. The reasons for this trend are complex, but they are related to the large number of women in the workforce, economic pressures, and the tendency for professionals to marry other professionals.

"Balancing the dual-career and family life can lead to conflict and create a considerable source of stress" (Thomas, 1990, p. 174). Such a situation is likely if one or both members of the couple are inflexible in redefining traditional gender roles related to their careers and family obligations. In the past, men have reported that their career interests interfered with their fathering roles, and women have stated that parenting interfered with their career roles (Gilbert, 1985; Nicola, 1980). Current research indicates that working women are more likely to experience conflict between their work and family roles than are working men (Blair-Loy, 2003; Werbel, 1998). Learning new skills, staying flexible, and continually assessing and revising work and family life are necessary if dual-career couples are to thrive. Because there are multiple variables in family life that affect the quality of these couples, their coping strategies over time must be dealt with, as well as their career and personal patterns.

Single-Parent Families

Single-parent families continue to be a challenge for marriage and family counselors. These families are often some of the poorest and neediest (Hansen, Heims, Julian, & Sussman, 1994; Waggonseller, Ruegamer, & Harrington, 1998). Although mothers predominantly head single-parent families (85%), each year there is an increasing number of fathers who gain custody of their children (Bumpass & Sweet, 1989; Davis & Borns, 1999).

The primary challenge for family counseling professionals is determining how to help these families find the support and services they need. The theoretical work of Nagy, which emphasizes community connectedness, is probably one of the most functional yet least utilized theories to date available for working with single-parent families (Boszormenyi-Nagy, 1987).

Childless Families

For many couples, the option of whether they will have a child (or children) is one they consciously make. For others, the decision is a result of chance (such as marrying late) or biology (infertility). For couples born between 1946 and 1955 (the initial wave of the baby boomers), "nearly one in five is childless. For college educated women in their 40s, the rate is one in four" (Shulins, 1992, p. 14). This significant rate of childlessness is expected to continue for women born in the 1960s. It is not an all-time high, but it is equal to the childless rate of "women born around World War I who matured during the Depression" (Usdansky, 1993, p. 8A).

Childless couples, especially women, face pressures related to electing to be childless. Women who are childless are sometimes stigmatized and made to feel out of place in social gatherings. Extended family relationships are sometimes strained, especially when siblings of the childless couple have children. Childless couples may also have difficulty in mourning the children they never had or in coming to terms with the choices they made not to have children (McGoldrick & Walsh, 1999).

In any of these situations, family counselors may need to involve other family members related to the couple. They may also need to emphasize the opportunities available to childless couples and advantages of being childless, such as having less stress, more discretionary income, and greater opportunities to serve in the community.

Remarried Families

Remarried families (along with first-married and single-parent families) are one of three predominant types of American families. One reason for the growth of this type of family is associated with the fact that approximately three out of every four people who divorce eventually remarry (Goldenberg & Goldenberg, 2008).

Overall, remarried families are quite complex in regard to relationships. Individuals within them often have to establish new roles and new rules. Family counselors need to be prepared to deal with the multifaceted nature of these families and help individual members bridge physical and psychological gaps in relating to each other.

Gay and Lesbian Families

During the past 20 years, there has been an increase in the number of openly gay and lesbian families in the United States. Gay and lesbian couples and families may come to therapy with concerns such as communication problems, parenting issues, or concerns related to intimacy, or they may come with concerns specifically related to being in a same-sex relationship. Counselors can be most effective by: (a) not assuming that the reason for therapy has to do with sexual orientation; (b) building awareness of personal prejudice and biases so that they are never imposed on clients (ACA Code of Ethics Standard A.5); (c) being knowledgeable about the political, social, and legal implications of being in a lesbian or gay family; and (d) being able to refer clients to places of support in the community (Nichols & Schwartz, 2007; Spitalnick & McNair, 2005).

Although research is lacking regarding the particular therapeutic needs of gay and lesbian families, the following concerns have been shown to be relevant (Falkner & Starkey, 2009; Nichols & Schwartz, 2007; Spitalnick & McNair, 2005): internalized homophobia, which can affect either the counselor or the couple or family; few role models either in the media or in the couple's family of origin, resulting in insufficient feedback and validation; traditional gender roles, which are often less useful in same-sex relationships; and systemic prejudice and heterosexism.

When working with a sexual minority couple, a social empowerment model may be helpful (Falkner & Starkey, 2009). The goal of *empowerment counseling* is to increase self-advocacy and to overcome inequities that may undermine the development of healthy relationships (Savage, Harley, & Nowak, 2005).

Aging Families

The American family is aging in proportion to the population of the United States. It is estimated that by the year 2020, the typical family will consist of at least four generations. Furthermore, by the year 2040, nearly a quarter of the population of the United States will be 65 years and older. Yet, the study of aging families is a new frontier that "still lacks identifiable landmarks and road maps" (Goldberg, 1992, p. 1).

What we do know is that with increased age, families become concerned with different personal, family, and societal issues. For instance, on an individual level there is more emphasis on physical health (Goldin & Mohr, 2000). This focus spills over into family and institutional relationships as well. In addition to health, aging families are involved with the launching or relaunching of their young adult children. This crisis is especially acute during hard financial times, such as recessions, when increasing numbers of young unmarried adults return to live with their parents.

Another factor associated with aging families is increased stress and rewards as elderly relatives move into their children's homes (Montalvo & Thompson, 1988). In these situations, couples and families have to change their household and community routines and sometimes become involved in the caretaking of their parents (Goeller, 2004). This type of situation can increase tension, anger, joy, guilt, gratitude, and grief among all involved. It is an uneven experience that fluctuates in its rewards and restrictions. It is a process that marriage and family counselors must become familiar with if they are to help aging families and their members cope.

Multigenerational Families

The number of multigenerational families has grown over the years (Anderson & Sabatelli, 2006). These are households that include a child, a parent, and a grandparent, according to the U.S. Bureau of the Census definition. Common before World War II, the number of multigenerational families decreased from that time until the 1980s. Now there are two factors influencing the increase in the number of these families. The first is economic, that is, when the economy is in recession, fewer people maintain separate households. The second factor is medical. The aging population of the United States is living longer because of advances in medicine. Many individuals, especially those past their mid-70s, cannot maintain a house by themselves and, therefore, move in with their children.

The advantages of multigenerational families are many. Different generations get to interact and enjoy each other more directly. There are often more people to help with household and child-care duties, which can lessen stress. However, the disadvantages of this type of arrangement can be considerable. For instance, there may be increased stress on the parent subunit to take care of children and grandparents. There can also be new financial and psychological difficulties as the parent subunit has to take care of more people with the same amount of money and is simultaneously squeezed to provide adequate living space.

Military Families

Over two million individuals serve in the U.S. armed forces at any one time. Many individuals who serve in the military are married and have children, whereas numerous others are the sons and daughters of families without direct connection to the military. Military families face special problems due to the nature of the work military personnel perform and the frequency of moves that personnel in the military have to make. Every few years, military families face the challenge of finding support, making adjustments, and building or rebuilding relationships and a sense of community (Kay, 2003). Military families also live with the uncertainty of how world or national events may unfold and have a direct impact on one or more family member, for example, being deployed to dangerous duty overseas (Pavlicin, 2003). In addition, military families face issues, such as stress, that dual-career couples and single parents encounter, but often in a more intense or crisis-oriented manner (Bowen & Orthner, 1990).

Current global events have increased the need for counseling services for military families (Hall, 2008). However, stigma associated with seeking mental health services continues to be a barrier for service members and their families. Civilian counselors can be trained to work effectively with military families, but as Hall pointed out, "It is essential that [counselors] understand the worldview, mind-set, and culture of the military before attempting to intervene and work with those families" (p. 5). Her book, *Counseling Military Families,* is one tool civilian counselors can use to gain a better understanding of how to work effectively with military personnel.

FAMILY LIFE STRESSORS

Stress is an inevitable part of life in all families. As with individuals, families attempt to keep stressful events from becoming distressful (Selye, 1976). They do this through a variety of means, some of which are healthier than others. The ways that families cope with stressors is sometimes related to whether they are prepared to deal with these situations.

Carter and McGoldrick (2005) have categorized family stressors into two types: vertical and horizontal (see Figure 10–2). Among the *vertical stressors* are those dealing with family patterns, myths, secrets, and legacies. These are stressors that are historical and that families inherit from previous generations. *Horizontal stressors* are those related to the present. Some horizontal stressors are developmental, such as life cycle transitions; others are unpredictable, such as an accident. The Carter and McGoldrick model is systemic and in line with how most family therapists view families.

Although families have universally expected stressors that accompany life transitions, families are unique too. For example, the rates at which families plan for their children to grow up, leave home, and start families of their own differ. Families with a British-American background usually expect a much faster shift in these events than Italian-American families. Anticipating when events may happen helps family members prepare themselves mentally and physically for changes and even failure. In many cases, family life stages and individual life stages complement each other (Bowen, 1978).

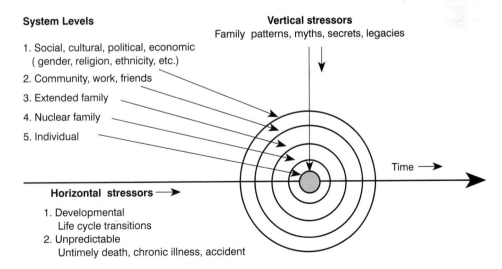

FIGURE 10–2   Horizontal and vertical stressors

Note. From *The Changing Family Life Cycle: A Framework for Family Therapy* (2nd ed.), by Betty Carter and Monica McGoldrick, 1989, Boston: Allyn & Bacon. © 1989 by Allyn & Bacon. Reprinted by permission.

Expected Life Stressors

There are a number of stressors that families can expect regardless of their level of functioning. Some are developmental stressors (i.e., age and life stage related), and others are situational stressors (i.e., interpersonal, such as dealing with feelings; Figley, 1989). Some stressors are related to present events such as work, school, and social functions (Kaslow, 1991); others are more historical in nature (i.e., family life heritage).

When surveyed, family members frequently cite prevalent stressors in their families as those associated with (a) economics and finances, (b) children's behaviors, (c) insufficient couple time, (d) communicating with children, (e) insufficient personal time, and (f) insufficient family play time (Curran, 1985). Some of these everyday stressors deal with deficiencies, such as not having enough time. In these types of stress situations, families can resolve problems through planning ahead, lowering their expectations, or both. They are then better able to cope. The flip side of this solution-based stress relief is that families and their members may experience stress from not accomplishing enough of what they planned and from overscheduling family calendars.

Unexpected Life Stressors

Some family life situations take family members by surprise or are beyond the control of the family. If life events come too soon, are delayed, or fail to materialize, the health, happiness, and well-being of all involved may be affected (Goodman, Schlossberg, & Anderson, 2006). Intensified emotionality and/or behavioral disorganization in families and their members are likely to occur as a result.

Timing is crucial to the functioning of families and their members, especially in dealing with the unexpected. If timing is off, families struggle. For example, if a first wedding is either relatively early in one's life (e.g., before age 20) or relatively late (after age 40), the difficulty of accepting or dealing with the circumstances surrounding the event, such as interacting with the new spouse, is increased for both the persons marrying and their families (Carter & McGoldrick, 2005).

Family development and environmental fit (Eccles et al., 1993) is a crucial variable in unexpected stress as well. Some environments are conducive to helping families develop and resolve unexpected crises; others are not. For example, a family that lives in an impoverished environment and experiences the loss of its major wage earner may not recover to its previous level of functioning, despite that family's best effort. Such would probably not be the case with a family experiencing the same circumstance but living in a more affluent and supportive environment.

Case Study: The Sanchez Family

Maria and Juan Sanchez met in high school and immediately fell in love. After their graduations, they decided to marry. Both wanted a large family. However, after years of trying without success, they went to a fertility clinic to get help. Unfortunately, 2 years of work with clinic personnel produced no results.

The Sanchezes have been referred to you for counseling. You recognize they are in a crisis because of the nonevent nature of their lives. Yet how do you convey to them that they are in crisis? In addition, how do you help them because you are not qualified to work with them on the physical aspects of their problem?

RESEARCH AND ASSOCIATIONS

Interest in marriage and family counseling has grown rapidly since the 1970s, and the number of individuals receiving training in this specialty has increased accordingly. One reason for these increases is the growing need for services. Gurman and Kniskern (1981) reported that approximately 50% of all problems brought to counselors are related to marriage and family issues. These issues include unemployment, poor school performance, spouse abuse, depression, rebellion, and self-concept.

Further, research studies summarized by Pinsof and Wynne (1995, 2000) report a number of interesting findings. First, family counseling interventions are at least as effective as individual interventions for most client complaints and lead to significantly greater durability of change. Second, some forms of family counseling (such as using structural–strategic family therapy with substance abusers) are more effective in treating problems than individual counseling approaches. Third, the presence of both parents, especially noncompliant fathers, in family counseling situations greatly improves the chances for success. Similarly, the effectiveness of marriage counseling when both partners meet conjointly with the counselor is nearly twice that of counselors working with just one spouse. Finally, when marriage and family counseling services are not offered to couples conjointly or to families systemically, the results of the intervention may be negative, and problems may worsen. Overall, the basic argument for using marriage and family counseling is its proven efficiency. This form of treatment is logical, fast, satisfactory, and economical.

Four major professional associations attract specialists in this area. The largest and oldest (established in 1942) is the American Association for Marriage and Family Therapy (AAMFT). The second association, the International Association of Marriage and Family Counselors (IAMFC), a division within the ACA, was chartered in 1986. The third association, Division 43 (Family Psychology), a division within the American Psychological Association (APA), was formed in 1984 to provide a professional affiliation for family practitioners who wanted to maintain their identity as psychologists (Kaslow, 1990). Finally, there is the American Family Therapy Association (AFTA), which was formed in 1977 and is identified as an academy of advanced professionals interested in the exchange of ideas (Gladding, 2007).

MARRIAGE COUNSELING

Couples seek marriage counseling for a wide variety of reasons, including issues of finance, children, fidelity, communication, and compatibility. Almost any situation can serve as the impetus to seek help.

Regardless of who initiates the request, it is crucial in almost all cases that the counselor sees both members of the couple from the beginning. Trying to treat one spouse alone for even one or two sessions increases both the other spouse's resistance to counseling and his or her anxiety. Also, if one member of a couple tries to change without the knowledge or support of the other, conflict is bound to ensue. Thus, Whitaker (1977) noted that if a counselor is not able to structure sessions so that both partners can attend, the counselor will probably not help the couple and possibly will do harm.

To combat possible negative results from occurring when one member of a couple is reluctant or refusing to attend counseling, Wilcoxon and Fenell (1983) developed a therapist-initiated letter explaining the process of marriage therapy to an absent partner. It outlines the perils of treating just one partner and is sent by counselors to the nonattending partner to

(Date)

Mr. John Jones
111 Smith Street
Anytown, USA 00000

Dear Mr. Jones,

As you may know, your wife, Jill, has requested therapy services for difficulties related to your marriage. However, she has stated that you do not wish to participate in marital therapy sessions.

As a professional marriage therapist, I have an obligation to inform each of you of the possible outcome of marital therapy services to only one spouse. The available research indicates that one-spouse marital therapy has resulted in reported increases in marital stress and dissatisfaction for both spouses in the marriage. On the other hand, many couples have reported that marital therapy which includes both spouses has been helpful in reducing marital stress and enhancing marital satisfaction.

These findings reflect general tendencies in marital research and are not absolute in nature. However, it is important for you and Jill to be informed of potential consequences which might occur through marital therapy in which only your spouse attends. Knowing this information, you may choose a course of action which best suits your intentions.

After careful consideration of this information, I ask that you and Jill discuss your options regarding future therapy services. In this way, all parties will have a clear understanding of another's intentions regarding your relationship.

As a homework assignment for Jill, I have asked that each of you read this letter and sign in the spaces provided below to verify your understanding of the potential consequences to your relationship by continuing one-spouse marital therapy. If you are interested in joining Jill for marital therapy, in addition to your signature below, please contact my office to indicate your intentions. If not, simply sign below and have Jill return the letter at our next therapy session. I appreciate your cooperation in this matter.
Sincerely,

Therapist X
_____

We verify by our signatures below that we have discussed and understand the potential implications of continued marital therapy with only one spouse in attendance.

_____	_____
Attending Spouse	Date
_____	_____
Non-Attending Spouse	Date

FIGURE 10–3 **Letter to engage a nonattending spouse**

Note. From "Engaging the Non-Attending Spouse in Marital Therapy Through the Use of Therapist-Initiated Written Communication," by A. Wilcoxon and D. Fenell, 1983, *Journal of Marital and Family Therapy, 9*(32), 199–203. © 1983 by the American Association for Marriage and Family Therapy/Wiley-Blackwell. Reprinted with permission.

help him or her see the possibilities that can accrue when working with both members of the couple (see Figure 10–3).

Depending on whether both partners decide to enter marriage counseling, a variety of approaches may be taken. Among the most popular approaches are psychoanalytic, social learning, Bowen family systems, structural–strategic, and rational emotive behavior therapy.

A number of other treatment methods will not be covered here because of their lack of proven effectiveness.

Psychoanalytic Theory

Psychoanalytical marriage counseling is based on the *theory of object relations,* a theory that addresses how relationships are developed across the generations (Scarf, 1995; Slipp, 1988). *Objects* are significant others in one's environment, such as a mother, with whom children form an interactive emotional bond. The basis of preferences for certain objects as opposed to others is developed in early childhood in parent–child interactions. Individuals bring these unconscious forces into a marriage relationship.

To help the marriage, the counselor focuses with each partner on obtaining emotional insight into early parent–child relationships. The treatment may be both individual and conjoint. The counselor uses the process of *transference,* where each partner restructures internally based perceptions of, expectations of, and reactions to self and others and projects them onto the counselor. Other techniques used in this approach include taking individual histories of each partner and taking a history of the marriage relationship. Interpretation, dream work, and an analysis of resistance are often incorporated into the treatment. *Catharsis,* the expression of pent-up emotion, is a must. The goal of this approach is for individuals and couples to gain new insights into their lives, leading to changed behaviors.

Social-Learning Theory

Social-learning theory is a form of behaviorism that stresses learning through modeling and imitation (Bandura, 1977b; Horne & Sayger, 2000). The premises underlying the theory are that behaviors are learned through observing others and that marriage partners either have a deficit or an excess of needed behaviors. A deficit may be the result of one or both partners never having witnessed a particular skill, such as how to fight fairly. An excess may come as a result of one or both partners' thinking that just a little more of a certain behavior will solve their problems. For example, one partner tells the other everything he or she likes and does not like in the marriage in the hope that honest communication will be beneficial. Although such honesty may be admired, research shows that marriages grow more through positive reciprocity than through negative feedback (Gottman & Silver, 2000). Selective communication and interaction with one's spouse seem to work best.

The focus in social-learning marriage counseling is on skill building in the present. Events that have disrupted the marriage in the past may be recognized but receive little focus. Within the treatment process, counselors may use a wide variety of behavioral strategies to help couples change, such as self-reports, observations, communication-enhancement training exercises, contracting, and homework assignments (Stuart, 1980, 1998). Much of social learning theory is based on linear thinking.

Bowen Family Systems Theory

The focus of Bowen family systems marital theory is on *differentiation,* or distinction, of one's thoughts from one's emotions and of one's self from others (Bowen, 1994; Kerr & Bowen, 1988). Couples marry at varying levels of emotional maturity, with those who are less mature having a more difficult time in their marriage relationships. When there is a great deal of friction within a marriage, the partners who compose it are characterized by a high degree of *fusion* (undifferentiated emotional togetherness) or *cutoff* (physical or psychological avoidance). They have not separated themselves from their families of origin in a healthy way nor have they formed stable self-concepts. When they experience stress within the marriage, they tend to *triangulate,* or focus on a third party (Aylmer, 1986; Gilbert, 2006). The third party can be the marriage itself, a child, an outside agency, or even a somatic complaint. Regardless, it leads to unproductive couple interactions.

Techniques used in this approach focus on ways to differentiate one's self from one's extended family-of-origin system. In the process, there is an attempt to create an individuated person with a healthy self-concept who can couple and not experience undue anxiety every time the relationship becomes stressful. Ways of achieving this goal include assessment of self and family through the use of a *genogram* (a visual representation of a person's family tree depicted in geometric figures, lines, and words) and a focus on *cognitive processes* such as asking content-based questions of one's family (Bowen, 1976). The sequencing and pacing of this process differ from spouse to spouse, and the therapeutic interaction takes place either with one spouse and the counselor or ideally with both spouses and the counselor together.

Structural–Strategic Theory

Structural–strategic theory is based on the belief that when dysfunctional symptoms occur in a marriage, they are an attempt to help couples adapt. This approach combines the best techniques of the structural and strategic schools of marriage and family therapy and sees problems as occurring within a developmental framework of the family life cycle. Marital difficulties are generated by the system the couple is in, and these symptoms consequently help maintain the marital system in which they operate (Todd, 1986). Therefore, the job of a structural–strategic marriage counselor is to get couples to try new behaviors because their old behaviors are not working. Usually, a specific behavior is targeted for change. If this behavior can be modified, it will tend to have a spillover effect, helping couples make other behavior changes as well.

To bring about change, counselors are active, direct, and goal oriented as well as problem focused, pragmatic, and brief (Todd, 1986). *Relabeling,* or giving a new perspective to a behavior, is frequently used, as are *paradoxing,* or insisting on just the opposite of what one wants, and *prescribing the symptom,* or having the couple display voluntarily what they had previously manifested involuntarily, such as fighting (Gladding, 2007). The counselor often asks clients to pretend to make changes or to carry out homework assignments (Madanes, 1984; Minuchin, 1974). The objective is to bring about new functional behaviors that will help couples achieve a specific goal.

Rational Emotive Behavior Theory (REBT)

The premise behind REBT is that couples, like individuals, often become disturbed because of what they think rather than because of specific actions that occur in the relationship (Ellis, 2000; Ellis & Dryden, 2007). *Irrational thinking* that is "highly exaggerated, inappropriately rigid, illogical, and especially absolutist" is what leads to neurosis and relationship disturbance (Ellis, Sichel, Yeager, DiMattia, & DiGiuseppe, 1989, p. 17). To combat disturbances, couples need to challenge and change their belief systems about activating events. Otherwise they continue to "awfulize" and "catastrophize" about themselves and their marriage. The essence of this theory is essentially what Ellis (1988) calls "double systems therapy," where emphasis is placed on personal and family systems change.

As with individual counseling, the REBT counselor concentrates on thinking, but within a couple context. The focus is on helping individuals first and marriages second (Ellis, 2000). After assessing what is occurring with the couple, the REBT counselor works with the individuals separately and together in the ABC method of REBT. There is a special emphasis, however, on some particular marital problems, such as jealousy and issues of sexuality.

FAMILY COUNSELING

Families enter counseling for a number of reasons. Usually, there is an identified patient, or an individual who is seen as the cause of trouble within the family structure, that family members use as their ticket of entry. Most family counseling practitioners do not view one member of a family as the problem but instead work with the whole family system. Occasionally, family therapy is conducted from an individual perspective.

Family counseling has expanded rapidly since the mid-1970s and encompasses many aspects of couples counseling. Seven of its main theoretical orientations will be covered here. Although some family counselors are linearly based and work on cause-and-effect relationships, most are not. Rather, the majority of family counselors operate from a general systems framework and conceptualize the family as an open system that evolves over the family life cycle in a sociocultural context. Functional families follow rules and are flexible in meeting the demands placed on them by family members and outside agencies. Family systems counselors stress the idea of *circular causality*; that is, family members affect each other for better or worse, and the family as a whole, through their multiple interactions. These counselors also emphasize the following concepts:

- **Nonsummativity.**   The family is greater than the sum of its parts. It is necessary to examine the patterns within a family rather than the actions of any specific member alone.
- **Equifinality.**   The same origin may lead to different outcomes, and the same outcome may result from different origins. Thus, the family that experiences a natural disaster may become stronger or weaker as a result. Likewise, healthy families may have quite dissimilar backgrounds. Therefore, the focus of treatment is on interactional family patterns rather than on particular conditions or events.
- **Communication.**   All behavior is seen as communicative. It is important to attend to the two functions of interpersonal messages: content (i.e., factual information) and relationship (i.e., how the message is to be understood). The *what* of a message is conveyed by how it is delivered.
- **Family Rules.**   A family's functioning is based on both explicit and implicit rules. Family rules provide expectations about roles and actions that govern family life. Most families operate on a small set of predictable rules, a pattern known as the *redundancy principle*. To help families change dysfunctional ways of working, family counselors have to help them define and/or expand the rules under which they operate.
- **Morphogenesis.**   The ability of the family to modify its functioning to meet the changing demands of internal and external factors is known as *morphogenesis*. Morphogenesis

usually requires a *second-order change* (i.e., the ability to make an entirely new response) instead of a *first-order change* (i.e., continuing to do more of the same things that have been done previously; Watzlawick, Weakland, & Fisch, 1974). Instead of just talking, family members may need to try new behaviors.

• **Homeostasis.** As with biological organisms, families have a tendency to remain in a steady, stable state of equilibrium unless otherwise forced to change. When a family member unbalances the family through his or her actions, other members quickly try to rectify the situation through *negative feedback loops* (morphostasis). The model of functioning is similar to a furnace that comes on when a house falls below a set temperature and cuts off once the temperature is reached. Sometimes homeostasis can be advantageous in helping a family achieve life cycle goals, but often it prevents the family from moving on to another stage in its development.

Counselors who operate from a family systems approach work according to the concepts just covered. For instance, if family rules are covert and cause confusion, the counselor helps the family make these regulations overt and clear. All members of the family are engaged in the process so that communication channels are opened. Often, a genogram is constructed to help family members and the counselor detect intergenerational patterns of family functioning that have an impact on the present (McGoldrick, Gerson, & Petry, 2008).

Overall, the popularity of family counseling may be attributed to the realization that persons become healthier when their families function better. The economy of using family counseling and its encompassing nature are intrinsically appealing and make it attractive for counselors who wish to work on complex, multifaceted levels within their communities.

Psychodynamic Family Counseling

As traditionally practiced, psychoanalysis concentrates on individuals instead of social systems such as the family. Ackerman (1966) broke with tradition by working with intact families. He believed that family difficulties resulted from *interlocking pathologies,* or unconscious and dysfunctional ways of acting, present in the couple and family system. An initial goal of psychodynamic family counseling is to change the personalities of family members so they can work with one another in a healthy and productive way. Nichols and Schwartz (2007) pointed out that psychodynamic counselors who follow Ackerman most often use an eclectic mix of psychoanalytic and systems concepts.

A unique contribution that psychodynamic practitioners have made to the field of family counseling is the use of *object relations* as a primary emphasis in treatment. Object relations, as mentioned previously, are internalized residues of early parent–child interactions. In dysfunctional families, object relations continue to exert a negative influence in present interpersonal relationships. Dysfunctional families are those with a greater degree of unconscious, unresolved conflict or loss (Paul & Paul, 1975). Three main ways of working with these families are (a) developing a stronger parent coalition, (b) defining and maintaining generation boundaries, and (c) modeling sex-linked roles.

Overall, psychodynamic family counselors concentrate on (a) helping family members obtain insight and resolve family-of-origin conflicts/losses, (b) eliminating distorted projections, (c) reconstructing relationships, and (d) promoting individual and family growth (Walsh, 2003). Prominent practitioners associated with this approach are Nathan Ackerman, James Framo, Theodore Lidz, and Norman Paul.

Experiential Family Counseling

Experientialist family counselors are concerned as much with individuals as with family systems and consider intrapsychic problems when explaining psychopathology. Unlike most other family counselors, experientialists describe patterns of family dysfunction using the individual or a dyad as the unit of analysis. They believe that dysfunctional families are made up of people who are unaware of their emotions, or if they are aware of their emotions, they suppress them, making real intimacy very difficult. This tendency not to feel or express feelings creates a climate of *emotional deadness.* Therefore, the goal of counseling is to emphasize sensitivity and feeling expression, thus opening family members to new experiences.

Two prominent practitioners in the experiential school are Virginia Satir and Carl Whitaker. Satir (1967, 1972) stresses the importance of clear communications in her approach. Whitaker (1976, 1977) is more of an existential maverick whose interactions with families have sometimes been unconventional but always are very creative. Satir believes that when family members are under stress, they may handle their communications in one of four nonproductive roles:

1. *Placater:*   agrees and tries to please
2. *Blamer:*   dominates and finds fault
3. *Responsible Analyzer:*   remains emotionally detached and intellectual
4. *Distractor:*   interrupts and constantly chatters about irrelevant topics.

Satir helps families by teaching members to own personal feelings and express them clearly, a process she calls *leveling.* Individuals are instructed to listen to one another to promote intimacy. Satir further stresses the importance of obtaining and providing feedback and negotiating differences when they arise. Her primary focus is on communication skills. She uses experiential exercises and props to help families and their members become more aware.

Whitaker, who takes a less structured approach to working with families, represents the extreme side of the experiential school. He advocates nonrational, creative experiences in family counseling and lets the form of his methods develop as he works. He is unconventional and sometimes uses *absurdity* (i.e., a statement that is half-truthful and even silly if followed out to its conclusion) in working with families. To be effective, Whitaker uses a cotherapist. He has been known to go to sleep, have a dream, and share it with a family. Messages that come from such events are hard for family members to dismiss or resist. Families begin to change their patterns of behaving and become more honest, open, and spontaneous with each other as a result. Overall, Whitaker (1989) emphasizes uncovering and utilizing the unconscious life of the family.

Behavioral Family Counseling

Behavioral family counselors use theory techniques originally devised for treating individuals. With the exception of functional family therapists (e.g., Alexander & Parsons, 1982), they are nonsystemic in conceptualizing and in clinically working with families. Instead, most behavioral family counselors stress the importance of learning. They emphasize the importance of family rules and skill training and believe that behaviors are determined by consequences rather than by antecedents (Gladding, 2007).

The goals of behavioral family counseling are specific and limited. Behaviorists try to modify troublesome behavior patterns to alleviate undesirable interactions. Much of their work focuses on changing dyadic interaction through teaching, modeling, and reinforcing new behaviors. Behaviorists believe that change is best achieved through accelerating positive behavior rather than decelerating negative behavior. Most of their work is concentrated in three main areas of (a) behavioral parent training (Patterson, 1971), (b) behavioral marriage counseling (Stuart, 1980), and (c) treatment of sexual dysfunctions (LoPiccolo, 1978; Masters & Johnson, 1970).

Structural Family Counseling

Structural family counseling, founded by Salvador Minuchin (1974), is based on general systems theory. Its practitioners advocate structural changes in the organization of the family unit, with particular attention on changing interactional patterns in subsystems of the family, such as the marital dyad, and establishing clear boundaries between family members (Minuchin, Montalvo, Guerney, Rosman, & Schumer, 1967).

In working with families, structural family counselors join with the family in a position of leadership. They try to formulate a structure in their minds of the family to determine how it is stuck in dysfunctional patterns. These counselors then use a number of techniques aimed at getting the family to change the way it operates (Minuchin & Fishman, 1981). One primary technique is to work with the family's interaction patterns. When family members repeat nonproductive sequences of behavior or demonstrate either a detached or enmeshed position in the family structure, the counselor will rearrange the physical environment so they have to act in a different way. The technique may be as simple as having people face each other when they talk. Structural family counselors also use *reframing,* or helping the family see its problem from a different and more positive perspective. For example, if a child is misbehaving, the behavior may be labeled "naughty" instead of "crazy." As a consequence, the child and actions will be viewed as less pathological. By helping families change their structure, reframe their problems, establish a hierarchy with the parents in charge, and create clear boundaries and appropriate ways of interacting, structuralists help families use their own inner resources to function in a productive and healthy way.

Strategic Family Counseling

Jay Haley (1973), Cloe Madanes (1991), and the Milan Group (Selvini-Palazzoli, Boscolo, Cecchin, & Prata, 1978) are prominent leaders within the strategic school of family counseling. Strategic counselors take a systemic view of problem behaviors and focus on the process rather than on the content of dysfunctional interactions. They strive to resolve presenting problems and pay little attention to instilling insight. One powerful technique often used by strategic counselors is to *prescribe the symptom.* This approach places targeted behaviors, such as family fights, under the control of the counselor by making a behavior voluntary if family members comply and eliminating a behavior if the family group resists the counselor's instructions. Strategic family counselors accept the presenting problems of families and view symptoms as serving the positive purpose of communication.

The Milan Group uses the technique of *ordeals:* for example, doing something a person does not want to do (such as buying a gift for somebody who is disliked), during the treatment process. The idea is that if families have to make sacrifices to get better, then the long-term improvements of treatment are enhanced. A major aspect of strategic family counseling is the assignment of original homework tasks, often given in the form of prescriptions that are to be completed between sessions. Many strategic counselors work in teams and limit the number of treatment sessions as a motivational factor. Overall, this treatment is short term and pragmatic.

Brief Solution-Focused Family Counseling

Brief solution-focused family counseling is both an extension of strategic family counseling and a distinct entity. It traces its roots to the work of Milton Erickson (1954), particularly his *utilization principle:* using whatever clients presented in counseling "as a basis and means for client solutions and change" (Lawson, 1994, p. 244). Erickson believed that people have within themselves the resources and abilities to solve their own problems. "Additionally, Erickson . . . believed that a small change in one's behavior is often all that is necessary to lead to more profound changes in a problem context" (Lawson, 1994, p. 244). This viewpoint was adopted from Erickson by Jay Haley and has been formulated into brief solution-focused family counseling by Steve deShazer and Bill O'Hanlon.

The essence of brief solution-focused family counseling is that clients create problems because of their perceptions, such as "I am always depressed." Brief solution-focused family counselors try to help clients get a different perspective on their situations through having them notice exceptions to the times they are distressed. Client families are then directed toward solutions to situations that already exist as found in these exceptions. Thus, the focus of sessions and homework is on positives and possibilities either now or in the future (Walter & Peller, 1992). One way to help individuals change perspective from concentrating on the negative to emphasizing the positive is by asking the *miracle question* (deShazer, 1991). In this intervention clients are asked to imagine that their problem is suddenly solved. What will then happen in regard to their behaviors, and how will they know the problem is solved?

Narrative Family Therapy

Narrative family therapy emphasizes the reauthoring by individuals and families of their life stories. The most prominent professionals associated with narrative family therapy are Michael White and David Epston from Australia and New Zealand, respectively. The approach distinguishes between logicoscientific reasoning, which is characterized by empiricism and logic, and narrative reasoning, which is characterized by stories, substories, meaningfulness, and liveliness. According to the narrative viewpoint, "people live their lives by stories" (Kurtz & Tandy, 1995, p. 177). Thus, the emphasis within narrative family therapy is helping people change their life stories (Figure 10–4).

The process of change in life stories is undertaken by externalization of the problem, which means that all family members can objectively address unproductive behaviors (White, 1995). In addition, the influence of the problem on a person or persons is noted as well as the influence of a person or persons on a problem. Narrative family therapists also predict setbacks in treatment so families and individuals can plan ahead for how they will act when those times come. As with solution-focused family counseling, there is a major focus on exceptions to the problem and on how families act when there is not a problem.

> I have found, both personally and professionally, that life is a series of losses and opportunities often reshaping the very structure of families. To learn about each family's *story* and community is a privilege, responsibility, and challenge. To effect positive change on individual, family, group, and community levels is intrinsically rewarding. My role as a practitioner is to restore or instill choice, help clients pass through transitions; and when appropriate, engage in advocacy. In working with problems relating to partner abuse, child abuse, suicide, physical health, and poverty, I have found that all problems have a family and social context; however, the appropriate treatment is not always couple/family therapy. Practicing in a time when services are limited by managed care requires the engagement of clients in understanding/creating their *story* (individual, couple, and family) while also problem-solving, and establishing links to community resources in a brief time-frame. As a social worker and educator with an interdisciplinary background, I have found that *joining* and *letting go* ultimately shapes the pain and the promise of working with couples and families.

FIGURE 10–4   Reflections: Working with Couples and Families

Nicholas Mazza, Ph.D., is a Professor of Social Work at Florida State University. He holds Florida licenses in clinical social work, marriage and family therapy, and psychology. He is the editor of the *Journal of Poetry Therapy* and serves on the editorial board of the *Journal of Family Social Work*. Dr. Mazza's integrative theoretical framework has a strengths perspective involving systems, narrative, and cognitive–behavioral components.

The goal is to challenge a family's view of the world and to offer them hope that their lives can be different because some changes have taken place and they are moving toward putting other changes in place.

When the family or individuals have been successful in overcoming the externalized problem, narrative family therapists offer them certificates of achievement and celebrations to signify their victory or achievement (White & Epston, 1990).

Case Study: Which Theory for the Thurbers?

John and Shelia Thurber are the parents of four children: John Jr. (age 18), Kathy (age 16), Tom (age 12), and Mimi (age 10). Kathy is struggling. She thinks her parents are not protecting her from the verbal insults of her older and younger brothers. She considers her sister a pest. Furthermore, Kathy is alienated from her former friends at school and has actually skipped school for the past week. She is now beginning to experiment with drugs, and her new friends are certainly not the type of people her parents want her hanging out with.

The Thurbers have come to you as a family, although it is obvious that they want you to "fix" Kathy and to do so quickly. You know the full range of theoretical approaches to working with a family like the Thurbers. At first you think you might work from a structural–strategic perspective. However, you are not quite sure that is a good fit.

How do you go about choosing a theoretical approach that will be helpful to a family such as the Thurbers? What if the approach you choose does not seem to work well? Is there any one approach that you think might be one you could drop back to if all else fails?

MARRIAGE AND FAMILY ENRICHMENT

Although the majority of this chapter focuses on different treatment modalities for working with couples and families, it ends on a positive note with a primary prevention emphasis—enrichment. The idea of marriage enrichment is based on the concept that couples, and consequently their families, stay healthy or get healthier by actively participating in certain activities with other couples (Mace & Mace, 1977). In such settings, couples learn about themselves; they also learn from other couples. There are over two dozen enrichment organizations in the United States on a national level, and the material in this field has mushroomed (Mace, 1987).

Couple retreats, engagement in interactive cooperative activities, and involvement in family councils are among the most recommended ways of achieving health in marriages and families. The research on enrichment shows that it can be helpful to couples and families who are not in distress. However, enrichment experiences, especially those involving marriage encounter weekends, can be quite disruptive and damaging to distressed couples and can lead to further deterioration of their relationships (Doherty, Lester, & Leigh, 1986). Care must be exercised in selecting couples and families to participate in these programs.

A part of marriage and family enrichment involves self- and couple help (Love & Stosny, 2007). This type of help is often in the form of information as well as structured exercises that theoretically and practically bring couples closer together through sharing experiences (Calvo, 1975; Guerney, 1977). For instance, couples may learn to give and receive nonverbal and verbal messages and to reflect on positive times in their life together. They may also be able to give and receive feedback on important relationship topics such as sexuality, finance, parenting, and household chores (Johnson, Fortman, & Brems, 1993).

Summary and Conclusion

Family life in the United States is very diverse with a number of family forms. Regardless of form, all families go through life cycles that influence their development. Expected and unexpected events can lead to stress and even distress. One way to help couples and families is through marriage and family counseling.

The professions of marriage and family counseling have grown rapidly in recent years for a number of reasons, including theory development, needs within the population, and proven research effectiveness. There are five main approaches to marriage counseling: psychoanalytic, social-learning, Bowen family systems, structural–strategic, and rational emotive behavior therapy. Family counseling has a wider range of approaches (e.g., behavioral, brief solution-focused, and narrative), but the dominant ones are family systems oriented.

In working as either a marriage counselor or a family counselor, the helping professional must be aware of the theoretical basis of the approach being implemented and must keep in mind where marriage and/or family members are in their individual and family life cycles. Counseling couples and families is important and gratifying for counselors. Likewise, primary prevention in the form of enrichment experiences can and should be a part of counselors' work in community settings. Through enrichment experiences and exercises, couples learn more about each other and how to relate to one another and their families.

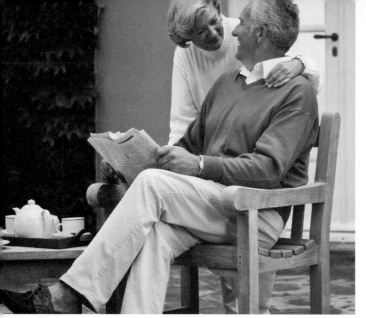

CHAPTER 11

Counseling Adults

My father tells me
  my mother is slowing down.
He talks deliberately and with deep feelings
  as stooped shouldered he walks to his garden
    behind the garage.
My mother informs me
  about my father's failing health.
"Not as robust as before," she explains,
  "Lower energy than in his 50s."
Her concerns arise as she kneads dough for biscuits.
Both express their fears to me
  as we view the present from the past.
In love, and with measured anxiety,
  I move with them into new patterns.

Gladding, S. T. (2008). *Family Therapy: History, Theory and Practice* (4th ed., p. 155). Upper Saddle River, NJ: Prentice Hall.

P eople are defined by their age, by the age in which they grew up, and by their gender. Thus, emphases and adjectives are attached to individuals and generations that may only partly be descriptive of them and may even discriminate against them. For example, Americans born between 1946 and 1964 ($n = 78$ million) are collectively known as "baby boomers," and those born between 1965 and 1976 ($n = 44$ million) are known as "baby busters," "Generation X," or "Thirteenth" generation (Dunn, 1993).

In working with adults of all ages and backgrounds, it is crucial that counselors keep in mind that individuals, as well as groups, change over time. What once may have been accurate in assessing a person or persons in a particular decade may lose validity over the years. Table 11–1 shows how generations in the 20th and 21st centuries have been characterized.

TABLE 11–1 The generational diagonal in twentieth-century America

	Inner-Driven Era 1901–24	Crisis Era 1925–42	Outer-Driven Era 1943–60	Awakening Era 1961–81	Inner-Driven Era 1982–2003
AGE 66+	PROGRESSIVE (Adaptive) sensitive	MISSIONARY (Idealist) visionary	LOST (Reactive) reclusive	G.I. (Civic) busy	SILENT (Adaptive) sensitive
AGE 44–65	MISSIONARY (Idealistic) moralistic	LOST (Reactive) pragmatic	G.I. (Civic) powerful	SILENT (Adaptive) indecisive	BOOM (Idealist) moralistic
AGE 22–43	LOST (Reactive) alienated	G.I. (Civic) heroic	SILENT (Adaptive) conformist	BOOM (Idealist) narcissistic	THIRTEENTH (Reactive) alienated
AGE 0–21	G.I. (Civic) protected	SILENT (Adaptive) suffocated	BOOM (Idealist) indulged	THIRTEENTH (Reactive) criticized	MILLENIAL (Civic) protected

Note. From William Strauss & Neil Howe. The cycle of generations. *American Demographics,* April 1991, p. 27. © American Demographics, Inc. Reprinted with permission.

Such a chart is useful in becoming more aware of people and the mind-sets that have accompanied the times in which they lived. Likewise gender roles for men and women have changed and will continue to do so. By being sensitive to both descriptors of persons and changes in them, counselors can remind themselves that collectively and individually people continue to grow throughout their lives—not just in childhood and adolescence.

To examine the development of adults and their needs in a clinical context, a counselor should begin by conceptually examining the word *development. Development* is traditionally defined as any kind of systematic change that is lifelong and cumulative (Papalia, Olds, & Feldman, 2007). Individuals develop throughout their lives on a number of levels: cognitively, emotionally, and physically. When events occur and develop within an expected time dimension, such as getting a first job somewhere in their 20s, individuals generally have only minor transitional or adjustment problems, if at all. However, if life events are accelerated, delayed, or fail to materialize (i.e., become nonevents) the well-being of persons and those associated with them may be negatively affected (Goodman, Schlossberg, & Anderson, 2006). For example, if individuals do not develop a positive self-esteem by young adulthood, they may act out in delinquent, defiant, and inappropriate ways. In contrast, adults entering middle age may experience a number of challenges, such as those described in The Case of Roger.

The Case of Roger

A 57-year-old Vietnam veteran with a diagnosis of PTSD has been brought to counseling by his wife, Betsy, prior to his next scheduled visit. Betsy complains that Roger has stopped listening to her and has become very forgetful. Roger is very frustrated because he doesn't think anything has changed and thinks Betsy is just "nagging a lot."

Roger's PTSD has been well managed up until this point by group and individual therapy and medications. According to Betsy, his nightmares and flashbacks have been getting progressively worse in the last few months. After further discussion, Roger admits the PTSD symptoms are increasing. He knows he is having more nightmares but doesn't always remember them by the time he awakens the next day.

After consultation about the case, Roger was sent for further medical analysis and was found to have early-onset Alzheimer's disease. Although Betsy seems to understand the diagnosis, she is in denial about what that means for the future. Roger is confused by the diagnosis and is angry about the turn his life has taken.

If you were Roger's individual counselor, how would you help him? What would be the best way to help Betsy? What developmental and clinical considerations are significant? Do you think that individual counseling, couples counseling, or a combination of both would be best at this point? Keep this case in mind as you read the rest of the chapter.

Theorists and researchers such as Jean Piaget, Lawrence Kohlberg, Erik Erikson, Carole Gilligan, Nancy Schlossberg, Elinor Waters, Jane Goodman, and Jane Myers have addressed issues associated with developmental stages of life. The Association for Adult Development and Aging (AADA), a division of the American Counseling Association, particularly focuses on chronological life span growth after adolescence for both men and women. In this chapter, developmental issues surrounding adults are addressed. At times, developmental issues related to adults are overlooked because it is sometimes assumed that growth prior to reaching adulthood is more important. However, life is a continuously evolving experience, and it is important that the developmental needs of adults are addressed by counselors.

YOUNG AND MIDDLE ADULTHOOD

Adulthood is a somewhat nebulous term (Broderick & Blewitt, 2006). It implies that a person has reached physical, mental, social, and emotional maturity. Yet, researchers, such as Levinson, Darrow, Klein, Levinson, and McKee (1978), have noted that adulthood is a multidimensional stage of growth characterized by a certain unevenness and unpredictability (Neugarten, 1979). There is little uniformity to it (Hudson, 2000). Indeed, as Allport (1955) stated, human beings are "always becoming," and what may be appropriate behavior in one period of adulthood may be considered inappropriate at a later time.

In this section, two periods of adulthood are considered: *young adulthood* and *middle adulthood*. During *young adulthood* (20 to 40 years), identity and intimacy are two primary developmental issues, whereas in *midlife* (40 to 65 years), needs related to generativity become the main focus (Erikson, 1963). Although it is somewhat artificial to divide adulthood into age categories, many counseling services for adults are conducted around themes that center on issues related to particular ages and issues in life. Therefore, in this section, these two divisions of adulthood are treated separately. Wrenn (1979) advised counselors to "learn to work more effectively with adults" (p. 88). This means understanding universal life stages as well as novel transitional experiences. Overall, aging is as much a mental process of considering one's self older as it is a biological phenomenon composed of physiological changes.

Young Adulthood

Young adults (those in their 20s and 30s) struggle with many issues. One of the most important, according to Erikson (1963), is establishing intimacy with the emphasis on achieving close interpersonal relationships. Other major concerns of young adults involve independence/dependence, choosing a career, deciding about marriage or partnership, developing a healthy lifestyle, finding meaning in life, and dealing with loneliness, disappointment, and potential (Corey & Corey, 2006; Robbins & Wilner, 2001).

Early in adult life, at least in the United States, the focus is on personal promise. Young adults are expected to live up to their potential by making good decisions, working hard, adjusting, and achieving proper roles and status. It is a time of maturation and transition. If all goes well, young adults usually make a smooth transition into gainful employment and into either single or couples life. Career development (which will be dealt with in a later chapter) is also important.

The three most prevalent lifestyles of young adults are singlehood, newly married, and parents of preschool children. Most young adults enter these lifestyles sequentially; however, circumstances such as separation and divorce may modify the order.

SINGLEHOOD. The first stage in the lives of most young adults is singlehood. It involves leaving home and initiating processes whereby one becomes independent. A major task of this period is to disconnect and reconnect with one's family on a different level while simultaneously establishing one's self as a person (Haley, 1980). This double focus is often difficult to achieve. Some young adults start the process by continuing their education, joining the armed forces, or getting their first job and moving in with other young people.

Being single requires a person to strike a balance between a number of choices, such as education, career, and/or marriage. Ambitions are continuously influenced by a desire for personal autonomy. In the past, singlehood was considered a transitional stage in life. However, being single is now a more accepted status than it was in the past, and its popularity as a lifestyle appears to be growing (Corey & Corey, 2005). For example, in 2000 the number of single adults over the age of 18 in the United States population living alone was approximately 25% of the population. At the same time only 52% of adult Americans were married (U.S. Census Bureau, 2000).

Therefore, singlehood is a viable alternative to marriage. Indeed, singles are usually the second-happiest group (married couples being the happiest), ranking above gay/lesbian couples, unmarried couples, and others. Singlehood can be as fulfilling as marriage, depending on the needs and interests of the individual (Gullotta, Adams, & Alexander, 1998). Being single and mentally healthy requires that individuals establish social networks, find meaning in their work or avocations, and live a balanced life physically and psychologically. Singles must also develop coping strategies to avoid becoming overwhelmed by stress, loneliness, or isolation (Kleinke, 2002). Living a healthy single life requires making adjustments to cultural demands and realizing that culture is a phenomenon to which one must accommodate. A major challenge for singles is overcoming internal and external pressures to marry or form partnerships, especially if they do not wish to or are not developmentally ready.

Because of the demands and pressures of singlehood, it is a challenge for community counselors to deal with this population. Mental health services to singles must be well thought out. The freedom to choose one's actions is a major attraction and benefit to this lifestyle and one that counselors, especially those from an existential background, can utilize in working with singles.

NEWLY MARRIED. The newly married lifestyle—less than 2 years of marriage—begins with courtship, where couples test their compatibility through dating. The process of dating and coupling may involve a number of partners before one becomes committed to marriage.

Generally, individuals tend to be most comfortable with those at the same or similar developmental level (Gladding, 2007; Rice, 2001). That is why relationships between dissimilar people rarely last.

As a group, single women usually have better mental and physical health than their counterparts (Apter, 1985). (The reason is related to a number of variables, including that some emotionally unstable women marry, whereas emotionally unstable men most likely do not because of the rejection power of women.) However, in new marriages, the mental health of men usually improves, and for women the reverse may occur. A factor influencing the mental health of newly married women and men is whether women cater to the wishes of their husbands at the expense of meeting their own needs or whether household duties are shared.

In general, the early stages of a couple's relationship are characterized by idealization and adjustment. Both men and women initially idealize each other and relate accordingly. This idealization is likely to dissipate naturally because of adjustments that must be made. If it does not, marital dissatisfaction and discord may occur. Overall, the new couple stage of the family life cycle in young adulthood is one filled with challenge and compromise. For example, new couples must learn how to share space, meals, work, leisure, and sleep activities. They must accommodate to each other's wishes, requests, and fantasies. The process takes time, energy, and goodwill. Couples that are most satisfied are those whose partners believe they are receiving as much as they are giving.

It is not surprising that the new couple stage of marriage is one of the most likely times for couples to divorce, due to an inability of individuals to resolve differences or make adaptations (Quinn & Odell, 1998). On the other hand, it is a time of life when couples may experience the greatest amount of satisfaction in their marriage, especially if they negotiate satisfactory arrangements early and have children later. The new couple is free to experiment with life and to engage freely in a wide variety of activities. Financial and time constraints are the two main limitations for couples during this period. Adjustment difficulties from the past or present circumstances, which are most often interpersonal, are the two primary reasons new couples seek counseling.

PARENTS WITH YOUNG CHILDREN.   Becoming a parent marks the beginning of a third phase of young adulthood. Parenting, especially when children are under 3 years old, is a physical, psychological, and social event that alters a couple's lifestyle dramatically (Bauman, 2002). The arrival of a child can have an impact on a couple's lifestyle (e.g., place of residence), marital relationship (e.g., sexual contact), and paternal/maternal stress (e.g., new demands; Hughes, 1999). When a newborn enters a family, the family becomes unbalanced, at least temporarily. Couples have to readjust the time they spend working outside the house, socializing with friends, and engaging in recreational activities. They also have to decide who will take responsibility for the child, when, where, and how. A rebalancing occurs in a couple's investment of time, energy, and focus (Bradt, 1988). The effect is often negative, especially after the first child (Kohler, Behrman, & Skytthe, 2005).

One of the most important tasks for young adult families is meeting the physical demands involved in having preschool children. This challenge becomes especially great when both partners are working outside the home, which is the case with a large percentage of couples in the United States with children under the age of 6 (Bauman, 2002). In such arrangements, child-care responsibilities are more likely to be shared to some extent, but women frequently are the primary caregivers (Darling-Fisher & Tiedje, 1990). Juggling multiple roles can lead to frustration and dissatisfaction, unless necessary adjustments are made. To increase marital and family satisfaction and fulfillment, it is important for partners to develop egalitarian gender-role expectations and negotiate effective methods of role sharing (Rosenbaum & Cohen, 1999).

Working with Young Adults

Regardless of the lifestyle chosen, many of the tasks engaged in during young adulthood, such as developing an identity and establishing intimacy, continue over the life span and influence future life outcomes. Therefore, young adults are under considerable pressure to do well. Although society will tolerate some delays in making adult commitments, young adults who do not respond appropriately in meeting the challenges of this time are discounted, disregarded, severely criticized, and/or ostracized.

It is little wonder, then, that many young adults attempt to avoid entering this life stage by staying at home in a delayed adolescence. Others fail to take calculated or needed risks and do not progress in forming a new or expanded identity. Yet a third group physically separates from their families of origin but simply flounders vocationally and interpersonally. A final unproductive strategy at this life stage is to short-circuit the developmental process of independence by marrying prematurely and assuming new and often overwhelming family responsibilities (Aylmer, 1988).

PREVENTION.   Prevention is one of the best ways to help young adults in any lifestyle. One way prevention can be implemented is through psychoeducation, where young adults are made aware of some of the normal and expected changes that may occur in their lives. For example, if young couples with preschool children expect their lives to be more hectic and less intimate, they may be prepared to deal with their circumstances, delay gratification, and not get discouraged with or withdraw from their relationship. Forewarning young adults of the consequences of too much change can also be helpful. Consequently, young adults may realize that they cannot do everything at once, thereby learning to decline as well as accept opportunities.

Another preventive strategy in working with young adults is to explore their personal, marital, and career ambitions and the changes that will have to occur in their lives to meet these goals, with a focus on growth and development. In most types of growth, there is "change in the direction of greater awareness, competence, and authenticity" (Jourard & Landsman, 1980, p. 238). Within individuals, regardless of their marital status, growth can be a conscious process that involves courage, that is, the ability to take calculated risks without knowing the exact consequences (Sweeney, 1999). When planned strategies and activities are outlined and accomplished as a part of growth, young persons understand the past more thoroughly, live actively and fully in the present, and envision possibilities of the future more clearly.

A third preventive strategy is to help young adults explore patterns within their families of origin, so they can understand and avoid making past mistakes as they develop their own lifestyles. One way to do this is to draw a genogram, such as the one shown in Figure 11–1.

A genogram is a visual representation of a person's family tree depicted in geometric figures, lines, and words (Gladding, 2007; Sherman, 1993). Genograms include information about items such as a family's employment, health, and marriage, as well as about family relationships over at least three generations. Genograms help people see and understand patterns in the context of historic and contemporary events (McGoldrick, Gerson, & Petry, 2008). The tangibility and nonthreatening nature of this process helps counselors and

FIGURE 11–1 Genogram: Three generations of the Smith family (as of 1965)

clients gather a large amount of information in a relatively brief period of time. Furthermore, genograms can increase "mutual trust and tolerance" among all involved in their construction (Sherman, 1993, p. 91).

Basically genograms allow young adults "to go 'back, back, back; and up, up, up' their family tree to look for patterns . . . getting not just information but a feel for the context and milieu that existed during each person's formative years" (White, 1978, pp. 25–26). This process promotes the shift from emotional reactivity to clear cognition. Data in a genogram are scanned for (a) repetitive patterns, such as triangles, cutoffs, and coalitions; (b) coincidences of dates, such as the death of members or the age of symptom onset; and (c) the impact of change and untimely life cycle transitions, such as "off-schedule" events like marriage, deaths, and the birth of children (McGoldrick et al., 2008).

A fourth preventive strategy helpful for young adults (and older adults) is group work. Within growth and support groups, young adults can gauge their own and other's reactions to issues related to the total process of being an adult. A group setting where people talk about and identify with others in similar situations usually helps young adults connect with peers. Psychoeducational and counseling groups are primarily used in exploring issues of young adulthood and the transitions that go with them. Group counseling with adults is essentially a process of using group facilitation to help adult group members deal with transitions relevant to their life cycle changes (Gladding, 2008).

Young adults experiencing life problems are also helped if they can be persuaded by counselors to make "a game" of them. Language games appear to be especially beneficial. Metaphorical language or concrete symbols are used in such games to enable the release of pent-up emotions; take more control of life; plan appropriate strategies for addressing predictable situations; and equally important, have fun and laugh at some less serious follies. Structured appropriately, games can help bring out the best in young adults and keep them from ruminating over situations they cannot control. Further, many games empower adults to take charge of the parts of their lives that parallel the games they have played and where they feel they can make positive contributions (Duhl, 1983).

TREATMENT.   As with other stages of life, young adults respond to a number of treatment modalities. Among the most prevalent are individual, group, or marriage/family counseling. Each has its place, depending on the problem or predicament. For instance, infidelity within a couple relationship might best be addressed with individual and marriage counseling, and career indecisiveness might be best addressed through an individual and a group approach.

A frequently used type of treatment for young adults is individual counseling. In one-on-one situations, young adults may evaluate their situations, put them in perspective, and also learn new skills either directly or indirectly. Sometimes individual counseling of this kind involves homework. One of the best examples of a playful counseling homework technique for young adults is a "shame attack" (Ellis & MacLaren, 1999). In shame attacks, people display behaviors of which they have been fearful. Clients frequently see that the world does not collapse or fall apart if they make a mistake or do not get what they want. For example, a young adult might ask for a glass of water in a restaurant without ordering food or might intentionally fall down at a shopping mall and see what happens.

In prison populations that contain a high percentage of young adults, one successful treatment modality that is similar to but more structured than a shame attack is drama therapy (Bergman, 2000). It can be conducted on either an individual or a group level. This type of counseling has been shown to be quite effective in reducing rates of recidivism. In it, inmates play out scenes they are likely to encounter and ways they may positively react to certain situations. Although the use of drama is not effective for all young adults who are incarcerated, Ryder (1976) reported a recidivism rate of about 15% for inmates who participated in a drama project he conducted. Such a rate is far below the national level.

Counselors in other agencies have also found drama techniques to be quite effective. Enactment is a major dramatic tool of most marriage and family counselors. In this process, a counselor "constructs an interpersonal scenario in the session in which dysfunctional transactions among family members are played out." Within this scenario the counselor can observe "the family members' verbal and nonverbal ways of signaling to each other and monitoring the range of tolerable transactions. The therapist can then intervene in the process by increasing its intensity, prolonging the time of transaction, involving other family members, indicating alternative transactions, and introducing experimental probes . . ." (Minuchin & Fishman, 1981, p. 79). The drama that occurs in presenting the problem and in finding successful resolutions decreases the power of symptoms and empowers the family of the young adult to be innovative and to change.

An interesting, interdisciplinary, positive-wellness model for self-selected young adults is the jogging group (Childers & Burcky, 1984). This approach is built on the premise that physical exercise is an important element that contributes to people's abilities to perform better in all areas of life (Freund & Seligman, 1982; Gerler, 1980; Gormley & Hussey, 2005). The jogging group combines an hour of exercise, in the form of walking, jogging, or running, with another hour of group process. The group is co-led by a counselor and a health facilitator (e.g., a physician or an exercise physiologist) and follows Lazarus's (1976, 1981) multimodal BASIC ID concept, which focuses on behavior, affect, sensation, imagery, cognition, interpersonal relationships, and drugs/biological factors. Jogging seems to hasten the group's developmental growth, and although research is lacking, the authors report that jogging groups function more like marathon groups than extended groups because of the high energy invested in the physical exercises before the group experience. Other exercise groups, such as Jazzercise, may well have a similar impact.

The Case of Milly, Barry, and Molly

Milly and Barry were "All World" academic and athletic achievers in college. When they married, they expected their children to be equally talented. However, their first child, Molly, was born with a number of physical and mental limitations. She is clumsy and slow to catch on. She also is strong-willed and has a terrible temper.

At age 5, Molly is now eligible to enter public kindergarten. Yet, Milly and Barry are embarrassed by her actions. They wonder whether they should homeschool Molly to keep her from reflecting badly on them and their former stellar reputations.

What would you advise Milly and Barry to do in regard to Molly? What counsel might you give them in regard to themselves? Do you think there are any preventive strategies that would help these parents deal productively with their situation? What treatment strategies might you employ with them should they approach you for help?

Middle Adulthood

Middle adulthood begins somewhere between the late 30s and the early 40s and ends in the early to mid-60s (Willis & Martin, 2005). Individuals at this time realize that life is half over and death is a reality. It is a time for evaluating, deciding, and making adjustments. This process is known as the *midlife transition*. It is a difficult time for many individuals as they give up the dreams of childhood and adolescence and come to terms with their own mortality (Marmor, 1982; Werner & Smith, 2001). Once they get through the thought process of having reached midlife, they typically settle down and enjoy themselves (Sheehy, 1976). However, those who do not successfully integrate the reality of this period into their lives will often try three other ways of coping:

1. Denial by escape (frantically engaging in activities)
2. Denial by overcompensation (engaging in sexual adventures)
3. Decompensation (being depressed and angry) (Marmor, 1982)

Overall, there is some physical decline in men and women during middle adulthood, including losses in hearing, sight, hormonal level, height, and attractiveness. Yet, there are some gains, too, including an improvement in crystallized intelligence (the ability to do something as a result of experience and education) and freedom from early child-rearing responsibilities and/or novice job demands (Kogan & Vacha-Haase, 2002). Women, as a group, become more assertive and achievement oriented, and men, as a group, become more nurturing and emotional (Neugarten, 1968). These behavioral changes support Jung's (1971) belief that men and women achieve a more balanced personality during this time. A prime developmental task for all individuals at this stage is to enhance their expression of generativity (creativity in their lives and work for the benefit of others) and to work toward self-actualization (realistically living up to their potential). A failure to do so results in stagnation and self-absorption (Erikson, 1963; Maslow, 1968).

Predictable crises that occur in midlife include coping with aging parents, the emancipation of children, reestablishing and/or evaluating one's work career, and bereavement (Kimmel, 1976; McCullough & Rutenberg, 1988; Werner & Smith, 2001). Midlifers are often sandwiched between caring for the needs of their children and those of their parents (Chisholm, 1999; Zal, 2001). They must constantly readjust to losses and gains in a manner secondary only to the rapid changes of adolescence. "For most people the middle years are quite busy, which may explain why some arrive at the end of this period with surprise that the journey is finished so quickly" (Worth, 1983, pp. 242–243).

PREVENTION.   A wide variety of approaches is available for working with adults in midlife. In the area of psychoeducation, N. Brown (2007) has provided a rich resource for working with adults in psychoeducational groups. Specifically, she addressed subjects adults, even in midlife, have difficulty with, such as listening, misunderstanding, and other forms of communication. In the medical area, Devine (2003) has found psychoeducational intervention helpful as an adjunction approach with midlife adults suffering from pain due to cancer. By sharing and learning about cancer, individuals are able to prevent some of the discomfort associated with it.

In everyday life, Parker (1975) reported on the use of systematic desensitization within a leadership group for the purpose of helping adult members become less anxious about public speaking. After participating in five sessions, participants noticed a decrease in anxiety about public speaking and a more relaxed attitude in their personal lives in general. Bisio and Crisan (1984) used a 1-day group workshop with adults to focus on nuclear anxiety and hidden stress in life. They emphasized principles of Victor Frankl's (1962) logotherapy and helped participants create a renewed sense of hope and purpose in life. Overall, psychoeducational groups are therapeutic in addressing areas of immediate and long-term concerns. By modifying the group format as needed, counselors can address a range of midlife issues.

Another way of promoting positive mental health and fostering the prevention of disorders in midlife is through the use of the creative arts, such as music, art, dramatic role play, and writing (Gladding, 2004). For instance, besides offering adults sounds to relax to, research suggests that music is an enhancer of physical endurance, especially if "movement is rhythmically coordinated with a musical stimulus" (Thaut, 1988, p. 129). Therefore, adults who are athletes or who regularly exercise can enhance their efforts by coordinating their physical movement with certain sounds. The reason for the positive effect of music is that it either distracts people's perceptions by causing them to selectively focus on pleasant stimuli or it physically inhibits negative feedback transmissions (i.e., fatigue) because of the pleasurable electrosensory reactions it generates. Regardless, music is a prime means of helping those in midlife maintain physical and mental health. Music also facilitates the enhancement of experiences. It promotes growth to the fullest (Maslow, 1968). Through music the rhythm of life events, and life itself, is appreciated more.

An interesting adaptation of music is the use of humorous rational songs. By employing these songs, overly serious adults are able to relax more and see their problems as more resolvable (Watzlawick, 1983). Ellis (1980) has written many humorous songs to familiar tunes. However, creative individuals can also write their own words and/or music. For example, to the tune "I've Been Working on the Railroad," an adult once wrote the following:

> I've been working on my problems/All the live long day/I've been working on my problems/Just to pass the time away/Can't you hear the problems growing/Rise up so early in the morn/Can't you hear me as I'm shouting/"I am so forlorn."

Regardless of the art form used by adults, actions that encourage creativity of any sort can be essential for adults in gaining insights and a healthy perspective on life (Csikszenmihalyi, 1996). Counseling prevention techniques with a playful quality are healthy and helpful for midlife individuals often squeezed between too many demands and not enough time or resources.

TREATMENT. A good deal of treatment for midlife adults is conducted in groups, although individual and family work are also a part of such efforts. Groups are used frequently because of the commonality of many problems that arise in midlife and the power of groups to help individuals struggling with these common concerns.

For adults who have grown up in families where at least one parent abused alcohol, heterogeneous groups based on Yalom and Leszcz's (2005) therapeutic factors, especially altruism and imitative behavior, can be empowering (Corazzini, Williams, & Harris, 1987). Such groups allow adults to question and change any of the four common roles (i.e., hero, scapegoat, lost child, and mascot) that adult children of alcoholics (ACOAs) tend to play out to survive the instability, confusion, and fear they experienced growing up (Wegscheider, 1981; Woititz, 2002). Groups of this nature also increase the support and reference network these individuals have within their lives.

Because alcoholic families tend to be rather isolated (Brown & Lewis, 1999; Steinglass, Bennett, Wolin, & Reiss, 1987), this extended system of group support is invaluable for ACOAs who wish to continue their growth toward more functional behavior and to break the three rules Black (1981) identified as universal for these individuals: (a) don't trust, (b) don't talk, and (c) don't feel. Corazzini et al. (1987) recommended that groups of this nature work best when conducted in an open format. Whitfield (1987) further noted that "many clinicians who work with ACOAs or other troubled or dysfunctional families believe that group therapy is the major choice for recovery work" (p. 142). Such work should be combined with a psychoeducational approach to the dynamics related to addiction, dysfunction, and recovery, as well as with individual and family counseling.

Individual clinical work (Farmer, 1990) as well as groups may be used to help grown-up abused children (Courtois & Leehan, 1982). Victims of abuse (whether physical, psychological, sexual, or neglect) have a number of common characteristics, such as low self-esteem, self-blame, unresolved anger, and an inability to trust (Courtois, 1999). Individual therapeutic work often focuses on specific exercises and journaling. Groups help survivors of abuse share their stories and feel emotional relief. In addition, group members can assist each other focus on resolving present, problematic behaviors that would be difficult to resolve individually. "The sharing and empathy derived from common experiences and reactions, as well as the analysis of the interactions between members, are of great therapeutic value" (Courtois, 1999, p. 244). Overall, individual and group work helps victims of abuse break the cycle of isolation so common to this population and to interrelate in a healthy, dynamic way. Particular to groups is that "many survivors come to view the group as a new family in which they are reparented as they help to reparent others" (Courtois, 1988, p. 247).

A final type of remedial service for adults in midlife that is both psychoeducational and psychotherapeutic involves career change (Bolles, 2008; J. Walker, 2000; Zimpfer & Carr, 1989). Midlifers are pressured both from within and without to advance in their life's work. Some midlife adults, especially those at the middle management level, think the best way to advance is to change careers. Persons who usually consider such a strategy have the following personal characteristics: high achievement motivation, a steady and successful work record, high need for advancement, career challenge and individual satisfaction, a positive self-image, a high energy level, and a sense of limited chances for advancement in their present position (Campbell & Cellini, 1980). They may also face increased pressure for different behavior from their spouses (McCullough & Rutenberg, 1988). Joining a career change group or working on career change individually with a counselor may help midlife participants sort out the reasons for pursuing a new career and evaluating whether some alternative course of action may be healthier for them. Effective career change treatment is holistic in nature and explores personal and professional aspects of individuals' lives.

LATE ADULTHOOD

Age 65 has traditionally marked the beginning of late adulthood because it is the time when people have, until recently, retired from work and collected Social Security or pension funds. However, old age is a concept that continues to change. According to some researchers (e.g., Neugarten, 1978), there are two major periods within this category. The first is the young–old: those between ages 55 and 75 who are still active physically, mentally, and socially, whether they are retired or not. The second period is the old–old: those individuals beyond age 75, whose physical activity is far more limited. The effects of decline with age are usually more apparent in the old–old population, though patterns of aging are clearly unique. Other developmental theorists categorize late adulthood according to functional age: the young–old elderly appear physically young for their age, and the old–old elderly appear frail and show signs of decline (Berk, 2001). Regardless of age or categorization, members of senior populations have developmental issues that collectively and individually are complex and in need of attention by community counselors and other mental health workers (Hill, Thorn, & Packard, 2000).

The need for counselors trained to work with older adults can be seen in recent and projected figures of their numbers. In 2008, persons over age 65 constituted approximately 12% of the U.S. population (U.S. Government, 2008). By the year 2030, the number of people aged 65 and older will constitute about 20% of the U.S. population (Administration on Aging, 2008; Sandberg, 2002). The growth of older Americans and their percentage of the total population are due primarily to the maturation of the so-called baby boomers of post–World War II and improved health care.

To work with older adults, counselors and other helpers need to know several prominent theories of aging. Birren and Schaie (2002) view aging from a biological, psychological, and social perspective, recognizing that the multidimensional process of this time may be uneven. Both Erikson (1963) and Havighurst (1959) have proposed that aging is a natural part of development. They believe also that individuals have specific tasks to accomplish as they grow older. For example, Erikson views late adulthood (after age 65) as a time when individuals enter a stage in which they either achieve integrity (i.e., an emphasis on integrating life activities and feeling worthwhile) or they become despairing. According to Havighurst (1959), older adults must learn to cope successfully with (a) the death of friends and/or spouses, (b) reduced physical vigor, (c) retirement and the reduction of income, (d) more leisure time and the making of new friends, (e) the development of new social roles, (f) dealing with grown children, and (g) changing living arrangements and/or making satisfactory living arrangements.

In general, older adults in the United States must deal with a broad range of complex issues in their transition from midlife to senior citizen status (Cox, 1985; Tinsley & Bigler, 2002). Some of the required changes associated with aging are gradual, such as the loss of physical strength. Others are abrupt, such as death. Transitions that involve a high level of stress are those connected with major loss, such as the death of a spouse, the loss of a job, or the contraction of a major illness (Sinick, 1979). In handling the death of a spouse, for instance, many older adults struggle due to the lack of a peer support group through which to voice their grief and work through emotions (Cicero, 2007; Morgan, 1994). Not all transitions are traumatic, however, and some may even involve a gain for the individual, such as becoming a grandparent. Regardless, the changes that are a part of aging have the potential to spark an identity crisis within the person for better or worse. Overall the developmental demands of older adults are probably second only to those of young children (Pulvino & Colangelo, 1980).

PREVENTION. To effectively offer preventive services to older adults, counselors must understand their needs. Old age is a unique life stage and involves continuous growth. When older clients are treated with respect and with empathy, services are more likely to be effective.

One preventive strategy for promoting positive mental health in older adults is to combat pervasive negative attitudes and messages about aging, such as viewing old age as an undesirable time of physical, cognitive, and emotional decline. These attitudes, also called *ageism,* influence older people's attitudes about themselves, creating a predisposition toward vulnerability (Nelson, 2002). Many older adults act old because their environments encourage and support such behavior. American society "equates age with obsolescence and orders its priorities accordingly" (Hansen & Prather, 1980, p. 74). Therefore, counselors must become educators and advocates for change in societal attitudes, if destructive age restrictions and stereotypes are to be overcome. "We need to develop a society that encourages people to stop acting their age and start being themselves" (Ponzo, 1978, pp. 143–144).

Counselors can also help older adults deal with specific and immediate environmental demands. Services for the aging are most helpful if they are portable and practical (Tomine, 1986). An educational, problem-solving model is very useful to this age group. Successful programs to help the elderly obtain employment are particularly noteworthy. A job club for older job seekers, where at regular meetings participants shared information about obtaining employment, has been found quite effective (Hitchcock, 1984; Rife & Belcher, 1994). Other useful prevention strategies include helping older adults find ways to reduce isolation through participating in community activities, engaging in physical exercise, being involved in church, and volunteering (Lee, 1999; Myers & Schwiebert, 1996).

A structured life review process has also proven beneficial in working with the elderly and may be a form of primary or secondary prevention (Haight & Haight, 2007; Haight, Michel, & Hendrix, 1998). This technique helps older adults integrate the past and prepare themselves for the future. It is particularly useful in fostering a sense of ego integrity (Myers, 1989; Sweeney, 1999). The use of photographs from the past is an excellent way to help the older clients participate in the life review process. The procedure used to introduce this activity can vary depending on the work setting. For example, a counselor employed in an older adult day care center can ask members to bring in photographs of their lives. However, a counselor employed in an inpatient facility where clients do not have ready access to their personal possessions may have to be more active and find some "representative photographs." Regardless of how it is done, the idea is to accentuate the positive and help clients recall early recollections. Negative experiences can be reframed by labeling them "learning times" instead of "failures" or "defeats." Through such means, self-esteem may be built.

Playing or making music with older adults is another preventive strategy. Its mental health benefits include the promotion of social interaction, the enhancement of self-worth, the facilitation of self-expression, and the recall of past events (Bruscia, 1987; Messinger, 2004; Osborn, 1989). Sessions may be conducted formally or informally, with either individuals or small groups. In formal sessions clients usually follow a schedule, and personal or interpersonal gains may become secondary to performance. In informal sessions, however, performance may become secondary to creativity and interaction. Music may also be used with older adults to help them achieve better functioning of their movements. Rhythmic music, for example, acts as a stimulus for helping older patients with gait disorders improve the flow of their movement (Staum, 1983). In this process, the beat of the music serves as a cue for individuals in anticipating a desired rate of movement.

TREATMENT.   Counseling with older adults historically has been a misunderstood and neglected area. For instance, Sadavoy, Jarvik, Grossberg, and Meyers (2004) estimated that approximately 3% of clinical services are provided to older adults, even though that group represents more than 12% of the population.

One reason older people do not receive more attention from counselors and other mental health specialists is due to the investment syndrome (Colangelo & Pulvino, 1980). The premise behind this syndrome is that some counselors feel their time and energy are better spent working with younger people "who may eventually contribute to society" (p. 69). Professionals who display this attitude are banking on future payoffs from the young and may have either misinformation about the elderly or an irrational fear of old age that keeps them at a psychological distance (Neugarten, 1971).

In treating older adults, it is important to recognize general concerns associated with aging as well as specific concerns germane to individual clients (Duffy, 1999). Five major problems associated with aging, most of which are treatable, include loneliness, physical illness, retirement, idleness, and bereavement (Shanks, 1982). In addition, a large number of persons over age 60 suffer some degree of depression, often related to these problems (Blazer, 2002; Myers & Schwiebert, 1996). Because older people may emphasize the physical signs of depression (e.g., lack of appetite, fatigue, headaches, and breathing difficulties) rather than feelings of sadness, depression may go undetected (Myers & Schwiebert, 1996). When depression is diagnosed, cognitive–behavioral interventions have been shown to be most successful (Lee, 1999). For example, rational emotive behavior therapy (REBT) and cognitive behavior therapy (CBT) can be used in a number of creative ways to combat potential disorders in thinking (Ellis, 1999).

Members of aging populations may suffer more incidents of psychosis as they grow older: 30% of the beds in psychiatric hospitals are occupied by the elderly. For older adults with Alzheimer's disease, counseling based on Rogers's theories and Carkhuff's practical application is beneficial in the early stages of the disease, whereas group counseling, based on Yalom's existential writings, may be productive in helping family members cope as the disease progresses (LaBarge, 1981).

A trend in working with the elderly is to get them physically, as well as emotionally, involved in their treatment. One way to do this is through developmental drama therapy. In this approach, the counselor works especially to help disoriented or depressed older adults connect with their past, their present, and each other in a positive way. A group format is used to implement this process, and group members are actively engaged in a sustained manner (Johnson, 1986). The developmental and sequential nature of drama progresses from a greeting stage, to unison activities, to the expression of group themes, to personification of images, to playing, to closing rituals. In this process, older adults are encouraged to interact with their fellow group members and to recognize and own their emotions through structured exercises, such as "phoning home." In phoning home a group member calls a significant person in his or her life and either resolves difficulties of the past or expresses gratitude.

In reminiscing or in present-oriented self/social treatment groups, music may be the key to encouraging the discussion of past or present feelings and thoughts about events, such as learning, romance, loss, and family life. Typically, music is initially played that revolves around a particular theme, but only after the group as a whole has warmed up by participating in a brief sing-along of familiar songs that includes their own accompaniment of clapping and foot-tapping sounds. In a maximum participation group, members select their own music and themes. In less democratic groups, much of the selection process is made by the leaders with particular foci in mind. Songs such as Barbara Streisand's "The Way We Were" and early American ballads like "My Old Kentucky Home" are used to set a tone and a mood that encourages talk and interaction after the singing has stopped.

Some popular group therapies that can be effective in the treatment of older adults include:

- *Reality-oriented groups* help orient confused group members to their surroundings.
- *Remotivation therapy groups* are aimed at helping older clients become more invested in both the present and the future.
- *Reminiscing groups* assist members in becoming more personally integrated through conducting life reviews.

- *Psychotherapy groups* are geared toward specific problems that often accompany aging, such as loss.
- *Member-specific groups* focus on particular transition concerns of individual members, such as hospitalization or dealing with in-laws. (Gladding, 2008)

In working with senior populations, counselors often become students of life, and older persons become their teachers (Kemp, 1984). When this type of open attitude is achieved, clients are more likely to deal with the events in their lives that are most important, and counselors are more prone to learn about a different dimension of life and be helpful in the process.

Case Study: Miss Blossom Emerges

Miss Blossom, age 82, has been a resident of the county retirement community for 12 years. She is physical capable but moves slowly. She has been depressed since the death of her best friend, Harriett, 5 years ago. Miss Blossom typically spends her days rocking in a chair or eating meals with the rest of the residents of the home in which they all reside. It does not appear that Miss Blossom is angry or has pent-up hostility. Therefore, you decide to try to help her.

Your plan for Miss Blossom and other residents is to have them role-play some scenes from popular movies and television shows, such as On Golden Pond *and* The Golden Girls. *After the role plays, which you think will energize them, you want Miss Blossom and the rest of the participants to reflect and reminisce about their lives and how the scene(s) they played was similar or different from earlier life experiences.*

Everything goes well during the enactment of scenes. However, Miss Blossom and several other cast members seem agitated and restless in the reminisce group. You try to calm them down by talking softly and slowly but your strategy does not work. What do you think is happening with the older adults with whom you are working? What do you think you should do now? What do you think their actions tell you about role playing in later sessions? If you did not engage your older adults in role plays, what else might you do to help them?

GENDER-BASED COUNSELING

Clients have distinct needs and concerns that are determined in part by their gender as well as the cultural climates and social groups in which they live and develop (Cook, 1993; Hoffman, 2006; Moore & Leafgren, 1990). Women and men are "basically cultural-social beings" (McFadden, 1999, p. 234). Counselors who are not fully aware of the influence of societal discrimination, stereotypes, and role expectations based on gender are not likely to succeed in helping their clients in counseling. Effective clinical counseling requires special knowledge and insight that focuses on particular and common aspects of sexuality. "This attention to unique and shared experiences of women and men is the paradoxical challenge of counseling" (Lee & Robbins, 2000, p. 488).

There is no longer any debate over the question of whether counselors need to possess specialized knowledge and skill in counseling women and men as separate groups as well as genders that have much in common. However, because women and men "experience different developmental challenges," they may need different styles of interaction from professionals (Nelson, 1996, p. 343). Furthermore, counselors who work more with one gender than another may need in-depth training and experience in particular areas. For example, women in the United States suffer from major depression at twice the rate of men (7 million compared with 3.5 million; Hart & Weber, 2002; McGrath, Keita, Strickland, & Russo, 1990). This finding holds true across cultures and countries, even when definitions of depression change (Shea, 1998). Part of the reason may be that women are socialized to suppress anger because it is seen as incompatible with the feminine gender role, whereas "anger has been hypothesized to be one of the few emotions that are compatible with the traditional masculine role" (Newman, Fuqua, Gray, & Simpson, 2006, p. 157).

Counseling Women

Women are the primary consumers of counseling services (Wastell, 1996). They have special needs related to biological differences and socialization patterns that make many of their counseling concerns different from men's (Cook, 1993; Hoffman, 2006; Huffman & Myers, 1999). Women still lack the degree of freedom, status, access, and acceptance that men possess, although their social roles and career opportunities have expanded considerably since the 1960s, when the women's movement influenced substantial changes (Kees, 2005).

As a group, women have quite different concerns than men in many areas. For instance, they differ in their interest and involvement in such fundamental issues as intimacy, career options, and life development (Kopla & Keitel, 2003). That is why the American Counseling Association and other professional helping associations have devoted special issues of their publications to the subject of women and counseling (see, for instance, the Summer 2005 issue of the *Journal of Counseling and Development*). "Women grow and/or develop in, through, and toward relationship" (Jordan, 1995, p. 52). When they feel connected with others, women have an increased sense of energy and a more accurate view of themselves and others. Furthermore, they feel empowered to act outside their relationships because they are active within them. They also feel a greater sense of worth and desire more connection (Miller & Stiver, 1997). Among the group's major concerns are development and growth, depression, eating disorders, sexual victimization, widowhood, and multiple roles.

Counseling women "is not a simple matter of picking a counseling theory or approach and commencing treatment" (Hanna, Hanna, Giordano, & Tollerud, 1998, p. 181). Rather, counselors' attitudes, values, and knowledge may either facilitate or impede the potential development of women clients, especially at an international level (Chung, 2005). Women are basically relational beings, and counselors' approaches should be geared toward that fact (Davenport & Yurich, 1991; Nelson, 1996). An examination of the literature indicates that professionals who counsel women should be "highly empathic, warm, understanding, and sufficiently well developed as a person to appreciate the predicament in which women find themselves" (Hanna et al., 1998, p. 167).

Unfortunately, evidence indicates that some counselors and health professionals still hold sex-role stereotypes of women (Mollen, 2006; Simon, Gaul, Friedlander, & Heatherington, 1992), and some counselors are simply uninformed about particular difficulties that women face in general or at different stages of their lives. On a developmental level, there is "a noticeable gap in the literature with respect to studies on women in midlife who are childless, single, disabled, lesbian, ethnic minorities, or members of extended family networks" (Lippert, 1997, p. 17). For example, in working with voluntarily child-free women, Mollen (2006) stressed the importance of acceptance and empowerment of these women as well as helping them manage the stigma they may face in society because of their choice.

False assumptions, inaccurate beliefs, and a lack of counselor understanding may all contribute to the problems of women clients (e.g., those who have primary or secondary infertility; Gibson & Myers, 2000). It is important that clinicians in mental health consider sociopolitical as well as other factors when counseling members of this population, for "regardless of the presenting problem, women often blame themselves for inadequacies that were [are] actually the products of unrecognized forced enculturation" (Petersen, 2000, p. 70).

CONCERNS IN COUNSELING WOMEN. One of the major concerns in counseling women revolves around the issue of adequate information about their lives. Many early theories of the nature and development of women, especially those based on psychoanalytic principles, tended to characterize women as innately "passive, dependent, and morally inferior to men" (Hare-Mustin, 1983, p. 594). Those theories promoted the status quo in regard to women and limited their available options (Lewis, Hayes, & Bradley, 1992). The general standard of healthy adult behavior came to be identified with men, and a double standard of mental health evolved with regard to adult females (Lawler, 1990; Nicholas, Gobble, Crose, & Frank, 1992). This double standard basically depicted adult female behavior as less socially desirable and healthy, a perception that lowered expectations for women's behavior and set up barriers against their advancement in nontraditional roles (Broverman, Broverman, Clarkson, Rosenkrantz, & Vogel, 1970).

However, the literature in the field of women's studies and female psychology has grown from only three textbooks in the early 1970s to a plethora of texts and articles today. Many of these publications have been written by women, for women, often from a feminist and feminist therapy perspective, to correct some older theoretical views generated by men without firsthand knowledge of women's issues (Axelson, 1999; Enns, 1993; Evans, Kincaide, Marbley, & Seem, 2005). For example, some theorists have proposed that women's development is in marked contrast to Erikson's psychosocial stages of development. These theorists stress the uniqueness of women and connectedness rather than separation. Furthermore, they outline female identity development from several points of view and compare and contrast it to ethnic identity models (Hoffman, 2006).

A second major concern in counseling women involves sexism, which Goldman (1972) described as "more deep rooted than racism" (p. 84). Sexism is the belief (and the behavior resulting from that belief) that females should be treated on the basis of their sex without regard to other criteria, such as interests and abilities. Such treatment is arbitrary, illogical, counterproductive, and self-serving. In the past, sexism has been blatant, such as limiting women's access to certain professions and encouraging them to pursue so-called pink-collar jobs that primarily employ women (e.g., nursing). Today, sexism is much more subtle, involving acts more of "omission rather than commission" (Leonard & Collins, 1979, p. 6). Many acts of omission result from a lack of information or a failure to change beliefs in light of new facts. In either case, sexism hurts not only women but society in general.

ISSUES AND THEORIES OF COUNSELING WOMEN. One of the main issues in counseling women involves the counselor's research knowledge about them and proven ways of responding to them as individuals and in groups (Leech & Kees, 2005). Women are diverse, and it is important for counselors to react to women in regard to their uniqueness as well as their similarity (Cook, 1993; Kopla & Keitel, 2003; Van Buren, 1992). Counselors should recognize that specialized knowledge is required for counseling women at various stages of life, such as childhood and adolescence, midlife, and old age. Counselors must also understand the dynamics of working with females under various conditions, such as eating disorders (Mendelsohn, 2007), sexual abuse and rape (Enns, 1996), and career development (Cook, Heppner, & O'Brien, 2002).

A number of excellent texts have been published on the psychology of women (e.g., Matlin 2008). A classic publication, Johnson and Scarato (1979), presented a model that outlines major areas of knowledge about the psychology of women that is still relevant. These authors proposed seven areas in which counselors should increase their knowledge of women and thereby decrease prejudice: (a) history and sociology of sex-role stereotyping, (b) psychophysiology of women and men, (c) theories of personality and sex-role development, (d) life span development, (e) special populations, (f) career development, and (g) counseling/psychotherapy. In the last area, the authors focused on alternatives to traditional counseling approaches as well as specific problems of women.

A major approach to working with women (and even some men) in counseling is feminist theory (Mejia, 2005). Feminist views of counseling sprang from the eruption of the women's movement in the 1960s. Initially, this movement was a challenge to patriarchal power; but as it grew, its focus centered on the development of females as persons with common and unique qualities (Okun, 1990). Beginning with the publication of Carol Gilligan's *In a Different Voice* (1982), there has been an increased integration of feminist theory into counseling. This approach encourages individuals to become more aware of socialization patterns and personal options in altering traditional gender roles as they make changes and encourages clients to become involved in social change activities that stress equality as a way of bringing about change (Enns & Hackett, 1993).

In many respects, feminist theory is more an approach to counseling rather than a well-formulated set of constructs. It is assertive in challenging and questioning attitudes of traditional counseling theories because these models often advocate the maintenance of the status quo of a male-dominated, hierarchical society. Two main emphases in the feminist position distinguish it from other forms of helping:

1. Its emphasis on equality in the helping relationship, which stems from a belief that women's problems are inseparable from society's oppression of women (Okun, 1997)
2. Its emphasis on valuing social, political, and economic action as a major part of the process of treatment

Androgyny, the importance of relationships, the acceptance of one's body "as is," and nonsexist career development are also stressed in feminist thought. Overall, "feminist theory starts with the experience of women and uses women's values and beliefs as the assumptive framework" (Nwachuku & Ivey, 1991, p. 106).

Counseling Men

An outgrowth of the focus on counseling women and eliminating sexism is new attention to the unique concerns and needs of men. In the early 1980s, Collison (1981) pointed out that "there seem to be fewer counseling procedures tailored to men than to women" (p. 220). Since that time, there has been an increase in conducting research on "men, masculinity, and the male experience" (Wade, 1998, p. 349) with the "the burgeoning interest in men's psychology" leading "to a greater demand for clinical services tailored explicitly for men"

(Johnson & Hayes, 1997, p. 302). Yet, most counselors lack formal education on men's issues (Gold & Pitariu, 2004).

CONCERNS IN COUNSELING MEN. Concerns related to counseling men often stem from their socialization. Part of men's general social behavior can be explained by the fact that men's traditional sex roles are more narrowly defined than women's and beginning in childhood there are "stricter sanctions against boys adopting feminine behaviors than exist among girls adopting those deemed as masculine" (Robinson & Howard-Hamilton, 2000, p. 196). In addition, during childhood, girls are rewarded for being emotionally or behaviorally expressive; boys are reinforced primarily for nonemotional physical actions. Thus, many men internalize their emotional reactions and seek to be autonomous, aggressive, and competitive (Scher & Stevens, 1987). They are oriented to display fighter rather than nurturing behavior, and they often "perceive themselves as losing power and status by changing in the direction of androgyny," especially in young adulthood (Brown, 1990, p. 11). Therefore, as a group, men operate primarily from a cognitive perspective (Levant & Pollack, 2003). Affective expression is usually eschewed because of a lack of experience in dealing with it and the anxiety it creates.

In such constrictive roles, insensitivity to the needs of others and self often develops, and a denial of mental and physical problems becomes lethal in the form of shorter life spans (Jourard, 1971). In addition, "men find psychological safety in independence and fear closeness" (Davenport & Yurich, 1991, p. 65). Therefore, counselors who work with men need to be aware that many of them will be loners and reticent to talk. Because of this isolation, they may well minimize their behaviors and others' actions. Most times they are not being obstinate but simply displaying behaviors for which they have been reinforced. Many men incorporate in childhood social taboos about self-disclosure, especially before other men, for it is not seen as "masculine" (Mejia, 2005).

Guidelines to assist counselors in understanding the realities of men's situations, including (a) an emphasis on the difficulty of change for most men, (b) the constraints imposed by sex-role stereotypes, (c) the importance of asking for assistance and dealing with affective issues, and (d) the need to distinguish between differences of roles and rules in one's personal and work life (Good & Brooks, 2005; Scher, 1981).

As a group, men are more reluctant than women to seek counseling (Gertner, 1994; Worth, 1983). Most men enter counseling only in crisis situations, such as in trauma, because they are generally expected to be self-sufficient, deny needs, and take care of others (Meija, 2005; Moore & Leafgren, 1990). Different age and stage levels of men may be especially relevant as to whether they consider counseling or not. Race may cause minority men to be particularly vulnerable, especially to gender role identity (Wester, Vogel, Wei, & McLain, 2006). Thus, when working with men, it is important to consult developmental models and culturally related research that underscore developmental and culture-specific themes.

ISSUES AND THEORIES IN COUNSELING MEN. Many myths as well as realities exist about counseling men (Good & Brooks, 2005; Kelly & Hall, 1994). When males are able to break through traditional restrictions, they usually work hard in counseling and see it as if it were another competition. They have high expectations of the process and want productive sessions. Thus, as a group, they are likely to be clear and sincere in the process and express themselves directly and honestly.

The dominance of cognitive functioning in men creates special challenges for counselors. Marino (1979) advised counselors to stay away from the cognitive domain in working with men and explore with them the feeling tones of their voices, the inconsistencies of their behaviors and feelings, and their ambivalence about control and nurturance. Scher (1979) also advised moving the client from the cognitive to the affective realm and recommended that the process be started by explaining to male clients the importance of owning feelings in overcoming personal difficulties and then working patiently with men to uncover hidden affect.

In contrast to eschewing the cognitive domain, Burch and Skovholt (1982) suggested that Holland's (1997) model of person–environment interaction may serve as the framework for understanding and counseling men. In this model, men are most likely to operate in the realistic dimension of functioning. Such individuals usually lack social skills but possess mechanical–technical skills; therefore, the authors recommended that counselors adopt a cognitive–behavioral approach to establish rapport and facilitate counseling. Giles (1983) disagreed with this idea, pointing out that no conclusive research supports it. He believes that counselors are not necessarily effective when they alter the counseling approach to fit the personal typology of clients.

Cultural, as well as cognitive, factors must be taken into consideration when working with men too. For instance, minority men, particularly African Americans, are often caught in a conundrum. If they attempt to meet one set of gender roles, such as those of the dominant European-American culture, "they likely frustrate the other set of gender roles (African American) while societal racism often does not allow them to fully meet either set" (Wester et al., 2006, p. 420). In such cases, counselors must work with the intersection of identities and male gender-role conflict (i.e., traditional versus nontraditional behaviors) such as that between work and interpersonal relationships.

Given the emphasis on interpersonal learning in groups, working with men in this way may be an effective intervention strategy (Andronico, 1996; Jolliff, 1994). The goals of men's groups are to increase personal awareness of sex-role conditioning, practice new desired behaviors, and promote a lifestyle based on the individual's needs. Three types of men—male sex offenders, gay men, and homeless men—may especially benefit from group work (DeAngelis, 1992). Men who do not do well in groups are those who are manic, very depressed, in severe crisis, addicted, inebriated, or paranoid (Horne & Mason, 1991).

Group work for men in general can be powerful in cutting through defenses, such as denial, and building a sense of community. To be effective, the counselor must publicize the availability of such a group, screen potential candidates carefully, identify specific behaviors on which to focus, institute opening and closing rituals, and develop intervention strategies aimed at resolving deep psychological issues such as conflict management (Hetzel, Barton, & Davenport, 1994; Horne & Mason, 1991).

In working with men in groups, Moore and Haverkamp (1989) found, in a well-controlled study, that "men age 30 to 50 are able to increase their level of affective expression, as measured by both self-report and behavioral tests" (p. 513). During this developmental stage of life, many men are seeking to become more intimate, deepen their relationships, and deal directly with their emotions. Thus, a group for men at this level of maturity can be very effective in producing change, especially, as the authors state, when it follows a social-learning paradigm in which other men serve as models and reinforcers for new behaviors. The impact of Robert Bly and the mythopoetic movement (the use of myths and poetry with men in groups) is one example of the power of such a paradigm for change (Erkel, 1990).

While promoting change and an exploration of affective issues, it is crucial that counselors be aware that rules within most men's world of work differ from those within the personal domain. Counselors must caution men not to naively and automatically introduce newly discovered behaviors that work in their personal lives into what may be a hostile environment—that is, the world of work.

Counseling with men, as with all groups, is a complex phenomenon, but the potential benefits are enormous. They include helping men develop productive strategies for dealing with expectations and changing roles (Moore & Leafgren, 1990). Through counseling, men may also develop new skills applicable to "marital communication, stress-related health problems, career and life decision making, and family interaction" (Moore & Haverkamp, 1989, p. 516). A particularly powerful procedure that may be used with select men involves having them interview their fathers. Using a series of structured, open-ended questions about family traditions, these men make discoveries about themselves by understanding their fathers more clearly. This new understanding can serve as a catalyst for implementing different behaviors within their own families.

Summary and Conclusion

In this chapter the issues and problems of adults throughout the life span have been examined on a number of levels. Prevention, treatment, concerns, issues, and theories associated with these problems have also been explored.

Specific developmental issues are associated with adulthood (ages 20 to 40) and midlife (ages 40 to 65). Each has a different focus: young adults concentrate on intimacy and becoming established in a productive lifestyle; midlifers face their own mortality, settle down, and work more toward generativity and self-actualization. Prevention activities for young adults include psychoeducation, exploration of goals, family-of-origin work, group work (such as support groups), and conceptualizing problematic situations as games or puzzles to be solved. Prevention activities for midlifers include psychoeducation, marriage and family enrichment, and use of the creative arts.

Treatment for young adults includes individual counseling situations, the use of drama, and jogging/exercise groups. Group treatment is especially effective for adults in midlife. Groups that focus on adult children of alcoholics, victims of abuse, and career change are popular.

Older adults are often misunderstood or avoided because of a lack of information or irrational fears. Yet, the elderly are an important and growing segment of the U.S. population (about 12%). Older adulthood can be divided into two groups: the young–old (ages 55 to 75) and the old–old (ages 75 and above). The young–old have more flexibility and are generally in better health than the old–old, but both groups need help from community counselors and others. Collectively and individually, older adults must work to achieve integrity in their lives and to deal with loss (of friends, physical strength, and/or spouse), as well as changing roles with their children and/or environments.

Preventive services for older adults can take many forms. Most important, however, is the need to treat older adults with respect and dignity. Counselors and others can advocate for the elderly by taking action to help modify the attitudes of nonsupportive people and systems that surround them. It is also beneficial to promote social interaction among older adults through activities such as art exercises (e.g., music, and life review groups). In treatment, cognitive theories may be helpful for some clients, and existential theories can be used with their families. Physical involvement as well as mental involvement of older adults facilitate treatment and may be achieved in a variety of ways, including the use of developmental drama. Various forms of group work with older adults can also be effective.

Just as childhood and adolescence are marked by unique developmental challenges and opportunities, so are the various stages of adulthood. In working with adults throughout the life span, counselors and community workers often learn as much as they teach and help themselves as much as they help others.

Likewise, working specifically with women and men is a challenge with its own issues. Paying attention to the unique and shared experiences of women and men is a major challenge in counseling. Women are the primary consumers of counseling services. They have special needs related to biological differences and socialization patterns that make many of their counseling concerns different from men's. One of the major concerns in counseling women revolves around the issue of adequate information about their lives. A major approach to working with women in counseling is feminist theory, which starts with the experience of women and uses women's values and beliefs as the assumptive framework.

Concerns related to counseling men often stem from their socialization. Many men internalize their emotional reactions and seek to be autonomous, aggressive, and competitive. Myths as well as realities exist about counseling men as a group, but men are more reluctant to seek counseling. When men do seek counseling, they tend to function more on a cognitive level than not, which creates special challenges for counselors. Counseling with men is a complex phenomenon. However, the potential benefits are enormous. They include helping men develop productive strategies for dealing with expectations and changing roles in society.

CHAPTER 12

Counseling Children and Adolescents

There you sit Alice Average
 midway back in the long-windowed classroom
  in the middle of Wednesday's noontime blahs,
Adjusting yourself to the sound of a lecture
 and the cold of the blue plastic desk that supports you.
In a world full of light words, hard rock, Madonnas,
 long hair, high tech, confusion, and change
  dreams fade like blue jeans
And "knowing" goes beyond the books and disks
 that are packaged for time-limited consumption
  and studied until the start of summer. . . .

Gladding, S. T. (1980/1995). Thoughts on Alice Average midway through the mid-day class on Wednesday. *Humanist Educator, 18,* 203. © 1980, 1986 by ACA. Reprinted with permission. No further reproduction authorized without written permission of ACA.

Poverty, violence, illness, school difficulties, and family disruption, as well as typical transitions associated with development, are factors that influence the mental health and well-being of a growing number of children and adolescents. Whether the increased prevalence of mental health issues in this population is due to a higher level of vulnerability or to increased efforts to identify problems, currently more young people are in need of mental health services than they were in years past (Kaffenberger & Seligman, 2003). According to the Surgeon General's Report (U.S. Department of Health and Human Services, 2000), approximately 20% of children and adolescents are estimated to have mental disorders of some type, and 5 to 9% of youth have serious emotional disturbances. However, an estimated 80% of young people who need treatment do not receive the mental health services they need.

Mental health problems appear in youth of all social classes and backgrounds. Some children are at greater risk than others because of a wide range of factors, including genetic

- Childhood is a time of transition and reorganization. It is important to assess children's mental health within the context of familial, social, and cultural expectations about age-appropriate thoughts, feelings, and behaviors.
- The range of "normal" is wide. Even so, there are children who develop mental disorders that fall out of the normal range. Approximately 20 percent of children and adolescents experience the signs and symptoms of a *DSM-IV* disorder during the course of a year. Only about 5 percent, however, experience "extreme functional impairment."
- Mental health problems appear in families of all social classes and of all backgrounds.
- A wide array of factors place children at risk for mental health problems, including intellectual disabilities, low birth weight, physical problems, family history of mental disorders, multigenerational poverty, and caregiver separation or abuse and neglect.
- Preventive interventions (e.g., educational programs for young children and parent education programs) help reduce the impact of risk factors and improve social and emotional development.
- Several efficacious psychosocial and pharmacological treatments exist for children's mental health problems, including ADHD, depression, and disruptive behavior disorders.
- Primary care facilities and schools are important settings in which professionals can recognize mental problems in young people. Options for referral to specialty care, however, are limited.
- For youth with "serious emotional disturbance," a systems approach in which multiple service sectors work collaboratively (i.e., systems of care) can be effective.
- Families are essential partners in the provision of mental health services to children and adolescents.
- Cultural differences can compound the general problems of access to appropriate mental health services.

FIGURE 12–1   Summary of the Surgeon General's Report on Children's Mental Health (U.S. Department of Health and Human Services, 2000)

vulnerability, temperament, family dysfunction, poverty, caregiver separation, and abuse (Surgeon General's Report, 2000; Figure 12–1). Clinical mental health counselors who work with children and adolescents need to be aware of these risk factors, as well as of the developmental factors that affect mental health. They also need to be skilled at implementing prevention and intervention strategies that target multiple levels, including the individual, the family, and the broader community.

We begin this chapter by describing developmental and bioecological influences on children's mental health. Next, we focus on the counseling process as it applies to children and adolescents. Following that, we provide an overview of some of the specific issues that affect children and adolescents living in today's society and describe treatment suggestions for working with those issues.

The Case of Brian

Four-year-old Brian is always on the go, according to his mother, Louise. He attends a local preschool for a half day, three days a week. Brian's preschool teacher says that he is "very active," and that he frequently interrupts other children when they are playing, often pushing them when they won't let him join them in their activities. Brian has one close friend, Luke, who tends to go along with whatever Brian wants to do. During circle time in preschool, Brian has trouble sitting still. He is easily distracted and will often try to leave the circle to go play with some of the toys in the room.

Brian has a new baby sister, Tamara, who is 3 months old. Louise, who is a single mother, enrolled Brian in preschool for the first time this fall, 2 months before Tamara was born. Tamara cries a lot and requires a lot of her mother's attention. Last week, Louise discovered Brian pinching Tamara, which made her cry. Distressed, Louise called Family Services, a community mental health agency in her town, to request help for Brian.

If you were one of the clinical mental health counselors at this agency, what would you want to know more about? What issues raise the biggest concerns for you? How would you conduct an intake interview with Brian and Louise? If counseling is warranted, what are some ways you might proceed?

DEVELOPMENTAL CONSIDERATIONS

Childhood and adolescence are characterized by dramatic developmental changes physically, cognitively, socially, and emotionally. To a large degree, mental health during these years is defined by achieving expected developmental milestones, establishing secure attachments, negotiating relationships with family members and peers, and learning effective coping skills. Mental health practitioners who work with young people need to be guided by developmental theory as they select strategies for prevention and treatment.

Development is multidimensional and complex and is marked by qualitative changes that occur in many different domains. A summary of developmental theories and counseling implications, which was adapted from several sources (e.g., Berk, 2007; Nystul, 2006) is presented in Table 12–1. Whereas it is not our intent to describe the full range of developmental characteristics associated with children and adolescents, in this next section, we provide an overview of some general characteristics of early childhood, middle childhood, and adolescence.

Early Childhood

Children between the ages of 2 and 6 are in the *early childhood stage,* sometimes called *the play years* (Berk, 2007). During this period, motor skills are refined, children begin to build ties with peers, and thought and language skills expand rapidly. To understand the way young children think and use language, it is helpful to refer to Jean Piaget's stage-constructed theory of cognitive development. Although current research indicates that the stages of cognitive development are not as discrete and clear-cut as Piaget hypothesized, his descriptions of cognitive development provide a relatively accurate picture of how children think and reason at different ages. (Bjorklund, 2000).

According to Piaget, children between 2 and 7 years of age are *preoperational,* which means they are developing the ability to represent objects and events through imitation, symbolic play, drawing, and spoken language. They are likely to be egocentric, implying that they cannot see the viewpoint of another. Preoperational children may attribute lifelike qualities to inanimate objects and have difficulty with abstract nouns and concepts, such as time and space (Vernon, 2004). For the first time, they are entering into a stage where they are able to represent and recall their feelings. As they near the end of the preoperational stage, their emotional self-regulation improves.

TABLE 12–1   Developmental theories and emerging developmental trends

Developmental Theories	Founder	Key Concepts	Implications for Counseling
Cognitive Theory	Piaget, Elkind	Conceptualized cognitive development into four stages: Sensorimotor (birth to 2), Preoperational (2 to 7), Concrete operations (7 to 11), Formal operations (usually begins after 11).	Counselors can adjust their approach and select interventions to match the child's level of cognitive functioning. For example, counselors working with young children will want to use some form of play media.
Moral Development	Kohlberg, Gilligan	Kohlberg identified three levels of moral development, beginning with a punishment and obedience orientation and progressing to higher stages of moral reasoning. Gilligan posited that feminine morality emphasizes an ethic of care, focusing on inter-personal relationships.	Counselors can use their understanding of moral reasoning to help children learn self-control and to help parents with discipline issues. Girls and boys may make moral judgments in different ways.
Sociocultural Theory	Vygotsky	Focused on the *zone of proximal development*, which emphasized a range of tasks too difficult for the child to complete alone but possible with the help of others.	Counselors can use groups to facilitate learning and accomplishment.
Psychosocial Development	Erikson	Identified seven psychosocial stages and their associated developmental tasks (for example, from birth to 1 year of age, the central task is trust).	Counselors can help clients obtain the coping skills necessary to master developmental tasks so they can move forward in their development.
Developmental Psychopathology	Kazdin, Kovacs, and others	Study of child and adolescent psychopathology in the context of maturational and develop-mental processes.	The theory provides a frame-work for understanding child psychopathology as unique from adult psychopathology, aiding in accurate assessment.
The Classic Theories	Freud, Adler, and Jung	The theories of personality Posited by the classic theorists emphasize the role of early life experiences on child and adolescent development.	The classic theories help counselors understand the dynamics of behavior *before* selecting counseling techniques to promote change.
Attachment Theory	Ainsworth, Bowlby, and others	Focuses on the relationship between the emotional bond between a parent and child and the child's psychosocial development over the life span.	An understanding of attachment relationships can provide useful insights into how to move toward optimal psychosocial development.
Emotional Intelligence	Salovey and Mayer	Focus is on the role that emotions play in social and psycho-logical functioning.	Counselors can help promote emotional intelligence through such activities as social skills training in groups.

Source: Adapted from *Introduction to Counseling: An Art and Science Perspective* (3rd ed., p. 303), by M. S. Nystul. Published by Allyn & Bacon, Boston, MA. Copyright 2006 by Pearson Education. Adapted by permission of the publisher.

Erik Erikson's psychosocial theory provides another way to understand children's development. Erikson described development as a series of psychological crises that occur at various stages. The way in which the crisis is resolved, along a continuum from positive to negative, influences healthy or maladaptive outcomes at each stage (Berk, 2007). Young children are in the process of resolving the developmental crisis of *initiative versus guilt*. *Initiative* refers to being enterprising, energetic, and purposeful. Children in this stage are discovering what kinds of people they are, particularly in regard to gender. Because of their increased language and motor skills, they are capable of imagining and trying out many new things. To navigate this period successfully, children need to be given a variety of opportunities to explore, experiment, and ask questions. The guidance of understanding adults can help young children develop self-confidence, self-direction, and emotional self-regulation.

Play is an extremely important activity for children in this age group. Through play, children find out about themselves and their world. Counselors who work with young children will want to use some form of play when counseling them. Play provides a way for children to express feelings, describe experiences, and disclose wishes. Although young children may not be able to articulate feelings, toys and other play media serve as the words they use to express emotions (Landreth, 1993). Materials used to facilitate play include puppets, art supplies, dolls and dollhouses, tools, and toy figures or animals.

Middle Childhood

Children between 7 and 11 years of age are in *middle childhood*. During this time period, children develop literacy skills and logical thinking. Cognitively, they are in Piaget's *concrete operational* stage, meaning that they are capable of reasoning logically about concrete, tangible information. Concrete operational children are able to mentally reverse actions, although they can only generalize from concrete experiences. They grasp logical concepts more readily than before, but they typically have difficulty reasoning about abstract ideas. Children in this stage learn best through questioning, exploring, manipulating, and doing (Flavell, 1985). As a rule, their increased reasoning skills enable them to understand the concept of intentionality and be more cooperative.

From a psychosocial perspective, children in this age group are in the process of resolving the crisis of *industry versus inferiority*. To maximize healthy development, they need opportunities to develop a sense of competence and capability. When adults provide manageable tasks, along with sufficient time and encouragement to complete the tasks, children are more likely to develop a strong sense of industry and efficacy (Thomas, 2005). Alternatively, children who do not experience feelings of competence and mastery may develop a sense of inadequacy and pessimism about their capabilities. Experiences with family, teachers, and peers all contribute to children's perceptions of efficacy and industry.

Negotiating relationships with peers is an important part of middle childhood. Acceptance in a peer group and having a "best friend" help children develop competence, self-esteem, and an understanding of others (Vernon, 2004). Some of the interpersonal skills children acquire during middle childhood include learning to get along with age mates, learning the skills of tolerance and patience, and developing positive attitudes toward social groups and institutions (Havighurst, 1972). Clinical mental health counselors can help children develop their interpersonal skills by implementing preventive strategies targeted toward social skills development.

Adolescence

Adolescence is the period when young people transition from childhood to adulthood. During adolescence, youth mature physically, develop an increased understanding of roles and relationships, and acquire and refine skills needed for performing successfully as adults (Crockett & Crouter, 1995). In many modern societies, the time span associated with adolescence can last for nearly a decade (Berk, 2007). Puberty marks the beginning of adolescence, with girls typically reaching puberty earlier than boys. As adolescence ends, young people ideally have constructed an identity, attained independence, and developed more mature ways of relating to others. Although in years past, adolescence was referred to as a time of *storm and stress,* current research indicates that although the period of adolescence can be emotionally turbulent for some young people, the term *storm and stress* exaggerates what most adolescents experience (Berk, 2007).

As young people enter adolescence, they begin to make the shift from concrete to formal operational thinking. The transition takes time and usually is not completed until at least age 15 (Schave & Schave, 1989). Adolescents moving into the *formal operational* stage are able to deal with abstractions, form hypotheses, engage in mental manipulation, and predict consequences. As formal operational skills develop, they become capable of reflective abstraction, which refers to the ability to reflect on knowledge, rearrange thoughts, and discover alternative routes to solving problems (Bjorklund, 2000). Consequently, counseling approaches that provide opportunities to generate alternative solutions are more likely to be effective with adolescents than with younger children. However, some adolescents and even adults do not become fully formal operational, due, perhaps, to restricted experiences (Lehman & Nisbett, 1990).

A new form of egocentrism often emerges during adolescence, characterized by a belief in one's uniqueness and invulnerability. This egocentricism may be reflected in reckless behavior and grandiose ideas. Consequently, preventive strategies addressing such issues as substance abuse, teenage pregnancy, reckless driving, and HIV/AIDS and other sexually transmitted diseases are warranted.

Also related to a heightened sense of uniqueness is the adolescent phenomenon of feeling constantly "on stage" or playing to an imaginary audience. It is not uncommon for adolescents to feel that everyone is looking at them, leading to increased anxiety and self-consciousness. These feelings tend to peak in early adolescence and then decline as formal operational skills improve (Bjorklund, 2000).

The onset of puberty often triggers the psychosocial crisis of *identity versus role confusion* (Erikson, 1968). A key challenge during adolescence is the formation of an identity, including self-definition and a commitment to goals, values, beliefs, and life purpose. To master this challenge, adolescents need opportunities to explore options, try on various roles and responsibilities, and speculate about possibilities. Sometimes adolescents enter a period of role confusion, characterized in part by overidentification with heroes or cliques, before they develop a true sense of individuality and recognize that they are acceptable to society (Thomas, 2005).

Spending time with peers continues to be important throughout adolescence. As they develop self-confidence and sensitivity, adolescents base their friendships on compatibility and shared experiences. Intimate friendships increase, as do dating and sexual experimentation. Counseling may involve helping these young people deal with issues of complex relationships and decision making about the future.

It is important to keep in mind that developmental generalizations may not be applicable to all ethnic or cultural groups. For example, the search for self-identity may be delayed, compounded by a search for ethnic identity, or even nonexistent among certain groups of adolescents (Herring, 1997). Also, research on Piagetian tasks suggests that some forms of logic do not emerge spontaneously according to stages but are socially generated, based on cultural experiences (Berk, 2007). Developmental theories provide useful guides for understanding children and adolescents; however, no theory provides a complete explanation of development, nor does any theory take into account all cultural perspectives. In the next section, we examine some of the biological, environmental, and sociocultural influences on child and adolescent adjustment.

BIOECOLOGICAL CONSIDERATIONS

The characteristics of the person at a given time in his or her life are a joint function of the characteristics of the person and of the environment over the course of that person's life up to that time.

(Bronfenbrenner, 1989, p. 190)

Bronfenbrenner's (1979, 1989, 1995) bioecological model illustrates the way development is influenced by multilayered interactions of specific characteristics of the child (e.g., genetic, biological, and psychological factors), the immediate environment (e.g., family, school, peers, neighborhood, and community), and the more global culture, or macrosystem, within which the young person lives. These systems are not static, but instead are constantly changing. To work effectively with children and adolescents, counselors need to assess individual, environmental, and cultural factors and their interactive effects on development and adjustment. Teasing the different influences apart can be difficult, if not impossible. In this section, specific influences on young people's mental health are described. Although the various factors are presented as separate entities, it is important to keep in mind the fact that influences are reciprocal and interactive.

Psychological, Biological, and Genetic Influences

A wide array of individual characteristics, including physical appearance, personality traits, cognitive functioning, and genetic predisposition, influence the manner in which children and adolescents adjust and adapt to their environments. A key factor affecting children's development is *temperament,* which refers to specific traits with which each child is born and which influence the way the child reacts to the surrounding environment (U.S. Department of Health and Human Services, 2000). Defined more simply, temperament refers to a person's *emotional style* (Berk, 2007). Temperament includes traits such as attention span, goal orientation, activity level, curiosity, and emotional self-regulation. Differences in temperament are evidenced when one child is easily excitable and impulsive, another is shy and withdrawn, and a third is calm and attentive. Although there is some continuity in temperamental traits across the life span, temperament may be modified during development, particularly through interaction with family members (Thomas & Chess, 1977).

In addition to temperament, cognitive factors, including intelligence, information processing skills, and neurological conditions, influence child and adolescent adjustment and well-being. Cognitive skills can serve as protective factors, increasing children's chances for success in school and ability to solve problems effectively. In contrast, neurological deficits and lower levels of intellectual functioning increase the risk of school failure, thereby placing youth at a greater risk for delinquency (Calhoun, Glaser, & Bartolumucci, 2001). Genetic factors and biological abnormalities of the central nervous system caused by injury, exposure to toxins, infection, or poor nutrition can lead to deficits in cognitive development.

Faulty cognitive processing skills, such as *attributional bias,* can adversely affect an individual's reactions to people and situations. For example, juvenile offenders often attribute hostility to others in neutral situations, resulting in unwarranted acts of aggression (Calhoun et al., 2001). As another example, depressed youth often have negative attributional styles, believing that they are helpless to influence events in their lives and that they are responsible for any failures or problems that are experienced. In contrast, young people with more accurate attributional styles tend to be more adaptable and less likely to form misperceptions, leading to more effective coping and adjustment.

Just as genetic inheritance influences individual characteristics such as temperament and cognitive functioning, it also has an influence on mental health. Although the precise manner in which heredity influences mental health is not fully understood, certain mental health illnesses, including depression, anxiety, and substance abuse, appear to have a genetic component. For example, children of depressed parents are three times as likely as children of nondepressed parents to experience a depressive disorder (U.S. Department of Health and Human Services, 2000). It is theorized that multiple gene variants act in conjunction with environmental factors and developmental events to make a person more likely to experience mental health problems (National Institute of Mental Health [NIMH], 2008a). Children and adolescents who are genetically vulnerable to specific conditions may benefit from prevention efforts targeted toward certain areas, such as increasing self-esteem or improving coping responses.

Contextual Influences

Whereas genetic inheritance and other biological factors help determine individual traits and set the stage for child development, they are not the only influences. The many contexts in which young people live and interact have powerful effects on their mental health and well-being. The family, school, and peers are examples of contextual factors that influence psychological adjustment.

FAMILY INFLUENCES. One of the most significant influences on the development of young people is the family, where interactions typically occur on a daily basis. Within the family, unique bonds are formed that serve as models for relationships in the greater community. Family relationships are complex and influence development both directly and indirectly. A number of family-related variables have been identified as risk factors for adverse mental health, including severe parental discord, parent psychopathology, overcrowding, and economic hardship (U.S. Department of Health and Human Services, 2000). In contrast, healthy interactions among family members can lead to positive outcomes as well as be a buffer against negative influences, such as illness or poverty, over which the family has little control.

The quality of the relationship between children and their caregivers is of principal importance to well-being across the life span. Parent–child interactions have been associated with a wide range of developmental outcomes, including self-confidence, academic achievement, psychological health, and conduct. In particular, parent–child interactions that are marked by high levels of parental support and behavioral control help children develop mastery and competence (Maccoby & Martin, 1983). Supportive behaviors are those that facilitate socialization through warmth, nurturance, responsiveness, and open communication. Controlling behaviors, including rule-setting, negotiating, and consistent discipline, help establish guidance and flexibility within the power hierarchy of the family. By combining the dimensions of support and control according to high and low extremes, parenting styles can be classified into four types: authoritative, authoritarian, indulgent, and neglecting (Baumrind, 1971; Maccoby & Martin, 1983). These four parenting types are depicted in Figure 12–2.

Authoritative families are characterized by emotional support, high standards, appropriate autonomy granting, and clear communication (Darling & Steinberg, 1993). Authoritative parents monitor their children and set clear standards for conduct. Disciplinary methods are inductive rather than punitive, and parental responses are consistent. Children are listened to and participate in family decision making. Goals for children in an authoritative family include social responsibility, self-regulation, and cooperation (Baumrind, 1991).

Authoritative parenting has been linked with a wide range of positive child outcomes, including social competence, psychological well-being, fewer conduct problems, and higher scholastic performance (e.g., Baumrind, 1991; Lamborn, Mounts, Steinberg, & Dornbusch, 1991; Supple & Small, 2006). Systematic efforts to educate parents about effective parenting processes and authoritative parenting practices can help improve the quality of family life and parent–child relationships. A variety of forums can be used to implement the teaching of parenting skills, including community-based parent education programs and school-sponsored clinics for parents.

In addition to parenting styles and practices, several other family-related factors influence child adjustment. Family structure (i.e., divorced, single-parent, married), family size, socioeconomic status, the amount of time family members spend together, and issues such

		Support	
		Accepting, responsive, child-centered	Rejecting, unresponsive, parent-centered
Control	**Demanding, Controlling**	AUTHORITATIVE Reciprocal, high in bidirectional communication	AUTHORITARIAN Power-assertive, high in control
	Undemanding, Low in control attempts	INDULGENT Permissive, warm, noncontrolling	NEGLECTING Ignoring, indifferent, uninvolved

FIGURE 12–2   A two-dimensional classification of parenting patterns
Source: Adapted from E. E. Maccoby and J. A. Martin, Socialization in the Context of the Family: Parent–Child Interaction, in E. M. Hetherington (Ed.), *Handbook of Child Psychology: Vol. 4, Socialization, Personality, and Social Development* (4th ed., p. 39), New York: Wiley. Copyright 1983. This material is used by permission of John Wiley & Sons, Inc.

as neglect and abuse all influence adjustment in various ways. Clinical mental health counselors who work with children and adolescents need to be aware of these influences, help families build on strengths, and target areas in which improvement is needed.

SCHOOL INFLUENCES.   The unique characteristics of the school context give it special prominence in child and adolescent development. Through interactions with peers, teachers, and other adults in the school, young people make judgments about themselves, their capabilities, and their goals for the future. Consequently, experiences in school play a major role in the development of individual differences in children and adolescents.

Schools in which support, trust, respect, optimism, and intentionality are demonstrated foster the development of positive student attitudes and behaviors (Purkey, 1991). In particular, supportive teachers can positively influence students' self-confidence and performance (Newsome, 1999). Also, schools that are orderly and organized, with consistent and fair enforcement of rules, are conducive to positive student behaviors, although excessive teacher control and discipline can be detrimental to adolescent adjustment and achievement (Eccles, Lord, & Midgley, 1991). Other factors that contribute to positive outcomes in youth include:

- Communication between teachers and parents
- Providing tasks that are challenging but not overwhelming
- Communicating the importance of effort in success
- Stressing individual progress and self-improvement
- Small classes that permit teachers to provide individualized support for mastery
- Cooperative learning and peer tutoring
- Accommodating individual and cultural differences in learning styles (Ames, 1992; Eccles, Wigfield, & Schiefele, 1998)

It is important for counselors to be aware of the powerful influence the school context has on young people. Community and agency counselors can work collaboratively with school counselors, teachers, and other school personnel to optimize child and adolescent development.

PEER INFLUENCES.   Relationships with peers—at home, at school, and in the community—become increasingly important as children grow older. Peer interaction plays a key role in helping children learn to take different perspectives and understand other points of view. Peer acceptance, which refers to being liked by other children, shapes the views children have of themselves as well as their views of others.

Whereas some children are well liked and make friends easily, others are rejected or neglected. Unfortunately, some children are the victims of frequent verbal and/or physical attacks by other children. Such victimization leads to a variety of adjustment difficulties, including depression, loneliness, and school avoidance (Ladd, Kochendorfer, & Coleman, 1997). Counselors can intervene at various levels to assist children who are having difficulties with peers. Depending on the situation, it may be necessary to help children develop social skills or assertiveness skills. Individual and group counseling interventions can include coaching, modeling, reinforcing positive social skills, and teaching perspective taking. Community and agency counselors can intervene systemically by working collaboratively with schools to develop codes against bullying and by conducting parent education groups to help ameliorate all forms of bullying.

During adolescence, young people begin spending more time with peers and less time with family members. Typically, friendships are formed with peers who have similar interests, values, and behaviors. Most often, peer group association positively influences well-being, as teenagers learn adaptive skills that benefit adjustment. In some cases, however, the peer group provides a negative context in which antisocial behaviors are the norm. For example, young people who were aggressive and rejected as children and who feel distanced from their families are likely to become involved with deviant peers and engage in antisocial behaviors (Berk, 2007). Difficult temperament, low intelligence, poor school performance, peer rejection in childhood, and being involved with antisocial peer groups are associated with juvenile delinquency, a widespread problem that affects a substantial proportion of criminal offenses committed in the United States. A comprehensive report about juvenile offenders was released by the U.S. Department of Justice in 2006, entitled *Juvenile Offenders and Victims: 2006 National Report*. This document, which can be accessed at www.ojjdp.ncjrs.gov/ojstatbb/nr2006/index.html, indicates that although the rate of juvenile violent crime arrests in the United States has decreased since 1994, a significant proportion (approximately 17%) of criminal activity continues to be attributed to juvenile offenders.

NORMATIVE AND NONNORMATIVE LIFE EVENTS. Many of the developmental challenges young people face are expected: physical changes, school transitions, emerging sexuality, changes in cognitive functioning, and changes in family and peer relationships. Developmental transitions of this nature are considered normative; that is, they are anticipated generic challenges that everyone encounters. In some contexts, developmental challenges are compounded by chronic stressors, which are enduring aspects of the environment that involve deprivation or hardship. Poverty, physical disability, and family dysfunction are examples of chronic stressors that can exert taxing demands on families.

Whereas normative life events are expected, nonnormative life events are those unexpected, acute demands that may alter the course of development, either directly or transactionally (Compas, 1987). Nonnormative life events include parental divorce, death of a family member, onset of illness or disability, and loss of a job. Catastrophic phenomena—sudden, powerful events that require major adaptive responses from the groups sharing the experience (e.g., natural disasters, accidents, and terrorism)—also are considered nonnormative events (McNamara, 2000). The devastation caused by Hurricane Katrina to residents in New Orleans and surrounding areas in 2005 exemplifies a nonnormative event that continues to have significant ramifications for over 15 million people (HurricaneKatrinaRelief.com, 2008). Nonnormative events are not always negative, however. Examples of positive events include inheriting a large amount of money or being selected for a coveted position.

Normative and nonnormative events occur in multiple contexts and have a wide range of effects on the people experiencing them. Frequency, intensity, and timing of the events can affect youth's mental health, with outcomes being moderated by subjective perceptions, parental and peer support, and coping skills (Newsome, Whitlatch, Southern, & Erford, in press). To understand young clients' developmental trajectories, counselors need to assess the normative and nonnormative life events they have experienced. They can help children handle negative life events more effectively by implementing stress management interventions that are tailored toward helping children use active, problem-focused coping strategies.

CULTURAL INFLUENCES.   Another ecological factor that exerts a strong influence on the development and adjustment of young people is the broader culture in which they live. Cultural beliefs, values, and institutions compose what Bronfenbrenner (1979, 1995) referred to as the *macrosystem*. In Chapter 4, we described the multidimensional aspects of culture. On one level, children are influenced by the dominant culture of a society: its values, laws, customs, and resources. When children are members of one or more minority groups, they are affected not only by the belief system of the dominant culture but also by the values that guide the minority cultures. The various sociocultural influences interact, and sometimes conflict, to shape the developing child's subjective worldview.

McClure and Teyber (2003) illustrated the effects cultural influences can have on the counseling process in the following examples:

> An adolescent, African American male who is "paranoid" around authority figures is often accurately discerning a persecutory or hostile environment given his life experiences. A counselor who diagnoses him as paranoid (which frequently occurs) and focuses on helping him see "reality" (i.e., the *counselor's* subjective worldview) would quickly lose credibility. Similarly, encouraging a young adult from a traditional Asian family to emancipate and become more autonomous from her family may only engender increased distress. (pp. 7–8)

Competent counselors are aware of the array of cultural issues that influence child and adolescent development. They recognize the importance of evaluating which cultural aspects are relevant to a particular individual and plan interventions that build on cultural strengths (Liu & Clay, 2002).

Summary

In this section, we have discussed developmental considerations that need to be taken into account when counseling children and adolescents. We also have described some of the bioecological factors that influence development. With that background in mind, we next focus on ways to counsel effectively with young people.

COUNSELING CONSIDERATIONS

Working effectively with young people requires a special knowledge of child development, contextual influences, and child-related counseling procedures. Children's needs, wishes, behaviors, and ways of viewing the world differ significantly from those of adults. Indeed, interventions that are appropriate for adults may be ineffective or even detrimental when applied to children and adolescents (Sherwood-Hawes, 1993). Through all stages of the counseling process, counselors need to take into account universal developmental principles as well as the unique, subjective way in which each child views the world.

Building a Counseling Relationship

The key to any successful counseling experience is developing an effective working relationship based on mutual trust and acceptance. Ways to go about establishing such a relationship with adults were described in Chapter 6. But how are therapeutic relationships built with children? Perhaps the most important first step is being willing to enter completely into the child's world, with no preconceptions, expectations, or agenda. All judgment needs to be suspended so that the counselor can remain open to what the child is sharing, either verbally or nonverbally. As the therapeutic relationship is being established, listening and observational skills are more important than questioning skills (Erdman & Lampe, 1996). By listening carefully to what young clients have to say, giving them undivided attention, and responding sensitively to feelings, reactions, and cultural cues, counselors can create bridges of trust and understanding.

ESTABLISHING RAPPORT. To build relationships successfully, counselors need to tailor their responses and interactions to fit the specific needs of each child, taking into account developmental experiences, sociocultural background, and reasons for referral (McClure & Teyber, 2003). With these considerations in mind, the counselor can select from a variety of approaches to help establish rapport. When working with young children who have difficulty verbalizing, play and art media can be especially effective. With older children, games like Jenga or "in-house" basketball can provide a nonthreatening introduction to the counseling process. I (DN) like to use a dry erase whiteboard and markers with children, inviting them to draw pictures or symbols that illustrate things they would like me to know about them. As a variation, I ask young clients to create an About Me collage by decoratively writing their names in the center of a piece of poster board. Then I invite them to draw or select magazine pictures that describe different aspects of themselves, including strengths, interests, relationships, or other characteristics they want to reveal at that point. Their choices serve as a springboard for further discussion and provide a lens for glimpsing their subjective worlds.

One of the factors that makes building a relationship with children different from building a relationship with adults is that children often do not understand what counseling is. They may be confused about the nature and process of counseling, fearful of being in an unknown situation, and/or resistant to talking about issues with a stranger. Typically, children are brought to counseling by parents or by other significant adults in their lives, and it is these adults, not the children, who want change to occur. This is particularly true when children or adolescents are referred because of behavioral patterns that bother adults (Sommers-Flanagan & Sommers-Flanagan, 2007). The counselor's task is to find ways to involve the child in the counseling process, first by clarifying the counseling role.

CLARIFYING THE COUNSELING ROLE. During the initial session, counselors need to find ways to explain to the child what counseling is all about. Any delay in getting to the reason for counseling can cause undue anxiety for children. After introducing myself, I (DN) try to find out why children think they are meeting with me. Although some children have had past experiences in counseling, many have not. Some of the responses children have given me include, "My mom said you are a doctor, but I'm not sick," "It's because I get mad too much," and the most frequent answer, "I don't know!" A short explanation of the counseling role can help establish structure, set expectations, and initiate the development of a collaborative therapeutic relationship. A counselor might say something like, "My job is to help children with lots of different things. Sometimes people have uncomfortable feelings they want to talk about. Other people might want help figuring out a problem. I wonder how I might be able to help you?"

Many times, parents or caregivers are included in the initial sessions with children. When this is the case, it is helpful to clarify the counseling role with everyone involved. It is especially important to dissipate any misconceptions about the purpose of counseling, such as beliefs that counseling will "fix" the child. It also is wise to let parents know that things may get worse before they get better. Depending on the child's age, it may be helpful to meet with everyone together at the outset and then meet separately with the child and the caregiver.

EXPLAINING CONFIDENTIALITY. Issues related to confidentiality can create challenging legal and ethical dilemmas for counselors who work with minors (Lawrence & Robinson Kurpius, 2000). As discussed in Chapter 3, the assurance of confidentiality is fundamental to the counseling process. Counselors have a responsibility to protect information received through confidential counseling relationships with all clients, including children. However, this responsibility often conflicts with legal rights of parents or guardians, which include the right to determine the need for counseling, the right to access pertinent information about their children's treatment, and the right to control the release of information that results from counseling (Glosoff, 2001). It is important to clarify with parents and their children the conditions and limits of confidentiality before counseling begins. Ethical and legal guidelines related to confidentiality and other topics pertinent to counseling with minors are presented in Figure 12–3.

BOX 12–1

Suggestions for Counselors Working with Minors

- Practice within the limits of your abilities, based on education, training, and supervised practice.
- Be thoroughly familiar with state statutes regarding privilege, informed consent, and child abuse reporting.
- Clarify policies regarding confidentiality with the child and the parents before beginning counseling. Ask everyone to sign a written statement of these policies.
- If you work with a minor without the parent's informed consent, ask the minor to provide informed assent in writing. Be aware of potential legal risks.
- Keep accurate and objective records of all counseling sessions, decisions, and interactions.
- Maintain adequate professional liability coverage.
- When in doubt, confer with other professionals and have legal assistance available.

Lawrence and Robinson Kurpius, 2000

In many cases, it is in the child's best interest to involve the parents in the counseling process. Taylor and Adelman (2001) maintain that keeping information from parents can impede the counselor's efforts to help the child. They recommend orienting the parents to the counseling process, educating them about confidentiality with minors, and letting them know that any vital information that affects their child's well-being will be shared. By orienting parents in this way, they are more likely to support the process and respect their child's right to privacy (Welfel, 2006).

The way a counselor approaches the issue of confidentiality with children depends on their age. Young children typically do not have an understanding of confidentiality or the need for it (Remley & Herlihy, 2010). It is important to explain the concept in words the

Professional Competence: The American Counseling Association (2005) *Code of Ethics* mandates that counselors practice only within their bounds of competence, based on education, training, supervised practice, and appropriate experience (ACA, 2005, C.2.a). Knowledge and skills needed to work effectively with minor clients differ from those needed to work with adult clients. Counselors who work with children need to be trained in child development and child counseling theory, as well as have an understanding of child psychopathology.

Informed Consent: Informed consent is "the formal permission given by a client that signals the beginning of the legal contractual agreement that allows treatment to be initiated" (Lawrence & Robinson Kurpius, 2000, p. 133). Legally, minor clients cannot enter into contracts. The ACA Code (2005) states that when minors or other individuals cannot give voluntary, informed consent, parents or guardians should be included in the counseling process (B.5). Ideally, if clients are minors, counselors should obtain signed informed *consent* from the parent(s) and *assent* from the minor client (Glosoff, 2001).

There are some instances in which minor clients can enter into treatment without parental consent, although the exceptions differ from state to state, depending on legal statutes. Typical exceptions include:

• Mature or emancipated minors: A mature minor is usually over the age of 16 (in some states, 14) and is capable of understanding the nature and consequences of agreeing to a proposed treatment. An emancipated minor is a child under the age of 18 who lives separately from parents or guardians and manages his or her own financial affairs (American Bar Association, 1980). Being head of a household, employed, in the armed forces, or married may constitute an exception in which the adolescent can give informed consent (Welfel, 2006).

• In some states, parental informed consent may not be required when the minor is in treatment for drugs or narcotics, for sexually transmitted diseases, for pregnancy and birth control counseling, or when waiting for parental consent would endanger the minor client's life or health.

Confidentiality: Counselors have the *ethical* obligation to protect minor clients' privacy. However, parents and guardians have the *legal* right to determine the need for treatment and the right to access pertinent information about their child's treatment. At times, ethical dilemmas arise trying to balance legal requirements and ethical responsibilities. Because state laws differ, counselors need to be familiar with the legal requirements of the state in which they practice. Counselors can motivate minor clients to disclose on their own when such disclosures would be beneficial and can involve the parents in creating mutually agreed on guidelines for disclosure (Lawrence & Robinson Kurpius, 2000).

Counselors need to discuss confidentiality and its limits with the parents and the child before counseling begins. Minor clients need to know that if they make a threat to hurt themselves or others, the counselor will be required to breach confidentiality. In some instances, duty to warn also applies to threats to destroy property (e.g., *Peck v. Counseling Service of Addison County,* 1985).

Reporting Abuse: All states have statutes requiring counselors and other professionals to report suspected child abuse and neglect (Kemp, 1998). Counselors are advised to become familiar with the wording of the statute for their particular state. In general, statutes require counselors to report if they have reason to believe that (a) a child is currently being abused or neglected, or (b) the child has been abused or neglected in the past. Requirements for reporting past abuse differ when the child is no longer in danger. Reporters are protected from liability as long as reports are made in good faith. When making the decision to report, it may be helpful to consult with professional colleagues or to gain legal advice. As with other counseling decisions, it is important to document the report and the reasons for making it.

FIGURE 12–3   Legal and ethical issues related to counseling minors

From Glosoff, 2001; Lawrence & Robinson Kurpius, 2000; and Remley & Herlihy, 2010.

child can understand. Therefore, the counselor might say, "Most of the things you and I talk about in here are between you and me, unless you tell me that you are planning to hurt yourself or someone else. If you tell me something that I think your mom (dad, other care-giver) needs to know, you and I will talk about it first."

Adolescents often have a heightened concern about privacy and confidentiality in the counseling relationship (Remley & Herlihy, 2010). Clinicians who work with adolescents can help adolescents understand confidentiality and its limits from the outset. It also is important for them to feel free to disclose their concerns in an atmosphere of trust. Balancing issues related to trust and minor consent laws can often be challenging.

It is not unusual for clinical mental health counselors to encounter dilemmas related to the requirements of confidentiality and the counselor's responsibilities to parents or other caregivers. By keeping the lines of communication open and taking responsibility for know-ing state and federal law, it may be possible to circumvent potential problems before they arise (Welfel, 2006). Also, some helpful references regarding minors' rights include the fol-lowing (cited in Thompson & Henderson, 2007):

- *State Minor Consent Laws: A Summary* (English & Kenney, 2003). Provides a state-by-state description of the legal status of minors.
- The Guttmacher Institute (www.guttmacher.org). Publishes policy briefs and summaries of laws that pertain to young people.
- The American Bar Association (www.abanet.org/public.html). Provides information about state laws and minors.
- Books on ethical and legal issues in counseling and psychotherapy (e.g., Remley & Herlihy, 2010; Welfel, 2006; Wheeler & Bertram, 2008).

In addition to consulting written materials related to minors and confidentiality, if you work with children, you will want to determine the policies that guide your work setting regarding confidentiality issues with minors (Salo, 2006).

Assessment and Evaluation

Assessment is an integral part of the counseling process. As described in Chapter 7, assessment is an ongoing process in which counselors gather information about clients from several different sources and then use that information to make decisions about treatment planning. Assessment also provides a way to evaluate counseling progress and outcomes. Assessment methods, which can be formal or informal, help counselors under-stand children's current problems or concerns within the context of their unique develop-mental histories.

INTERVIEWS.   Initial assessment typically begins with an intake that involves the child and the child's parents or guardians. The amount of time spent with everyone together versus time spent with each individual depends on the age of the child, the nature of the problem, the family dynamics, agency policy, and the particular work setting (e.g., an inpa-tient setting will differ from a private practice setting). During the intake session, the types of rapport-building activities described earlier in the chapter can be used to gather impor-tant information about the child. In many agencies, intake forms are available for use with children and families.

Early and ongoing assessment is necessary for accurate case conceptualization and effective intervention planning. Orton (1997) suggests conducting a complete developmental assessment that provides counselors with the following information:

- **The Specific Concerns That Brought the Child to Counseling.** The manifestation, intensity, frequency, and duration of the concerns should be explored. In what settings or around which individuals are the concerns evidenced? Expression, manifestation, and course of a disorder in children may be quite different from adults (U.S. Department of Health and Human Services, 2000). Certain behaviors may be normal at one age but represent a problem at another age (e.g., temper tantrums exhibited by a 3-year-old child versus tantrums exhibited by a 6-year-old). Assessment, diagnosis, and treatment planning need to occur within the context of the child's overall development.
- **Physical, Cognitive, Emotional, and Social Development.** Evaluating each of these areas of development is essential to conducting a thorough assessment. When possible, counselor will want to obtain information about the child's medical history, perinatal history, motor development, cognitive functioning, and ability to express and regulate emotions. They also will want to gather information about socioeconomic and sociocultural factors that have affected development. To facilitate information gathering, counselors can ask parents or guardians to complete an information form, which includes questions about the child's physical, cognitive, emotional, and social development, prior to or immediately following the initial counseling session (Orton, 1997). The counselor can use the form to guide exploration of any areas that may be contributing to the problem.
- **Relationships Between the Child and His or Her Parents, Siblings, and Peers.** Understanding the nature and quality of relationships the child has with family members and peers is a key component of child assessment. Topics to be addressed include the child's living arrangements, home responsibilities, parental methods of discipline, the child's response to discipline, and typical family activities, and a "typical day." Interview questions or qualitative assessment methods such as the genogram or the Kinetic Family Drawing (i.e., asking the child to draw a picture of everyone in the family doing something) can provide rich information about relationships, as can ongoing observation of interactions as the counselor works with the child and the family.
- **The Child's School Experiences, Including Academics, Attendance, and Attitude.** Academic and social successes or failures play an important part in children's overall development. Children who experience repeated failures often have poor self-esteem and may engage in disruptive behaviors as a way of compensating. Also, school failure may signify a learning disorder that typically requires formal testing for diagnosis. Because of the pervasive effect school has on children's lives, it is advisable to ask parents to sign a consent form for release of information so that the school can be contacted early in the counseling process.
- **The Child's Strengths, Talents, and Support System.** Implementing a strengths-based approach to assessment can help take the focus off the problem so that it is possible to begin moving toward solutions. Creative activities, checklists, and various qualitative assessment methods provide useful tools for evaluating strengths and supports. After learning about children's special skills and interests, counselors can incorporate them into treatment planning. For example, if a child enjoys art, the counselor can select expressive art interventions to facilitate the change process.

INFORMAL AND FORMAL ASSESSMENT. Informal assessment includes direct observation and qualitative assessment methods. As we discussed in Chapter 7, qualitative assessment emphasizes holistic procedures that typically are not standardized and do not produce quantitative raw scores. A variety of qualitative assessment methods can be used with children and adolescents, including informal checklists, unfinished sentences, decision-making dilemmas, writing activities, games, expressive arts, storytelling, role-play activities, and play therapy strategies (Vernon, 2004). Informal assessment procedures of this nature can reveal patterns of thoughts and behaviors relevant to concerns and issues. Such methods are especially helpful with young children, who may not know exactly what is bothering them or lack the words to express their concerns verbally (Orton, 1997).

Formal assessment instruments that have been standardized and have sound psychometric properties provide a way for counselors to gain a somewhat more objective view of children's behaviors or attributes than do informal methods of assessment (Orton, 1997). Whereas some instruments are designed to assess specific disorders (e.g., the *Children's Depression Inventory,* Kovacs, 1992), others assess a full range of behavioral and emotional symptoms and disorders (e.g., *Achenbach System of Empirically Based Assessment*). A number of questionnaires, scales, and checklists designed to assess attributes, behaviors, interests, and emotional states of children and adolescents have been published in recent years. To learn about different options, counselors can refer to resources such as the *Mental Measurements Yearbook,* published by the Buros Institute, which provides descriptions and reviews of a wide range of published instruments. Carefully selected formal assessment tools can supplement and enhance the information counselors gather through less formal methods of assessment.

By appraising children's therapeutic needs through interviews, informal assessment, and formal assessment, the counselor gains a better understanding of the child's development and concerns. This understanding can then be used to set goals, design and implement interventions, and evaluate the counseling process. As with adults, the information gained through assessment sometimes leads to a diagnosis, using an established diagnostic classification system, such as the *Diagnostic and Statistical Manual of Mental Disorders* (*DSM-IV-TR;* American Psychiatric Association [APA], 2000; see Chapter 7). However, the criteria for diagnosing many mental disorders in children are derived from adult criteria, and less research has been conducted on children to verify their validity (U.S. Department of Health and Human Services, 2000). Consequently, diagnosing childhood mental disorders is a challenging task and requires training and supervision.

Designing and Implementing a Treatment Plan

Several factors affect treatment planning for child and adolescent clients. The age and characteristics of the child; the nature of the presenting issue; and the counselor's theoretical approach, past training, and current skills all influence the selection of interventions. Competent counselors take each of these factors into consideration. If they realize that the presenting issue is out of their bounds of competence, they take steps to match the child with a counselor who is prepared to work with the issue.

INTENTIONALITY AND FLEXIBILITY. Counselors who work with children and adolescents need to be intentional and flexible as they conceptualize cases and design interventions. Being intentional refers to taking steps to set counseling goals collaboratively with the child and, in many cases, the child's parents or caregivers. Being flexible refers to the counselor's ability to adapt strategies to meet the specific needs of the child in his or her context. No single counseling approach is best for all children or all problems. Counselors who are familiar with a wide array of interventions and child-based counseling strategies can personalize the treatment plan so that the possibility of a positive outcome is enhanced. Also, to work effectively with children (as well as with adults), counselors need to be cognizant of ethnicity, gender, socioeconomic status, and other areas of diversity.

One way counselors can intentionally plan interventions is by asking specific questions related to the following areas (Vernon, 1993):

a. ***Vision.*** What could be different? How could things be better? What would be ideal?
b. ***Goal Setting.*** What is going well? What needs to be worked on?
c. ***Analysis.*** What is enabling or interfering with achieving these goals? What is getting in the way of solving the problem?
d. ***Objective.*** What specifically does the child want to change?
e. ***Exploration of Interventions.*** What has already been tried, and how did it work? Who else will be involved in the counseling process? What types of activities does the child respond to best? What has research shown to be the most effective interventions for this type of concern?

SELECTING INTERVENTIONS. Using information gathered through assessment and goal setting, counselors can begin making decisions about which intervention to implement. No one theoretical approach to counseling children and adolescents has been found to be generally more effective than another (Sexton, Whiston, Bleuer, & Walz, 1997). Instead, a systematic, eclectic approach enables counselors to work constructively with the many different needs and concerns that bring young people to counseling.

Although more outcome-based research has been conducted with adults than with children, a body of information is beginning to accumulate matching efficacious interventions with specific concerns and needs. Consequently, clinical mental health counselors will want to be familiar with current outcome research on effective treatment when selecting interventions. For example, an empirically supported approach to providing treatment for children with attention-deficit/hyperactivity disorder (ADHD) is a multimodal, multisystemic approach that involves parent training, counseling, and school interventions (Edwards, 2002). For adolescents with conduct disorder, a promising treatment is multisystemic therapy (MST), an intensive home- and family-focused treatment (U.S. Department of Health and Human Services, 2000). MST integrates empirically based treatment approaches such as cognitive skills training into an ecological framework that addresses the family, peer, school, and community context (Schoenwald, Brown, & Henggeler, 2000). Other examples of efficacious treatments include play or art therapy for sexually abused children and cognitive–behavioral approaches for children who are depressed or anxious. It is the counselor's responsibility to keep up with current research to provide the best possible care for their young clients.

Creative Interventions

USING EXPRESSIVE ARTS WITH CHILDREN AND FAMILIES. Counseling young people effectively often requires a departure from traditional talk therapy. In many cases, an integrative approach that uses a variety of techniques, including art, music, clay, puppetry, storytelling, drama, bibliotherapy, sand play, and other forms of directive and nondirective play therapy can guide the counseling process and promote healing and growth. Counselors who work with children are encouraged to refer to the many excellent resources that are available to enhance their expertise in using play and expressive arts in counseling.

BOX 12–2

Expressive arts have been a part of my counseling since I began working as a counselor. I have worked with different ages and in different settings, and I have found that expressive arts easily transfer everywhere. My clients quickly come to understand that I may ask them to draw, paint, string beads, tell stories, act things out, or play, in addition to traditional talking. I may initially encounter surprise, disbelief, reluctance, or fear, but I have yet to be turned down.

What I have found by using creative arts is that my clients relax, have a sense of playfulness, and open up more quickly. I have used creative arts to draw out depressed clients who are locked up in their despair; gain trust with a mistrustful child; help a family learn to positively interact with one another; give an adolescent a chance to express herself in new ways; calm an anxious parent; and join a group together. The possibilities are only as limited as my mind. When I encounter my own limitations, I ask my clients for options. They often come up with the most creative ideas.

There are also personal advantages for me in using expressive arts as a counselor. I find my sessions to be exciting and packed with energy. I look forward to helping people find new ways to express themselves. As a counselor, I feel it is important to be myself. Being creative is a natural part of who I am. Using expressive arts in counseling is a perfect match for me.

Elizabeth Vaughan, M.A. Ed., LPC

CONCERNS AFFECTING CHILDREN AND ADOLESCENTS

Clinical counselors who work with children and adolescents are likely to see a wide range of presenting problems, including mood disorders, anxiety disorders, attention-deficit/hyperactivity disorder (ADHD), aggressive or antisocial behaviors, learning disorders, and eating disorders. They also are likely to work with young people coping with family disruption, abuse, violence, unemployment, and grief. In this section, we provide an overview of three disorders that may be experienced by young people: depression, eating disorders, and ADHD. We also describe three common concerns associated with childhood and adolescence: parental divorce, death of a loved one, and child maltreatment. Other childhood disorders and concerns are listed in Appendix B. To work effectively with the many issues that affect children and adolescents, counselors need to consult resources that deal specifically with children's mental health issues and participate in additional educational experiences, training, and supervision.

Depression[1]

Depression is a mood disorder that can affect thoughts, feelings, behaviors, and overall health. It can affect relationships, academic performance, sleeping, appetite, self-esteem, and thought processes. A depressed child may pretend to be sick, refuse to go to school, cling to caretakers, or worry that a caretaker may die (National Institute of Mental Health [NIMH], 2008a). The onset

---

[1]Portions of this section were taken from the chapter, *Helping Students with Depression,* written by Newsome, Southern, & Erford, which is in the book, *Handbook of Professional School Counseling* (2nd ed.), edited by B. T. Erford (in press).

of major depressive disorders typically is between the ages of 13 and 19, with depression being one of the most common psychological problems of adolescence (Birmaher, Ryan, & Williamson, 1996). Unless treated, early onset of depression can predict more severe and negative symptoms later in life. Untreated mood disorders also increase the risk of suicide, particularly during the adolescent years (U.S. Department of Health and Human Services, 2000). The Child Welfare League of America (2008) reported that suicide is the third leading cause of death for 15- to 24-year-olds and the sixth leading cause of death for 5- to 14-year-olds and that attempted suicides are even more common.

MANIFESTATION OF DEPRESSION. Levels of depression in young people can vary, ranging from depressed mood, which is not a clinical disorder, to more severe diagnosable mood disorders. Approximately one third of adolescents experience depressed mood for short or extended periods of time. Depressed mood is characterized by negative emotions, which may include sadness, anxiety, guilt, disgust, anger, and fear (Petersen, Compas, & Brooks-Gunn, 1992).

For depression to be considered a clinical disorder, a collection of symptoms must be evidenced that meet specific diagnostic criteria according to standardized classification systems, such as the *DSM-IV-TR* (APA, 2000). Diagnosis is based on the intensity and duration of a set of symptoms serious enough to interfere with one's level of functioning. Examples of depressive disorders include major depressive disorder and dysthymic disorder. Adjustment disorder with depressed mood (or mixed anxiety and depressed mood) also is marked by depressive symptoms, as are bipolar disorder, cyclothymic disorder, and mood disorder due to medical condition or substance abuse.

Identifying depression in young people may be challenging because the symptoms are often masked. Although the key defining features of major depressive disorder are the same for youth as for adults, it may be difficult for young people to identify or describe their feelings (NIMH, 2008a). Instead, depressed children and adolescents may appear irritable, act out, or withdraw from family and friends. Also, they may display more anxiety symptoms and somatic complaints than adults. A list of common signs and symptoms of depression in young people is presented in Figure 12–4.

Some two thirds of children and adolescents with clinical depression also have another clinical disorder (U.S. Department of Health and Human Services, 2000). The most commonly associated disorders include anxiety disorders, disruptive disorders, eating disorders, substance abuse, and personality disorders. When a young person has more than one disorder, depression is more likely to begin after the onset of the other disorder, with the exception of substance abuse. Counselors will want to be alert to the possibility of dual or multiple diagnoses and be prepared to plan interventions accordingly.

ETIOLOGY AND RISK FACTORS. Several factors are associated with the etiology (causes) of depression, including biological, cognitive, and environmental variables. Biological explanations focus on the role of genetics and biochemical factors associated with depression. It is theorized that multiple gene variants, rather than a single gene, act in conjunction with environmental factor and developmental events, thus making a person more likely to experience depressive symptoms (NIMH, 2008a). Various neurotransmitters, including serotonin, norepinephrine, and dopamine, are associated with depression. These neurotransmitters function within structures of the brain that regulate emotions, reactions to stress, and various physical drives (e.g., sleep, appetite, and sexuality).

FIGURE 12–4 Signs and symptoms of depression in children and adolescents

From NIMH, 2008; and Rice & Leffert, 1997

- Feeling sad, empty, or hopeless
- Increased emotional sensitivity
- Lack of interest or ability to engage in pleasurable activities
- Decreased energy level
- Physical complaints (headaches, stomachaches, tiredness)
- Frequent absences from school (or poor performance)
- Outbursts (shouting, complaining, crying)
- Being bored
- Substance abuse
- Fear of death
- Suicidal ideation
- Sleep/appetite disturbances
- Reduced ability to think clearly and make decisions
- Increased irritability, anger, or restlessness
- Failure to make expected weight gains
- Reckless behavior
- Difficulty with relationships

Cognitive theory describes a strong link between an individual's cognitions, emotions, and behaviors. According to cognitive theory, people's interpretations of events, rather than the events themselves, trigger emotional upsets and mood disturbances (e.g., Beck, 1976). Such interpretations affect one's view of self, the world, and the future. Inaccurate interpretations, or faulty information processing, can lead to depressive symptoms in young people (Kendall, 2006). Examples of faulty information processing include negative attributions (e.g., when children believe they are helpless to influence events in their lives) and cognitive distortions (e.g., minimizing positive accomplishments and maximizing negative events).

Other explanations of depression emphasize the role played by stressful life events. Youth who experience numerous stressors may be more likely to experience depression than those who do not. Stressors can be categorized as normative life events (expected changes, such as school entry and puberty), nonnormative events (divorce, abuse, moving away), and daily hassles (conflict with friends, excessive schoolwork). Exposure to stress triggers several physical, emotional, and cognitive changes in the body, and long-term exposure can lead to physical and psychosocial difficulties, including depression (Sharrer & Ryan-Wenger, 2002). The manner in which stress is experienced varies greatly from child to child. Preventive strategies, such as teaching constructive coping skills, can help children manage stress more effectively.

OTHER RISK FACTORS. A number of other factors have been linked with depression, including family conflict, the emotional unavailability of parents, poor peer relationships, being considered "different," loss of a loved one, breakup of a relationship, chronic illness, and abuse (NIMH, 2008a; Rice & Leffert, 1997). A thorough developmental assessment can alert counselors to the presence of conditions that might make children more vulnerable to depression and thus can inform treatment planning.

TREATMENT STRATEGIES. Counselors who work with depressed young people typically involve both the individual and the family (McWhirter & Burrow, 2001). In some settings, counselors conduct group interventions, which can be especially effective with older children and adolescents.

Research has demonstrated the efficacy of certain approaches, especially cognitive–behavioral therapy (CBT), in alleviating depressive symptoms in young people (NIMH, 2008a; Reinecke, Ryan, & DuBois, 1998). The goal of CBT is to help clients develop cognitive structures that will positively influence their future experiences (Kendall, 2006). The cognitive component of CBT helps individuals identify and change negative, pessimistic thinking, biases, and attributions. Examples of cognitive based strategies include:

1. Recognizing the connections among thoughts, feelings, and behaviors
2. Monitoring negative automatic thoughts
3. Examining evidence that refutes distorted automatic cognitions
4. Substituting more realistic interpretations for distorted cognitions
5. Regulating emotions and controlling impulses (McWhirter & Burrow, 2001, pp. 201–202)

The behavioral component, also important to the process, focuses on increasing positive behavior patterns and improving social skills (Asarnow, Jaycox, & Tompson, 2001). Other behavioral strategies include relaxation training, social skills training, and behavioral rehearsal (McWhirter & Burrow, 2001).

Another type of counseling, interpersonal therapy for adolescents (IPT-A), was adapted from IPT for adults (Mufson, Moreau, Weissman, & Klerman, 1993). Depression is viewed as a conflict taking place in the context of interpersonal relationships (Mufson & Fairbanks, 1996). The two primary goals of IPT are to reduce depressive symptoms and to improve disturbed relationships that may contribute to depression. In treatment, five potential areas of concern are addressed: grief, interpersonal role disputes, role transitions, deficits in interpersonal skills, and single-parent families.

FAMILY INTERVENTIONS. Concurrent family consultation or family counseling is nearly always indicated when working with depressed children and adolescents (McWhirter & Burrow, 2001). Frequently, counselors need to consult with parents to educate them about depression and help them learn ways to encourage their child's use of new skills (Stark et al., 2006). At times, family counseling is required to make systemic changes to factors that are contributing to the child's depression. Significant goals may include developing communication skills, enhancing family interactions, and sharing information about specific issues.

ANTIDEPRESSANT MEDICATIONS. Certain antidepressant medications—usually selective serotonin reuptake inhibitors (SSRIs)—may benefit children and adolescents with depression (NIMH, 2008a). However, our knowledge of the ways antidepressants affect young people, as compared to adults, is limited. The NIMH recently published research, the Treatment of Adolescents with Depression Study (TADS), in *The Archives of General Psychiatry*. In this study (2007), a combination of psychotherapy and antidepressant medication appeared to be the most effective treatment for adolescents with major depressive disorder. However, because some studies have suggested that SSRIs and other antidepressants may have adverse effects on young people, in particular an increased risk in suicidal thinking, in 2004 the Food and Drug Administration (FDA) adopted a *black box warning label* on antidepressant medications. The black box warning label emphasizes that children, adolescents, and young adults (up through age 24) taking antidepressants should be closely monitored for adverse side effects of the medication, including suicidal ideation (NIMH, 2008a).

Child and adolescent depression is a serious but treatable condition that has received considerable attention during the past three decades. Early identification and treatment of depression can help alleviate symptoms and put young people on a healthy developmental trajectory. Through individual, group, and family counseling, clinical mental health counselors can help depressed youth address depressive symptoms and meet the challenges of development in ways that provide positive mental health.

Eating Disorders

The Case of Seema

Seema is an 18-year-old Pakistani female whose family moved to the United States from Pakistan a year ago. She has just started college as a freshman. Carmen, a clinical mental health counselor, first met Seema when she was referred by the university nurse following an incident in which Seema passed out in class. The nurse suspected that Seema might be anorexic. Seema admitted that she had skipped breakfast and dinner the night before. Her move to the United States has been hard on her. The pressure to fit into the image of an ideal body type has led her to try several diets over the last several months. In addition, the pressure of juggling separate cultural lives—at home and at the university—has progressively led Seema to feel out of control.

Seema talked with Carmen about the conflict she experiences in leading separate lives—a conservative Muslim girl at home and a young teen at the university dating and socializing at parties with her friends. Seema feels pressured to fit in and be accepted at the university. Initially, she was concerned that she was heavier than most of her friends. Her roommate introduced her to the Ana Web sites to help Seema "lose weight fast." Seema states that for the first time in ages she feels in control. She denies being anorexic and believes that she is finally looking her best. She carefully restricts food consumption and exercises for at least an hour each day. She has lost a significant amount of weight during the past 2 months.

Over the next several meetings Carmen has noticed that Seema is losing weight at an alarming rate. Her face looks sunken and hollow, and though she has not had another fainting incident during class, Seema's hair is losing its luster, her nails are brittle, and she has a layer of fine hair on her arms and face that was not noticeable earlier.

Discuss the primary issues Seema is facing. What would you do if you were Carmen? Who else would you want to involve in Seema's treatment plan? Would you disclose information to her parents? What are the dangers associated with continuing to work with Seema without involving others?

Eating disorders often appear for the first time in pre- or early adolescence or during the transition to young adulthood, although some reports indicate that they can develop during childhood or later in adolescence (NIMH, 2008a). Eating disorders involve serious disturbances in eating behaviors (e.g., unhealthy reduction of body weight or extreme overeating) as well as feelings of distress or excessive concern about body shape or weight (NIMH, 2007). Girls and young women tend to exhibit eating problems at a much higher frequency than do boys or young men, although the prevalence rate in males has increased in recent years (Kalodner & Van Lone, 2001). Also, although eating disorders have been more frequently associated with young, affluent, white females, it appears that disorders exist among various ethnic and cultural minority groups (Kalodner & Van Lone, 2001). Counselors need to be aware of early warning signs in all populations so that preventive interventions can be implemented when necessary.

TYPES OF EATING DISORDERS.   The two main types of eating disorders are anorexia nervosa and bulimia nervosa. Anorexia typically arises during the transition to adolescence, whereas bulimia is more likely to develop during the transition to young adulthood (Attie & Brooks-Gunn, 1995). A third category, eating disorders not otherwise specified (EDNOS), includes several variations of eating disorders that do not fit the criteria for the other two diagnoses. Binge-eating disorder is one example of an EDNOS.

Individuals with anorexia nervosa weigh less than 85% of what is considered normal for their age and height (APA, 2000). They have a resistance to maintaining minimally normal weight, an intense fear of gaining weight or becoming fat, and a distorted view of their own bodies and weight. Youth with anorexia often stop (or fail to start) menstruating. Unusual eating habits develop, such as avoiding food, picking out only a few foods and eating them in small quantities, or weighing food servings. Whereas some young people with anorexia severely restrict eating, others engage in compulsive exercise or purge by means of vomiting or use of laxatives. Youth with anorexia tend to deny that they have a problem, making treatment difficult.

Bulimia nervosa is characterized by recurrent episodes of binge eating, typically twice a week or more, followed by attempts at compensating by purging or exercising (APA, 2000). Binge eating is defined by excessive, rapid overeating, often to the point of becoming uncomfortably full. An episode of binge eating is usually accompanied by a sense of lack of control, as well as by feelings of disgust, depression, or guilt (Kalodner & Van Lone, 2001). Subsequently, the individual engages in activities to compensate for overeating: vomiting or laxative use for the purging type of bulimia and excessive exercise or fasting for the nonpurging type. Youth with bulimia do not meet the severe underweight criterion associated with anorexia; indeed, they may appear to be within the normal weight range for their age and height. However, they are dissatisfied with their bodies and desire to lose weight or fear gaining weight.

Binge-eating disorder—an EDNOS—is characterized by recurrent binge-eating episodes with no purging, excessive exercise, or fasting. Consequently, young people with this disorder may be overweight or obese. They also are likely to experience guilt, shame, and distress about their binge-eating (NIMH, 2007).

Youth with eating disorders tend to be high achievers and sensitive to rejection. Eating disorders often coexist with other disorders, including depression, substance abuse, and anxiety disorders. They are considered medical illnesses with complex psychological and biological causes (NIMH, 2007). To make sure that these issues are addressed in treatment, clinicians need to conduct a thorough developmental assessment.

A number of physical complications are associated with eating disorders. In anorexia, the physical problems are related to malnutrition and starvation. Common physical symptoms include fatigue, brittle hair and nails, cold intolerance, and abdominal pain. In more severe cases, major organ systems in the body are affected. The mortality rate associated with anorexia is 10%—higher than almost any other psychiatric problem (APA, 2000). In bulimia, the medical complications are due to vomiting or the use of laxatives or diuretics and can include dental problems, esophageal inflammation, and metabolic imbalances.

ETIOLOGY AND RISK FACTORS.   An interplay of biological, psychological, and sociocultural factors are thought to contribute to the development of disordered eating. As stated earlier, anorexia often arises during the transition to adolescence, when young people are undergoing intense physical and psychological changes. During this time, the chief developmental task is identity formation—a task that can be perceived as extremely challenging. Peer pressure, puberty, self-esteem issues, and societal messages that glorify thinness may all coalesce to trigger problematic eating patterns in young people. Some of the factors that appear to be linked to eating disorders include:

- Media promotion of thinness as healthy and a sign of success
- Perfectionism
- Highly competitive environments that stress body thinness and high performance (e.g., gymnastics, dancing)
- Experiences of loss in personal relationships (e.g., family breakups or death)
- A low sense of self-esteem
- Heightened concern for appearance and body shape during adjustment to the changes associated with puberty (Manley, Rickson, & Standeven, 2000, p. 228)

Eating disorders often reflect struggles with unmet needs, including the need to be loved, cared for, and respected. Eating problems may stem from an individual's desire to be perfect, compliant, or highly regarded. Regulating food intake may represent a way to exert control and meet those needs. People with eating disorders often have difficulty acknowledging and expressing feelings, and in some cases, disordered eating becomes a means of coping with feelings that are painful (McClure & Teyber, 2003).

Family theorists describe eating disorders as symptoms of family dysfunction (e.g., Minuchin, Rosman, & Baker, 1978; Schwartz, Barrett, & Saba, 1984). Family characteristics associated with anorexia in young people include enmeshment, overprotectiveness, and rigidity. Boundaries are not well established, and the child may feel unable to individuate. Such families also do not tolerate conflict or disagreement well and may avoid topics that are controversial. Consequently, family therapy is often the preferred treatment for adolescents who live at home (Kalodner & Von Lone, 2001).

TREATMENT STRATEGIES.   When eating disorders are treated early, positive outcomes are more likely. A comprehensive treatment plan is required that involves medical care and monitoring, counseling, nutritional consultation, and at times, medication management. In some cases, when body weight is dangerously low, hospitalization is required. Treatment involves a team process, with the counselor working closely with the young person's physician and nutritionist. Counseling can take place individually, with families, in groups, or in some combination of the three methods.

To treat anorexia, the National Institute of Mental Health (2007) recommends three phases:

1. Restoring the person to a healthy weight
2. Treating psychological disturbances, including body image distortion, self-esteem issues, and interpersonal conflicts
3. Reducing or eliminating thoughts and behaviors that lead to disordered eating, and preventing relapse.

Families are often included in the counseling process. Often, family members are distressed about the issue of low weight and food refusal. The responsibility to gain weight needs to be put on the individual with anorexia. To help, family members can be encouraged to allow the young person to eat foods that he or she selects (Kalodner & Van Lone, 2001). Other studies suggest family-based interventions in which the parents assume responsibility for feeding their child or adolescent, especially in nonchronic cases (NIMH, 2007).

For bulimia, the primary treatment goal is to reduce or eliminate binge eating and purging behaviors (NIMH, 2007). Nutritional counseling and psychotherapy can be used to help the young person develop healthier patterns of thinking, feeling, and behaving. The counselor works collaboratively with the client to

1. Establish a pattern of regular, nonbinge meals
2. Improve attitudes related to the eating disorder
3. Encourage healthy but not excessive exercise
4. Alleviate co-occurring conditions such as mood or anxiety disorders

Cognitive–behavioral approaches, interpersonal psychotherapy, and group counseling that uses a cognitive–behavioral approach can be used effectively to help young people with bulimia. At times, medication may be prescribed. At this point, fluoxetine (Prozac) is the only FDA-approved medication for treating bulimia (NIMH, 2007).

Interventions for binge-eating disorder are similar to those used to treat bulimia. In addition, young people with binge-eating disorder are sometimes prescribed appetite suppressants (NIMH, 2007).

Boys and Young Men with Eating Disorders

Although eating disorders are more likely to affect young women, boys and men are also vulnerable. In some cases, males with the disorder may want to loose weight. In other cases, young men may want to gain weight or muscle mass. Issues related to self-esteem, anxiety, and control, as well as body image distortions, are evidenced in boys as well as girls with eating disorders.

Young clients with eating disorders usually enter treatment reluctantly, denying the extent of their problems and reluctant to give up their primary method of coping. The counseling process can be challenging, as the counselor helps the young person accept the reality of the problem, feel accepted, and develop new, more flexible ways of coping with feelings and relating to others. Counselors who work with young people with eating disorders need to participate in training and supervision to ensure that they are providing the most efficacious treatment.

Attention-Deficit/Hyperactivity Disorder

Attention-deficit/hyperactivity disorder (ADHD), the most common neurologically based disorder of childhood, can influence children's emotional, behavioral, and social adjustment. ADHD typically first appears in early childhood, with children exhibiting symptoms of inattention, impulsivity, and hyperactivity (APA, 2000). An estimated 3 to 7% of school-age children have the disorder, with boys diagnosed more frequently than girls. (Ratios vary from 2:1 to 9:1, depending on the subtype.) Fifty to 80% of children with ADHD will continue to have symptoms of the disorder through adolescence, and many will carry the symptoms into adulthood (Barkley, 1996).

The *DSM-IV-TR* (APA, 2000) identifies three types of ADHD: *predominantly inattentive type, predominantly hyperactive–impulsive type,* or a *combined type* (APA, 2000). The two symptom clusters used to diagnose ADHD are the *inattention cluster* and the *hyperactivity–impulsivity cluster* (Figure 12–5). A child must exhibit at least six of the nine behaviors in the cluster to be considered significantly inattentive or hyperactive (APA, 2000; Brown, 2000).

Inattentive Type

Six (or more) of the following symptoms of **inattention** have persisted for at least 6 months to a degree that is maladaptive and inconsistent with developmental level:

a) often fails to give close attention to details or makes careless mistakes in schoolwork, work, or other activities
b) often has difficulty sustaining attention in tasks or play activities
c) often does not seem to listen when spoken to directly
d) often does not follow through on instructions and fails to finish schoolwork, chores, or duties in the workplace (not due to oppositional behavior or failure to understand instructions)
e) often has difficulty organizing tasks and activities
f) often avoids, dislikes, or is reluctant to engage in tasks that require sustained mental effort (such as schoolwork or homework)
g) often loses things necessary for tasks or activities (e.g., toys, school assignments, pencils, books, or tools)
h) is often easily distracted by extraneous stimuli
i) is often forgetful in daily activities

Hyperactive-impulsive type

Six (or more) of the following symptoms of **hyperactivity-impulsivity** have persisted for at least 6 months to a degree that is maladaptive and inconsistent with developmental level:

Hyperactivity

a) often fidgets with hands or feet or squirms in seat
b) often leaves seat in classroom or in other situations in which remaining seated is expected
c) often runs about or climbs excessively in situations in which it is inappropriate (in adolescents or adults, may be limited to subjective feelings of restlessness)
d) often has difficulty playing or engaging in leisure activities quietly
e) is often "on the go" or often acts as if "driven by a motor"
f) often talks excessively

Impulsivity

a) often blurts out answers before questions have been completed
b) often has difficulty awaiting turn
c) often interrupts or intrudes on others (e.g., butts into conversations or games)

FIGURE 12–5 Two symptom clusters for attention-deficit/hyperactivity disorder

Source: From *Diagnostic and Statistical Manual of Mental Disorders* (4th ed., text rev., p. 92). Copyright 2000 American Psychiatric Association. Reprinted with permission.

Children with the combined subtype of ADHD, which is the most common presentation, exhibit six or more symptoms in both categories. For all subtypes, symptoms must be evidenced for at least 6 months in two or more settings, with some of the symptoms present before the age of 7 years (APA, 2000).

Children with ADHD are thought to have an underdeveloped inhibition of behavior, thus making it a disorder of impulse control (Barkley, 1997). They typically have difficulty staying on task for more than a few minutes, are disorganized, and often ignore social rules. Children who have the inattentive type have difficulty focusing (e.g., listening, following directions) and sustaining attention (staying on task, completing assignments). They frequently lose things and are forgetful. Children who have the hyperactive–impulsive type may act as though they are "always on the go." They have difficulty sitting still and taking turns. Their social skills tend to be impaired, as evidenced by excessive talking, interrupting, and blurting out answers in class (McClure & Teyber, 2003).

ADHD can create numerous difficulties for children, their families, and their teachers. Due to impaired social skills and lack of behavioral control, children with ADHD may experience peer rejection, academic difficulties, and negative family interactions. Coexisting conditions associated with ADHD include oppositional–defiant disorder, conduct disorder, anxiety or depressive symptoms, substance abuse, and learning disabilities (Brown, 2000). Careful assessment is needed to ensure that counselors "look beyond the hallmark symptoms of the disorder and consider interventions that address comorbid problems as well" (Nigg & Rappley, 2001, pp. 183–184).

ETIOLOGY AND RISK FACTORS. Despite years of research, there is still no conclusive proof of what causes ADHD (McClure & Teyber, 2003). Some of the causal factors attributed to the development of ADHD include neurological factors, hereditary factors, pre- and postnatal factors, and toxic influences (Brown, 2000; NIMH, 2008a). In particular, physical differences in brain structure and brain chemistry appear to play roles in the myriad symptoms associated with ADHD (Lyoo et al., 1996). Family factors also have been attributed to the development of ADHD; however, stressful home life does not cause ADHD. Instead, the disruptions brought about in the family as a result of the expression of ADHD symptoms can cause family stress and disorganization, which can then exacerbate the preexisting symptoms.

TREATMENT STRATEGIES. A multimodal, multicomponent approach to treatment is recommended for children with ADHD (e.g., Brown, 2000; Edwards, 2002; NIMH, 2008a). Prior to treatment, a comprehensive assessment is conducted that includes a developmental history, interviews with the child and significant adults, child observation, and a medical examination by the child's physician. Typically, behavior rating scales such as the Conners–3 (Conners, 2008) or the Behavior Assessment System for Children–2 (BASC–2; Reynolds & Kamphaus, 2004) are used with parents and teachers to supplement information gathered during clinical interviews. If the assessment indicates that the child has ADHD, multimodal interventions that address the child, the family, and the environment are suggested. To develop a comprehensive treatment program, the following areas should be considered:

- Behavioral interventions in the family that include parent and child education about ADHD, parent training for behavior management, and ancillary family counseling when necessary are essential to treatment (Nigg & Rappley, 2001). Helping families develop predictable daily routines, organized households, and firm but affectionate discipline can improve family functioning. Barkley (2005) has developed a comprehensive training program for parents that can be especially helpful.

- Individual and group counseling can provide a setting in which children feel understood and where issues of self-esteem and social relationships can be addressed. In particular, *cognitive–behavioral self-regulation approaches* to help children control their behavior and *social-skills training* to help children learn to take turns, follow rules, and develop hobbies or sports activities can be helpful (McClure & Teyber, 2003).

- Medication can be particularly effective in addressing the core symptoms of ADHD, although it is a controversial intervention for some educational and mental health professionals (Edwards, 2002). The medications that appear to most effective are stimulant medications. A list of stimulant medications used to treat ADHD can be accessed through the NIMH Web site at www.nimh.nih.gov/health/publications/adhd/treatment.shtml. One medication that is not a stimulant that recently was approved by the FDA for ADHD is Strattera (atomoxetine), which affects the neurotransmitter norepinephrine. (Stimulant medications primarily target dopamine.) Not all children with ADHD need medication, and the decision to use it depends on several factors. Physicians who prescribe medication follow up with the child to determine whether the medication is working and to monitor potential side effects (NIMH, 2008a).

- School interventions are often instigated by clinical counselors as they work with teachers and school counselors to coordinate the child's treatment plan (Edwards, 2002). Counselors can consult with teachers about behavior management and academic interventions. Pfiffner and Barkley (1998) have suggested a number of classroom interventions that can help children with ADHD experience school success.

- Intensive summer camp programs may benefit children with ADHD (Edwards, 2002). Such programs include sports-skill training, behavior management interventions, and opportunities for positive peer interactions.

As with any disorder, training is needed for counselors to work effectively with children who have ADHD and with their families. With training, clinical mental health counselors can coordinate multimodal, multicomponent treatment approaches that include parent management training, counseling, school interventions, and medication.

Specific Issues of Concern

Young people in today's society are faced with myriad issues that can affect development and adjustment. Child abuse, drug and alcohol abuse, changing family situations, life-threatening illnesses, trauma, and the death of loved ones are just some of the many concerns that may affect children and precipitate a need for counseling.

CHILDREN OF DIVORCE.   Postdivorce family relationships are among the most common issues seen by counselors who work with young people (McClure & Teyber, 2003). Nearly half of all first marriages end in divorce, affecting over 1 million children (Thompson & Henderson, 2007). Research indicates the children involved are often confronted with a wide range of adjustment challenges. Many studies document negative consequences for children whose parents divorce, particularly in regard to psychological adjustment, academic achievement, and behavior problems (e.g., Amato, 1993; Hetherington, 1993; Zill, Morrison, & Coiro, 1993). However, there is a marked variability in children's responses to divorce, with some children adjusting well and even showing improved behavior after the breakup, particularly if there has been a lot of conflict in the home (Amato, 1993).

Some of the factors that influence young people's responses to divorce include their developmental level at the time of the separation, social support systems, individual resilience and coping styles, the level of parental conflict prior to and during the divorce, parenting quality after the divorce, and the degree of economic hardship experienced. There also may be gender differences in responses, with some studies indicating that boys appear to experience greater adjustment difficulties (e.g., Morrison & Cherlin, 1995; Wallerstein & Blakeslee, 1989).

Although responses vary, the initial experience of family disruption is painful for most children. Their responses to the experience tend to differ based on their developmental level. Preschoolers may feel frightened and insecure, experience nightmares, and regress to more infantile behaviors. Children between the ages of 6 and 8 may experience pervasive sadness, view the divorce as their fault, feel rejected, fear abandonment, and hold unrealistic hopes for reconciliation. Older children are more likely to feel anger and anxiety, develop psychosomatic symptoms, blame one parent or the other, and engage in troublesome behavior. Responses vary even more in adolescents than in younger children. Some adolescents feel betrayed, disengage from the family, and become depressed. Others show a positive developmental spurt and demonstrate maturity, compassion, and helpfulness toward their parents and younger siblings (McClure & Teyber, 2003).

It is important for counselors and parents to remember that adjusting to divorce takes time and requires continued efforts of patience and reassurance. During the adjustment period, children may benefit from individual or group counseling. Counselors can help children with the adjustment process by giving them opportunities to express their feelings and concerns. They also can assist children as they work through the following psychological tasks (Thompson & Henderson, 2007; Wallerstein & Blakeslee, 2003):

- Acknowledging the reality of the marital breakup
- Disengaging from parental conflict and distress and resuming typical activities
- Resolving the loss of what used to be
- Resolving anger and self-blame
- Accepting the permanence of the divorce
- Achieving realistic hope regarding the relationship

Counselors may also work with the parents of children involved in divorce. Parent support groups and counselor–parent consultation can help parents cope more effectively with the changes brought about by the divorce. Counselors can encourage parents to

- Talk with children about the divorce in a way that is developmentally appropriate, making sure that they do not consider the divorce their fault.
- Plan for ways to make the child's life as stable and consistent as possible.
- Arrange for regular visits from the absent parent to assure the child that they are loved by both parents.
- Talk with children about the future. Involve them in the planning, without overwhelming them.
- Avoid asking children to take on responsibilities beyond their capabilities. (Thompson & Henderson, 2007, p. 367)

GRIEF AND LOSS.   At one time or another, all children are affected by death, either of a pet, a grandparent, a parent or sibling, or a friend. Accepting the reality of death as part of life is a developmental task that often needs to be facilitated in counseling.

Children may experience a range of physical and emotional responses to grief experiences. Some of the physical reactions to loss include headaches, chest pains, or stomachaches. The child may experience a distortion in time or find it difficult to start new projects or begin new relationships. Some children regress to an earlier period in development, in which they felt safer. Emotional responses may vary widely, ranging from feelings of anger or guilt to those of sadness, fear, or denial of pain.

As with divorce, several factors influence children's responses to death, including their developmental level, support systems, and the manner in which the adults in their lives deal with grieving. The grief process is unique for each individual, and it is important not to assume that children in the same age group will respond in the same manner. Counselors can let children take the lead in sharing their grief experiences by requesting, "Help me find ways to help you tell me about what you feel." One of the most beneficial things a counselor can do is listen carefully to the child, trusting the child's wisdom and giving him or her unhurried time to express thoughts, feelings, and concerns.

In addition to listening carefully, the following counseling strategies can help children dealing with loss through death:

• Focus on what the child shares about specific thoughts, feelings, and concerns. Respond clearly and thoughtfully, keeping in mind the child's cognitive level.

• Allow children to express their grief, talk freely, and ask questions. Play therapy, creative expression, puppetry, bibliotherapy, imagery, and letter writing are just a few of the methods that facilitate children's expression of death.

• Help the child commemorate the loss and say good-bye, perhaps through compiling a scrapbook of their loved one or memorializing the loss in some significant way.

• Work collaboratively with parents to help the child learn more about the process of death and dying. Child-appropriate books about death, which are available in most libraries, can help answer questions, stimulate conversation, and provide new understanding (Redcay, 2001).

• Help families work to reduce stress in the child's life by maintaining structure and being aware of the possibility of regression. Family counseling may be needed.

• Be aware of triggers of grief, including birthdays, holidays, and the anniversary of the death.

• Help children give themselves permission to go on with life without feeling guilty (Thompson & Henderson, 2007).

CHILD MALTREATMENT.   Child maltreatment, which refers to abuse and neglect, is one of our nation's most serious concerns. Approximately 905,000 cases of substantiated maltreatment were documented in 2006, with an estimated 1,530 fatalities (Child Welfare Information Gateway, 2008). Over 3,570,000 cases of maltreatment were reported that received an investigation and/or assessment. Child abuse and neglect occur at all levels of socioeconomic and educational levels (Thompson & Henderson, 2007). Maltreatment categories and associated statistics include *neglect* (64%), *physical abuse* (16%), *sexual abuse* (8.8%), and psychological or emotional maltreatment (6.6%). Rates of maltreatment have fluctuated only slightly during the decade. Descriptions of each maltreatment category are presented in Figure 12–6.

Child Neglect	Physical Abuse
• Deliberate failure by a caretaker to provide a child with shelter, food, clothing, education, supervision, medical care, and other basic necessities.	• Any act which results in a non-accidental physical injury. Such acts include punching, beating, mkicking, burning, cutting, twisting limbs, or otherwise harming a child.
• Represents an ongoing pattern of inadequate care.	• Often represents unreasonable and unjustified punishment to a child from a caregiver.
• Physical signs and symptoms: poor hygiene, poor weight gain, inadequate medical care, dressing inadequately for weather, chronically late or absent from school, constant complaints of hunger, severe developmental lags.	• Physical signs and symptoms: bruises, burns, and fractures.
• Affective-behavioral signs and symptoms: low self-esteem, aggression, anger, frustration, conduct problems.	• Affective-behavioral signs and symptoms: aggression, hope lessness, depression, low self-esteem, defiance, running away, property offenses, delinquency, substance abuse.
Sexual Abuse	**Psychological Maltreatment**
• Any act of a person that forces, coerces, or threatens a child to have any form of sexual contact or engage in any type of sexual activity.	• A pattern of behavior that can seriously interfere with a child's positive emotional development.
• Includes both touching and non-touching offenses (e.g., indecent exposure).	• Acts that communicate to a child that he or she is worthless, unloved, or unwanted.
• Physical signs and symptoms: genital bleeding, odors, eating or sleep disturbances, somatic complaints, enuresis or encopresis.	• Includes emotionally neglectful behaviors and emotionally abusive behaviors.
• Affective-behavioral signs and symptoms: anxiety, nightmares, guilt, anger/hostility, depression, low self-esteem, sexualized behavior, aggression, regression, hyperactivity, self-injurious behavior, delinquency, running away, substance abuse.	• Affective-behavioral signs and symptoms: self-abusive behavior, aggression, anxiety, shame, guilt, anger/hostility, pessimism, dependency
	• Social deficits: insecure attachments, poor social adjustment

FIGURE 12–6 Definitions, signs, and symptoms of child maltreatment

From American Humane Association, 1996; and Miller-Perrin, 2001.

Every state has laws requiring professionals who work with children to report suspected child abuse or neglect to local child protective services (see Figure 12–3). Also, each state and most counties have social services agencies that provide protective services to children. Counselors who work with children need to be aware of the agencies in their region to contact in cases of suspected abuse.

Victims of child maltreatment differ in regard to their preabuse histories, the nature of the abuse experiences, family and system responses to the abuse, available social supports, and individual coping resources (Miller-Perrin, 2001). They also differ in regard to the types of symptoms displayed, with some children displaying many symptoms and others displaying few or none. Consequently, there is no single treatment approach that is appropriate or effective for all clients. Depending on the individual client's presentation, clinicians should consider treatment approaches that include the following (Miller-Perrin, 2001):

• **Managing Negative Thoughts and Feelings Associated with the Maltreatment, Including Guilt, Anxiety, Shame, Fear, and Stigmatization.**   Counseling can give children opportunities to diffuse negative feelings by confronting the abuse experience within the safety of the therapeutic relationship. Older children and adolescents may be able to talk about their experience. For younger children, reenacting the experience through play or art may be helpful.

• **Providing Clarification of Cognitions and Beliefs That Might Lead to Negative Attributions.**   Confronting issues of secrecy and stigmatization are important. Cognitive–behavioral approaches that help children restructure their beliefs about themselves (e.g., being "different," being at fault) can be effective. Group counseling may facilitate cognitive restructuring.

• **Reducing Problem Behavior.**   Behavioral problems such as impulsivity, aggression, and sexualized behavior often need to be addressed in counseling. Parent training typically accompanies the counseling process in cases where the parent is not the perpetrator.

• **Empowering the Child Survivor.**   Prevention training that includes self-protection skills is often necessary. Self-protection skills include teaching children to identify potential abuse situations, providing them with protective responses, and encouraging them to disclose any abuse experiences.

• **Enhancing Developmental Skills.**   Children may have deficits in problem-solving skills and social skills. Depending on the age of the child when the abuse occurred, there also may be developmental lags in regard to psychosocial development (e.g., learning to trust). Individual and group counseling can facilitate growth in these areas.

• **Improving Parenting Skills.**   In many cases of child maltreatment, parent-focused interventions are warranted. Such interventions include educating parents about developmental processes to correct misperceptions and unrealistic expectations, teaching parents about appropriate disciplinary techniques, and teaching anger management and stress reduction skills.

Due to the complex nature of child maltreatment, counselors should consider accessing community resources and services to help families manage difficult situations more effectively. Examples of such services include substance abuse treatment, money management training, crisis hotlines, respite care services, preschool services, and parent education classes.

OTHER ISSUES.   Divorce, grief, and abuse are just a few of the many issues with which children and adolescents may struggle. Other issues include living in chemically dependent families, being homeless, living with chronic or terminal illness, adjusting to blended families, managing teenage pregnancy, dealing with bullying or violence, and engaging in delinquent activities. Although it would be beyond the scope of this chapter to cover all the concerns faced by young people, counselors who work with this population are encouraged to develop the expertise needed to meet the needs of their young clients in the most effective way possible.

BOX 12–3

My first counseling job was as a drug prevention and intervention counselor in a small, rural school district in North Carolina. My individual involvement with a client named "Carl" (not his real name) began soon after he started high school. He was flunking his classes, defying his parents, and usually finding better things to do with his day than attend school . . . such as getting stoned or drunk. What set Carl apart from the other "users" I worked with were his intelligence and his wit. His test scores were off the charts, and his humor was sharp, sarcastic, and biting (just like mine!). After a drug offense at school, Carl became involved in a group of mine and became an individual client as well. For whatever reason, Carl formed a real attachment to me during this time. He would hang out in my office before school, seek me out at lunch, and give me "high fives" in the hallway between classes. He was never a great group member, usually choosing to sabotage a serious discussion with a well-placed but inappropriate joke. I found that my best individual sessions with Carl were not ones where we talked about his using, or getting in trouble, or even what things were like at home. The best sessions were when he read me a poem he'd written over the weekend entitled, "What It's REALLY Like To Be Me"; or when we talked about his favorite rock group; or his "secret" dreams for what he would do with his life after high school (he thought he'd make a good lawyer or maybe a stand-up comedian); or the 10 reasons he felt his friends were such losers (his words, not mine). I tried different "traditional" counseling interventions with him, but he would usually tell me to "stop trying to fix him," and we'd go back to just shooting the breeze.

By the end of his freshman year, Carl's grades started going up. He started going to school more, and I heard less and less about drug offenses. He was more likely to be seen hanging around the basketball court than spending time on the skipping trail. At the end of the year, which was also my last year in this particular job, Carl came by to shoot the breeze for a while. We talked about his summer plans (he was going to be a camp counselor) and how he was going to "survive" a summer at home with his parents. "So where does hanging out with your friends and getting high fit into this summer?" I asked. Carl just shrugged, and said that probably wasn't going to be a big priority. "I think I have better things to do," he said. As he got up to leave, we shook hands. "Thanks," he said, and left.

As with most counseling outcomes, I never know what to attribute change to; or if I even had a hand in it at all. With Carl, I certainly felt my curricula and interventions were not terribly effective. I did, however, feel that I showed Carl respect. I showed him that I valued his sense of humor, and that I recognized his possibilities. I didn't lecture, I didn't judge, and I didn't tell him "NOT" to do anything. He came to that on his own. I learned from Carl that counseling is less about "doing," and more about "being." Thanks, Carl.

Kelly Coker, Ph.D., LPC, Counselor Educator

Summary and Conclusion

Working with children and adolescents provides unique and exciting challenges for community and agency counselors. Clinicians who work with this population need to have a comprehensive understanding of the developmental issues that influence young people's well-being. They also need to be aware of the various contextual influences on development, including the family, school, peers, life events, and culture.

Counselors use their knowledge of development and bioecological influences to frame the manner in which they counsel children and adolescents. When counseling young people, special attention needs to be given to building a therapeutic relationship, assessing and evaluating, and selecting and implementing developmentally appropriate interventions. For many children, the use of expressive arts or play in counseling can be especially effective.

Young people in today's society are confronted with a wide array of issues, ranging from diagnosable mental health disorders to specific concerns related to life events. Some of the disorders discussed in this chapter included depression, eating disorders, and ADHD. Other concerns that may precipitate the need for counseling include parental divorce, death of a loved one, and child maltreatment. These are just a few of the multiple concerns that may bring young people to counseling. We encourage counselors who plan to work with children and adolescents to participate in ongoing training, education, and supervision so that they are equipped to provide effective prevention and intervention services for this population.

PART 4

Clinical Mental Health Counseling: Settings and Services

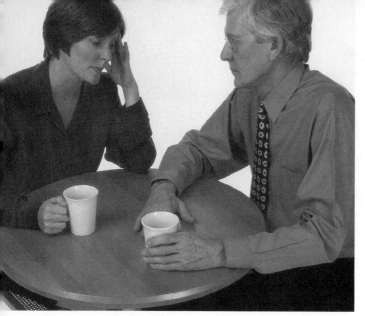

CHAPTER 13

Community Agencies, Medical Settings, and Other Specialized Clinical Settings

As our sessions go on you speak of your scars
  and show me the places where you have been burned.
Sadly, I hear your fiery stories
  reliving with you, through your memories and words,
  all of the tension-filled blows and events
  that have beaten and shaped your life.
"I wish I were molten steel," you say,
"And you were a blacksmith's hammer.
  Maybe then, on time's anvil, we could structure together
    a whole new person, with soft smooth sounds,
    inner strength and glowing warmth."

Gladding, S. T. (1977). Scars. *Personnel and Guidance Journal, 56,* 246. © 1977 by ACA. Reprinted with permission. No further reproduction authorized without written permission of ACA.

During the past four decades, professional counselors' opportunities for employment have increased significantly. Prior to the passage of the Community Mental Health Act of 1963 (Title II, Public Law 88-164), counselors worked primarily in educational settings. With the passage of the Community Mental Health Act, funding was provided for the nationwide establishment of community mental health centers, thereby opening the door for large numbers of counselors to work in agency settings. Today, community and agency counselors are employed in many different clinical sites, including government-funded agencies, hospitals, rehabilitation agencies, family service agencies, shelters for victims of domestic violence, and probation settings, to name just a few. Within these settings, counselors provide a wide range of direct and indirect services to people of all ages who struggle with problems ranging from developmental transitions to serious mental disorders.

In this chapter, we describe some of the publicly and privately funded settings in which clinical mental health counselors might be employed: community agencies, health-care facilities, child and family agencies, and specialized clinical sites. In the next chapter, we describe additional settings, including career counseling centers, employment assistance programs, and private practices.

COMMUNITY MENTAL HEALTH CENTERS AND AGENCIES

Evolution of Community Mental Health Centers

Prior to 1963, people with mental illness were primarily hospitalized in state institutions. Unsafe and inhumane conditions in many of these institutions precipitated a reform movement that led to the enactment of the Community Mental Health Centers Act (CMHC Act) of 1963, resulting in the *deinstitutionalization* of people with chronic and severe mental illness. The purpose of deinstitutionalization was to remove people with severe mental health issues from state institutions and public hospitals and to provide them with quality care in their communities. The CMHC Act provided federally matched funds for the state construction of community mental health centers in *catchment* areas—geographic areas of 75,000 to 200,000 people (MacCluskie & Ingersoll, 2001). These community-based agencies were expected to provide a comprehensive continuum of care to all Americans in need of mental health services. Five core elements of service were identified: outpatient, inpatient, consultation and education, partial hospitalization, and emergency/crisis intervention. In addition to providing a comprehensive system of care, community agencies were expected to engage in outreach to the community and form linkages with other service providers. A primary purpose of community mental health centers was to serve as many clients as possible in the least-restrictive setting.

In subsequent years, funding of community mental health centers (CMHCs) shifted primarily from federal monies to state and local funding. By 1981, with the passage of the Omnibus Budget Reconciliation Act, federal funding of mental health services was allocated through block grants "to be used by states as they saw fit" (MacCluskie & Ingersoll, 2001, p. 230). Block grants were grouped into nine areas of preventive health, with one of the largest being the alcohol, drug abuse, and mental health block grant (ADAMHA). In 1992, Congress passed the ADAMHA Reorganization Act, which abolished ADAMHA and replaced it with a new federal organization called Substance Abuse and Mental Health Services Administration (SAMHSA) (www.samhsa.gov/), which is a division of the Department of Health and Human Services (DHHS). Currently, although states still bear the primary funding burden for mental health services, federal government funds help finance mental health care through Medicaid, Medicare, and federally funded special programs for adults with serious mental illness and children with serious emotional disability (Surgeon General Report, 2000). Medicaid is unique in that it is funded by federal, state, and local funds; is run by state guidelines; and is designed to assist low-income persons by paying for most medical expenses.

Although community mental health centers were designed to provide a broad range of community care, community members often needed more support than the CMHCs could provide, resulting in many people not receiving treatment and increased rates of homelessness and rehospitalization. The Surgeon General Report on Mental Health (2000) stated that approximately one in five Americans experiences a mental disorder, and 15% of the adult population uses mental health services in any given year. The report described the community mental health system as "multifaceted and complex, comprised of public and private sectors, general health and specialty mental health providers, and social services, housing, criminal justice, and education agencies," which do not always provide the coordinated service delivery system of care they were designed to provide (Surgeon General Report, 2000, p. 11). Providing adequate support to all people in need of mental health assistance continues to be a challenge for community mental health service providers.

Many state and community mental health programs currently are in a state of organizational transition, as attempts are made to manage human and financial resources while providing quality mental health services. However, good intentions do not always lead to positive results. For example, in 2001 the General Assembly of North Carolina voted for mental-health reform in the state, which was designed "to tear down, then rebuild the way the state treats mentally ill people, about 210,000 of whom seek state help each year" (Stith & Raynor, 2008, p. 2). Instead of providing services through traditional community mental health centers, the state was divided into geographic areas served by 25 local management entities (LMEs). The LMEs serve as administrative behavioral health authorities that outsource treatment to a network of providers in the area, some of which are more successful than others in providing an effective system of care for individuals with mental health needs. Many of the LME providers hired high school graduates, rather than licensed professionals, to provide services at a rate of up to $61 per hour (Stith & Raynor, 2008). In addition, more than 500 hospital beds were eliminated, the cost of mental health care to the state increased, and many people needing mental health services did not receive—and still are not receiving—the treatment they needed. The importance of mental health advocacy becomes even more vital when plans to improve mental health treatment are not executed successfully.

Service Delivery

The way in which community mental health services are delivered varies from state to state, especially due to national, state, and local budgeting concerns. In some states, community mental health centers (CMHCs) still exist and are required to provide certain core services. In other states, such as North Carolina, community-based mental health services are delivered through state-endorsed providers. Still other states use different methods of mental health service delivery. The National Association of State Mental Health Program Directors (NASMHPD; www.nasmhpd.org) provides summaries of the various ways states use Mental Health Block Grants to deliver mental health services. Each state is required to develop a comprehensive mental health plan and to demonstrate how funds are being used (NASMHPD, 2008).

The goal of community-based mental health is to provide a comprehensive system of care designed in partnership with the community, service providers, and payers. The following principles guide community mental health practices:

1. Services should be accessible and culturally sensitive to those who seek treatment.
2. Services should be accountable to the entire community, including the at-risk and underserved.
3. Services should be comprehensive, flexible, and coordinated.
4. Continuity of care should be assured.
5. Treatment providers should utilize a multidisciplinary team approach to care (Administration on Aging [AOA], 2001).

Multidisciplinary teams that provide services typically include psychiatrists, psychologists, counselors, social workers, psychiatric nurses, and paraprofessionals. The following areas of service are frequently offered by community mental-health providers:

- **Outpatient Counseling Services.** The goal of outpatient services is to help clients improve personal and social functioning through the use of individual, group, and/or family counseling, and possibly medication management. Most often, social workers, counselors, and psychologists provide these services, which address both acute and chronic mental health needs.
- **Day Programs.** Day programs provide intensive treatment to clients who do not need 24-hour care but have significant impairment due to psychiatric, emotional, behavioral, and/or addictive disorders. These programs provide a combination of individual and group therapy, psychoeducation, recreational therapy, life-skills training, vocational rehabilitation, medication management, and other activities designed to help participants acquire skills needed for adjustment to everyday-life tasks and roles (Hershenson, Power, & Waldo, 1996; Viger, 2001). In many community agencies, day programs include two types of service: *partial hospitalization programs* (PHPs) and *intensive outpatient programs* (IOPs). PHPs provide brief, intensive structured treatment for clients who need a high level of care, whereas IOPs usually serve more stable individuals who still need structured treatment programs but on a more flexible basis.
- **Emergency Services/Crisis Intervention.** These services provide for the delivery of center- and community-based crisis intervention in psychiatric emergencies. Community members experiencing acute distress can contact emergency and crisis intervention agencies and receive immediate crisis intervention assistance (Staton et al., 2007). Services are available on a 24-hour basis through telephone crisis lines, walk-in treatment, or agencies specifically designated to provide emergency care.
- **Substance Abuse Services.** Substance abuse services address the recovery of individuals who are dealing with addiction, dependence, or abuse of substances. Addictive substances can include alcohol, prescription medication, or illegal drugs. Because recovery is an ongoing process, treatment may include outpatient services, residential care, inpatient treatment, emergency care, and the coordination of community drug abuse resources. In addition, counseling and educational programs for family members are usually available to help the family understand and cope with the effects of a substance abuse environment.
- **Case Management and Outreach.** Case management links clients to essential services and supports in the community. Essential services include securing financial benefits, health care, and psychiatric treatment. Goals of case management include preventing hospitalization, improving quality of life and levels of functioning, and empowering clients to maximize their independence (MacCluskie & Ingersoll, 2001). Outreach involves engaging people in need of services who are unable or unwilling to seek services on their own (Viger, 2001).

Because clients with severe mental health conditions may require a variety of services but do not have a central location in which those services are delivered (such as long-term-care mental institutions), finding ways to meet the needs of chronically mentally ill clients is challenging. One case management model that is designed to assist clients in accessing, coordinating, and integrating mental health services is called Assertive Community Treatment (ACT). ACT programs typically share six common elements (Gerig, 2007, p. 225):

1. Low case-manager-to-client ratios
2. Community-based treatments

3. Shared caseloads
4. Continuous coverage 24 hours a day, 7 days a week
5. The majority of services provided by the ACT team
6. Time-unlimited services

• **Education and Consultation.**   These services include support for family members of clients who are mentally ill, communitywide education programs on the nature of mental health, preventive programs that teach participants about skills such as stress management, and informational programs describing ways to link with various community resources (Lewis, Lewis, Daniels, & D'Andrea, 2003). Education and consultation play key roles in primary and secondary prevention, which are geared toward promoting and maintaining mental health. Funding challenges can impede the delivery of education and consultation services, which may not translate into billable hours. However, grants, contracts with other organizations, and pro bono work can help ensure that these crucial service components are delivered (Staton et al., 2007).

• **Residential Programs.**   Residential programs include transitional facilities where individuals recently discharged from hospitals learn to function in the community, youth homes for troubled or delinquent adolescents, homes for individuals with developmental delays, and other residential homes that vary in the degree to which clients are supervised. Residential supervision can range from 24-hour staffed supervision to independent living options that allow participants to receive care based on their level of functioning. In some cases, intensive outpatient programs for substance abuse and other disorders provide a temporary residential option for clients during the course of treatment.

• **Inpatient Services.**   Most community mental health agencies are affiliated with either community or state hospitals that provide intensive, inpatient mental health services to stabilize symptoms of acute mental illness and prepare clients to return to community-based care. During the past several decades, the number of state psychiatric institutions providing inpatient services has shrunk dramatically, resulting in the discharge of many individuals who are severely mentally ill from hospitals into nursing homes or board-and-care homes that are inadequately prepared to provide necessary services (Duffy & Wong, 2003). The average length of stay in state mental hospitals is less than 8 days. In contrast, the average length of stay in psychiatric facilities was 189 days (Levine, Perkins, & Perkins, 2005). Although reducing the length of time in psychiatric facilities is one way to support the contemporary mental health philosophy of least-restrictive treatment to maximize the client's personal freedom, there have been serious consequences for shortened stays. "Some clients are admitted, stabilized, released to outpatient care, and then readmitted," resulting in the "revolving door" phenomenon (Gerig, 2007, p. 225). Lack of sufficient treatment can lead to increased hospital emergency room visits or incarceration.

BOX 13–1

Negative Consequences of Early Release from Inpatient Treatment

. . . [L]ack of proper treatment is causing more people who are mentally ill or who have a substance-abuse problem to be taken to hospital emergency rooms—or jail. And they're rotating in and out of the state's psychiatric hospitals. On some days, state hospitals are so full, they are refusing to accept new patients.

Since 2001 [in North Carolina], at least 13 people committed suicide or overdosed on drugs less than a week after being discharged from state hospitals. Some died within hours.

(Stith & Raynor, 2008, p. 2)

TABLE 13–1 Direct and indirect community and client services in community mental health agencies

	Community Services	Client Services
Direct	Educational programs on the nature of mental health Preventive education programs that teach about mental health and life skills	Counseling and crisis intervention services Outreach programs for persons dealing with life transitions and other high-risk situations
Indirect	Helping the local community organize to work for positive environmental change Taking action on policies affecting community mental health	Advocacy for groups such as people who have experienced chronic mental health problems Consultation within clients' helping networks Promoting self-help programs Linkage with other helping systems in the community

Source: From *Community Counseling: Empowerment Strategies for a Diverse Society* (3rd ed.), by J. A. Lewis, M. D. Lewis, J. A. Daniels, and M. J. D'Andrea, 2003, Pacific Grove, CA: Brooks/Cole. Adapted with permission of Wadsworth, a division of Thomson Learning: www.thomsonrights.com. Fax 800 730-2215.

Direct and Indirect Services

Clinical mental health counselors who work in community agencies provide services that focus on prevention and promotion of mental health as well as on treatment of mental disorders and dysfunctions. Lewis et al. (2003, p. 259) categorized the services as *direct* and *indirect,* some of which are targeted toward individual clients and others that are targeted toward the community at large. Examples of direct and indirect services that might be provided by clinical mental health counselors are illustrated in Table 13–1.

To provide direct and indirect services effectively, counselors who work in community mental health centers must have basic counseling skills as well as specialty skills related to particular populations and problems. They need to be skilled in assessment and diagnosis, which includes having a comprehensive knowledge of the *DSM-IV-TR* (American Psychiatric Association [APA], 2000) and its classifications. They also need to be familiar with medications used to treat mood, anxiety, substance abuse, and psychotic disorders, and these medications' common side effects. Knowledge and skills related to evidence-based treatment services are indispensable. Other essential skills include being able to plan, implement, and evaluate prevention programs designed for individuals, groups, and the community at large. Community mental health agencies treat a diverse set of clients, many of whom come from lower socioeconomic backgrounds and present with a broad spectrum of issues. Consequently, multicultural awareness, knowledge, and skills are necessary for effective service delivery.

In most community mental health sites, counselors are expected to meet the organization's productivity expectations, which vary from agency to agency (MacCluskie & Ingersoll, 2001). *Productivity* refers to the number of "billable hours" a clinician generates. Many agencies have a specified number of client hours that must be averaged over a period of time and often affect salary and promotion. Being able to meet productivity expectations, complete paperwork requirements, provide crisis intervention when needed, and attend staff meetings and supervision can prove to be challenging, making it all the more necessary for counselors to practice self-care to maintain wellness and avoid burnout (Figure 13–1).

The greatest challenge of working in a community mental health center (CMHC) is to effectively meet administrative (agency) and clinical (consumer) needs without burning out over time. All settings have paperwork and difficult clients, yet a CMHC, as a public agency, is subject to a high volume of documentation requirements and high volume of clients. There is also the burden of meeting productivity expectations (quotas) each month. This is not an easy task when 50 percent of new clients no-show for first appointments. The challenge is to work with as many clients as you can, as skillfully as you can, and not get behind in paperwork, productivity, or passion.

Many days the benefits of working in a CMHC setting outweigh the struggles. These include the ease of consulting with, and referring clients to, colleagues under the same roof; stable work hours; and no personal responsibility for emergency crisis coverage. Additionally, the pay is good, the organization values high practice standards, and clients do improve. A CMHC is a great place to grow professionally and make a difference in the lives of those who seek therapy.

Ellen Nicola, Ph.D.
Senior Psychologist/Team Leader at a community mental health center

Figure 13–1   Urban community mental health: Adult outpatient services

Professional Affiliation and Certification

Counselors who work in mental health settings may choose to affiliate with the American Mental Health Counselors Association (AMHCA), a division of the American Counseling Association (ACA). Members of AMHCA have been active in supporting federal and state legislation that recognizes mental health counselors as core practitioners, or reimbursable providers of services. They also have helped define the areas in which mental health counselors work and establish guidelines for involvement in those areas. AMHCA has initiated several different task forces that focus on prevention and treatment in relation to specific populations and concerns. Such concentrations are important because they enable counselors who work in mental health settings to obtain in-depth knowledge and skills in particular areas. The organization also publishes a quarterly periodical, the *Journal of Mental Health Counseling,* which provides readers with up-to-date information on prevention, treatment, and emerging issues in the mental health field.

AMHCA was instrumental in establishing the certified clinical mental health counseling credential (CCMHC), a specialty credential within the field of professional counseling. Professionals seeking this credential first need to be National Certified Counselors (NCCs). Requirements for the CCMHC credential include:

- Sixty semester hours of graduate coursework including theories of counseling, psychotherapy, and personality; abnormal psychology and psychopathology; human growth and development; career development; professional orientation and ethics for counselors; research; appraisal; and social/cultural foundations.
- An academic course of study that included 9 to 15 semester hours of clinical training in supervised practicum/internship relevant to the practice of clinical mental health counseling.
- A minimum of 2 years of supervised postmaster's clinical practice, which includes 3,000 hours of direct client contact in a clinical setting with 100 hours of face-to-face clinical counseling supervision over 2 years.

- A passing score on the Examination of Clinical Counseling Practice (ECCP). (If an applicant passed the NCMHCE for state credentialing, he or she will not be required to taken the ECCP.) The ECCP consists of 10 clinical vignettes typically encountered by clinical mental health counselors.
- Submission of an audio- or videotape of a clinical counseling session for review following receipt of a passing score on the ECCP.

National Board for Certified Counselors (NBCC), 2008

For counselors who work in community agencies and other settings, becoming a certified clinical mental health counselor may enhance employability by authorizing them to be qualified mental health providers.

HOSPITALS AND HEALTH-CARE SETTINGS

Many clinical mental health counselors work in hospitals and other health-care facilities, which are essential components of community health-care systems (Browers, 2005). Medical facilities may be public or private and may operate for profit or not for profit. Most hospitals offer behavioral health-care or psychiatric services to assist people struggling with mental health issues, and many provide preventive and maintenance programs for patients with cardiac disease, diabetes, stroke, and other illnesses (Browers, 2005). Hospitals and other health care settings also provide counseling through programs such as cancer patient support, rehabilitation services, HIV/AIDS clinics, and hospice care. People receiving care in health care facilities are usually referred to as *patients* rather than *clients*. Using that terminology may be uncomfortable for counselors initially but can facilitate communication with other helping professionals (Barker, 2001). Many behavioral health-care systems demonstrate their commitment to quality standards by seeking accreditation from organizations such as the Joint Commission on Accreditation of Healthcare Organizations (JCAHO) or the Commission on Accreditation of Rehabilitation Facilities (CARF).

Inpatient Medical Settings

Inpatient services are designed to treat patients with mental health disorders such as major depression, bipolar disorder, schizophrenia, substance abuse, and dementia. Inpatient services provide crisis stabilization, evaluation, and intensive monitoring based on medical assessment conducted by a multidisciplinary team. Team members include psychiatrists, psychiatric nurses, social workers, counselors, occupational therapists, and other health professionals. Usually within 24 hours of admission, patients are given a complete medical, nursing, and psychosocial assessment. Each team member participates in the assessment process and then works collaboratively to formulate a diagnosis and treatment plan.

When possible, the patient and the patient's family members work with the interdisciplinary team in developing a treatment plan (Barker, 2001). The treatment plan, which is reviewed periodically, includes a description of patient problems and assets, goals and objectives, target dates, interventions and outcomes, and discharge information. Interventions may include medication; individual, group, and/or family counseling; psychoeducation; recreation therapy; and support groups. To provide a continuum of care, after patients have been stabilized in an inpatient setting, they may be discharged and then moved to another level of treatment, such as the ones described in the next section.

Other Behavioral Health/Psychiatric Services

Many hospitals offer a broad spectrum of treatment options that represent a continuum of care, ranging from outpatient services to more intensive services. Treatment options include several of the services that were described in the previous section. For example, partial hospital programs (PHPs) and intensive outpatient programs (IOPs) provide services to patients who continue to need intensive treatment but do not need 24-hour supervised care. An additional service, the 23-hour observation bed, is an option for intensive monitoring and evaluation without formal admission into the inpatient unit and associated expensive inpatient costs. Residential treatment programs provide supervised housing and treatment for specific problems, particularly for substance abuse. Outpatient clinics or services provide individual, group, and/or family counseling, based on the patient's need. Examples of outpatient, partial hospitalization, and residential treatment services that may be found in hospitals include:

- Marital and family therapy clinics, providing services to families and couples
- Memory disorders clinics, which assist in the evaluation of individuals with declines in memory, concentration, and thinking, followed by appropriate referral
- Sleep centers, which evaluate sleep disorders and recommend treatment
- Substance abuse intensive outpatient programs, which help patients recovering from chemical abuse or dependency. Services may include detoxification, medication management, dual diagnosis treatment, 12-step orientation, family education, and relapse prevention
- Child and adolescent outpatient services, which use multimodal approaches to treat the needs of youth and their families
- Child and adolescent partial hospitalization services, which help reduce psychological symptoms and improve the psychosocial functioning of troubled youth
- Residential treatment for sexually aggressive children and adolescents, where treatment focuses on relapse prevention in a safe, structured, supportive environment
- Sexual abuse clinics, which provide evaluation and treatment for children who may have been abused sexually, prevention services for preschool youth, and education to the community
- Geriatric outreach services, in which health-care professions specializing in geriatric mental health offer services to seniors in their homes and work with family members to access community resources (Wake Forest Baptist Medical Center, 2008)

The Case of Anna

Anna is an 18-year-old female who has a history of bipolar disorder with severe manic episodes. When she was 15, she was hospitalized for attempting to commit suicide by taking over 50 Tylenol capsules. Six days ago, she was taken to the emergency room by her mother, who found her unconscious on the bathroom floor with deep cuts in both wrists.

After Anna was stabilized, she was assessed by one of the hospital psychiatrists. He recommended inpatient hospitalization. Anna was then evaluated by an interdisciplinary team consisting of a psychiatric nurse, the psychiatrist, and a clinical social worker. During the assessment, Anna revealed that she had not been taking her medication for the past 2 months and that her suicide attempt came after breaking up with her boyfriend. After Anna was released from the inpatient program, she began attending daily outpatient treatment, where you work as a clinical mental health counselor. The outpatient treatment program includes group counseling, recreation therapy, and some individual counseling.

What goals might be part of Anna's treatment plan? What would be some ways to help her achieve those goals? What resources can she access as she learns to develop new coping mechanisms? What do you consider to be the top priority regarding her treatment?

Whereas the services provided through hospitals' psychiatric and behavioral health-care programs are geared toward helping people with chronic or acute mental health disorders, other services offered in hospital and health-care facilities are geared toward patients and family members dealing with physical illnesses. An example of this type of service is cancer patient support, which is described next.

Cancer Patient Support Services

> **BOX 13–2**
>
> *Receiving a diagnosis of cancer is a little like being pushed out of a helicopter into a jungle war without any training, any familiarity with the terrain, or any sense of how to survive.*
>
> (Lerner, 1994, p. 28)

> **BOX 13–3**
>
> *The ultimate goal of successful treatment for cancer is not just survival but a quality of survival, which is the ability to transcend the trauma of being diagnosed and treated for cancer, to create a lifestyle that is compatible with having a chronic illness, and to renew the process of achieving life goals.*
>
> (Henderson, 1997, p. 188)

Statistics indicate that men have a one in two risk and women a one in three risk of developing cancer during the course of a lifetime, with three out of four families in the United States being affected by some form of cancer (American Cancer Society, 2008). Cancer accounts for approximately one quarter of all deaths in the United States, exceeded only by cardiac disease. When cancer is diagnosed, feelings of fear, anxiety, and confusion often emerge, placing the patient and frequently the entire family in a state of crisis (Johnson, 1997). In many medical settings, oncology clinics provide counseling and other forms of psychosocial support to help families through the diagnosis, treatment, and posttreatment process. Examples of the services provided by cancer-patient-support programs include:

- New patient orientation services that provide information about the oncology center, treatment procedures, and support services.
- Individual counseling to help the patient cope with the cancer diagnosis, treatment ramifications, and related life issues.
- Family counseling that focuses on helping family members learn ways to help the patient and themselves as they cope with new stresses on the family system.
- Support and educational groups for caregivers, cancer patients, and cancer survivors. For example, a Coping with Breast Cancer group can help group members with lifestyle adjustments specific to breast cancer.

- Appearance consultation to assist patients receiving chemotherapy who may need help with various appearance-related issues, including the provision of wigs, turbans, and hats.
- Resource rooms that provide information for patients and family members on all aspects of cancer care, including diagnosis, treatment, and coping strategies. Resources may include books, brochures, videotapes, and computer access to Internet information.

Many cancer-patient-support programs use mental health professionals and volunteers as service providers. Mental health professionals can recognize the psychosocial, spiritual, and other concerns that come with a cancer diagnosis and respond accordingly. For example, we interviewed the associate director of a local cancer-patient-support program who has worked with cancer patients and their families for over 20 years. When we asked her to describe her work, she stressed the importance of just being there to listen—to let people tell their stories. She explained, "You just see them visibly relax. Telling their stories gives them a sense of control: It is something that they need to do time and time again." She went on to say, "Even though many people in today's society are cancer survivors, there is still a feeling in the general public that a diagnosis of cancer is a death sentence. A lot of what I do is to normalize what they are experiencing" (DeChatelet, personal communication, July 15, 2001).

Counselors who work with cancer patients and their families need to be aware that the impact cancer has on the family system varies, depending on the nature of the cancer diagnosis, the phase of the clinical course of the cancer, and the developmental stage of the family (Veach & Nicholas, 1998). Counselors also need to have worked through their own issues related to cancer, illness, and loss so that they are capable of helping others facing difficult circumstances.

Other Hospital-Based Counseling Services

Other counseling services offered in hospital settings include pastoral counseling, caregiver support programs, patient support groups, rehabilitation facilities, and trauma centers (see Box 13–4).

BOX 13–4

Level I Trauma Centers, Alcohol Screening, and Brief Counseling Interventions

In 2007 the American College of Surgeons (ACS) Committee on Trauma changed its standards and now requires alcohol screening and brief counseling interventions for accrediting Level I Trauma Centers (ACS, 2006). The National Highway Traffic Safety Administration (2007) notes that someone suffers an alcohol-related injury every 2 minutes in an automobile crash. Up to half of hospitalized trauma patients test positive for alcohol-related concerns (Saitz, 2005). Patients experiencing alcohol-related trauma injuries may be at a point where they are ready to consider the impact alcohol is having on their lives. Offering screening and brief counseling interventions in trauma centers can lead to the prevention of future alcohol problems.

Mary Claire O'Brien, M.D., and Laura J. Veach, Ph.D., Recipients of the Robert Wood Johnson Foundation Grant for Substance Abuse Policy Research Programs, September, 2008

In addition to hospital settings, counselors work in a variety of public and private non-profit agencies or clinics that have a medical connection, including HIV/AIDS clinics, retirement or assisted-living homes, geriatric outreach programs, hospice programs, and substance abuse agencies. A brief overview of programs offering hospice care and substance abuse treatment is provided next.

Hospice and Palliative Care

BOX 13–5

The great events of life, as we observe them, are still clearly recognizable as journeys. . . . Out of centuries of experience has come the repeated observation that death appears to be a process rather than an event, a form of passage for human life.

Sandol Stoddard (The Hospice Movement: A Better Way of Caring for the Dying, 1992)

Although hospice and palliative care programs function outside hospitals, they are connected with the medical world and hence are included in this section. Hospice and palliative care programs assist individuals and their families as they cope with grief, loss, and change. *Hospice care* specifically refers to the care needed by an individual during the last months or weeks of his or her life. *Palliative care* includes hospice care and refers to a compassionate, comprehensive team approach to care that focuses on quality of life for anyone coping with a serious illness, including the patient and the family members (Hospice and Palliative Care Center, 2008). Hospice and palliative care centers provide help to families dealing with many different diseases, including Alzheimer's, arterial lateral sclerosis (ALS), cancer, chronic lung disease, AIDS, pediatric conditions, and congestive heart failure. Hospice team members traditionally include nurses, physicians, social workers, counselors, clergy, art and music therapists, physical and occupational therapists, nutritionists, pharmacists, and trained volunteers (Stoddard, 1992).

An important role of hospice and palliative care centers is to provide bereavement support services, including counseling, to individuals and families who are facing or have faced the death of a loved one. The types of bereavement support services offered through the centers vary, depending on the resources available at the particular site. Support can include home visits, grief workshops, support groups, individual counseling, telephone calls, and the provision of brochures and other materials that describe how individuals deal with the sorrow and uncertainty surrounding death (Foliart, Clausen, & Siljestrom, 2001; Figure 13–2). Hospice services also include partnerships with other community organizations to help families engage in advanced planning end-of-life care issues.

A noteworthy example of a specialized bereavement program is the Grief Counseling Center (GCC), which is part of the Hospice and Palliative Care Center in Winston-Salem, North Carolina. The GCC offers programs specifically designed to meet the needs of individuals and families experiencing a death-related loss, an anticipated death, or a life-limiting illness. Established in 1990, the GCC provides ongoing grief and bereavement counseling to children and adults and offers art therapy, play therapy, support groups, and a summer camp for children and adults in the community who are grieving the loss of a loved one. Other services include community educational presentations and a bereavement library with books, videos, articles, and other resources on grief and loss. Due to community donations and memorials, services are provided at no charge. The staff at the Grief Counseling Center includes a board-certified art therapist and master's-level, licensed professional counselors. Susanna Lund, a licensed professional counselor and registered art therapist in the GCC, described her work with grieving children in this way:

> Children go through a grieving process just like adults, but often are not sure how to
> verbally connect the emotional dots. Expression through art gives them another way to
> express and understand their feelings. Art is recognized as being less threatening than

Unhelpful Comments	Helpful Comments
I know exactly how you're feeling.	I am sorry that you are going through this painful process.
I can imagine how you are feeling.	It must be hard to accept that this has happened.
I understand how you are feeling.	It's okay to grieve and be really angry with God and anyone else.
You should be over it by now. It's time you moved on.	Grieving takes time. Don't feel pushed to hurry through it.
You had so many years together. You are so lucky.	I did not know _____; will you tell me about him? What was your relationship like?
You're young; you'll meet someone else.	What is the scariest part about facing the future alone without _____?
At least her suffering is over. She is in a better place now.	You will never forget _____, will you?
He lived a really long and full life.	It's not easy for you, is it? What part of your relationship will you miss the most?
How old was he?	He meant a lot to you.

FIGURE 13–2   Unhelpful and helpful comments in speaking with the bereaved

Source: From *Heavenly hurts: Surviving AIDS-related deaths and losses*, by S. Klein, 1998, New York: Baywood Publishing Company. Adapted with permission.

> words, therefore providing a safe outlet for expression of feelings. Art can allow for the cathartic expression of emotions of grief, allowing the healing process to begin.
>
> (Art from the Heart, 2002, p. 1)

Counselors working in hospice programs need to be skilled in grief and bereavement counseling, knowledgeable about death education, aware of their own feelings and beliefs about death, and capable of maintaining personal and professional boundaries. Issues related to countertransference, dealing with the loss of a client, and fostering overdependence can be especially difficult to manage. Counselors working in hospice programs can navigate boundary issues more effectively by asking themselves the following questions (Hampton, 2002):

- Have I experienced less patience and increased irritability?
- Am I giving out any telephone number other than my work number?
- Is the family becoming overly dependent on me? (or vice versa)
- Do I feel like no one can support the family like I can?

By maintaining healthy boundaries, working as part of a team, and engaging in consultation or supervision when needed, clinical mental health counselors can play vital roles in meeting the needs of hospice patients and their families.

OTHER SPECIALIZED CLINICAL SETTINGS

Whereas centralized community mental health centers and medical facilities provide a wide array of treatment options, other agencies intentionally provide a narrower range of specialized services. Specialized agencies usually focus on a specific problem (e.g., domestic violence, substance abuse) or a specific group (e.g., older adults, children, at-risk youth; Lewis et al., 2003), or both. Examples of specialized services include support for Alzheimer's patients and their caregivers, AIDS care centers, child abuse prevention services, drop-in crisis counseling centers, child and family services, homeless shelters, and services for at-risk youth, to name just a few. In this section, we describe services offered in substance abuse treatment programs and child and family service agencies. We conclude the chapter by highlighting some of the other specialized clinical settings in which clinical mental health counselors practice.

Substance Abuse Treatment Programs

Substance-related disorders represent the most commonly occurring mental health problem in the United States (Vuchinich, 2002). It is estimated that approximately 25% of the patients seen by primary care physicians have an alcohol or drug problem (cited in Doweiko, 2009). An estimated 1 in 10 adults has significant problems related to the use of alcohol, with rates being higher among certain ethnic groups (Miller & Brown, 1997). Other substances that frequently are abused include marijuana, cocaine, heroin, and a wide range of prescription drugs. Problems related to substance use transcend gender, ethnicity, socioeconomic levels, geography, and almost all other domains (Stevens-Smith & Smith, 1998). Substance abuse is the number one cause of preventable death in the United States, and between 20% and 50% of all hospital admissions are related to the effects of substance abuse and addiction (cited in Doweiko, 2009, p. 1). We could continue to cite statistics, but the numbers alone do not tell the complete story. Unfortunately, many people with substance use problems are in denial, and their conditions often go undiagnosed and untreated.

When people with substance use disorders do present for treatment, either voluntarily or involuntarily, they typically are diagnosed with either a *substance abuse* or a *substance dependency* disorder. *Substance abuse* is characterized by continued use of a substance in the presence of significant adverse consequences. An individual who exhibits one or more of the following symptoms within a 12-month period is considered to have a substance abuse problem:

- Substance use is responsible for failure to fulfill major role obligations at work, school, or home.
- Recurrent substance use occurs in situations in which it is physically hazardous.
- Legal problems related to substance use recur.
- Continued substance use occurs despite the difficulties it is causing in significant relationships (APA, 2000).

Substance dependence refers to the repeated, nonmedical use of a substance that harms the user or precipitates behavior in the user that harms others and is characterized by physical or psychological dependence. Dependence is diagnosed when three or more of the following symptoms are evidenced:

- Tolerance (increased amounts of the substance are needed to experience the desired effect).
- Withdrawal (when withdrawal symptoms occur or when individuals continue to use the substance to avoid withdrawal symptoms).

- The substance is taken in larger amounts or over a longer period of time than was intended.
- There is a persistent desire to cut down or control substance use.
- A lot of time is spent trying to acquire the substance.
- Important work, social, or leisure activities are given up or reduced because of the substance use.
- Substance use continues despite knowledge of recurrent physical or psychological consequences (APA, 2000).

Frequently, individuals with substance-related disorders have co-occurring mental health issues, including mood disorders, anxiety, personality disorders, sleep disorders, posttraumatic stress disorder, psychotic disorders, and other psychological disorders. The coexistence of substance abuse and mental disorders is referred to as *dual diagnosis,* a condition that can be particularly intractable to treatment. Clients with a dual diagnosis are at greater risk for relapse, and those who do relapse are more likely to develop depression (Pidcock & Polansky, 2001). Another condition that makes the already complex issue of substance use disorders more difficult to assess, diagnose, and treat is *polysubstance abuse,* which refers to the abuse of two or more substances simultaneously.

People with a substance dependency are considered to have an *addiction.* Addiction is a complex, progressive behavior pattern with biological, psychological, sociological, and behavioral components (Scott, 2000). It has been defined as "a persistent and intense involvement with and stress upon a single behavior pattern, with a minimization or even exclusion of other behaviors, both personal and interpersonal" (L'Abate, 1992, p. 2). Addictive disorders, which can include gambling, workaholism, sexual addictions, Internet addictions, and compulsive behaviors continue to be major problems in the United States (Doweiko, 2009). Counselors may work in sites that specialize in treating any of these addictions. In this section, however, the focus is on the treatment of addictions to or abuse of chemical substances, including alcohol, illegal drugs, and prescription drugs.

In the 1980s, the primary mode of treatment for addiction was residential care. However, now, the more frequently used level of care, after a client has been through detoxification and is stabilized, is intensive outpatient treatment (Veach & Madwid, 2005). Treatment for individuals who abuse substances primarily occurs in two general settings: substance abuse treatment facilities and community mental health centers or agencies (Von Steen, Vacc, & Strickland, 2002). Some facilities provide public or nonprofit services, whereas others provide for-profit services. Professionals and paraprofessionals, including rehabilitation counselors and other professional counselors, often are employed in substance abuse treatment centers. Many agencies provide education, prevention, and consultation services about substance use as well as about treatment and rehabilitation services for substance abuse.

Although it is important for all clinical mental health counselors to have some training in addictions and substance abuse, counselors who work in substance abuse treatment facilities need specialized training and certification (e.g., licensed clinical addiction specialist, certified clinical addiction specialist, certified substance abuse counselor, and certified substance abuse prevention consultant). The number of academic programs that educate counselors with an emphasis on substance abuse is growing, and since 1994, the National Board of Certified Counselors (NBCC) has provided a certification process for becoming a certified master addictions counselor (MAC).

The Council for Accreditation of Counseling and Related Educational Programs (CACREP) (2009) has created a new specialty area for counselors who want to work in the addictions field.

For the first time, counselor education programs can offer the specialty area of addiction counseling. Students preparing to work as addiction counselors will develop knowledge and skills "necessary to work in a wide range of addiction counseling, treatment, and prevention programs, as well as in a mental health context" (CACREP, 2009, p. 17).

The dominant model for treating chemical dependence is the Minnesota Model of Chemical Dependency Treatment (Doweiko, 2009; Benshoff & Janikowski, 2000). The Minnesota Model was designed in the 1950s and has evolved over time, particularly due to changes in reimbursement policies in the 1990s (Doweiko, 2009). The model is based on the disease concept of dependency, which asserts that chemical addiction is a treatable disease with specific origins, symptoms, progression, and outcomes. The multidisciplinary model ascertains that recovery is only possible through abstinence accompanied by major emotional and spiritual changes, a belief that has been disputed by some professionals but serves as the underpinning for most treatment programs. The model uses a *treatment team* comprised of health professionals with different specialty areas, including physicians, counselors, nurses, and clergy. In addition to advocating abstinence, the model places a strong emphasis on life change utilizing 12-step programs (e.g., Alcoholics Anonymous [AA] and Narcotics Anonymous [NA]); provides a combination of didactic, educational, and psychotherapeutic interventions; and values personal confrontation. Initially designed for the treatment of alcoholism, the model is now used to treat all forms of chemical dependency. It is characterized by a continuum of care that includes detoxification, inpatient and outpatient services, and aftercare services (Benshoff & Janikowski, 2000).

- *Detoxification* is the first phase of dependency treatment. Three forms include *medical detoxification* (when withdrawal can be life threatening, thus requiring the help of medical professionals), *social detoxification* (when withdrawal symptoms are less severe, enabling detoxification to occur in a residential, nonmedical setting), and *self-detoxification* (unmanaged, unsupervised detoxification that often is unsuccessful). Detoxification serves as a gateway to treatment, with formal detoxification typically lasting from 3 to 5 days.
- *Residential treatment* can occur in medical or nonmedical residential facilities, halfway houses, and therapeutic communities. Two widely recognized residential settings are the Betty Ford Center and Hazelden, which utilize the Minnesota Model of Treatment.

> The programs [at Hazelden] are not defined by a number of days, but rather by individual needs. Lengths of stay in both outpatient and residential programs are dependent on the needs of the individual and are determined through an assessment and evaluation process. For most people, an average length of stay in primary care is four to six weeks but longer-term programs—often two or three months—are beneficial to some. Successful treatment is the ultimate goal, and time is necessary to win the battle.
>
> (Hazelden, 2008, www.hazelden.org/web/public/faqtreatment.page)

Other settings, which are less costly, are referred to as freestanding programs. They offer residential care in community-based settings with lower levels of direct medical monitoring. During the course of treatment, abstinence is required, and group therapy and psychoeducation are emphasized, although some programs also provide individual counseling. Residential programs focus on the attainment of short-term goals in treatment and the development of longer term goals for posttreatment. In these confrontational but supportive environments, clients have an opportunity to live and act productively in a drug-free manner.

- *Outpatient treatment* is designed to follow more intensive inpatient or residential treatment as part of the continuum of care plan. In the past, outpatient treatment for substance abuse was either unlimited or had very liberal limits, allowing clients to continue in treatment for an indefinite period of time. However, insurance companies and funding agencies now impose stricter limits on the number of outpatient visits covered per year or per policy. An additional problem associated with outpatient treatment, particularly if it is not preceded by more intensive forms of treatment, is a high rate of missed appointments and relapse because the individual has not been removed from the pressures of the drinking or drug-using environment in which he or she lives. To address this problem, many sites offer intensive outpatient programs (IOPs), which may provide temporary housing for people in treatment. IOPs are the predominant level of care for clients in treatment for chemical dependency and consist of 3 to 5 days or evenings per week, ranging from 3 to 10 weeks of care. Counseling and psychoeducation in IOPs tend to be group focused, intensive, and multidimensional, in accordance with the Minnesota Model. Family members often are encouraged to participate, and clients are asked to attend AA or NA meetings during and after treatment.

- *Aftercare.* When a client successfully completes a chemical dependency treatment program, he or she is not *cured*; instead, recovery has just begun and is considered to be a lifelong process. According to Prochaska, DiClemente, and Norcross's (1992) *transtheoretical model of change* (described in Chapter 6), clients who successfully complete treatment are in the *maintenance stage,* in which there is still much work to accomplish. During the first few months of maintenance, clients are especially vulnerable to relapse. Continued vigilance and support are needed to help clients maintain their new lifestyle. Many treatment programs offer aftercare support groups that meet on a weekly basis. To help with recovery and to prevent relapse, 95% of inpatient addiction treatment programs in the United States incorporate AA and NA into plans for treatment and follow-up care (Bristow-Braitman, 1995). These peer support groups provide guidance, support, sustenance, and solace to individuals seeking help with substance-related disorders (Benshoff, 1996). Typically, AA, NA, and other support groups, which are adjunctive to a comprehensive continuum of care, have at their foundation the 12 Steps, which are listed in Figure 13–3. The 12 Steps utilize important counseling concepts, including *problem recognition* (Step 1), *hope* (Step 2), *help seeking* (Steps 3, 5, and 7), *insight development* (Steps 4, 6, and 10), *restitution* (Steps 8 and 9), and *adoption of new consciousness and forms of behavior* (Step 12; Benshoff & Janikowski, 2000).

Working with clients who have substance-related disorders can be challenging for many reasons. *Denial,* which involves minimizing the effects of substance abuse on oneself or others, is a common defense mechanism and can sabotage successful treatment. Related to denial is the client's degree of motivation, or readiness for change. When clients are court ordered to receive treatment for substance use, they may not be at a point where they are willing to acknowledge that they have a problem or consider changing their behaviors. According to Prochaska et al. (1992), such individuals are in the *precontemplation stage* of change. Counselors working with clients in this stage are advised to use strategies such as motivational interviewing to help clients become more aware of their emotional response to the negative consequences associated with their substance use habits (Prochaska & Norcross, 1999). Various forms of client resistance, unhealthy family dynamics, negative environmental influences, and stressful living conditions are other factors that can make working with this population problematic. Counselors who work with clients struggling with substance use will want to seek ongoing consultation and supervision so that they can provide optimal services to their clients and avoid burnout.

1. We admitted that we were powerless over alcohol—that our lives had become unmanageable.
2. Came to believe that a Power greater than ourselves could restore us to sanity.
3. Made a decision to turn our will and our lives over to God *as we understood Him*.
4. Made a searching and fearless moral inventory of ourselves.
5. Admitted to God, to ourselves and to another human being the exact nature of our wrongs.
6. Were entirely ready to have God remove all these defects of character.
7. Humbly asked Him to remove our shortcomings.
8. Made a list of all persons we had harmed and became willing to make amends to all of them.
9. Made direct amends to such people wherever possible, except when to do so would injure them or others.
10. Continued to take personal inventory, and when we were wrong promptly admitted it.
11. Sought through prayer and meditation to improve our conscious contact with God *as we understood Him,* praying only for the knowledge of His will and the power to carry that out.
12. Having had a spiritual awakening as a result of these steps, we tried to carry this message to alcoholics and to practice these principles in all our affairs (Alcoholics Anonymous, 2001, pp. 2–3).

FIGURE 13–3   The 12 Steps of Alcoholics Anonymous

BOX 13–6

Chemical Dependency Treatment Center

The challenges of work in chemical dependency counseling are often mixed with the rewards. What may be frustrating suddenly leads to a breakthrough insight. Never boring, chemical dependency counseling often presents the counselor with many opportunities. Relapses are prevalent and knowing some clients lose their life while relapsing is perhaps one of the hardest aspects of chemical dependency work. Skillful preparation, teamwork, and helpful supervision are invaluable, as the nature of addiction challenges the counseling relationship.

The benefits of chemical dependency counseling include being a part of a person's discovery of sobriety. Recovery from chemical dependency is often a difficult struggle, and as a counselor in that process, it is both an honor and a daunting responsibility to provide our best work. Helping people learn how to live life on life's terms, take responsibility for their own recovery, and make amends to loved ones equally scarred by addiction are just the beginning. Other benefits involve leading group processes where clients share and thereby lessen pain, conducting family counseling that leads to a better understanding of enabling behaviors, and facilitating sessions with clients who had been obsessively ruled by chemicals as they sense their new freedom to live clean and sober. Just being a part of the many miracles of those whose lives change as they discover, sometimes for the first time, the joy of being alive makes chemical dependency counseling a rewarding occupation.

Laura Veach, Ph.D., LPC, NCC
Certified Clinical Addiction Specialist, Certified Clinical Supervisor
Associate Professor, Department of Counseling, Wake Forest University

---

Although we are aware of the challenges of working with people who are chemically dependent, we also recognize that recovery is both a goal and a reality for many clients. The term *recovery* is frequently used in the chemical dependency world, as well as in the broader world of mental health. Recovery refers to "a process, a new way to live one's life beyond mere abstinence from alcohol and other drugs. Recovery defines how one lives life today, implying hope, healing, and restoration" (Adams & Grieder, 2005, p. 17). Recovery is a priority promoted by the President's New Freedom Commission on Mental Health, which released its final report in July 2003 (see www.mentalhealthcommission.gov/). The Commission defined recovery as the ability to live a full and productive life—for individuals with disabilities and for individuals for whom reduction or remission of symptoms is the goal. In a transformed mental health world, which has been called for both by state commissions and the New Freedom Commission, mental health professionals adopt a person-centered and recovery-oriented approach to services (Adams & Grieder, 2005).

Child and Family Service Agencies

Many communities have nonprofit agencies that specialize in treating the needs of children, couples, and families. Funding sources for child and family service agencies vary, with many of the private agencies getting support from the United Way, religiously affiliated organizations, charities, private endowments, or grants (Browers, 2005; Rheineck, 2009). Counselors with a background in family counseling may find excellent opportunities in agencies that specialize in child and family services. Depending on the agency, family services may include combinations of any of the following services:

- Child and family assessment
- Individual counseling
- Couples counseling
- Family counseling
- Parent education
- Pregnancy testing and support/education services
- Adoption support services
- Domestic violence and rape crisis hotlines
- Shelters for women and children who are victims of domestic violence or sexual assault
- Victim assistance counseling
- Counseling and support groups for abusers
- Counseling and support groups for adult survivors of sexual abuse or incest
- Supervised, structured visitation for parents who are not allowed to be alone with their children
- Family preservation programs
- Counseling and support for abusive or potentially abusive families
- Community education programs to help prevent abuse and neglect

Counselors who work in child and family settings need to have a comprehensive understanding of systems-based counseling. Systems-based counseling, as described in Chapter 10, embraces a circular causality approach and assumes that interactions within families are dynamic rather than static or linear. For counseling to be effective, both the family system and the larger systems within which the family is embedded need to be taken into account. Popular family counseling approaches include structural, strategic, experiential, solution focused, and narrative.

DOMESTIC VIOLENCE.   Domestic violence is a pervasive problem that affects spouses, partners, children, and seniors. Intimate partner violence (IPV) is a form of domestic violence that occurs between two people in a close relationship and can include physical abuse, emotional abuse, and/or sexual abuse (Centers for Disease Control [CDC], 2006). Women are more likely than men to be victims of IPV (Catalano, 2007), although there are many instances in which men are abused. Approximately 4.8 million women experience IPV related to physical assaults and rapes. Men experience about 2.9 million intimate partner-related physical assaults (CDC, 2006). These figures should be viewed as conservative estimates because many incidents of IPV go unreported (James, 2008). In addition to IPV, domestic violence includes abusive treatment of elders or children and the witnessing of violence by children.

Victims of violence are at increased risk for mental health problems as well as for physical injury and death (CDC, 2006; Surgeon General Report, 2000). Anxiety, posttraumatic stress disorder (PTSD), depression, suicide, eating disorders, and substance abuse are among the many mental health issues associated with being abused. Children who witness abuse are at a greater risk for short- or long-term emotional disturbances, including nightmares, PTSD, depression, learning difficulties, and aggressive behavior.

Due to the prevalence and severity of domestic violence, many family service agencies include services designed to prevent domestic violence from occurring or recurring and to protect victims of domestic violence. To accomplish these goals, comprehensive family service agency programs may provide anger management programs, counseling groups for abusers, support groups for people who have been abused, and protective shelters for women and children.

WHAT IS ABUSE? According to the National Coalition Against Domestic Violence (NCADV, 2005), *abuse* is a pattern of behavior used to establish power and control over another person through the use of fear and intimidation. Abuse occurs when one person believes that he or she is entitled to control another person. Three major categories of abuse are

a. ***Physical Abuse,*** which can range from bruising to murder. Many times, physical abuse begins with trivial injuries that then escalate over time.
b. ***Sexual Abuse,*** which refers to any forced sexual activity.
c. ***Psychological or Emotional Abuse,*** which includes constant verbal abuse, harassment, extreme possessiveness, deprivation of resources, isolation, and the destruction of physical property.

A number of social, psychological, and cultural theories have been posited to explain battering and abuse. Among the more prominent of those theories are attachment theory, feminist theory, social learning theory, and systems theory (James, 2008; James & Gilliland, 2005). Counselors providing domestic violence services will want to be familiar with theoretical frameworks about causes of battering so that they can work more effectively with perpetrators and victims.

WHO ARE BATTERERS? Domestic violence cuts across socioeconomic, geographic, cultural, and religious barriers. Several psychological and behavioral characteristics are associated with batterers, although no single typology characterizes all people who abuse. Men who abuse women may exhibit some of the following characteristics, attitudes, and behaviors:

- Objectify women. Women are not respected but instead are viewed as property.
- Exhibit low self-esteem. Batterers often feel inadequate or powerless.
- Blame their behavior on external causes. They may blame their behaviors on a "bad day," alcohol, or drugs.
- Deny the severity of the problem and its effects on their families.

- Be characterized as jealous, possessive, demanding, and aggressive.
- Abuse alcohol or other drugs.
- Were abused as children or saw their mothers abused.
- Have strong, traditional, patriarchal beliefs.
- Tend to overreact; have a short fuse.
- Be likely to use force or violence to solve problems.
- Cycle from being hostile, aggressive, and cruel to being charming, manipulative, and seductive, depending on the situation.
- Have unrealistic expectations of marriage, their spouses, and relationships in general (James, 2008; NCADV, 2005).

WHY DO WOMEN STAY?   Reasons to remain in or terminate a relationship are seldom simple. In cases of domestic violence, reasons typically are quite complex. Often, the act of leaving is dangerous, as many batterers will attempt to retaliate (Walker, 2000). It has been noted that most women leave an abusive relationship an average of three to six times, with varying degrees of permanency (James, 2008). Some of the reasons a woman might choose to stay in an abusive relationship include:

- She would suffer shame, embarrassment, and humiliation if her secret were revealed.
- She fears repercussion from her partner.
- Financial circumstances make leaving difficult.
- Early role models of an abusive parent may have warped her view of the nature of relationships.
- She may not have access to safety or support.
- She may hold strong beliefs against separation or divorce.
- She may believe that her partner will reform.
- She may focus on the good times rather than the battering (James, 2008; NCADV, 2005).

WHAT SERVICES ARE AVAILABLE?   During the last 30 years, as consciousness about domestic violence has been raised, programs have been established that target both the victim and the abuser. Crisis lines, shelters, and support groups are common forms of assistance for victims. Counselors who work with domestic violence issues need to be well trained in crisis intervention as well as in other forms of intervention appropriate for victims of violence. Examples of knowledge and skills that should be acquired by counselors who work with this population are listed in Figure 13–4. Ensuring the victim's safety is of primary concern, regardless of the setting. Counselors also often serve as victim advocates by providing assistance with legal, economic, housing, and parenting issues (NCADV, 2005). To advocate effectively, counselors need to understand the legal system and have a strong networking alliance so that help can be obtained quickly (James, 2008).

Many communities have created programs to treat people who have abused their partners, recognizing that treatment is necessary for change to occur. Although not all counselors who work in family services will choose to work with those who victimize, it is important to be aware of the types of services available to domestic abusers. Most batterers (those who inflict physical abuse), especially those who are adjudicated, do not enter intervention programs willingly and often exhibit denial, minimization, justification, or projection of blame (James, 2008). The prevalent mode of intervention for batterers is court-ordered group counseling,

- Knowledge about the phenomenon of partner abuse (definitions, prevalence rates, types of abuse, dynamics and consequences of abuse)
- Knowledge of the explanatory theories of abuse and violence
- Knowledge of feminist-informed and culturally sensitive theories and practices pertaining to partner abuse
- Effective assessment protocols for partner abuse
- Knowledge of the experiences, needs, and risks faced by battered individuals (including symptoms of PTSD)
- Key principles and practices for individual treatment
- Services and resources available for victims and abusers

FIGURE 13–4   Knowledge and skills needed to work with victims of domestic violence

From Haddock, 2002.

which provides opportunities for social learning, anger management, confrontation, and support. Groups typically are designed to help abusers learn to accept responsibility for their behavior, recognize the spectrum of abuse, resolve conflict without violence or abuse, and address personal concerns (Golden & Frank, 1994; James, 2008). Two counselors who worked with batterers during their clinical internships describe their experiences in Figure 13–5 and Figure 13–6.

CHILD ABUSE SERVICES.   In Chapter 12, we described some of the issues related to child abuse and neglect. In many communities, specialized agencies focus on the prevention and

"They" were not the people I expected to meet. I expected "them" to be the stereotype—uncaring, manipulative, harsh, and antisocial. I took the assignment because I needed the hours. I was already working with sexually and physically abused boys. I told myself I would only do the groups for a short time, just until the end of my internship. My first group was almost 7 years ago and I am still with the program.

Some male batterers personify the stereotype—a noxious soup of bullying, selfishness, narcissism, and sociopathology. They always try to tell me what they think I want to hear. They always think they can hide their true selves. They can't see themselves accurately, and they assume that I am similarly impaired. Their problems are always caused by others and the deck is always stacked against them.

The majority of male batterers I encounter, however, value family, love their partners, and acknowledge that some of their behaviors are inappropriate. Many of these men enter the group believing that control will prevent abandonment, and the opposite is true. Many batterers enter the group believing that "taking care of her" is respectful and appropriate, and the opposite is true. Intimate relationships produce a frustrating paradox for most of these men. The harder they try, the more conflict, frustration, and failure they experience.

The purpose of the program is to produce a safer world for women and children. The goal is to educate and change beliefs. The process is one of engagement, confrontation, and encouragement. Success is measured with attendance, homework returned, and in-session behavior. Throughout the process, I always hope for healing and changes of heart.

Robin Daniel, Ph.D., LPC, NCC

FIGURE 13–5   Group counseling with male batterers

Rivett and Rees (2004) describe working with domestic violence offenders as "dancing on a razor's edge" because it is both "unsettling" and "humbling" (p. 143). I couldn't agree more. I have learned more than I could have imagined from the members of the group I've helped lead this semester. I've shed many of my preconceptions and judgments about this population and have built bonds with them through group process. The moral complexities I witnessed in being part of the group have tempered my initial evaluations of interventions for batterers, which studies suggest have little impact on recidivism rates. Dealing with domestic violence is not easy; there is no clear solution or treatment. Instead raising awareness, providing a balance of support and confrontation, encouraging male bonding, teaching new skills, listening, providing my experience as a woman, and letting members know how I learn from them all contribute to positive growth, and that has to be worth something.

Elisabeth Harper, M.A.T.S., Counseling Intern

FIGURE 13–6   Working with male batterers during an initial clinical experience

treatment of child abuse. These agencies provide support services for abusive or potentially abusive families, parent training programs, and community education programs regarding the recognition of abuse and neglect (Figure 13–7). Lewis et al.'s (2003) community counseling model, which was described earlier, provides a helpful framework for conceptualizing the types of services that might be offered at a child abuse prevention and treatment agency (see Table 13–2).

HOME-BASED SERVICES.   Home-based services provide intensive interventions within the homes of children and youth with emotional disturbances. In most cases, home-based services are provided through the child welfare, juvenile justice, or community mental health systems (Surgeon General Report, 2000). Three major goals of home-based services are to

Working with victims is an ultimate challenge, considering that their need for therapy is always the result of their exposure to some trauma. Some of the challenges to be dealt with in therapy are lack of trust, low self-esteem and the absence of autonomy, fear of reprisal from the person or persons responsible for the trauma, and the possible absence of a viable and healthy support system. An additional hidden challenge is the possibility that, in an effort to survive, the victims may have acquired some of the characteristics of the person or persons responsible for the trauma; i.e., they may be cunning, manipulative, and coercive. The challenge then is for the therapist to recognize these behaviors in the clients, help the clients to recognize these behaviors in themselves and acknowledge the source of the behaviors, and help the client adapt more appropriate coping skills.

The rewards of working with this population are many, including seeing the victims learn to trust; witnessing their elevated self-esteem and evidence, though small at times, of their movement toward self-nurturing; and observing the growth of courage to assign responsibility for their trauma to its rightful owner. The ultimate reward is when they no longer see themselves as victims but as survivors.

Dorothy Walton Walker, M.S., LPC, NCC
Director, StaSafe (Systemic Treatment after Sexual Abuse for Families) Exchange/SCAN

FIGURE 13–7   Counseling with victims of sexual abuse

TABLE 13–2 Direct and indirect community and client services in a child abuse prevention and treatment agency

	Community Services	Client Services
Direct	Community education programs regarding the recognition of abuse and neglect. Parent training classes offered to the community-at-large.	Individual and family counseling for children and parents. Assessment of and treatment for sexual offenders.
Indirect	Sponsoring community awareness events to make families aware of abuse and neglect issues. Working with local and state legislators to advance children's rights.	Sponsoring parent support groups that focus on effective parenting skills. Working with DSS to provide supervision and structured intervention for visits between children and parents who are not allowed to be alone with their children.

Source: From *Community Counseling: Empowerment Strategies for a Diverse Society* (3rd ed.), by J. A. Lewis, M. D. Lewis, J. A. Daniels, and M. J. D'Andrea, 2003, Pacific Grove, CA: Brooks/Cole. Adapted with permission of Wadsworth, a division of Thomson Learning: www.thomsonrights.com. Fax 800 730-2215.

(a) prevent out-of-home placements; (b) connect youth and their families with community resources, thereby creating an outside support system; and (c) strengthen the family's coping skills and capacity after crisis treatment is completed (Stroul, 1988). Services provided through these programs include evaluation, assessment, counseling, skills training, and coordination of services.

Two primary types of home-based services are family preservation programs and multisystemic therapy programs (MST; Promising Practices Network on Children, Families, and Communities, 2004; Surgeon General Report, 2000). Family preservation programs provide family-based services designed to keep dysfunctional families together. For example, the Surgeon General Mental Health Report (2000) describes the Homebuilders Program in Tacoma, Washington, and family reunification programs in both Washington State and Utah. The success of these programs was attributed to

- Delivering services in a home and community setting
- Viewing family members as colleagues in defining a service plan
- Making backup services available 24 hours a day
- Building life skills based on individual needs of family members
- Offering marital and family interventions
- Efficiently coordinating community services
- Assisting with basic needs, such as clothing, food, and housing

MST programs (Henggeler, Schoenwald, Borduin, Rowland, & Cunningham, 1998) are intensive, short-term, home- and family-focused treatment services for youth with behavioral and emotional disturbances. MST is based on Bronfenbrenner's (1979, 1995) bioecological theory, which was described in Chapters 2 and 12. Originally implemented with juvenile delinquents, MST intervenes directly in the young person's family, school, neighborhood, and peer group by identifying factors that contribute to the problem behaviors (Surgeon General Report, 2000). Major goals of MST are to (a) empower caregivers with the skills needed to address the difficulties that accompany parenting youth with behavior problems and (b) empower youth to cope more effectively with family, peer, school, and neighborhood difficulties. By working intensively with the young person, the family, and the larger community, skills are developed across all groups that lead to improved behaviors and mental health. The efficacy of MST has been attributed to the fact that it is clearly specified, is based on solid empirical research, and uses quality assurance mechanisms to ensure that treatment protocol is followed (Schoenwald, Brown, & Henggeler, 2000).

OTHER CLINICAL SERVICES.   Opportunities for community-based mental health counselors exist in many different settings, depending on the counselor's training, skills, interests, and professional certification. In addition to the sites already mentioned, opportunities for employment include wellness centers, for-profit agencies, faith-based counseling centers, career centers, private practice, correctional facilities, school-based mental health settings, colleges and universities, and government agencies. In particular, there is a growing need for civilian counselors to work with military personnel (Hall, 2008). Although legislation has now recognized licensed professional counselors as "legitimate providers" of mental health services within the Veteran's Healthcare Administration, there still are issues to be worked our regarding supervision and level of pay.

The settings in which clinical mental health counselors work are numerous, and the varying needs for services are great. We conclude this section with narratives from counselors working in two diverse settings: an ecumenical, not-for-profit, counseling center and a state prison. Both counselors describe some of the challenges and rewards that are inherent in their work.

BOX 13–7

Directing and Counseling in a Private, Nonprofit Community Counseling Center

Trinity Center, Inc. is a small, ecumenical community counseling center that operates on a budget of approximately $575,000 annually. Trinity Center is staffed by 3 full-time and 1 half-time administrative and support staff; four clinical employees, one of whom works also as part-time administrator; 14 part-time contract clinicians; 1 part-time (5 hours per week) medical director and 1 part-time (3.5 hours per week) behavioral pediatrician; and a 16-member Board of Directors. One of the rewards of directing Trinity Center is working alongside talented, committed professionals who bring creativity and energy into the work they do with their clients, each other's lives and the life of the Center. An ongoing challenge is continually adapting to changes that come from professionals' evolving interests and the profession's evolving standards of acceptable practice. It is a challenge to hold both of these goals in balance—sacrificing neither procedural predictability and accountability nor professional creativity and growth.

Another challenge is maintaining financial stability as we combine the model of a standard private practice (clients able to pay the full fee for services either through insurance or self-pay) with that of a nonprofit agency (serve appropriate clients, regardless of ability to pay, soliciting missing revenue from donors and foundations). The richness inherent in the variety of client issues and the reward of bringing professional expertise and talent to the community continue to make this the model of choice for those of us involved at Trinity Center. For over 25 years, we have shared the financial challenges as well as the professional enrichment—learning and adapting as we have grown.

Ann Dixon Coppage, M.A. Ed., LPC

BOX 13–8

Group Counseling in a Prison Setting

There are some barriers to providing an effective group experience to inmates in a prison setting. For instance, a disadvantage is the limited amount of privacy, with closed-circuit television and windowed doors. Institutional furniture in a room with tables and no carpeting ordinarily are not conducive to physical comfort and emotional closeness. Materials used in the group must be approved in advance and examined by prison guards. Out-of-group contact also can be a problem, even in a very large institution.

Some counselors might be reluctant to hold groups in this milieu due to concerns for personal safety. Though unfounded, these fears may be difficult to overcome until trust has been established. Also, there is ambivalence in society as to whether an inmate, who is in prison for punishment, is entitled to grief groups.

The advantages, however, greatly outweigh the disadvantages. The prison chaplains publicize the group, interview prospective members, and collect evaluations after the group ends. A mixture of self-referrals and men encouraged by the psychologist or social worker brings a variety of experiences and awareness to the group. Many of the participants have experience with groups and have learned to communicate directly and with great insight. They are enthusiastic about (and have time for) homework assignments, often taking great care with written activities such as letter writing and closing comments. They are open to experiential exercises, genuine with each other, and appreciative of facilitators who treat them as "real people." Our experience with these groups has been growth promoting for the facilitators as well as the participants.

Margaret (Peg) J. Olson, Ph.D., Counselor Educator;
Margaret (Peg) A. McEwen, MSN, Family Nurse Practitioner

Summary and Conclusion

In this chapter, we have described a variety of settings in which clinical mental health counselors may be employed. Some of the venues, such as community mental health centers and hospitals, provide many different treatment options to diverse clientele who present with a spectrum of issues. Other settings, including family service agencies, hospice programs, and substance abuse agencies, allow counselors to focus on a specific population or mental health issue. Services in CMHCs, hospitals, clinics, and agencies can include inpatient treatment and day programs, residential treatment, outpatient services, home visits, prevention efforts, and multisystemic interventions.

Regardless of the setting in which they practice, counselors will want to engage in ongoing training and supervision to update knowledge, skills, and professional certifications. The counseling profession and community mental health service programs continue to evolve, both as a result of changes in the profession itself and as a consequence of government and public policy. It is incumbent on counseling professionals to be cognizant of those changes, remaining open to new approaches, interventions, and service options.

CHAPTER 14

Career Counseling, Employee Assistance Programs, and Private Practice

Far in the back of his mind he harbors thoughts
   like small boats in a quiet cove
      ready to set sail at a moment's notice.
I, seated on his starboard side,
   listen for the winds of change
      ready to lift anchor with him
         and explore the choppy waves of life ahead.
Counseling requires a special patience
   best known to seamen and navigators—
      courses are only charted for times
         when the tide is high and the breezes steady.

From "Harbor Thoughts," by S. T. Gladding, 1985, *Journal of Humanistic Education and Development, 23,* p. 68. © 1985 by ACA. Reprinted with permission. No further reproduction authorized without written permission of the American Counseling Association.

This chapter examines three counseling specialties that appeal to many clinical mental health counselors—career counseling, employee assistance program (EAP) counseling, and private practice. The activities of counselors who engage in these specialties are conducted in a variety of settings ranging from those that are primarily educational to those that are affiliated with business or government agencies.

Career counselors help clients to "clarify, specify, implement, and adjust to work-related decisions" (Amundson, Harris-Bowlsbey, & Niles, 2009). Settings in which career counselors work include school systems, higher education systems, unemployment centers, community agencies, and private practices. EAP counselors work with companies and institutions, sometimes operating within a particular company and sometimes operating on a referral basis. Their activities may include personal counseling, referral, and prevention-based initiatives to workers in employment settings. Finally, private practitioners are counselors who work independently or in a group with other clinicians. Some private practitioners are generalists, whereas others specialize in helping people with specific disorders or concerns, including grief, depression, anxiety, eating disorders, and family transitions, to name just a few.

In this chapter, we focus primarily on career counseling, which takes place in a variety of settings. We also provide an overview of the purposes and challenges associated with EAP and private practice settings.

CAREER COUNSELING

The Case of Jeremy

Jeremy has worked as a computer analyst for a major company for 23 years. Recently, the company decided to outsource its Information Technology department, and Jeremy was told that he would lose his job in 6 months. During the past several years, Jeremy has considered pursuing another career, but he wondered how to go about making a change. He likes interacting with people, and he does not have many opportunities to do that in his current position. He views the layoff as an opportunity to train for a new career, possibly in education or the health-care field. His severance package will be significant; however, he is concerned that changing careers at this stage of life is too risky. His current company is providing career counseling for employees who will be laid off.

If you were his career counselor, what approach would you take to assist Jeremy? How would you help him with the transition? What factors might you and he discuss during the process? What additional information would you like to have to work effectively with Jeremy?

Choosing a career is more than simply deciding what one will do to earn a living. Occupations influence a person's whole way of life, including physical, mental, and emotional health. Work roles and other life roles are often interconnected (Imbimbo, 1994). Thus, income, stress, social identity, meaning, education, clothes, hobbies, interests, friends, lifestyle, place of residence, and even personality characteristics are linked to one's work life (Herr, Cramer, & Niles, 2004). In some cases, work groups serve as cultures in which social needs are met and values are developed. The nature and purpose of a person's work are related to his or her sense of identity, well-being, and life satisfaction (Burlew, 1992). Qualitative research indicates that individuals who appear most happy in their work are committed to following their interests; exhibit a breadth of personal competencies and strengths; and function in work environments that are characterized by freedom, challenge, meaning, and a positive social atmosphere (Henderson, 2000).

Yet, despite evidence highlighting the importance of work, many individuals do not systematically explore and choose their careers. In surveys commissioned by the National Career Development Association (NCDA) and the National Occupational Information Coordinating Committee (NOICC), it was found that approximately 40% of adults selected their careers by conscious planning and nearly 70% of adults would investigate job options more thoroughly if they were starting the process over again (cited in Brown, 2007). Therefore, it is important that individuals obtain career information early and enter the job market with knowledge and flexibility in regard to their plans.

BOX 14–1

"It is so important to plan your career and not drift wherever the wind blows," says Friedberg, who is a New York-based career coach with the Five O'Clock Club, a national career counseling organization, and has a private practice in the city. "You must do some careful long-term strategic assessment, think about what you might need at each stage of your life, commit to a plan, and accept the fact that there will be some trade-off along the way. Too often, people try to fit themselves into a job and end up patterning their lives after it. What they should do instead is find a job that fits them and fits into their lives."

(cited in Hayes, 2001)

A variety of factors influence the process of career development. For instance, personality styles, developmental stages, values, skills, and cultural factors all affect career development and career choice (Drummond & Ryan, 1995). Serendipity and happenstance (Guindon & Hanna, 2002), family background (Chope, 2006), gender (Hotchkiss & Borow, 1996), giftedness (Maxwell, 2007), and age (Canaff, 1997) may also influence career options and choices. Other important factors include local and global economic conditions, trends in the workplace, and the accessibility of career information (Borgen, 1997; Brown, 2007).

The world of work, and the importance work plays in clients' lives, has changed tremendously throughout history, as has the process of career counseling. Career counselors in contemporary society need to have skills in personal counseling, an understanding of career development theories, knowledge about projections for occupational opportunities, and an ability to use technology to assist clients with career-related decisions. They also need to possess multicultural competencies and follow the ethical codes that guide the practice of career counseling, such as the ACA *Code of Ethics* (2005), NCDA *Code of Ethics* (2007), and the NCDA *Guidelines for Use of the Internet for Career Information and Planning Services* (available online at www.ncda.org).

The National Career Development Association (NCDA; formerly the National Vocational Guidance Association [NVGA]) and the National Employment Counselors Association (NECA) are the two divisions within the American Counseling Association (ACA) primarily devoted to career development and career counseling. The NCDA, the oldest division within the ACA, traces its roots back to 1913. The association is made up of professionals in business and industry, rehabilitation agencies, government, private practice, and educational settings. Its mission is to promote career development across the life span by providing services to the public through career development professionals. Services include professional development activities, publications, research, public information, professional standards, advocacy, and professional recognition for achievement (NCDA, 2008). Among its publications is a description of career counseling competencies, adopted by the NCDA in 1997. These competencies can be accessed through the NCDA Web site (www.ncda.org). NECA was founded to offer professional leadership to people who counsel in employment services or career development settings and to people employed in related areas of counselor education, research, administration, or supervision. Its mission is to help people plan for, enter, understand, and progress in the world of work through legislative advocacy, establishing standards and guidelines, showcasing best practices, and networking (NECA, 2008). Both divisions publish quarterly journals: the *Career Development Quarterly* (formerly the *Vocational Guidance Quarterly*) and the *Journal of Employment Counseling,* respectively.

Another group that promotes career development is the National Occupational Information Coordinating Committee (NOICC). NOICC is not a professional counseling organization; instead, it is a federal interagency organization that works with the Department of Defense, the Department of Labor, and the Department of Education to promote excellence in the way occupational information is compiled and delivered (Brown, 2007). A State Occupational Information Coordinating Committee (SOICC) exists in each state and works in conjunction with NOICC to accomplish overarching national goals.

Career Counseling and Related Terminology

Changes that have taken place in society and the world of work have resulted in changes in the practice and definition of career counseling. Several current definitions of career counseling are worth examining. The NCDA (1997) defines *career counseling* as "the process of assisting individuals in the development of a life-career with focus on the definition of the worker role and how that role interacts with other roles" (p. 1). Niles and Harris-Bowlsbey (2005) described career counseling as a formal relationship in which a counselor helps a client or group of clients find ways to cope more effectively with career concerns, including making a career choice, handling career transitions, and managing job-related stress. Career counseling can also be viewed as "a series of general and specific interventions throughout the life span" dealing with issues pertaining to self-understanding, work selection and satisfaction, work site behavior, and life style issues (e.g., balancing work, family, and leisure; Engels, Minor, Sampson, & Splete, 1995, p. 134).

Each of the preceding definitions illustrates the broad scope of career counseling—a complex process that is both a counseling specialty and a core element of general counseling practice. By necessity, career counselors possess a wide range of competencies that encompass general counseling skills as well as skills, knowledge, and awareness specific to the career domain (Niles & Harris-Bowlsbey, 2005). Career counseling may include any combination of the following activities:

- Administering and interpreting assessments to help clients clarify and specify relevant self-characteristics, including values, skills, interests, and personality traits
- Encouraging career exploration activities, such as job shadowing, internships (or externships), and occupational information interviews
- Using career planning systems and occupational information systems to help individuals understand the world of work
- Providing opportunities for improving decision-making skills
- Assisting in the development of individualized career plans
- Teaching job-search strategies, interview skills, and resume development skills
- Helping resolve potential personal conflicts on the job through practice in developing relevant interpersonal skills, such as assertiveness training or anger management
- Providing support for clients experiencing job stress, job loss, and/or career transition (www.ncda.org)

Throughout its history, career development and career counseling have been known by several different names, including *vocational guidance, occupational counseling,* and *vocational counseling.* Differences in terminology reflect changes in viewpoints about the meaning of work and its significance in our society. To understand the process of career counseling as it is conceptualized in the 21st century, it is first important to clarify terms associated with *career* and *career counseling.*

Three terms associated with the term *career* are *job, occupation,* and *vocation.* A *job* is merely an activity undertaken for economic returns (Fox, 1994), whereas an *occupation* may be defined as a group of similar jobs found in different industries or organizations (Herr et al., 2004). The term *vocation,* which is sometimes used synonymously with *occupation,* implies a psychological commitment or calling to a particular field. Each of these terms is somewhat limited in scope. In contrast, the term *career* is broader, more modern, and more inclusive than other terminology and is discussed next.

Career development specialists have defined *career* in a number of ways. According to Sears (1982), a career is the totality of work one does in a lifetime. It is a lifelong process that encompasses psychological, sociological, educational, economic, physical, and chance factors. Brown (2007) added to Sears's definition by emphasizing the relevance of cultural factors to the career development process. Super's (1976) classic definition of *career* incorporates many of these same factors. Super defined *career* as:

> . . . the course of events that constitutes a life; the sequence of occupations and other life roles which combine to express one's commitment to work in his or her total pattern of self-development; the series of remunerated and nonremunerated positions occupied by a person from adolescence through retirement, of which occupation is only one. A career includes work-related roles such as those of student, employee, and pensioner together with complementary avocational, familial, and civic roles. Careers exist only as people pursue them; they are person-centered. (p. 4)

McDaniels (1984) emphasized the interaction of work and leisure in relation to career and expressed that interaction in a formula: "Career equals Work plus Leisure" ($C = W + L$). Similarly, Liptak (2001) described the interaction between work and leisure activities, maintaining that effective career counseling involves helping clients fuse work and leisure experiences to gain greater life satisfaction.

Five additional terms related to the process of career counseling include *career education, career information, career intervention, career development facilitator,* and *career coaching.* To help build a foundation for what follows, we define each term briefly here and then provide elaboration in subsequent sections of the chapter:

- **Career Education:** a systematic attempt to influence the career development of students and adults through various educational strategies, including providing occupational information, infusing career-related concepts into the academic curriculum, and offering career planning courses (Brown, 2007).
- **Career Information:** information about the labor market, including job trends, industries, and comprehensive information systems. Career counselors need to be aware of where to acquire occupational information and how to assess the quality of that information. The Internet provides a wealth of career-related information. The U.S. Department of Labor (www.dol.gov), as well as other government departments, is a premier source of occupational information that publishes numerous resources (Duggan & Jurgens, 2007).
- **Career Intervention:** a deliberate act designed to empower people to cope effectively with career development tasks (Spokane, 1991). Career interventions include individual and group career counseling, career development programs, computer information delivery systems, and career education (Niles & Harris-Bowlsbey, 2005).

- **Career Development Facilitator (CDF):**   an occupational title that designates individuals working in a variety of career development settings. These individuals may or may not be professional counselors and have participated in at least 120 hours of career development training. A CDF may serve as a career group facilitator, job search trainer, career resource center coordinator, career coach, career development case manager, intake interviewer, occupational and labor market information resource person, human resource career development coordinator, employment/placement specialist, or workforce development staff person (from www.ncda.org, 2008).
- **Career Coaching:**   an interactive process that helps individuals and organizations improve their performances. Career coaches work with clients in many areas, including business, career, finances, health, and relationships. Through the process of career coaching, clients learn skills such as goal setting, taking positive action, decision making, and building on their natural strengths (International Coach Foundation, 2008).

Comments from the Field of Executive Coaching

Executive coaching, as I see it, comprises personal counseling, business advice, and advice about managing for people who are in executive management. More generally, "executive coaching" comprises a one-to-one helping relationship between the coach and the client. It is understood that the major aim of the relationship is to help the executive perform her own duties more effectively. In each case, there are problems the client has encountered which require changes in the client's behaviors. My own practice of executive coaching has led me to expect to deal with a combination of personal advice about styles of interaction, discussion of personal problems which impede my clients' accomplishment of their executive duties, and even receiving spreadsheets while on the road myself for inspection and comment to my clients.

John P. Anderson, LPC, Executive Coach

Just as it is important for counselors to be familiar with current terminology related to career development and career counseling, it also is essential for them to be informed about the different theories of career development that guide career counseling practice. Although it would be beyond the scope and purpose of this text to elaborate on each of the theories that has contributed to our knowledge about career development, in the next section, we summarize the central concepts of four theories that have influenced past and current research and practice.

Career Development Theories

Career development theories try to explain why individuals choose careers. They also deal with the career adjustments people make over time, because people living in the 21st century are likely to change jobs several times over their life span. Some of the more prominent career development theories, which are broad and comprehensive in regard to individual and occupational development, began appearing in the literature in the 1950s (Gysbers, Heppner, & Johnston, 2003). The theories of Donald Super and John Holland are perhaps the most utilized and/or recognized theories of career development (Weinrach, 1996), although a number of other career theories have been generated, and some are currently

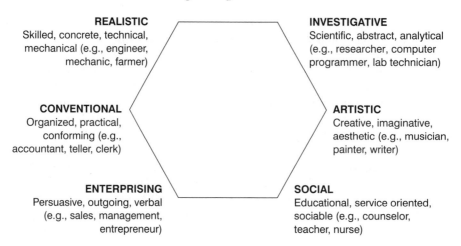

FIGURE 14–1 **Holland's six categories of personality and occupation**

Note: Reproduced by special permission of the publisher, Psychological Assessment Resources, Inc., from *Making Vocational Choices: A Theory of Careers,* 3rd ed., copyright by J. L. Holland. © 1973, 1985, 1992, 1997 by Psychological Assessment Resources, Inc. All rights reserved.

evolving. In this section, we provide an overview of four prominent theories of career development that have been extensively researched and often guide career counseling practice.

TRAIT-AND-FACTOR THEORY.   Trait-and-factor theory, which currently is also referred to as trait-and-type theory, originated with Frank Parsons (1909). The theory stresses that the traits of clients should first be assessed and then systematically matched with factors inherent in various occupations. Its most widespread influence occurred during the Great Depression, when E. G. Williamson (1939) championed its use. Trait-and-factor theory fell out of favor during the 1950s and 1960s but has resurfaced in a more modern form, which is reflected in John Holland's (1997) Theory of Vocational Choice.

Holland's Theory of Vocational Choice stresses the interpersonal nature of careers and associated lifestyles as well as the performance requirements of a work position. Holland (1997) identified six categories in which personality types and job environments can be classified: Realistic, Investigative, Artistic, Social, Enterprising, and Conventional (RIASEC) (see Figure 14–1). Individuals of a particular type are attracted to environments of similar types. People typically achieve the most work satisfaction when their work environment matches their personality type (McWhirter, Joyce, & Aranda, 2009).

Counselors grounded in Holland's approach use instruments to assess a client's personality type and then explore corresponding work orientations (McWhirter et al., 2009). The *Strong Interest Inventory,* the *Self Directed Search,* and the *Kuder Career Search with Person Match* are examples of instruments that are frequently used to assess personality type. These assessment tools provide clients with a three-letter personality code that, according to Holland (1997), represents their modal personality orientation. For example, a person's code might be *SAE* (Social, Artistic, Enterprising). A person with this code would have interests in helping others (S), using creative talents (A), and leading or influencing others (E). Holland codes for multiple occupations can be found in the *O*Net* occupational database, which is the official online publication of the U.S. Department of Labor (www.online.

onetcenter.org). Holland's *Occupations Finder* (Holland, 1994) and the *Dictionary of Holland Occupational Titles* (Gottfredson & Holland, 1996) can also be used to help clients find occupations that are similar to their codes.

Three constructs that are central to the Theory of Vocational Choice are *congruence, consistency,* and *differentiation* (Holland, 1997). *Congruence* refers to a match between personality type and work environment type. For example, a counselor, whose code might be *SAE*, would be in a profession considered congruent with her type. *Consistency* is a little more challenging to define briefly. It refers to the relative proximity, in regard to the arrangement of the letters on the Holland hexagon (see Figure 14–1), of a person's three-letter personality code. People with letters that are adjacent, such as *SA* or *SE*, are more likely to find working environments that are consistent with their interests than individuals whose code letters are inconsistent (i.e., the first two letters are opposite to each other on the hexagon, such as *SR*). *Differentiation* indicates the degree to which an individual's interests are defined. For example, a person who has a clearly differentiated profile will demonstrate at least one code letter that is markedly higher than the lowest code letter. Someone with clearly differentiated interests is likely to have less dificulty making career decisions than an undifferentiated person (Duggan & Jurgens, 2007). Work environments also differ in regard to levels of differentiation, with some environments providing more flexibility in regard to various environments than others. Career counselors who utilize Holland's theory consider these constructs as they explore career options with their clients.

DEVELOPMENTAL THEORIES. Two of the most widely known developmental theories are those associated with Donald Super and Eli Ginzberg. Both theories focus on personal growth and development. The original developmental theory proposed by Ginzberg and his associates has had great influence and has been revised to reflect a more comprehensive life span approach (Ginzberg, 1972). Super's theory is examined in detail here because it has been researched and implemented more extensively.

Compared to other career approaches, developmental theories are generally more inclusive, more concerned with longitudinal expression of career behavior, and more inclined to highlight the importance of self-concept. Super's life-span, life-space approach (1957, 1980, 1990) posits that career development is the lifelong process of implementing a self-concept. Self-concept evolves throughout a lifetime and is influenced by biological, psychological, and support factors (McWhirter et al., 2009). People's views of themselves are reflected in what they do. Super suggested that vocational development unfolds in five stages, each of which contains a developmental task to be completed. The five stages also consist of substages, which are described in most career counseling textbooks but will not be discussed here.

The first stage, according to Super, is the *growth* stage (from birth to age 14). During this stage, children form a mental picture of themselves in relation to others. They develop interests and skills, and their self-concept begins to develop. Throughout the *growth* stage, children become oriented to the world of work.

The second stage, *exploration*, takes place during latter adolescence and early adulthood. The major tasks of this stage include a general exploration of the world of work and the initial specification of a career preference. With the current *millennial generation* (i.e., young people born in the early 1980s through the late 1990s), specification appears to be less common than it was during the time Super developed his theory. A minority of millennials have prior job experience as they enter young adulthood, and many lack the basic knowledge of the world of work that young people from previous generations typically possessed (Kennedy, 2008).

The third stage is known as *establishment* (ages 25–44). During this stage, adults choose and implement a career and become established in that career. According to Super, once a career is selected, persons can concentrate on advancement until they reach the top of the professions, tire of their job, or are forced to change jobs. Again, in contemporary society, people are expected to change jobs several times over the course of a lifetime. Therefore, the *establishment* stage may look quite different now than it did a few decades ago.

The fourth stage, *maintenance* (ages 45–64), has the major task of preserving what one has already achieved. Continued efforts to improve skills and knowledge and to keep up with technological advancements are especial critical during this stage. The final stage, *disengagement* (formerly called *decline*—a rather negative term that, fortunately, was re-named) was theorized to occur from the age of 65 and above. Major tasks of this stage include detaching from work and aligning with other sources of life satisfaction. Activities associated with this stage include deceleration, retirement planning, and retirement living (Niles & Harris-Bowlsbey, 2005).

Super (1990) suggested that people often *recycle* through stages at various points in life, particularly when they are considering career changes and/or are destabilized by down-sizing, illness, injury, or other socioeconomic or personal events. For example, if a 40-year-old woman loses the job she has had with a particular company for the past 20 years, she is likely to reenter the *exploration* stage, as she reexamines options and opportunities.

Whereas Super's concept of *life span* is characterized by five stages and recycling, the concept of *life space* refers to the combination of life roles in which people participate (Super, 1980). These roles include those of son or daughter, student, leisurite, citizen, worker, spouse or partner, homemaker, parent, and pensioner (a person who is retired). People participate in various roles in specific arenas, such as the home, the school, the workplace, and the community. Super's *Life-Career Rainbow* illustrates how six life roles might be depicted within a person's life space (see Figure 14–2). The degree of salience people attach to different roles, the amount of time allotted to each, and the extent to which life-roles overlap and/or interact all influence life satisfaction. When life seems out of bal-ance or stressful, it may be due to attempts at balancing multiple roles in a manner that is not satisfying. Issues of stress related to balancing roles and expectations can be a source of angst that leads people to seek career counseling.

The major contributions of developmental career counseling theories are their emphases on the importance of the life span development in career decision making and on career de-cisions that are influenced by other processes and events in a person's life. This "life pattern paradigm for career counseling encourages counselors to consider a client's aptitudes and interests in a matrix of life experiences, not just in comparison to some normative group" (Savickas, 1989, p. 12).

Career counselors using Super's developmental theory may include any of the follow-ing in their work with clients:

- Identifying the client's level of career maturity (i.e., the readiness of a client to make sound career choices)
- Attempting to reduce potential deficits in regard to needed attitudes, skills, knowl-edge, and accomplishment of career development tasks

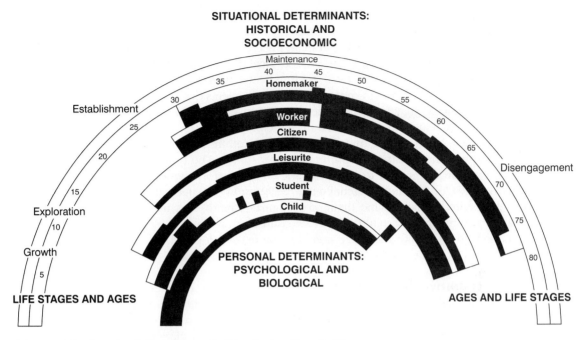

FIGURE 14–2 Super's rainbow theory: Six life roles in schematic life space

Source: From "Career and Life Development," by D. F. Super, 1990, *Career Choice and Development: Applying Contemporary Theories to Practice* (2nd ed.) San Francisco: Jossey-Bass. © 1990 by Donald Super. Used with permission of Jossey-Bass.

- Analyzing the client's self-concept and strengthening it through assessment and counseling, if needed
- Identifying interests, abilities, and values and helping the client examine how they are distributed across life roles
- Understanding that a career is a combination of interacting life roles and assisting clients define those roles and their salience as they attempt to achieve balance in life.

(Amundson et al., 2009, p. 22)

LEARNING THEORY OF CAREER COUNSELING. A third influential career development theory was originally proposed by John Krumboltz in 1979, at which time it was called the *social learning theory* of career decision making and was based on Bandura's (1977b, 1986) social cognitive theory. In recent years, Krumboltz and his colleagues have expanded the theory to include specific applications of social learning theory to the practice of career counseling. The expanded theory is called the *learning theory of career counseling* (LTCC).

According to LTCC (Mitchell & Krumboltz, 1996), four factors influence a person's career decision making: genetic endowment (innate traits and abilities), environmental conditions and events (which may be planned or unplanned), learning experiences (instrumental and associative learning), and task-approach skills (work habits, expectations of performance, cognitive processes, and emotional response patterns). Through the interaction of these four factors, people form beliefs about their own abilities (self-observation generalizations) and beliefs about the world (worldview generalizations). These generalizations affect actions and decisions relevant to the career-planning process.

The goal of career counseling from an LTCC perspective is to help clients develop skills, interests, beliefs, values, work habits, and personal qualities that will enable them to have satisfying lives within a dynamic work environment (Swanson & Fouad, 1999). Often, career counselors serve as coaches or mentors as they help clients develop new beliefs, attitudes, and skills. Interventions may be developmental and preventive (e.g., career education, job clubs) or targeted and remedial (directed toward unhelpful cognitions and behaviors).

Mitchell, Levin, and Krumboltz (1999) amended the learning theory of career counseling to include the construct of *planned happenstance.* The term, which at first glance appears oxymoronic, refers to the "creating and transforming of unplanned events into opportunities for learning" (Mitchell et al., 1999, p. 117). Career counselors can help clients develop attitudes that enable them to recognize, create, and use events that happen by chance as career opportunities. Moreover, counselors can help their clients learn to be comfortable with ambiguity and indecision, thereby making it possible for them to capitalize on unforeseen future events.

SOCIAL COGNITIVE CAREER THEORY.   An emerging theory of career development that has been the subject of much current research is social cognitive career theory (SCCT). Proposed by Lent, Brown, and Hackett (1994), SCCT provides a framework for explaining career development that focuses on the "(a) formation and elaboration of career-relevant interests, (b) the selection of academic and career choice options, and (c) performance and persistence in educational and occupational pursuits" (Lent et al., 1994, p. 79). Like Krumboltz's LTCC theory, SCCT derived from Bandura's (1977, 1986) social cognitive theory. As with LTCC, a primary assumption of SCCT is that a complex array of factors, including culture, gender, genetic endowment, and health, affect people's beliefs, interests, and subsequent career decision-making behaviors. However, Lent et al. emphasized two additional constructs—self-efficacy beliefs and outcome expectations—in a manner that differs from Krumboltz's approach.

Self-efficacy refers to an individual's beliefs about his or her ability to successfully perform a particular task (Bandura, 1977, 1986). Outcome expectations are the consequences a person expects to occur following a particular course of action (Bandura, 1986). According to SCCT, self-efficacy beliefs and outcome expectations influence the development of career-related interests. These interests, in turn, influence the development of career-related aspirations and goals (Lent et al., 1994).

Two other key constructs believed to influence career interests and goals are people's perceptions of barriers and their perceptions of supports (Lent, Brown, & Hackett, 2000). To illustrate, even if a person possesses high levels of self-efficacy, high expectations, and interests that match a particular career, that person may avoid pursuing the career if barriers toward that pursuit appear insurmountable. For example, a person may lower his or her aspirations because of financial concerns or perceived discrimination. In contrast, an individual's perception of certain supports (e.g., family, community) may enhance the likelihood that he or she will embark on a particular career path.

SCCT has particular relevance for addressing the unique factors that shape the career development of women, ethnic minorities, gay and lesbian individuals, and others who are members of cultural minorities (e.g., Fouad, 2007; Leong & Gupta, 2007; McWhirter & Flojo, 2001). Career counselors who follow an SCCT approach acknowledge the influence of contextual factors on cognitions, interests, and goals. Counselors working from this perspective may implement interventions that help clients:

- Identify options that may have been foreclosed due to unrealistic or faulty self-efficacy beliefs or outcome expectations.
- Identify perceived barriers that may have led clients to eliminate career possibilities prematurely and then examine how realistic those perceptions of barriers are.
- Modify and counteract faulty beliefs and expectations as well as faulty occupational information (Swanson & Fouad, 1999).

Theories of career development serve as road maps to help counselors understand their clients' career-related beliefs, behaviors, and aspirations (Krumboltz, 1994). Theoretical approaches help career counselors make sense of the information clients bring them about work-related issues. Many career counselors adopt a holistic approach to career counseling that integrates key constructs from various theories that have particular relevance for particular clients dealing with particular issues. A strong understanding of career development theories and their applications guides counselors as they become skilled in implementing effective career interventions.

Career Counseling Process and Skills

As mentioned previously, career counseling is a complex process that has evolved throughout the years. A number of factors have contributed to rapid change in the world of work and the delivery of career counseling services, including

- An interdependent global economy and other economic factors
- Evolving occupational projections and trends
- Continued advancement in technology, especially Internet services
- An increasingly diverse workforce
- Higher levels of unemployment
- Corporate downsizing
- An increased number of dual-career families and number of people working from locations away from the workplace (Duggan & Jurgens, 2007; Niles & Harris-Bowlsbey, 2005)

BOX 14–2

Career Coaching by Telephone

As a part of the relocation package offered to employees of our client companies, my job was to contact the "trailing" spouse and offer assistance in his or her own career move. The service was available without charge to the spouse and could include any or all of the following: the Myers-Briggs Type Indicator (MBTI) and Strong Interest Inventory (SII) administration and interpretation, résumé critiques, practice interviews, job search strategies and contact information for potential employers. All of the services were provided over the telephone—in the vast majority of cases, I never met the client in person.

That was the primary challenge—establishing rapport with the client via the telephone. Also, because some clients were only available at night or on weekends, it was hard to separate working hours and personal time.

The benefits included the ability to work from home and in one's casual clothes or even pajamas. The company that employed me provided great support in the form of test administration

(continued)

and research about targeted industries. There were personal rewards as well. Often the spouse was surprised and pleased to find out there was someone interested in his or her own employment challenges and personal reaction to the upcoming move.

Pamela Karr, M.A. Ed., NCC, LPC

The NCDA developed a set of career counseling competency statements designed to guide the practice of professional career counselor. The competency statements, which can be accessed through the NCDA Web site (www.ncda.org/), focus on a broad range of general counseling and specific career-related skills. In this section, we highlight three essential skill areas: conducting career-related assessment, providing career information, and counseling diverse clientele.

CAREER ASSESSMENT.   It is not uncommon for clients to enter career counseling with the misconception that the counselor will give them tests that will magically reveal the perfect career match. Perhaps this misconception stems from the early days of trait-and-factor theory, when Frank Parson's model of career counseling predominated. The Parsonian model encouraged career counselors "to objectify interests, values, and abilities through the use of standardized assessment to guide people in identifying where they fit within the occupational structure" (Niles & Harris-Bowlsbey, 2005, p. 15). In today's society, the complex process of career counseling goes well beyond the "test and tell" method, and counselors recognize the limitations associated with standardized testing. Therefore, it is important for career counselors to clarify their role from the outset, so that the client understands the purposes and limits of career counseling and assessment.

Although career assessment does not act as a crystal ball, it does serve a key role in career counseling. As stated in Chapter 7, assessment is an ongoing activity that takes place throughout the entire counseling process, from referral to follow-up (Hohenshil, 1996). Formal and informal methods of assessment help counselors gather information to determine the nature of clients' issues, the prevalence of their problems, and their strengths and skills, (Whiston, 2009). Similarly, career-related assessment may be formal or informal, is used to gather client information, and helps evaluate individual strengths and areas of concern. The purposes of career assessment are to help clients examine career possibilities, assess personal strengths, acquire a structure for evaluating career alternatives, clarify expectations, and implement plans of action (Spokane, 1991).

Conceptually, it is helpful to divide career assessment into two major categories: assessment of individual differences and assessment of the career choice process (see Betz, 1992 and Whiston, 2009). Assessment of individual differences is conducted to increase client self-awareness in multiple areas, including interests, values, needs, personality attributes, and abilities. In contrast, assessing the career choice process involves measuring where clients are in the decision-making process. Assessment in this area may include measuring degree of career maturity or level of decidedness. Many different career assessment instruments have been published during the past several decades, some of which have stronger psychometric properties than others. Publications such as *A Counselor's Guide to Career Assessment Instruments* (Kapes & Whitfield, 2002) and *Using Assessment Results for Career Development* (Osborn & Zunker, 2005) can be especially helpful in describing characteristics of various instruments, including purpose, reading level, validity, reliability, and cultural fairness.

Computer-assisted assessment in career counseling has become even more prevalent during the past decade. Career assessment can be conducted online, or instruments can be purchased for computerized administration and interpretation. When computers are used in career assessment, scoring errors are avoided and results are obtained quickly, thus saving time for professionals and eliminating the wait period for clients. However, several concerns have been raised in regard to computer-assisted assessment. Whiston (2009) summarized some of those concerns by stating,

> With the ease of computer-generated reports, clinicians may be lulled into a false sense of security and use the computer-generated results without becoming educated about the instrument. Instruments used in counseling are validated for specific purposes; therefore, a counselor cannot use a general computer-generated report in isolation. The American Counseling Association's (2005) *Code of Ethics* states that counselors confirm the validity of assessment scoring and interpretation if they use such assessment services. . . . Simply using a computer-generated report without knowledge of the instrument's strengths and limitations would be considered by the courts to be negligent and unprofessional. Computer-generated reports are designed to supplement or complement the clinician's interpretation of the results, not replace them. (pp. 398–399)

Qualitative methods of assessment, which encourage active client participation, are especially applicable to career counseling. Qualitative approaches can be used alone or in conjunction with quantitative instruments (McWhirter & Flojo, 2001). Through qualitative assessment procedures, clients have opportunities to tell their stories and explore the meaning they take from those stories (McMahon, Patton, & Watson, 2003). There are several examples of qualitative assessment processes, including card sorts, lifelines, and career genograms. The career genogram is similar to the family genogram described in Chapter 10 in that it creates a graphic representation of a client's family spanning three generations. It "is particularly useful because it provides a direct and relevant framework for use with clients to shed light on many topics, including their worldviews, possible environmental barriers, personal–work–family role conflicts, racial identity status and issues, and levels of acculturation" (Gysbers, Heppner, & Johnston, 2003, p. 202). The career genogram provides a venue through which the client can describe family relationships and prevailing attitudes about the various occupations that have been charted.

Qualitative and quantitative forms of career assessment can help clients clarify values, interests, skills, and personality traits that affect career development and choice. In summarizing important points related to the use of assessment in career counseling, Niles and Harris-Bowlsbey (2005) remind us that:

- The results of assessment tools are only one piece of data that the client and counselor use to consider career options. They should be interpreted in conjunction with other data, including the client's self-knowledge, past experiences, and knowledge about world of work.
- Using assessment to identify new concepts of self, areas of potential growth, and possibilities for exploration is preferable to using assessment for making predictions.
- It is best to work collaboratively with the client in making decisions about whether to engage in assessment, in determining what procedures to use, and in interpreting results.

CAREER INFORMATION AND PLANNING. Career information refers to the many types of resources available in print and electronic form that can be used to help clients make informed career choices (Niles & Harris-Bowlsbey, 2005). The NCDA has developed a comprehensive set of guidelines describing counselors' responsibilities in regard to selecting high-quality information resources of all types. These guidelines can be accessed through the NCDA Web site (www.ncda.org/) under the section titled *NCDA Guidelines: Evaluations of Literature, Video, and Software.*

In the past, *The Dictionary of Occupational Titles* (*DOT*), published by the U.S. Department of Labor, was considered the definitive source of occupational information. In 1994, the U.S. Department of Labor began the process of developing a new occupational classification scheme to replace the *DOT*. The new system, called the *Occupational Information Network* (*O*NET*), replaced the *DOT* in 2001. *O*NET* is a computer-based career information system that provides the most up-to-date occupational information available (Brown, 2007). It can be accessed at the following Web site: www.onetcenter.org/. The Department of Labor now places all its major publications, such as the *Occupational Outlook Handbook,* and the *Bureau of Labor Statistics Employment and Unemployment Data,* online.

Although many people have ready access to computers and the Internet, technology is not the only source of career information. Many print resources that provide valuable career information are available through libraries, bookstores, and educational sites. Some self-help books, such as Bolles and Nelson's (2007) *What Color Is Your Parachute?*, outline practical steps that most individuals, from late adolescence on, can follow to define personal values and successfully complete career-seeking tasks, such as writing a résumé. These books also provide a wealth of information on how to locate positions of specific interest.

In addition to selecting high-quality career-related resource materials, career counselors also are responsible for making the resources known to clients in as user-friendly a manner as possible. Moreover, they are responsible for helping clients process the information that has been gathered (Niles & Harris-Bowlsbey, 2005). When career information is not processed accurately or adequately, clients may have difficulty making career decisions effectively. It also is important for counselors to discuss the nature of the career decision process with their clients, reminding them that career decidedness develops over time and that the decision-making process is complex, not simple (Krieshok, 1998). Knowledge of career information and of the processes associated with it does not guarantee self-exploration in career development, but good career decisions cannot be made without these data. A lack of sufficient or up-to-date information is one reason that individuals fail to make career decisions or make unwise choices.

A number of *computer-assisted career guidance systems* (CACGSs) offer career information and help individuals sort through their values and interests or just find job information. One of the beauties of computer-based career planning systems is their accessibility: they are available in many settings and to diverse clientele across cultures and the life span (Harris-Bowlsbey, 1992; Sampson & Bloom, 2001). Two of the better known CACGSs include SIGI-Plus (*System of Interactive Guidance and Information,* with "Plus" indicating a refinement of the system) and DISCOVER, which has been adapted for varying age levels. Ways of enhancing computer-assisted career guidance systems are constantly being implemented. No matter how sophisticated the programs are, however, it is wise to have trained career counselors available to assist people who may make use of this technology but still have questions about its applicability to their lives (Walker-Staggs, 2000).

Skilled career counselors know how to access, evaluate, and utilize various types of printed and electronic career-related resources. Knowledge alone, however, is not sufficient. Effective career counselors also are able to work collaboratively with the client so that the information retrieved can be translated into something that is meaningful and useful.

Career counselors are likely to work in any number of settings, including job placement services, rehabilitation facilities, employment offices, businesses and industries, or in private practice (Brown, 2007). Typically, career counselors in community and agency settings work with adults, rather than children, whereas counselors in educational settings focus on career development interventions and activities for young people. Regardless of the setting, being able to counsel effectively with diverse populations is an essential skill needed by career counselors.

CAREER COUNSELING WITH DIVERSE POPULATIONS.   Many of the assumptions inherent in traditional theories of career development were based on working with heterosexual, able-bodied, middle- to upper-class white men and fall short in their application to diverse populations (McWhirter et al., 2009; Luzzo & McWhirter, 2001). Social activism, combined with a growing body of research, helps challenge constraining negative forces and create models of career counseling for diverse groups (Peterson & Gonzalez, 2000). A career counselor's ability to work effectively with diverse populations is dependent on a willingness to reflect carefully on the appropriateness of any assumption, theory, or intervention when working with specific individuals.

Several current career development textbooks and journals provide excellent suggestions for conducting career counseling with diverse populations. For example, Duggan and Jurgens (2007) focused on career development and counseling with the following groups:

- Single parents
- Homemaker reentering the workforce
- Welfare-to-work clients
- The working poor
- Victims of intimate partner violence
- Dislocated or displaced workers
- Homeless individuals
- Older adults
- Offenders and ex-offenders
- People with physical and/or mental disabilities
- People with chemical dependencies
- Veterans
- The newly immigrated

In addition to these groups, issues related to gender, sexual orientation, and ethnicity need to be taken into consideration, as those issues may relate to career development, choice, and advancement. To this end, McWhirter et al. (2009) asserted the following:

> Is it possible to be knowledgeable about all cultures and all types of disability or to fully understand the complexities of gender and sexual orientation as they interact with career development? Of course, the answer to this question is no. It certainly is possible, and in fact is a professional obligation, to develop an approach to all clients that explores and honors their multiple identities and orientations. Such an approach requires continuous education through reading, contact with diverse clientele, consultation with colleagues, seminars and workshops, and ongoing critical self-reflection. (p. 273)

Summary

Career counseling is a complex process that combines general counseling skills with specific, career-related skills. Many changes in society and in the workplace have affected the delivery of career counseling services, making it essential for career counselors to affiliate with professional organizations such as the NCDA or NCEA to stay abreast of current developments and emerging trends in the field. Effective career counselors have a strong understanding of career development theories, are skilled in career assessment and interpretation, and know how to implement career-related interventions. They also are able to access and evaluate career information resources and are accomplished at counseling clients from diverse backgrounds.

Before concluding this section on career counseling, we want to add a note about the importance of integrating career counseling with personal counseling—a topic that has been the focus of much research and dialog during the past decades (e.g., Imimbo, 1994; Krumboltz, 1993; Manuele-Adkins, 1992; Maxwell, 2007). Although distinctions are sometimes drawn between career counseling and personal counseling, the two processes are not dichotomous but instead are intricately related. Often, a client will present with a career-related issue that is rooted in personal problems (for example, anger management problems leading to job loss). Or the reverse can occur, where stress brought on by a toxic work environment results in decreased coping skills that negatively affect family interactions. Competent career counselors are able to work holistically with clients, helping them deal effectively with personal issues and career-related issues that arise during the counseling process (Liptak, 2001).

EMPLOYEE ASSISTANCE PROGRAMS

For many years, business, industry, government, educational, and private/public institutions in the United States have exhibited a strong interest in the overall health of their employees (Herlihy, 2000). Many corporate organizations now include mental health services as part of their employee benefits programs. (Del Campo, Del Campo, & Gorman, 2002). *Employee assistance programs* (EAPs) provide mental health services to employees, recognizing that personal and professional issues can affect work performance, health, and general well-being. EAPs are designed to assist individual employees, their families, and work organizations.

The EAP field was established 50 years ago and has undergone significant evolution. The early focus of EAP work was to identify, intervene with, and assist employees with alcohol-related problems. The service has evolved to address a multitude of mental health issues, including the following (Employee Assistance Professionals Association [EAPA], 2008):

- Emotional and mental distress (e.g., anxiety, grief, depression)
- Stress at home or work
- Family/personal relationship issues
- Work relationship issues
- Substance abuse and addictions
- Career issues
- Financial and legal concerns
- Child and elder care concerns
- Health and wellness
- Critical incidents (e.g., exposure to crises and trauma)
- Violence
- Company reorganization and change

EAP services are provided by approximately 10,000 mental health professionals, including counselors and social workers. Many of these professionals are represented by membership organizations such as the Employee Assistance Professional Association (EAPA; www.eapassn.org), the Employee Assistance Society of North America (EASNA; www.easna.org), and the Occupational Program Consultants Association. About 5,000 professionals are Certified

Employee Assistance Professionals (CEAP), a certification that is provided by EAPA (EAPA, 2008). Virtually all the *Fortune* 500 companies in the United States have EAP programs, with most EAP programs offering *fourth-party payments* (from companies themselves) to counselors. According to the 2008 National Study of Employers, 65% of employers provided EAPs in 2008, up from 56% in 1998 (Families and Work Institute, 2008).

The EAP profession has positively affected the productivity of employees, resulting in savings to employers and healthier lifestyles for employees (EAPA, 2008). Employees and their household members have the opportunity to use EAPs to manage professional and personal issues that may affect their work performance. Typically, there is no charge for these services because they have been prepaid by the employer. Confidentiality is maintained in accordance with privacy laws and ethical guidelines. In self-referred cases, employers do not know who is using EAP services, unless there are extenuating services and written release forms have been signed. In cases of formal referrals (i.e., supervisory referrals made for employees who are experiencing job performance problems), the client who was referred may be asked to sign a release form indicating that counseling appointments were kept; however, information about the content of the counseling sessions remains confidential unless otherwise specified.

In addition to providing direct services to individual clients, EAPs also provide services to their *corporate client*—the organization that either contracts with the EAP externally or has an in-house EAP provisions. Examples of services an EAP might provide to an organization include:

- **Workplace consultation:** Providing consultation to supervisors, work groups, union officials, and other individuals in the organization regarding performance issues and recommended approaches to specific situations.
- **Policy consultation:** Providing consultation to the organization regarding organizational policies that address human factors in the workplace (e.g., responding to violence, drug testing, work teams, managing an aging workforce).
- **Training:** Skill building for supervisors, managers, and executive on topics such as conflict management, communication skills, performance management, violence prevention, and diversity.
- **Information and education activities:** Sharing information with workplace personnel through such activities as seminars, employee orientation, mailings, and e-mails.
- **Critical incident management:** Responding to traumatic events that affect the workplace. Services may include situation assessment, debriefing, defusing, and family information management.
- **Special situations:** Providing services that address specific company events, including downsizing, mergers, and celebratory events.
- **Program implementation and management:** Managing the programs provided by the EAP or other vendors. This service promotes the efficient implementation and ongoing operation of the EAP and related workplace activities. (EAPA, 2008)

The Case of Peter

Peter is a 42-year-old, Caucasian car sales manager who lives in a suburban West Coast town. His ex-wife, Lisa, divorced him 10 months ago. Since then, Peter has been living alone in an apartment and seeing his teenage son very occasionally. Peter and Lisa avoid each other as much as possible despite living in the same town. Meanwhile, Peter's parents, older sister, and extended family all live on the East Coast.

Peter moved across the country in his early 20s to pursue a job in acting. After years of playing bit parts, he began working at a car dealership to have a regular income. He met Lisa when he was 26, and they were married a year later. Peter stayed in car sales, getting promoted to manager of one shop and then district manager.

Lately, Peter has been having difficulty in his role at work. Two direct reports have quit in response to Peter's angry outbursts and increasingly unrealistic sales goals. His drinking, one of the reasons for the divorce, is escalating in quantity and frequency. Peter has been spending his weekends bar-hopping with younger, unmarried coworkers and occasionally driving home intoxicated.

Peter's boss mandated he seek counseling after Peter walked into a meeting still hung over from the night before. For Peter to keep his job, he must pass a sobriety test and complete a specified number of counseling sessions through his company's employee assistance program.

If you were Peter's EAP counselor, what would your responsibilities be to Peter? To his supervisor? To the company? Which issue do you think needs to be addressed first? Can you work with Peter in a short period of time (i.e., six sessions)? Do you need to refer him to a substance abuse agency? What other factors will you want to consider?

Becoming an EAP Counselor

In a national survey of EAP programs, over 60% of the externally administered programs reported hiring counseling graduates with master's and doctoral degrees (Hosie & Spruill, 1990). This percentage was topped only slightly by EAP programs hiring master's-level social workers. From these statistics, it is evident that the need exists for counselors to provide preventive and remedial services to employees and to train supervisors to recognize troubled workers and refer them for help. Counselors can also actively contribute to the conceptual development of EAP prevention and intervention programs. For many clinical mental health counselors, EAPs represent an alternative to traditional community mental health agencies and provide a way for counselors to interact with the mental health world and the corporate world.

Employee assistance utilizes knowledge about human behavior and behavioral health to improve personal and professional productivity. The EAP profession integrates organizational development, behavioral health, human resources, and business management (EAPA, 2008). EAP professionals come from diverse professional backgrounds, including the fields of counseling and social work, substance abuse and addictions counseling, and human resources and organizational development. Many EAP organizations expect their mental health professionals to understand organizational practice and have competencies in consultation, program management, evaluation, and marketing (Hosie, West, & Mackey, 1993).

Although some universities offer formal EAP training, most professional development for EAP workers comes through continuing education offered through EAPA and its local chapters. Joining EAPA provides a sense of professional identity as well as access to information and resources available to members. Among those resources is the *Journal of Employee Assistance*, which is published quarterly. The journal addresses a plethora of organizational- and employee-related topics. For example, the featured topics in the four 2008 journals include:

- Managing multiple generations in the workplace
- EAPs and the electronic society
- The integration of physical and mental health
- Fee systems for EAPs

(a) emphasize positive, life-enhancing activities; (b) alter traditional screening to include more emphasis on overall health; (c) highlight the importance of physical fitness as it relates to overall well-being, and (d) continue to conduct research studies to evaluate the effectiveness of wellness programs and other holistic approaches.

PRIVATE PRACTICE COUNSELING

BOX 14–5

Working in a Private Practice Setting

Being in private practice means living in two worlds. The first is the world of the clinician. It's the delight of working with clients, being challenged by them and sometimes being inspired by them. Part of my focus is figuring out what sort of client I work best with—who is a good match for my skills, training, and interests? Knowing this helps refine my message when I'm getting the word out about my work. Being in solo practice, I also have to be intentional about finding support, connecting with formal or peer supervision groups.

As a counselor in private practice, I have the freedom to set my own hours, deciding what time in the morning to start and how late in the evening to work. I can block out time to tend to the demands of my own life, whether that means finding time for exercise or taking care of family commitments.

The other world I work in is the world of business. As a small business owner (my practice is a small business) I have to deal with the administrative side of the work. I choose to make my own appointments and file insurance claims. I keep records not only of my income but also of my business expenses.

As a business owner, I also have to market my practice, letting people know who I am and what kind of work I offer. One day I may work on a brochure about my practice. Another day I meet with my networking group or speak to a community group. Another day I may work on my Web site or send thank-you cards to professionals (such as doctors) who refer clients to me. For me, the variety of tasks is part of what I enjoy.

Being in private practice requires having an entrepreneurial personality and being comfortable with a certain level of risk. Income may vary from week to week and can be impacted by snowstorms or flu epidemics. Being self-employed means being responsible for your health insurance and retirement benefits. Being in private practice requires that you become comfortable with promoting yourself and dealing with money issues. Fortunately, there are more and more resources out there for people who are looking for help in building a practice.

For those of us who love private practice, the freedom that we have in working with our clients and creating the shape of our practices outweighs the risks and demands.

Peggy Haymes, M.Div., M.A., LPC

Private practice counselors have a less formalized history than either career or EAP counselors. The involvement of mental health practitioners in private practice predates the existence of licensed professional counselors (LPCs; Ginter, 2001). Currently, however, most counselors involved in private practice are licensed professional counselors (LPCs), licensed mental health counselors (LMHCs), or licensed clinical professional counselors (LCPCs).

Private practitioners work for themselves in an individual or group practice unaffiliated with an agency. Many private practitioners specialize in distinct areas of treatment, such as helping clients with depression, anxiety, or grief issues. Others take a more generalist approach that may involve working with children, adolescents, or adults and working with them "in the context of individual, couple, family, or group counseling" (Ginter, 2001, p. 356).

In decades past—before insurance, third-party payments, managed care, and HIPAA—the professional lives of private practitioners were less complex than they are today. Clinicians were reimbursed on a fee-for-service basis, comparable to the way in which physicians were reimbursed. They operated a counseling business and did so for the freedom and opportunity it afforded them. That arrangement changed dramatically in the 1980s as managed care began to replace fee-for-service arrangements.

Despite changes in the ways clinicians are now reimbursed for service, many practitioners choose to work in private practice settings. Indeed, doctoral graduates of counseling programs have indicated that private practice is their preferred venue of service delivery (Zimpfer, 1996; Zimpfer & DeTrude, 1990). Often counselors conceptualize that a private practice setting will give them more control over their lives and will be more rewarding financially. Indeed, a private practice can be a wonderful experience. However, it usually takes a great deal of work to begin such a practice unless a professional buys into or is invited into an already established practice.

Difficulties Setting Up a Private Practice

To be successful as a private practitioner, a counselor needs a number of abilities beyond clinical expertise. Some of the most salient of those abilities include the following:

- Being able to balance business skills with counseling skills or able to find a competent business manager.
- Being able to build support networks in the community. Such networks are less necessary in agencies, where one is often surrounded by colleagues who can supply needed information on treatment plans or give referrals to appropriate specialists.
- Being able to overcome or avoid the use of restrictive covenants or noncompetitive agreements that some agencies put in their contracts with counselors. Such contracts prohibit counselors from setting up a private practice within a certain geographic area or within a certain time period after leaving the agency (Wyatt, Daniels, & White, 2000).
- Being willing to invest time and hard work in "pull marketing" relationships (i.e., in making oneself attractive by offering services to specialized groups and meeting regularly with other community professionals to increase referral possibilities; Crodzki, 2002).
- Being willing to donate services and participate in endeavors for the public good to build up a reputation and a practice, for as Allen Ivey remarked: "There is just a very small window for private practitioners to make big money" (Littrell, 2001, p. 117).

Advantages in Establishing a Private Practice

There are opportunities for counselors to enter private practice and succeed. Indeed, mental health agency administrators view "private practitioners . . . as the greatest competitors for insured clients" (Wyatt, et al., 2000, p. 19). Among the advantages private practitioners have are the following:

- A growing dissatisfaction among consumers with mental health managed care. In such an environment, consumers are most likely to begin paying directly for services when they can afford it and not go through a managed care arrangement. Such an arrangement may benefit counselors in private practice and portions of the public.

- A chance to become known in their communities as professionals who provide quality service and thus to gain excellent reputations.
- An opportunity to set up their office hours for times that are most convenient for them.
- A chance for counselors to become specialists in treatment, especially if they live in large urban areas where there are abundant numbers of clients dealing with specific problems.

Overall, although private practice can be challenging, it will continue to be a setting in which clinical mental health counselors elect to work. The ACA monthly publication, *Counseling Today*, regularly includes a column that focuses on private practice in counseling and addresses topics such as extending client coverage, electronic communication, renting office space, and other practical issues relevant to private practice counseling. The column is edited by Norman Dasenbrook and Robert Walsh, who coauthored the book, *The Complete Guide to Private Practice for Licensed Mental Health Professionals* (2007). ACA members can e-mail questions about private practice to walshgasp@aol.com and access a series of "Private Practice Pointers" on the ACA Web site (www.counseling.org).

Summary and Conclusion

This chapter has covered information on various aspects of career counseling, employee assistance programs, and private practice. Influential theories of career counseling—trait-and-factor, developmental, learning, and social-cognitive—were reviewed. Specific skills associated with career counseling were described, with a focus on conducting career assessment, providing career information, and working with diverse groups of clients. Among the many functions that career counselors perform are

- Administering and interpreting tests and inventories
- Conducting personal counseling sessions
- Developing individualized career plans
- Helping clients integrate vocational and avocational life roles
- Facilitating decision-making skills
- Providing support for persons experiencing job stress, job loss, or career transitions

Employee assistance program services are becoming increasingly widespread in the United States and around the world. An EAP is a worksite-based program designed to assist employees and organizations with a multitude of issues that may affect work performance. EAP professionals integrate organizational development, behavioral health, human resources, and business management as they work with employees and their work sites.

The final group discussed in this chapter, private practitioners, shares common interests with career counselors and EAP counselors in that they may deal with vocational and general counseling concerns. Many counselors in private practice choose to align themselves with one or more specialty areas. However, private practitioners are unique in that they must be strong business managers as well as skilled counselors. Practitioners who are energetic, disciplined, and able to balance the demands of running a business with the demands of counseling are likely to find private practice a fulfilling venue in which to work.

EPILOGUE

Maintaining Effectiveness as a Counselor: Managing Stress and Avoiding Burnout

Exhausted, Tanya climbed into her car and began the long drive home. Her day had been filled with back-to-back clients and staff meetings. One of her clients was suicidal and had to be involuntarily hospitalized. Another client lost his temper during the session, demanding to know why insurance wouldn't pay for continued counseling, which, according to him, "wasn't really helping, anyway." During the staff meeting, the agency director admonished clinicians to do a better job of meeting productivity quotas. "How can I possibly see more clients?" Tanya thought. "I haven't even finished writing today's case notes." Finding the time to catch up tonight wasn't going to be easy. After all, Nicholas and Anthony deserved at least some of her attention, and Anthony would probably need help with that English assignment. Maybe they'd just eat out again this evening—or order pizza. Just thinking about trying to cook and clean up made Tanya feel even wearier. As she braked suddenly to avoid hitting the car that stopped unexpectedly in front of her, Tanya felt like crying. She wondered what had happened to her energy, her concentration, her enthusiasm, and the passion she used to have for counseling.

Clinical mental health counseling provides challenges and opportunities that can be rewarding and life enhancing. However, working therapeutically with clients day after day can also be emotionally draining and stressful. How do counselors effectively balance the taxing demands of the profession with personal needs and responsibilities? As we near the end of this text, we address ways counselors can successfully manage stress, avoid burnout, and maximize life satisfaction both personally and professionally.

STRESS AND BURNOUT IN COUNSELING

A growing body of evidence suggests that human service workers, including counselors, experience high levels of stress in the workplace (e.g., Edwards, Burnard, Coyle, Fothergill, & Hannigan, 2000; James, 2008; Kottler & Schofield, 2001; Patrick, 2007b). In addition to the "typical" stressors associated with everyday living, clinicians encounter challenges unique to mental health professionals. A full day of counseling clients can stretch one's emotional and mental resources, particularly when clients are dealing with traumatic problems such as assault, disease, and abuse (MacCluskie & Ingersoll, 2001). Other stressors that often are present in community mental health environments include long work hours, low pay, organizational demands, paperwork deadlines, and hassles related to insurance reimbursement. When professional demands are coupled with personal pressures, finding ways to cope effectively can be especially challenging.

Stress is experienced when a substantial imbalance exists between real or perceived environmental demands and an individual's response capabilities (Baird, 2008; Lazarus & Folkman, 1984). When stress is not dealt with effectively and the imbalance is not corrected, counselors may experience *burnout*. James (2008) described *burnout* as "a state of physical, mental, and emotional exhaustion caused by long-term involvement in emotionally demanding situations" (p. 521). It is the single-most common personal consequence of working as a counselor (Kottler, 1993). People experiencing burnout are emotionally or physically drained to the point that they cannot perform functions meaningfully. Symptoms of excessive stress and burnout can be manifested in several areas, including the following (James & Gilliland, 2005; James, 2008; Kottler & Schofield, 2001; Patrick, 2007b):

- *Cognitive Functioning.* Individuals may experience confusion, memory problems, organizational difficulties, irrational thinking, negativity, rigidity, disillusionment, and decreased creativity.
- *Emotional Functioning.* Common emotional expressions associated with burnout include irritability, sadness, anxiety, numbness, apathy, and a sense of being "out of control," or "emotionally drained," or "not oneself."
- *Behavioral Functioning.* People may withdraw from colleagues, friends, and activities; be critical or detached; and engage in inappropriate risk taking. Struggles with interpersonal relationships may be evidenced, and productivity may decrease.
- *Physical Functioning.* A host of physical problems are associated with burnout, including headaches, sleep problems, nervousness, addictions, fatigue, chest or back pains, loss of appetite, increased blood pressure levels, and lowered resistance to illness.

Kottler and Schofield (2001) categorized sources of counselor stress and burnout into four primary areas: the *work environment, specific events, client-induced stress,* and *self-induced stress.* Stressors associated with the work environment include excessive paperwork, demanding time pressures, inflexible rules and regulations, unsupportive colleagues, and incompetent supervisors. Event-related stressors tend to stem from individuals' personal lives and may include developmental transitions (e.g., getting married, having children, entering midlife), health-related issues, and financial concerns. In contrast, client-induced stressors include difficult or resistant clients, clients experiencing trauma or crisis, and clients who terminate prematurely. Finally, examples of self-induced stressors include perfectionism, unrealistic expectations, an unhealthy lifestyle, exhaustion, and fear of failure on the part of the clinician. Kottler and Schofield (2001) remind us that all counselors will experience stress of some type. The question is not whether stress will be experienced, but instead, how counselors will choose to cope with it.

MANAGING STRESS AND AVOIDING BURNOUT

Counselors are in the business of helping clients improve their quality of life. However, to be effective helpers, it is essential for counselors to find ways to take care of themselves (Baird, 2008). Just as prevention in counseling is preferable to remediation, a proactive approach to managing stress and avoiding burnout can help counselors balance professional and personal challenges more effectively. In this section, we address four areas in which clinical mental health counselors can take steps to achieve that balance: establishing limits, modeling self-care, cultivating self-awareness, and maintaining a sense of humor.

Establishing Limits

Some of the very characteristics that inspire people to become counselors—wanting to help others, idealism, and high motivation—can lead them to taking on more responsibilities than can be managed realistically or effectively. In addition to serving the needs of clients, counselors often work extra hours, engage in volunteer activities, and make themselves accessible to clients and others long after the "normal" workday is finished. Swenson (1998) labeled the tendency to take on too much and continually push personal limits as *overload syndrome.* Many of us are not very adept at defining our personal limits, and consequently, it is easy to overextend them. However, living in a state of constant overload, with no margins or buffers to protect our time and energy, can lead to exhaustion and stagnation. Setting limits at work and elsewhere is essential to healthy, effective living. The following suggestions, made by various authors (e.g., Baird, 2008; MacCluskie & Ingersoll, 2001; Patrick, 2007b; Swenson, 1998) can help counselors establish and maintain limits in their personal and professional lives.

• **Use appropriate assertiveness by saying no** (MacCluskie & Ingersoll, 2001). Many people set unrealistic expectations for themselves, believing that they can accomplish more in a 24-hour period than is feasible. Other people accept additional responsibilities because they fear the repercussions of declining them. Setting necessary limits involves prioritizing what is important, recognizing that we have more control over our schedules than we realize, and learning how to say no, even to good things, to avoid overcommitment.

• **Consider doing less, not more** (Swenson, 1998). It is easy to saturate our schedules, leaving little room for empty space or margins. Overly packed schedules provide the fuel for stress responses. Counselors can intentionally create margins in their schedules by (a) ending sessions on time; (b) building in breaks during the day for note writing, physical activity, and rejuvenation; and (c) periodically pruning, or cutting out, activities that are unnecessary or unrewarding.

• **Create boundaries around the private spaces of life** (Swenson, 1998). Often, the boundary between work and home becomes blurred or even nonexistent, making burnout more likely. Belson (1992) facetiously advised counselors who want to "achieve" burnout to

    a. Work long hours, especially weekends and evenings, telling yourself that this doesn't interfere with family relationships.

    b. Think about your most difficult cases, even when you are not at work.

    c. Worry continually about what you are not doing that you should be doing.

In contrast, counselors who maintain healthy boundaries recognize that it is desirable to establish and defend perimeters around their homes, communities, and leisure activities. Protecting boundaries provides ways to nurture relationships with family members and friends, which are essential to healthy living.

Modeling Self-Care

In addition to setting limits, counselors can model physical, mental, emotional, and spiritual self-care. The counselor who pursues a wellness-oriented lifestyle is in a better position to provide services to clients and help them engage in their own self-care plans (MacCluskie & Ingersoll, 2001).

• **Physical Self-Care.** Often, counselors place their own physical self-care on the back burner as they attempt to meet the multiple demands of clients and organizations. However, the cost of physical neglect can be high, resulting in outcomes such as illness, hypertension, bodily aches and pains, fatigue, and other forms of physical or mental malaise. Engaging in physical self-care is essential to one's personal health and effectiveness as a counselor.

Sleep, nutrition, and exercise are three areas that need ongoing attention to maintain optimal health. Many of us consistently chip away at the hours needed for rest to "catch up." We allow insufficient time for sleep, relying on alarm clocks to wake us. Ongoing sleep deprivation can lead to poor concentration, disorganization, and exhaustion. Prioritizing the need for sleep and guarding that time are essential to stress management. Similarly, carving out time to exercise regularly and eat nutritiously yields physical, emotional, and cognitive benefits. The sedentary nature of counseling combined with busy schedules that may not include formal lunch breaks increase the need for ongoing physical exercise and attention to nutrition. Counselors also will want to monitor physical tension associated with stress and find healthy ways to alleviate tension through such activities as controlled breathing, relaxation exercises, yoga, and other physical activities that are stress-reducing.

As a side note, I (Newsome) have made physical exercise a priority for the past 30 years. For me, running, swimming, and working out relieve stress and leave me reenergized. Although at times I feel guilty for spending time doing what is "fun," when I know that the demands of my work schedule are great, I know that without the time out to exercise, I will not be able to concentrate or perform my job effectively.

- **Cognitive Self-Care.** The beliefs counselors hold about themselves, their clients, and the counseling process may promote health and well-being or create stress. Evaluating and modifying irrational stress-inducing cognitions promote positive mental health (Baird, 2008). Several authors have identified faulty beliefs that may negatively affect counselor effectiveness (e.g., Baird, 2008; Freemont & Anderson, 1986; James, 2008; Kottler & Schofield, 2001). Examples of irrational beliefs associated with stress and burnout include the following:

  - My job is my life; what I do is who I am.
  - I must be totally competent and knowledgeable.
  - I must help everyone all the time.
  - I must be a model of mental health.
  - I need to be available at all times.
  - No one can do the job like I can.
  - I am responsible for client change.
  - I should not be anxious or uncertain.
  - Any negative feedback indicates that there is something wrong with me.
  - The client is in counseling to change or get better. (Although this sometimes is the case, it is not necessarily so.)
  - The client should appreciate the counselor's efforts.
  - The client should be different from what he or she is.

Taking the time to evaluate one's beliefs about self, the counseling process, and clients is the first step toward enhancing cognitive functioning. Counselors may want to work with a supervisor or colleague as they strive to identify and modify faulty beliefs and expectations.

- **Emotional and Spiritual Self-care.** Some of the qualities that help make counselors effective—being empathic, sensitive, humane, people-oriented, and highly committed—also can lead to difficulties and stress. For example, empathic, sensitive counselors may also be anxious, obsessive, overly conscientious, overly enthusiastic, and susceptible to identifying too closely with clients (James, 2008). Counselors who work with traumatized clients may be vulnerable to experiencing vicarious traumatization, also called *compassion fatigue*. Consequently, it is crucial for counselors to monitor their emotional reactions on an ongoing basis. Baird (2008) suggested engaging in "cleansing rituals" after demanding sessions. These rituals may include stretching, walking, splashing water on one's face, or deep breathing exercises. Moreover, counselors can symbolize leaving clients at work by placing client files in the file cabinet, closing the door to the office, and literally and figuratively leaving them there.

Seeking support from friends, family members, and colleagues is a key element of emotional self-care. Taking time to nurture personal relationships with loved ones provides an important source of support. However, one of the difficulties related to counseling is the need to keep clients' stories confidential, which means that much of what goes on during the day cannot be shared with those closest to us. Consequently, having a professional colleague or supervisor with whom one can discuss difficult or unsettling cases can be an invaluable resource. Another source of support, especially when counselors are dealing with difficult personal issues, comes through personal counseling or therapy. Ironically, many counselors are reluctant or unwilling to seek help for themselves, even though they recommend it for others (Kottler & Schofield, 2001). However, participating in counseling can help counselors deal with personal issues, the stresses of practice, and their understanding of the therapeutic practice (Baird, 2008).

In addition to emotional self-care, spiritual nurturing can help counselors manage stress more effectively. Myers and Williard (2003) defined *spirituality* as "the capacity and tendency present in all human beings to find and construct meaning about life and existence and to move toward personal growth, responsibility, and relationship with others" (p. 149). We discussed spirituality in Chapter 5. Although religion is a form of spirituality, the construct of spirituality encompasses more than religion or religious practices (Myers & Williard, 2003). Finding ways to nurture and enhance one's spiritual development—whether through prayer, meditation, mindfulness, worship, or some other practice—can promote personal growth and facilitate optimal functioning.

Cultivating Self-Awareness

One of the key characteristics of effective counselors is self-awareness. Counselors who are self-aware have an in-depth knowledge of their attitudes, values, and feelings, as well as the ability to recognize ways situations and events affect them. Self-awareness enables counselors to identify early symptoms of stress and overload and then select coping responses more effectively. Kottler and Schofield (2001) suggested that counselors use the following questions to guide reflection and increase self-awareness:

- What haunts you the most and continues to plague you during vulnerable moments?
- In what ways are you less than fully functioning in your personal and professional life?
- What are some aspects of your lifestyle that are unhealthy?
- What are your most difficult, conflicted, and dysfunctional relationships?
- How does all of this impact your work with clients? (p. 429).

Counselors can increase personal self-awareness by creating *reflective structures,* which allow time and space for self-examination (Boyatzis, McKee, & Goleman, 2002). Reflective structures provide time away from work and responsibilities for the purpose of being alone with one's thoughts. Reflection involves a conscious, disciplined effort at self-examination. It provides an opportunity to contemplate past experiences, current relationships, and future hopes. Through reflection, counselors may encounter themselves and their deepest feelings in ways that are surprising, unexpected, and perhaps a little frightening. Such encounters put counselors in a better position to take stock and move in directions that are personally and professionally enhancing.

Maintaining a Sense of Humor

The physiological benefits of humor were extolled in Norman Cousins' (1979) *Anatomy of an Illness*. Having a sense of humor—being able to laugh at oneself and one's situations—can be a primary source of energy for rejuvenation. As Oscar Wilde once stated, "Life is too important to be taken seriously." Or, to paraphrase the title and content of a book by Paul Watzlawick (1983), humor allows one to know that many human problems are "hopeless but not serious" or "serious but not hopeless" and, therefore, solvable.

Humor has the remarkable ability to promote insight, generate creativity, and defuse tense situations (Gladding, 1995). It can help regulate anxiety, relieve boredom, dispel fear, boost performance, and build group cohesion (Weaver & Wilson, 1997). Laughter can stimulate the immune system and help reduce stress (Goldin & Bordan, 1999). Being able to laugh at oneself and one's mistakes can help put things in perspective and create pathways for healing.

In the following narrative, Gladding shares an example of how humor sometimes arises unexpectedly in counseling situations.

BOX 1
Maintaining Effectiveness as a Counselor

I learned about the value of humor in counseling during my first years of work as a counselor. I had completed intake information on a man and asked him what he would like to work on in the session. He looked at me a bit negatively and simply stated: "I am not talking until you get rid of the rabbits in this room."

We were in a rural area, so I surveyed our surroundings. Not seeing any rabbits, I asked where they were. He pointed to an imaginary hare (that I assumed was wild), and I went over, grabbed it by its invisible ears, then opened the door, and threw it outside. As I went to sit down, he pointed to a second imaginary furry creature, so I proceeded to do the same thing. Again, as I went back to my chair, he pointed to a third unseeable furry critter with long ears and a cotton tail (so he said). As I approached this third imaginary hare and started to grab it by its long ears and toss it out with a flare, I suddenly stopped and thought: "Who really needs help here?" I laughed to myself and proceeded to get my client the help he needed.

From that experience, I began to develop better confrontation skills. I probably would have eventually learned these necessary helping techniques in counseling, but the bizarre nature of my client's experience accelerated the process and gave me a laugh at myself in the process. Levity can sometimes be enlightening, and there often is a humorous side to even the most serious of situations.

Counseling is serious business. However, it also provides multiple opportunities for joy, enthusiasm, and continued mastery of personal and professional skills. As you develop that mastery, it is helpful to keep in mind the words of Robert Brown, a leader in the counseling profession, who died of cancer several years ago:

> What do I have to say to counselors in the field who are trying to find their way, to create meaning in their lives? Don't take yourself seriously, but take yourself measurably. Don't take yourself in a manner that is cavalier, but take yourself in a manner that has sincerity and thoughtfulness about it. (Kottler & Brown, 2000, p. 383)

As we conclude this text, we encourage you to engage in lifelong learning, ask questions, take risks, and build professional relationships. We also encourage you to find ways to balance your professional and personal endeavors, manage stress effectively, grow in self-awareness, learn from your mistakes, and remember to laugh. In so doing, may the contributions you give to the community not only enrich the clients you serve but also rejuvenate and enhance your personal and professional experiences on multiple levels.

APPENDIX A

DSM-IV-TR Classification

NOS = Not Otherwise Specified.

An *x* appearing in a diagnostic code indicates that a specific code number is required.

An ellipsis (. . .) is used in the names of certain disorders to indicate that the name of a specific mental disorder or general medical condition should be inserted when recording the name (e.g., 293.0 Delirium Due to Hypothyroidism).

Numbers in parentheses are page numbers.

If criteria are currently met, one of the following severity specifiers may be noted after the diagnosis:

Mild

Moderate

Severe

If criteria are no longer met, one of the following specifiers may be noted:

In Partial Remission

In Full Remission

Prior History

Disorders Usually First Diagnosed in Infancy, Childhood, or Adolescence (39)

MENTAL RETARDATION (41)

Note: These are coded on Axis II.

317   Mild Mental Retardation (43)

318.0   Moderate Mental Retardation (43)

318.1   Severe Mental Retardation (43)

318.2   Profound Mental Retardation (44)

319   Mental Retardation, Severity Unspecified (44)

LEARNING DISORDERS (49)

315.00   Reading Disorder (51)

315.1   Mathematics Disorder (53)

Source: Diagnostic and Statistical Manual of Mental Disorders (4th ed., text rev.). Copyright 2000 American Psychiatric Association, 1994. Reprinted with permission.

TIC DISORDERS (108)

307.23 Tourette's Disorder (111)

307.22 Chronic Motor or Vocal Tic Disorder (114)

307.21 Transient Tic Disorder (115)

> *Specify if:* Single Episode/Recurrent

307.20 Tic Disorder NOS (116)

ELIMINATION DISORDERS (116)

___.__ Encopresis (116)

787.6 With Constipation and Overflow Incontinence

307.7 Without Constipation and Overflow Incontinence

307.6 Enuresis (Not Due to a General Medical Condition) (118)

> *Specify type:* Nocturnal Only/Diurnal Only/Nocturnal and Diurnal

OTHER DISORDERS OF INFANCY, CHILDHOOD, OR ADOLESCENCE (121)

309.21 Separation Anxiety Disorder (121)

> *Specify if:* Early Onset

313.23 Selective Mutism (125)

313.89 Reactive Attachment Disorder of Infancy or Early Childhood (127)

> *Specify type:* Inhibited Type/Disinhibited Type

307.3 Stereotypic Movement Disorder (131)

> *Specify if:* With Self-Injurious Behavior

313.9 Disorder of Infancy, Childhood, or Adolescence NOS (134)

Delirium, Dementia, and Amnestic and Other Cognitive Disorders (135)

DELIRIUM (136)

293.0 Delirium Due to . . . *[Indicate the General Medical Condition]* (141)

___.__ Substance Intoxication Delirium *(refer to Substance-Related Disorders for substance-specific codes)* (143)

___.__ Substance Withdrawal Delirium *(refer to Substance-Related Disorders for substance-specific codes)* (143)

___.__ Delirium Due to Multiple Etiologies *(code each of the specific etiologies)* (146)

___.__ Delirium NOS (147)

DEMENTIA (147)

294.xx* Dementia of the Alzheimer's Type, With Early Onset *(also code 331.0 Alzheimer's disease on Axis III)* (154)

.10   Without Behavioral Disturbance

.11   With Behavioral Disturbance

294.xx* Dementia of the Alzheimer's Type, With Late Onset *(also code 331.0 Alzheimer's disease on Axis III)* (154)

.10   Without Behavioral Disturbance

.11   With Behavioral Disturbance

290.xx   Vascular Dementia (158)

.40   Uncomplicated

.41   With Delirium

.42   With Delusions

.43   With Depressed Mood

Specify if: With Behavioral Disturbance

Code presence or absence of a behavioral disturbance in the fifth digit for Dementia Due to a General Medical Condition:

0 = Without Behavioral Disturbance

1 = With Behavioral Disturbance

294.1x* Dementia Due to HIV Disease *(also code 042 HIV on Axis III)* (163)

294.1x* Dementia Due to Head Trauma *(also code 854.00 head injury on Axis III)* (164)

294.1x* Dementia Due to Parkinson's Disease *(also code 332.0 Parkinson's disease on Axis III)* (164)

294.1x* Dementia Due to Huntington's Disease *(also code 333.4 Huntington's disease on Axis III)* (165)

294.1x* Dementia Due to Pick's Disease *(also code 331.1 Pick's disease on Axis III)* (165)

294.1x* Dementia Due to Creutzfeldt-Jakob Disease *(also code 046.1 Creutzfeldt-Jakob disease on Axis III)* (166)

294.1x* Dementia Due to . . . *[Indicate the General Medical Condition not listed above] (also code the general medical condition on Axis III)* (167)

___.__   Substance-Induced Persisting Dementia *(refer to Substance-Related Disorders for substance-specific codes)* (168)

___.__   Dementia Due to Multiple Etiologies *(code each of the specific etiologies)* (170)

294.8   Dementia NOS (171)

AMNESTIC DISORDERS (172)

294.0   Amnestic Disorder Due to . . . *[Indicate the General Medical Condition]* (175)

Specify if: Transient/Chronic

---

*ICD-9-CM code valid after October 1, 2000.

___.___ Substance-Induced Persisting Amnestic Disorder *(refer to Substance-Related Disorders for substance-specific codes)* (177)

294.8 Amnestic Disorder NOS (179)

OTHER COGNITIVE DISORDERS (179)

294.9 Cognitive Disorder NOS (179)

Mental Disorders Due to a General Medical Condition Not Elsewhere Classified (181)

293.89 Catatonic Disorder Due to . . . *[Indicate the General Medical Condition]* (185)

310.1 Personality Change Due to . . . *[Indicate the General Medical Condition]* (187)

Specify type: Labile Type/Disinhibited Type/Aggressive Type/Apathetic Type/Paranoid Type/Other Type/Combined Type/Unspecified Type

293.9 Mental Disorder Nos Due to . . .*[Indicate the General Medical Condition]* (190)

Substance-Related Disorders (191)

The following specifiers apply to Substance Dependence as noted:

[a]With Physiological Dependence/Without Physiological Dependence

[b]Early Full Remission/Early Partial Remission/

Sustained Full Remission/Sustained Partial Remission

[c]In a Controlled Environment

[d]On Agonist Therapy

The following specifiers apply to Substance-Induced Disorders as noted:

[1]With Onset During Intoxication/[W]With Onset During Withdrawal

ALCOHOL-RELATED DISORDERS (212)

Alcohol Use Disorders (213)

303.90 Alcohol Dependence[a,b,c] (213)

305.00 Alcohol Abuse (214)

Alcohol-Induced Disorders (214)

303.00 Alcohol Intoxication (214)

291.81 Alcohol Withdrawal (215)

Specify if: With Perceptual Disturbances

291.0   Alcohol Intoxication Delirium (143)

291.0   Alcohol Withdrawal Delirium (143)

291.2   Alcohol-Induced Persisting Dementia (168)

291.1   Alcohol-Induced Persisting Amnestic Disorder (177)

291.x   Alcohol-Induced Psychotic Disorder (338)

   .5   With Delusions[I,W]

   .3   With Hallucinations[I,W]

291.89   Alcohol-Induced Mood Disorder[I,W] (405)

291.89   Alcohol-Induced Anxiety Disorder[I,W] (479)

291.89   Alcohol-Induced Sexual Dysfunction[I] (562)

291.89   Alcohol-Induced Sleep Disorder[I,W] (655)

291.9   Alcohol-Related Disorder NOS (223)

AMPHETAMINE-(OR AMPHETAMINE-LIKE) RELATED DISORDERS (223)

Amphetamine Use Disorders (224)

304.40   Amphetamine Dependence[a,b,c] (224)

305.70   Amphetamine Abuse (225)

Amphetamine-Induced Disorders (226)

292.89   Amphetamine Intoxication (226)

       Specify if: With Perceptual Disturbances

292.0   Amphetamine Withdrawal (227)

292.81   Amphetamine Intoxication Delirium (143)

292.xx   Amphetamine-Induced Psychotic Disorder (338)

   .11   With Delusions[I]

   .12   With Hallucinations[I]

292.84   Amphetamine-Induced Mood Disorder[I,W] (405)

292.89   Amphetamine-Induced Anxiety Disorder[I] (479)

292.89   Amphetamine-Induced Sexual Dysfunction[I] (562)

292.89   Amphetamine-Induced Sleep Disorder[I,W] (655)

292.9   Amphetamine-Related Disorder NOS (231)

CAFFEINE-RELATED DISORDERS (231)

Caffeine-Induced Disorders (232)

305.90   Caffeine Intoxication (232)

292.89   Caffeine-Induced Anxiety Disorder[I] (479)

292.89   Caffeine-Induced Sleep Disorder[I] (655)

292.9   Caffeine-Related Disorder NOS (234)

CANNABIS-RELATED DISORDERS (234)

Cannabis Use Disorders (236)

304.30   Cannabis Dependence[a,b,c] (236)

305.20   Cannabis Abuse (236)

Cannabis-Induced Disorders (237)

292.89   Cannabis Intoxication (237)

   Specify if: With Perceptual Disturbances

292.81   Cannabis Intoxication Delirium (143)

292.xx   Cannabis-Induced Psychotic Disorder (338)

   .11   With Delusions[I]

   .12   With Hallucinations[I]

292.89   Cannabis-Induced Anxiety Disorder[I] (479)

292.9   Cannabis-Related Disorder NOS (241)

COCAINE-RELATED DISORDERS (241)

Cocaine Use Disorders (242)

304.20   Cocaine Dependence[a,b,c] (242)

305.60   Cocaine Abuse (243)

Cocaine-Induced Disorders (244)

292.89   Cocaine Intoxication (244)

   Specify if: With Perceptual Disturbances

292.0   Cocaine Withdrawal (245)

292.81   Cocaine Intoxication Delirium (143)

292.xx   Cocaine-Induced Psychotic Disorder (338)

   .11   With Delusions[I]

   .12   With Hallucinations[I]

292.84   Cocaine-Induced Mood Disorder[I,W] (405)

292.89   Cocaine-Induced Anxiety Disorder[I,W] (479)

292.89   Cocaine-Induced Sexual Dysfunction[I] (562)

292.89   Cocaine-Induced Sleep Disorder[I,W] (655)

292.9   Cocaine-Related Disorder NOS (250)

HALLUCINOGEN-RELATED DISORDERS (250)

Hallucinogen Use Disorders (251)

304.50   Hallucinogen Dependence[b,c] (251)

305.30   Hallucinogen Abuse (252)

Hallucinogen-Induced Disorders (252)

292.89   Hallucinogen Intoxication (252)

292.89   Hallucinogen Persisting Perception Disorder (Flashbacks) (253)

292.81   Hallucinogen Intoxication Delirium (143)

292.xx   Hallucinogen-Induced Psychotic Disorder (338)

   .11   With Delusions[I]

   .12   With Hallucinations[I]

292.84   Hallucinogen-Induced Mood Disorder[I] (405)

292.89   Hallucinogen-Induced Anxiety Disorder[I] (479)

292.9   Hallucinogen-Related Disorder NOS (256)

INHALANT-RELATED DISORDERS (257)

Inhalant Use Disorders (258)

304.60   Inhalant Dependence[b,c] (258)

305.90   Inhalant Abuse (259)

Inhalant-Induced Disorders (259)

292.89   Inhalant Intoxication (259)

292.81   Inhalant Intoxication Delirium (143)

292.82   Inhalant-Induced Persisting Dementia (168)

292.xx   Inhalant-Induced Psychotic Disorder (338)

   .11   With Delusions[I]

   .12   With Hallucinations[I]

292.84   Inhalant-Induced Mood Disorder[I] (405)

292.89   Inhalant-Induced Anxiety Disorder[I] (479)

292.9   Inhalant-Related Disorder NOS (263)

NICOTINE-RELATED DISORDERS (264)

Nicotine Use Disorder (264)

305.1   Nicotine Dependence[a,b] (264)

Nicotine-Induced Disorder (265)

292.0   Nicotine Withdrawal (265)

292.9   Nicotine-Related Disorder NOS (269)

OPIOID-RELATED DISORDERS (269)

Opioid Use Disorders (270)

304.00   Opioid Dependence[a,b,c,d] (270)

305.50   Opioid Abuse (271)

Opioid-Induced Disorders (271)

292.89   Opioid Intoxication (271)

            Specify if: With Perceptual Disturbances

292.0   Opioid Withdrawal (272)

292.81   Opioid Intoxication Delirium (143)

292.xx   Opioid-Induced Psychotic Disorder (338)

  .11   With Delusions[I]

  .12   With Hallucinations[I]

292.84   Opioid-Induced Mood Disorder[I] (405)

292.89   Opioid-Induced Sexual Dysfunction[I] (562)

292.89   Opioid-Induced Sleep Disorder[I,W] (655)

292.9   Opioid-Related Disorder NOS (277)

PHENCYCLIDINE-(OR PHENCYCLIDINE-LIKE) RELATED DISORDERS (278)

Phencyclidine Use Disorders (279)

304.60   Phencyclidine Dependence[b,c] (279)

305.90   Phencyclidine Abuse (279)

Phencyclidine-Induced Disorders (280)

292.89   Phencyclidine Intoxication (280)

            Specify if: With Perceptual Disturbances

292.81   Phencyclidine Intoxication Delirium (143)

292.xx   Phencyclidine-Induced Psychotic Disorder (338)

  .11   With Delusions[I]

  .12   With Hallucinations[I]

292.84   Phencyclidine-Induced Mood Disorder[I] (405)

292.89   Phencyclidine-Induced Anxiety Disorder[I] (479)

292.9   Phencyclidine-Related Disorder NOS (283)

SEDATIVE-, HYPNOTIC-, OR ANXIOLYTIC-RELATED DISORDERS (284)

Sedative, Hypnotic, or Anxiolytic Use Disorders (285)

304.10   Sedative, Hypnotic, or Anxiolytic Dependence[a,b,c] (285)

305.40   Sedative, Hypnotic, or Anxiolytic Abuse (286)

Sedative-, Hypnotic-, or Anxiolytic-Induced Disorders (286)

292.89   Sedative, Hypnotic, or Anxiolytic Intoxication (286)

292.0   Sedative, Hypnotic, or Anxiolytic Withdrawal (287)
         Specify if: With Perceptual Disturbances

292.81   Sedative, Hypnotic, or Anxiolytic Intoxication Delirium (143)

292.81   Sedative, Hypnotic, or Anxiolytic Withdrawal Delirium (143)

292.82   Sedative-, Hypnotic-, or Anxiolytic-Induced Persisting Dementia (168)

292.83   Sedative-, Hypnotic-, or Anxiolytic-Induced Persisting Amnestic Disorder (177)

292.xx   Sedative-, Hypnotic-, or Anxiolytic-Induced Psychotic Disorder (338)

   .11   With Delusions[I,W]

   .12   With Hallucinations[I,W]

292.84   Sedative-, Hypnotic-, or Anxiolytic-Induced Mood Disorder[I,W] (405)

292.89   Sedative-, Hypnotic-, or Anxiolytic-Induced Anxiety Disorder[W] (479)

292.89   Sedative-, Hypnotic-, or Anxiolytic-Induced Sexual Dysfunction[I] (562)

292.89   Sedative-, Hypnotic-, or Anxiolytic-Induced Sleep Disorder[I,W] (655)

292.9   Sedative-, Hypnotic-, or Anxiolytic-Related Disorder NOS (293)

POLYSUBSTANCE-RELATED DISORDER (293)

304.80   Polysubstance Dependence[a,b,c,d] (293)

OTHER (OR UNKNOWN) SUBSTANCE-RELATED DISORDERS (294)

Other (or Unknown) Substance Use Disorders (295)

304.90   Other (or Unknown) Substance Dependence[a,b,c,d] (192)

305.90   Other (or Unknown) Substance Abuse (198)

Other (or Unknown) Substance-Induced Disorders (295)

292.89   Other (or Unknown) Substance Intoxication (199)

   Specify if: With Perceptual Disturbances

292.0   Other (or Unknown) Substance Withdrawal (201)

   Specify if: With Perceptual Disturbances

292.81   Other (or Unknown) Substance-Induced Delirium (143)

292.82   Other (or Unknown) Substance-Induced Persisting Dementia (168)

292.83   Other (or Unknown) Substance-Induced Persisting Amnestic Disorder (177)

292.xx   Other (or Unknown) Substance-Induced Psychotic Disorder (338)

   .11   With Delusions[I,W]

   .12   With Hallucinations[I,W]

292.84   Other (or Unknown) Substance-Induced Mood Disorder[I,W] (405)

292.89   Other (or Unknown) Substance-Induced Anxiety Disorder[I,W] (479)

292.89   Other (or Unknown) Substance-Induced Sexual Dysfunction[I] (562)

292.89   Other (or Unknown) Substance-Induced Sleep Disorder[I,W] (655)

292.9   Other (or Unknown) Substance-Related Disorder NOS (295)

Schizophrenia and Other Psychotic Disorders (297)

295.xx   Schizophrenia (274)

   The following Classification of Longitudinal Course applies to all subtypes of Schizophrenia:

   Episodic With Interepisode Residual Symptoms (*specify if:* With Prominent Negative Symptoms)/Episodic With No Interepisode Residual Symptoms

   Continuous (*specify if:* With Prominent Negative Symptoms)

   Single Episode In Partial Remission (*specify if:* With Prominent Negative Symptoms)/Single Episode in Full Remission

   Other or Unspecified Pattern

   .30   Paranoid Type (313)

   .10   Disorganized Type (314)

   .20   Catatonic Type (315)

   .90   Undifferentiated Type (316)

   .60   Residual Type (316)

295.40   Schizophreniform Disorder (317)

   Specify if: Without Good Prognostic Features/With Good Prognostic Features

295.70   Schizoaffective Disorder (319)

   Specify type: Bipolar Type/Depressive Type

297.1   Delusional Disorder (323)

     Specify type: Erotomanic Type/Grandiose Type/Jealous Type/Persecutory Type/Somatic Type/Mixed Type/Unspecified Type

298.8   Brief Psychotic Disorder (329)

     Specify if: With Marked Stressor(s)/Without Marked Stressor(s)/With Postpartum Onset

297.3   Shared Psychotic Disorder (332)

293.xx   Psychotic Disorder Due to . . .*[Indicate the General Medical Condition]* (334)

  .81   With Delusions

  .82   With Hallucinations

___.__   Substance-Induced Psychotic Disorder *(refer to Substance-Related Disorders for substance-specific codes)* (338)

     Specify if: With Onset During Intoxication/With Onset During Withdrawal

298.9   Psychotic Disorder NOS (343)

Mood Disorders (345)

Code current state of Major Depressive Disorder or Bipolar I Disorder in fifth digit:

    1 = Mild

    2 = Moderate

    3 = Severe Without Psychotic Features

    4 = Severe With Psychotic Features

    Specify: Mood-Congruent Psychotic Features/Mood-Incongruent Psychotic Features

    5 = In Partial Remission

    6 = In Full Remission

    0 = Unspecified

    The following specifiers apply (for current or most recent episode) to Mood Disorders as noted:

[a]Severity/Psychotic/Remission Specifiers/[b]Chronic/[c]With Catatonic Features/[d]With Melancholic Features/[e]With Atypical Features/[f]With Postpartum Onset

    The following specifiers apply to Mood Disorders as noted:

[g]With or Without Full Interepisode Recovery/[h]With Seasonal Pattern/[i]With Rapid Cycling

DEPRESSIVE DISORDERS (369)

296.xx   Major Depressive Disorder (369)

  .2x   Single Episode[a,b,c,d,e,f]

  .3x   Recurrent[a,b,c,d,e,f,g,h]

300.4   Dysthymic Disorder (376)

        Specify if: Early Onset/Late Onset

        Specify: With Atypical Features

311   Depressive Disorder NOS (381)

BIPOLAR DISORDERS (382)

296.xx   Bipolar I Disorder (382)

    .0x   Single Manic Episode[a,c,f]

        Specify if: Mixed

    .40   Most Recent Episode Hypomanic[g,h,i]

    .4x   Most Recent Episode Manic[a,c,f,g,h,i]

    .6x   Most Recent Episode Mixed[a,c,f,g,h,i]

    .5x   Most Recent Episode Depressed[a,b,c,d,e,f,g,h,i]

    .7   Most Recent Episode Unspecified[g,h,i]

296.89   Bipolar II Disorder[a,b,c,d,e,f,g,h,i] (392)

        Specify (current or most recent episode): Hypomanic/Depressed

301.13   Cyclothymic Disorder (398)

296.80   Bipolar Disorder NOS (400)

293.83   Mood Disorder Due to . . . *[Indicate the General Medical Condition]* (401)

        Specify type: With Depressive Features/With Major Depressive-Like Episode/With Manic Features/With Mixed Features

___.___   Substance-Induced Mood Disorder *(refer to Substance-Related Disorders for substance-specific codes)* (405)

        Specify type: With Depressive Features/With Manic Features/With Mixed Features

        Specify if: With Onset During Intoxication/With Onset During Withdrawal

296.90   Mood Disorder NOS (410)

Anxiety Disorders (429)

300.01   Panic Disorder Without Agoraphobia (433)

300.21   Panic Disorder With Agoraphobia (433)

300.22   Agoraphobia Without History of Panic Disorder (441)

300.29   Specific Phobia (443)

        Specify type: Animal Type/Natural Environment Type/Blood-Injection-Injury Type/Situational Type/Other Type

300.23   Social Phobia (450)

        Specify if: Generalized

300.3   Obsessive-Compulsive Disorder (456)

Specify if: With Poor Insight

309.81   Posttraumatic Stress Disorder (463)

Specify if: Acute/Chronic

Specify if: With Delayed Onset

308.3   Acute Stress Disorder (469)

300.02   Generalized Anxiety Disorder (472)

293.84   Anxiety Disorder Due to . . . *[Indicate the General Medical Condition]* (476)

Specify if: With Generalized Anxiety/With Panic Attacks/With Obsessive-Compulsive Symptoms

___.___   Substance-Induced Anxiety Disorder *(refer to Substance-Related Disorders for substance-specific codes)* (479)

Specify if: With Generalized Anxiety/With Panic Attacks/With Obsessive-Compulsive Symptoms/With Phobic Symptoms

Specify if: With Onset During Intoxication/With Onset During Withdrawal

300.0   Anxiety Disorder NOS (484)

Somatoform Disorders (485)

300.81   Somatization Disorder (486)

300.82   Undifferentiated Somatoform Disorder (490)

300.11   Conversion Disorder (492)

Specify type: With Motor Symptom or Deficit/With Sensory Symptom or Deficit/With Seizures or Convulsions/With Mixed Presentation

307.xx   Pain Disorder (498)

.80   Associated With Psychological Factors

.89   Associated With Both Psychological Factors and a General Medical Condition

Specify if: Acute/Chronic

300.7   Hypochondriasis (504)

Specify if: With Poor Insight

300.7   Body Dysmorphic Disorder (507)

300.82   Somatoform Disorder NOS (511)

Factitious Disorders (513)

300.xx   Factitious Disorder (513)

.16   With Predominantly Psychological Signs and Symptoms

.19   With Predominantly Physical Signs and Symptoms

.19   With Combined Psychological and Physical Signs and Symptoms

300.19   Factitious Disorder NOS (517)

Dissociative Disorders (519)

300.12   Dissociative Amnesia (520)

300.13   Dissociative Fugue (523)

300.14   Dissociative Identity Disorder (526)

300.6   Depersonalization Disorder (530)

300.15   Dissociative Disorder NOS (532)

Sexual and Gender Identity Disorders (535)

SEXUAL DYSFUNCTIONS (535)

The following specifiers apply to all primary Sexual Dysfunctions:

Lifelong Type/Acquired Type

Generalized Type/Situational Type

Due to Psychological Factors/Due to Combined Factors

Sexual Desire Disorder (539)

302.71   Hypoactive Sexual Desire Disorder (539)

302.79   Sexual Aversion Disorder (541)

Sexual Arousal Disorders (543)

302.72   Female Sexual Arousal Disorder (543)

302.72   Male Erectile Disorder (545)

Orgasmic Disorders (547)

302.73   Female Orgasmic Disorder (547)

302.74   Male Orgasmic Disorder (550)

302.75   Premature Ejaculation (552)

Sexual Pain Disorders (554)

302.76   Dyspareunia (Not Due to a General Medical Condition) (554)

306.51   Vaginismus (Not Due to a General Medical Condition) (556)

Sexual Dysfunction Due to a General Medical Condition (558)

625.8   Female Hypoactive Sexual Desire Disorder Due to . . . *[Indicate the General Medical Condition]* (558)

608.89   Male Hypoactive Sexual Desire Disorder Due to . . . *[Indicate the General Medical Condition]* (558)

607.84   Male Erectile Disorder Due to . . . *[Indicate the General Medical Condition]* (558)

625.0   Female Dyspareunia Due to . . . *[Indicate the General Medical Condition]* (558)

608.89   Male Dyspareunia Due to . . . *[Indicate the General Medical Condition]* (558)

625.8   Other Female Sexual Dysfunction Due to . . . *[Indicate the General Medical Condition]* (558)

608.89   Other Male Sexual Dysfunction Due to . . . *[Indicate the General Medical Condition]* (558)

___.__   Substance-Induced Sexual Dysfunction *(refer to Substance-Related Disorders for substance-specific codes)* (562)

          Specify if: With Impaired Desire/With Impaired Arousal/With Impaired Orgasm/With Sexual Pain

          Specify if: With Onset During Intoxication

302.70   Sexual Dysfunction NOS (565)

PARAPHILIAS (566)

302.4   Exhibitionism (569)

302.81   Fetishism (569)

302.89   Frotteurism (570)

302.2   Pedophilia (571)

          Specify if: Sexually Attracted to Males/Sexually Attracted to Females/Sexually Attracted to Both

          Specify if: Limited to Incest

          Specify type: Exclusive Type/Nonexclusive Type

302.83   Sexual Masochism (572)

302.84   Sexual Sadism (573)

302.3   Transvestic Fetishism (574)

          Specify if: With Gender Dysphoria

302.82   Voyeurism (575)

302.9   Paraphilia NOS (576)

GENDER IDENTITY DISORDERS (576)

302.xx   Gender Identity Disorder (576)

   .6   in Children

   .85   in Adolescents or Adults

Specify if: Sexually Attracted to Males/Sexually Attracted to Females/Sexually Attracted to Both/Sexually Attracted to Neither

302.6   Gender Identity Disorder NOS (582)

302.9   Sexual Disorder NOS (582)

Eating Disorders (583)

307.1   Anorexia Nervosa (583)

Specify type: Restricting Type; Binge-Eating/Purging Type

307.51   Bulimia Nervosa (589)

Specify type: Purging Type/Nonpurging Type

307.50   Eating Disorder NOS (594)

Sleep Disorders (597)

PRIMARY SLEEP DISORDERS (598)

Dyssomnias (598)

307.42   Primary Insomnia (599)

307.44   Primary Hypersomnia (604)

Specify if: Recurrent

347   Narcolepsy (609)

780.59   Breathing-Related Sleep Disorder (615)

307.45   Circadian Rhythm Sleep Disorder (622)

Specify type: Delayed Sleep Phase Type/Jet Lag Type/Shift Work Type/Unspecified Type

307.47   Dyssomnia NOS (629)

Parasomnias (630)

307.47   Nightmare Disorder (631)

307.46   Sleep Terror Disorder (634)

307.46   Sleepwalking Disorder (639)

307.47   Parasomnia NOS (644)

SLEEP DISORDERS RELATED TO ANOTHER MENTAL DISORDER (645)

307.42   Insomnia Related to . . . *[Indicate the Axis I or Axis II Disorder]* (645)

307.44   Hypersomnia Related to . . . *[Indicate the Axis I or Axis II Disorder]* (645)

OTHER SLEEP DISORDERS (651)

780.xx   Sleep Disorder Due to . . .*[Indicate the General Medical Condition]* (651)

   .52   Insomnia Type

   .54   Hypersomnia Type

   .59   Parasomnia Type

   .59   Mixed Type

___.__   Substance-Induced Sleep Disorder *(refer to Substance-Related Disorders for substance-specific codes)* (655)

      Specify type: Insomnia Type/Hypersomnia Type/Parasomnia Type/Mixed Type

      Specify if: With Onset During Intoxication/With Onset During Withdrawal

Impulse-Control Disorders Not Elsewhere Classified (663)

312.34   Intermittent Explosive Disorder (663)

312.32   Kleptomania (667)

312.33   Pyromania (669)

312.31   Pathological Gambling (671)

312.39   Trichotillomania (674)

312.30   Impulse-Control Disorder NOS (677)

Adjustment Disorders (679)

309.xx   Adjustment Disorder (679)

   .0   With Depressed Mood

   .24   With Anxiety

   .28   With Mixed Anxiety and Depressed Mood

   .3   With Disturbance of Conduct

   .4   With Mixed Disturbance of Emotions and Conduct

   .9   Unspecified

      Specify if: Acute/Chronic

Personality Disorders (685)

Note: These are coded on Axis II.

301.0   Paranoid Personality Disorder (690)

301.20   Schizoid Personality Disorder (694)

301.22   Schizotypal Personality Disorder (697)

301.7   Antisocial Personality Disorder (701)

301.83   Borderline Personality Disorder (706)

301.50   Histrionic Personality Disorder (711)

301.81   Narcissistic Personality Disorder (714)

301.82   Avoidant Personality Disorder (718)

301.6   Dependent Personality Disorder (721)

301.4   Obsessive-Compulsive Personality Disorder (725)

301.9   Personality Disorder NOS (729)

Other Conditions That May be a Focus of Clinical Attention (731)

PSYCHOLOGICAL FACTORS AFFECTING MEDICAL CONDITION (731)

316   . . . *[Specified Psychological Factor]*

Affecting . . . [Indicate the General Medical Condition] (731) *Choose name based on nature of factors:*

Mental Disorder Affecting Medical Condition

Psychological Symptoms Affecting Medical Condition

Personality Traits or Coping Style Affecting Medical Condition

Maladaptive Health Behaviors Affecting Medical Condition

Stress-Related Physiological Response Affecting Medical Condition

Other or Unspecified Psychological Factors Affecting Medical Condition

MEDICATION-INDUCED MOVEMENT DISORDERS (734)

332.1   Neuroleptic-Induced Parkinsonism (735)

333.92   Neuroleptic Malignant Syndrome (735)

333.7   Neuroleptic-Induced Acute Dystonia (735)

333.99   Neuroleptic-Induced Acute Akathisia (735)

333.82   Neuroleptic-Induced Tardive Dyskinesia (736)

333.1   Medication-Induced Postural Tremor (736)

333.90   Medication-Induced Movement Disorder NOS (736)

OTHER MEDICATION-INDUCED DISORDER (736)

995.2   Adverse Effects of Medication NOS (736)

RELATIONAL PROBLEMS (736)

V61.9   Relational Problem Related to a Mental Disorder or General Medical Condition (737)

V61.20   Parent–Child Relational Problem (737)

V61.10   Partner Relational Problem (737)

V61.8   Sibling Relational Problem (737)

V62.81   Relational Problem NOS (737)

PROBLEMS RELATED TO ABUSE OR NEGLECT (738)

V61.21   Physical Abuse of Child (738) *(code 995.54 if focus of attention is on victim)*

V61.21   Sexual Abuse of Child (738) *(code 995.53 if focus of attention is on victim)*

V61.21   Neglect of Child (738) *(code 995.52 if focus of attention is on victim)*

___.___   Physical Abuse of Adult (738)

V61.12   (if by partner)

V62.83   (if by person other than partner) *(code 995.81 if focus of attention is on victim)*

___.___   Sexual Abuse of Adult (738)

V61.12   (if by partner)

V62.83   (if by person other than partner) *(code 995.83 if focus of attention is on victim)*

ADDITIONAL CONDITIONS THAT MAY BE A FOCUS OF CLINICAL ATTENTION (739)

V15.81   Noncompliance With Treatment (739)

V65.2   Malingering (739)

V71.01   Adult Antisocial Behavior (740)

V71.02   Child or Adolescent Antisocial Behavior (740)

V62.89   Borderline Intellectual Functioning (740)

Note: This is coded on Axis II.

780.9   Age-Related Cognitive Decline (740)

V62.82   Bereavement (740)

V62.3   Academic Problem (741)

V62.2   Occupational Problem (741)

313.82   Identity Problem (741)

V62.89   Religious or Spiritual Problem (741)

V62.4   Acculturation Problem (741)

V62.89   Phase of Life Problem (742)

Additional Codes (743)

300.9   Unspecified Mental Disorder (nonpsychotic) (743)

V71.09 No Diagnosis or Condition on Axis I (743)

799.9   Diagnosis or Condition Deferred on Axis I (743)

V71.09 No Diagnosis on Axis II (743)

799.9   Diagnosis Deferred on Axis II (743)

Multiaxial System

Axis I   Clinical Disorders Other Conditions That May Be a Focus of Clinical Attention

Axis II   Personality Disorders Mental Retardation

Axis III General Medical Conditions

Axis IV Psychosocial and Environmental Problems

Axis V   Global Assessment of Functioning

APPENDIX B

DSM-IV-TR Classification of Disorders and Conditions That Affect Children and Adolescents

DISORDERS USUALLY FIRST DIAGNOSED IN INFANCY, CHILDHOOD, OR ADOLESCENCE

Mental Retardation (Axis II)

317	Mild Mental Retardation (50–59 to 69–70 IQ)
318.0	Moderate Mental Retardation (35–40 to 50–55 IQ)
318.1	Severe Mental Retardation (20–25 to 35–40 IQ)
318.2	Profound Mental Retardation (below 20–25 IQ)
319	Mental Retardation, Severity Unspecified

Learning Disorders

315.00	Reading Disorder
315.1	Mathematics Disorder
315.2	Disorder of Written Expression
315.9	Learning Disorder NOS

Motor Skills Disorders

315.4	Developmental Coordination Disorder

Communication Disorders

315.31	Expressive Language Disorder
315.31	Mixed Receptive/Expressive Language Disorder
315.39	Phonological Disorder
307.0	Stuttering
307.9	Communication Disorder NOS

Pervasive Developmental Disorders

299.00 Autistic Disorder

299.80 Rett's Disorder

299.10 Childhood Disintegrative Disorder

299.80 Asperger's Disorder

299.80 Pervasive Developmental Disorder

Attention-Deficit and Disruptive Behavior Disorders

314.xx Attention-Deficit/Hyperactivity Disorder

   .01 Combined Type

   .00 Predominantly Inattentive Type

   .01 Predominantly Hyperactive-Impulsive Type

314.9 Attention-Deficit/Hyperactivity Disorder NOS

312.xx Conduct Disorder

   .81 Childhood-Onset Type

   .82 Adolescent-Onset Type

   .89 Unspecified Onset

313.81 Oppositional Defiant Disorder

312.9 Disruptive Behavior Disorder NOS

Feeding and Eating Disorders of Infancy or Early Childhood

307.52 Pica

307.53 Rumination Disorder

307.59 Feeding Disorder of Infancy or Early Childhood

Tic Disorders

307.23 Tourette's Disorder

307.22 Chronic Motor or Vocal Tic Disorder

307.21 Transient Tic Disorder

307.20 Tic Disorder NOS

Elimination Disorders

787.6 Encopresis With Constipation and Overflow Incontinence

307.7 Encopresis Without Constipation and Overflow Incontinence

307.6 Enuresis (Not Due to a General Medical Condition)

Other Disorders of Infancy, Childhood, or Adolescence

309.21   Separation Anxiety Disorder

313.23   Selective Mutism

313.89   Reactive Attachment Disorder of Infancy or Early Childhood

307.3   Stereotypic Movement Disorder

313.9   Disorder of Infancy, Childhood, or Adolescence NOS

OTHER CONDITIONS THAT MAY BE EVIDENCED IN CHILDHOOD AND ADOLESCENCE

Relational Problems

V61.20   Parent–Child Relational Problem

V61.8   Sibling Relational Problem

V62.81   Relational Problem NOS

Child or Adolescent Antisocial Behavior

V71.02   (The antisocial behavior is not due to conduct disorder or another mental disorder. Examples include isolated antisocial acts of children or adolescents.)

Borderline Intellectual Functioning

V62.89   (Coded on Axis II. 71 to 84 IQ)

Bereavement

V62.82   Reaction to the Death of a Loved One

Academic Problem

V62.3   Focus of attention is an academic problem that is not due to a mental disorder, or if due to a mental disorder, is sufficiently severe to warrant independent attention.

Abuse or Neglect

995.54   Physical abuse of a child, with focus on the victim

995.53   Sexual abuse of a child, with focus on the victim

995.52   Neglect of a child, with focus on the victim

Substance-Related Disorders
Mood Disorders

For example, major depressive disorder, dysthymic disorder, bipolar disorder, cyclothymic disorder, substance-induced mood disorder, and mood disorder NOS. Irritability rather than depressed mood may characterize children and adolescents who are depressed.

Anxiety Disorders

For example, panic disorder, specific phobias, social phobia, obsessive compulsive disorder, posttraumatic stress disorder, acute stress disorder, generalized anxiety disorder

Somatoform Disorders
Dissociative Disorders
Eating Disorders

Anorexia nervosa, bulimia nervosa, eating disorder NOS

Sleep Disorders
Impulse Control Disorders (not classified elsewhere)

Pyromania, trichotillomania, kleptomania

Adjustment Disorders

The development of emotional or behavioral symptoms in response to an identifiable stressor occurring within 3 months of the onset of the stressor. The nature of the stressor can be listed on Axis IV.

Personality Disorders (Axis II)

Personality disorders typically first appear during adolescence or earlier, but the diagnosis is not made until adulthood.

Schizophrenia and Related Disorders

Schizophrenia is usually manifested in adolescence or early adulthood.

APPENDIX C

American Counseling Association
Code of Ethics (2005)

The new ethics code of the American Counseling Association (ACA) is the most comprehensive the association has ever produced. It is binding on all counselors who are ACA members. The code is divided into eight (8) sections that represent the ideals that should guide counselors in their interactions with clients. These sections are:

- The Counseling Relationship
- Confidentiality, Privileged Communication, and Privacy
- Professional Responsibility
- Relationships with Other Professionals
- Evaluation, Assessment, and Interpretation
- Supervision, Training, and Teaching
- Research and Publication
- Resolving Ethical Issues

New areas in the 2005 *Code of Ethics* that distinguish it from the 1995 *Code of Ethics and Standards of Practice* include sections on potentially beneficial interactions, end-of-life care for terminally ill clients, technological applications, counselor incapacitation, historical and social prejudices in the diagnosis of pathology, and innovative theories and techniques. Also, in regard to research, the term "subjects" has been replaced by the word "participants" (Herlihy & Corey, 2006). Overall, the 2005 ACA *Code of Ethics* is much more thorough and user friendly than the 1995 *Code of Ethics and Standards of Practice*.

REFERENCE

Herlihy, B., & Corey, G. (2006). *ACA ethical standards casebook* (6th ed.). Alexandria, VA: American Counseling Association

AMERICAN COUNSELING ASSOCIATION CODE OF ETHICS
PREAMBLE

The American Counseling Association is an educational, scientific, and professional organization whose members work in a variety of settings and serve in multiple capacities. ACA members are dedicated to the enhancement of human development throughout the life span. Association members recognize diversity and embrace a cross cultural approach in support of the worth, dignity, potential, and uniqueness of people within their social and cultural contexts.

Source: Reprinted from *Code of Ethics* (2005). American Counseling Association. Reprinted with permission. No further reproduction authorized without written permission from the American Counseling Association.

Professional values are an important way of living out an ethical commitment. Values inform principles. Inherently held values that guide our behaviors or exceed prescribed behaviors are deeply ingrained in the counselor and developed out of personal dedication, rather than the mandatory requirement of an external organization.

ACA CODE OF ETHICS PURPOSE

The *ACA Code of Ethics* serves five main purposes:

1. The *Code* enables the association to clarify to current and future members, and to those served by members, the nature of the ethical responsibilities held in common by its members.
2. The *Code* helps support the mission of the association.
3. The *Code* establishes principles that define ethical behavior and best practices of association members.
4. The *Code* serves as an ethical guide designed to assist members in constructing a professional course of action that best serves those utilizing counseling services and best promotes the values of the counseling profession.
5. The *Code* serves as the basis for processing of ethical complaints and inquiries initiated against members of the association.

The *ACA Code of Ethics* contains eight main sections that address the following areas:

Section A: The Counseling Relationship

Section B: Confidentiality, Privileged Communication, and Privacy

Section C: Professional Responsibility

Section D: Relationships with Other Professionals

Section E: Evaluation, Assessment, and Interpretation

Section F: Supervision, Training, and Teaching

Section G: Research and Publication

Section H: Resolving Ethical Issues

Each section of the *ACA Code of Ethics* begins with an Introduction. The introductions to each section discuss what counselors should aspire to with regard to ethical behavior and responsibility. The Introduction helps set the tone for that particular section and provides a starting point that invites reflection on the ethical mandates contained in each part of the *ACA Code of Ethics.*

When counselors are faced with ethical dilemmas that are difficult to resolve, they are expected to engage in a carefully considered ethical decision-making process. Reasonable differences of opinion can and do exist among counselors with respect to the ways in which values, ethical principles, and ethical standards would be applied when they conflict. While there is no specific ethical decision-making model that is most effective, counselors are expected to be familiar with a credible model of decision making that can bear public scrutiny and its application.

Through a chosen ethical decision-making process and evaluation of the context of the situation, counselors are empowered to make decisions that help expand the capacity of people to grow and develop.

A brief glossary is given to provide readers with a concise description of some of the terms used in the *ACA Code of Ethics.*

Section A: The Counseling Relationship

INTRODUCTION. Counselors encourage client growth and development in ways that foster the interest and welfare of clients and promote formation of healthy relationships. Counselors actively attempt to understand the diverse cultural backgrounds of the clients they serve. Counselors also explore their own cultural identities and how these affect their values and beliefs about the counseling process.

Counselors are encouraged to contribute to society by devoting a portion of their professional activity to services for which there is little or no financial return (pro bono publico).

A.1. WELFARE OF THOSE SERVED BY COUNSELORS

A.1.a. *Primary Responsibility.* The primary responsibility of counselors is to respect the dignity and to promote the welfare of clients.

A.1.b. *Records.* Counselors maintain records necessary for rendering professional services to their clients and as required by laws, regulations, or agency or institution procedures. Counselors include sufficient and timely documentation in their client records to facilitate the delivery and continuity of needed services. Counselors take reasonable steps to ensure that documentation in records accurately reflects client progress and services provided. If errors are made in client records, counselors take steps to properly note the correction of such errors according to agency or institutional policies. (See A.12.g.7., B.6., B.6.g., G.2.j.)

A.1.c. *Counseling: Plans.* Counselors and their clients work jointly in devising integrated counseling plans that offer reasonable promise of success and are consistent with abilities and circumstances of clients. Counselors and clients regularly review counseling plans to assess their continued viability and effectiveness, respecting the freedom of choice of clients. (See A.2.a., A.2.d., A.12.g.)

A.1.d. *Support Network Involvement.* Counselors recognize that support networks hold various meanings in the lives of clients and consider enlisting the support, understanding, and involvement of others (e.g., religious/spiritual/community leaders, family members, friends) as positive resources, when appropriate, with client consent.

A.1.e. *Employment Needs.* Counselors work with their clients considering employment in jobs that are consistent with the overall abilities, vocational limitations, physical restrictions, general temperament, interest and aptitude patterns, social skills, education, general qualifications, and other relevant characteristics and needs of clients. When appropriate, counselors appropriately trained in career development will assist in the placement of clients in positions that are consistent with the interest, culture, and the welfare of clients, employers, and/or the public.

A.2. INFORMED CONSENT IN THE COUNSELING RELATIONSHIP. (See A.12.g., B.5., B.6.b., E.3., E.13.b., F.1.c., G.2.a.)

A.2.a. *Informed Consent.* Clients have the freedom to choose whether to enter into or remain in a counseling relationship and need adequate information about the counseling process and the counselors. Counselors have an obligation to review in writing and verbally with clients the rights and responsibilities of both the counselor and the client. Informed consent is an ongoing part of the counseling process, and counselors appropriately document discussions of informed consent throughout the counseling relationship.

A.2.b. **Types of Information Needed.**   Counselors explicitly explain to clients the nature of all services provided. They inform clients about issues such as, but not limited to, the following: the purposes, goals, techniques, procedures, limitations, potential risks, and benefits of services; the counselor's qualifications, credentials, and relevant experience; continuation of services upon the incapacitation or death of a counselor; and other pertinent information. Counselors take steps to ensure that clients understand the implications of diagnosis, the intended use of tests and reports, fees, and billing arrangements. Clients have the right to confidentiality and to be provided with an explanation of its limitations (including how supervisors and/or treatment team professionals are involved); to obtain clear information about their records; to participate in the ongoing counseling plans; and to refuse any services or modality change and to be advised of the consequences of such refusal.

A.2.c. **Developmental and Cultural Sensitivity.**   Counselors communicate information in ways that are both developmentally and culturally appropriate. Counselors use clear and understandable language when discussing issues related to informed consent. When clients have difficulty understanding the language used by counselors, they provide necessary services (e.g., arranging for a qualified interpreter or translator) to ensure comprehension by clients. In collaboration with clients, counselors consider cultural implications of informed consent procedures and, where possible, counselors adjust their practices accordingly.

A.2.d. **Inability to Give Consent.**   When counseling minors or persons unable to give voluntary consent, counselors seek the assent of clients to services, and include them in decision making as appropriate. Counselors recognize the need to balance the ethical rights of clients to make choices, their capacity to give consent or assent to receive services, and parental or familial legal rights and responsibilities to protect these clients and make decisions on their behalf.

A.3. CLIENTS SERVED BY OTHERS.   When counselors learn that their clients are in a professional relationship with another mental health professional, they request release from clients to inform the other professionals and strive to establish positive and collaborative professional relationships.

A.4. AVOIDING HARM AND IMPOSING VALUES

A.4.a. **Avoiding Harm.**   Counselors act to avoid harming their clients, trainees, and research participants and to minimize or to remedy unavoidable or unanticipated harm.

A.4.b. **Personal Values.**   Counselors are aware of their own values, attitudes, beliefs, and behaviors and avoid imposing values that are inconsistent with counseling goals. Counselors respect the diversity of clients, trainees, and research participants.

A.5. ROLES AND RELATIONSHIPS WITH CLIENTS.   (See F.3., F.10., G.3.)

A.5.a. **Current Clients.**   Sexual or romantic counselor–client interactions or relationships with current clients, their romantic partners, or their family members are prohibited.

A.5.b. **Former Clients.**   Sexual or romantic counselor–client interactions or relationships with former clients, their romantic partners, or their family members are prohibited for a period of 5 years following the last professional contact. Counselors, before engaging in sexual or romantic interactions or relationships with clients, their romantic partners, or client family members after 5 years following the last professional contact, demonstrate forethought and document (in written form) whether the interactions or relationship can be viewed as exploitive in some way and/or whether there is still potential to harm the former client; in cases of potential exploitation and/or harm, the counselor avoids entering such an interaction or relationship.

A.5.c.   *Nonprofessional Interactions or Relationships (Other Than Sexual or Romantic Interactions or Relationships).*   Counselor–client nonprofessional relationships with clients, former clients, their romantic partners, or their family members should be avoided, except when the interaction is potentially beneficial to the client. (See A.5.d.)

A.5.d.   *Potentially Beneficial Interactions.*   When a counselor–client nonprofessional interaction with a client or former client may be potentially beneficial to the client or former client, the counselor must document in case records, prior to the interaction (when feasible), the rationale for such an interaction, the potential benefit, and anticipated consequences for the client or former client and other individuals significantly involved with the client or former client. Such interactions should be initiated with appropriate client consent. Where unintentional harm occurs to the client or former client, or to an individual significantly involved with the client or former client, due to the nonprofessional interaction, the counselor must show evidence of an attempt to remedy such harm. Examples of potentially beneficial interactions include, but are not limited to, attending a formal ceremony (e.g., a wedding/commitment ceremony or graduation); purchasing a service or product provided by a client or former client (excepting unrestricted bartering); hospital visits to an ill family member; mutual membership in a professional association, organization, or community. (See A.5.c.)

A.5.e.   *Role Changes in the Professional Relationship.*   When a counselor changes a role from the original or most recent contracted relationship, he or she obtains informed consent from the client and explains the right of the client to refuse services related to the change. Examples of role changes include:

1. changing from individual to relationship or family counseling, or vice versa;
2. changing from a nonforensic evaluative role to a therapeutic role, or vice versa;
3. changing from a counselor to a researcher role (i.e., enlisting clients as research participants), or vice versa; and
4. changing from a counselor to a mediator role, or vice versa.

Clients must be fully informed of any anticipated consequences (e.g., financial, legal, personal, or therapeutic) of counselor role changes.

A.6. ROLES AND RELATIONSHIPS AT INDIVIDUAL, GROUP, INSTITUTIONAL, AND SOCIETAL LEVELS

A.6.a.   *Advocacy.*   When appropriate, counselors advocate at individual, group, institutional, and societal levels to examine potential barriers and obstacles that inhibit access and/or the growth and development of clients.

A.6.b.   *Confidentiality and Advocacy.*   Counselors obtain client consent prior to engaging in advocacy efforts on behalf of an identifiable client to improve the provision of services and to work toward removal of systemic barriers or obstacles that inhibit client access, growth, and development.

A.7. MULTIPLE CLIENTS.   When a counselor agrees to provide counseling services to two or more persons who have a relationship, the counselor clarifies at the outset which person or persons are clients and the nature of the relationships the counselor will have with each involved person. If it becomes apparent that the counselor may be called upon to perform potentially conflicting roles, the counselor will clarify, adjust, or withdraw from roles appropriately. (See A.8.a., B.4.)

A.8. GROUP WORK.   (See B.4.a.)

A.8.a.   *Screening.* Counselors screen prospective group counseling/therapy participants. To the extent possible, counselors select members whose needs and goals are compatible with goals of the group, who will not impede the group process, and whose well-being will not be jeopardized by the group experience.

A.8.b.   *Protecting Clients.* In a group setting, counselors take reasonable precautions to protect clients from physical, emotional, or psychological trauma.

A.9. END-OF-LIFE CARE FOR TERMINALLY ILL CLIENTS

A.9.a.   *Quality of Care.* Counselors strive to take measures that enable clients

1. to obtain high quality end-of-life care for their physical, emotional, social, and spiritual needs;
2. to exercise the highest degree of self-determination possible;
3. to be given every opportunity possible to engage in informed decision making regarding their end-of-life care; and
4. to receive complete and adequate assessment regarding their ability to make competent, rational decisions on their own behalf from a mental health professional who is experienced in end-of-life care practice.

A.9.b.   *Counselor Competence, Choice, and Referral.* Recognizing the personal, moral, and competence issues related to end-of-life decisions, counselors may choose to work or not work with terminally ill clients who wish to explore their end-of-life options. Counselors provide appropriate referral information to ensure that clients receive the necessary help.

A.9.c.   *Confidentiality.* Counselors who provide services to terminally ill individuals who are considering hastening their own deaths have the option of breaking or not breaking confidentiality, depending on applicable laws and the specific circumstances of the situation and after seeking consultation or supervision from appropriate professional and legal parties. (See B.5.c., B.7.c.)

A.10. FEES AND BARTERING

A.10.a.   *Accepting Fees From Agency Clients.* Counselors refuse a private fee or other remuneration for rendering services to persons who are entitled to such services through the counselor's employing agency or institution. The policies of a particular agency may make explicit provisions for agency clients to receive counseling services from members of its staff in private practice. In such instances, the clients must be informed of other options open to them should they seek private counseling services.

A.10.b.   *Establishing Fees.* In establishing fees for professional counseling services, counselors consider the financial status of clients and locality. In the event that the established fee structure is inappropriate for a client, counselors assist clients in attempting to find comparable services of acceptable cost.

A.10.c. *Nonpayment of Fees.* If counselors intend to use collection agencies or take legal measures to collect fees from clients who do not pay for services as agreed upon, they first inform clients of intended actions and offer clients the opportunity to make payment.

A.10.d. *Bartering.* Counselors may barter only if the relationship is not exploitive or harmful and does not place the counselor in an unfair advantage, if the client requests it, and if such arrangements are an accepted practice among professionals in the community. Counselors consider the cultural implications of bartering and discuss relevant concerns with clients and document such agreements in a clear written contract.

A.10.e. *Receiving Gifts.* Counselors understand the challenges of accepting gifts from clients and recognize that in some cultures, small gifts are a token of respect and showing gratitude. When determining whether or not to accept a gift from clients, counselors take into account the therapeutic relationship, the monetary value of the gift, a client's motivation for giving the gift, and the counselor's motivation for wanting or declining the gift.

A.11. TERMINATION AND REFERRAL

A.11.a. *Abandonment Prohibited.* Counselors do not abandon or neglect clients in counseling. Counselors assist in making appropriate arrangements for the continuation of treatment, when necessary, during interruptions such as vacations, illness, and following termination.

A.11.b. *Inability to Assist Clients.* If counselors determine an inability to be of professional assistance to clients, they avoid entering or continuing counseling relationships. Counselors are knowledgeable about culturally and clinically appropriate referral resources and suggest these alternatives. If clients decline the suggested referrals, counselors should discontinue the relationship.

A.11.c. *Appropriate Termination.* Counselors terminate a counseling relationship when it becomes reasonably apparent that the client no longer needs assistance, is not likely to benefit, or is being harmed by continued counseling. Counselors may terminate counseling when in jeopardy of harm by the client, or another person with whom the client has a relationship, or when clients do not pay fees as agreed upon. Counselors provide pretermination counseling and recommend other service providers when necessary.

A.11.d. *Appropriate Transfer of Services.* When counselors transfer or refer clients to other practitioners, they ensure that appropriate clinical and administrative processes are completed and open communication is maintained with both clients and practitioners.

A.12. TECHNOLOGY APPLICATIONS

A.12.a. *Benefits and Limitations.* Counselors inform clients of the benefits and limitations of using information technology applications in the counseling process and in business/billing procedures. Such technologies include but are not limited to computer hardware and software, telephones, the World Wide Web, the Internet, online assessment instruments and other communication devices.

A.12.b. *Technology-Assisted Services.* When providing technology-assisted distance counseling services, counselors determine that clients are intellectually, emotionally, and physically capable of using the application and that the application is appropriate for the needs of clients.

A.12.c. *Inappropriate Services.*   When technology-assisted distance counseling services are deemed inappropriate by the counselor or client, counselors consider delivering services face to face.

A.12.d. *Access.*   Counselors provide reasonable access to computer applications when providing technology-assisted distance counseling services.

A.12.e. *Laws and Statutes.*   Counselors ensure that the use of technology does not violate the laws of any local, state, national, or international entity and observe all relevant statutes.

A.12.f. *Assistance.*   Counselors seek business, legal, and technical assistance when using technology applications, particularly when the use of such applications crosses state or national boundaries.

A.12.g. *Technology and Informed Consent.*   As part of the process of establishing informed consent, counselors do the following:

1. Address issues related to the difficulty of maintaining the confidentiality of electronically transmitted communications.
2. Inform clients of all colleagues, supervisors, and employees, such as Informational Technology (IT) administrators, who might have authorized or unauthorized access to electronic transmissions.
3. Urge clients to be aware of all authorized or unauthorized users including family members and fellow employees who have access to any technology clients may use in the counseling process.
4. Inform clients of pertinent legal rights and limitations governing the practice of a profession over state lines or international boundaries.
5. Use encrypted Web sites and e-mail communications to help ensure confidentiality when possible.
6. When the use of encryption is not possible, counselors notify clients of this fact and limit electronic transmissions to general communications that are not client specific.
7. Inform clients if and for how long archival storage of transaction records are maintained.
8. Discuss the possibility of technology failure and alternate methods of service delivery.
9. Inform clients of emergency procedures, such as calling 911 or a local crisis hotline, when the counselor is not available.
10. Discuss time zone differences, local customs, and cultural or language differences that might impact service delivery.
11. Inform clients when technology-assisted distance counseling services are not covered by insurance. (See A.2.)

A.12.h. *Sites on the World Wide Web.*   Counselors maintaining sites on the World Wide Web (the Internet) do the following:

1. Regularly check that electronic links are working and professionally appropriate.
2. Establish ways clients can contact the counselor in case of technology failure.

3. Provide electronic links to relevant state licensure and professional certification boards to protect consumer rights and facilitate addressing ethical concerns.

4. Establish a method for verifying client identity.

5. Obtain the written consent of the legal guardian or other authorized legal representative prior to rendering services in the event the client is a minor child, an adult who is legally incompetent, or an adult incapable of giving informed consent.

6. Strive to provide a site that is accessible to persons with disabilities.

7. Strive to provide translation capabilities for clients who have a different primary language while also addressing the imperfect nature of such translations.

8. Assist clients in determining the validity and reliability of information found on the World Wide Web and other technology applications.

Section B: Confidentiality, Privileged Communication, and Privacy

INTRODUCTION.   Counselors recognize that trust is a cornerstone of the counseling relationship. Counselors aspire to earn the trust of clients by creating an ongoing partnership, establishing and upholding appropriate boundaries, and maintaining confidentiality. Counselors communicate the parameters of confidentiality in a culturally competent manner.

B.1. RESPECTING CLIENT RIGHTS

B.1.a.   Multicultural/Diversity Considerations.   Counselors maintain awareness and sensitivity regarding cultural meanings of confidentiality and privacy. Counselors respect differing views toward disclosure of information. Counselors hold ongoing discussions with clients as to how, when, and with whom information is to be shared.

B.1.b.   Respect for Privacy.   Counselors respect client rights to privacy. Counselors solicit private information from clients only when it is beneficial to the counseling process.

B.1.c.   Respect for Confidentiality.   Counselors do not share confidential information without client consent or without sound legal or ethical justification.

B.1.d.   Explanation of Limitations.   At initiation and throughout the counseling process, counselors inform clients of the limitations of confidentiality and seek to identify foreseeable situations in which confidentiality must be breached. (See A.2.b.)

B.2. EXCEPTIONS

B.2.a.   Danger and Legal Requirements.   The general requirement that counselors keep information confidential does not apply when disclosure is required to protect clients or identified others from serious and foreseeable harm or when legal requirements demand that confidential information must be revealed. Counselors consult with other professionals when in doubt as to the validity of an exception. Additional considerations apply when addressing end-of-life issues. (See A.9.c.)

B.2.b.   Contagious, Life-Threatening Diseases.   When clients disclose that they have a disease commonly known to be both communicable and life threatening, counselors may be justified in disclosing information to identifiable third parties, if they are known to be at demonstrable and high risk of contracting the disease. Prior to making a disclosure, counselors confirm that there is such a diagnosis and assess the intent of clients to inform the third parties about their disease or to engage in any behaviors that may be harmful to an identifiable third party.

B.2.c. ***Court-Ordered Disclosure.*** When subpoenaed to release confidential or privileged information without a client's permission, counselors obtain written, informed consent from the client or take steps to prohibit the disclosure or have it limited as narrowly as possible due to potential harm to the client or counseling relationship.

B.2.d. ***Minimal Disclosure.*** To the extent possible, clients are informed before confidential information is disclosed and are involved in the disclosure decision-making process. When circumstances require the disclosure of confidential information, only essential information is revealed.

B.3. INFORMATION SHARED WITH OTHERS

B.3.a. ***Subordinates.*** Counselors make every effort to ensure that privacy and confidentiality of clients are maintained by subordinates, including employees, supervisees, students, clerical assistants, and volunteers. (See F.1.c.)

B.3.b. ***Treatment Teams.*** When client treatment involves a continued review or participation by a treatment team, the client will be informed of the team's existence and composition, information being shared, and the purposes of sharing such information.

B.3.c. ***Confidential Settings.*** Counselors discuss confidential information only in settings in which they can reasonably ensure client privacy.

B.3.d. ***Third-Party Payers.*** Counselors disclose information to third-party payers only when clients have authorized such disclosure.

B.3.e. ***Transmitting Confidential Information.*** Counselors take precautions to ensure the confidentiality of information transmitted through the use of computers, electronic mail, facsimile machines, telephones, voicemail, answering machines, and other electronic or computer technology. (See A.12.g.)

B.3.f. ***Deceased Clients.*** Counselors protect the confidentiality of deceased clients, consistent with legal requirements and agency or setting policies.

B.4. GROUPS AND FAMILIES

B.4.a. ***Group Work.*** In group work, counselors clearly explain the importance and parameters of confidentiality for the specific group being entered.

B.4.b. ***Couples and Family Counseling.*** In couples and family counseling, counselors clearly define who is considered "the client" and discuss expectations and limitations of confidentiality. Counselors seek agreement and document in writing such agreement among all involved parties having capacity to give consent concerning each individual's right to confidentiality and any obligation to preserve the confidentiality of information known.

B.5. CLIENTS LACKING CAPACITY TO GIVE INFORMED CONSENT

B.5.a. ***Responsibility to Clients.*** When counseling minor clients or adult clients who lack the capacity to give voluntary, informed consent, counselors protect the confidentiality of information received in the counseling relationship as specified by federal and state laws, written policies, and applicable ethical standards.

B.5.b. ***Responsibility to Parents and Legal Guardians.*** Counselors inform parents and legal guardians about the role of counselors and the confidential nature of the counseling relationship. Counselors are sensitive to the cultural diversity of families and respect the inherent rights and responsibilities of parents/guardians over the welfare of their children/charges according to law. Counselors work to establish, as appropriate, collaborative relationships with parents/guardians to best serve clients.

B.5.c. ***Release of Confidential Information.***   When counseling minor clients or adult clients who lack the capacity to give voluntary consent to release confidential information, counselors seek permission from an appropriate third party to disclose information. In such instances, counselors inform clients consistent with their level of understanding and take culturally appropriate measures to safeguard client confidentiality.

B.6. RECORDS

B.6.a. ***Confidentiality of Records.***   Counselors ensure that records are kept in a secure location and that only authorized persons have access to records.

B.6.b. ***Permission to Record.***   Counselors obtain permission from clients prior to recording sessions through electronic or other means.

B.6.c. ***Permission to Observe.***   Counselors obtain permission from clients prior to observing counseling sessions, reviewing session transcripts, or viewing recordings of sessions with supervisors, faculty, peers, or others within the training environment.

B.6.d. ***Client Access.***   Counselors provide reasonable access to records and copies of records when requested by competent clients. Counselors limit the access of clients to their records, or portions of their records, only when there is compelling evidence that such access would cause harm to the client. Counselors document the request of clients and the rationale for withholding some or all of the record in the files of clients. In situations involving multiple clients, counselors provide individual clients with only those parts of records that related directly to them and do not include confidential information related to any other client.

B.6.e. ***Assistance With Records.***   When clients request access to their records, counselors provide assistance and consultation in interpreting counseling records.

B.6.f. ***Disclosure or Transfer.***   Unless exceptions to confidentiality exist, counselors obtain written permission from clients to disclose or transfer records to legitimate third parties. Steps are taken to ensure that receivers of counseling records are sensitive to their confidential nature. (See A.3., E.4.)

B.6.g. ***Storage and Disposal After Termination.***   Counselors store records following termination of services to ensure reasonable future access, maintain records in accordance with state and federal statutes governing records, and dispose of client records and other sensitive materials in a manner that protects client confidentiality. When records are of an artistic nature, counselors obtain client (or guardian) consent with regards to handling of such records or documents. (See A.1.b.)

B.6.h. ***Reasonable Precautions.***   Counselors take reasonable precautions to protect client confidentiality in the event of the counselor's termination of practice, incapacity, or death. (See C.2.h.)

B.7. RESEARCH AND TRAINING

B.7.a. ***Institutional Approval.***   When institutional approval is required, counselors provide accurate information about their research proposals and obtain approval prior to conducting their research. They conduct research in accordance with the approved research protocol.

B.7.b. ***Adherence to Guidelines.***   Counselors are responsible for understanding and adhering to state, federal, agency, or institutional policies or applicable guidelines regarding confidentiality in their research practices.

B.7.c. ***Confidentiality of Information Obtained in Research.***   Violations of participant privacy and confidentiality are risks of participation in research involving human participants. Investigators maintain all research records in a secure manner. They explain to participants the risks of violations of privacy and confidentiality and disclose to participants any limits of confidentiality that reasonably can be expected. Regardless of the degree to which confidentiality will be maintained, investigators must disclose to participants any limits of confidentiality that reasonably can be expected. (See G.2.e.)

B.7.d. ***Disclosure of Research Information.***   Counselors do not disclose confidential information that reasonably could lead to the identification of a research participant unless they have obtained the prior consent of the person. Use of data derived from counseling relationships for purposes of training, research, or publication is confined to content that is disguised to ensure the anonymity of the individuals involved. (See G.2.a., G.2.d.)

B.7.e. ***Agreement for Identification.***   Identification of clients, students, or supervisees in a presentation or publication is permissible only when they have reviewed the material and agreed to its presentation or publication. (See G.4.d.)

B.8. CONSULTATION

B.8.a. ***Agreements.***   When acting as consultants, counselors seek agreements among all parties involved concerning each individual's rights to confidentiality, the obligation of each individual to preserve confidential information, and the limits of confidentiality of information shared by others.

B.8.b. ***Respect for Privacy.***   Information obtained in a consulting relationship is discussed for professional purposes only with persons directly involved with the case. Written and oral reports present only data germane to the purposes of the consultation, and every effort is made to protect client identity and to avoid undue invasion of privacy.

B.8.c. ***Disclosure of Confidential Information.***   When consulting with colleagues, counselors do not disclose confidential information that reasonably could lead to the identification of a client or other person or organization with whom they have a confidential relationship unless they have obtained the prior consent of the person or organization or the disclosure cannot be avoided. They disclose information only to the extent necessary to achieve the purposes of the consultation. (See D.2.d.)

Section C: Professional Responsibility

INTRODUCTION.   Counselors aspire to open, honest, and accurate communication in dealing with the public and other professionals. They practice in a nondiscriminatory manner within the boundaries of professional and personal competence and have a responsibility to abide by the *ACA Code of Ethics*. Counselors actively participate in local, state, and national associations that foster the development and improvement of counseling.

Counselors advocate to promote change at the individual, group, institutional, and societal levels that improves the quality of life for individuals and groups and removes potential barriers to the provision or access of appropriate services being offered. Counselors have a responsibility to the public to engage in counseling practices that are based on rigorous research methodologies. In addition, counselors engage in self-care activities to maintain and promote their emotional, physical, mental, and spiritual well-being to best meet their professional responsibilities.

C.1. KNOWLEDGE OF STANDARDS.   Counselors have a responsibility to read, understand, and follow the *ACA Code of Ethics* and adhere to applicable laws and regulations.

C.2. PROFESSIONAL COMPETENCE

C.2.a.   ***Boundaries of Competence.***   Counselors practice only within the boundaries of their competence, based on their education, training, supervised experience, state and national professional credentials, and appropriate professional experience. Counselors gain knowledge, personal awareness, sensitivity, and skills pertinent to working with a diverse client population. (See A.9.b., C.4.e., E.2., F.2., F.11.b.)

C.2.b.   ***New Specialty Areas of Practice.***   Counselors practice in specialty areas new to them only after appropriate education, training, and supervised experience. While developing skills in new specialty areas, counselors take steps to ensure the competence of their work and to protect others from possible harm. (See F.6.f.)

C.2.c.   ***Qualified for Employment.***   Counselors accept employment only for positions for which they are qualified by education, training, supervised experience, state and national professional credentials, and appropriate professional experience. Counselors hire for professional counseling positions only individuals who are qualified and competent for those positions.

C.2.d.   ***Monitor Effectiveness.***   Counselors continually monitor their effectiveness as professionals and take steps to improve when necessary. Counselors in private practice take reasonable steps to seek peer supervision as needed to evaluate their efficacy as counselors.

C.2.e.   ***Consultation on Ethical Obligations.***   Counselors take reasonable steps to consult with other counselors or related professionals when they have questions regarding their ethical obligations or professional practice.

C.2.f.   ***Continuing Education.***   Counselors recognize the need for continuing education to acquire and maintain a reasonable level of awareness of current scientific and professional information in their fields of activity. They take steps to maintain competence in the skills they use, are open to new procedures, and keep current with the diverse populations and specific populations with whom they work.

C.2.g.   ***Impairment.***   Counselors are alert to the signs of impairment from their own physical, mental, or emotional problems and refrain from offering or providing professional services when such impairment is likely to harm a client or others. They seek assistance for problems that reach the level of professional impairment, and, if necessary, they limit, suspend, or terminate their professional responsibilities until such time it is determined that they may safely resume their work. Counselors assist colleagues or supervisors in recognizing their own professional impairment and provide consultation and assistance when warranted with colleagues or supervisors showing signs of impairment and intervene as appropriate to prevent imminent harm to clients. (See A.11.b., F.8.b.)

C.2.b.   ***Counselor Incapacitation or Termination of Practice.***   When counselors leave a practice, they follow a prepared plan for transfer of clients and files. Counselors prepare and disseminate to an identified colleague or "records custodian" a plan for the transfer of clients and files in the case of their incapacitation, death, or termination of practice.

C.3. ADVERTISING AND SOLICITING CLIENTS

C.3.a.   ***Accurate Advertising.***   When advertising or otherwise representing their services to the public, counselors identify their credentials in an accurate manner that is not false, misleading, deceptive, or fraudulent.

C.3.b.   ***Testimonials.***   Counselors who use testimonials do not solicit them from current clients nor former clients nor any other persons who may be vulnerable to undue influence.

C.3.c.   ***Statements by Others.***   Counselors make reasonable efforts to ensure that statements made by others about them or the profession of counseling are accurate.

C.3.d.   ***Recruiting Through Employment.***   Counselors do not use their places of employment or institutional affiliation to recruit or gain clients, supervisees, or consultees for their private practices.

C.3.e.   ***Products and Training Advertisements.***   Counselors who develop products related to their profession or conduct workshops or training events ensure that the advertisements concerning these products or events are accurate and disclose adequate information for consumers to make informed choices. (See C.6.d.)

C.3.f.   ***Promoting to Those Served.***   Counselors do not use counseling, teaching, training, or supervisory relationships to promote their products or training events in a manner that is deceptive or would exert undue influence on individuals who may be vulnerable. However, counselor educators may adopt textbooks they have authored for instructional purposes.

C.4. PROFESSIONAL QUALIFICATIONS

C.4.a.   ***Accurate Representation.***   Counselors claim or imply only professional qualifications actually completed and correct any known misrepresentations of their qualifications by others. Counselors truthfully represent the qualifications of their professional colleagues. Counselors clearly distinguish between paid and volunteer work experience and accurately describe their continuing education and specialized training. (See C.2.a.)

C.4.b.   ***Credentials.***   Counselors claim only licenses or certifications that are current and in good standing.

C.4.c.   ***Educational Degrees.***   Counselors clearly differentiate between earned and honorary degrees.

C.4.d.   ***Implying Doctoral-Level Competence.***   Counselors clearly state their highest earned degree in counseling or closely related field. Counselors do not imply doctoral-level competence when only possessing a master's degree in counseling or a related field by referring to themselves as "Dr." in a counseling context when their doctorate is not in counseling or related field.

C.4.e.   ***Program Accreditation Status.***   Counselors clearly state the accreditation status of their degree programs at the time the degree was earned.

C.4.f.   ***Professional Membership.***   Counselors clearly differentiate between current, active memberships and former memberships in associations. Members of the American Counseling Association must clearly differentiate between professional membership, which implies the possession of at least a master's degree in counseling, and regular membership, which is open to individuals whose interests and activities are consistent with those of ACA but are not qualified for professional membership.

C.5. NONDISCRIMINATION.   Counselors do not condone or engage in discrimination based on age, culture, disability, ethnicity, race, religion/spirituality, gender, gender identity, sexual orientation, marital status/partnership, language preference, socioeconomic status, or any basis proscribed by law. Counselors do not discriminate against clients, students, employees, supervisees, or research participants in a manner that has a negative impact on these persons.

C.6. PUBLIC RESPONSIBILITY

C.6.a.   ***Sexual Harassment.***   Counselors do not engage in or condone sexual harassment. Sexual harassment is defined as sexual solicitation, physical advances, or verbal or nonverbal conduct that is sexual in nature, that occurs in connection with professional activities or roles, and that either

1. is unwelcome, is offensive, or creates a hostile workplace or learning environment, and counselors know or are told this; or
2. is sufficiently severe or intense to be perceived as harassment to a reasonable person in the context in which the behavior occurred.

Sexual harassment can consist of a single intense or severe act or multiple persistent or pervasive acts.

C.6.b.   ***Reports to Third Parties.***   Counselors are accurate, honest, and objective in reporting their professional activities and judgments to appropriate third parties, including courts, health insurance companies, those who are the recipients of evaluation reports, and others. (See B.3., E.4.)

C.6.c.   ***Media Presentations.***   When counselors provide advice or comment by means of public lectures, demonstrations, radio or television programs, prerecorded tapes, technology-based applications, printed articles, mailed material, or other media, they take reasonable precautions to ensure that

1. the statements are based on appropriate professional counseling literature and practice,
2. the statements are otherwise consistent with the *ACA Code of Ethics,* and
3. the recipients of the information are not encouraged to infer that a professional counseling relationship has been established.

C.6.d.   ***Exploitation of Others.***   Counselors do not exploit others in their professional relationships. (See C.3.e.)

C.6.e.   ***Scientific Bases for Treatment Modalities.***   Counselors use techniques/ procedures/ modalities that are grounded in theory and/or have an empirical or scientific foundation. Counselors who do not must define the techniques/procedures as "unproven" or "developing" and explain the potential risks and ethical considerations of using such techniques/procedures and take steps to protect clients from possible harm. (See A.4.a., E.5.c., E.5.d.)

C.7. RESPONSIBILITY TO OTHER PROFESSIONALS

C.7.a. *Personal Public Statements.*   When making personal statements in a public context, counselors clarify that they are speaking from their personal perspectives and that they are not speaking on behalf of all counselors or the profession.

Section D: Relationships with Other Professionals

INTRODUCTION.   Professional counselors recognize that the quality of their interactions with colleagues can influence the quality of services provided to clients. They work to become knowledgeable about colleagues within and outside the field of counseling. Counselors develop positive working relationships and systems of communication with colleagues to enhance services to clients.

D.1. RELATIONSHIPS WITH COLLEAGUES, EMPLOYERS, AND EMPLOYEES

D.1.a. *Different Approaches.*   Counselors are respectful of approaches to counseling services that differ from their own. Counselors are respectful of traditions and practices of other professional groups with which they work.

D.1.b. *Forming Relationships.*   Counselors work to develop and strengthen interdisciplinary relations with colleagues from other disciplines to best serve clients.

D.1.c. *Interdisciplinary Teamwork.*   Counselors who are members of interdisciplinary teams delivering multifaceted services to clients keep the focus on how to best serve the clients. They participate in and contribute to decisions that affect the well-being of clients by drawing on the perspectives, values, and experiences of the counseling profession and those of colleagues from other disciplines. (See A.1.a.)

D.1.d. *Confidentiality.*   When counselors are required by law, institutional policy, or extraordinary circumstances to serve in more than one role in judicial or administrative proceedings, they clarify role expectations and the parameters of confidentiality with their colleagues. (See B.1.c., B.1.d., B.2.c., B.2.d., B.3.b.)

D.1.e. *Establishing Professional and Ethical Obligations.*   Counselors who are members of interdisciplinary teams clarify professional and ethical obligations of the team as a whole and of its individual members. When a team decision raises ethical concerns, counselors first attempt to resolve the concern within the team. If they cannot reach resolution among team members, counselors pursue other avenues to address their concerns consistent with client well-being.

D.1.f. *Personnel Selection and Assignment.*   Counselors select competent staff and assign responsibilities compatible with their skills and experiences.

D.1.g. *Employer Policies.*   The acceptance of employment in an agency or institution implies that counselors are in agreement with its general policies and principles. Counselors strive to reach agreement with employers as to acceptable standards of conduct that allow for changes in institutional policy conducive to the growth and development of clients.

D.1.b.   Negative Conditions.   Counselors alert their employers of inappropriate policies and practices. They attempt to effect changes in such policies or procedures through constructive action within the organization. When such policies are potentially disruptive or damaging to clients or may limit the effectiveness of services provided and change cannot be effected, counselors take appropriate further action. Such action may include referral to appropriate certification, accreditation, or state licensure organizations, or voluntary termination of employment.

D.1.i.   Protection From Punitive Action.   Counselors take care not to harass or dismiss an employee who has acted in a responsible and ethical manner to expose inappropriate employer policies or practices.

D.2. CONSULTATION

D.2.a.   Consultant Competency.   Counselors take reasonable steps to ensure that they have the appropriate resources and competencies when providing consultation services. Counselors provide appropriate referral resources when requested or needed. (See C.2.a.)

D.2.b.   Understanding Consultees.   When providing consultation, counselors attempt to develop with their consultees a clear understanding of problem definition, goals for change, and predicted consequences of interventions selected.

D.2.c.   Consultant Goals.   The consulting relationship is one in which consultee adaptability and growth toward self-direction are consistently encouraged and cultivated.

D.2.d.   Informed Consent in Consultation.   When providing consultation, counselors have an obligation to review, in writing and verbally, the rights and responsibilities of both counselors and consultees. Counselors use clear and understandable language to inform all parties involved about the purpose of the services to be provided, relevant costs, potential risks and benefits, and the limits of confidentiality. Working in conjunction with the consultee, counselors attempt to develop a clear definition of the problem, goals for change, and predicted consequences of interventions that are culturally responsive and appropriate to the needs of consultees. (See A.2.a., A.2.b.)

Section E: Evaluation, Assessment, and Interpretation

INTRODUCTION.   Counselors use assessment instruments as one component of the counseling process, taking into account the client personal and cultural context. Counselors promote the well-being of individual clients or groups of clients by developing and using appropriate educational, psychological, and career assessment instruments.

E.1. GENERAL

E.1.a.   Assessment.   The primary purpose of educational, psychological, and career assessment is to provide measurements that are valid and reliable in either comparative or absolute terms. These include, but are not limited to, measurements of ability, personality, interest, intelligence, achievement, and performance. Counselors recognize the need to interpret the statements in this section as applying to both quantitative and qualitative assessments.

E.1.b.   Client Welfare.   Counselors do not misuse assessment results and interpretations, and they take reasonable steps to prevent others from misusing the information these techniques provide. They respect the client's right to know the results, the interpretations made, and the bases for counselors' conclusions and recommendations.

E.2. COMPETENCE TO USE AND INTERPRET ASSESSMENT INSTRUMENTS

E.2.a. ***Limits of Competence.***   Counselors utilize only those testing and assessment services for which they have been trained and are competent. Counselors using technology assisted test interpretations are trained in the construct being measured and the specific instrument being used prior to using its technology based application. Counselors take reasonable measures to ensure the proper use of psychological and career assessment techniques by persons under their supervision. (See A.12.)

E.2.b. ***Appropriate Use.***   Counselors are responsible for the appropriate application, scoring, interpretation, and use of assessment instruments relevant to the needs of the client, whether they score and interpret such assessments themselves or use technology or other services.

E.2.c. ***Decisions Based on Results.***   Counselors responsible for decisions involving individuals or policies that are based on assessment results have a thorough understanding of educational, psychological, and career measurement, including validation criteria, assessment research, and guidelines for assessment development and use.

E.3. INFORMED CONSENT IN ASSESSMENT

E.3.a. ***Explanation to Clients.***   Prior to assessment, counselors explain the nature and purposes of assessment and the specific use of results by potential recipients. The explanation will be given in the language of the client (or other legally authorized person on behalf of the client), unless an explicit exception has been agreed upon in advance. Counselors consider the client's personal or cultural context, the level of the client's understanding of the results, and the impact of the results on the client. (See A.2., A.12.g., F.1.c.)

E.3.b. ***Recipients of Results.***   Counselors consider the examinee's welfare, explicit understandings, and prior agreements in determining who receives the assessment results. Counselors include accurate and appropriate interpretations with any release of individual or group assessment results. (See B.2.c., B.5.)

E.4. RELEASE OF DATA TO QUALIFIED PROFESSIONALS.   Counselors release assessment data in which the client is identified only with the consent of the client or the client's legal representative. Such data are released only to persons recognized by counselors as qualified to interpret the data. (See B.1., B.3., B.6.b.)

E.5. DIAGNOSIS OF MENTAL DISORDERS

E.5.a. ***Proper Diagnosis.***   Counselors take special care to provide proper diagnosis of mental disorders. Assessment techniques (including personal interview) used to determine client care (e.g., locus of treatment, type of treatment, or recommended follow-up) are carefully selected and appropriately used.

E.5.b. ***Cultural Sensitivity.***   Counselors recognize that culture affects the manner in which clients' problems are defined. Clients' socioeconomic and cultural experiences are considered when diagnosing mental disorders. (See A.2.c.)

E.5.c.   ***Historical and Social Prejudices in the Diagnosis of Pathology.***   Counselors recognize historical and social prejudices in the misdiagnosis and pathologizing of certain individuals and groups and the role of mental health professionals in perpetuating these prejudices through diagnosis and treatment.

E.5.d.   ***Refraining From Diagnosis.***   Counselors may refrain from making and/or reporting a diagnosis if they believe it would cause harm to the client or others.

E.6. INSTRUMENT SELECTION

E.6.a.   ***Appropriateness of Instruments.***   Counselors carefully consider the validity, reliability, psychometric limitations, and appropriateness of instruments when selecting assessments.

E.6.b.   ***Referral Information.***   If a client is referred to a third party for assessment, the counselor provides specific referral questions and sufficient objective data about the client to ensure that appropriate assessment instruments are utilized. (See A.9.b., B.3.)

E.6.c.   ***Culturally Diverse Populations.***   Counselors are cautious when selecting assessments for culturally diverse populations to avoid the use of instruments that lack appropriate psychometric properties for the client population. (See A.2.c., E.5.b.)

E.7. CONDITIONS OF ASSESSMENT ADMINISTRATION.   (See A.12.b., A.12.d.)

E.7.a.   ***Administration Conditions.***   Counselors administer assessments under the same conditions that were established in their standardization. When assessments are not administered under standard conditions, as may be necessary to accommodate clients with disabilities, or when unusual behavior or irregularities occur during the administration, those conditions are noted in interpretation, and the results may be designated as invalid or of questionable validity.

E.7.b.   ***Technological Administration.***   Counselors ensure that administration programs function properly and provide clients with accurate results when technological or other electronic methods are used for assessment administration.

E.7.c.   ***Unsupervised Assessments.***   Unless the assessment instrument is designed, intended, and validated for self-administration and/or scoring, counselors do not permit inadequately supervised use.

E.7.d.   ***Disclosure of Favorable Conditions.***   Prior to administration of assessments, conditions that produce most favorable assessment results are made known to the examinee.

E.8. MULTICULTURAL ISSUES/DIVERSITY IN ASSESSMENT.   Counselors use with caution assessment techniques that were normed on populations other than that of the client. Counselors recognize the effects of age, color, culture, disability, ethnic group, gender, race, language preference, religion, spirituality, sexual orientation, and socioeconomic status on test administration and interpretation and place test results in proper perspective with other relevant factors. (See A.2.c., E.5.b.)

E.9. SCORING AND INTERPRETATION OF ASSESSMENTS

E.9.a.   ***Reporting.***   In reporting assessment results, counselors indicate reservations that exist regarding validity or reliability due to circumstances of the assessment or the inappropriateness of the norms for the person tested.

E.9.b.   *Research Instruments.*   Counselors exercise caution when interpreting the results of research instruments not having sufficient technical data to support respondent results. The specific purposes for the use of such instruments are stated explicitly to the examinee.

E.9.c.   *Assessment Services.*   Counselors who provide assessment scoring and interpretation services to support the assessment process confirm the validity of such interpretations. They accurately describe the purpose, norms, validity, reliability, and applications of the procedures and any special qualifications applicable to their use. The public offering of an automated test interpretations service is considered a professional-to-professional consultation. The formal responsibility of the consultant is to the consultee, but the ultimate and overriding responsibility is to the client. (See D.2.)

E.10. ASSESSMENT SECURITY.   Counselors maintain the integrity and security of tests and other assessment techniques consistent with legal and contractual obligations. Counselors do not appropriate, reproduce, or modify published assessments or parts thereof without acknowledgment and permission from the publisher.

E.11. OBSOLETE ASSESSMENTS AND OUTDATED RESULTS.   Counselors do not use data or results from assessments that are obsolete or outdated for the current purpose. Counselors make every effort to prevent the misuse of obsolete measures and assessment data by others.

E.12. ASSESSMENT CONSTRUCTION.   Counselors use established scientific procedures, relevant standards, and current professional knowledge for assessment design in the development, publication, and utilization of educational and psychological assessment techniques.

E.13. FORENSIC EVALUATION: EVALUATION FOR LEGAL PROCEEDINGS

E.13.a.   *Primary Obligations.*   When providing forensic evaluations, the primary obligation of counselors is to produce objective findings that can be substantiated based on information and techniques appropriate to the evaluation, which may include examination of the individual and/or review of records. Counselors are entitled to form professional opinions based on their professional knowledge and expertise that can be supported by the data gathered in evaluations. Counselors will define the limits of their reports or testimony, especially when an examination of the individual has not been conducted.

E.13.b.   *Consent for Evaluation.*   Individuals being evaluated are informed in writing that the relationship is for the purposes of an evaluation and is not counseling in nature, and entities or individuals who will receive the evaluation report are identified. Written consent to be evaluated is obtained from those being evaluated unless a court orders evaluations to be conducted without the written consent of individuals being evaluated. When children or vulnerable adults are being evaluated, informed written consent is obtained from a parent or guardian.

E.13.c.   *Client Evaluation Prohibited.*   Counselors do not evaluate individuals for forensic purposes they currently counsel or individuals they have counseled in the past. Counselors do not accept as counseling clients individuals they are evaluating or individuals they have evaluated in the past for forensic purposes.

E.13.d. Avoid Potentially Harmful Relationships.   Counselors who provide forensic evaluations avoid potentially harmful professional or personal relationships with family members, romantic partners, and close friends of individuals they are evaluating or have evaluated in the past.

Section F: Supervision, Training, and Teaching

INTRODUCTION.   Counselors aspire to foster meaningful and respectful professional relationships and to maintain appropriate boundaries with supervisees and students. Counselors have theoretical and pedagogical foundations for their work and aim to be fair, accurate, and honest in their assessments of counselors-in-training.

F.1. COUNSELOR SUPERVISION AND CLIENT WELFARE

F.1.a.   Client Welfare.   A primary obligation of counseling supervisors is to monitor the services provided by other counselors or counselors-in-training. Counseling supervisors monitor client welfare and supervisee clinical performance and professional development. To fulfill these obligations, supervisors meet regularly with supervisees to review case notes, samples of clinical work, or live observations. Supervisees have a responsibility to understand and follow the *ACA Code of Ethics*.

F.1.b.   Counselor Credentials.   Counseling supervisors work to ensure that clients are aware of the qualifications of the supervisees who render services to the clients. (See A.2.b.)

F.1.c.   Informed Consent and Client Rights.   Supervisors make supervisees aware of client rights including the protection of client privacy and confidentiality in the counseling relationship. Supervisees provide clients with professional disclosure information and inform them of how the supervision process influences the limits of confidentiality. Supervisees make clients aware of who will have access to records of the counseling relationship and how these records will be used. (See A.2.b., B.1.d.)

F.2. COUNSELOR SUPERVISION COMPETENCE

F.2.a.   Supervisor Preparation.   Prior to offering clinical supervision services, counselors are trained in supervision methods and techniques. Counselors who offer clinical supervision services regularly pursue continuing education activities including both counseling and supervision topics and skills. (See C.2.a., C.2.f.)

F.2.b.   Multicultural Issues/Diversity in Supervision.   Counseling supervisors are aware of and address the role of multiculturalism/diversity in the supervisory relationship.

F.3. SUPERVISORY RELATIONSHIPS

F.3.a.   Relationship Boundaries With Supervisees.   Counseling supervisors clearly define and maintain ethical professional, personal, and social relationships with their supervisees. Counseling supervisors avoid nonprofessional relationships with current supervisees. If supervisors must assume other professional roles (e.g., clinical and administrative supervisor, instructor) with supervisees, they work to minimize potential conflicts and explain to supervisees the expectations and responsibilities associated with each role. They do not engage in any form of nonprofessional interaction that may compromise the supervisory relationship.

F.3.b.   ***Sexual Relationships.***   Sexual or romantic interactions or relationships with current supervisees are prohibited.

F.3.c.   ***Sexual Harassment.***   Counseling supervisors do not condone or subject supervisees to sexual harassment. (See C.6.a.)

F.3.d.   ***Close Relatives and Friends.***   Counseling supervisors avoid accepting close relatives, romantic partners, or friends as supervisees.

F.3.e.   ***Potentially Beneficial Relationships.***   Counseling supervisors are aware of the power differential in their relationships with supervisees. If they believe nonprofessional relationships with a supervisee may be potentially beneficial to the supervisee, they take precautions similar to those taken by counselors when working with clients. Examples of potentially beneficial interactions or relationships include attending a formal ceremony; hospital visits; providing support during a stressful event; or mutual membership in a professional association, organization, or community. Counseling supervisors engage in open discussions with supervisees when they consider entering into relationships with them outside of their roles as clinical and/or administrative supervisors. Before engaging in nonprofessional relationships, supervisors discuss with supervisees and document the rationale for such interactions, potential benefits or drawbacks, and anticipated consequences for the supervisee. Supervisors clarify the specific nature and limitations of the additional role(s) they will have with the supervisee.

F.4. SUPERVISOR RESPONSIBILITIES

F.4.a.   ***Informed Consent for Supervision.***   Supervisors are responsible for incorporating into their supervision the principles of informed consent and participation. Supervisors inform supervisees of the policies and procedures to which they are to adhere and the mechanisms for due process appeal of individual supervisory actions.

F.4.b.   ***Emergencies and Absences.***   Supervisors establish and communicate to supervisees procedures for contacting them or, in their absence, alternative on-call supervisors to assist in handling crises.

F.4.c.   ***Standards for Supervisees.***   Supervisors make their supervisees aware of professional and ethical standards and legal responsibilities. Supervisors of postdegree counselors encourage these counselors to adhere to professional standards of practice. (See C.1.)

F.4.d.   ***Termination of the Supervisory Relationship.***   Supervisors or supervisees have the right to terminate the supervisory relationship with adequate notice. Reasons for withdrawal are provided to the other party. When cultural, clinical, or professional issues are crucial to the viability of the supervisory relationship, both parties make efforts to resolve differences. When termination is warranted, supervisors make appropriate referrals to possible alternative supervisors.

F.5. COUNSELING SUPERVISION EVALUATION, REMEDIATION, AND ENDORSEMENT

F.5.a.   ***Evaluation.***   Supervisors document and provide supervisees with ongoing performance appraisal and evaluation feedback and schedule periodic formal evaluative sessions throughout the supervisory relationship.

F.5.b.   ***Limitations.***   Through ongoing evaluation and appraisal, supervisors are aware of the limitations of supervisees that might impede performance. Supervisors assist supervisees in securing remedial assistance when needed. They recommend dismissal from training programs, applied counseling settings, or state or voluntary professional credentialing processes when those supervisees are unable to provide competent professional services. Supervisors seek consultation and document their decisions to dismiss or refer supervisees for assistance. They ensure that supervisees are aware of options available to them to address such decisions. (See C.2.g.)

F.5.c.   *Counseling for Supervisees.* If supervisees request counseling, supervisors provide them with acceptable referrals. Counselors do not provide counseling services to supervisees. Supervisors address interpersonal competencies in terms of the impact of these issues on clients, the supervisory relationship, and professional functioning. (See F.3.a.)

F.5.d.   *Endorsement.* Supervisors endorse supervisees for certification, licensure, employment, or completion of an academic or training program only when they believe supervisees are qualified for the endorsement. Regardless of qualifications, supervisors do not endorse supervisees whom they believe to be impaired in any way that would interfere with the performance of the duties associated with the endorsement.

F.6. RESPONSIBILITIES OF COUNSELOR EDUCATORS

F.6.a.   *Counselor Educators.* Counselor educators who are responsible for developing, implementing, and supervising educational programs are skilled as teachers and practitioners. They are knowledgeable regarding the ethical, legal, and regulatory aspects of the profession, are skilled in applying that knowledge, and make students and supervisees aware of their responsibilities. Counselor educators conduct counselor education and training programs in an ethical manner and serve as role models for professional behavior. (See C.1., C.2.a., C.2.c.)

F.6.b.   *Infusing Multicultural Issues/Diversity.* Counselor educators infuse material related to multiculturalism/diversity into all courses and workshops for the development of professional counselors.

F.6.c.   *Integration of Study and Practice.* Counselor educators establish education and training programs that integrate academic study and supervised practice.

F.6.d.   *Teaching Ethics.* Counselor educators make students and supervisees aware of the ethical responsibilities and standards of the profession and the ethical responsibilities of students to the profession. Counselor educators infuse ethical considerations throughout the curriculum. (See C.1.)

F.6.e.   *Peer Relationships.* Counselor educators make every effort to ensure that the rights of peers are not compromised when students or supervisees lead counseling groups or provide clinical supervision. Counselor educators take steps to ensure that students and supervisees understand they have the same ethical obligations as counselor educators, trainers, and supervisors.

F.6.f.   *Innovative Theories and Techniques.* When counselor educators teach counseling techniques/procedures that are innovative, without an empirical foundation, or without a well-grounded theoretical foundation, they define the counseling techniques/procedures as "unproven" or "developing" and explain to students the potential risks and ethical considerations of using such techniques/procedures.

F.6.g.   *Field Placements.* Counselor educators develop clear policies within their training programs regarding field placement and other clinical experiences. Counselor educators provide clearly stated roles and responsibilities for the student or supervisee, the site supervisor, and the program supervisor. They confirm that site supervisors are qualified to provide supervision and inform site supervisors of their professional and ethical responsibilities in this role.

F.6.b.   ***Professional Disclosure.***   Before initiating counseling services, counselors-in-training disclose their status as students and explain how this status affects the limits of confidentiality. Counselor educators ensure that the clients at field placements are aware of the services rendered and the qualifications of the students and supervisees rendering those services. Students and supervisees obtain client permission before they use any information concerning the counseling relationship in the training process. (See A.2.b.)

F.7. STUDENT WELFARE

F.7.a.   ***Orientation.***   Counselor educators recognize that orientation is a developmental process that continues throughout the educational and clinical training of students. Counseling faculty provide prospective students with information about the counselor education program's expectations:

1. the type and level of skill and knowledge acquisition required for successful completion of the training;
2. program training goals, objectives, and mission, and subject matter to be covered;
3. bases for evaluation;
4. training components that encourage self-growth or self-disclosure as part of the training process;
5. the type of supervision settings and requirements of the sites for required clinical field experiences;
6. student and supervisee evaluation and dismissal policies and procedures; and
7. up-to-date employment prospects for graduates.

F.7.b.   ***Self-Growth Experiences.***   Counselor education programs delineate requirements for self-disclosure or self-growth experiences in their admission and program materials. Counselor educators use professional judgment when designing training experiences they conduct that require student and supervisee self-growth or self-disclosure. Students and supervisees are made aware of the ramifications their self-disclosure may have when counselors whose primary role as teacher, trainer, or supervisor requires acting on ethical obligations to the profession. Evaluative components of experiential training experiences explicitly delineate predetermined academic standards that are separate and do not depend on the student's level of self-disclosure. Counselor educators may require trainees to seek professional help to address any personal concerns that may be affecting their competency.

F.8. STUDENT RESPONSIBILITIES

F.8.a.   ***Standards for Students.***   Counselors-in-training have a responsibility to understand and follow the *ACA Code of Ethics* and adhere to applicable laws, regulatory policies, and rules and policies governing professional staff behavior at the agency or placement setting. Students have the same obligation to clients as those required of professional counselors. (See C.1., H.1.)

F.8.b.   ***Impairment.***   Counselors-in-training refrain from offering or providing counseling services when their physical, mental, or emotional problems are likely to harm a client or others. They are alert to the signs of impairment, seek assistance for problems, and notify their program supervisors when they are aware that they are unable to effectively provide services. In addition, they seek appropriate professional services for themselves to remediate the problems that are interfering with their ability to provide services to others. (See A.1., C.2.d., C.2.g.)

F.9. EVALUATION AND REMEDIATION OF STUDENTS

F.9.a. **Evaluation.** Counselors clearly state to students, prior to and throughout the training program, the levels of competency expected, appraisal methods, and timing of evaluations for both didactic and clinical competencies. Counselor educators provide students with ongoing performance appraisal and evaluation feedback throughout the training program.

F.9.b. **Limitations.** Counselor educators, throughout ongoing evaluation and appraisal, are aware of and address the inability of some students to achieve counseling competencies that might impede performance. Counselor educators:

1. assist students in securing remedial assistance when needed,
2. seek professional consultation and document their decision to dismiss or refer students for assistance, and
3. ensure that students have recourse in a timely manner to address decisions to require them to seek assistance or to dismiss them and provide students with due process according to institutional policies and procedures. (See C.2.g.)

F.9.c. **Counseling for Students.** If students request counseling or if counseling services are required as part of a remediation process, counselor educators provide acceptable referrals.

F.10. ROLES AND RELATIONSHIPS BETWEEN COUNSELOR EDUCATORS AND STUDENTS

F.10.a. **Sexual or Romantic Relationships.** Sexual or romantic interactions or relationships with current students are prohibited.

F.10.b. **Sexual Harassment.** Counselor educators do not condone or subject students to sexual harassment. (See C.6.a.)

F.10.c. **Relationships With Former Students.** Counselor educators are aware of the power differential in the relationship between faculty and students. Faculty members foster open discussions with former students when considering engaging in a social, sexual, or other intimate relationship. Faculty members discuss with the former student how their former relationship may affect the change in relationship.

F.10.d. **Nonprofessional Relationships.** Counselor educators avoid nonprofessional or ongoing professional relationships with students in which there is a risk of potential harm to the student or that may compromise the training experience, or grades assigned. In addition, counselor educators do not accept any form of professional services, fees, commissions, reimbursement, or remuneration from a site for student or supervisee placement.

F.10.e. **Counseling Services.** Counselor educators do not serve as counselors to current students unless this is a brief role associated with a training experience.

F.10.f. **Potentially Beneficial Relationships.** Counselor educators are aware of the power differential in the relationship between faculty and students. If they believe a nonprofessional relationship with a student may be potentially beneficial to the student, they take precautions similar to those taken by counselors when working with clients. Examples of potentially beneficial interactions or relationships include, but are not limited to, attending a formal ceremony; hospital visits; providing support during a stressful event; or mutual membership in a professional association, organization, or community. Counselor educators engage in open discussions with students when they consider entering into relationships with students outside of their roles as teachers and supervisors. They discuss with students the rationale for such interactions, the potential benefits and drawbacks, and the anticipated consequences for the student. Educators clarify the specific nature and limitations of the additional role(s) they will have with the student prior to engaging in a nonprofessional relationship. Nonprofessional relationships with students should be time-limited and initiated with student consent.

F.11. MULTICULTURAL/DIVERSITY COMPETENCE IN COUNSELOR EDUCATION AND TRAINING PROGRAMS

F.11.a. Faculty Diversity.   Counselor educators are committed to recruiting and retaining a diverse faculty.

F.11.b. Student Diversity.   Counselor educators actively attempt to recruit and retain a diverse student body. Counselor educators demonstrate commitment to multicultural/ diversity competence by recognizing and valuing diverse cultures and types of abilities students bring to the training experience. Counselor educators provide appropriate accommodations that enhance and support diverse student well-being and academic performance.

F.11.c. Multicultural/Diversity Competence.   Counselor educators actively infuse multicultural/diversity competency in their training and supervision practices. They actively train students to gain awareness, knowledge, and skills in the competencies of multicultural practice. Counselor educators include case examples, role-plays, discussion questions, and other classroom activities that promote and represent various cultural perspectives.

Section G: Research and Publication

INTRODUCTION.   Counselors who conduct research are encouraged to contribute to the knowledge base of the profession and promote a clearer understanding of the conditions that lead to a healthy and more just society. Counselors support efforts of researchers by participating fully and willingly whenever possible. Counselors minimize bias and respect diversity in designing and implementing research programs.

G.1. RESEARCH RESPONSIBILITIES

G.1.a. Use of Human Research Participants.   Counselors plan, design, conduct, and report research in a manner that is consistent with pertinent ethical principles, federal and state laws, host institutional regulations, and scientific standards governing research with human research participants.

G.1.b. Deviation From Standard Practice.   Counselors seek consultation and observe stringent safeguards to protect the rights of research participants when a research problem suggests a deviation from standard or acceptable practices.

G.1.c.   Independent Researchers.   When independent researchers do not have access to an Institutional Review Board (IRB), they should consult with researchers who are familiar with IRB procedures to provide appropriate safeguards.

G.1.d.   Precautions to Avoid Injury.   Counselors who conduct research with human participants are responsible for the welfare of participants throughout the research process and should take reasonable precautions to avoid causing injurious psychological, emotional, physical, or social effects to participants.

G.1.e.   Principal Researcher Responsibility.   The ultimate responsibility for ethical research practice lies with the principal researcher. All others involved in the research activities share ethical obligations and responsibility for their own actions.

G.1.f.   Minimal Interference.   Counselors take reasonable precautions to avoid causing disruptions in the lives of research participants that could be caused by their involvement in research.

G.1.g.   Multicultural/Diversity Considerations in Research.   When appropriate to research goals, counselors are sensitive to incorporating research procedures that take into account cultural considerations. They seek consultation when appropriate.

G.2. RIGHTS OF RESEARCH PARTICIPANTS.   (See A.2, A.7.)

G.2.a.   Informed Consent in Research.   Individuals have the right to consent to become research participants. In seeking consent, counselors use language that:

1. accurately explains the purpose and procedures to be followed,
2. identifies any procedures that are experimental or relatively untried,
3. describes any attendant discomforts and risks,
4. describes any benefits or changes in individuals or organizations that might be reasonably expected,
5. discloses appropriate alternative procedures that would be advantageous for participants,
6. offers to answer any inquiries concerning the procedures,
7. describes any limitations on confidentiality,
8. describes the format and potential target audiences for the dissemination of research findings, and
9. instructs participants that they are free to withdraw their consent and to discontinue participation in the project at any time without penalty.

G.2.b.   Deception.   Counselors do not conduct research involving deception unless alternative procedures are not feasible and the prospective value of the research justifies the deception. If such deception has the potential to cause physical or emotional harm to research participants, the research is not conducted, regardless of prospective value. When the methodological requirements of a study necessitate concealment or deception, the investigator explains the reasons for this action as soon as possible during the debriefing.

G.2.c.   Student/Supervisee Participation.   Researchers who involve students or supervisees in research make clear to them that the decision regarding whether or not to participate in research activities does not affect one's academic standing or supervisory relationship. Students or supervisees who choose not to participate in educational research are provided with an appropriate alternative to fulfill their academic or clinical requirements.

G.2.d. ***Client Participation.***   Counselors conducting research involving clients make clear in the informed consent process that clients are free to choose whether or not to participate in research activities. Counselors take necessary precautions to protect clients from adverse consequences of declining or withdrawing from participation.

G.2.e. ***Confidentiality of Information.***   Information obtained about research participants during the course of an investigation is confidential. When the possibility exists that others may obtain access to such information, ethical research practice requires that the possibility, together with the plans for protecting confidentiality, be explained to participants as a part of the procedure for obtaining informed consent.

G.2.f. ***Persons Not Capable of Giving Informed Consent.***   When a person is not capable of giving informed consent, counselors provide an appropriate explanation to, obtain agreement for participation from, and obtain the appropriate consent of a legally authorized person.

G.2.g. ***Commitments to Participants.***   Counselors take reasonable measures to honor all commitments to research participants. (See A.2.c.)

G.2.h. ***Explanations After Data Collection.***   After data are collected, counselors provide participants with full clarification of the nature of the study to remove any misconceptions participants might have regarding the research. Where scientific or human values justify delaying or withholding information, counselors take reasonable measures to avoid causing harm.

G.2.i. ***Informing Sponsors.***   Counselors inform sponsors, institutions, and publication channels regarding research procedures and outcomes. Counselors ensure that appropriate bodies and authorities are given pertinent information and acknowledgment.

G.2.j. ***Disposal of Research Documents and Records.***   Within a reasonable period of time following the completion of a research project or study, counselors take steps to destroy records or documents (audio, video, digital, and written) containing confidential data or information that identifies research participants. When records are of an artistic nature, researchers obtain participant consent with regard to handling of such records or documents. (See B.4.a, B.4.g.)

G.3. RELATIONSHIPS WITH RESEARCH PARTICIPANTS (WHEN RESEARCH INVOLVES INTENSIVE OR EXTENDED INTERACTIONS)

G.3.a. ***Nonprofessional Relationships.***   Nonprofessional relationships with research participants should be avoided.

G.3.b. ***Relationships With Research Participants.***   Sexual or romantic counselor–research participant interactions or relationships with current research participants are prohibited.

G.3.c. ***Sexual Harassment and Research Participants.***   Researchers do not condone or subject research participants to sexual harassment.

G.3.d. ***Potentially Beneficial Interactions.***   When a nonprofessional interaction between the researcher and the research participant may be potentially beneficial, the researcher must document, prior to the interaction (when feasible), the rationale for such an interaction, the potential benefit, and anticipated consequences for the research participant.

Such interactions should be initiated with appropriate consent of the research participant. Where unintentional harm occurs to the research participant due to the nonprofessional interaction, the researcher must show evidence of an attempt to remedy such harm.

G.4. REPORTING RESULTS

G.4.a. ***Accurate Results.***   Counselors plan, conduct, and report research accurately. They provide thorough discussions of the limitations of their data and alternative hypotheses. Counselors do not engage in misleading or fraudulent research, distort data, misrepresent data, or deliberately bias their results. They explicitly mention all variables and conditions known to the investigator that may have affected the outcome of a study or the interpretation of data. They describe the extent to which results are applicable for diverse populations.

G.4.b. ***Obligation to Report Unfavorable Results.***   Counselors report the results of any research of professional value. Results that reflect unfavorably on institutions, programs, services, prevailing opinions, or vested interests are not withheld.

G.4.c. ***Reporting Errors.***   If counselors discover significant errors in their published research, they take reasonable steps to correct such errors in a correction erratum, or through other appropriate publication means.

G.4.d. ***Identity of Participants.***   Counselors who supply data, aid in the research of another person, report research results, or make original data available take due care to disguise the identity of respective participants in the absence of specific authorization from the participants to do otherwise. In situations where participants self-identify their involvement in research studies, researchers take active steps to ensure that data is adapted/changed to protect the identity and welfare of all parties and that discussion of results does not cause harm to participants.

G.4.e. ***Replication Studies.***   Counselors are obligated to make available sufficient original research data to qualified professionals who may wish to replicate the study.

G.5. PUBLICATION

G.5.a. ***Recognizing Contributions.***   When conducting and reporting research, counselors are familiar with and give recognition to previous work on the topic, observe copyright laws, and give full credit to those to whom credit is due.

G.5.b. ***Plagiarism.***   Counselors do not plagiarize, that is, they do not present another person's work as their own work.

G.5.c. ***Review/Republication of Data or Ideas.***   Counselors fully acknowledge and make editorial reviewers aware of prior publication of ideas or data where such ideas or data are submitted for review or publication.

G.5.d. ***Contributors.***   Counselors give credit through joint authorship, acknowledgment, footnote statements, or other appropriate means to those who have contributed significantly to research or concept development in accordance with such contributions. The principal contributor is listed first, and minor technical or professional contributions are acknowledged in notes or introductory statements.

G.5.e. ***Agreement of Contributors.***   Counselors who conduct joint research with colleagues or students/supervisees establish agreements in advance regarding allocation of tasks, publication credit, and types of acknowledgment that will be received.

G.5.f.   ***Student Research.***   For articles that are substantially based on students' course papers, projects, dissertations or theses, and on which students have been the primary contributors, they are listed as principal authors.

G.5.g.   ***Duplicate Submission.***   Counselors submit manuscripts for consideration to only one journal at a time. Manuscripts that are published in whole or in substantial part in another journal or published work are not submitted for publication without acknowledgment and permission from the previous publication.

G.5.h.   ***Professional Review.***   Counselors who review material submitted for publication, research, or other scholarly purposes respect the confidentiality and proprietary rights of those who submitted it. Counselors use care to make publication decisions based on valid and defensible standards. Counselors review article submissions in a timely manner and based on their scope and competency in research methodologies. Counselors who serve as reviewers at the request of editors or publishers make every effort to only review materials that are within their scope of competency and use care to avoid personal biases.

Section H: Resolving Ethical Issues

INTRODUCTION.   Counselors behave in a legal, ethical, and moral manner in the conduct of their professional work. They are aware that client protection and trust in the profession depend on a high level of professional conduct. They hold other counselors to the same standards and are willing to take appropriate action to ensure that these standards are upheld.

Counselors strive to resolve ethical dilemmas with direct and open communication among all parties involved and seek consultation with colleagues and supervisors when necessary. Counselors incorporate ethical practice into their daily professional work. They engage in ongoing professional development regarding current topics in ethical and legal issues in counseling.

H.1. STANDARDS AND THE LAW.   (See F.9.a.)

H.1.a.   ***Knowledge.***   Counselors understand the *ACA Code of Ethics* and other applicable ethics codes from other professional organizations or from certification and licensure bodies of which they are members. Lack of knowledge or misunderstanding of an ethical responsibility is not a defense against a charge of unethical conduct.

H.1.b.   ***Conflicts Between Ethics and Laws.***   If ethical responsibilities conflict with law, regulations, or other governing legal authority, counselors make known their commitment to the *ACA Code of Ethics* and take steps to resolve the conflict. If the conflict cannot be resolved by such means, counselors may adhere to the requirements of law, regulations, or other governing legal authority.

H.2. SUSPECTED VIOLATIONS

H.2.a.   ***Ethical Behavior Expected.***   Counselors expect colleagues to adhere to the *ACA Code of Ethics*. When counselors possess knowledge that raises doubts as to whether another counselor is acting in an ethical manner, they take appropriate action. (See H.2.b., H.2.c.)

H.2.b.   ***Informal Resolution.***   When counselors have reason to believe that another counselor is violating or has violated an ethical standard, they attempt first to resolve the issue informally with the other counselor if feasible, provided such action does not violate confidentiality rights that may be involved.

H.2.c. Reporting Ethical Violations.   If an apparent violation has substantially harmed, or is likely to substantially harm a person or organization and is not appropriate for informal resolution or is not resolved properly, counselors take further action appropriate to the situation. Such action might include referral to state or national committees on professional ethics, voluntary national certification bodies, state licensing boards, or to the appropriate institutional authorities. This standard does not apply when an intervention would violate confidentiality rights or when counselors have been retained to review the work of another counselor whose professional conduct is in question.

H.2.d. Consultation.   When uncertain as to whether a particular situation or course of action may be in violation of the *ACA Code of Ethics,* counselors consult with other counselors who are knowledgeable about ethics and the *ACA Code of Ethics,* with colleagues, or with appropriate authorities

H.2.e. Organizational Conflicts.   If the demands of an organization with which counselors are affiliated pose a conflict with the *ACA Code of Ethics,* counselors specify the nature of such conflicts and express to their supervisors or other responsible officials their commitment to the *ACA Code of Ethics.* When possible, counselors work toward change within the organization to allow full adherence to the *ACA Code of Ethics.* In doing so, they address any confidentiality issues.

H.2.f. Unwarranted Complaints.   Counselors do not initiate, participate in, or encourage the filing of ethics complaints that are made with reckless disregard or willful ignorance of facts that would disprove the allegation.

H.2.g. Unfair Discrimination Against Complainants and Respondents.   Counselors do not deny persons employment, advancement, admission to academic or other programs, tenure, or promotion based solely upon their having made or their being the subject of an ethics complaint. This does not preclude taking action based upon the outcome of such proceedings or considering other appropriate information.

H.3. COOPERATION WITH ETHICS COMMITTEES.   Counselors assist in the process of enforcing the *ACA Code of Ethics.* Counselors cooperate with investigations, proceedings, and requirements of the ACA Ethics Committee or ethics committees of other duly constituted associations or boards having jurisdiction over those charged with a violation. Counselors are familiar with the *ACA Policy and Procedures for Processing Complaints of Ethical Violations* and use it as a reference for assisting in the enforcement of the *ACA Code of Ethics.*

REFERENCES

Ackerman, N. W. (1966). *Treating the troubled family.* New York: Basic Books.

Adams, N., & Grieder, D. M. (2005). *Treatment planning for person-centered care: The road to mental health and addiction recovery.* Burlington, MA: Elsevier.

Administration on Aging (AOA). (2001). Community mental health services. Retrieved December 28, 2002, from http://www.aoa.dhhs.gov/mh/report2001/chapter2.html

Administration on Aging (AOA). (2008). *Profile of older Americans.* Washington, DC: Author.

Aguilera, D. C., & Messick, J. M. (1982). *Crisis intervention: Theory and methodology* (4th ed.). St. Louis, MO: Mosby.

Albee, G. W. (2000). Commentary on prevention in counseling psychology. *Counseling Psychologist, 28,* 845–853.

Albee, G. W., & Gullotta, T. P. (1997). *Primary prevention works.* Thousand Oaks, CA: Sage.

Albee, G. W., & Ryan-Finn, K. D. (1993). An overview of primary prevention. *Journal of Counseling and Development, 72,* 115–123.

Alcoholics Anonymous World Services, Inc. (2001). *AA fact sheet.* Grand Central Station, NY: Author.

Alexander, J., & Parsons, B. V. (1982). *Functional family therapy.* Pacific Grove, CA: Brooks/Cole.

Allport, G. W. (1954). *The nature of prejudice.* Reading, MA: Addison-Wesley.

Allport, G. W. (1955). *Becoming: Basic considerations for a psychology of personality.* New Haven, CT: Yale University Press.

Amato, P. R. (1993). Children's adjustment to divorce: Theories, hypotheses, and empirical support. *Journal of Marriage and the Family, 55,* 23–38.

American Association of State Counseling Boards. (2008). Retrieved January 5, 2008, from http://www.aascb.org

American Bar Association. (1980). *Standards relating to the rights of minors.* Cambridge, MA: Ballinger.

American Cancer Society. (2008). *Statistics for 2007.* Retrieved September 6, 2008, from http://www.cancer.org/

American College of Surgeons Committee on Trauma. (2006). *Resources for optimal care of the injured patient.* Chicago: ACS.

American Counseling Association. (2003). Counselor licensure legislation: Protecting the public. Retrieved May 4, 2003, from http://www.counseling.org/resources/licensure.htm

American Counseling Association. (2005). *ACA code of ethics.* Alexandria, VA: Author.

American Counseling Association. (2007). Retrieved January 5, 2008, from http://www.counseling.org

American Counseling Association Governing Council. (2005). *Policies and procedures for processing complaints of ethical violations.* Alexandria, VA: Author, July 1, 2008, from http://www.counseling.org

American Educational Research Association, American Psychological Association, and National Council on Measurement in Education. (1999). *Standards for educational and psychological testing* (2nd ed.). Washington, DC: American Educational Research Association.

American Humane Association: Children's Division. (1996). *Fact sheets.* Englewood, CO: Author.

American Mental Health Counselors Association. (2000). *Code of ethics of the American Mental Health Counselors Association—2000 revision.* Alexandria, VA: Author.

American Mental Health Counselors Association. (2009). Why use a mental health counselor? Retrieved February 19, 2009, from http://www.amhca.org/why/

American Psychiatric Association (APA). (1968). *Diagnostic and statistical manual of mental disorders* (2nd ed.). Washington, DC: Author.

American Psychiatric Association (APA). (2000). *Diagnostic and statistical manual of mental disorders* (4th ed., text rev.). Washington, DC: Author.

American Psychological Association. (2003). *Ethical principles of psychologists and code of conduct.* Washington DC: Author.

American Rehabilitation Counseling Association. (2008). *Mission* and *Scope of Practice.* Retrieved July 26, 2008, from http://www.arcaweb.org/

Ames, C. (1992). Classrooms: Goals, structures, and student motivation. *Journal of Educational Psychology, 84,* 261–271.

Amos, W. E., & Williams, D. E. (1972). *Community counseling: A comprehensive model for developmental services.* St. Louis, MO: Warren H. Green.

Amundson, N. E., Harris-Bowlsbey, J., & Niles, S. G. (2009). *Essential elements of career counseling: Processes and techniques* (2nd ed.). Upper Saddle River, NJ: Merrill/Pearson Education.

Anatasi, A., & Urbina, S. (1997). *Psychological testing* (7th ed.). Upper Saddle River, NJ: Prentice Hall.

Anderson, B. S. (1996). *The counselor and the law* (4th ed.). Alexandria, VA: American Counseling Association.

Anderson, C. E. (2000). Dealing constructively with managed care: Suggestions from an insider. *Journal of Mental Health Counseling, 22,* 343–353.

Anderson, D., & Swanson, C. D. (1994). *Legal issues in licensure.* Alexandria, VA: American Counseling Association.

Anderson, S. A., & Sabatelli, R. M. (2006). *Family interaction: A multigenerational developmental perspective* (4th ed.). Boston: Allyn & Bacon.

Andronico, M. P. (Ed.). (1996). *Men in groups: Insights, interventions, and psychoeducational work.* Washington, DC: American Psychological Association.

Apter, T. (1985). *Why women don't have wives.* New York: Schocken.

Armour, D. J. (1969). *The American counselor.* New York: Russell Sage.

Arredondo, P., Toporek, R., Brown, S., Jones, J., Locke, D. C., Sanchez, J., & Stadler, H. (1996). *Operationalization of the multicultural counseling competencies.* Alexandria, VA: Association for Multicultural Counseling and Development.

Art from the Heart. (2002, Fall/Winter). *The Circular* (Hospice and Palliative Care Center), *1,* 7.

Asarnow, J. R., Jaycox, L. H., & Tompson, M. C. (2001). Depression in youth: Psychosocial interventions. *Journal of Clinical Child Psychology, 30,* 33–45.

Association for Assessment in Counseling. (2003, January). *Applying the standards for educational and psychological testing—what a counselor needs to know.* Baltimore: Author.

Association for Specialists in Group Work (ASGW). (1990). *Standards for training group workers.* Alexandria, VA: Author.

Association for Specialists in Group Work (ASGW). (1992). Professional standards for the training of group workers. *Journal for Specialists in Group Work, 17,* 12–19.

Association for Specialists in Group Work (ASGW). (1998). *Best practice guidelines.* Alexandria, VA: Author.

Association for Specialists in Group Work (ASGW). (2000). *Professional standards for the training of group workers.* Alexandria, VA: Author.

Attie, I., & Brooks-Gunn, J. (1995). The development of eating regulation across the life span. In D. Cicchetti & D. J. Cohen (Eds.), *Developmental psychopathology, Vol. 2: Risk, disorder, & adaptation* (pp. 332–368). New York: Wiley.

Attkisson, C. C., & Greenfield, T. K. (1994). Client Satisfaction Questionnaire-8 and Service Satisfaction Scale-30. In M. Maruish (Ed.), *The use of psychological testing for treatment planning and outcome assessment* (pp. 402–422). Hillsdale, NJ: Erlbaum.

Attneave, C. (1982). American Indian and Alaskan native families: Emigrants in their own homeland. In M. McGoldrick, J. Pearce, & J. Giordano (Eds.), *Ethnicity and family therapy* (pp. 55–83). New York: Guilford Press.

Aubrey, R. F. (1977). Historical development of guidance and counseling and implications for the future. *Personnel and Guidance Journal, 55,* 288–295.

Aubrey, R. F. (1982). A house divided: Guidance and counseling in twentieth century America. *Personnel and Guidance Journal, 60,* 198–204.

Aubrey, R. F. (1983). The odyssey of counseling and images of the future. *Personnel and Guidance Journal, 61,* 78–82.

Austad, C. S., & Berman, W. H. (1991). Managed care and the evolution of psychotherapy. In C. S. Austad & W. H. Berman (Eds.), *Psychotherapy in managed health care: The optimal use of time and resources* (pp. 3–18). Washington, DC: American Psychological Association.

Austin, J. T. (1994). Minnesota Multiphasic Personality Inventory (MMPI–2). *Measurement* and Evaluation in Counseling and Development, 27, 178–185.

Avasthi, S. (1990). Native American students targeted for math and sciences. *Guidepost, 33*(6), 1, 6, 8.

Axelson, J. A. (1999). *Counseling and development in a multicultural society* (3rd ed.). Pacific Grove, CA: Brooks/Cole.

Aylmer, R. C. (1986). Bowen family systems marital therapy. In N. S. Jacobson & A. S. Gurman (Eds.), *Clinical handbook of marital therapy* (pp. 107–148). New York: Guilford Press.

Aylmer, R. C. (1988). The launching of the single young adult. In B. Carter & M. McGoldrick (Eds.), *The changing family life cycle* (2nd ed., pp. 191–208). New York: Gardner.

Bacon, S. F., Collins, M. J., & Plake, E. V. (2002). Does the global assessment of functioning assess functioning? *Journal of Mental Health Counseling, 24,* 202–212.

Bagheri, H., Memarian, R., & Alhani, F. (2007). Evaluation of the effect of group counselling on post myocardial infarction patients: Determined by an analysis of quality of life. *Journal of Clinical Nursing, 16*(2), 402–406.

Baird, B. N. (2008). *The internship, practicum, and field placement handbook: A guide for the helping professions* (5th ed.). Upper Saddle River, NJ: Prentice Hall.

Bandura, A. (1977a). Self-efficacy: Toward a unifying theory of behavioral change. *Psychological Review, 84,* 191–215.

Bandura, A. (1977b). *Social learning theory.* Upper Saddle River, NJ: Prentice Hall.

Bandura, A. (1986). *Social foundations of thought and action.* Upper Saddle River, NJ: Prentice Hall.

Barker, S. B. (2001). Counseling in medical settings. In D. C. Locke, J. E. Myers, & E. L. Herr (Eds.), *The handbook of counseling* (pp. 373–390). Thousand Oaks, CA: Sage.

Barkley, R. A. (1996). Attention deficit hyperactivity disorder. In E. J. Marsh & R. A. Barkley (Eds.), *Child psychopathology* (pp. 63–112). New York: Guilford Press.

Barkley, R. A. (1997). Behavioral inhibition, sustained attention, and executive functions: Constructing a unifying theory of ADHD. *Psychological Bulletin, 121,* 65–94.

Barkley, R. A. (2005). *Attention deficit hyperactivity disorder: A handbook for diagnosis and treatment* (3rd ed.). New York: Guilford Press.

Barnett, J. E. (1998). Confidentiality in the age of managed care. *The Clinical Psychologist, 51,* 30–33.

Barstow, S. (1998, June). Managed care debate heats up in Congress. *Counseling Today, 1,* 26.

Baruth, L. G., & Huber, C. H. (1985). *Counseling and psychotherapy.* Columbus, OH: Merrill.

Bauer, A. (2001). Responding to a community crisis: Frontline counseling. In E. R. Welfel & R. Elliott Ingersoll (Eds.), *The mental health desk reference* (pp. 239–245). New York: Wiley.

Bauman, S. S. M. (2002). Promoting parenting and child-rearing skills. In C. L. Juntenen & D. R. Atkinson (Eds.), *Counseling across the lifespan* (pp. 227–242). Thousand Oaks, CA: Sage.

Baumrind, D. (1971). Current patterns of parental authority. *Developmental Psychology Monographs, 4,* 1–103.

Baumrind, D. (1991). The influence of parenting style on adolescent competence and substance use. *Journal of Early Adolescence, 11,* 56–95.

Beamish, P. M., Granello, D. H., & Belcastro, A. L. (2002). Treatment of panic disorder: Practical guidelines. *Journal of Mental Health Counseling, 24,* 224–246.

Beck, A. T. (1976). *Cognitive therapy and the emotional disorders.* New York: International Universities.

Beck, J. S. (1995). *Cognitive therapy: Basics and beyond.* New York: Guilford Press.

Becvar, D. S., & Becvar, R. J. (2009). *Family therapy: A systematic integration* (7th ed.). Boston: Allyn & Bacon.

Beers, C. (1908). *A mind that found itself.* New York: Longman Green.

Belkin, G. S. (1984). *Introduction to counseling* (2nd ed.). Dubuque, IA: Wm. C. Brown.

Belson, R. (1992, September/October). Ten tried-and-true methods to achieve therapist burnout. *Family Therapy Networker, 22.*

Bemak, F. (1998, February 13). *Counseling at-risk students.* Presentation at Wake Forest University Institute for Ethics and Leadership in Counseling, Winston-Salem, NC.

Benjamin, A. (1987). *The helping interview* (4th ed.). Boston: Houghton Mifflin.

Bennett, J. B., & Lehman, W. E.-K. (Eds.). (2003). *Preventing workplace substance abuse: Beyond drug testing to wellness.* Washington, DC: American Psychological Association.

Benshoff, J. J. (1996). Peer self-help groups. In W. Crimando & T. F. Riggar (Eds.), *Utilizing community resources: An overview of human services* (pp. 57–66). Delray Beach, FL: St. Lucie Press.

Benshoff, J. J., & Janikowski, T. P. (2000). *The rehabilitation model of substance abuse counseling.* Belmont, CA: Wadsworth.

Berecz, J. M., & Helm, H. W., Jr. (1998). Shame: The underside of Christianity. *Journal of Psychology and Christianity, 17*(1), 5–14.

Bergin, A. E. (1985). Proposed values for guiding and evaluating counseling and psychotherapy. *Counseling and Values, 29,* 99–115.

Bergin, A. E. (1992). Three contributions of a spiritual perspective to counseling, psychotherapy, and behavior change. In M. T. Burke & J. G. Miranti (Eds.), *Ethical and spiritual values in counseling* (pp. 5–15). Alexandria, VA: American Counseling Association.

Bergman, J. (2000). Creating new cultures: Using drama therapy to build therapeutic communities in prisons. In P. Lewis & D. R. Johnson (Eds.), *Current approaches to drama therapy* (pp. 303– 330). Springfield, IL: Charles C Thomas.

Berk, L. E. (2001). *Development through the lifespan* (2nd ed.). Needham Heights, MA: Allyn & Bacon.

Berk, L. E. (2007). *Development through the lifespan* (4th ed.). Boston: Pearson Allyn & Bacon.

Betz, N. E. (1992). Career assessment: A review of critical issues. In S. D. Brown & R. W. Lent (Eds.), *Handbook of counseling psychology* (2nd ed., pp. 453–484). New York: Wiley.

Birmaher, B., Ryan, N. D., & Williamson, D. E. (1996). Depression in children and adolescents: Clinical features and pathogenesis. In K. Shulman, M. Tohen, & S. P. Kutcher (Eds.), *Mood disorders across the life span* (pp. 51–82). New York: Wiley.

Birren, J. E., & Schaie, K. W. (Eds.). (2002). *Handbook of the psychology of aging* (5th ed.). New York: Academic Press.

Bisio, T. A., & Crisan, P. (1984). Stress management and nuclear anxiety: A structured group experience. *Journal of Counseling and Development, 63,* 108–109.

Bjorklund, D. F. (2000). *Children's thinking: Developmental function and individual differences* (3rd ed.). Belmont, CA: Wadsworth.

Black, C. (1981). *It will never happen to me.* Denver: M.A.C. Printing.

Black, J., & Underwood, J. (1998). Young, female, and gay: Lesbian students and the school environment. *Professional School Counseling, 1,* 15–21.

Blair-Loy, M. (2003). *Competing devotions: Career and family among women executives.* Cambridge, MA: Harvard University Press.

Blatter, C. W., & Jacobsen, J. J. (1993). Older women coping with divorce: Peer support groups. *Women and Therapy, 14,* 141–154.

Blazer, D. (2002). *Depression in late life* (3rd ed.). New York: Springer.

Bloom, M. (1996). *Primary prevention practices.* Thousand Oaks, CA: Sage.

Boeree, C. G. (2002). *General psychology: Limbic system.* Retrieved August 24, 2008, from http://webspace.ship.edu/cgboer/limbicsystem.html

Boeree, C. G. (2003). *General psychology: Neurotransmitters.* Retrieved August 24, 2008, from http://webspace.ship.edu/cgboer/genpsyneurotransmitters.html

Bolles, R. N. (2008). *What color is your parachute? 2008: A practical manual for job-hunters and career-changers.* Berkeley, CA: Ten Speed Press.

Bolles, R. N., & Nelson, J. E. (2007). *What color is your parachute?* Berkeley, CA: Ten Speed Press.

Bolton, R. (1979). *People skills: How to assert yourself, listen to others, and resolve conflicts.* Upper Saddle River, NJ: Prentice Hall.

Borgen, W. A. (1997). People caught in changing career opportunities: A counseling perspective. *Journal of Employment Counseling, 34,* 133–143.

Borrell-Carrió, F., Suchman, A. L., & Epstein, R. M. (2004). The biopsychosocial model

25 years later: Principles, practice, and scientific inquiry. *Annals of Family Medicine, 2,* 576–582.

Boszormenyi-Nagy, I. (1987). *Foundations of contextual therapy.* New York: Brunner/Mazel.

Bowen, G. L., & Orthner, D. (1990). *The organization family: Work and family linkages in the U.S. military.* New York: Praeger.

Bowen, M. (1976). Theory in the practice of psychotherapy. In P. J. Guerin, Jr. (Ed.), *Family therapy: Theory and practice* (pp. 42–90). New York: Gardner Press.

Bowen, M. (1978). *Family therapy in clinical practice.* New York: Jason Aronson.

Bowen, M. (1994). *Family therapy in clinical practice.* New York: Jason Aronson.

Boyatzis, R., McKee, A., & Goleman, D. (2002). Reawakening your passion for work. *Harvard Business Review, 80,* 86–93.

Bradley, L. J. (1995). Certification and licensure issues. *Journal of Counseling and Development, 74,* 185–186.

Bradt, J. O. (1988). Becoming parents: Families with young children. In B. Carter & M. McGoldrick (Eds.), *The changing family life cycle* (2nd ed.; pp. 235–254). New York: Gardner.

Brammer, L. M. (1985). *The helping relationship: Process and skills* (3rd ed.). Upper Saddle River, NJ: Prentice Hall.

Brammer, L. M. (1993). *The helping relationship* (5th ed.). Boston: Allyn & Bacon.

Brandt, R. (1959). *Ethical theory.* Upper Saddle River, NJ: Prentice Hall.

Braun, S. A., & Cox, J. A. (2005). Managed mental health care: Intentional misdiagnosis of mental disorders. *Journal of Counseling and Development, 83,* 425–433.

Brewer, J. M. (1932). *Education as guidance.* New York: Macmillan.

Briggs, M. K. (2008, April). *Consult, consult, consult! A collaborative approach to working through ethical dilemmas using the 2005 ACA Code of Ethics.* Workshop presentation at Wake Forest University, Winston-Salem, NC.

Bringaze, T. B., & White, L. J. (2001). Living out proud: Factors contributing to healthy identity development in lesbian leaders. *Journal of Mental Health Counseling, 23,* 162–173.

Brinson, J. A. (1996). Cultural sensitivity for counselors: Our challenge for the twenty-first century. *Journal of Humanistic Education and Development, 34,* 195–206.

Bristow-Braitman, A. (1995). Addiction recovery: 12-step programs and cognitive-behavioral psychology. *Journal of Counseling and Development, 73,* 414–418.

Broderick, P. C., & Blewitt, P. (2006). *The life span: Human development for helping professionals* (2nd ed.). Upper Saddle River, NJ: Prentice Hall.

Bronfenbrenner, U. (1979). *The ecology of human development.* Cambridge, MA: Harvard University Press.

Bronfenbrenner, U. (1989). Ecological systems theory. In R. Vasta (Ed.), *Six theories of child development: Revised formulations and current issues* (pp. 187–249). London: Jessica Kingsley.

Bronfenbrenner, U. (1995). The bioecological model from a life course perspective: Reflections of a participant observer. In P. Moen, G. H. Elder, & K. Luscher (Eds.), *Examining lives in context: Perspectives on the ecology of human development* (pp. 599–647). Washington, DC: American Psychological Association.

Broverman, I., Broverman, D., Clarkson, F., Rosenkrantz, P., & Vogel, S. (1970). Sex role stereotypes and clinical judgments of mental health. *Journal of Consulting and Clinical Psychology, 34,* 1–7.

Browers, R. T. (2005). Counseling in mental health and private practice settings. In D. Capuzzi & D. R. Gross (Eds.), *Introduction to the counseling profession* (4th ed., pp. 357–380). Needham Heights, MA: Pearson/Allyn & Bacon.

Brown, D. (2007). *Career information, career counseling, and career development* (9th ed.). Boston: Pearson/Allyn & Bacon.

Brown, M. B. (2000). Diagnosis and treatment of children and adolescents with attention-deficit hyperactivity disorder. *Journal of Counseling and Development, 78,* 195–203.

Brown, N. M. (1990). Men nurturing men. *Family Therapy Networker, 14,* 11.

Brown, N. W. (2007). *Psychoeducational groups: Process and practice* (2nd ed.). Philadelphia: Taylor and Francis (Kindle Edition).

Brown, S., & Lewis, V. M. (1999). *The alcoholic family in recovery: A developmental model.* New York: Guilford Press.

Bruff v. North Mississippi Health Services, Inc., 244F.3d 495 (5th Cir. 2001).

Bruscia, K. E. (1987). *Improvisational models of music therapy.* Springfield, IL: Charles C. Thomas.

Bubenzer, D. L., Zimpfer, D. G., & Mahrle, C. L. (1990). Standardized individual appraisal in agency and private practice: A survey. *Journal of Mental Health Counseling, 12,* 51–66.

Bumpass, L. L., & Sweet, J. A. (1989). Children's experience in single-parent families: Implications of cohabitation and marital transitions. *Family Planning Perspectives, 21,* 256–260.

Bunch, B. J., Lund, N. L., & Wiggins, F. K. (1983). Self-disclosure and perceived closeness in the development of group process. *Journal for Specialists in Group Work, 8,* 59–66.

Burch, M. A., & Skovholt, T. M. (1982). Counseling services and men in need: A problem in person-environment matching. *AMHCA Journal, 4,* 89–96.

Burck, H. D., & Peterson, G. W. (1975). Needed: More evaluation, not research. *Personnel and Guidance Journal, 53,* 563–569.

Burke, M. T., Chauvin, J. C., & Miranti, J. G. (2005). *Religious and spiritual issues in counseling: Applications across diverse populations.* New York: Brunner-Routledge.

Burke, M. T., Hackeny, H., Hudson, P., Miranti, J., Watts, G. A., & Epp, L. (1999). Spirituality, religion, and CACREP curriculum standards. *Journal of Counseling and Development, 77,* 251–257.

Burlew, L. (1992, Winter). My job, my mind. *American Counselor, 1,* 24–27.

Butcher, J. N., Dahlstrom, W. G., Graham, J. R., Tellegen, A., & Kaemmer, B. (1989). *Minnesota Multiphasic Personality Inventory-2 (MMPI-2): Manual for administration and scoring.* Minneapolis: University of Minnesota Press.

Butler, K. (1994, July/August). Duty of care. *Family Therapy Networker, 18,* 10–11.

Cadwallader, E. H. (1991). Depression and religion: Realities, perspectives, and directions. *Counseling & Values, 35,* 83-92.

Calhoun, G. B., Bartolomucci, C. L., & McLean, B. A. (2005). Building connections: Relational group work with female adolescent offenders. *Women & Therapy, 28*(2), 17–29.

Calhoun, G. B., Glaser, B. A., & Bartolomucci, C. L. (2001). The juvenile counseling and assessment model and program: A conceptualization and intervention for juvenile delinquency. *Journal of Counseling and Development, 79,* 131–141.

Calvo, G. (1975). *Marriage encounter: Official national manual.* St. Paul, MN: Marriage Encounter.

Cameron, S., & turtle-song, i. (2002). Learning to write case notes using the SOAP format. *Journal of Counseling and Development, 80,* 286–292.

Campbell, R. E., & Cellini, J. V. (1980). Adult career development. *Counseling and Human Development, 12,* 1–8.

Canaff, A. L. (1997). Later life career planning: A new challenge for career counselors. *Journal of Employment Counseling, 34,* 85–93.

Caplan, G. (1964). *Principles of preventive psychiatry.* New York: Basic Books.

Capuzi, D., & Gross, D. R. (2004). Prevention: An overview. In D. Capuzzi & D. R. Gross (Eds.). *Youth at risk: A prevention resource for counselors, teachers, and parents* (4th ed.). Alexandria, VA: American Counseling Association.

Carkhuff, R. R. (1969). *Helping and human relations.* New York: Holt, Rinehart & Winston.

Carkhuff, R. R. (1972). *The art of helping.* Amherst, MA: Human Resource Development Press.

Carlson, J., & Ardell, D. B. (1988). Physical fitness as a pathway to wellness and effective counseling. In R. Hayes & R. Aubrey (Eds.), *New directions for counseling and human development* (pp. 383– 396). Denver: Love.

Carroll, L., Gilroy, P. J., & Ryan, J. (2002). Counseling transgendered, transsexual, and gender-variant clients. *Journal of Counseling and Development, 80,* 131–139.

Carroll, M., Bates, M. M., & Johnson, C. D. (2004). *Group leadership: Strategies for group counseling leaders* (4th ed.). Denver: Love.

Carroll, M. R., & Levo, L. (1985). The association for specialists in group work. *Journal for Counseling and Development, 63,* 453–454.

Carter, B., & McGoldrick, M. (Eds.). (2005). *Expanded family life cycle: Individual, family, and social perspectives* (3rd ed.). Boston: Allyn & Bacon.

Carter, R. T. (1990). The relationship between racism and racial identity among white Americans: An exploratory investigation. *Journal of Counseling and Development, 69,* 46–50.

Casas, J. M. (2005). Race and racism: The efforts of counseling psychology to understand and address the issues associated with these terms. *The Counseling Psychologist, 33,* 501–512.

Casey, J. A. (2000). Managing technology wisely: A new counselor competency. In J. W. Bloom & G. R. Walz (Eds.), *Cybercounseling and cyberlearning: Strategies and resources for the new millennium* (pp. 17–28). Alexandria, VA: American Counseling Association.

Casey, J. A. (2001). Counseling and technology. In D. Capuzzi & D. R. Gross (Eds.), *Introduction to the counseling profession* (3rd ed.; pp. 106–120). Needham Heights, MA: Allyn & Bacon.

Cashwell, C. S., & Young, J. S. (Eds.). (2005). *Integrating spirituality and religion into counseling: A guide to competent practice.* Alexandria, VA: American Counseling Association.

Cass, V. C. (1979). Homosexual identity formation: A theoretical model. *Journal of Homosexuality, 4,* 219–235.

Cass, V. C. (1984). Homosexual identity formation: A concept in need of definition. *Journal of Homosexuality, 10,* 105–126.

Catalano, S. (2007). *Intimate partner violence in the United States.* [Electronic copy]. Retrieved June 21, 2007, from http://www.ojp.usdoj.gov/bjs/pub/pdf/ipvus.dpd. Washington, DC: U.S. Department of Justice, Bureau of Justice Statistics.

Center for Credentialing and Education. (2008). Retrieved January 4, 2008, from http://www.cce-global.org

Centers for Disease Control (CDC). (2006). *Understanding intimate partner violence.* Retrieved August 25, 2008, from http://www.cdc.gov/injury

Chen-Hayes, S. F. (2000). Social justice advocacy with lesbian, bisexual, gay and transgendered persons. In J. Lewis & L. Bradley (Eds.), *Advocacy in counseling: Counselors, clients, and community* (pp. 89–98). Greensboro, NC: ERIC/CASS.

Cheung, F. K. (1991). The use of mental health services by ethnic minorities. In H. F. Myers, P. Wholford, L. P. Guzman, & R. J. Echemendia (Eds.), *Ethnic minority perspectives on clinical training and services in psychology* (pp. 23–31). Washington, DC: American Psychological Association.

Child Welfare Information Gateway. (2008). *Child abuse and neglect statistics.* Retrieved August 3, 2008, from http://www.childwelfare.gov/systemwide/statistics/can.cfm

Child Welfare League of America. (2008). *Child, youth, and family development: Childhood depression.* Retrieved July 29, 2008, from http://www.cwla.org/programs/health/healthtipschilddepression.htm

Childers, G. H., Jr., & Burcky, W. D. (1984). The jogging group: A positive-wellness strategy. *AMHCA Journal, 6,* 118–125.

Childers, J. H., Jr., & Couch, R. D. (1989). Myths about group counseling: Identifying and challenging misconceptions. *Journal for Specialists in Group Work, 14,* 105–111.

Chisholm, J. F. (1999). The sandwich generation. *Journal of Social Distress and the Homeless, 8,* 177–191.

Chope, R. C. (2006). *Family matters: The influence of the family in career decision making.* Austin, TX: Pro-Ed.

Chung, R., C.-Y. (2005). Women, human rights, and counseling: Crossing international boundaries. *Journal of Counseling & Development, 83,* 262–268.

Chung, R. C.-Y., & Bemak, F. (2002). The relationship of culture and empathy in cross-cultural counseling. *Journal of Counseling and Development, 80,* 154–159.

Chung, Y. B., & Baird, M. K. (1999). Physical exercise as a counseling intervention. *Journal of Mental Health Counseling, 21,* 124–135.

Cicero, J. K. (2007). *Waking up alone: Grief and healing.* Bloomington, IN: AuthorHouse.

Clark, W. (2003, November/December). Substance abuse and evidence-based family interventions. *Family Therapy Magazine, 2*(6), 15–19.

Cohen, J., Marecek, J., & Gillham, J. (2006). Is three a crowd? Clients, clinicians, and managed care. *American Journal of Orthopsychiatry, 76,* 251–259.

Cohen, M. N. (1998, April 17). Culture, not race, explains human diversity. *Chronicle of Higher Education,* B4–B5.

Colangelo, N. (1985). Overview. *Elementary School Guidance and Counseling, 19,* 244–245.

Colangelo, N., & Pulvino, C. J. (1980). Some basic concerns in counseling the elderly. *Counseling and Values, 24,* 68–73.

Coleman, H. L. K. (1998). General and multicultural counseling competency: Apples and oranges? *Journal of Multicultural Counseling and Development, 26,* 147–156.

Collie, K. R., Mitchell, D., & Murphy, L. (2000). Skills for online counseling: Maximum impact at minimum bandwidth. In J. W. Bloom & G. R. Walz (Eds.), *Cybercounseling and cyberlearning: Strategies and resources for the new millennium* (pp. 219–236). Alexandria, VA: American Counseling Association.

Collison, B. B. (1981). Counseling adult males. *Personnel and Guidance Journal, 60,* 219–222.

Compas, B. E. (1987). Stress and life events during childhood and adolescence. *Clinical Psychology Review, 7,* 275–302.

Conners, C. K. (1996). *Conners' Rating Scales—Revised.* Minneapolis: Pearson Assessments.

Conners, C. K. (2008). *Conners Third Edition.* Los Angeles: Western Psychological Services.

Conyne, R. K. (1991). Gains in primary prevention: Implications for the counseling profession. *Journal of Counseling and Development, 69,* 277–279.

Conyne, R. K. (2000). Prevention in counseling psychology: At long last, has the time now come? *Counseling Psychologist, 28,* 838–844.

Cook, E. P. (Ed.). (1993). *Women, relationships, and power: Implications for counseling.* Alexandria, VA: American Counseling Association.

Cook, E. P., Heppner, M. J., & O'Brien, K. M. (2002). Career development of women of color and White women: Assumptions, conceptualizations, and interventions from an ecological perspective. *Career Development Quarterly, 50,* 291–305.

Cooper, C. C., & Gottlieb, M. C. (2000). Ethical issues with managed care: Challenges facing counseling psychology. *The Counseling Psychologist, 28,* 179–236.

Corazzini, J. G., Williams, K., & Harris, S. (1987). Group therapy for adult children of alcoholics: Case studies. *Journal for Specialists in Group Work, 12,* 156–161.

Corey, G. (2008). *Theory and practice of group counseling* (7th ed.). Belmont, CA: Thomson/Brooks/Cole.

Corey, G. (2009). *The art of integrative counseling* (2nd ed.). Belmont, CA: Brooks/Cole.

Corey, G., & Corey, M. S. (2005). *I never knew I had a choice* (8th ed.). Belmont, CA: Thomson/Brooks/Cole.

Corey, G., Corey, M. S., & Callanan, P. (1998). *Issues and ethics in the helping professions* (5th ed.). Pacific rove, CA: Brooks/Cole.

Corey, G., Corey, M. S., & Callanan, P. (2007). *Issues and ethics in the helping professions* (7th ed.). Belmont, CA: Brooks/Cole.

Corey, M. S., & Corey, G. (2006). *Groups: Process and practice* (7th ed.). Belmont, CA: Thomson/Brooks/Cole.

Cormier, L. S., & Hackney, H. (2008). *Counseling strategies and interventions* (7th ed.). Boston: Pearson/Allyn & Bacon.

Cormier, W. H., & Cormier, L. S. (1998). *Interviewing strategies for helpers: Fundamental skills and cognitive behavioral interventions* (4th ed.). Pacific Grove, CA: Brooks/Cole.

Corsini, R. J. (2008). Introduction. In R. J. Corsini & D. Wedding (Eds.), *Current psychotherapies* (8th ed., pp. 1–13). Belmont, CA: Thomson Brooks/Cole

Corsini, R. J., & Wedding, D. (Eds.). (2008). *Current psychotherapies* (8th ed.). Belmont, CA: Thompson Brooks/Cole.

Costa, L., & Altekruse, M. (1994). Duty-to-warn guidelines for mental health counselors. *Journal of Counseling and Development, 72,* 346–350.

Cottone, R. R., & Claus, R. E. (2000). Ethical decision-making models: A review of the literature. *Journal of Counseling and Development, 78,* 275–283.

Cottone, R. R., & Tarvydas, V. M. (2007). *Counseling ethics and decision making* (3rd ed.). Upper Saddle River, NJ: Merrill/Prentice Hall.

Council for Accreditation of Counseling and Related Educational Programs. (2008). *Directory of accredited programs.* Retrieved July 5, 2008, from http://www.cacrep.org/directory

Council for Accreditation of Counseling and Related Educational Programs. (2009). *CACREP standards.* Retrieved August 31, 2008, from http://www.cacrep.org/2009standards.html

Council on Licensure, Enforcement and Regulation (CLEAR). (1993). *The directory of professional and occupational regulation in the United States and Canada.* Lexington, KY: Author.

Counselors for Social Justice. (2007). CSJ mission statement. Retrieved July 28, 2008, from http://www.counselorsforsocialjustice.com/

Courtois, C. A. (1988). *Healing the incest wound: Adult survivors in therapy.* New York: Norton.

Courtois, C. A. (1999). *Recollections of sexual abuse: Treatment principles and guidelines.* New York: Norton.

Courtois, C. A., & Leehan, J. (1982). Group treatment for grown-up abused children. *Personnel and Guidance Journal, 60,* 564–566.

Cousins, N. (1979). *Anatomy of an illness.* New York: Norton.

Cowan, E. W., & Presbury, J. H. (2000). Meeting client resistance and reactance with reverence. *Journal of Counseling and Development, 78,* 411–419.

Cowger, E. L., Hinkle, J. S., DeRidder, L. M., & Erk, R. R. (1991). CACREP community counseling programs: Present status and implications for the future. *Journal of Mental Health Counseling, 13,* 172–186.

Cox, B. J., & Waller, L. L. (1991). *Bridging the communication gap with the elderly.* Chicago: American Hospital Association.

Cox, H. G. (1985). *Later life: The realities of aging.* Upper Saddle River, NJ: Prentice Hall.

Crawford, R. L. (1994). *Avoiding counselor malpractice.* Alexandria, VA: American Counseling Association.

Crockett, L. J., & Crouter, A. C. (1995). Pathways through adolescence: An overview. In L. J. Crockett & A. C. Crouter (Eds.), *Pathways through adolescence* (pp. 1–12). Mahwah, NJ: Erlbaum.

Crodzki, L. (2002, May/June). Practice strategies. *Family Therapy Magazine, 1,* 43–44.

Csikszenmihalyi, M. (1996). *Creativity: Flow and the psychology of discovery and invention.* New York: Harper

Cuellar, I. (2000). Acculturation and mental health: Ecological transactional relations of adjustment. In I. Cuellar & F. A. Paniagua (Eds.), *Handbook of multicultural mental health: Assessment and treatment of diverse populations* (pp. 45–62). New York: Academic Press.

Curran, D. (1985). *Stress and the healthy family.* San Francisco: Harper & Row.

D'Andrea, M., & Daniels, J. (2001). Facing the changing demographic structure of our society. In D. C. Locke, J. E. Myers, & E. L. Herr (Eds.), *The handbook of counseling* (pp. 529–540). Thousand Oaks, CA: Sage.

D'Andrea, M., & Heckman, E. F. (2008). Contributing to the ongoing evolution of the multicultural counseling movement: An introduction to the special issue. *Journal of Counseling & Development, 86,* 259–260.

Daniels, J. A. (2001). Managed care, ethics, and counseling. *Journal of Counseling and Development, 79,* 119–122.

Daniels, J. A. (2002). Assessing threats of school violence: Implications for counselors. *Journal of Counseling and Development, 80,* 215–218.

Daniluk, J. C., & Haverkamp, B. E. (1993). Ethical issues in counseling adult survivors of incest. *Journal of Counseling and Development, 72,* 16–22.

Danzinger, P. R., & Welfel, E. R. (2001). *Journal of Mental Health Counseling, 23,* 137–150.

Darden, C. A., Gazda, G. M., & Ginter, E. J. (1996). Life-skills and mental health counseling. *Journal of Mental Health Counseling, 18,* 134–141.

Darling, N., & Steinberg, L. (1993). Parenting style as context: An integrative model. *Psychological Bulletin, 188,* 487–496.

Darling-Fisher, C. S., & Tiedje, L. B. (1990). The impact of maternal employment characteristics on fathers' participation in child care. *Family Relations, 39,* 20–26.

Dasenbrook, N. C., & Walsh, R. (2007). *The complete guide to private practice for licensed mental health professionals* (4th ed.). Rockford, IL: Crysand Press.

Davenport, D. S., & Yurich, J. M. (1991). Multicultural gender issues. *Journal of Counseling and Development, 70,* 64–71.

Davis, H. V. (1988). *Frank Parsons: Prophet, innovator, counselor.* Carbondale: University of Southern Illinois Press.

Davis, R. F., & Borns, N. E. (1999). *Solo dad survival guide: Raising your kids on your own.* New York: NTC/Contemporary Publishing.

Davis, S. R., & Meier, S. T. (2001). *The elements of managed care.* Belmont, CA: Wadsworth.

DeAngelis, T. (1992, November). Best psychological treatment for many men: Group therapy. *APA Monitor, 23,* 31.

Degges-White, S., Rice, B., & Myers, J. E. (2000). Revisiting Cass's theory of sexual identity formation: A study of lesbian development. *Journal of Mental Health Counseling, 22,* 318–333.

Del Campo, R. L., Del Campo, D. S., & Gorman, D. (2002). Employee assistance: Some background and employment opportunities. *Annals of the American Psychotherapy Association, 5,* 15–17.

DePauw, M. E. (1986). Avoiding ethical violations: A timeline perspective for individual counseling. *Journal of Counseling and Development, 64,* 303–305.

Derogatis, L. R. (1993). *The Brief Symptom Inventory (BSI): Administration, scoring, and procedures.* Minneapolis, MN: Pearson Assessments.

Derogatis, L. R. (1994). *The SCL-90-R: Administration, scoring and procedures manual* (3rd ed.). Minneapolis, MN: Pearson Assessments.

Derogatis, L. R., & Lazarus, L. (1994). SCL-90-R, Brief Symptom Inventory, and Matching Clinical Rating Scales. In M. Maruish (Ed.), *The use of psychological testing for treatment planning and outcome assessment* (pp. 217–248). Hillsdale, NJ: Erlbaum.

deShazer, S. (1991). *Putting differences to work.* New York: Norton.

Devine, E. C. (2003). Meta-analysis of the effect of psychoeducational interventions on pain in adults with cancer. *Ontological Nursing Forum, 30*(1), 75–89.

Dinkmeyer, D. C., & Muro, J. J. (1979). *Group counseling: Theory and practice* (2nd ed.). Itasca, IL: F. E. Peacock.

Doan, R. E., & Scherman, A. (1987). The therapeutic effect of physical fitness on measures of personality: A literature review. *Journal of Counseling and Development, 66,* 28–36.

Doherty, W. J., Lester, M. E., & Leigh, G. (1986). Marriage encounter weekends: Couples who win and couples who lose. *Journal of Marital and Family Therapy, 12,* 49–61.

Donigian, J. (1994, Fall). Group reflections. *Together, 23,* 6.

Donigian, J., & Hulse-Killacky, D. (1999). *Critical incidents in group therapy* (2nd ed.). Pacific Grove, CA: Brooks/Cole.

Dorn, F. J. (1984). The social influence model: A social psychological approach to counseling. *Personnel and Guidance Journal, 62,* 342–345.

Dougherty, A. M. (2008). *Psychological consultation and collaboration in school and community settings* (5th ed.). Belmont, CA: Brooks/Cole.

Doweiko, H. E. (2009). *Concepts of chemical dependency* (7th ed.). Belmont, CA: Brooks/Cole, Cengage Learning.

Dreikurs, R. R., & Mosak, H. H. (1966). The task of life. I: Adler's three tests. *Individual Psychologist, 4,* 18–22.

Drummond, R. J., & Ryan, C. W. (1995). *Career counseling: A development approach.* Upper Saddle River, NJ: Merrill/Prentice Hall.

Duffy, K. G., & Wong, F. Y. (2003). *Community psychology* (3rd ed.). Needham Heights, MA: Allyn & Bacon.

Duffy, M. (Ed.). (1999). *Handbook of counseling and psychotherapy with older adults.* New York: Wiley.

Duggan, M. H., & Jurgens, J. C. (2007). *Career interventions and techniques: A complete guide for human service professionals.* Boston: Pearson/Allyn & Bacon.

Duhl, B. S. (1983). *From the inside out and other metaphors.* New York: Brunner/Mazel.

Dunn, W. (1993). *The baby bust: A generation comes of age.* New York: American Demographic Books.

Dyer, W. W., & Vriend, J. (1977). *Counseling techniques that work.* New York: Funk & Wagnalls.

Eccles, J. S., Lord, S., & Midgley, C. (1991). What are we doing to early adolescents? The impact of educational contexts on early adolescents. *American Journal of Education, 44,* 521–542.

Eccles, J. S., Midgley, C., Wigfield, A., Buchanan, C. M., Reuman, D., Flanagan, C., & MacIver, D.

(1993). Development during adolescence: The impact of stage–environment fit on young adolescents' experiences in schools and families. *American Psychologist, 48,* 90–101.

Eccles, J. S., Wigfield, A., & Schiefele, U. (1998). Motivation to succeed. In N. Eisenberg (Ed.), *Handbook of child psychology: Vol. 3. Social, emotional, and personality development* (5th ed., pp. 1017–1095). New York: Wiley.

Edwards, D., Burnard, P., Coyle, D., Fothergill, A., & Hannigan, B. (2000). Stress and burnout in community mental health nursing: A review of the literature. *Journal of Psychiatric and Mental Health Nursing, 7,* 7–14.

Edwards, J. H. (2002). Evidence-based treatment for child ADHD: "Real-world" practice implications. *Journal of Mental Health Counseling, 24,* 126–139.

Egan, G. (2007). *The skilled helper* (8th ed.). Belmont, CA: Thomson/Brooks/Cole.

Elkind, D. (1984). *All grown up and no place to go: Teenagers in crisis.* Reading, MA: Addison-Wesley.

Ellis, A. (1980). *Rational humorous songs: A garland of rational songs.* New York: Institute of Rational Emotive Therapy.

Ellis, A. (1988). *How to stubbornly refuse to make yourself miserable about anything— yes, anything!* Secaucus, NJ: Lyle Stuart.

Ellis, A. (1999). Rational Emotive Behavior Therapy and Cognitive Behavior Therapy for elderly people. *Journal of Rational- Emotive & Cognitive-Behavior Therapy, 17*(1), 5–18.

Ellis, A. (2000). Rational–emotive behavior in marriage and family therapy. In A. M. Horne (Ed.), *Family counseling and therapy* (3rd ed., pp. 489–514). Itasca, IL: F. E. Peacock.

Ellis, A., & Dryden, W. (Eds.). (2007). *The practice of rational emotive behavior therapy* (2nd ed.). New York: Springer.

Ellis, A., & MacLaren, C. (1999). *Rational emotive behavior therapy: A therapist's guide.* New York: Impact Publishers.

Ellis, A., Sichel, J. L., Yeager, R. J., DiMattia, D. J., & DiGiuseppe, R. (1989). *Rational- emotive couples therapy.* New York: Pergamon Press.

Employee Assistance Professionals Association (EAPA). Retrieved August 16, 2008, from http://www.eapassn.org

Engel, G. (1977). The need for a new medical model. *Science, 196,* 129–136.

Engels, D. W., Minor, C. W., Sampson, J. P., Jr., & Splete, H. H. (1995). Career counseling specialty: History, development, and prospect. *Journal of Counseling and Development, 74,* 134–138.

English, A., & Kenney, K. E. (2003). *State minor consent laws: A summary* (2nd ed.). Chapel Hill, NC: Center for Adolescent Health and the Law.

Enns, C. Z. (1993). Twenty years of feminist counseling and therapy. *Counseling Psychologist, 21,* 3–87.

Enns, C. Z. (1996). Counselors and the backlash: "Rape hype" and "false-memory syndrome." *Journal of Counseling and Development, 74,* 358–367.

Enns, C. Z., & Hackett, G. (1993). A comparison of feminist and nonfeminist women's and men's reactions to nonsexist and feminist counseling: A replication and extension. *Journal of Counseling and Development, 71,* 499–509.

Epp, L. R. (1998). The courage to be an existential counselor: An interview with Clemmont E. Vontress. *Journal of Mental Health Counseling, 20,* 1–12.

Erdman, P., & Lampe, R. (1996). Adapting basic skills to counsel children. *Journal of Counseling and Development, 74,* 374–377.

Erickson, M. (1954). Special techniques of brief hypnotherapy. *Journal of Clinical and Experimental Hypnosis, 2,* 109–129.

Erikson, E. H. (1959). *Identity and the life cycle: Psychological issues.* New York: International Universities Press.

Erikson, E. H. (1963). *Childhood and society* (2nd ed.). New York: Norton.

Erikson, E. H. (1968). *Identity: Youth and crisis.* New York: Norton.

Erk, R. R. (2008). *Counseling treatment for children and adolescents with DSM-IV-TR disorders* (2nd ed.), Upper Saddle River, NJ: Pearson Education.

Erkel, R. T. (1990, May/June). The birth of a movement. *Family Therapy Networker, 14,* 26–35.

Evans, K. M., Kincade, E. A., Marbley, A. F., & Seem, S. R. (2005). Feminism and feminist therapy: Lessons from the past and hopes for the future. *Journal of Counseling and Development, 83,* 269–277.

Everly, G. S., & Mitchell, J. T. (n.d.). *A primer on Critical Incident Stress Management (CISM).* Retrieved August 1, 2008, from http://www.icisf.org/

Exner, J. E. (1995). Why use personality tests? A brief historical view. In J. N. Butcher (Ed.), *Clinical personality assessment: Practical approaches* (pp. 10–18). New York: Oxford University Press.

Ezell, M. (2001). *Advocacy in the human services.* Belmont, CA: Wadsworth.

Falkner, J., & Starkey, D. (2009). Counseling lesbian, gay, bisexual, transgender, and questioning clients. In D. Capuzzi & D. R. Gross (Eds.), *Introduction to the counseling profession* (5th ed., pp. 501–529). Boston: Pearson/Allyn & Bacon.

Families and Work Institute. (2008). Retrieved August 17, 2008, from http://www.familiesandwork.org

Farmer, S. (1990). *Adult children of abusive parents: a healing program for those who have been physically, sexually, or emotionally abused.* New York: Ballantine Books.

Faustman, W. O. (1994). Brief psychiatric rating scale. In M. Maruish (Ed.), *The use of psychological testing for treatment planning and outcome assessment* (pp. 371–401). Hillsdale, NJ: Erlbaum.

Figley, C. R. (1989). *Helping traumatized families.* San Francisco: Jossey-Bass.

Firestone, R. W., & Firestone, L. A. (1998). Voices in suicide: The relationship between self-destructive thought processes, maladaptive behavior, and self-destructive manifestations. *Death Studies, 22,* 411–433.

First Line. (2001). *Directory of community resources.* Winston-Salem, NC: United Way of Forsyth County, NC.

Flavell, J. H. (1985). *Cognitive development* (2nd ed.). Upper Saddle River, NJ: Prentice Hall.

Foliart, D. E., Clausen, M., & Siljestrom, C. (2001). Bereavement practices among California hospices: Results of a statewide survey. *Death Studies, 25,* 461–467.

Fong, M. L. (1995). Assessment and *DSM-IV* diagnosis of personality disorders: A primer for counselors. *Journal of Counseling and Development, 73,* 635–639.

Fong, M. L., & Silien, K. A. (1999). Assessment and diagnosis of *DSM-IV* anxiety disorders. *Journal of Counseling and Development, 77,* 209–217.

Foos, J. A., Ottens, A. J., & Hill, L. K. (1991). Managed mental health: A primer for counselors. *Journal of Counseling and Development, 69,* 332–336.

Ford, D., & Urban, H. (1963). *Systems of psychotherapy: A comparative study.* New York: Wiley.

Forester-Miller, H., & Davis, T. D. (1998). *A practitioner's guide to ethical decision making.* Alexandria, VA: American Counseling Association. Retrieved July 1, 2008, from http://www.counseling.org/Counselors/PractitionersGuide.aspx

Forsyth, D. R. (2006). *Group dynamics* (4th ed.). Belmont, CA: Thomson/Wadsworth.

Foster, S. (1996). October is National Disability Employment Awareness Month. *Counseling Today, 39*(4), 18.

Fouad, N. A. (2007). Work and vocational psychology: Theory, research, and applications. *Annual Review of Psychology, 58*(5), 1–22.

Fox, M. (1994). *The reinvention of work: A new vision of livelihood for our time.* San Francisco: Harper.

Frankl, V. (1962). *Man's search for meaning: An introduction to logo-therapy.* New York: Washington Square Press.

Freemont, S., & Anderson, W. (1986). What client behaviors make counselors angry? An exploratory study. *Journal of Counseling and Development, 65,* 67–70.

Freund, P., & Seligman, M. (1982). Group jogging and emotionally disturbed clients. *Journal for Specialists in Group Work, 7,* 194–198.

Frey, D. H. (1972). Conceptualizing counseling theories. *Counselor Education and Supervision, 11,* 243–250.

Fujiura, G. T. (2001). Emerging trends in disability. *Population Today, 29,* 9–10.

Gary, J. M., & Remolino, L. (2000). Coping with loss and grief through online support groups. In J. W. Bloom & G. R. Walz (Eds.), *Cybercounseling and cyberlearning: Strategies and resources for the new millennium* (pp. 95–114). Alexandria, VA: American Counseling Association.

Gazda, G. M. (1989). *Group counseling: A developmental approach* (4th ed.). Boston: Allyn & Bacon.

Gazda, G. M., Balzer, F. J., Childers, W. C., Nealy, A., Phelps, R. E., & Walters, R. P. (2005). *Human relations development: A manual for educators* (7th ed.). Boston: Allyn & Bacon.

Gazda, G. M., Ginter, E. J., & Horne, A. M. (2001). *Theory and practice of group psychotherapy*. Boston: Allyn & Bacon.

Geertz, C. (1973). *The interpretation of cultures*. New York: Basic Books.

Gerig, M. S. (2007). *Foundations for mental health and community counseling: An introduction to the profession*. Upper Saddle River, NJ: Merrill/Prentice Hall.

Gerler, E. R., Jr. (1980). Physical exercise and multimodal counseling groups. *Journal for Specialists in Group Work, 5,* 157–162.

Gertner, D. M. (1994). Understanding and serving the needs of men. *Counseling and Human Development, 27,* 1–16.

Gibson, D. M., & Myers, J. E. (2000). Gender and infertility: A relational approach to counseling women. *Journal of Counseling and Development, 78,* 400–410.

Gilbert, L. A. (1985). *Men in dual-career families: Current realities and future prospects*. Hillsdale, NJ: Erlbaum.

Gilbert, R. M. (2006). *The eight concepts of Bowen theory*. Falls Church, VA: Leading Systems Press.

Giles, T. A. (1983). Counseling services and men in need: A response to Burch and Skovholt. *AMHCA Journal, 5,* 39–43.

Gill, J. G., & Barry, R. A. (1982). Group focused counseling: Classifying the essential skills. *Personnel and Guidance Journal, 60,* 302–305.

Gilligan, C. (1982). *In a different voice: Psychological theory and women's development*. Cambridge, MA: Harvard University Press.

Ginter, E. J. (1999). David K. Brooks' contribution to the developmentally based life-skills approach. *Journal of Mental Health Counseling, 21,* 191–202.

Ginter, E. J. (2001). Private practice: The professional counselor. In D. C. Locke, J. E. Myers, & E. L. Herr (Eds.), *The handbook of counseling* (pp. 355– 372). Thousand Oaks, CA: Sage.

Ginzberg, E. (1972). Toward a theory of occupational choice: A restatement. *Vocational Guidance Quarterly, 20,* 169–176.

Gladding, S. T. (1973). Reality sits in a green-cushioned chair. *Personnel and Guidance Journal, 54,* 222.

Gladding, S. T. (1974). Without applause. *Personnel and Guidance Journal, 52,* 586.

Gladding, S. T. (1975). Autumn storm. *Personnel and Guidance Journal 54,* 149.

Gladding, S. T. (1978). In the midst of the puzzles and counseling journey. *Personnel and Guidance Journal, 57,* 148.

Gladding, S. T. (1979). A restless presence: Group process as a pilgrimage. *The School Counselor, 27,* 126–127.

Gladding, S. T. (1984). Bittersweet. *Counseling and Values, 28,* 146.

Gladding, S. T. (1990). Coming full cycle: Reentry after the group. *Journal for Specialists in Group Work, 15,* 130–131.

Gladding, S. T. (1995). Humor in counseling: Using a natural resource. *Journal of Humanistic Education and Development, 34,* 3–12.

Gladding, S. T. (2004). *Counseling as an art: The creative arts in counseling* (3rd ed.). Alexandria, VA: American Counseling Association.

Gladding, S. T. (2006). *The counseling dictionary: Concise definitions of frequently used terms*. Upper Saddle River, NJ: Prentice Hall.

Gladding, S. T. (2007). *Family therapy: History, theory, and practice* (4th ed.). Upper Saddle River, NJ: Prentice Hall.

Gladding, S. T. (2008). *Group work: A counseling specialty* (5th ed.). Upper Saddle River, NJ: Prentice Hall.

Gladstein, G. A., & Apfel, F. S. (1987). A theoretically based adult career counseling center. *Career Development Quarterly, 36,* 178–185.

Glosoff, H. L. (1992). Accrediting and certifying professional counselors. *Guidepost, 34*(12), 6–8.

Glosoff, H. L. (1997). Multiple relationships in private practice. In B. Herlihy & G. Corey (Eds.), *Boundary issues in counseling* (pp. 114–120). Alexandria, VA: American Counseling Association.

Glosoff, H. L. (1998). Managed care: A critical ethical issue for counselors. *Counseling and Human Development, 31,* 1–16.

Glosoff, H. L. (2001, November). *Ethical practice in a complex era: Clients' rights, counselors' responsibilities.* Workshop presentation at Wake Forest University, Winston-Salem, NC.

Glosoff, H. L., Garcia, J., Herlihy, B., & Remley, T. P. (1999). Managed care: Ethical considerations for counselors. *Counseling and Values, 44,* 8–16.

Glosoff, H. L., Herlihy, B., & Spence, E. B. (2000). Privileged communication in the counselor–client relationship. *Journal of Counseling and Development, 78,* 454–462.

Goeller, G. (2004). *Coming of age with aging parents.* Spokane, WA: Patina.

Gold, J., & Pitariu, G. V. (2004). Opening the eyes of counselors to the emotional abuse of men: An overlooked dynamic in dysfunctional families. *Journal of Humanistic Counseling, Education and Development, 43,* 178–187.

Goldberg, J. R. (1992, August). The new frontier: Marriage and family therapy with aging families. *Family Therapy News, 23,* 1, 14, 21.

Golden, G. K., & Frank, P. B. (1994). When 50-50 isn't fair: The case against couple counseling in domestic abuse. *Social Work, 39,* 636–637.

Goldenberg, H., & Goldenberg, I. (2008). *Counseling today's families* (7th ed.). Belmont, CA: Thomson/Brooks/Cole.

Goldin, E., & Bordan, T. (1999). The use of humor in counseling: The laughing cure. *Journal of Counseling and Development, 77,* 405–410.

Goldin, E., & Mohr, R. (2000). Issues and techniques for counseling long-term, later-life couples. *The Family Journal, 8,* 229–235.

Goldman, L. (1972a). Introduction. *Personnel and Guidance Journal, 51,* 85.

Goldman, L. (1990). Qualitative assessment. *The Counseling Psychologist, 18,* 205–213.

Goldstein, A. (1971). *Psychotherapeutic attraction.* New York: Pergamon.

Good, G. E., & Brooks, G. R. (2005). *The new handbook of psychotherapy and counseling with men: a comprehensive guide to settings, problems, and treatment approaches* (Rev. ed.). Hoboken, NJ: Wiley.

Goodman, J. E., Schlossberg, N. K., & Anderson, M. (2006). *Counseling adults in transition: Linking practice with theory* (3rd ed.). New York: Springer.

Goodyear, R. K. (1981). Termination as a loss experience for the counselor. *Personnel and Guidance Journal, 59,* 349–350.

Goodyear, R. K. (1984). On our journal's evolution: Historical developments, transitions, and future directions. *Journal of Counseling and Development, 63,* 3–9.

Goodyear, R. K., & Bradley, F. O. (1980). The helping process as contractual. *Personnel and Guidance Journal, 58,* 512–515.

Gormley, J., & Hussey, J. (2005). Exercise therapy: Prevention and treatment of disease. Boston: Wiley-Blackwell

Gottfredson, G. D., & Holland, J. L. (1996). *Dictionary of Holland occupational codes* (3rd ed.). Odessa, FL: Psychological Assessment Resources.

Gottman, J., & Silver, N. (2000). *The seven principles of making marriage work.* New York: Three Rivers Press.

Granello, D. H., & Granello, P. F. (2007). *Suicide: An essential guide for helping professionals and editors.* Boston: Allyn & Bacon.

Granello, P. F. (2000). Historical context: The relationship of computer technologies and counseling. In J. W. Bloom & G. R. Walz (Eds.), *Cybercounseling and cyberlearning: Strategies and resources for the new millennium* (pp. 3–16). Alexandria, VA: American Counseling Association.

Granello, P. F., & Witmer, J. M. (1998). Standards of care: Potential implications for the counseling profession. *Journal of Counseling and Development, 76,* 371–380.

Grant, B. (1992). The moral nature of psychotherapy. In M. T. Burke & J. G. Miranti (Eds.), *Ethical and spiritual values in counseling* (pp. 27–35). Alexandria, VA: American Counseling Association.

Greenan, D. E., & Tunnell, G. (2003). *Couple therapy with gay men.* New York: Guilford Press.

Guerney, B. (1977). *Relationship enhancement.* San Francisco: Jossey-Bass.

Guindon, M. H., & Hanna, F. J. (2002). Coincidence, happenstance, serendipity, fate, or the hand of God: Case studies in synchronicity. *Career Development Quarterly, 50,* 195–208.

Gullotta, T., Adams, G., & Alexander, S. (1998). *Today's marriages and families: A wellness approach*. Pacific Grove, CA: Brooks/Cole.

Gurman, A., & Kniskern, D. (1981). Family therapy outcome research: Knowns and unknowns. In A. Gurman & D. Kniskern (Eds.), *Handbook of family therapy* (pp. 742–775). New York: Brunner/Mazel.

Gysbers, N. C., Heppner, J. A., & Johnston, J. A. (2003). *Career counseling: Process, issues, & techniques* (2nd ed.). Boston: Allyn & Bacon.

Hackney, H., & Cormier, L. S. (1996). *The professional counselor* (4th ed.). Boston: Allyn & Bacon.

Hackney, H., & Wrenn, C. G. (1990). The contemporary counselor in a changed world. In H. Hackney (Ed.), *Changing contexts for counselor preparation in the 1990s* (pp. 1–20). Alexandria, VA: Association for Counselor Education and Supervision.

Haddock, S. A. (2002). Training family therapists to assess for and intervene in partner abuse: A curriculum for graduate courses, professional workshops, and self-study. *Journal of Marital and Family Therapy, 28,* 193–202.

Hadley, R. G., & Mitchell, L. K. (1995). *Counseling research and program evaluation*. Pacific Grove, CA: Brooks/Cole.

Haight, B. K., & Haight, B. S. (2007). *The handbook of structured life review*. Baltimore: Health Professions Press.

Haight, B. K., Michel, Y., & Hendrix, K. (1998). Life review: Preventing despair in newly relocated nursing home residents: Short- and long-term effects. *International Journal of Aging and Human Development, 47,* 119–142.

Haley, J. (1973). *Uncommon therapy*. New York: Norton.

Haley, J. (1980). *Leaving home: The therapy of disturbed young people*. New York: McGraw-Hill.

Haley, M. (2004). Risk and protective factors. In D. Capuzzi (Ed.), *Suicide across the life span: Implications for counselors* (pp. 95–138). Alexandria, VA: American Counseling Association.

Haley, M., & Vasquez, J. (2009). Technology and counseling. In D. Capuzzi & D. R. Gross (Eds.), *Introduction to the counseling profession* (5th ed., pp. 156–186). Boston: Pearson/Allyn & Bacon.

Hall, L. K. (2008). *Counseling military families: What mental health professionals need to know*. New York: Routledge/Taylor & Francis Group.

Hamachek, D. E. (1988). Evaluating self-concept and ego development within Erikson's psychosocial framework: A formulation. *Journal of Counseling and Development, 66,* 354–360.

Hampson, R. B., Beavers, W. R., & Hulgus, Y. (1990). Cross-ethnic family differences: Interactional assessment of white, black, and Mexican-American families. *Journal of Marital and Family Therapy, 16,* 307–319.

Hampton, D. (2002). *Grief counseling: It's all about loss*. Unpublished manuscript.

Hanna, C. A., Hanna, F. J., Giordano, F. G., & Tollerud, T. (1998). Meeting the needs of women in counseling: Implications of a review of the literature. *Journal of Humanistic Education and Development, 36,* 160–170.

Hansen, J. C., & Prather, F. (1980). The impact of values and attitudes in counseling the aged. *Counseling and Values, 24,* 74–85.

Hansen, J. C., Rossberg, R. H., & Cramer, S. H. (1994). *Counseling: Theory and process* (5th ed.). Boston: Allyn & Bacon.

Hansen, J. C., Warner, R. W., & Smith, E. J. (1980). *Group counseling* (2nd ed.). Chicago: Rand McNally.

Hansen, S. M. H., Heims, M. L., Julian, D. J., & Sussman, M. B. (Eds.). (1994). *Single parent families* New York: Haworth.

Harding, A. K., Gray, L. A., & Neal, M. (1993). Confidentiality limits with clients who have HIV: A review of ethical and legal guidelines and professional policies. *Journal of Counseling and Development, 71,* 297–304.

Hare-Mustin, R. T. (1983). An appraisal of the relationship between women and psychotherapy. *American Psychologist, 38,* 593–599.

Harold, M. (1985). Council's history examined after 50 years. *Guidepost, 27*(10), 4.

Harper, E. (2007). *A review of the literature pertaining to the effects of religious rejection on the mental health of lesbian, gay, and bisexual individuals*. Unpublished manuscript.

Harper, E., & Varner, K. (2008). *Counseling concerns of lesbian, gay, and bisexual university students*. Unpublished manuscript.

Harris, A. H. S., Thoresen, C. E., & Lopez, S. J. (2007). Integrating positive psychology into counseling: Why and (when appropriate) how. *Journal of Counseling & Development, 85,* 3–13.

Harris-Bowlsbey, J. (1992, December). Building blocks of computer-based career planning systems. *CAPS Digest,* EDO-CG-92-7.

Hart, A., & Weber, C. H. (2002). *A woman's guide to overcoming depression.* Grand Rapids, MI: Revell.

Hartung, P. J., & Blustein, D. L. (2002). Reason, intuition, and social justice: Elaborating on Parsons' career decision-making model. *Journal of Counseling and Development, 80,* 41–47.

Hattie, J. A., Myers, J. E., & Sweeney, T. J. (2004). A factor structure of wellness: Theory, assessment, analysis, and practice. *Journal of Counseling and Development, 82,* 354–364.

Havighurst, R. J. (1959). Social and psychological needs of the aging. In L. Gorlow & W. Katkovsky (Eds.), *Reading in the psychology of adjustment* (pp. 443–447). New York: McGraw-Hill.

Havighurst, R. J. (1972). *Developmental tasks and education* (3rd ed.). New York: David McKay.

Hazelden. (2008). *What is treatment like at Hazelden and how is it done?* Retrieved September 8, 2008, from http://www.hazelden .org/web/public/faqtreatment.page

Hay, C. E., & Kinnier, R. T. (1998). Homework in counseling. *Journal of Mental Health Counseling, 20,* 122–132.

Hayes, C. (2001). Choosing the right path. *Black Enterprise, 31,* 108–112.

Hayes, P. A. (1996). Addressing the complexities of culture and gender in counseling. *Journal of Counseling and Development, 74,* 332–338.

Hayes, R. L. (1984, March). Report on community counseling. *ACES Newsletter,* 15.

Henderson, P. A. (1997). Psychosocial adjustment of adult cancer survivors: Their needs and counselor interventions. *Journal of Counseling and Development, 75,* 188–194.

Henderson, S. J. (2000). "Follow your bliss": A process for career happiness. *Journal of Counseling and Development, 78,* 305–315.

Henggeler, S. W., Schoenwald, S. K., Borduin, C. M., Rowland, M. D., & Cunningham, P. B. (1998). *Multisystemic treatment of antisocial behavior in children and adolescents.* New York: Guilford Press.

Heppner, P. P. (1990). Life lines: Institutional perspectives [Feature editor's introduction]. *Journal of Counseling and Development, 68,* 246.

Herlihy, B., & Corey, G. (2006). *ACA ethical standards casebook* (6th ed.). Alexandria, VA: American Counseling Association.

Herlihy, B., & Remley, T. P., Jr. (1995). Unified ethical standards: A challenge for professionalism. *Journal of Counseling and Development, 74,* 130–133.

Herlihy, P. A. (2000). Employee assistance and work/family programs: Friends or foes? *Employee Assistance Quarterly, 16,* 33–52.

Hermann, M. A., & Herlihy, B. R. (2006). Legal and ethical implications of refusing to counsel homosexual clients. *Journal of Counseling & Development, 84,* 414–418.

Herr, E. L. (1985). AACD: An association committed to unity through diversity. *Journal of Counseling and Development, 63,* 395–404.

Herr, E. L., Cramer, S. H., & Niles, S. G. (2004). *Career guidance and counseling through the lifespan: Systematic approaches* (6th ed.). Boston: Allyn & Bacon.

Herr, E. L., & Fabian, E. S. (1993). The *Journal of Counseling and Development*: Its legacy and its aspirations. *Journal of Counseling and Development, 72,* 3–4.

Herring, R. D. (1997). *Multicultural counseling in schools.* Alexandria, VA: American Counseling Association.

Hershenson, D. B. (1998). Systemic, ecological model for rehabilitation counseling. *Rehabilitation Counseling Bulletin, 42,* 40–50.

Hershenson, D. B., & Berger, G. P. (2001). The state of community counseling: A survey of directors of CACREP-accredited programs. *Journal of Counseling and Development, 79,* 188–193.

Hershenson, D. B., Power, P. W., & Waldo, M. (1996). *Community counseling: Contemporary theory and practice.* Needham Heights, MA: Allyn & Bacon.

Hertz, R., & Marshall, N. L. (2001). *Working families: The transformation of the American home.* Berkeley: University of California Press.

Hetherington, E. M. (1993). An overview of the Virginia longitudinal study of divorce and re-marriage with a focus on early adolescence. *Journal of Family Psychology, 7,* 39–56.

Hettler, W. (1984). Wellness: Encouraging a life-time pursuit of excellence. *Health Values: Achieving High Level Wellness, 8,* 13–17.

Hetzel, R. D., Barton, D. A., & Davenport, D. S. (1994). Helping men change: A group counseling model for male clients. *Journal for Specialists in Group Work, 19,* 52–64.

Hill, N. R., & Beamish, P. M. (2007). Treatment outcomes for obsessive-compulsive disorder: A critical review. *Journal of Counseling and Development, 85,* 504–510.

Hill, R. D., Thorn, B. L., & Packard, T. (2000). Counseling older adults: Theoretical and empirical issues in prevention and intervention. In S. D. Brown & R. W. Lent (Eds.), *Handbook of counseling psychology* (3rd ed.; pp. 499–531). New York: Wiley.

Hines, M. (1988). Similarities and differences in group and family therapy. *Journal for Specialists in Group Work, 13,* 173–179.

Hinkle, J. S. (1992). The mental status examination via computer: An evaluation of the mental status checklist computer report. *Measurement and Evaluation in Counseling and Development, 24,* 188–189.

Hinkle, J. S. (1999). A voice from the trenches: A reaction to Ivey and Ivey (1998). *Journal of Counseling and Development, 77,* 474–483.

Hitchcock, A. A. (1984). Work, aging, and counseling. *Journal of Counseling and Development, 63,* 258–259.

Hobson, C. J., Delunas, L., & Kesic, D. (2001). Compelling evidence of the need for corporate work/life balance initiatives: Results from a national survey of stressful life-events. *Journal of Employment Counseling, 38,* 38–44.

Hoffman, R. M. (2006). Gender self-definition and gender self-acceptance in women: Intersections with feminist, womanist, and ethnic identities. *Journal of Counseling & Development, 84,* 358–372.

Hohenshil, T. H. (1996). Role of assessment and diagnosis in counseling. *Journal of Counseling and Development, 75,* 64–67.

Holland, J. L. (1994). *The occupations finder.* Odessa, FL: Psychological Assessment Resources.

Holland, J. L. (1997). *Making vocational choices: A theory of vocational preferences and work environments* (3rd ed.). Odessa, FL: Psychological Assessment Resources.

Hollis, J. W. (2000). *Counselor preparation 1999–2001: Programs, faculty, trends* (10th ed.). Philadelphia: Taylor & Francis.

Hollis, J. W., & Wantz, R. A. (1980). *Counselor preparation.* Muncie, IN: Accelerated Development.

Holmes, J. F. (1999). U.S. population, a profile of America's diversity: The view from the Census Bureau, 1998. In *The world almanac and book of facts.* Mahwah, NJ: Primedia Reference.

Hood, A. B., & Johnson, R. W. (2007). *Assessment in counseling: A guide to the use of psychological assessment procedures* (4th ed.). Alexandria, VA: American Counseling Association.

Horne, A. M., & Mason, J. (1991, August). *Counseling men.* Paper presented at the Annual Convention of the American Psychological Association, San Francisco.

Horne, A. M., & Sayger, T. V. (2000). Behavioral approaches to couple and family therapy. In A. M. Horne (Ed.), *Family counseling and therapy* (3rd ed., pp. 454–488). Itasca, IL: F. E. Peacock.

Horowitz, J. L., & Newcomb, M. D. (1999). Bisexuality, not homosexuality: Counseling issues and treatment approaches. *Journal of College Counseling, 2,* 148–164.

Hosie, T. W. (1991). Historical antecedents and current status of counselor licensure. In F. Bradley (Ed.), *Credentialing in counseling* (pp. 23–52). Alexandria, VA: American Counseling Association.

Hosie, T. W., & Spruill, D. (1990, November). *Counselor employment and roles in three major types of EAP organizations.* Paper presented at the Southern Association for Counselor Education and Supervision Convention, Norfolk, VA.

Hosie, T. W., West, J. D., & Mackey, J. A. (1993). Employment and roles of counselors in employee assistance programs. *Journal of Counseling and Development, 71,* 355–359.

Hospice and Palliative Care Center. (2008). Retrieved September 6, 2008, from http://www.hospicecarecenter.org/

Hotchkiss, L., & Borow, H. (1996). Sociological perspective on work and career development. In D. Brown, L. Brooks, & Associates (Eds.), *Career choice and development* (3rd ed.). San Francisco: Jossey-Bass.

Howard, K. I., Orlinsky, D. E., & Bankoff, E. A. (1994). The research project on long-term psychotherapy: A qualitative analysis. *Journal of Counseling Psychology, 43,* 207–217.

Hoyt, M. F. (1995). *Brief therapy and managed care: Readings for contemporary practice.* San Francisco: Jossey-Bass.

Huber, C. H. (1994). *Ethical, legal and professional issues in the practice of marriage and family therapy* (2nd ed.). New York: Macmillan.

Hudson, F. (2000). *The adult years: Mastering the art of self-renewal.* San Francisco: Jossey-Bass.

Huffman, S. B., & Myers, J. E. (1999). Counseling women in midlife: An integrative approach to menopause. *Journal of Counseling and Development, 77,* 258–266.

Hughes, F. P. (1999). *Human development across the life span* (Rev. ed.). Upper Saddle River, NJ: Merrill/Prentice Hall.

Hughes, R. S. (2000). Cybercounseling and regulations: Quagmire or quest? In J. W. Bloom & G. R. Walz (Eds.), *Cybercounseling and cyberlearning: Strategies and resources for the new millennium* (pp. 321–338). Alexandria, VA: American Counseling Association.

Hulse-Killacky, D. (1993). Personal and professional endings. *Journal of Humanistic Education and Development, 32,* 92–94.

Hulse-Killacky, D., Killacky, J., & Donigian, J. (2001). *Making task groups work in your world.* Upper Saddle River, NJ: Prentice Hall.

Hummell, D. L., Talbutt, L. C., & Alexander, M. D. (1985). *Law and ethics in counseling.* New York: Van Nostrand Reinhold.

HurricaneKatrinaRelief.com. (2008). Frequently asked questions. Retrieved July 29, 2008, from http://ojjdp.ncjrs.gov/ojstatbb/nr2006/index.html

Hutchins, D. E., & Vaught, C. G. (1997). *Helping relationships and strategies* (3rd ed.). Pacific Grove, CA: Brooks/Cole.

Imbimbo, P. V. (1994). Integrating personal and career counseling: A challenge for counselors. *Journal of Employment Counseling, 31,* 50–59.

Ingersoll, R. E. (1994). Spirituality, religion, and counseling: Dimensions and relationships. *Counseling and Values, 38,* 98–111.

International Coach Foundation. (2008). *What is coaching?* Retrieved August 16, 2008, from http://www.coachfederation.org/ICF/For+Coaching+Clients/

International Society for Mental Health Online (ISMHO). (2000). *Suggested principles for the online provision of mental health services.* Retrieved August 31, 2008, from http://www.ismho.org/builder/?p =page&id=214

Ivey, A. E. (1971). *Microcounseling: Innovations in interviewing training.* Springfield, IL: Charles C Thomas.

Ivey, A. E. (1973). Demystifying the group process: Adapting microcounseling procedures to counseling in groups. *Educational Technology, 13,* 27–31.

Ivey, A. E., & Ivey, M. B. (1999). Toward a developmental diagnostic and statistical manual: The vitality of a contextual framework. *Journal of Counseling and Development, 77,* 484–490.

Ivey, A. E., & Ivey, M. B. (2007). *Intentional interviewing and counseling* (7th ed.). Belmont, CA: Thomson Brooks/Cole.

Jacobs, E. E., Masson, R. L., & Harvill, R. L. (2009). *Group counseling* (6th ed.). Belmont, CA: Thomson/Brooks/Cole.

Jaffee v. Redmond, WL 314841 (U.S. June 13, 1996).

James, M. D., & Hazler, R. J. (1998). Using metaphors to soften resistance in chemically dependent clients. *Journal of Humanistic Education and Development, 36,* 122–133.

James, R. K. (2008). *Crisis intervention strategies* (6th ed.). Belmont, CA: Thompson Brooks/Cole.

James, R. K., & Gilliland, B. E. (2005). *Crisis intervention strategies* (5th ed.). Pacific Grove, CA: Brooks/Cole.

Johnson, D. R. (1986). The developmental method in drama therapy: Group treatment with the elderly. *Arts in Psychotherapy, 13,* 17–33.

Johnson, D. W., & Johnson, F. P. (2009). *Joining together: Group theory and group skills* (10th ed.). Boston: Allyn & Bacon.

Johnson, L. S. (1997). Developmental strategies for counseling the child whose parent or sibling has cancer. *Journal of Counseling and Development, 75,* 417–427.

Johnson, M., & Scarato, A. M. (1979). A knowledge base for counselors of women. *Counseling Psychologist, 8,* 14–16.

Johnson, M. E., Fortman, J. B., & Brems, C. (1993). *Between two people: Exercises toward intimacy.* Alexandria, VA: American Counseling Association.

Johnson, T. W., & Colucci, P. (1999). Lesbian, gay men, and the family life cycle. In B. Carter & M. McGoldrick (Eds.), *The expanded family life cycle* (3rd ed., pp. 346–361). Boston: Allyn & Bacon.

Johnson, W. B., & Hayes, D. N. (1997). An identity-focused counseling group for men. *Journal of Mental Health Counseling, 19,* 295–303.

Jolliff, D. (1994). Group work with men. *Journal for Specialists in Group Work, 19,* 50–51.

Jordan, J. V. (1995). A relational approach to psychotherapy. *Women and Therapy, 16,* 51–61.

Jourard, S. M. (1971). *The transparent self.* Princeton, NJ: Van Nostrand.

Jourard, S. M., & Landsman, T. (1980). *Healthy personality* (4th ed.). New York: Macmillan.

Jung, C. G. (1971). The stages of life. In J. Campbell (Ed.), *The portable Jung.* New York: Viking.

Kabat-Zinn, J. (1990). *Full catastrophe living.* New York: Delta.

Kabat-Zinn, J. (1994). *Wherever you go there you are: Mindfulness meditation in everyday life.* New York: Hyperion.

Kaffenberger, C. J., & Seligman, L. (2003). Helping students with mental and emotional disorders. In B. T. Erford (Ed.), *Transforming the school counseling profession* (pp. 249–284). Upper Saddle River, NJ: Prentice Hall.

Kalodner, C. R., & Van Lone, J. S. (2001). Eating disorders: Guidelines for assessment, treatment, and referral. In E. R. Welfel & R. E. Ingersoll (Eds.), *The mental health desk reference: A sourcebook for counselors and therapists* (pp. 119–128). New York: Wiley.

Kapes, J. T., & Whitfield, E. A. (Eds.). (2002). *A counselor's guide to career assessment instruments* (4th ed.). Broken Arrow, OK: National Career Development Association.

Kaplan, D. M. (2002, July). Celebrating 50 years of excellence. *Counseling Today, 1,* 45.

Kaplan, D. M., & Coogan, S. L. (2005). The next advancement in counseling: the bio-psycho-social model. In G. R. Walz & R. K. Yep (Eds.), *VISTAS: Compelling perspectives on counseling, 2005* (pp. 17–25). Alexandria, VA: American Counseling Association.

Kaplan, R. (2000). Two pathways to prevention. *American Psychologist, 55,* 382–396.

Kaslow, F. W. (1990). *Voices in family psychology.* Newbury Park, CA: Sage.

Kaslow, F. W. (1991). The art and science of family psychology. *American Psychologist, 46,* 621–626.

Kay, E. (2003). *Heroes at home.* Minneapolis, MN: Bethany House.

Kees, N. L. (2005). Women's voices, women's lives: An introduction to the special issue on women and counseling. *Journal of Counseling & Development, 83,* 259–261.

Kelly, E. W., Jr. (1995). *Spirituality and religion in counseling and psychotherapy.* Alexandria, VA: American Counseling Association.

Kelly, K. R., & Hall, A. S. (1994). Affirming the assumptions of the developmental model for counseling men. *Journal of Mental Health Counseling, 16,* 475–482.

Kelly, K. R., & Stone, G. L. (1982). Effects of time limits on the interview behavior of type A and B persons within a brief counseling analog. *Journal of Counseling Psychology, 29,* 454–459.

Kemp, A. (1998). *Abuse in the family: An introduction.* Pacific Grove, CA: Brooks/Cole.

Kemp, J. T. (1984). Learning from clients: Counseling the frail and dying elderly. *Personnel and Guidance Journal, 62,* 270–272.

Kendall, P. C. (2006). Guiding theory for therapy with children and adolescents. In P. C. Kendall (Ed.), *Child and adolescent therapy: Cognitive-behavioral procedures* (3rd ed., pp. 3–31). New York: Guilford Press.

Kennedy, A. (2008, July). Next stop, adulthood. *Counseling Today, 51*(1), 42–45.

Kennedy, S. (2001). Organizational change affects work stress and work-family balance.

Australian and New Zealand Journal of Family Therapy, 22, 105–106.

Kerr, B. A., Claiborn, C. D., & Dixon, D. N. (1982). Training counselors in persuasion. *Counselor Education and Supervision, 22,* 138–147.

Kerr, M. E., & Bowen, M. (1988). *Family evaluation: An approach based on Bowen theory.* New York: Norton.

Kiesler, C. A. (2000). The next wave of change for psychology and mental health services in the health care revolution. *American Psychologist, 55,* 481–487.

Kimmel, D. C. (1976). Adult development: Challenges for counseling. *Personnel and Guidance Journal, 55,* 103–105.

Kinnier, R. T., Brigman, S. L., & Noble, F. C. (1990). Career indecision and family enmeshment. *Journal of Counseling and Development, 68,* 309–312.

Kinsey, A. C., Pomeroy, W. B., & Martin, C. E. (1948). *Sexual behavior in the human male.* Philadelphia: Saunders.

Kiselica, M. S., & Look, C. T. (1993). Mental health counseling and prevention: Disparity between philosophy and practice? *Journal of Mental Health Counseling, 15,* 3–14.

Kiselica, M. S., & Robinson, M. (2001). Bringing advocacy counseling to life: The history, issues, and human dramas of social justice work in counseling. *Journal of Counseling and Development, 79,* 387–397.

Kitchener, K. S. (1984). Intuition, critical evaluation, and ethical principles: The foundation for ethical decisions in counseling psychology. *The Counseling Psychologist, 12,* 43–55.

Kitchener, K. S. (1994, May). Doing good well—The wisdom behind ethical supervision. *Counseling and Human Development, 1–8.*

Kleinke, C. L. (2002). *Coping with life challenges* (2nd ed.). Prospect Height, IL: Waveland.

Kleist, D. M. (1999). The state of prevention in mental health counseling and counselor education. In J. S. Hinkle (Ed.), *Promoting optimum mental health through counseling: An overview* (pp. 35–40). Greensboro, NC: ERIC/CASS.

Kogan, L. R., & Vacha-Haase, T. (2002). Supporting adaptation to new family roles in middle age. In C. L. Juntenen & D. R. Atkinson (Eds.), *Counseling across the lifespan* (pp. 299–327). Thousand Oaks, CA: Sage.

Kohler, H. P., Behrman, J. R., & Skytthe, A. (2005). Partner + Children = Happiness? The effects of partnerships and fertility on well-being. *Population and Development Review, 31,* 407–445.

Kopla, M., & Keitel, M. A. (Eds.). (2003). *Handbook of counseling women.* Thousand Oaks, CA: Sage.

Kottler, J. A. (1993). *On being a therapist.* San Francisco: Jossey-Bass.

Kottler, J. A. (1994). Working with difficult group members. *Journal for Specialists in Group Work, 19,* 3–10.

Kottler, J. A., & Brown, R. W. (2000). *Introduction to therapeutic counseling: Voices from the field* (4th ed.). Belmont, CA: Wadsworth.

Kottler, J. A., & Schofield, M. (2001). When therapists face stress and crisis: Self-initiated coping strategies. In E. R. Welfel & R. Elliott Ingersoll (Eds.), *The mental health desk reference* (pp. 426–431). New York: Wiley.

Kottler, J. A., Sexton, T. L., & Whiston, S. C. (1994). *The heart of healing.* San Francisco: Jossey-Bass.

Kovacs, M. (1992). *Children's Depression Inventory.* North Tonawanda, NY: Multi-Health Systems.

Krause, K. (1995). The Group. *Together, 23*(3), 2.

Krieshok, T. S. (1998). An anti-introspectivist view of career decision making. *Career Development Quarterly, 46,* 210–229.

Krumboltz, J. D. (Ed.). (1966). *Revolution in counseling.* Boston: Houghton Mifflin.

Krumboltz, J. D. (1979). *Social learning and career decision making.* New York: Carroll.

Krumboltz, J. D. (1993). Integrating career and personal counseling. *Career Development Quarterly, 42,* 143–148.

Krumboltz, J. D. (1994). Integrating career and personal counseling. *Career Development Quarterly, 42,* 143–148.

Kurpius, D. J., & Rozecki, T. G. (1992). Outreach, advocacy, and consultation: A framework for prevention and intervention. *Elementary School Guidance and Counseling, 26,* 176–189.

Kurtz, P. D., & Tandy, C. C. (1995). Narrative family interventions. In A. C. Kilpatrick & T. P. Holland (Eds.), *Working with families* (pp. 177–197). Boston: Allyn & Bacon.

L'Abate, L. (1992). Introduction. In L. L'Abate, G. E. Farrar, & D. A. Serritella (Eds.), *Handbook of differential treatments for addiction* (pp. 1–4). Boston: Allyn & Bacon.

LaBarge, E. (1981). Counseling patients with senile dementia of the Alzheimer type and their families. *Personnel and Guidance Journal, 60,* 139–142.

Ladd, G. W., Kochenderfer, B. J., & Coleman, C. C. (1997). Classroom peer acceptance, friendship, and victimization: Distinct relational systems that contribute uniquely to children's school adjustment? *Child Development, 68,* 1181–1197.

Lambert, M. J., & Bergin, A. E. (1994). The effectiveness of psychotherapy. In A. E. Bergin & S. L. Garfield (Eds.), *Handbook of psychotherapy and behavior change* (pp. 143–189). New York: Wiley.

Lamborn, S. D., Mounts, N. S., Steinberg, L., & Dornbusch, S. M. (1991). Patterns of competence and adjustment among adolescents from authoritative, authoritarian, indulgent, and neglectful families. *Child Development, 62,* 1049–1065.

Landreth, G. (1993). Child-centered play therapy. *Elementary School Guidance and Counseling, 28,* 17–29.

Lapsley, D. K., & Quintana, S. M. (1985). Recent approaches to the moral and social education of children. *Elementary School Guidance and Counseling, 19,* 246–259.

Laux, J. M. (2002). A primer on suicidology: Implications for counselors. *Journal of Counseling and Development, 80,* 380–383.

Lawler, A. C. (1990). The healthy self: Variations on a theme. *Journal of Counseling and Development, 68,* 652–654.

Lawless, L. L., Ginter, E. J., & Kelly, K. R. (1999). Managed care: What mental health counselors should know. *Journal of Mental Health Counseling, 21,* 50–65.

Lawrence, G., & Robinson Kurpius, S. E. (2000). Legal and ethical issues involved when counseling minors in nonschool settings. *Journal of Counseling and Development, 78,* 130–136.

Lawson, D. (1994). Identifying pretreatment change. *Journal of Counseling and Development, 72,* 244–248.

Lazarus, A. A. (1976). *Multimodal behavior therapy.* New York: Springer.

Lazarus, A. A. (1981). *The practice of multimodal therapy.* New York: McGraw-Hill.

Lazarus, R. S., & Folkman, S. (1984). *Stress, appraisal and coping.* New York: Springer.

Lease, S. H., Horne, S. G., & Noffsinger-Frazier, N. (2005). Affirming faith experiences and psychological health for Caucasian lesbian, gay, and bisexual individuals. *Journal of Counseling Psychology, 52,* 378–388.

Lee, C. C. (1997). The promise and pitfalls of multicultural counseling. In C. C. Lee (Ed.), *Multicultural issues in counseling* (2nd ed., pp. 3–13). Alexandria, VA: American Counseling Association.

Lee, C. C. (2001). Defining and responding to racial and ethnic diversity. In D. C. Locke, J. E. Myers, & E. L. Herr (Eds.), *The handbook of counseling* (pp. 581–588). Thousand Oaks, CA: Sage.

Lee, C. C. (Ed.). (2006a). *Counseling for social justice* (2nd ed.). Alexandria, VA: American Counseling Association..

Lee, C. C. (Ed.). (2006b). *Multicultural issues in counseling: New approaches to diversity* (3rd ed.). Alexandria, VA: American Counseling Association.

Lee, C. C., & Walz, G. R. (Eds.). (1998). *Social action: A mandate for counselors.* Alexandria, VA: American Counseling Association.

Lee, J. M. (1966). Issues and emphases in guidance: A historical perspective. In J. M. Lee & N. J. Pallone (Eds.), *Readings in guidance and counseling.* New York: Sheed & Ward.

Lee, R. M., & Robbins, S. B. (2000). Understanding social connectedness in college women and men. *Journal of Counseling and Development, 78,* 484–491.

Lee, W. M. L. (1999). *An introduction to multicultural counseling.* Ann Arbor, MI: Taylor & Francis.

Lee, W. M. L. (2007). *An introduction to multicultural counseling* (2nd ed.). New York: Taylor & Francis/Routledge.

Leech, N. L., & Kees, N. L. (2005). Researching women's groups: Findings, limitations, and recommendations. *Journal of Counseling and Development, 83,* 367–373.

Lehman, D. R., & Nisbett, R. E. (1990). A longitudinal study of the effects of undergraduate training on reasoning. *Developmental Psychology, 26,* 952–960.

Leibert, T. W. (2006). Making change visible: The possibilities of assessing mental health counseling outcomes. *Journal of Counseling and Development, 84,* 108–113.

Lemoire, S. J., & Chen, C. P. (2005). Applying person-centered counseling to sexual minority adolescents. *Journal of Counseling & Development, 83,* 146–154.

Lent, R. W., Brown, S. D., & Hackett, G. (1994). Toward a unifying social cognitive theory of career and academic interest, choice, and performance. *Journal of Vocational Behavior, 45,* 79–122.

Lent, R. W., Brown, S. D., & Hackett, G. (2000). Contextual supports and barriers to career choice: A social cognitive analysis. *Journal of Counseling Psychology, 47,* 36–49.

Leonard, M. M., & Collins, A. M. (1979). Woman as footnote. *Counseling Psychologist, 8,* 6–7.

Leong, F. T., & Gupta, A. (2007). Career development and vocational behaviors of Asian Americans. In F. T. Leong, A. Ebreo, L. Kinoshita, A. G. Inman, & L. H. Yang (Eds.), *Handbook of Asian American psychology* (2nd ed., pp. 159–178). Thousand Oaks, CA: Sage.

Lerner, M. (1994). Training for cancer: An interview with Michael Lerner. *The Journal of Mind-Body Health, 10,* 27–37.

Levant, R. F., & Pollack, W. S. (2003). *A new psychology of men.* New York: Basic Books.

Levine, M., Perkins, D. D., & Perkins, D. V. (2005). *Principles of community psychology: Perspectives and applications* (3rd ed.). New York: Oxford University Press.

Levinson, D. J., Darrow, C. N., Klein, E. B., Levinson, M. H., & McKee, B. (1978). *The seasons of a man's life.* New York: Knopf.

Lewis, J. A., & Bradley, L. (2000). Introduction. In J. Lewis & L. J. Bradley (Eds.), *Advocacy in counseling: Counselors, clients, and community* (pp. 3–4). Greensboro, NC: Caps Publications.

Lewis, J. A., Hayes, B. A., & Bradley, L. J. (Eds.). (1992). *Counseling women over the life span.* Denver: Love.

Lewis, J. A., & Lewis, M. D. (1977). *Community counseling: A human services approach.* New York: Wiley.

Lewis, J. A., Lewis, M. D., Daniels, J. A., & D'Andrea, M. J. (2003). *Community counseling: Empowerment strategies for a diverse society* (3rd ed.). Pacific Grove, CA: Brooks/Cole.

Lewis, J. A., Lewis, M. D., Packard, T., & Souflee, F., Jr. (2001). *Management of human service programs* (3rd ed.). Belmont, CA: Wadsworth.

Lieberman, J. A., III, & Stuart, M. R. (1999). The BATHE method: Incorporating counseling and psychotherapy into the everyday management of patients. *Primary Care Companion to The Journal of Clinical Psychiatry, 1,* 35–38.

Lieberman, M. A., Yalom, I. D., & Miles, M. B. (1973). *Encounter groups: First facts.* New York: Basic Books.

Linehan, M. M. (1997). *Suicidal behaviors questionnaire.* Unpublished inventory. Department of Psychology, University of Washington, Seattle, WA.

Linehan, M. M., & Comtois, K. (1997). *Lifetime parasuicide count.* Unpublished instrument. University of Washington, Seattle, WA.

Lippert, L. (1997). Women at midlife: Implications for theories of women's adult development. *Journal of Counseling and Development, 76,* 16–22.

Liptak, J. J. (2001). *Treatment planning in career counseling.* Pacific Grove, CA: Brooks/Cole.

Littrell, J. M. (2001). Allen E. Ivey: Transforming counseling theory and practice. *Journal of Counseling and Development, 79,* 105–118.

Liu, W. M., & Clay, D. L. (2002). Multicultural counseling competencies: Guidelines for working with children and adolescents. *Journal of Mental Health Counseling, 24,* 177–187.

Livneh, H., & Antonak, R. F. (2005). Psychosocial adaptation to chronic illness and disability: A primer for counselors. *Journal of Counseling & Development, 83,* 12–20.

Livneh, H., & Evans, J. (1984). Adjusting to disability: Behavioral correlates and intervention strategies. *Personnel and Guidance Journal, 62,* 363–368.

Livneh, H., & Wosley-George, E. T. (2001). Counseling clients with disabilities. In D. Capuzzi & D. R. Gross (Eds.), *Introduction to the counseling profession* (3rd ed., pp. 435–462). Needham Heights, MA: Allyn & Bacon.

Locke, D. C. (1990). A not so provincial view of multicultural counseling. *Counselor Education and Supervision, 30,* 18–25.

Locke, D. C. (2001). ACES at its best: Celebrating the human spirit. *Counselor Education and Supervision, 40,* 242–251.

Loesch, L. C. (2001). Counseling program evaluation: Inside and outside the box. In D. C. Locke, J. E. Myers, & E. L. Herr (Eds.), *The handbook of counseling* (pp. 513–525). Thousand Oaks, CA: Sage.

Lopez, F. G. (1986). Family structure and depression: Implications for the counseling of depressed college students. *Journal of Counseling and Development, 64,* 508–511.

LoPiccolo, J. (1978). Direct treatment of sexual dysfunction. In J. LoPiccolo & L. LoPiccolo (Eds.), *Handbook of sex therapy.* New York: Plenum.

Love, P., & Stosny, S. (2007). *How to improve your marriage without talking about it.* New York: Broadway.

Luck, R. S. (1999). Rehabilitation counseling credentialing as a professional specialty. In G. L. Gandy, E. D. Martin, & R. E. Hardy (Eds.), *Counseling in the rehabilitation process: Community services for mental and physical disabilities* (2nd ed.; pp. 271–288). Springfield, IL: Charles C Thomas.

Lusky, M. B., & Hayes, R. L. (2001). Collaborative consultation and program evaluation. *Journal of Counseling and Development, 79,* 26–38.

Lustig, D. C., Rosenthal, D. A., Strauser, D. R., & Haynes, K. (2000, Spring). The relationship between sense of coherence and adjustment in persons with disabilities. *Rehabilitation Counseling Bulletin, 43,* 134–141.

Luzzo, D. A., & McWhirter, E. H. (2001). Sex and ethnic differences in the perception of educational and career-related barriers and levels of coping efficacy. *Journal of Counseling and Development, 79,* 61–67.

Lynch, R. K., & Maki, D. (1981). Searching for structure: A trait-factor approach to vocational rehabilitation. *Vocational Guidance Quarterly, 30,* 61–68.

Lynn, S. J., & Frauman, D. (1985). Group psychotherapy. In S. J. Lynn & J. P. Garske (Eds.), *Contemporary psychotherapies: Models and methods* (pp. 419– 458). Columbus, OH: Merrill.

Lyoo, K., Noam, G. G., Lee, C. K., Lee, H. K., Kennedy, B. P., & Renshaw, P. F. (1996). The corpus callosum and lateral ventricles in children with attention-deficit hyperactivity disorder: A brain magnetic resonance imaging study. *Biological Psychiatry, 40,* 1060–1063.

Mabe, A. R., & Rollin, S. A. (1986). The role of a code of ethical standards in counseling. *Journal of Counseling and Development, 64,* 294–297.

MacCluskie, K. C., & Ingersoll, R. E. (2001). *Becoming a 21st century agency counselor: Personal and professional explorations.* Belmont, CA: Wadsworth.

Maccoby, E. E., & Martin, J. A. (1983). Socialization in the context of the family: Parent–child interaction. In R. H. Mussen (Series Ed.) & E. M. Hetherington (Vol. Ed.), *Handbook of child psychology: Vol. 4. Socialization, personality, and social development* (pp. 1–101). New York: Wiley.

Mace, D. (1987). Three ways of helping married couples. *Journal of Marital and Family Therapy, 13,* 179–186.

Mace, D., & Mace, V. (1977). *How to have a happy marriage: A step-by-step guide to an enriched relationship.* Nashville, TN: Abington.

Madanes, C. (1984). *Behind the one-way mirror: Advances in the practice of strategic therapy.* San Francisco: Jossey-Bass.

Madanes, C. (1991). Strategic family therapy. In A. S. Gurman & D. P. Kniskern (Eds.), *Handbook of family therapy* (Vol. II, pp. 396–416). New York: Brunner/Mazel.

Madonna, T. I. (2000). Providing mental health services under managed care arrangements: The challenges. *Hospital Topics, 78,* 23–27.

Mahaffy, K. A. (1996). Cognitive dissonance and its resolution: A study of lesbian Christians. *Journal for the Scientific Study of Religion, 35,* 392–402.

Manderscheid, R. W., & Sonnenschein, M. A. (1992). *Mental health in the United States,*

1992 (DHHS Publication No. [SMA] 92–1942). Washington, DC: U.S. Government Printing Office.

Manley, R. S., Rickson, H., & Standeven, B. (2000). Children and adolescents with eating disorders: Strategies for teachers and school counselors. *Intervention in School and Clinic, 35,* 228–231.

Manuele-Adkins, C. (1992). Career counseling is personal counseling. *Career Development Quarterly, 40,* 313–323.

Maples, M. F., & Han, S. (2008). Cybercounseling in the United States and South Korea: Implications for counseling college students of the millennial generation and the networked generation. *Journal of Counseling & Development, 86,* 178–183.

Marino, T. M. (1979). Resensitizing men: A male perspective. *Personnel and Guidance Journal, 58,* 102–105.

Marmor, J. (1982). Transition to the empty nest. In L. Allman & D. Gaffe (Eds.), *Reading in adult psychology: Contemporary perspectives.* New York: Harper & Row.

Martin, E. D., Jr. (1999). Foundations of rehabilitation. In G. L. Gandy, E. D. Martin, Jr., & R. E. Hardy (Eds.), *Counseling in the rehabilitation process: Community services for mental and physical disabilities* (2nd ed., pp. 5–31). Springfield, IL: Charles C Thomas.

Maslow, A. H. (1968). *Toward a psychology of being* (2nd ed.). New York: Van Nostrand Reinhold.

Masters, W. H., & Johnson, V. E. (1970). *Human sexual inadequacy.* Boston: Little, Brown.

Matlin, M. W. (2008). *The psychology of women* (6th ed.). Belmont, CA: Wadsworth.

Matthews, D. A., McCollough, M. E., Larson, D. B., Koenig, H. G., & Swyer, J. P. (1998). Religious commitment and health status: A review of the research and implications for family medicine. *Archives in Family Medicine, 7,* 118–124.

Matthews, G. G. (2001). *Neurobiology: Molecules, cells and systems.* Malden, MA: Blackwell Science.

Maxmen, J. S., & Ward, N. G. (1995). *Essential psychopathology and its treatment* (2nd ed.). New York: Norton.

Maxwell, M. (2007). Career counseling is personal counseling: A constructivist approach to nurturing the development of gifted female adolescents. *Career Development Quarterly, 55,* 206–224.

May, K. M. (1996). Naturalistic inquiry and counseling: Contemplating commonalities. *Counseling and Values, 40,* 219–229.

Maynard, P. E., & Olson, D. H. (1987). Circumplex model of family systems: A treatment tool in family counseling. *Journal of Counseling and Development, 65,* 502–504.

McCarn, S. R., & Fassinger, R. E. (1996). Revisioning sexual minority identity formation: A new model of lesbian identity and its implications for counseling and research. *The Counseling Psychologist, 24,* 508–534.

McClure, B. A. (1990). The group mind: Generative and regressive groups. *Journal for Specialists in Group Work, 15,* 159–170.

McClure, B. A. (1994). The shadow side of regressive groups. *Counseling and Values, 38,* 77–89.

McClure, F. H., & Teyber, E. (2003). *Casebook in child and adolescent treatment: Cultural and familial contexts.* Pacific Grove, CA: Brooks/Cole.

McCoy, G. A. (1994, April). A plan for the first group session. *The ASCA Counselor, 31,* 18.

McCulloch, J., Ramesar, S., & Peterson, H. (1998). Psychotherapy in primary care: The BATHE technique. *American Family Physician.* Retrieved August 25, 2008, from http://www.aafp.org/afp/980501ap/mcculloc.html

McCullough, P. G., & Rutenberg, S. K. (1988). Launching children and moving on. In B. Carter & M. McGoldrick (Eds.), *The changing family life cycle* (2nd ed.; pp. 285–309). New York: Gardner.

McDaniels, C. (1984). The work/leisure connection. *Vocational Guidance Quarterly, 33,* 35–44.

McFadden, J. (Ed.). (1999). *Transcultural counseling* (2nd ed.). Alexandria, VA: American Counseling Association.

McGoldrick, M., Gerson, R., & Petry, S. (2008). *Genograms: Assessment and intervention* (3rd ed.). New York: Norton.

McGoldrick, M., Giordano, J., & Garcia-Preto, N. (Eds.). (2005). *Ethnicity and family therapy.* New York: Guilford Press.

McGoldrick, M., & Walsh, F. (1999). Death and the family life cycle. In B. Carter & M. McGoldrick (Eds.), *The expanded family life cycle* (3rd ed., pp. 185– 201). Boston: Allyn & Bacon.

McGrath, E., Keita, G. F., Strickland, N. R., & Russo, N. (1990). *Women and depression*. Washington, DC: American Psychological Association.

McMahon, M., Patton, W., & Watson, M. (2003). Developing qualitative career assessment processes. *Career Development Quarterly, 51,* 194–202.

McNamara, S. (2000). *Stress in young people: What's new and what can we do?* New York: Continuum.

McReynolds, C. J., & Garske, G. G. (1999, Oct.–Dec.). Psychiatric rehabilitation: A survey of rehabilitation counseling education programs. *Journal of Rehabilitation, 65,* 45–49.

McWhirter, B. T., & Burrow, J. J. (2001). Assessment and treatment recommendations for children and adolescents with depression. In E. R. Welfel & R. E. Ingersoll (Eds.), *The mental health desk reference* (pp. 199–205). New York: Wiley.

McWhirter, E. H. (1994). *Counseling for empowerment*. Alexandria, VA: American Counseling Association.

McWhirter, E. H. (1997). Empowerment, social activism, and counseling. *Counseling and Human Development, 29,* 1–14.

McWhirter, E. H., & Flojo, J. R. (2001). Career counseling: Counseling for life. In D. Capuzzi & D. R. Gross (Eds.), *Introduction to the counseling profession* (3rd ed., pp. 188–207). Needham Heights, MA: Allyn and Bacon.

McWhirter, E. H., Joyce, J., & Aranda, C. L. (2009). An introduction to career counseling. In D. Capuzzi & D. R. Gross (Eds.), *Introduction to the counseling profession* (5th ed., pp. 263–291). Upper Saddle River, NJ: Merrill/Pearson Education.

Mead, M. A., Hohenshil, T. H., & Singh, K. (1997). How the *DSM* system is used by clinical counselors: A national study. *Journal of Mental Health Counseling, 19,* 383–401.

Meisenhelder, J. B., & Chandler, E. N. (2002). Spirituality and health outcomes in the elderly. *Journal of Religion and Health, 42,* 243–252.

Mejia, X. E. (2005). Gender matters: Working with adult male survivors of trauma. *Journal of Counseling and Development, 83,* 29–40.

Mendelsohn, S. J. (2007). *It's not about the weight: Attacking eating disorders from the inside out*. Bloomington, IN: iUniverse, Inc.

Messinger, B. (2004). *Melody lingers on: A complete music activities program for older adults*. State College, PA: Venture Publishing.

Meyers, H. H. (2007). Counseling and spirituality: Integrating wellness into practice. In P. K. S. Patrick (Ed.), *Contemporary issues in counseling* (pp. 320–338). New York: Pearson/ Allyn & Bacon.

Middleton, R. A., Rollins, C. W., & Harley, D. A. (1999). The historical and political context of the civil rights of persons with disabilities: A multicultural perspective for counselors. *Journal of Multicultural Counseling and Development, 27,* 105–120.

Miller, I. J. (1996). Managed care is harmful to outpatient mental health services: A call for accountability. *Professional Psychology: Research and Practice, 27,* 349–363.

Miller, J. B., & Stiver, I. R. (1997). *The healing connection: How women form relationships in therapy and in life*. Northvale, NJ: Jason Aronson.

Miller, J. L., & House, R. M. (2005). Counseling gay, lesbian, and bisexual clients. In D. Capuzzi & D. R. Gross (Eds.), *Introduction to the counseling profession* (4th ed., pp. 430–464). Boston: Pearson/Allyn & Bacon.

Miller, W. R., & Brown, S. A. (1997). Why psychologists should treat alcohol and drug problems. *American Psychologist, 52,* 1269–1279.

Miller-Perrin, C. L. (2001). Child maltreatment: Treatment of child and adolescent victims. In E. R. Welfel & R. E. Ingersoll (Eds.), *The mental health desk reference* (pp. 169–177). New York: Wiley.

Minuchin, S. (1974). *Families and family therapy*. Cambridge, MA: Harvard University Press.

Minuchin, S., & Fishman, C. H. (1981). *Family therapy techniques*. Cambridge, MA: Harvard University Press.

Minuchin, S., Montalvo, B., Guerney, B., Rosman, B., & Schumer, F. (1967). *Families of the slums.* New York: Basic Books.

Minuchin, S., Rosman, B., & Baker, L. (1978). *Psychosomatic families: Anorexia in context.* Cambridge, MA: Harvard University Press.

Mitchell, T., & Everly, G. S. (1996). *Critical Incident Stress Debriefing: An operations manual.* Ellicott City, MD: Chevron.

Mitchell, C. G. (1998). Perceptions of empathy and client satisfaction with managed behavioral health care. *Social Work, 43,* 404–411.

Mitchell, D. (2007). *About therapy online.* Retrieved August 31, 2008, from http://www.therapyonline.ca/aboutclt.htm

Mitchell, K. E., Levin, A. S., & Krumboltz, J. D. (1999). Planned happenstance: Constructing unexpected career opportunities. *Journal of Counseling and Development, 77,* 115–124.

Mitchell, L. K., & Krumboltz, J. D. (1996). Krumboltz's learning theory of career choice and counseling. In D. Brown, L. Brooks, & Associates (Eds.), *Career choice and development* (3rd ed., pp. 233–280). San Francisco: Jossey-Bass.

Mitchell, R. M. (2007). *Documentation in counseling records: An overview of ethical, legal, and clinical issues* (3rd ed.). Alexandria, VA: American Counseling Association.

Mollen, D. (2006). Voluntarily childfree women: Experiences and counseling considerations. *Journal of Mental Health Counseling, 28,* 269–284.

Montalvo, B., & Thompson, R. F. (1988, July/August). Conflicts in the caregiving family. *Family Therapy Networker, 12,* 30–35.

Moore, D. L. (2005). Expanding the view: The lives of women with severe work disabilities in context. *Journal of Counseling & Development, 83,* 343–348.

Moore, D., & Haverkamp, B. E. (1989). Measured increases in male emotional expressiveness following a structured group intervention. *Journal of Counseling and Development, 67,* 513–517.

Moore, D., & Leafgren, F. (Eds.). (1990). *Problem solving strategies and interventions for men in conflict.* Alexandria, VA: American Counseling Association.

Morgan, J. (1995). American Red Cross disaster mental health services: Implementation and recent developments. *Journal of Mental Health Counseling, 17,* 291–300.

Morgan, J. P., Jr. (1994). Bereavement in older adults. *Journal of Mental Health Counseling, 16,* 318–326.

Morran, D. K. (1982). Leader and member self-disclosing behavior in counseling groups. *Journal for Specialists in Group Work, 7,* 218–223.

Morrison, D. R., & Cherlin, A. J. (1995). The divorce process and young children's well-being: A prospective analysis. *Journal of Marriage and the Family, 57,* 800–812.

Mostade, J. (2009). Affirmative counseling with transgendered persons. In C. Lee (Ed.), *Multicultural issues in counseling: New approaches to diversity* (3rd ed., pp. 303–318). Alexandria, VA: American Counseling Association.

Moursund, J., & Kenny, M. C. (2002). *The process of counseling and therapy* (4th ed.). Upper Saddle River, NJ: Prentice Hall.

Mufson, L., & Fairbanks, J. (1996). Interpersonal psychotherapy for depressed adolescents: A one-year naturalistic follow-up study. *Journal of the American Academy of Child and Adolescent Psychiatry, 35,* 1145–1155.

Mufson, L., Moreau, D., Weissman, M. M., & Klerman, G. L. (1993). *Interpersonal psychotherapy for depressed adolescents.* New York: Guilford Press.

Murphy, L., & Mitchell, D. (1998). When writing helps to heal: E-mail as therapy. *British Journal of Guidance and Counselling, 26,* 21–32.

Muse v. Charter Hospital of Winston-Salem, Inc., 117 N.C. App.468 (1995).

Myer, R. A. (2001). *Assessment for crisis intervention: A triage assessment model.* Belmont, CA: Wadsworth.

Myer, R. A., Williams, R. C., Ottens, A. J., & Schmidt, A. E. (1992). Crisis assessment: A three-dimensional model for triage. *Journal of Mental Health Counseling, 14,* 137–148.

Myers, I. B., McCaulley, M. H., Quenk, N. L., & Hammer, A. L. (1998). *MBTI manual: A guide to the development and use of the Myers-Briggs Type Indicator* (3rd ed.). Palo Alto, CA: Consulting Psychologists Press.

Myers, J. E. (1989). *Infusing gerontological counseling into counselor preparation.* Alexandria, VA: American Association for Counseling and Development.

Myers, J. E. (1992). Wellness, prevention, development: The cornerstone of the profession. *Journal of Counseling and Development, 71,* 136–138.

Myers, J. E., & Schwiebert, V. L. (1996). *Competencies for gerontological counseling.* Alexandria, VA: American Counseling Association.

Myers, J. E., & Sweeney, T. J. (1999). *The five factor Wel (Wel-J).* Greensboro, NC: Authors.

Myers, J. E., & Sweeney, T. J. (2005a). *Counseling for wellness: Theory, research, and practice.* Alexandria, VA: American Counseling Association.

Myers, J. E., & Sweeney, T. J. (2005b). *Manual for the five factor wellness inventory, elementary.* Palo Alto, CA: Mindgarden, Inc.

Myers, J. E., & Sweeney, T. J. (2008). Wellness counseling: The evidence base for practice. *Journal of Counseling & Development, 87*(4), 482–493.

Myers, J. E., Sweeney, T. J., & White, V. E. (2002). Advocacy for counseling and counselors: A professional imperative. *Journal of Counseling and Development, 80,* 394–402.

Myers, J. E., Sweeney, T. J., & Witmer, J. M. (2000). The wheel of wellness counseling for wellness: A holistic model for treatment planning. *Journal of Counseling and Development, 78,* 251–266.

Myers, J. E., Sweeney, T. J., & Witmer, J. M. (2001). Optimization of behavior. In D. C. Locke, J. E. Myers, & E. L. Herr (Eds.), *The handbook of counseling* (pp. 641–652). Thousand Oaks, CA: Sage.

Myers, J. E., & Truluck, M. (1998). Human beliefs, religious values, and the counseling process: A comparison of counselors and other mental health professionals. *Counseling and Values, 42,* 106–123.

Myers, J. E., & Williard, K. (2003). Integrating spirituality into counselor preparation: A developmental, wellness approach. *Counseling and Values, 47,* 142–155.

Myers, S. (2000). Empathetic listening: Reports on the experience of being heard. *Journal of Humanistic Psychology, 40,* 148–173.

National Association of Social Workers. (1999). *Code of ethics of the National Association of Social Workers.* Washington, DC: Author.

National Association of State Mental Health Program Directors (NASMHPD). (2008, April). *Testimony on FY 2009 federal funding for mental health services.* Retrieved September 9, 2008, from http://www.nasmhpd.org/

National Board for Certified Counselors (NBCC). (2005). *NBCC code of ethics.* Retrieved July 4, 2008, from http://www.nbcc.org/

National Board for Certified Counselors (NBCC). (2007). *Standards for the ethical practice of Internet counseling.* Retrieved August 31, 2008, from http://www.nbcc.org/webethics2

National Board for Certified Counselors (NBCC). (2008). Retrieved September 4, 2008, from http://www.nbcc.org/

National Career Development Association (NCDA). (1990). *National survey of working America, 1990: Selected findings.* Alexandria, VA: Author.

National Career Development Association (NCDA). (1997a). *Career counseling competencies.* Columbus, OH: Author.

National career Development Association (NCDA). (1997b). *NCDA guidelines for the use of the Internet for the provision of career information and planning services.* Alexandria, VA: Author.

National Career Development Association (NCDA). (2008). Retrieved August 13, 2008, from http://www.ncda.org/

National Child Traumatic Stress Network and National Center for PTSD. (2006, July). *Psychological first aid: Field operations guide* (2nd ed.). Retrieved August 1, 2008, from http://www.ncptsd.va.gov

National Clearinghouse on Child Abuse and Neglect Information. (2002). *In focus: The risk and prevention of maltreatment of children with disabilities.* Retrieved November 26, 2002, from http://www.calib.com/nccanch/pubs/prevenres/focus.cfm

National Coalition Against Domestic Violence (NCADV). (2002). *National Coalition Against Domestic Violence Web site.* Retrieved December 30, 2002, from http://www.ncadv.org/

National Employment Counseling Association (NECA). (2008). *National Employment Counseling Association*. Retrieved August 13, 2008, from http://www.geocities.com/employment-counseling/neca.html

National Fair Access Coalition on Testing. (2007). [On-line]. Retrieved on December 31, 2007, from http://www.fairaccess.org/

National Highway Traffic Safety Administration. (2007). *Traffic safety facts DOT HS 810 631*. Retrieved March 1, 2007, from www-nrd .nhtsa.dot.gov/pdf/nrd-30/NCSA/TSFAnn/ html/TSF2005.htm

National Institute of Mental Health (NIMH). (2007). *Eating disorders*. Retrieved July 31, 2008, from http://www.nimh.nih.gov/health/ publications/eating-disorders/nimheatingdis-orders.pdf

National Institute of Mental Health (NIMH). (2008a). *Child and adolescent mental health*. Retrieved July 31, 2008, from http://www .nimh.nih.gov/health/topics/child-and-adolescent-mental-health/ndex.shtml

National Institute of Mental Health (NIMH). (2008b). *The numbers count: Mental disorders in America*. Retrieved July 13, 2008, from http://www.nimh.nih.gov/health/ publications/the-numbers-count-mental-disorders-in-america.shtml

National Occupational Information Coordinating Committee (NOICC). (1994). *Program guide: Planning to meet career development needs in school-to-work transition programs*. Washington, DC: U.S. Government Printing Office.

National Organization on Disability. (2000). *Survey of the status of people with disabilities in the United States: Employment*. Washington, DC: Author.

National Organization on Disability. (2004). *Harris Survey on Americans with disabilities*. Retrieved on July 26, 2008, from http://www .disabilityfunders.org/system/files/harris2004_ pres.ppt.

National Victim Assistance Academy (NVAA). (2002). *Victimization of individuals with disabilities*. Retrieved on July 24, 2008, from http://www.ojp.usdoj.gov/ovc/assist/ nvaa2002/chapter15.html

National Wellness Institute. (n.d.). *Dimensions of wellness*. Retrieved August 30, 2008, from http://www.nationalwellness.org/index .php?id_tier = 2&id_c = 25

Nations, R. (2006, November 2006). *Spirituality issues in counseling: Applying attachment theory in understanding spirituality and counseling*. Paper presented at Wake Forest University, Winston-Salem, NC.

Nauert, R. (2008). Stress hormone affects immune system. *PsychCentral*. Retrieved August 24, 2008, from http://psychcentral .com/news/2008/07/15/stress-hormone-affects-immune-system/2608.html

Nelligan, A. (1994, Fall). Balancing process and content: A collaborative experience. *Together, 23*, 8–9.

Nelson, M. L. (1996). Separation versus connection: The gender controversy: Implications for counseling women. *Journal of Counseling and Development, 74*, 339–344.

Nelson, T. D. (2002). *Ageism: Stereotyping and prejudice against older persons*. Cambridge, MA: MIT Press

Neugarten, B. L. (Ed.). (1968). *Middle age and aging*. Chicago: University of Chicago Press.

Neugarten, B. L. (1971, December). Grow old along with me! The best is yet to be. *Psychology Today, 48*–56.

Neugarten, B. L. (1978). The wise of the young-old. In R. Gross, B. Gross, & S. Seidman (Eds.), *The new old: Struggling for decent aging* (pp. 47–49). New York: Doubleday.

Neugarten, B. L. (1979). Time, age and the life cycle. *American Journal of Psychiatry, 136*, 887–894.

Neukrug, E. S. (2007). *The world of the counselor: An introduction to the counseling profession* (3rd ed.). Belmont, CA: Thomson Brooks/Cole.

Neukrug, E. S., & Fawcett, R. C. (2006). *Essentials of testing and assessment: A practical guide for counselors, social workers, and psychologists*. Belmont, CA: Brooks/Cole.

Newman, J. L., Fuqua, D. R., Gray, E. A., & Simpson, D. B. (2006). Gender differences in the relationship of anger and depression in a clinical sample. *Journal of Counseling & Development, 84*, 157–162.

Newsome, D. W. (1999). *Parental and school influences on adolescent academic achievement*. Unpublished doctoral dissertation, University of North Carolina, Greensboro.

Newsome, D. W., Southern, J. A., & Erford, B. T. (in press). Helping students with depression. In B. T. Erford (Ed.), *Professional school counseling: A handbook of theories, programs and practices* (2nd ed.). Austin, TX: Pro-Ed.

Newsome, D. W., Whitlatch, N. H., Southern, J. A., & Erford, B. T. (in press). Helping students manage stress. In B. T. Erford (Ed.), *Professional school counseling: A handbook of theories, programs and practices* (2nd ed.). Austin, TX: Pro-Ed.

Nicholas, D. R., Gobble, D. C., Crose, R. G., & Frank, B. (1992). A systems view of health, wellness, and gender: Implications for mental health counseling. *Journal of Mental Health Counseling, 14,* 8–19.

Nichols, M., & Schwartz, R. C. (2007). *Family therapy: Concepts and methods* (8th ed.). Boston: Allyn & Bacon.

Nichols, W. C. (1993). *The AAMFT: 50 years of marital and family therapy.* Washington, DC: AAMFT.

Nicola, J. S. (1980). *Career and family roles of dual-career couples: Women in academia and their husbands.* Ann Arbor, MI: University Microfilms International.

Nigg, J. T., & Rappley, M. D. (2001). Interventions for attention-deficit/hyperactivity disorder. In E. R. Welfel & R. E. Ingersoll (Eds.), *The mental health desk reference* (pp. 183–190). New York: Wiley.

Niles, S. G., & Harris-Bowlsbey, J. H. (2005). *Career development interventions in the 21st century* (2nd ed.). Upper Saddle River, NJ: Merrill/Prentice Hall.

Nugent, F. A. (1981). *Professional counseling.* Monterey, CA: Brooks/Cole.

Nugent, F. A., & Jones, K. D. (2005). *An introduction to the profession of counseling* (4th ed.). Upper Saddle River, NJ: Merrill/Prentice Hall.

Nwachuku, U., & Ivey, A. (1991). Culture-specific counseling: An alternative model. *Journal of Counseling and Development, 70,* 106–111.

Nystul, M. S. (2006). *Introduction to counseling: An art and science perspective* (3rd ed.). Boston: Allyn & Bacon.

Oestmann, J. (2007). The bio-psycho-social model: Integrating science and practice. In P. K. S. Patrick (Ed.), *Contemporary issues in counseling* (pp. 122–155). New York: Pearson/Allyn & Bacon.

Ohlsen, M. M. (1977). *Group counseling* (2nd ed.). New York: Holt, Rinehart & Winston.

Ohlsen, M. M. (1983). *Introduction to counseling.* Itasca, IL: F. E. Peacock.

Okonski, V. O. (2003). Exercise as a counseling intervention. *Journal of Mental Health Counseling, 25,* 45–56.

Okun, B. F. (1990). *Seeking connections in psychotherapy.* San Francisco: Jossey-Bass.

Okun, B. F. (1997). *Effective helping: Interviewing and counseling techniques* (5th ed.). Belmont, CA: Thomson.

Okun, B. F., Fried, J., & Okun, M. L. (1999). *Understanding diversity: A learning-as-practice primer.* Pacific Grove, CA: Brooks/Cole.

Okun, B. F., & Kantrowitz, R. E. (2008). *Effective helping: Interviewing and counseling techniques* (7th ed.). Belmont, CA: Thompson Brooks/Cole.

Olsen, L. D. (1971). Ethical standards for group leaders. *Personnel and Guidance Journal, 50,* 288.

Olson, D. H. (1986). Circumplex model VII: Validation studies and FACES III. *Family Process, 25,* 337–351.

Olson, D. H., & Gorall, D. M. (2003). Circumplex model of marital and family systems. In F. Walsh (Ed.). *Normal family processes* (3rd ed.; pp. 514–548). New York: Guilford Press.

O'Neil, J. M., & Carroll, M. R. (1988). A gender role workshop focused on sexism, gender role conflict, and the gender role journey. *Journal of Counseling and Development, 67,* 193–197.

Oravec, J. A. (2000). Online counselling and the Internet: Perspectives for mental health care supervision and education. *Journal of Mental Health, 9,* 121–135.

Orton, G. L. (1997). *Strategies for counseling with children and their parents.* Pacific Grove, CA: Brooks/Cole.

Osborn, C. (1989). Reminiscence: When the past eases the present. *Journal of Gerontological Nursing, 15,* 6–12.

Osborne, D. S., & Zunker, V. G. (2005). *Using assessment results for career development* (7th ed.). Boston: Thompson-Wadsworth.

Osman, A., Gutierrez, P. M., Kopper, B. A., Barrios, F. X., & Chiros, C. E. (1998). The Positive and Negative Suicide Ideation Inventory: Development and validation. *Psychological Reports, 82,* 783–793.

Otani, A. (1989). Client resistance in counseling: Its theoretical rationale and taxonomic classification. *Journal of Counseling and Development, 67,* 458–461.

Ottens, A. J., & Klein, J. F. (2005). Common factors: Where the soul of counseling and psychotherapy resides. *Journal of Humanistic Counseling, Education, and Development, 44,* 32–45.

Page, B. J., Delmonico, D. L., Walsh, J., L'Amoreaux, N. A., Danninhirsh, C., & Thompson, R. S. (2000). Setting up on-line support groups using The Palace software. *Journal for Specialists in Group Work, 25,* 133–145.

Page, R. C., & Chandler, J. (1994). Effects of group counseling on ninth-grade at-risk students. *Journal of Mental Health Counseling,* 340–351.

Palma, T. V., & Stanley, J. L. (2002). Effective counseling with lesbian, gay, and bisexual clients. *Journal of College Counseling, 5,* 74–89.

Papalia, D. E., Olds, S. W., & Feldman, R. D. (2007). *Human development* (10th ed.). Boston: McGraw-Hill.

Parker, C. L. (1975). A desensitization group for adult community leaders. *Personnel and Guidance Journal, 54,* 48–49.

Parsons, F. (1909). *Choosing a vocation.* Boston: Houghton Mifflin.

Patrick, P. K. S. (2007a). *Contemporary issues in counseling.* New York: Pearson/Allyn & Bacon.

Patrick, P. K. S. (2007b). Stress-induced challenges to the counselor role: Burnout, compassion fatigue, and vicarious traumatization. In P. K. S. (Ed.), *Contemporary issues in counseling* (pp. 210–250). Boston: Pearson/Allyn & Bacon.

Patterson, G. R. (1971). *Families: Applications of social learning to family life.* Champaign, IL: Research Press.

Paul, N. L., & Paul, B. B. (1975). *A marital puzzle: Transgenerational analysis in marriage.* New York: Norton.

Paulson, B. L., & Worth, M. (2002). Counseling for suicide: Client perspectives. *Journal of Counseling and Development, 80,* 86–93.

Paulson, R. I. (1996). Swimming with the sharks or walking in the Garden of Eden: Two visions of managed care and mental health practice. In P. R. Raffoul & C. A. McNeece (Eds.), *Future issues of social work practice* (pp. 85–96). Needham Heights, MA: Allyn & Bacon.

Pavlicin, K. M. (2003). *Surviving deployment: A guide for military families.* St. Paul, MN: Elva Resa Publishing.

Pearson, J. E. (1988). A support group for women with relationship dependency. *Journal of Counseling and Development, 66,* 394–396.

Peck v. Counseling Service of Addison County, 499 A.2d (Vt. 1985).

Pedersen, P. B. (1990). The constructs of complexity and balance in multicultural counseling theory and practice. *Journal of Counseling and Development, 68,* 550–554.

Pedersen, P. B. (1997). The cultural context of the American Counseling Association code of ethics. *Journal of Counseling and Development, 76,* 23–28.

Pedersen, P. B. (2002). Ethics, competence, and other professional issues in culture-centered counseling. In P. B. Pedersen, J. G. Draguns, W. J. Lonner, & J. E. Trimble (Eds.), *Counseling across cultures* (5th ed., pp. 3–27). Thousand Oaks, CA: Sage.

Perls, F. S. (1969). *Gestalt therapy verbation.* Lafayette, CA: Real People Press.

Perry, W. G. (1955). The findings of the commission in counseling and guidance. *Annals: New York Academy of Science, 63,* 396–407.

Petersen, A. C., Compas, B. E., & Brooks-Gunn, J. (1992). *Depression in adolescence: Current knowledge, research directions, and implications for programs and policy.* New York: Carnegie Corporation (ERIC Document Reproduction Service No. ED358384).

Petersen, S. (2000). Multicultural perspective on middle-class women's identity development. *Journal of Counseling and Development, 78,* 63–71.

Peterson, N., & Gonzalez, R. C. (Eds.). (2000). *Career counseling models for diverse populations.* Pacific Grove, CA: Brooks/Cole.

Peterson, N., & Priour, G. (2000). Battered women: A group vocational counseling model. In N. Peterson & R. C. González (Eds.), *Career counseling models for diverse populations* (pp. 205–218). Pacific Grove, CA: Brooks/Cole.

Petrocelli, J. V. (2002). Processes and stages of change: Counseling with the transtheoretical model of change. *Journal of Counseling and Development, 80,* 22–30.

Pew Internet & American Life Project. (2008). *New report on libraries and the digital divide.* Retrieved August 31, 2008, from http://www .pewinternet.org/press_release.asp?r = 74

Pfiffner, L. J., & Barkley, R. A. (1998). Treatment of ADHD in school settings. In R. A. Barkley (Ed.), *Attention deficit hyperactivity disorder: A handbook for diagnosis and treatment* (pp. 458–490). New York: Guilford Press.

Phelps, R., Eisman, E. J., & Kohout, J. (1998). Psychological practice and managed care: Results of the CAPP practitioner study. *Professional Psychology: Research and Practice, 29,* 31–36.

Piazza, N. J., & Baruth, N. D. (1990). Client record guidelines. *Journal of Counseling and Development, 68,* 313–316.

Pidcock, B. W., & Polansky, J. (2001). Clinical practice issues in assessing for adult substance use disorders. In E. R. Welfel & R. E. Ingersoll (Eds.), *The mental health desk reference: A sourcebook for counselors and therapists* (pp. 128–135). New York: Wiley.

Pietrofesa, J. J., Hoffman, A., & Splete, H. H. (1984). *Counseling: An introduction* (2nd ed.). Boston: Houghton Mifflin.

Pinsof, W. M., & Wynne, L. C. (Eds.). (1995). Special issue: The effectiveness of marital and family therapy. *Journal of Marital and Family Therapy, 21,* 339–613.

Pinsof, W. M., & Wynne, L. C. (2000). Toward progress research: Closing the gap between family therapy practice and research. *Journal of Marital and Family Therapy, 26,* 1–8.

Pinterits, E. J., & Atkinson, D. R. (1998). The diversity video forum: An adjunct to diversity sensitive training in the classroom. *Counselor Education and Supervision, 37,* 203–216.

Polanski, P. J., & Hinkle, J. S. (2000). The mental status examination: Its use by professional counselors. *Journal of Counseling and Development, 78,* 357–364.

Polkinghorne, D. E. (2001). Managed care programs: What do clinicians need? In B. D. Slife, R. N. Williams, & S. H. Barlow (Eds.), *Critical issues in psychotherapy: Translating new ideas into practice* (pp. 121–140). Thousand Oaks, CA: Sage.

Ponterotto, J. G., & Casas, J. M. (1987). In search of multicultural competence within counselor education programs. *Journal of Counseling and Development, 65,* 430–434.

Ponzo, Z. (1978). Age prejudice of "act your age." *Personnel and Guidance Journal, 57,* 140–144.

Pope, K. S., & Wedding, D. (2008). Current issues in psychotherapy. In R. J. Corsini & D. Wedding (Eds.), *Current psychotherapies* (8th ed., pp. 512–540). Belmont, CA: Thomson Brooks Cole.

Pope, M., Barret, B., Szymanski, D. M., Chung, Y. B., Singaravelu, H., McLean, R., & Sanabria, S. (2004). Culturally appropriate career counseling with gay and lesbian clients. *The Career Development Quarterly, 53,* 158–177.

Pope, M., & Sweinsdottir, M. (2005). *Frank,* we hardly knew ye: The very personal side of *Frank Parsons. Journal of Counseling and Development, 83,* 105–115.

Prediger, D. J. (1994). Multicultural assessment standards: Compilation for counselors. *Measurement and Evaluation in Counseling and Development, 27,* 68–73.

Pressly, P. K. & Heesacker, M. (2001). The physical environment and counseling: A review of theory and research. *Journal of Counseling and Development, 79,* 148–160.

Price, R., Cowen, E., Lorion, R., & Ramos-McKay, J. (Eds.). (1988). *14 ounces of prevention: A casebook for practitioners.* Washington, DC: American Psychological Association.

Prieto, L. R., & Scheel, K. R. (2002). Using case documentation to strengthen trainees' case conceptualization skills. *Journal of Counseling and Development, 80,* 11–21.

Prochaska, J. O., DiClemente, C. C., & Norcross, J. C. (1992). In search of how people change: Applications to addictive behaviors. *American Psychologist, 47,* 1102–1114.

Prochaska, J. O., & Norcross, J. C. (1999). *Systems of psychotherapy: A transtheoretical analysis.* Pacific Grove, CA: Brooks/Cole.

Prochaska, J. O., & Norcross, J. C. (2003). *Systems of psychotherapy: A transtheoretical analysis* (5th ed.). Pacific Grove, CA: Brooks/Cole.

Promising Practices Network on Children, Families, and Communities. (2004). *Multisystemic therapy.* Retrieved September 9, 2008, from http://www.promisingpractices.net/program.asp?programid=81

Prosser, J. (1997). Transgender. In A. Medhurst & S. R. Munt (Eds.), *Lesbian and gay studies: A critical introduction* (pp. 309–326). Herndon, VA: Cassell.

Pulvino, C. J., & Colangelo, N. (1980). Counseling the elderly: A developmental perspective. *Counseling and Values, 24,* 139–147.

Purkey, W. W. (1991). *What is invitational education and how does it work?* Paper presented at the Annual California State Conference on Self-Esteem, Santa Clara, CA. (ERIC Document Reproduction Service No. ED 334 488).

Quenk, N. (2000). *Essentials of Myers-Briggs Type Indicator assessment.* New York: Wiley.

Quinn, W. H., & Odell, M. (1998). Predictors of marital adjustment during the first two years. *Marriage and Family Review, 27,* 113–130.

Rajeski, W. J. (2008). Mindfulness: Reconnecting the body and mind in geriatric medicine and gerontology. *The Gerontologist, 48,* 135–141.

Redcay, S. (2001). Helping children deal with loss. *The Counseling Corner from the American Counseling Association.* Retrieved July 24, 2002, from http://www.counseling.org/site/PageServer?pagename = publications_ccorner_corner801

Reinecke, M. A., Ryan, N. E., & DuBois, D. L. (1998). Cognitive–behavioral therapy of depression and depressive symptoms during adolescence: A review and meta-analysis. *Journal of the American Academy of Child and Adolescent Psychiatry, 37,* 26–34.

Remley, T. P., Jr. (1991). *Preparing for court appearances.* Alexandria, VA: American Counseling Association.

Remley, T. P., Jr. (1992, Spring). You and the law. *American Counselor, 1,* 33.

Remley, T. P., Jr., & Herlihy, B. (2010). *Ethical, legal, and professional issues in counseling* (3rd ed.). Upper Saddle River, NJ: Merrill/Prentice Hall.

Remley, T. P., Jr., Herlihy, B., & Herlihy, S. B. (1997). The U.S. Supreme Court decision in *Jaffee v. Redmond:* Implications for counselors. *Journal of Counseling and Development, 75,* 213–218.

Reynolds, C. R., & Kamphaus, R. W. (2004). *Behavior assessment system for children* (2nd ed.). Circle Pines, MN: Pearson Assessment Group.

Rheineck, J. E. (2009). Counseling in mental health and private practice settings. In D. Capuzzi & D. R. Gross (Eds.), *Introduction to the counseling profession* (5th ed., pp. 421–444). Needham Heights, MA: Pearson/Allyn & Bacon.

Rice, F. P. (2001). *Human development: A life-span approach* (4th ed.). Upper Saddle River, NJ: Prentice Hall.

Rice, K. G., & Leffert, N. (1997). Depression in adolescence: Implications for school counselors. *Canadian Journal of Counselling, 31,* 18–34.

Richards, P. S., & Bergin, A. E. (1997). *A spiritual strategy for counseling and psychotherapy.* Washington, DC: American Psychological Association.

Richardson, B. K., & Bradley, L. J. (1986). *Community agency counseling: An emerging specialty in counselor preparation programs.* Alexandria, VA: American Association for Counseling and Development Foundation.

Riemer-Reiss, M. L. (2000). Utilizing distance technology for mental health counseling. *Journal of Mental Health Counseling, 22,* 189–203.

Rife, J. C., & Belcher, J. R. (1994). Assisting unemployed older workers to become reemployed: An experimental evaluation. *Research on Social Work Practice, 4*(1), 3–13.

Riordan, R. J., & Beggs, M. S. (1987). Counselors and self-help groups. *Journal of Counseling and Development, 65,* 427–429.

Ritchie, M. H. (1986). Counseling the involuntary client. *Journal of Counseling and Development, 64,* 516–518.

Ritter, K. Y. (1982). Training group counselors: A total curriculum perspective. *Journal for Specialists in Group Work, 7,* 266–274.

Ritter, K. Y., & Terndrup, A. I. (2002). *Handbook of affirmative psychotherapy with lesbians and gay men*. New York: Guilford Press.

Rivett, M., & Rees, A. (2004). Dancing on a razor's edge: Systemic group work with batterers. *The Association for Family Therapy and Systemic Practice, 26,* 142–162.

Robbins, A., & Wilner, A. (2001). *Quarterlife crisis: The unique challenges of life in your twenties.* New York: Penguin.

Robinson, T. L., & Howard-Hamilton, M. (2000). *The convergence of race, ethnicity, and gender: Multiple identities in counseling.* Upper Saddle River, NJ: Merrill/Prentice Hall.

Robinson-Wood, T. L. (2009). *The convergence of race, ethnicity, and gender: Multiple identities in counseling* (3rd ed.). Upper Saddle River, NJ: Merrill/Prentice Hall.

Rodriguez, C. P. (2004, September). *The biopsychosocial model.* Paper presented at Wake Forest University, Winston-Salem, NC.

Rogers, C. R. (1942). *Counseling and psychotherapy.* Boston: Houghton Mifflin.

Rogers, C. R. (1987). The underlying theory: Drawn from experience with individuals and groups. *Counseling and Values, 32,* 38–46.

Rogers, J. R. (2001). Suicide risk assessment. In E. R. Welfel & R. E. Ingersoll (Eds.), *The mental health desk reference: A sourcebook for counselors and therapists* (pp. 259–264). New York: Wiley.

Roland, J. (1994). *Families, illness and disability.* New York: Basic Books.

Rollins, J. (2008, July). Emerging client issues. *Counseling Today. 51*(1), 30–41.

Romano, G. (1992, Spring). AACD's 40th anniversary. *American Counselor, 1,* 18–26.

Romano, J. L. (2001). Stress, coping, and well-being: Applications of theory to practice. In E. R. Welfel & R. Elliott Ingersoll (Eds.), *The mental health desk reference* (pp. 44–50). New York: Wiley.

Romano, J. L., & Hage, S. M. (2000). Prevention and counseling psychology: Revitalizing commitments for the 21st century. *Counseling Psychologist, 28,* 733–763.

Rosenbaum, M., & Cohen, E. (1999). Egalitarian marriages, spousal support, resourcefulness, and psychological distress among Israeli working women. *Journal of Vocational Behavior, 54,* 102–113.

Ross, C. E. (1990). Religion and psychological distress. *Journal for the Scientific Study of Religion, 29,* 236–245.

Rothrock, J. A. (1999). A personal experience of acceptance and adjustment to disability. In G. L. Gandy, E. D. Martin, Jr., & R. E. Hardy (Eds.), *Counseling in the rehabilitation process: Community services for mental and physical disabilities* (2nd ed., pp. 204–217). Springfield, IL: Charles C Thomas.

Rudd, M. D. (1989). The prevalence of suicidal ideation among college students. *Suicide & Life-Threatening Behavior, 19,* 173–183.

Rueth, T., Demmitt, A., & Burger, S. (1998, March). *Counselors and the DSM-IV: Intentional and unintentional consequences of diagnosis.* Paper presented at the American Counseling Association World Conference, Indianapolis, IN.

Ryder, P. (1976). Theatre as prison therapy. *Drama Review, 20,* 60–66.

Sack, R. T. (1988). Counseling responses when clients say "I don't know." *Journal of Mental Health Counseling, 10,* 179–187.

Sadavoy, J., Jarvik, L. E., Grossberg, G. T., & Meyers, B. S. (Eds.). (2004). *Comprehensive textbook of geriatric psychiatry* (3rd ed.). New York: Norton.

Sager, J. B. (2001). Latin American lesbian, gay, and bisexual clients: Implications for counseling. *Journal of Humanistic Counseling, Education, and Development, 40,* 13–33.

Saidla, D. D. (1990). Cognitive development and group stages. *Journal for Specialists in Group Work, 15,* 15–20.

Saitz, R. (2005). Clinical practice: Unhealthy alcohol use. *New England Journal of Medicine, 10,* 596–607.

Salo, M. (2006). Counseling minor clients. In B. Herlihy & G. Corey, *ACA Ethical standards casebook* (6th ed., pp. 201–203). Alexandria, VA: American Counseling Association.

Sampson, J. P., Jr., & Bloom, J. W. (2001). The potential for success and failure of computer applications in counseling and guidance. In D. C. Locke, J. E. Myers, & E. L. Herr (Eds.), *The handbook of counseling* (pp. 613–627). Thousand Oaks, CA: Sage.

Sampson, J. P., Jr., Kolodinsky, R. W., & Greeno, B. P. (1997). Counseling on the information highway: Future possibilities and potential problems. *Journal of Counseling and Development, 75,* 203–212.

Sandberg, J. (2002). Our aging selves. *Family Therapy Magazine, 1*(6), 10–15.

Sandhu, D. S. (Ed.). (2002). *Counseling employees: A multifaceted approach.* Alexandria, VA: American Counseling Association.

Santos, P. J. (2004). Career dilemmas in career counseling groups: Theoretical and practical issues. *Journal of Career Development, 31*(1), 31–44.

Satir, V. M. (1967). *Conjoint family therapy.* Palo Alto, CA: Science and Behavior Books.

Satir, V. M. (1972). *Peoplemaking.* Palo Alto: Science and Behavior Books.

Savage, T. A., Harley, D. A., & Nowak, T. M. (2005). Applying social empowerment strategies as tools for self-advocacy in counseling lesbian and gay male clients. *Journal of Counseling & Development, 83,* 131–137.

Savickas, M. L. (1989). Annual review: Practice and research in career counseling and development, 1988. *Career Development Quarterly, 38,* 100–134.

Savolaine, J., & Granello, P. F. (2002). The function of meaning and purpose for individual wellness. *Journal of Humanistic Counseling, Education and Development, 41,* 178–189.

Scarf, M. (1995). *Intimate worlds: Life inside the family.* New York: Random House.

Schave, D., & Schave, B. F. (1989). *Early adolescence and the search for self: A developmental perspective.* New York: Praeger.

Scher, M. (1979). On counseling men. *Personnel and Guidance Journal, 57,* 252–254.

Scher, M. (1981). Men in hiding: A challenge for the counselor. *Personnel and Guidance Journal, 60,* 199–202.

Scher, M., & Stevens, M. (1987). Men and violence. *Journal of Counseling and Development, 65,* 351–355.

Schmitt, S. M. (2002). Kaplan takes over as ACA president. *Counseling Today, 1,* 45.

Schoenwald, S. K., Brown, T. L., & Henggeler, S. W. (2000). Inside multisystemic therapy: Therapist, supervisory, and program practices. *Journal of Emotional and Behavioral Disorders, 8,* 113–127.

Schure, M. B., Christopher, J., & Christopher, S. (2008). Mind-body medicine and the art of self-care: Teaching mindfulness to counseling students through yoga, meditation, and qigong. *Journal of Counseling and Development, 86,* 47–56.

Schwartz, R. C., Barrett, M. J., & Saba, G. (1984). Family therapy for bulimia. In D. M. Garner & P. E. Garfinkel (Eds.), *Handbook of psychotherapy for anorexia nervosa and bulimia* (pp. 280–307). New York: Guilford Press.

Scileppi, J. A., Teed, E. L., & Torres, R. D. (2000). *Community psychology: A common sense approach to mental health.* Upper Saddle River, NJ: Prentice Hall.

Scott, C. G. (2000). Ethical issues in addiction counseling. *Rehabilitation Counseling Bulletin, 43,* 209–214.

Sears, S. (1982). A definition of career guidance terms: A National Vocational Guidance Association perspective. *Vocational Guidance Quarterly, 31,* 137–143.

Seiler, G., Brooks, D. K., Jr., & Beck, E. S. (1987). Training standards of the American Mental Health Counselors Association: History, rationale, and implications. *Journal of Mental Health Counseling, 9,* 199–209.

Seligman, L. (1999). Twenty years of diagnosis and the DSM. *Journal of Mental Health Counseling, 21,* 229–239.

Seligman, L. (2004). *Diagnosis and treatment planning in counseling* (3rd ed.). New York: Kluwer Academic/Plenum.

Seligman, L. (2006). *Systems, strategies, and skills of counseling and psychotherapy.* Upper Saddle River, NJ: Merrill/Prentice Hall.

Seligman, L. (2009). Diagnosis in counseling. In D. Capuzzi & D. R. Gross (Eds.), *Introduction to the counseling profession* (5th ed., pp. 373– 394). Needham Heights, MA: Allyn & Bacon.

Selvini-Palazzoli, M., Boscolo, L., Cecchin, G., & Prata, G. (1978). *Paradox and counterparadox.* New York: Monson.

Selye, H. (1976). *The stress of life* (2nd ed.). New York: Guilford Press.

Sexton, T. L. (2001). Evidence-based counseling intervention programs. In D. C. Locke, J. E. Myers, & E. L. Herr (Eds.), *The handbook of counseling* (pp. 499–512). Thousand Oaks, CA: Sage.

Sexton, T. L., & Whiston, S. C. (1996). Integrating counseling research and practice. *Journal of Counseling and Development, 74,* 588–589.

Sexton, T. L., Whiston, S. C., Bleuer, J. C., & Walz, G. R. (1997). *Integrating outcome research into counseling practice and training.* Alexandria, VA: American Counseling Association.

Shanker, T. (2008, April 6). Army is worried by rising stress of return tours to Iraq. *New York Times.* Retrieved September 3, 2008, from http://www.nytimes.com/2008/04/06/washington/06military.html?

Shanks, J. L. (1982). Expanding treatment for the elderly: Counseling in a private medical practice. *Personnel and Guidance Journal, 61,* 553–555.

Sharrer, V. W., & Ryan-Wenger, N. A. (2002). School-age children's self-reported stress symptoms. *Pediatric Nursing, 28,* 21–27.

Shaw, H., & Shaw, S. F. (2006). Critical ethical issues in online counseling: Assessing current practices with an ethical intent checklist. *Journal of Counseling and Development, 84,* 41–53.

Shea, C. (1998, January 30). Why depression strikes more women than men: "Ruminative coping" may provide answers. *Chronicle of Higher Education, 44,* A14.

Sheehy, G. (1976). *Passages: Predictable crises of adult life.* New York: Dutton.

Sherman, R. (1993). The intimacy genogram. *The Family Journal, 1,* 91–93.

Shertzer, B., & Stone, S. (1980). *Fundamentals of counseling* (3rd ed.). Boston: Houghton Mifflin.

Shertzer, B., & Stone, S. C. (1981). *Fundamentals of guidance* (4th ed.). Boston: Houghton Mifflin.

Sherwood-Hawes, A. (1993). Individual counseling: Process. In A. Vernon (Ed.), *Counseling children and adolescents* (pp. 19–50). Denver, CO: Love.

Shulins, N. (1992, June 27). Baby-boomers are waking up to childlessness. *Winston-Salem Journal, 14,* 17.

Shulman, L. (1999). *The skills of helping individuals and groups.* Itasca, IL: F. E. Peacock.

'Simon, L., Gaul, R., Friedlander, M. L., & Heatherington, L. (1992). Client gender and sex role: Predictors of counselors' impressions and expectations. *Journal of Counseling and Development, 71,* 48–52.

Simpson, L. R. (2009). Counseling and spirituality. In D. Capuzzi & D. R. Gross (Eds.), *Introduction to the counseling profession* (5th ed., pp. 292–313). Boston: Pearson/Allyn & Bacon.

Sinick, D. (1979). Adult developmental changes and counseling challenges. In M. L. Ganikos, K. A. Grady, & J. B. Olson (Eds.), *Counseling the aged, a training syllabus for educators* (pp. 31–44). Washington, DC: American Personnel and Guidance Association.

Skinner, A., & Zack, J. S. (2004). Counseling and the Internet. *American Behavioral Scientist, 48,* 434–446.

Sklare, G., Keener, R., & Mas, C. (1990). Preparing members for "here-and-now" group counseling. *Journal for Specialists in Group Work, 15,* 141–148.

Sklare, G., Petrosko, J., & Howell, S. (1993). The effect of pregroup training on members' level of anxiety. *Journal for Specialists in Group Work, 18,* 109–114.

Slater, S. (1999). *The lesbian family life cycle.* New York: The Free Press.

Sleek, S. (1995, July). Group therapy: Tapping the power of teamwork. *APA Monitor, 26*(1), 38–39.

Slipp, S. (1988). *The technique and practice of object relations family therapy.* New York: Aronson.

Smart, J. F., & Smart, D. W. (2006). Models of disability: Implications for the counseling profession. *Journal of Counseling & Development, 84,* 29–40.

Smith, E. M. J., & Vasquez, M. J. T. (1985). Introduction. *Counseling Psychologist, 13,* 531–536.

Smith, H. B. (1999). Managed care: A survey of counselor educators and counselor practitioners. *Journal of Mental Health Counseling, 21,* 270–283.

Society of Counseling Psychology. (2007). Retrieved December 31, 2007, from http://www.div17.org

Sommers-Flanagan, J., & Sommers-Flanagan, R. (2007). *Tough kids, cool counseling* (2nd ed.). Alexandria, VA: American Counseling Association.

Sophie, J. (1987). Internalized homophobia and lesbian identity. *Journal of Homosexuality, 14*, 53–65.

Spitalnick, J. S., & McNair, L. D. (2005). Couples therapy with gay men and lesbian clients: An analysis of important clinical issues. *Journal of Sex and Marital Therapy, 31*, 43–56.

Spokane, A. R. (1991). *Career intervention.* Upper Saddle River, NJ: Prentice Hall.

Stadler, H. (1986). Preface to the special issue. *Journal of Counseling and Development, 64*, 291. Stanton, M. D. (1999, May). Alcohol use disorders. *AAMFT Clinical Update, 1*(3), 1–8. Stark, D. D., Hargrave, J., Sander, J. B., Custer, G., Schnoebelen, S., Simpson, J., & Molnar, J. (2006). Treatment of childhood depression: The ACTION treatment program. In P. C. Kendall (Ed.), *Child and adolescent therapy: Cognitive–behavioral procedures* (3rd ed., pp. 160–216). New York: Guilford Press.

Staton, A. R., Benson, A. J., Briggs, M. K., Cowan, E. Echterling, L. G., Evans, W. F., et al. (2007). *Becoming a community counselor: Personal and professional explorations.* Boston: Lahaska Press.

Staum, M. (1983). Music and rhythmic stimuli in the rehabilitation of gait disorders. *Journal of Music Therapy, 20*, 69–87.

Steenbarger, B. N., & Smith, H. B. (1996). Assessing the quality of counseling services: Developing accountable helping systems. *Journal of Counseling and Development, 75*, 145–150.

Steinglass, P., Bennett, L. A., Wolin, S. J., & Reiss, D. (1987). *The alcoholic family.* New York: Perseus.

Steinhauser, L. (1985). A new PhD's search for work: A case study. *Journal of Counseling and Development, 63*, 300–303.

Steinhauser, L., & Bradley, R. (1983). Accreditation of counselor education programs. *Counselor Education and Supervision, 25*, 98–108.

Stelmachers, Z. T. (1995). Assessing suicidal clients. In J. N. Butcher (Ed.), *Clinical personality assessment: Practical approaches* (pp. 367–379). New York: Oxford University Press.

Stevens-Smith, P., & Smith, R. L. (1998). *Substance abuse counseling: Theory and practice.* Upper Saddle River, NJ: Merrill/Prentice Hall.

St. Germaine, J. (1993). Dual relationships: What's wrong with them? *American Counselor, 2*, 25–30.

Stinnett, N., & DeFrain, J. (1985). *Secrets of strong families.* Boston: Little, Brown.

Stith, P., & Raynor, D. (2008, February 26). Reform wastes millions, fails mentally ill. *The News and Observer.* Retrieved September 3, 2008, from http://www.newsobserver.com/2771/v-print/story/962049.html

Stockton, R., Barr, J. E., & Klein, R. (1981). Identifying the group dropout: A review of the literature. *Journal for Specialists in Group Work, 6*, 75–82.

Stoddard, S. (1992). *The hospice movement: A better way of caring for the dying* (Rev. ed.). New York: Random House.

Stripling, R. O. (1978). ACES guidelines for doctoral preparation in counselor education. *Counselor Education and Supervision, 17*, 163–166.

Strong, B., DeVault, C., & Sayad, B. W. (2008). *The marriage and family experience: Intimate relationships in a changing society* (10th ed.). Belmont, CA: Wadsworth.

Strong, E. K., Jr. (1943). *Vocational interests of men and women.* Stanford, CA: Stanford University Press.

Strong, S. R. (1982). Emerging integrations of clinical and social psychology: A clinician's perspective. In G. Weary & H. Mirels (Eds.), *Integrations of clinical and social psychology* (pp. 181–213). New York: Oxford University Press.

Stroul, B. A. (1988). *Series on community-based services for children and adolescents who are severely emotionally disturbed, Vol. I: Home-based services.* Washington, DC: CASSP Technical Assistance Center, Georgetown University Child Development Center.

Stuart, R. B. (1980). *Helping couples change: A social learning approach to marital therapy.* New York: Guilford Press.

Stuart, R. B. (1998). Updating behavior therapy with couples. *The Family Journal: Counseling and Therapy for Couples and Families, 6*, 6–12.

Stude, E. W., & McKelvey, J. (1979). Ethics and the law: Friend or foe? *Personnel and Guidance Journal, 57*, 453–456.

Sue, D. W. (1981). *Counseling and the culturally different: Theory and practice.* New York: Wiley.

Sue, D. W. (1992, Winter). The challenge of multiculturalism. *American Counselor, 1,* 6–14.

Sue, D. W., Arredondo, P., & McDavis, R. J. (1992). Multicultural counseling competencies and standards: A call to the profession. *Journal of Counseling and Development, 70,* 477–486.

Sue, D. W., Ivey, A. E., & Pedersen, P. (1996). *A theory of multicultural counseling and therapy.* Pacific Grove, CA: Brooks/Cole.

Sue, D. W., & Sue, D. (2003). *Counseling the culturally diverse: Theory and practice* (4th ed.). New York: Wiley.

Summit results in formation of spiritual competencies. (1995, December). *Counseling Today, 30.*

Super, D. E. (1954). Career patterns as a basis for vocational counseling. *Journal of Counseling Psychology, 1,* 12–19.

Super, D. E. (1955). Transition: From vocational guidance to counseling psychology. *Journal of Counseling Psychology, 2,* 3–9.

Super, D. E. (1957). *The psychology of careers.* New York: Harper.

Super, D. E. (1976). *Career education and the meaning of work* [Monograph]. Washington, DC: Office of Career Education, U.S. Office of Education.

Super, D. E. (1980). A life-span, life space approach to career development. *Journal of Vocational Behavior, 16,* 282–298.

Super, D. E. (1990). A life-span, life-space approach to career development. In D. Brown, L. Brooks, & Associates (Eds.), *Career choice and development: Applying contemporary theories to practice* (2nd ed., pp. 197–261). San Francisco: Jossey-Bass.

Supple, A. J., & Small, S. A. (2006). The influence of parental support, knowledge, and authoritative parenting among Hmong and European American adolescent development. *Journal of Family Issues, 27,* 1214–1232.

Surgeon General. (2002). Overview of cultural diversity and mental health services. Retrieved May 30, 2002, from http://www .surgeongeneral.gov/library/mentalhealth/ chapter3/sec5.html

Surgeon General Report. (2000). *Mental health: A report of the Surgeon General.* Retrieved December 1, 2002, from http://www .surgeongeneral.gov/Library/MentalHealth

Survey says. (2005). *Gay and Lesbian Review Worldwide, 12*(1), 17–21.

Sussman, R. J. (1998). *Counseling online.* Retrieved January 14, 2003, from *CTOnline,* http://www.counseling.org

Suzuki, L. A., & Kugler, J. F. (2001). Multicultural assessment. In E. R. Welfel & R. E. Ingersoll (Eds.), *The mental health desk reference: A sourcebook for counselors and therapists* (pp. 279–286). New York: Wiley.

Suzuki, L. A., Ponterotto, J. G., & Meller, P. J. (Eds.). (2008). *Handbook of multicultural assessment: Clinical, psychological, and educational applications* (3rd ed.). San Francisco: Jossey-Bass.

Swanson, C. D. (1983a). Ethics and the counselor. In J. A. Brown & R. H. Pate, Jr. (Eds.), *Being a counselor* (pp. 47–65). Monterey, CA: Brooks/Cole.

Swanson, C. D. (1983b). The law and the counselor. In J. A. Brown & R. H. Pate, Jr. (Eds.), *Being a counselor* (pp. 26–46). Monterey, CA: Brooks/Cole.

Swanson, J. L., & Fouad, N. A. (1999). *Career theory and practice: Learning through case studies.* Thousand Oaks, CA: Sage.

Swartz-Kulstad, J. L., & Martin, W. E., Jr. (1999). Impact on culture and context on psychosocial adaptation: The cultural and contextual guide process. *Journal of Counseling and Development, 77,* 281–293.

Sweeney, T. J. (1989). Excellence vs. elitism. *Newsletter of Chi Sigma Iota, 5,* 1, 11.

Sweeney, T. J. (1991). Counseling credentialing: Purpose and origin. In F. O. Bradley (Ed.), *Credentialing in counseling* (pp. 1–12). Alexandria, VA: Association for Counselor Education and Supervision.

Sweeney, T. J. (1995). Accreditation, credentialing, professionalization: The role of specialties. *Journal of Counseling & Development, 74,* 117–125.

Sweeney, T. J. (1999). *Adlerian counseling: A practitioner's approach.* Philadelphia: Taylor & Francis.

Sweeney, T. J. (2001). Counseling: Historical origins and philosophical roots. In D. C. Locke,

J. E. Myers, & E. L. Herr (Eds.), *The handbook of counseling* (pp. 3–26). Thousand Oaks, CA: Sage.

Sweeney, T. J., & Witmer, J. M. (1991). Beyond social interest: Striving toward optimal health and wellness. *Individual Psychology, 47,* 527–540.

Swenson, R. A. (1998). *The overload syndrome: Learning to live within your limits.* Colorado Springs, CO: NavPress.

Tait, A. (1999). Face-to-face and at a distance: The mediation of guidance and counselling through the new technologies. *British Journal of Guidance and Counselling, 27,* 113–122.

Talbott, J. A. (2001). The economics of mental health care in the USA as the potential for managed care to expand to Europe. *Current Opinion in Psychiatry, 14*(4), 279–285.

Tanigoshi, H., Kontos, A. P., & Remley, T. P., Jr. (2008). The effectiveness of individual wellness counseling on the wellness of law enforcement officers. *Journal of Counseling and Development, 86,* 64–74.

Tarasoff v. Board of Regents of the University of California. (1976). 551 p2d 334, 131, Cal Rptr 14 (Cal. Sup. Ct. 1976).

Taylor, L., & Adelman, H. (2001). Enlisting appropriate parental cooperation and involvement in children's mental health treatment. In E. R. Welfel & R. E. Ingersoll (Eds.), *The mental health desk reference: A sourcebook for counselors and therapists* (pp. 219–224). New York: Wiley.

Terres, C. K., & Larrabee, M. J. (1985). Ethical issues and group work with children. *Elementary School Guidance and Counseling, 19,* 190–197.

Thaut, M. H. (1988). Rhythmic intervention techniques in music therapy with gross motor dysfunctions. *Arts in Psychotherapy, 15,* 127–137.

Thomas, R. (2002). Supreme Court limits ADA disability definition. Retrieved November 15, 2002, from http://www.ppspublishers.com/biz/ada.htm

Thomas, R. M. (2005). *Comparing theories of child development* (6th ed.). Belmont, CA: Wadsworth.

Thomas, R. M., & Chess, S. (1977). *Temperament and development.* New York: Brunner/Mazel.

Thomas, V. G. (1990). Determinants of global life happiness and marital happiness in dual-career black couples. *Family Relations, 39,* 174–178.

Thompson, A. (1990). *Guide to ethical practice in psychotherapy.* New York: Wiley.

Thompson, C. L., & Henderson, D. H. (2007). *Counseling children* (7th ed.). Belmont, CA: Thomson Brooks/Cole.

Tinsley, D. J., & Bigler, M. (2002). Facilitating transition in retirement. In C. L. Juntunen & D. R. Atkinson (Eds.), *Counseling across the lifespan* (pp. 375– 397). Thousand Oaks, CA: Sage.

Todd, T. C. (1986). Structural-strategic marital therapy. In N. S. Jacobson & A. S. Gurman (Eds.), *Clinical handbook of marital therapy* (pp. 71–105). New York: Guilford Press.

Tomine, S. (1986). Private practice in gerontological counseling. *Journal of Counseling and Development, 64,* 406–409.

Toporek, R. L. (2000). Developing a common language and framework for understanding advocacy in counseling. In J. Lewis & L. J. Bradley (Eds.), *Advocacy in counseling: Counselors, clients, and community* (pp. 5–14). Greensboro, NC: Caps Publications.

Trotzer, J. P. (1988). Family theory as a group resource. *Journal for Specialists in Group Work, 13,* 180–185.

Truax, C. B., & Carkhuff, R. R. (1967). *Toward effective counseling and psychotherapy: Training and practice.* Chicago: Aldine.

Trzepacz, P. T., & Baker, R. W. (1993). *The psychiatric mental status examination.* New York: Oxford University Press.

Tuckman, B. W. (1965). Developmental sequence in small groups. *Psychological Bulletin, 63,* 384–399.

Tuckman, B. W., & Jensen, M. A. (1977). Stages of small group development revisited. *Group and Organizational Studies, 2,* 419–427.

Tyiska, C. (1998). Working with victims with disabilities. *Office for Victims of Crime Bulletin,* Washington, DC: U.S. Department of Justice, Office for Victims of Crimes.

U.S. Census Bureau. (2000). Retrieved December 8, 2002, from http://landview.census.gov/population/www.cen2000/phc-t1.html

U. S. Census Bureau. (2000, April 1). *Census 2000*. Retrieved March 25, 2009, from http://www.census.gov/

U.S. Census Bureau. (2007). The American community—Hispanics: 2004. *American Community Survey Reports*. Washington, DC: U.S. Department of Commerce.

U.S. Department of Health and Human Services. (2000). Mental health: A report of the Surgeon General—Executive summary. Retrieved July 28, 2008, from http://www.surgeongeneral.gov/library/mentalhealth/summary.html

U.S. Employment Service. (1939). *Dictionary of occupational titles*. Washington, DC: Author.

U.S. Government. (2008). *Older Americans 2008: Key indicators of well-being*. Retrieved August 31, 2008, from http://agingstats.gov

Usdansky, M. L. (1993, July 14). Many women in 30s won't have kids. *USA Today*, 8A.

Utsey, S. O., Ponterotto, J. G., & Porter, J. S. (2008). Prejudice and racism, year 2008—still going strong: Research on reducing prejudice with recommended methodological advances. *Journal of Counseling & Development, 86,* 339–347.

Vacc, N. A., & Juhnke, G. A. (1997). The use of structured clinical interviews for assessment in counseling. *Journal of Counseling and Development, 75,* 470–480.

Vacc, N. A., & Loesch, L. (2000). *Professional orientation to counseling* (3rd ed.). Philadelphia: Brunner-Routledge.

Van Buren, J. (1992). Gender-fair counseling. In J. A. Lewis, B. Hayes, & L. J. Bradley (Eds.), *Counseling women over the life span* (pp. 271–289). Denver: Love.

Van Hoose, W. H., & Kottler, J. (1985). *Ethical and legal issues in counseling and psychotherapy* (2nd ed.). San Francisco: Jossey-Bass.

VanZandt, C. E. (1990). Professionalism: A matter of personal initiatives. *Journal of Counseling and Development, 68,* 243–245.

Veach, L. J., & Madwid, R. (2005). Older adults and the issue of addiction. In V. A. Kelly & G. A. Juhnke (Eds.), *Critical incidents in addictions counseling*. Alexandria, VA: American Counseling Association.

Veach, T. A., & Nicholas, D. R. (1998). Understanding families of adults with cancer: Combining the clinical course of cancer and

stages of family development. *Journal of Counseling and Development, 76,* 144–156.

Vera, E. M. (2000). A recommitment to prevention work in counseling psychology. *Counseling Psychologist, 28,* 829–837.

Vernon, A. (1993). *Developmental assessment and intervention with children and adolescents*. Alexandria, VA: American Counseling Association.

Vernon, A. (2004). Working with children, adolescents, and their parents: Practical application of developmental theory. In A. Vernon (Ed.), *Counseling children and adolescents* (3rd ed., pp. 1–34). Denver, CO: Love.

Vickio, C. J. (1990). The goodbye brochure: Helping students to cope with transition and loss. *Journal of Counseling and Development, 68,* 575–577.

Viger, J. (2001). Community mental health centers. Retrieved December 28, 2002, from http://www.echoman.com/knowledgesource/Community_Mental_Health_Centers.htm

Von Steen, P. G., Vacc, N. A., & Strickland, I. M. (2002). The treatment of substance-abusing clients in multiservice mental health agencies: A practice analysis. *Journal of Addictions and Offender Counseling, 22,* 61–71.

Vontress, C. E. (1996). A personal retrospective on cross-cultural counseling. *Journal of Multicultural Counseling and Development, 16,* 73–83.

Vriend, J., & Dyer, W. W. (1973). Counseling the reluctant client. *Journal of Counseling Psychology, 20,* 240–246.

Vuchinich, R. E. (2002). President's column. *Addictions Newsletter, 10*(1), 1, 5.

Wade, J. C. (1998). Male reference group identity dependence: A theory of male identity. *Counseling Psychologist, 26,* 349–383.

Waggonseller, B. R., Ruegamer, L. C., & Harrington, M. C. (1998). *Coping in a single-parent home*. New York: Rosen.

Wake Forest University Baptist Medical Center. (2008). *Department of psychiatry and behavioral medicine*. Retrieved September 7, 2008, from http://www1.wfubmc.edu/psychiatry/

Waldo, M. (1985). Curative factor framework for conceptualizing group counseling. *Journal for Counseling and Development, 64,* 52–58.

Waldo, M., & Bauman, S. (1998). Regrouping the categorization of group work: A goal and process (GAP) matrix for groups. *Journal for Specialists in Group Work, 23,* 164–176.

Walker, J. E. (2000). *The age advantage: Making the most of your mid-life career transition.* New York: Berkley.

Walker, L. E. (2000). *Battered woman syndrome* (2nd ed.). New York: Springer.

Walker-Staggs, J. (2000). Discover. In N. Peterson & R. C. Gonzalez (Eds.), *Career counseling models for diverse populations* (pp. 112–120). Pacific Grove, CA: Brooks/Cole.

Wallace, B. A., & Shapiro, S. L. (2006). Mental balance and well-being: Building bridges between Buddhism and Western psychology. *American Psychologist, 61,* 690–701.

Wallerstein, J. S., & Blakeslee, S. (1989). *Second chances.* New York: Ticknor & Fields.

Wallerstein, J. S., & Blakeslee, S. (2003). *What about the kids?* New York: Hyperion.

Walsh, F. (2003). Changing families in a changing world: Reconstructing family normality In F. Walsh (Ed.), *Normal family processes* (3rd ed.; pp. 3–26). New York: Guilford Press.

Walsh, R. (2000). Asian psychotherapies. In R. J. Corsini & D. Wedding (Eds.), *Current psychotherapies* (6th ed., pp. 407–444). Itasca, IL: F. E. Peacock.

Walter, J., & Peller, J. (1992). *Becoming solution-focused in brief therapy.* New York: Brunner/Mazel.

Walz, G. R. (2000). Preface. In J. W. Bloom & G. R. Walz (Eds.), *Cybercounseling and cyberlearning: Strategies and resources for the new millennium* (pp. xi–xvii). Alexandria, VA: American Counseling Association.

Walz, G. R., & Kirkman, C. J. (Eds.). (2002). *Helping people cope with tragedy and grief.* Greensboro, NC: ERIC/CASS and NBCC.

Ward, D. E. (1982). A model for the more effective use of theory in group work. *Journal for Specialists in Group Work, 7,* 224–230.

Ward, D. E. (1984). Termination of individual counseling: Concepts and strategies. *Journal of Counseling and Development, 63,* 21–25.

Wastell, C. A. (1996). Feminist development theory: Implications for counseling. *Journal of Counseling and Development, 74,* 575–581.

Watts, R. E. (1999). Confidentiality and duty to report: A case study. *Family Journal, 7,* 65–67.

Watts, R. E., Trusty, J., & Lim, M.-G. (2000). Characteristics of healthy families as a model of social interest. *Canadian Journal of Adlerian Psychology, 26,* 1–12.

Watzlawick, P. (1983). *The situation is hopeless, but not serious.* New York: Norton.

Watzlawick, P., Weakland, J., & Fisch, R. (1974). *Change: Principles of problem formation and problem resolution.* New York: Norton.

Weaver, S. T., & Wilson, C. N. (1997). Addiction counselors can benefit from appropriate humor in the work setting. *Journal of Employment Counseling, 34,* 108–114.

Webb, L. D., Brigman, G. A., & Campbell, C. (2005). Linking school counselors and student success: A replication of the student success skills approach targeting the academic and social competence of students. *Professional School Counseling, 8*(5), 407–413.

Webber, J., Bass, D. D., & Yep, R. (Eds.). (2005). *Terrorism, trauma, and tragedies: A counselor's guide to preparing and responding* (2nd ed.). Alexandria, VA: American Counseling Association.

Wegscheider, S. (1981). *Another chance: Hope and health for the alcoholic family.* Palo Alto, CA: Science & Behavior Books.

Weikel, W. J. (1996). The mental health counselors association. In W. J. Weikel & A. J. Palmo (Eds.), *Foundations of mental health counseling* (2nd ed.). Springfield, IL: Charles C. Thomas.

Weinrach, S. G. (1987). Microcounseling and beyond: A dialogue with Allen Ivey. *Journal of Counseling and Development, 65,* 532–537.

Weinrach, S. G. (1996). The psychological and vocational interest patterns of Donald Super and John Holland. *Journal of Counseling and Development, 75,* 5–16.

Weinrach, S. G., & Thomas, K. R. (1998). Diversity sensitive counseling today: A postmodern clash of values. *Journal of Counseling and Development, 76,* 115–122.

Weitzman, J. (2006). The family's role in adolescent depression and treatment: Recent findings. *Journal of Psychotherapy and the Family, 17,* 37–48.

Welfel, E. R. (2006). *Ethics in counseling and psychotherapy: Standards, research, and emerging issues* (3rd ed.). Pacific Grove, CA: Brooks/Cole.

Welfel, E. R., & Patterson, L. E. (2005). *The counseling process: A multitheoretical integrative approach* (6th ed.). Belmont, CA: Thomson Brooks/Cole.

Werbel, J. (1998). Intent and choice regarding maternal employment following childbirth. *Journal of Vocational Behavior, 53,* 372–385.

Werner, E. E., & Smith, R. S. (2001). *Journeys from childhood to midlife: Risk, resilience, and recovery.* Ithaca, NY: Cornell University Press.

Wester, S. R., Vogel, D. L., Wei, M., & McLain, R. (2006). African American men, gender role conflict, and psychological distress: The role of racial identity. *Journal of Counseling and Development, 84,* 419–429.

West-Olatunji, C. A. (2001). Counseling ethnic minority clients. In D. Capuzzi & D. R. Gross (Eds.), *Introduction to the counseling profession* (3rd ed., pp. 415–434). Needham Heights, MA: Allyn & Bacon.

Wheeler, A. M., & Bertram, B. 2008). *The counselor and the law: A guide to legal and ethical practice* (5th ed.). Alexandria, VA: American Counseling Association.

Whiston, S. C. (2009). *Principles and applications of assessment in counseling* (3rd ed.). Belmont, CA: Brooks/Cole.

Whitaker, C. (1976). The hindrance of theory in clinical work. In P. J. Guerin (Ed.), *Family therapy: Theory and practice* (pp. 154–164). New York: Gardner Press.

Whitaker, C. (1977). Process techniques of family therapy. *Interaction, 1,* 4–19.

Whitaker, C. (1989). *Midnight musings of a family therapist.* New York: Norton.

White, H. (1978). Exercises in understanding your family. In *Your family is good for you.* New York: Random House.

White, M. (1995). *Re-authoring lives.* Adelaide, South Australia: Dulwich Centre Publications.

White, M., & Epston, D. (1990). *Narrative means to therapeutic ends.* New York: Norton.

White, V. E. (2002). Developing counseling objectives and empowering clients: A strength-based intervention. *Journal of Mental Health Counseling, 24,* 270–279.

Whitely, J. M. (1984). Counseling psychology: A historical perspective. *Counseling Psychologist, 12,* 2–109.

Whitfield, C. L. (1987). *Healing the child within: Discovery and recovery for adult children of dysfunctional families.* Pompano Beach, FL: Health Communications.

Whitman, J. S., Glosoff, H. L., Kocet, M. M., & Tarvydas, V. (2006). *Ethical issues related to conversion or reparative therapy.* Retrieved July 20, 2008, from http://www.counseling.org/PressRoom/NewsReleases.aspx

Wickline v. State of California, 239 Cal. Rptr. 805, 741 P.2d 613 (1987).

Wilcoxon, S. A. (1985). Healthy family functioning: The other side of family pathology. *Journal of Counseling and Development, 63,* 495–499.

Wilcoxon, S. A., & Fenell, D. (1983). Engaging the non-attending spouse in marital therapy through the use of therapist-initiated written communication. *Journal of Marital and Family Therapy, 9,* 199–203.

Wilcoxon, S. A., Remley, T. P., Jr., Gladding, S. T., & Huber, C. H. (2007). *Ethical, legal and professional issues in the practice of marriage and family therapy* (4th ed.). Upper Saddle River, NJ: Merrill/Prentice Hall.

Williamson, E. G. (1939). *How to counsel students: A manual of techniques for clinical counselors.* New York: McGraw-Hill.

Williamson, E. G., & Biggs, D. A. (1979). Trait-factor theory and individual differences. In H. M. Burks, Jr., & B. Stefflre (Eds.), *Theories of counseling* (3rd ed., pp. 91–131). New York: McGraw-Hill.

Willis, S. L., & Martin, M. (Eds.). (2005). *Middle adulthood: A lifespan perspective.* Thousand Oaks, CA: Sage.

Wilmarth, R. R. (1985, Summer). Historical perspective, part two. *AMHCA News, 8,* 21.

Winegar, N. (1993). Managed mental health care: Implications for administrators and managers of community-based agencies. *Families in Society: The Journal of Contemporary Human Services, 74,* 171–178.

Winegar, N., & Hayter, L. M. (1998). *Guidebook to managed care and practice management terminology.* New York: Haworth Press.

Winter, J. M. (February 2002). *Counseling lesbian, gay, and bisexual clients.* Paper presented at the North Carolina Counseling Association Annual Conference, Greensboro, NC.

Witmer, J. M., & Sweeney, T. J. (1992). A holistic model for wellness and prevention over the life span. *Journal of Counseling and Development, 71,* 140–148.

Woititz, J. (2002). *The complete ACOA sourcebook: Adult children of alcoholics at home, at work and in love.* Deerfield Beach, FL: Health Communications.

Woods, T. E., Antoni, M. H., Ironson, G. H., & Kling, D. W. (1999). Religiosity is associated with affective status in symptomatic HIV-infected African-American women. *Journal of Health Psychology, 4,* 317–326.

Worth, M. R. (1983). Adults. In J. A. Brown & R. H. Pate, Jr. (Eds.), *Being a counselor: Directions and challenges* (pp. 230–252). Pacific Grove, CA: Brooks/Cole.

Worthington, R. L., Dillon, F. R., & Becker-Schutte, A. M. (2005). Development, reliability, and validity of the lesbian, gay, and bisexual knowledge and attitudes scale for heterosexuals. *Journal of Counseling Psychology, 52,* 104–118.

Wrenn, C. G. (1962a). *The counselor in a changing world.* Washington, DC: American Personnel and Guidance Association.

Wrenn, C. G. (1962b). The culturally encapsulated counselor. *Harvard Educational Review, 32,* 444–449.

Wrenn, C. G. (1979). Proposed changes in counselor attitudes: Toward your job. *School Counselor, 27,* 81–90.

Wright, K. C., & Martin, E. D., Jr. (1999). The rehabilitation process: A perspective for the rehabilitation counselor. In G. L. Gandy, E. D. Martin, Jr., & R. E. Hardy (Eds.), *counseling in the rehabilitation process: Community services for mental and physical disabilities* (2nd ed., pp. 117–129). Springfield, IL: Charles C Thomas.

Wyatt, T., Daniels, M. H., & White, L. J. (2000). Noncompetition agreements and the counseling profession: An unrecognized reality for private practitioners. *Journal of Counseling and Development, 78,* 14–20.

Wylie, M. S. (1995, May/June). The power of the *DSM-IV*: Diagnosing for dollars. *Networker,* 22–32.

Wyndzen, M. H. (2008). *DSM-V* workgroup for sexual & gender identity disorders appoint-ment of Kenneth Zucker & Ray Blanchard. Retrieved July 10, 2008, from http://genderpsychology.org/psychology/dsm_v_workgroup.html

Yakushko, O. (2005). Influence of social support, existential well-being, and stress over sexual orientation on self esteem of gay, lesbian, and bisexual individuals. *International Journal for the Advancement of Counselling, 27*(1), 131–143.

Yalom, I. D., & Leszcz, M. (2005). *The theory and practice of group psychotherapy* (5th ed.). New York: Basic Books.

Yalom, I. D., & Lieberman, M. (1971). A study of encounter group casualties. *Archives of General Psychiatry, 25,* 16–30.

Yeh, C. J., & Hwang, M. Y. (2000). Interdependence in ethnic identity and self: Implications for theory and practice. *Journal of Counseling and Development, 78,* 420–429.

Young, J. S., Wiggins-Frame, M., & Cashwell, C. S. (2007). Spirituality and counselor competence: A national survey of American Counseling Association Members. *Journal of Counseling and Development, 85,* 47–52.

Young, M. E. (2009). *Learning the art of helping: Building blocks and techniques* (4th ed.). Upper Saddle River, NJ: Merrill/Prentice Hall.

Zal, H. M. (2001). *The sandwich generation: Caught between growing children and aging parents.* New York: Da Capo Press.

Zill, N., Morrison, D., & Coiro, M. (1993). Long-term effects of parental divorce on parent–child relationships, adjustment, and achievement in young adulthood. *Journal of Family Psychology, 7,* 1–13.

Zimpfer, D. G. (1996). Five-year follow-up of doctoral graduates in counseling. *Counselor Education and Supervision, 35,* 218–229.

Zimpfer, D. G., & Carr, J. J. (1989). Groups for midlife career change: A review. *Journal for Specialists in Group Work, 14,* 1–8.

Zimpfer, D. G., & DeTrude, J. (1990). Follow-up of doctoral graduates in counseling. *Journal of Counseling and Development, 69,* 51–56.

Zytowski, D. (1985). Frank! Frank! Where are you now that we need you? *The Counseling Psychologist, 13,* 129–135.

NAME INDEX

SUBJECT INDEX